The Wiley Blackwell Handbook of Forensic Neuroscience

The Wiley Blackwell Handbook of Forensic Neuroscience

Volume 2

Edited by

Anthony R. Beech
Adam J. Carter
Ruth E. Mann
Pia Rotshtein

WILEY Blackwell

This edition first published 2018
© 2018 John Wiley & Sons Ltd

All rights reserved. No part of this publication may be reproduced, stored in a retrieval system, or transmitted, in any form or by any means, electronic, mechanical, photocopying, recording or otherwise, except as permitted by law. Advice on how to obtain permission to reuse material from this title is available at http://www.wiley.com/go/permissions.

The right of Anthony R. Beech, Adam J. Carter, Ruth E. Mann and Pia Rotshtein to be identified as the authors of the editorial material in this work has been asserted in accordance with law.

Registered Offices
John Wiley & Sons, Inc., 111 River Street, Hoboken, NJ 07030, USA
John Wiley & Sons Ltd, The Atrium, Southern Gate, Chichester, West Sussex, PO19 8SQ, UK

Editorial Office
111 River Street, Hoboken, NJ 07030, USA

For details of our global editorial offices, customer services, and more information about Wiley products visit us at www.wiley.com.

Wiley also publishes its books in a variety of electronic formats and by print-on-demand. Some content that appears in standard print versions of this book may not be available in other formats.

Limit of Liability/Disclaimer of Warranty
While the publisher and authors have used their best efforts in preparing this work, they make no representations or warranties with respect to the accuracy or completeness of the contents of this work and specifically disclaim all warranties, including without limitation any implied warranties of merchantability or fitness for a particular purpose. No warranty may be created or extended by sales representatives, written sales materials or promotional statements for this work. The fact that an organization, website, or product is referred to in this work as a citation and/or potential source of further information does not mean that the publisher and authors endorse the information or services the organization, website, or product may provide or recommendations it may make. This work is sold with the understanding that the publisher is not engaged in rendering professional services. The advice and strategies contained herein may not be suitable for your situation. You should consult with a specialist where appropriate. Further, readers should be aware that websites listed in this work may have changed or disappeared between when this work was written and when it is read. Neither the publisher nor authors shall be liable for any loss of profit or any other commercial damages, including but not limited to special, incidental, consequential, or other damages.

Library of Congress Cataloging-in-Publication Data

Names: Beech, Anthony R., editor. | Carter, Adam J., 1968– editor. | Mann, Ruth E., 1965– editor. | Rotshtein, Pia, editor.
Title: The Wiley Blackwell handbook of forensic neuroscience / edited by Anthony R. Beech, Adam J. Carter, Ruth E. Mann, Pia Rotshtein.
Description: First edition. | Hoboken, NJ : John Wiley & Sons, 2018. | Includes index. |
Identifiers: LCCN 2017034459 (print) | LCCN 2017044364 (ebook) | ISBN 9781118650905 (pdf) | ISBN 9781118650912 (epub) | ISBN 9781118650929 (cloth-set)
Subjects: LCSH: Forensic neuropsychology.
Classification: LCC RA1147.5 (ebook) | LCC RA1147.5 .W55 2018 (print) | DDC 614/.15–dc23
LC record available at https://lccn.loc.gov/2017034459

Cover image: © Sergey7777/Gettyimages
Cover design: Wiley

Set in 10/12pt GalliardStd by Aptara Inc., New Delhi, India

10 9 8 7 6 5 4 3 2 1

For Dawn who has had to put up with me through the long gestation of this volume – AB

For Anne and Leslie and the wonderful Ruby – AC

In memory of Ralph Mann 1927-2014 – RM

For my parents Alice and Gadi – PR

Contents

VOLUME 1

About the Editors   xi

List of Contributors   xiii

Part I   Introduction   1

1   Neuroscience in Forensic Settings: Origins and Recent Developments   3
Anthony R. Beech and Dawn Fisher

2   A Brief Introduction to Neuroscience   25
Pia Rotshtein and Ian J. Mitchell

Part II   General Neuroscience Research   59

3   The Neurobiology of Aggressive Behavior   61
Jens Foell and Christopher J. Patrick

4   The Neurobiology of Sexual Behavior and Sexual Attraction   83
Anders Ågmo

5   Reward Sensitivity and Behavioral Control: Neuroimaging Evidence for
Brain Systems Underlying Risk-Taking Behavior   105
Renate L. E. P. Reniers, Ulrik R. Beierholm, and Stephen J. Wood

6   The Neurobiology of Emotion Regulation   125
Catherine L. Sebastian and Saz P. Ahmed

7   The Social Neuroscience of Empathy and its Relationship to
Moral Behavior   145
Jean Decety and Jason M. Cowell

8   The Neuroscience of Deception   171
Jennifer M. C. Vendemia and James M. Nye

viii   *Contents*

Part III   Neurobiology of Offending   **189**

9   The Neurobiological Underpinnings of Psychopathy   191
    Stéphane A. De Brito and Ian J. Mitchell

10 Antisocial Personality Disorder   229
    Sheilagh Hodgins, Dave Checknita, Philip Lindner, Boris Schiffer, and
    Stéphane A. De Brito

11 Offenders with Autism Spectrum Disorder   273
    Björn Hofvander

12 The Neuroscience of Violent Offending   301
    Heather L. McLernon, Jeremy A. Feiger, Gianni G. Geraci, Gabriel
    Marmolejo, Alexander J. Roberts, and Robert A. Schug

13 The Neuroscience of Sexual Offending   333
    Andreas Mokros

14 The Neuroscience of Acquisitive/Impulsive Offending   359
    Claire Nee and Stephanos Ioannou

15 Neurobiology of Brain Injury and its Link with Violence and Extreme
    Single and Multiple Homicides   385
    Clare S. Allely

16 The Neurobiology of Offending Behavior in Adolescence   421
    Graeme Fairchild and Areti Smaragdi

17 Alcohol-Related Aggression and Violence   455
    Stefan Gutwinski, Adrienne J. Heinz, and Andreas Heinz

VOLUME 2

About the Editors   xi

List of Contributors   xiii

Part IV   Neurobiological Bases to Risk Factors for Offending   **481**

18 Genetic Contributions to the Development of Psychopathic Traits and
    Antisocial Behavior in Youths   483
    Nathalie M. G. Fontaine, Eamon J. McCrory, and Essi Viding

19 Developmental Risk Factors   507
    Anthony R. Beech, Ben Nordstrom, and Adrian Raine

20 Mental Illness as a Putative Risk Factor for Violence and Aggression   531
    Ahmad Abu-Akel and Sune Bo

21 Modifying Risk Factors: Building Strengths   553
    Corine de Ruiter

Contents ix

Part V   Rehabilitation 575

22   Engaging with Forensic Populations: A Biologically Informed Approach 577
Fiona Williams and Adam J. Carter

23   Brain Scanning and Therapeutics: How Do You Know Unless You
Look? Neuroimaging Guided Treatment in Forensic Settings 601
Daniel G. Amen and Kristen Willeumier

24   Therapy for Acquired Brain Injury 631
Nick Alderman, Caroline Knight, Jennifer Brooks

25   The Impact of Physical Exercise on Antisocial Behavior:
A Neurocognitive Perspective 659
Dylan B. Jackson and Kevin M. Beaver

26   Treating Emotion Dysregulation in Antisocial Behavior:
A Neuroscientific Perspective 677
Steven M. Gillespie and Anthony R. Beech

27   The Pharmacological Treatment of Sex Offenders 703
Don Grubin

28   Understanding and Using Compassion-Focused Therapy in
Forensic Settings 725
Russell Kolts and Paul Gilbert

29   The Neurobiology of Eye Movement Desensitization
Reprocessing Therapy 755
Derek Farrell

30   Adjusting the Lens: A Developmental Perspective for Treating Youth
with Sexual Behavior Problems 783
Kevin Creeden

Part VI   Ethical, Legal, and Political Implications 813

31   The Impact of Neglect, Trauma, and Maltreatment on
Neurodevelopment: Implications for Juvenile Justice Practice, Programs,
and Policy 815
*Bruce D. Perry, Gene Griffin, George Davis, Jay A. Perry, and
Robert D. Perry*

32   Forensic Neuropsychology and Violence: Neuroscientific and
Legal Implications 837
John Matthew Fabian

33   Forensic Neuropsychology in the Criminal Court: A Socio-legal
Perspective 889
Leon McRae

34   Forensic Neuropsychology: Social, Cultural, and Political Implications 917
Jessica Pykett

Contents

Part VII Conclusions   **937**

35 Explanation in Forensic Neuroscience   939
    Tony Ward and Carolyn E. Wilshire

36 Considerations for the Forensic Practitioner   947
    Adam J. Carter and Ruth E. Mann

Index   959

About the Editors

Anthony R. Beech is an emeritus professor in criminological psychology at the University of Birmingham, UK and a fellow of the BPS. He has authored over 190 peer-reviewed articles, 50 book chapters and six books in the area of forensic science/criminal justice. In 2009 he received the Significant Achievement Award from the Association for the Treatment of Sexual Abusers in Dallas, and the Senior Award from the Division of Forensic Psychology, British Psychological Society. His particular areas of research interests are: risk assessment; the neurobiological bases of offending; reducing online exploitation of children; and increasing psychotherapeutic effectiveness of the treatment given to offenders. His recent research has examined: Internet offending; new approaches to treatment of offenders; and the neurobiological basis of offending.

Adam J. Carter is a chartered and registered forensic psychologist with over 20 years' experience working in National Offender Management Service (NOMS) and Her Majesty's Prison Service, predominantly in the assessment and treatment of sexual offending. Adam has a number of book chapters and journal articles published on the subject of the assessment and treatment of sexual offending, and is committed to improving practice in these areas. He received his Ph.D. from Leicester University in 2009 and is currently Head of Offence Specialism for Extremism Offending in Interventions Services, Her Majesty's Prison and Probation Service, UK.

Ruth E. Mann is employed by Her Majesty's Prison and Probation Service, England and Wales. As Head of Evidence-Based Practice, she monitors and translates research literature and oversees research projects designed to improve criminal justice processes. Previously Ruth managed the national strategy for the assessment and treatment of sexual offending in the prison and probation services. In 2010, Ruth received the BPS Division of Forensic Psychology Senior Award for her contribution to forensic psychology in the UK. Ruth has authored or co-authored over 70 scholarly publications on topics related to the treatment of sexual offending, program evaluations and large-scale studies of risk factors for crime.

Pia Rotshtein is a lecturer at the School of Psychology, University of Birmingham, UK. She has authored over 70 peer-reviewed publications. Her research interest focuses on understating the neuroscience of complex behaviors and cognition, like those involved in social cognition and emotional processing.

The editors would like to thank Francesca White and Fiona Screen for their hard work on the text, Jane Read for the index, and Baljinder Kaur at Aptara for the typesetting.

List of Contributors

Ahmad Abu-Akel is a research fellow at the Institute of Psychology, University of Lausanne, Switzerland. His research focuses on the neural bases of attentional and socio-cognitive abilities, and the relationship between autism and schizophrenia spectrum disorders using behavioral and neuroimaging paradigms.

Anders Ågmo is professor of psychobiology at the University of Tromsø, Norway. He has spent part of his career in France (Université Paris VI and Université de Tours) and Mexico (Universidad Anáhuac), and been a guest professor at the University of Düsseldorf, the Rockefeller University, the University of Nebraska at Omaha, and the University of Tsukuba, Japan. Professor Ågmo has published extensively on rodent sexual behavior and motivation, and on the potential usefulness of animal models for understanding human behavior.

Saz P. Ahmed recently completed her doctoral studies at the Department of Psychology, Royal Holloway, University of London, UK. Her research interests include cognitive and neural processes underpinning emotion regulation.

Nick Alderman is Director of Clinical Services & Consultant Clinical Neuropsychologist, Brain Injury Services, Partnerships in Care. He is acknowledged as one of the UK's foremost experts in the management of challenging behavior secondary to acquired brain injury and has over 30 years' experience working in and leading neurobehavioral rehabilitation services.

Clare S. Allely is a lecturer in psychology at the University of Salford in Manchester, UK, and is an affiliate member of the Gillberg Neuropsychiatry Centre at Gothenburg University, Sweden. Clare is also an Honorary Research Fellow in the College of Medical, Veterinary and Life Sciences affiliated to the Institute of Health and Wellbeing at the University of Glasgow. Dr. Allely holds a Ph.D. in psychology from the University of Manchester and has previously graduated with an M.A. (hons.) in Psychology from the University of Glasgow, an M.Res. in Psychological Research Methods from the University of Strathclyde, and an M.Sc. degree in Forensic Psychology from Glasgow Caledonian University. Between June 2011 and June 2014, Dr. Allely worked at the University of Glasgow as a postdoctoral researcher. Current research projects and interests include the path to intended violence in mass shooters; autism spectrum disorders in the criminal justice system (police, courts, prisons); the psychology of terrorism and research into brain injury or neurodevelopmental disorders in forensic populations.

Daniel G. Amen is the founder of Amen Clinics in Costa Mesa and San Francisco, CA, Bellevue, WA, Reston, VA, Atlanta, GA, and New York, NY. Amen Clinics have the world's largest database of functional brain scans relating to behavior, totaling more than 125,000 scans on patients from 111 countries. He is the lead researcher on the world's largest brain imaging and rehabilitation study on professional football players. He is the author or co-author of 70 professional articles, seven book chapters, and over 30 books, including the number one *New York Times* bestseller *The Daniel Plan* and *Change Your Brain, Change Your Life, Healing ADD*, and *The Brain Warrior's Way*. Dr. Amen's published scientific articles have appeared in a number of journal including: Molecular Psychiatry, PLOS One, and Nature's Translational Psychiatry, and his research teams' work was honored by *Discover* Magazine as one of the top 100 stories in science for 2015.

Kevin M. Beaver is a professor in the College of Criminology and Criminal Justice at Florida State University and a visiting distinguished professor in the Center of Social and Humanities Research at King Abdulaziz University. His research examines the development of antisocial behaviors from a biosocial perspective.

Anthony R. Beech is an emeritus professor in criminological psychology at the University of Birmingham, UK, and a fellow of the BPS. He has authored over 190 peer-reviewed articles, 50 book chapters, and six books in the area of forensic science/criminal justice. In 2009 he received the Significant Achievement Award from the Association for the Treatment of Sexual Abusers in Dallas, and the Senior Award from the Division of Forensic Psychology, British Psychological Society. His particular areas of research interests are: risk assessment; the neurobiological bases of offending; reducing online exploitation of children; and increasing psychotherapeutic effectiveness of the treatment given to offenders. His recent research has examined: Internet offending; new approaches to treatment of offenders; and the neurobiological basis of offending.

Ulrik R. Beierholm is assistant professor in psychology at the University of Durham, UK. He is a computational neuroscientist developing and testing theoretical models of information processing in the human brain, taking inspiration from economics and machine learning to explain human perception, learning, and decision making.

Sune Bo is a clinical psychologist at the Child and Adolescent Psychiatry and Psychiatric Research Unit, Region Zealand, Denmark. His research focuses on personality disorders, mentalizing, and psychotherapy treatment.

Jennifer Brooks is consultant clinical psychologist for Brain Injury Services, Partnerships in Care and has worked within neurobehavioral rehabilitation for ten years. She has delivered various conference papers on the assessment and treatment of challenging behavior after acquired brain injury and published clinical papers on risk assessment and rehabilitation approaches.

Adam J. Carter is a chartered and registered forensic psychologist with over 20 years' experience working in National Offender Management Service (NOMS) and Her

Majesty's Prison Service, predominantly in the assessment and treatment of sexual offending. Adam has a number of book chapters and journal articles published on the subject of the assessment and treatment of sexual offending, and is committed to improving practice in these areas. He received his Ph.D. from Leicester University in 2009 and is currently Head of Offence Specialism for Extremism Offending in Interventions Services, HMPPS UK.

Dave Checknita is a Ph.D. student in neuroscience at Uppsala University whose research examines how early life adversity associates with genetic and epigenetic factors to influence risk for mental disorders and antisocial behavior in adulthood.

Jason M. Cowell is a developmental psychologist (Ph.D. from the University of Minnesota). He is an associate professor of psychology at the University of Wisconsin at Green Bay, US. Dr. Cowell studies the development of moral cognition and behavior in young children across cultures.

Kevin Creeden, M.A., LMHC, is the Director of Assessment and Research at the Whitney Academy in East Freetown, MA. He has over 35 years of clinical experience treating children, adolescents, and their families, working extensively with sexually and physically aggressive youth. Over the past 25 years, his primary focus has been on issues of trauma and attachment difficulties, especially with regard to the neurological impact of trauma on behavior. He has authored articles and book chapters on the neuro-developmental impact of trauma on sexual behavior problems and sexual offending behavior. Mr. Creeden trains and consults nationally and internationally to youth service, community, mental health, and forensic service programs.

George Davis is a child and adolescent psychiatrist who currently serves as the Director of Psychiatry for the New Mexico Department of Children, Youth and Families. Dr. Davis previously served on faculty at the University of New Mexico School of Medicine as Residency Director, Division Director and Vice Chair of the Division of Child and Adolescent Psychiatry, and continues to teach and supervise there on a limited basis as adjunct faculty. In addition to the university and state service, Dr. Davis previously worked for five years at the Indian Health Service, providing care for several of the pueblos and tribal hospitals and clinics in New Mexico. He became a Fellow of the ChildTrauma Academy in 2011. His primary areas of interest are delinquency as an outcome of early neglect and abuse, extreme behavior disorders in young children, psychopharmacology, and systems of care for severely disabled and underserved populations.

Stéphane A. De Brito is a Birmingham Fellow in the School of Psychology at the University of Birmingham, UK. His research focuses on the social, cognitive, affective, and neurocognitive factors implicated in the development and persistence of antisocial and aggressive behavior. A second strand of his research examines those factors among youths who have experienced early adversity. A common goal across these two strands of research is to understand how environmental and individual factors interact throughout the lifespan to increase risks for poor outcomes or promote resilience.

Jean Decety is Irving B. Harris Distinguished Service Professor of Psychology and Psychiatry at the University of Chicago and the College. He is the director of the Child Neurosuite and the Social Cognitive Neuroscience Laboratory. He is a leading scholar on the social neuroscience of empathy, morality, and prosocial behavior. Dr. Decety is the co-founder of the *Society for Social Neuroscience*. He recently edited the *Oxford Handbook of Social Neuroscience* (2011), *Empathy from Bench to Bedside* (2012), *New Frontiers in Social Neuroscience* (2014), and *The Moral Brain – A Multidisciplinary Perspective* (2015).

Corine de Ruiter, Ph.D., is professor of Forensic Psychology at Maastricht University, the Netherlands. Her research interests include the relationship between mental disorders and violence, and the assessment and management of risk for future violence. She has authored more than 200 peer-reviewed publications and was one of the developers of the Structured Assessment of Protective Factors for violence risk (SAPROF). From 2009 to 2014, she served as Associate Editor of the *International Journal of Forensic Mental Health*. In 2015 she and Dr. Nancy Kaser-Boyd published *Forensic Psychological Assessment in Practice: Case Studies*. Her website is http://www.corinederuiter.eu.

John Matthew Fabian, PSY.D., J.D., ABPP, is a board-certified forensic and clinical psychologist and fellowship-trained clinical neuropsychologist. Dr. Fabian has a national practice specializing in criminal and civil forensic psychological and neuropsychological evaluations including competency to stand trial, insanity, death penalty litigation, sexually violent predator civil commitment, internet pornography/solicitation, and juvenile homicide, sentencing, and waiver cases. Dr. Fabian was formerly director of a state court psychiatric clinic, and he has worked and testified in adult and juvenile court psychiatric clinics, state forensic hospital, federal prison forensic psychiatric settings, and university medical school and VA Polytrauma center. In addition to teaching courses in forensic psychology, neuropsychology and the law, and violence risk assessment, he is published in law review, peer-reviewed, and bar journals. Dr. Fabian lectures at the University of Texas Dell Medical School Department of Psychiatry and the Department of Psychiatry at the University of Texas Health Sciences Center San Antonio.

Graeme Fairchild is senior lecturer in clinical psychology at the University of Southampton, UK. He did his Ph.D. in Neuroscience at the University of Newcastle and then moved to the University of Cambridge to carry out postdoctoral research on stress reactivity in adolescents with severe antisocial behavior. This led to a second project funded by the Wellcome Trust investigating brain structure and function in adolescents with conduct disorder using magnetic resonance imaging techniques. He was appointed as a lecturer in abnormal psychology at the University of Southampton in 2010 and became an associate professor in 2014. His research interests include the neurobiological basis of violence and antisocial behavior, sex differences in antisocial behavior, the impact of early adversity on brain development, and the cognitive neuroscience of emotion recognition and empathy.

Derek Farrell is a principal lecturer in psychology, and EMDR Therapy Europe accredited trainer and consultant, a chartered psychologist with the British Psychological Society, and an accredited psychotherapist with the British Association of Cognitive & Behavioural Psychotherapies (BABCP). He is currently president of the EMDR UK and Ireland Board, president of Trauma Aid Europe, co-vice president of EMDR Europe Board and chair of the EMDR Europe practice committee. He is involved in a number of humanitarian trauma capacity building projects in Pakistan, Turkey, India, Cambodia, Myanmar, Thailand, Indonesia, Lebanon, Poland, Palestine and Iraq. His

Ph.D. in psychology was researching survivor's experiences of sexual abuse perpetrated by clergy and consequently he has written several publications on this subject matter. In 2013, Derek was the recipient of the "David Servan Schreiber Award" for Outstanding Contribution to EMDR Therapy. In addition, Derek was also shortlisted for the prestigious *Times Higher Education Supplement* (TES) Awards (2017) for "International Impact" due to his humanitarian trauma capacity building work in Iraq with the Free Yezidi Foundation and the Jiyan Foundation for Torture and Human Rights.

Jeremy A. Feiger is a master of arts in psychological research candidate in the Department of Psychology at California State University, Long Beach, US. His research interests include investigating the neurocognitive factors – including brain injury – that contribute to aggressive and violent behaviors as well as mental illness.

Dawn Fisher is a chartered forensic and clinical psychologist and is head of psychology at St Andrews Healthcare Birmingham, UK. She has worked with offenders for over 30 years, and has written over 60 publications (book chapters, academic papers, and one book).

Jens Foell is a postdoctoral associate in Dr. Christopher Patrick's Clinical Neuroscience Laboratory at Florida State University. His expertise is in experimental clinical and cognitive neuroscience and his interests focus on brain processes and how they relate to personality traits and perception in differing modalities. He trained at Heidelberg University in Germany with eminent cognitive neuroscientist Dr. Herta Flor, where he collected data for his dissertation study – an award-winning fMRI investigation of the neural basis and amelioration of phantom limb pain in patients undergoing amputations. Topics of his publications include chronic pain treatment, psychopathy, externalizing, body perception, emotion processing, and borderline personality disorder, using a wide range of methods including neuroimaging, electrocortical measurements, virtual reality and augmented reality environments, fear conditioning, and body illusion experiments.

Nathalie M. G. Fontaine is an associate professor in the School of Criminology at the Université de Montréal. Her research focuses on the development and the prevention of antisocial behavior and related disorders using longitudinal and experimental designs.

Gianni G. Geraci graduated from California State University, Long Beach, US, with her master's degree in psychology. Presently, she conducts psychiatric and neurological evaluations of patients with severe mental illness who are participating in clinical trials. Her research interests aim to understand abnormal brain functioning in those with severe mental illness and that impact on subsequent aggression and/or criminal behavior.

Paul Gilbert, Ph.D., O.B.E., is the founder of Compassion-Focused Therapy and is world renowned for his work on depression, shame, and self-criticism. He is head of the mental health research unit at the University of Derby in the United Kingdom. Professor Gilbert is the author of *Mindful Compassion, The Compassionate Mind, Overcoming Depression*, and numerous other books and scholarly articles.

Steven M. Gillespie, Ph.D., is a lecturer in clinical psychology at the Institute of Psychology, Health and Society, University of Liverpool, UK. Before joining Liverpool in 2017 Steven worked as a lecturer in forensic psychology at Newcastle University and as a research fellow at the University of Birmingham. Steven has also worked as a research psychologist for the Lucy Faithfull Foundation, a UK-based charitable organization dedicated to preventing child sexual abuse. Steven uses laboratory-based methods, including eye tracking and tests of emotional face processing, to examine cognitive-affective functioning in psychopathic personality, and in men convicted of sexual and violent offenses. Steven's other research interests include female sexual offenders, Internet sexual offending, and the effectiveness of treatment given to sexual offenders.

Gene Griffin, J.D., Ph.D., is a clinical psychologist and attorney who works in the fields of child trauma, child welfare, children's mental health, and juvenile justice. He presently serves as the Director of Research for the ChildTrauma Academy. He retired in 2013 from Northwestern University's Feinberg School of Medicine in Chicago, where he was co-director of a project funded by the National Child Traumatic Stress Network. He was also the lead developer of the MacArthur Foundation Models for Change Action Network on Mental Health and Juvenile Justice's curriculum and was awarded the Network's 2012 Champion for Change award. Dr. Griffin has served as an expert witness and offered testimony to legislative bodies. As a clinician he was unit chief of adolescent, inpatient psychiatric units. He has also worked as an assistant public defender in Juvenile Court in Chicago.

Don Grubin is professor of forensic psychiatry at Newcastle University and (Hon) consultant forensic psychiatrist in the Northumberland, Tyne & Wear NHS Foundation Trust. He trained in psychiatry at the Institute of Psychiatry, and the Maudsley and Broadmoor Hospitals. He moved to Newcastle in 1994, and took up the Chair of Forensic Psychiatry in 1997. He has been psychiatric adviser to the English National Offender Management Service Sex Offender Treatment Programs and a member of the Ministry of Justice Correctional Services Accreditation Panel. He led the trials of sex offender polygraph testing that resulted in the introduction in England and Wales of mandatory testing for high-risk sex offenders on parole.

Stefan Gutwinski, M.D., Dr. med., is a consultant in the Department of Psychiatry and Psychotherapy, Charité Campus St. Hedwig Hospital, Berlin, Germany. He is head of the research group Psychotropic Substances. His main field of research is treatment and epidemiology of addiction.

Adrienne J. Heinz, Ph.D., is clinical research psychologist, Substance and Anxiety Intervention Laboratory, National Center for Posttraumatic Stress Disorder and Center for Innovation to Implementation, VA Palo Alto Health Care System. Dr. Heinz's research focuses on social and neurocognitive mechanisms that frustrate recovery from substance use disorders and post-traumatic stress and on improving existing evidence-based treatments for these conditions.

Andreas Heinz, M.D., Ph.D., is a full professor of psychiatry, Charité Universitätsmedizin Berlin, Germany. Director of the Department of Psychiatry and Psychotherapy, Charité Campus Mitte and Campus St. Hedwig Hospital, Berlin. His main field of research is transcultural psychiatry, etiology, treatment, and neurobiology of psychosis and addiction.

List of Contributors

Sheilagh Hodgins, Ph.D., F.R.S.C., is currently professor at the Département de Psychiatrie, Université de Montréal and the Institut Universitaire de Santé Mentale de Montréal, Canada, and the Department of Clinical Neuroscience at the Karolinska Institutet, Sweden. Professor Hodgins has been studying antisocial behavior for many decades. She has published numerous studies focusing on the development and etiology of persons with antisocial personality disorder, conduct disorder, and psychopathy, and antisocial and violent behavior of individuals who develop severe mental illness. Presently, she is working on prospective, longitudinal studies, in Canada and in Sweden, that aim to unravel the complex interplay between genetic and environmental factors that impact the developing brain to promote antisocial and aggressive behavior.

Björn Hofvander, Ph.D., is a senior lecturer at Lund University, Sweden and clinical psychologist. His research focuses on the developmental aspects and longitudinal outcomes of aggressive and antisocial behavior.

Stephanos Ioannou is an assistant professor of physiology at Alfaisal University, Saudi Arabia. He holds a B.Sc. in psychology, an M.Sc. in functional neuroimaging, and a Ph.D. in neuroscience from the University of Parma, Italy. His interests lie in the domain of brain and behavior, currently he is investigating cognitive development through the peripheral nervous system while most of his recent work has focused on the psychophysiology of emotions.

Dylan B. Jackson is an assistant professor in the Department of Criminal Justice at the University of Texas at San Antonio. His research focuses on the developmental precursors to antisocial and criminal behaviors, including factors related to child neuropsychological functioning and health.

Caroline Knight is Lead Consultant Clinical Neuropsychologist for Brain Injury Services, Partnerships in Care. She has over 20 years' experience working with people with neurological conditions and challenging behavior. Her research has contributed to the development of bespoke assessment tools in challenging behavior and neuropsychological assessment and which are recognized nationally and internationally.

Russell Kolts, Ph.D., is a professor of psychology at Eastern Washington University and is a licensed clinical psychologist. He has authored or co-authored numerous books and scholarly articles, including CFT Made Simple and The Compassionate Mind Guide to Managing Your Anger. An international expert on CFT, Kolts developed the True Strength manualized group treatment of anger based on CFT principles, which has been run in a US prison for the past several years.

Philip Lindner is a clinical psychologist and clinical neuroscientist, currently working as a post-doctoral researcher at the Department of Psychology at Stockholm University. His research focus is using diffusion tensor imaging to investigate how abnormalities of the white matter tracts that connect different regions of the brain are associated with antisocial behavior, common psychiatric comorbidities, psychopathy, and personality traits, particularly in women.

Ruth E. Mann is employed by Her Majesty's Prison and Probation Service, England and Wales. As Head of Evidence-Based Practice, she monitors and translates research literature and oversees research projects designed to improve criminal justice processes.

Previously Ruth managed the national strategy for the assessment and treatment of sexual offending in the prison and probation services. In 2010, Ruth received the BPS Division of Forensic Psychology Senior Award for her contribution to forensic psychology in the UK. Ruth has authored or co-authored over 70 scholarly publications on topics related to the treatment of sexual offending, program evaluations and large-scale studies of risk factors for crime.

Gabriel Marmolejo graduated with his Master of Social Work degree from California State University, Los Angeles. He currently works as an emergency response social worker for Child Protection Services.

Eamon J. McCrory is a clinical psychologist and a professor of developmental neuroscience and psychopathology in the Division of Psychology and Language Sciences at University College London. His research focuses on the impact of early adversity on development and the mechanisms underlying childhood resilience.

Heather L. McLernon graduated with her masters in 2015 from California State University, Long Beach. She currently works as a survey manager for the US Census Bureau. Her interests continue to lie in research and statistics.

Leon McRae was most recently a lecturer in criminal law and mental health law (criminal context) at the Dickson Poon School of Law, King's College London. His research interests are in mental health law, criminal law, criminal justice, and aspects of health care law. He is especially interested in legal and medical responses to psychopathy, and the application of exculpatory defenses in criminal courts. Between 2007 and 2010, he was principal investigator on an Economic and Social Research Council (ESRC)-funded study looking into the therapeutic, legal and relational consequences of treating criminal psychopaths in secure hospital settings under the Mental Health Act 1983.

Ian J. Mitchell is a senior lecturer in psychology at the University of Birmingham, UK. His research focuses on how cortical, limbic and subcortical systems interact to affect social and antisocial behavior.

Andreas Mokros graduated with a Diploma degree (German Master's equivalent) in psychology, an M.Sc. in investigative psychology, and a Ph.D. in psychology, from the universities of Bochum, Germany, Liverpool, UK, and Wuppertal, Germany, respectively. In 2013 he was appointed adjunct professor ("Privatdozent") of psychology at the University of Regensburg, Germany. He is currently Chair of Personality Psychology, Assessment, and Consulting, Department of Psychology, University of Hagen. His main research topics are: experimental assessment of disorders of sexual preference using attentional methods; etiology and assessment of psychopathy; assessment of sexual sadism; forensic risk evaluation; and quantitative methods.

Claire Nee is a reader in forensic psychology and Director of the International Centre for Research in Forensic Psychology, University of Portsmouth, UK. She holds a B.A. and a Ph.D. in applied psychology from University College, Cork, Ireland. Her research interests lie in the development of criminality in children and in the offender's perspective of their cognition, emotion, and behavior leading up to, during, and after the criminal act. She has spent most of her academic career focusing on acquisitive offenders, particularly burglars.

List of Contributors

Ben Nordstrom is a diplomate of the American Board of Psychiatry and Neurology and is board certified in both psychiatry and addiction psychiatry. He received his degree from Dartmouth Medical School and his Ph.D. in criminology from the University of Pennsylvania. He completed his training in psychiatry at the Columbia University Medical Center/New York State Psychiatric Institute where he was selected to be Chief Resident. Following his general training, Ben stayed at Columbia and completed a research and clinical fellowship in addiction psychiatry. He is currently an assistant professor of psychiatry at the Geisel School of Medicine at Dartmouth and the Director of Addiction Services and the Director of the Addiction Psychiatry Fellowship at Dartmouth-Hitchcock Medical Center.

James M. Nye is a doctoral candidate working under the mentorship of Jennifer M. C. Vendemia at the University of South Carolina, US. James's research on deception considers theories of cognitive psychology and language comprehension in order to examine the processes of planning and performing deceptive behavior.

Christopher J. Patrick is a professor of clinical psychology at Florida State University, US. His scholarly interests include psychopathy, antisocial behavior, substance abuse, personality, fear and fearlessness, psychophysiology, and affective and cognitive neuroscience. He is author of more than 220 articles and book chapters, and editor of the *Handbook of Psychopathy* (Guilford Press, 2006; 2nd ed. in press). He served in 2010 as a Workgroup Member for the National Institute of Mental Health's Research Diagnostic Criteria (RDoC) initiative, and from 2008 to 2013 as a scientific advisor to the DSM-5 Personality and Personality Disorders (PPD) Work Group. A recipient of Early Career awards from the American Psychological Association (APA; 1993) and the Society for Psychophysiological Research (SPR; 1995) and a Lifetime Career Contribution award from the Society for Scientific Study of Psychopathy (SSSP; 2013), Dr. Patrick is a past president of both SPR and SSSP, and a fellow of APA and the Association for Psychological Science.

Bruce D. Perry is the senior fellow of The ChildTrauma Academy, a not-for-profit organization based in Houston, TX and adjunct professor in the Department of Psychiatry and Behavioral Sciences at the Feinberg School of Medicine at Northwestern University in Chicago. Dr. Perry served as the Trammell Research Professor of Child Psychiatry at Baylor College of Medicine in Houston, Texas. During this time, Dr. Perry also was Chief of Psychiatry for Texas Children's Hospital and Vice-Chairman for Research within the Department of Psychiatry. Dr. Perry has conducted both basic neuroscience and clinical research. This work has examined the cognitive, behavioral, emotional, social, and physiological effects of neglect and trauma in children, adolescents and adults. This work has been instrumental in describing how childhood experiences, including neglect and traumatic stress, change the biology of the brain – and, thereby, the health of the child.

Jay A. Perry, J.D., is an attorney specializing in criminal defense. He is based in Chattanooga, Tennessee. He is a graduate of Sewanee (B.S) and the University of Colorado School of Law. Among his areas of interest and expertise are juvenile justice and child welfare law.

Robert D. Perry, B.S., is a graduate of the University of North Carolina-Chapel Hill (biology and psychology). He served as a Robin Fancourt Research Intern at The

ChildTrauma Academy in Houston, Texas where he is examined the role of relational health in buffering the adverse effects of traumatic experiences.

Jessica Pykett is a senior lecturer in human geography at the University of Birmingham. Her research interests are in social and political geography, including citizenship, governance, education, behavior change, welfare, and wellbeing. Her recent books on the role of the behavioral sciences, psychology and neurosciences in policy and practice include *Emotional States: Sites and Spaces of Affective Governance*, edited with Eleanor Jupp and Fiona Smith (2017, Routledge); *Brain Culture: Shaping Policy through Neuroscience* (2015, Policy Press); and *Changing Behaviors: On the Rise of the Psychological State*, with Rhys Jones and Mark Whitehead (2013, Edward Elgar Publishing).

Adrian Raine is visiting professor in the Department of Psychology at Nanyang Technological University, and the Richard Perry University Professor of Criminology, Psychiatry, and Psychology at the University of Pennsylvania. He gained his undergraduate degree in experimental psychology at the University of Oxford, and his Ph.D. in psychology from the University of York. His interdisciplinary research focuses on the etiology and prevention of antisocial, violent, and psychopathic behavior in children and adults. He has published 375 journal articles and book chapters, 7 books, and given 335 invited presentations in 26 countries. His latest book, *The Anatomy of Violence* (2013, Pantheon and Penguin), reviews the brain basis to violence and draws future implications for the punishment, prediction, and prevention of offending, as well as the neuroethical concerns surrounding this work. He is past-president of the Academy of Experimental Criminology, and received an honorary degree from the University of York (UK) in 2015.

Renate L. E. P. Reniers is a lecturer in Psychiatry at the University of Birmingham, UK. She is a research psychologist investigating the interplay between neurobiological, clinical, and behavioral aspects of adolescent development and youth mental health.

Pia Rotshtein is a lecturer at the School of Psychology, University of Birmingham, UK. She has authored over 70 peer-reviewed publications. Her research interest focuses on understanding the neuroscience of complex behaviors and cognition, such as those involved in social cognition and emotional processing.

Boris Schiffer, Ph.D., is currently professor of forensic psychiatry at LWL-University Hospital Bochum, Department of Psychiatry and Psychotherapy, University Bochum, Germany and Executive Clinical Director of the LWL-Hospital of Forensic Psychiatry, Herne, Germany. Professor Schiffer has been studying antisocial behavior for many years. He has published studies focusing on the neural correlates of pedophilia and child sexual abuse as well as antisocial and violent behavior in people with conduct disorder and antisocial personality disorder, substance use disorders and schizophrenia. Presently, he is working on cross sectional brain imaging studies, that aim to disentangle alterations in social brain functioning as well as the psychobiological stress regulation in men with antisocial personality disorder or substance use disorders.

Robert A. Schug is an associate professor of criminology, criminal justice, and forensic psychology. Dr. Schug's area of specialization is the biology and psychology of the criminal mind. His research interests are predominantly focused upon understanding the relationship between extreme forms of psychopathology and antisocial, criminal, and violent behavior from a bio-psycho-social perspective – with the application of advanced neuroscience techniques from areas such as neuropsychology, psycho-physiology, and brain imaging. He is particularly interested in the etiological mechanisms, risk factors, and developmental progression of antisocial behavior within major mental disorders such as psychopathy and schizophrenia, as well as the ability to predict antisocial behavioral outcomes within mentally ill individuals. It is his hope that a better understanding of the relationship between these disorders and antisociality will have important implications in research, treatment, and forensic arenas; and will help to reduce the negative stigma often associated with mentally ill individuals who are not criminal or violent, while contributing to more effective treatment and management strategies for those who are.

Catherine L. Sebastian is a reader in psychology at Royal Holloway University of London, UK. Her research focuses on the development of emotion processing and regulation in adolescence, using techniques from developmental psychology and cognitive neuroscience. Her particular interest is in mechanisms underpinning aggressive behaviour.

Areti Smaragdi is a Ph.D. student in developmental cognitive neuroscience at the University of Southampton, UK. She did her masters in cognitive neuroscience at the University of York, UK where she became familiar with several different neuroimaging methods. Her research interests include sex differences in antisocial behavior, the neurobiological basis of different types of aggression, and the relationship between antisocial behavior and psychopathy.

Jennifer M. C. Vendemia is an associate professor of psychology at the University of South Carolina and is Director of the Center for Advanced Technologies for Deception Detection, US. Her current research follows multiple threads which interweave deceptive behaviors, executive functions, memory, and emotional processes. Because deception represents a complex social behavior that recruits multiple regions of the brain, Dr. Vendemia's research examines how these distinct components are integrated together in order to bring about deceptive behavior.

Essi Viding is a professor of developmental psychopathology in the Division of Psychology and Language Sciences at University College London. Her research is combining cognitive experimental measures, twin model-fitting, brain imaging, and genotyping to study different developmental pathways to persistent antisocial behavior.

Tony Ward received his Ph.D. and trained as a clinical psychologist at Canterbury University, Christchurch, New Zealand. Tony was the former Director of the Kia Marama Sexual Offenders' Unit at Rolleston Prison in New Zealand and has taught clinical and forensic psychology at Victoria, Deakin, Canterbury, and Melbourne Universities. Tony is currently Professor of Clinical Psychology at Victoria University of Wellington, New Zealand. He is particularly interested in the critique and generation of theory within forensic and correctional psychology as well as the examination of ethical constructs in practice.

Kristen Willeumier, Ph.D., is the Director of Research at the Amen Clinics. She conducted her graduate research in neurophysiology at the University of California, Los Angeles and in Neurogenetics at Cedars-Sinai Medical Center using live cell imaging to investigate mechanisms of synaptic signaling in Parkinson's disease. She received

M.Sc. degrees in physiological science and neurobiology and a Ph.D. degree in neurobiology from the University of California, Los Angeles. She was a postdoctoral fellow in the Department of Neurology at Cedars-Sinai Medical Center where she continued her work in the field of neurodegenerative disease. She was the recipient of an NIH fellowship from the National Institute of Mental Health to study the molecular mechanisms underlying Parkinson's disease and has presented her work at national and international scientific meetings including the Society for Neuroscience, Gordon Conference and the World Brain Mapping Conference. Dr. Willeumier's published scientific articles have appeared in the Journal of Neuroscience, the Journal of Alzheimer's Disease, Brain Imaging and Behavior, Nature's Obesity, and the Archives of Clinical Psychiatry, among many others.

Fiona Williams is a chartered and registered forensic psychologist and is the Head of Interventions Services in HM Prison and Probation Service. She is responsible for the design, development, training, and quality assurance of offending behavior treatment programmes and services delivered across custody and in the community. Fiona has over 25 years' experience in the assessment and development of offending behavior programmes and has particular expertise in working with learning disabled offenders.

Carolyn E. Wilshire received her Ph.D. From the University of Cambridge in the area of neuropsychology. She is currently a senior lecturer in cognitive neuropsychology in the School of Psychology at Victoria University of Wellington, New Zealand. Carolyn's research primarily focuses on examining language in special populations, such as dyslexia and aphasia. She is also interested in the application of this understanding to the diagnosis and treatment of language disorders. Carolyn is currently working on a project examining the nature of explanation in psychopathology and neurology.

Professor Stephen J. Wood is associate director of research, and Head of Clinical Translational Neuroscience at Orygen, the National Centre of Excellence in Youth Mental Health; and at the Centre for Youth Mental Health, University of Melbourne, Australia. He explores the clinical, cognitive, and neurobiological predictors of severe mental illness in young people.

The unnumbered images in this book have been selected by the editors who take full responsibility for their content and also thank their students Safa Kaptan and Yang Pu who helped in selecting and organizing the images.

Part IV
Neurobiological Bases to Risk Factors for Offending

18

Genetic Contributions to the Development of Psychopathic Traits and Antisocial Behavior in Youths

Nathalie M. G. Fontaine, Eamon J. McCrory, and Essi Viding

> **Key points**
>
> - This chapter provides an overview of recent twin and molecular genetic studies that have the potential to inform a model of developmental vulnerability to adult psychopathy and offending.
> - It is noted that studies examining callous-unemotional traits (e.g., lack of empathy, shallow emotions) in youths are of particular interest, given that these traits have been found to be associated with severe and persistent antisocial behavior and adult psychopathy.
> - Existing studies suggest that youths with high levels of callous-unemotional traits are genetically vulnerable to developing psychopathic and antisocial behavior.
> - Genetic factors appear to be important in explaining the stability of callous-unemotional traits across development, possibly more so in boys than in girls.
> - There is also evidence indicating that environmental influences can drive change in callous-unemotional traits.
> - It is argued that a better understanding of the specific mechanistic pathways from genetic vulnerability to behavioral outcomes has the potential to shed light on effective interventions and inform policy in the future.

The Wiley Blackwell Handbook of Forensic Neuroscience, First Edition. Edited by Anthony R. Beech, Adam J. Carter, Ruth E. Mann and Pia Rotshtein.
© 2018 John Wiley & Sons Ltd. Published 2018 by John Wiley & Sons Ltd.

Terminology Explained

Those that exhibit **antisocial behaviors** break rules or transgress social conventions, threaten/intimidate others, cause injury to others and/or damage property. Such behaviors can be categorized as premeditated or impulsive/reactive.

Callous-unemotional traits are distinguished by a persistent pattern of behavior that reflects a disregard for others, and also a lack of empathy and generally deficient affect (empathetic responding). The interplay between genetic and environmental risk factors may play a role in the expression of these traits as conduct disorder (CD).

Conduct disorder (CD) is the term given to a repetitive, and persistent, pattern of behavior in childhood in which the basic rights of others or societal conventions are violated. Children with CD often show antisocial personality disorder (ASPD) as adults.

Genetic and environmental contributions can be assessed by using a twin study design to decompose variance to "A" = additive genetic influences; "C" = shared environmental influences that impact the family members in a same way; "E" = environmental risk factors unique to the individual.

Genome-wide association is a technique that searches complete sets of genes of a number of people to identify common genetic variations.

H^2_g refers to group heritability, h^2 is individual differences in heritability.

A **phenotype** results from the expression of an organism's genes as well as the influence of environmental factors and the interactions between the two.

Limited pro-social emotions specifier is a specific indicator for CD. The fifth edition of the *Diagnostic and Statistical Manual of Mental Disorders* (*DSM-5*)(American Psychiatric Association, 2013, pp. 470–471) provides the following definition: "to qualify … an individual must have displayed at least two of the following (over the last 12 months) … lack of remorse/guilt … callous lack of empathy … unconcerned about performance … shallow/deficient affect."

Psychopaths' personality characteristics can be broadly described as the following: criminally minded; glib/superficially charming; manipulative; having a lack of remorse or guilt/conscience; pathological liars; having a lack of emotional depth; being irresponsible and impulsiveness; being sexually promiscuous; and having a history of childhood (antisocial) problems.

The Twins Early Development Study (**TEDS**) examines how an individual's genes and the environment they experience shape who that individual becomes, through the lifespan.[1]

Introduction

Antisocial behavior is associated with substantial social and economic costs. Individuals with psychopathic traits are particularly prone to violent behavior, which can cause severe harm and significant emotional distress. Most of these individuals started to get involved in antisocial behavior early in life, which has led several researchers to extend the study of psychopathic traits to youths (Frick & Viding, 2009). Notwithstanding certain qualms about describing children and adolescents as having psychopathic traits (Salekin, 2006), several regard research in this field as a necessary step if we are to shed light on the vulnerabilities associated with severe and persistent antisocial behavior in adulthood and develop more effective prevention and intervention strategies (Frick & Viding, 2009; Lynam, Caspi, Moffit, Loeber, & Stouthamer-Loeber, 2007).

Psychopathic traits in youths and adults encompass affective (e.g., lack of empathy, lack of guilt, shallow emotions) and interpersonal deficits (e.g., superficial charm) as well as overt impulsive, irresponsible, and antisocial behavior (Cooke, Michie, & Hart, 2006; Frick & Viding, 2009). The affective dimension, often termed as callous-unemotional traits, has been posited as the central feature of psychopathy (Cleckley, 1976; Frick & Viding, 2009). Callous-unemotional traits can distinguish a subgroup of youths with conduct problems who show a more severe and stable pattern of antisocial behavior (Viding, Fontaine, & McCrory, 2012). Given the evidence for a distinctive subgroup of youths with callous-unemotional traits, the fifth edition of the *Diagnostic Statistical Manual of Mental Disorders* (*DSM-5*) (American Psychiatric Association, 2013) now includes callous-unemotional traits as a specific indicator of conduct disorder (CD), denoted as the *limited pro-social emotions specifier*.

Youths with antisocial behavior and callous-unemotional traits are disposed to pre-meditated violent behavior and are at an elevated risk for developing psychopathy in adulthood (Frick & Viding, 2009; Lynam et al., 2007). Longitudinal research suggests that youths showing antisocial behavior with callous-unemotional traits have a more severe behavioral profile and more long-term adjustment problems than youths who have antisocial behavior with lower levels of callous-unemotional traits (Fontaine, McCrory, Boivin, Moffitt, & Viding, 2011; Frick & Viding, 2009). In addition, youths showing antisocial behavior with callous-unemotional traits appear resistant to some forms of traditional interventions prescribed for antisocial behavior, such as time-out disciplinary strategies (Hawes & Dadds, 2005). They also appear emotionally under-reactive, particularly to others' distress, whereas youths showing antisocial behavior without callous-unemotional traits may be emotionally over-reactive, particularly to perceived threat (Jones, Laurens, Herba, Barker, & Viding, 2009; Marsh et al., 2008; Sebastian et al., 2012; Viding, Sebastian et al., 2012).

Theoretical explanations of antisocial behavior combined with callous-unemotional traits propose that socialization processes are disturbed in these youths because they do not form adequate associations between their wrongdoings and punishment consequences, they have a fearless temperament and they do not find others' distress aversive, and consequently have problems developing empathy (Blair, Peschardt, Budhani, Mitchell, & Pine, 2006; Frick & Viding, 2009). This affective profile is different than the one usually found for youths showing antisocial behavior without callous-unemotional traits, who are often hypervigilant to threat emotions and appear capable of empathy (Frick & Viding, 2009; Jones, Happé, Gilbert, Burnett, & Viding, 2010; Schwenck et al., 2012; Viding, Sebastian et al., 2012).

Research also suggests that youths with callous-unemotional traits may be genetically vulnerable to antisocial behavior, whereas the etiology of antisocial behavior in youths without high levels of callous-unemotional traits may be primarily environmental (Viding, Fontaine et al., 2012).[2] Taking genetic information into consideration adds an important level of analysis when examining callous-unemotional/psychopathic traits as a potential risk factor for persistent antisocial behavior. Genetic information can be useful to differentiate homogenous groups of youths with antisocial behavior. Such research has scope to be informative not just about genetic risk, but also about the nature of the environmental risk associated with callous-unemotional/psychopathic traits and antisocial behavior. Genetically informative studies of youths on callous-unemotional/psychopathic traits and antisocial behavior also have a great potential to provide relevant knowledge for prevention and treatment.

In this chapter, we review the current research on the genetic contributions to the development of callous-unemotional/psychopathic traits and antisocial behavior in youths. In addition, we address environmental risk factors in the context of genetically informative studies. The review concentrates on twin studies, given that they have led the genetic research within this area. First, we will review twin research on the etiology of callous-unemotional/psychopathic traits. Second, we will briefly and selectively review molecular genetic studies on the topic. Finally, we will address the implications for intervention strategies and policy making.

Etiology of Callous-Unemotional/Psychopathic Traits from Twin Studies

Genetic and environmental contributions

A number of twin studies have examined the etiology of callous-unemotional/ psychopathic traits in youths. The current review focuses more specifically on genetically informative data on callous-unemotional traits or antisocial behavior with callous-unemotional traits, as callous-unemotional traits represent the core affective features of psychopathy (Cleckley, 1976; Frick & Viding, 2009). The studies are based on samples of youths from the USA, Sweden, and the UK. The samples used in these studies vary in size from moderate (398 twin pairs) to large (more than 3,500 twin pairs), encompass different age groups (7–24 years old), and have used a range of measures of callous-unemotional traits that have relied on both self and other (parent or teacher) ratings. Table 18.1 presents a summary of these studies.

Twin studies estimate heritability (genetic contributions) by assessing the degree to which identical twins (who share 100% of their polymorphic genes) compared with non-identical twins (who on average share 50% of their polymorphic genes) are similar to each other. Heritability is inferred when a greater resemblance on a trait or behavior is observed between identical twins than between non-identical twins. Findings from extant studies, which were conducted across different countries, different age groups, and using different measures of callous-unemotional traits, are remarkably consistent. These studies show moderate to strong heritability of callous-unemotional traits in youths, with estimates indicating that 40–78% of the variation in callous-unemotional traits across the population was due to genetic contributions (e.g., Bezdjian, Raine, Baker, & Lynam, 2011; Blonigen, Hicks, Krueger, Patrick, & Iacono, 2005, 2006; Fontaine, Rijsdijk, McCrory, & Viding, 2010; Larsson, Andershed, & Lichtenstein, 2006; Taylor, Loney, Bobadilla, Iacono, & McGue, 2003; Viding, Frick, & Plomin, 2007). Data from the TEDS also have indicated that high levels of

Table 18.1 Summary of twin studies on callous-unemotional traits/antisocial behavior in youths

Sample	Authors	N youths (sex)	Age (years) at assessment	Measure of callous-unemotional Traits	Key findings[1]
Minnesota Twin Family Study	Taylor et al. (2003)	398 pairs (all males)	16–18	Items from the Minnesota Temperament Inventory (self-reports)	– Genetic contributions: 42% of the variance in callous-unemotional traits – Non-shared environmental contributions: 58% of the variance in callous-unemotional traits – High genetic correlation between callous-unemotional traits and antisocial behavior ($r_g = 0.74$)
	Blonigen et al. (2005)	626 pairs (46% males)	17	Items from the Multidimensional Personality Questionnaire (self-reports)	– Genetic contributions: 45% of the variance in callous-unemotional traits – Non-shared environmental contributions: 55% of the variance in callous-unemotional traits – Modest genetic overlap between callous-unemotional traits and externalizing behavior ($r_g = 0.16$)
	Blonigen et al. (2006)	626 pairs (46% males)	2 time points: 17 and 24	Items from the Multidimensional Personality Questionnaire (self-reports)	– Genetic contributions: 48% and 42% of the variance in callous-unemotional traits at 17 and 24 years old, respectively – Non-shared environmental contributions: 52% and 58% of the variance in callous-unemotional traits at 17 and 24 years old, respectively – Stability of callous-unemotional traits influenced by genetic factors (58% of the variance)

(*continued*)

Table 18.1 (*Continued*)

Sample	Authors	N youths (sex)	Age (years) at assessment	Measure of callous-unemotional Traits	Key findings[1]
Southern California Twin Project	Bezdjian, Raine et al. (2011)	605 pairs (49% males)	9–10	Child Psychopathy Scale (caregiver reports)	– Genetic contributions: 64% and 49% of the variance in callous-unemotional traits, for males and females, respectively – Non-shared environmental contributions: 36% and 44% of the variance in callous-unemotional traits, for males and females, respectively
	Bezdjian, Tuvblad et al. (2011)	605 pairs (49% males)	9–10	Child Psychopathy Scale (caregiver reports and self-reports)	– Important genetic overlap between callous-unemotional traits and aggression, especially between self-reported callous-unemotional traits and proactive aggression ($r_g = 0.76$)
Swedish Twin Study of Child and Adolescent Development	Larsson et al. (2006)	1,090 pairs (48% males)	16–17	Youth Psychopathic Traits Inventory (self-reports)	– Genetic contributions: 43% of the variance in callous-unemotional traits – Non-shared environmental contributions: 57% of the variance in callous-unemotional traits
	Larsson et al. (2007)	2,387 twins (48% males)	2 time points: 13–14 and 16–17	Youth Psychopathic Traits Inventory (self-reports)	– Genetic overlap between psychopathic dimensions (including callous-unemotional traits) and antisocial behavior – Shared environmental contributions to antisocial behavior, but not psychopathic dimensions

	Forsman et al. (2007)	Over 2,000 twins (about 50% males)	3 time points: 8–9, 13–14, and 16–17	Youth Psychopathic Traits Inventory (self-reports)	– Genetic contributions explained the longitudinal association between externalizing behavior and psychopathic traits in boys
	Forsman et al. (2008)	1,467 twins (40% males)	2 time points: 16 and 19	Youth Psychopathic Traits Inventory (self-reports)	– Test-retest correlation of the higher order psychopathic traits factor was high ($r = 0.60$), and as much as 90% of the test-retest correlation was explained by genetic factors – Evidence for specific genetic stability of callous-unemotional traits
	Forsman et al. (2010)	2,255 twins (48% males)	4 time points: 8–9, 13–14, 16–17, and 19–20	Youth Psychopathic Traits Inventory (self-reports)	– Psychopathic traits (including callous-unemotional traits) in adolescence predicted antisocial behavior in early adulthood – Genetic contributions explained the association between psychopathic traits in adolescence and antisocial behavior in adulthood – Genetic contributions explained the association between persistent antisocial behavior (from childhood to adolescence) and psychopathic traits in adulthood
Twins Early Development Study	Viding et al. (2005)	3,687 pairs (about 50% males)	7	Items from the Antisocial Process Screening Device (callous-unemotional traits) and the Strengths and Difficulties Questionnaire (teacher reports)	– High group heritability of callous-unemotional traits ($h^2_g = 0.67$) – Antisocial behavior in children with high levels of callous-unemotional traits was under strong genetic influence ($h^2_g = 0.81$) and no influence of shared environment – Antisocial behavior in children with low levels of callous-unemotional traits showed moderate genetic ($h^2_g = 0.30$) and shared environmental contributions ($c^2_g = 0.34$)

(*continued*)

Table 18.1 (*Continued*)

Sample	Authors	N youths (sex)	Age (years) at assessment	Measure of callous-unemotional Traits	Key findings[1]
	Viding et al. (2007)	3,434 pairs (about 50% males)	7	Items from the Antisocial Process Screening Device (callous-unemotional traits) and the Strengths and Difficulties Questionnaire (teacher reports)	– No qualitative sex differences – Quantitative sex differences: higher heritability of callous-unemotional traits for males (67%) compared to females (48%) – Substantial genetic overlap between callous-unemotional traits and antisocial behavior ($r_g = 0.57$ for boys and $r_g = 0.65$ for girls)
	Larsson et al. (2008)	4,430 twins (53% males)	7	Items from the Antisocial Process Screening Device (callous-unemotional traits) and the Strengths and Difficulties Questionnaire (teacher reports)	– The heritability estimates of elevated levels of callous-unemotional traits were high regardless of the presence of antisocial behavior ($h^2_g = 0.80$, for callous-unemotional traits with antisocial behavior; $h^2_g = 0.68$, for callous-unemotional traits without antisocial behavior)
	Viding et al. (2008)	1,865 pairs (about 50% males)	9	Items from the Antisocial Process Screening Device (callous-unemotional traits) and the Strengths and Difficulties Questionnaire (teacher reports)	– Replication of the finding of different heritability estimates for antisocial behavior with ($h^2_g = 0.75$) versus without ($h^2_g = 0.53$) high levels of callous-unemotional traits – The heritability difference was more pronounced in magnitude when controlling for hyperactive symptoms

Viding et al. (2009)	2,254 pairs, identical twins only (46% males)	2 time points: 7 and 12	Items from the Antisocial Process Screening Device (callous-unemotional traits) and the Strengths and Difficulties Questionnaire (parent and teacher reports)	–	Negative parental discipline was a non-shared environmental risk factor for conduct problems, but not for callous-unemotional traits
Fontaine et al. (2010)	9,462 twins (47% males)	3 time points: 7, 9 and 12	Items from the Antisocial Process Screening Device (callous-unemotional traits) and the Strengths and Difficulties Questionnaire (teacher reports)	– –	Trajectory modeling from the ages of 7 to 12 Quantitative sex differences: stable high callous-unemotional traits highly heritable for males (78%), but mainly driven by shared environmental contributions for females (75%)

Notes:

[1] Authors have occasionally used a different label than callous-unemotional traits, e.g., "detachment." Interested readers should consult the individual papers for further details on the specific labels used.

c^2_g = group shared environment (the degree of group differences due to shared environmental contributions).

h^2_g = group heritability (the degree of group differences due to genetic contributions).

r_g = genetic correlation (the degree of genetic overlap).

callous-unemotional traits (top 10%) are under important genetic influences ($h_g^2 = 0.67$) (Viding, Blair, Moffitt, & Plomin, 2005). High heritability has been found whether or not callous-unemotional traits were combined with ($h_g^2 = 0.80$) or without ($h_g^2 = 0.68$) high levels of antisocial behavior (Larsson, Viding, & Plomin, 2008).

Twin studies are also central for documenting the extent to which environmental factors contribute to the variation in callous-unemotional traits. Shared environment in twin studies refers to environmental experiences that make family members similar to one another, and is evident when non-identical twin similarity is greater than 50% that of identical twin resemblance (i.e., greater than expected by genetic relatedness alone). Non-shared environment refers to the unique environmental experiences that make family members dissimilar from one another, and is manifest when identical twins do not resemble each other by 100%, as expected by genetic relatedness. Shared environmental contributions for callous-unemotional traits were found in a small number of studies (Fontaine et al., 2010; Viding et al., 2007). Our longitudinal data suggest that such contributions may be particularly important for a small group of girls with stable and high levels of callous-unemotional traits (Fontaine et al., 2010; see below for greater detail).

Moreover, all studies have demonstrated that non-shared environmental contributions are particularly important to explain variation in callous-unemotional traits. These results do not suggest that family, school, or neighborhood environments are insignificant factors in relation to the development of callous-unemotional traits. Environmental factors, including the ones from the family context, can promote differences between members of the same family. For example, a parent could show less affection toward one twin compared to the other one, and this difference in parenting could differentially affect the development of callous-unemotional traits in each twin (this would correspond to non-shared environment in a twin model). Further research is much needed to understand better the specific environmental factors that can impact the development of callous-unemotional traits (Viding, Fontaine, Oliver, & Plomin, 2009; see below for a discussion of this). Still, it is important to note that the heritability and environmental estimates for callous-unemotional traits in youth samples are in line with estimates found in adult twin data on psychopathic traits (Blonigen, Carlson, Krueger, & Patrick, 2003).

Sex differences in the etiology of callous-unemotional traits

Although most of the research on callous-unemotional/psychopathic traits is largely based on male samples, there is little evidence suggesting that these traits are any less relevant to females than they are to males (Marsee, Silverthorn, & Frick, 2005). The prevalence of high levels of callous-unemotional/psychopathic traits is greater in males than in females, however, phenotypic analyses on risk factors associated with these traits have not revealed clear sex differences (Fontaine et al., 2011). Only a small number of twin studies to date (e.g., Bezdjian, Raine et al., 2011; Blonigen et al., 2006; Fontaine et al., 2010; Larsson et al., 2006; Viding et al., 2007) have explored potential sex differences in the etiology of callous-unemotional/psychopathic traits. Research has not revealed qualitative sex differences for callous-unemotional traits, which suggests that the same genetic and environmental factors influence phenotypic variation in callous-unemotional traits for males and females (Viding et al., 2007).

Research has found little evidence of quantitative sex differences (i.e., the same genetic and environmental factors influencing males and females to a different magnitude) for callous-unemotional traits (Blonigen et al., 2006; Larsson et al., 2006). Still, there is preliminary support for a higher heritability of callous-unemotional traits in males than in females (Bezdjian, Raine et al., 2011; Fontaine et al., 2010; Viding et al., 2007). For example, using data from 9,462 youths involved in the TEDS, Fontaine et al. (2010) found that following a trajectory of stable high callous-unemotional traits (between 7 and 12 years old) was under strong heritability ($h^2 = 0.78$) for males, whereas for females, stable high callous-unemotional traits were mainly driven by shared environmental contributions ($c^2 = 0.75$). Replication of this finding is needed considering the small number of youths who followed the trajectory of stable high callous-unemotional traits, especially females (less than 1% of the total sample).

The extant findings indicate that even if mean differences in callous-unemotional trait scores at the phenotypic level are observed between males and females, the same genetic and environmental contributions appear important to explain individual differences in callous-unemotional traits for both sexes. More specifically, research suggests that although the same genetic contributions are important for both sexes, these may have a greater influence on individual differences in callous-unemotional traits in males than in females. However, shared environmental factors appear important primarily for females. It could be that factors such as maltreatment or abuse impact the development of callous-unemotional traits particularly in females (Odgers, Reppucci, & Moretti, 2005). Negligible contributions of shared environmental factors do not mean that family, school or neighborhood environments are not relevant for the development of callous-unemotional traits in males. Rather, for males the environmental risk factors appear to increase differences between members of the same family (non-shared environment in a twin model). Additional investigations with measured environmental factors within twin designs are needed to explore this further. These studies could also provide evidence on the potential distinct etiology of heterogeneous groups of callous-unemotional traits, namely primary callous-unemotional traits, which may be particularly driven by genetic factors, and secondary callous-unemotional traits, which may be especially influenced by environmental factors such as childhood maltreatment (Fanti, Demetriou, & Kimonis, 2013; Kahn et al., 2013). After knowing more about the specific genetic and environmental contributions and how they operate for males and females, policy implications with regard to more targeted prevention and treatment strategies for at-risk males and females could be developed.

Contributions accounting for the stability and change in callous-unemotional traits

Few twin studies to date have investigated the genetic and environmental contributions accounting for the stability and change in callous-unemotional traits in youths. In one study, Forsman, Lichtenstein, Andershed, and Larsson (2008) assessed callous-unemotional traits (as well as impulsivity/irresponsible and grandiosity/manipulative dimensions) and investigated the genetic and environmental contributions to the stability of these traits between two time points (ages 16 and 19). Forsman and colleagues (2008) used a hierarchical model of psychopathic personality wherein a higher order general factor substantively explained the variation in the three psychopathic personality dimensions in mid- and late adolescence. They found a high test-retest correlation ($r = 0.60$) of the higher order psychopathic personality factor, and that as high as 90% of this correlation was explained by genetic influences. They also reported evidence for specific genetic stability in callous-unemotional traits, namely that a relatively important proportion of the unique genetic contributions in callous-unemotional traits at age 19 (13%) was shared with unique genetic contributions at age 16. This study therefore provides evidence for etiologic generality (together with other dimensions of psychopathic personality) and etiologic specificity for the stability of callous-unemotional traits between the ages of 16 and 19.

In another study, Blonigen et al. (2006) used data on callous-unemotional traits collected at two time points (i.e., when the twins were 17 and 24 years old) to examine the contributions of genetic and environmental factors on the continuity and change in these traits. They found that heritability of callous-unemotional traits remained constant across time and that 58% of the stability in callous-unemotional traits was due to genetic contributions. Their findings indicated that the stability in callous-unemotional traits was substantially influenced by genetic factors. Change in callous-unemotional traits over time, on the other hand, was influenced by greater non-shared environmental contributions.

As discussed earlier in this chapter, Fontaine et al. (2010) reported that stable high trajectory of callous-unemotional traits in youths (between 7 and 12 years) was strongly heritable in males ($h^2 = 0.78$), but not in females for which stable high callous-unemotional traits were substantially influenced by shared environmental contributions ($h^2 = 0.00$, $c^2 = 0.75$). This suggests that during childhood/early adolescence genetic influences may drive the stability of high levels of callous-unemotional traits for males in particular. Findings from this study also highlighted the malleability of callous-unemotional traits, namely that callous-unemotional traits could increase or decrease over time for some youths, instead of remaining at constant high or low levels. Analyses revealed that both genetic and environmental contributions accounted for increasing or decreasing levels of callous-unemotional traits. This may reflect interplay between environmental and genetic risk factors that could promote or inhibit the development of callous-unemotional traits, and therefore trajectories of increasing or decreasing callous-unemotional traits. The challenge for researchers and clinicians is to identify the key environmental factors associated with the development of callous-unemotional traits, which could be targeted in interventions aimed at reducing callous-unemotional traits and thereby reducing the risk for maladaptive outcomes such as severe and persistent antisocial behavior.

In sum, results from longitudinal twin studies suggest that the stability in callous-unemotional traits during childhood (in males particularly) and from adolescence to early adulthood is substantively driven by genetic contributions. Future longitudinal twin research should explore: 1) the genetic and environmental factors influencing callous-unemotional traits during the transition from childhood to adolescence; 2) how genetic and environmental factors influence different developmental trajectories for antisocial youths with or without callous-unemotional traits; and 3) developmental hypotheses about gene and environment interplays (e.g., different patterns of gene-environment correlations and gene–environment interactions) in the stability and change of callous-unemotional traits.

Twin studies *Twin studies examine how individuals' genes and the environment they experience shape who they become, through the lifespan. Data from a UK twin study, the Twins Early Development Study (TEDS), showed that children with high levels of callous-unemotional traits were highly likely to have conduct problems.*

Source: © Kangheungbo. Used under license from 699pic.

Overlap in the etiology of callous-unemotional traits and antisocial behavior

Research has shown overlap between callous-unemotional traits and antisocial behavior at the phenotypic level. Findings have highlighted the asymmetrical relationship between callous-unemotional traits and conduct problems in youths (Fontaine et al., 2011), which is in line with the literature on psychopathy/antisocial behavior in adulthood (Hart & Hare, 1997). Analyses using data from the TEDS showed that youths with high levels of callous-unemotional traits were highly likely to have conduct problems, whereas youths with high levels of conduct problems were only moderately likely to have high levels of callous-unemotional traits (Fontaine et al., 2011). Twin models have been used to explore the etiologic overlap between callous-unemotional traits and antisocial behavior. Multivariate genetic models are useful to estimate the magnitude of genetic/environmental correlations, which refers to the degree of overlap between genetic/environmental contributions on different traits or behaviors.

Multivariate twin studies to date have shown modest ($r_g = 0.16$) (Blonigen et al., 2005) but also moderate to high genetic correlations between callous-unemotional traits and antisocial behavior/aggression (range of $r_g = 0.41–0.76$) (Bezdjian, Tuvblad et al., 2011; Taylor et al., 2003; Viding et al., 2007) when co-variation is assessed in the whole sample. The genetic commonality may be slightly stronger at the extreme high end of both callous-unemotional traits and antisocial behavior distributions (Viding et al., 2007). Genetic overlap between callous-unemotional traits and different types of aggression has been reported. Bezdjian, Tuvblad, Raine, and Baker (2011) found that callous-unemotional traits shared genetic influences with both reactive and proactive aggression, and that the genetic correlation was particularly strong between self-reports of callous-unemotional traits and proactive aggression ($r_g = 0.76$).

A few studies using data from the Swedish Twin Study of Child and Adolescent Development focused on the genetic commonality between psychopathic traits and antisocial behavior. In one study, Larsson et al. (2007) examined the genetic overlap between three psychopathic dimensions (grandiose-manipulative, callous-unemotional traits, and impulsive-irresponsible dimensions) and antisocial behavior measured at 13–14 and 16–17 years old. They found that a common genetic factor loaded substantively on both psychopathic traits and antisocial behavior. In another study, Forsman, Larsson, Andershed, and Lichtenstein (2007) found that genetic factors explained the association between persistent externalizing behavior (from age 8–9 to age 13–14) and higher levels of psychopathic traits in adolescence (age 16–17) in boys. Finally, Forsman, Lichtenstein, Andershed, and Larsson (2010) reported that psychopathic traits in adolescence (age 16–17) predicted antisocial behavior in early adulthood (age 19–20), over and above pre-existing and concomitant levels of antisocial behavior. Genetic effects primarily explained the association between psychopathic traits in adolescence and antisocial behavior in adulthood. This therefore appears in line with a genetically influenced personality driven process, namely that individuals may be genetically predisposed to antisocial behavior because of their psychopathic personality.

Although research suggests that genetic factors are important in explaining the overlap between callous-unemotional traits and antisocial behavior, this does not seem to be the case for environmental factors. Only modest to moderate non-shared environmental correlations have been reported between callous-unemotional traits and antisocial behavior/aggression (e.g., Bezdjian, Tuvblad et al., 2011; Viding et al., 2007). This suggests that the child specific environmental contributions important for callous-unemotional traits are largely independent from those that contribute to the development of antisocial behavior/aggression. Using data from the TEDS, we conducted a longitudinal monozygotic twin difference study to examine whether or not negative parental discipline (e.g., shouting and harsh discipline) was a non-shared environmental factor for callous-unemotional traits and antisocial behavior in youths (Viding et al., 2009). We found a phenotypic association between negative parental discipline at age 7 and both callous-unemotional traits and antisocial behavior at age 12. However, negative parental discipline emerged as a non-shared environmental factor for antisocial behavior only. Stated in a different way, the members of the monozygotic twin pair who received more negative parental discipline at age 7 were also more likely to show antisocial behavior at age 12, even after taking into account the differences in the baseline levels of antisocial behavior. This was not the case of callous-unemotional traits. We proposed that the phenotypic association between negative parental discipline and callous-unemotional traits could reflect the genetic endowment within those families with youths displaying callous-unemotional traits, rather than an environmentally driven negative parenting process that increases the risk for callous-unemotional traits.

Etiology of antisocial behavior with and without callous-unemotional traits

Twin studies have also been useful in exploring the utility of callous-unemotional traits as a subtyping characteristic for youths with antisocial behavior. Viding et al. (2005) used data from the TEDS sample to investigate if the etiology of antisocial behavior varied as a function of callous-unemotional traits at age 7. Youths with elevated levels of antisocial behavior (top 10% for the TEDS sample) were separated into two groups according to their score of callous-unemotional traits (top 10% or not). Extreme levels of antisocial behavior in youths with callous-unemotional traits were under strong genetic influences ($h_g^2 = 0.81$) and no contribution of shared environment. On the other hand, extreme levels of antisocial behavior in youths without callous-unemotional traits were under important environmental influences, shared as well as non-shared, and only moderate genetic influences ($h_g^2 = 0.30$). Viding, Jones, Frick, Moffitt, and Plomin (2008) replicated the finding of different heritability estimates for antisocial behavior with or without callous-unemotional traits using the TEDS data when the twins were at the age of nine.

Molecular Genetic Studies and Callous-Unemotional Traits/Antisocial Behavior

In spite of the extensive research showing that callous-unemotional traits in youths are driven by genetic factors, only a handful of published candidate gene association studies have focused on callous-unemotional traits in children or adolescents and these studies have tentatively implicated variants in genes, in particular the serotonin and oxytocin genes (e.g., Beichtman et al., 2012; Fowler et al., 2009; Malik, Zai, Abu, Nowrouzi, & Beitchman, 2012; Moul, Dobson-Stone, Brennan, Hawes, & Dadds, 2013; see Table 18.2 for a list of molecular genetic studies).

The current candidate gene studies need to be replicated in larger samples to evaluate whether or not they report true, replicable associations. Picking candidate genes is not straightforward and can lead to unadjusted multiple testing. Because genetic risk may in many cases only "penetrate" in the presence of environmental risk, genetic studies should carefully document the environmental risk factors in their samples to increase interpretability of the findings and consequently, our understanding of how genetic risk translates to a disorder outcome. A recent study reported that the long allele of a serotonin transporter polymorphism, the allele reported to confer low amygdala reactivity, was associated with callous-unemotional traits in adolescents from low socioeconomic backgrounds, a finding which was observed in two independent community samples, both rural and urban (Sadeh et al., 2010). These findings suggest that genetic vulnerability to callous-unemotional traits may only express under unfavorable environmental conditions (e.g., low socioeconomic resources, maltreatment, or victimization).

Table 18.2 Summary of molecular genetic studies on callous-unemotional traits/antisocial behavior in youths

Sample	Authors	N youths (sex)	Age (years) at assessment	Measure of callous-unemotional traits	Key findings
Youths from a genetic study of ADHD	Fowler et al. (2009)	147 (93% males)	12–19	Psychopathy Checklist Youth Version (emotional dysfunction component)	– COMT val/val, 5-HTTLPRs, and MAOA-L genotypes associated with increased callous-unemotional traits in youths with ADHD
Study 1: Rural sample of youths recruited from treatment/legal agencies and from the community Study 2: Community sample from urban setting	Sadeh et al. (2010)	Study 1: 118 (42% males) Study 2: 178 (55% males)	Study 1: 14 Study 2: 11	Study 1: Antisocial Process Screening Device (self-reports) Study 2: Inventory of Callous-unemotional Traits (self-reports)	– Callous-unemotional traits increased as socioeconomic resources decreased among youths with the 5-HTTLPRl genotype in both study samples
Boys with antisocial behavior problems referred to clinics	Moul et al. (2013)	258 (100% males)	3–16	Items from the Antisocial Process Screening Device and the Strengths and Difficulties Questionnaire (parent reports)	– Functional single nucleotide polymorphisms from the serotonin 1b receptor gene (HTR1B) and 2a receptor gene (HTR2A) associated with callous-unemotional traits – Serum serotonin levels associated with callous-unemotional traits (levels were significantly lower in boys with high callous-unemotional traits than in boys with low callous-unemotional traits)
Youths with aggressive behavior recruited through referral from health/treatment centers	Beitchman et al. (2012)	162 (65% males; each youth was matched with a healthy adult control)	6–16	Psychopathy Screening Device (parent reports)	– OXTR_rs237885 AA genotype carriers scored higher than AC or CC genotype carriers on callous-unemotional traits – Haplotype consisting of the OXTR_rs237885 A allele and OXTR_rs2268493 A allele was associated with significantly higher callous-unemotional traits than other haplotypes

	Malik et al. (2012)	236 (69% males; 160 youths were matched with a healthy adult control)	6–16	Psychopathy Screening Device (parent reports)	– OXTR SNPs rs6770632 and rs1042778 may be associated with severe and persistent aggressive behavior in females and males, respectively – No significant differences were detected with respect to callous-unemotional traits
Youths from the Twins Early Development Study	Viding et al. (2010)	Stage 1: 600 (69% males); Stage 2: 586 (71% males)	7	Items from the Antisocial Process Screening Device (callous-unemotional traits) and the Strengths and Difficulties Questionnaire (teacher reports)	– Two-stage GWA study of pooled DNA (Stage 1, screening; Stage 2, test of the strongest associations based on Stage 1) – None of the associations reached genome-wide significance – Tentative hits near neurodevelopmental genes such as ROBO2
	Viding et al. (2013)	2,930 (about 46% males)	3 time points: 7, 9, and 12	Items from the Antisocial Process Screening Device (callous-unemotional traits) and the Strengths and Difficulties Questionnaire (teacher reports)	– New DNA method (Genome-wide Complex Trait Analysis; GCTA) and genome-wide association (GWA) analysis were used to examine the genetics of callous-unemotional traits in youths – No significant associations were found in the GWA analysis – GCTA estimates of heritability were near zero, despite that twin analysis of callous-unemotional traits in the sample confirmed the high heritability of callous-unemotional traits reported in previous studies

The association studies only considered a limited number of candidate genes. However, a growing number of genome-wide association (GWA) studies for psychiatric phenotypes have shown that genome-wide "hits" are often in genes not previously hypothesized to influence the phenotype or not in traditional genes at all (Visscher, Brown, McCarthy, & Yang, 2012). GWA studies systematically scan the genome with hundreds of thousands of DNA markers, made possible by DNA arrays. GWA studies of callous-unemotional traits suggest that much larger samples will be needed to detect novel associations that account for far less than 1% of the variance (Viding et al., 2010, 2013).

Methods to identify gene–gene and gene–environment interactions (that more than likely account for a proportion of the heritability estimate for callous-unemotional traits in youths) are also required, as is whole-genome sequencing to detect rare variants. Genetic research is likely to advance greatly in the coming decade, including studies using novel epigenetic approaches that may help uncover mechanisms of gene–environment interaction, but it is of critical importance to keep in mind that there are no genes for callous-unemotional traits. Genes code for proteins that influence characteristics such as neurocognitive vulnerabilities that may in turn increase risk for developing callous-unemotional traits. Genetic variants that are implicated as risk genes for callous-unemotional traits are likely to include several common polymorphisms that confer advantages, as well as disadvantages, depending on the environmental context. The neurocognitive vulnerabilities associated with callous-unemotional traits are at least partially distinct from those associated with conduct problems in general (e.g., Sebastian et al., 2012; Viding, Sebastian et al., 2012). This suggests that the risk alleles for callous-unemotional traits or conduct problems that co-occur with callous-unemotional traits may not always be the same as risk alleles for conduct problems in the absence of callous-unemotional traits.

Implications for Interventions and Policy Making

The extant studies suggest a degree of genetic vulnerability to callous-unemotional traits, as well as etiological differences between antisocial youths with or without callous-unemotional traits. Given distinct patterns of etiological vulnerability, youths with antisocial behavior and callous-unemotional traits may respond to interventions differently than youths with antisocial behavior without callous-unemotional traits. For example, there is evidence that youths with antisocial behavior and callous-unemotional traits have genetic vulnerability that may predispose them to altered development of emotion processing, reinforcement learning, and empathy, which could affect their response to treatment.

Few studies have provided data on how treatment outcome may vary in relation to a youth's levels of callous-unemotional traits and if different forms of intervention may be more or less effective in promoting change in youths with high callous-unemotional traits (e.g., Hawes & Dadds, 2005). However, there is preliminary evidence that young people with high levels of callous-unemotional traits benefit significantly from standard interventions (Caldwell, Skeem, Salekin, & van Ryoboek, 2006; Waller, Gardner, & Hyde, 2013). While they are likely to enter and finish treatment with more pronounced behavioral and social difficulties, they can show real improvements. For example, Kolko and Pardini (2010) found that a sample of clinic-referred children with conduct problems and high callous-unemotional traits who received a wide range of individualized and modular interventions (e.g., parent training, cognitive behavioral therapy, peer relationship development, medication for ADHD) improved at a similar rate to other children with conduct problems. More recently, White, Frick, Lawing, and Bauer (2013) have reported significant improvements in behavioral and emotional domains following an evaluation of functional family therapy delivered over three to five months (average of ten sessions) in adolescents with high levels of conduct problems and callous-unemotional traits.

Although some traditional treatments appear to work with youths who have conduct problems and high levels of callous-unemotional traits, these youths typically enter treatment with the most severe behavioral presentations and even after improvement following treatment often continue to present with ongoing problematic and concerning behaviors. More systematic research is required to pinpoint the specific components of existing treatments that work more or less effectively for these youths in order to optimize and improve current clinical practice. For example, new treatment modules focusing on specific areas of functioning known to be problematic in youths with high levels of callous-unemotional traits appear promising. In a recent randomized controlled trial by Dadds, Cauchi, Wimalaweera, Hawes, & Brennan (2012), treatment-as-usual (TAU) was evaluated with or without the adjunctive emotion recognition training (ERT), where the TAU comprised a fully manualized parent training program based on well-established parenting components. While ERT did not have an effect on the group as a whole, youths with higher levels of callous-unemotional traits (even those without a diagnosis of CD) showed more improvement in affective empathy and reduced conduct problems in response to ERT. Such preliminary findings provide a promising basis for future programs to incorporate tailored treatment strategies for youths with higher levels of callous-unemotional traits where specific components are added or removed from traditional treatment protocols.

When thinking about intervention for these youths more broadly, it may be helpful to bear in mind a number of important points. First, *genetic vulnerability does not signify immutability*. Levels of callous-unemotional traits can be malleable during childhood (Fontaine et al., 2011) and there are data showing that callous-unemotional traits can change in response to interventions that focus on rewarding good behavior (e.g., Hawes & Dadds, 2005). The current findings suggest, however, that understanding the nature of genetic vulnerability and how it may differ between individuals may provide important information for adapting interventions to individual needs. Second, *behavioral genetic studies suggest that environment may drive change*. Genetic risk associated with the development of callous-unemotional traits or antisocial behavior with callous-unemotional traits could be buffered by prevention and treatment, which could be considered as positive gene–environment interaction. For example, data suggest that warm parenting can reduce the risk for conduct problems in children with high levels of callous-unemotional traits (Pasalich, Dadds, Hawes, & Brennan, 2011). Treatments promoting positive child–parent interactions may therefore be helpful. Future research is needed to inform what environmental factors may exert maximal influence on the change of callous-unemotional traits in youths. These are likely to be behavioral and multisystemic interventions specifically tailored to the youths' characteristics (e.g., deficits in empathic arousal). Third, *gene therapy is not an appropriate form of intervention.* We sometimes hear concerns with regard to gene therapy, that is, insertion, alteration, or removal of genes within an individual's cells to treat disease. Such an approach does not appear to be a viable option for the treatment of complex, polygenic traits, such as antisocial behavior/callous-unemotional traits. This appears particularly important given that "risk" genes are usually common polymorphisms involved in a range of normative developmental processes. Moreover, these genes are hypothesized to confer only a small increase in probability of behavior problems. Although the current data suggest that there is genetic vulnerability for callous-unemotional traits, it is important to consider that there are no *genes* for callous-unemotional traits. Instead, it appears that genes act in a probabilistic manner and in concert with environmental factors to increase the vulnerability for developing callous-unemotional traits (see e.g., Moffitt, 2005).

Policy-making changes should proceed with extensive ethical consultation and issues such as discrimination, stigma, and labeling should be considered (see Singh & Rose, 2009). Research on genetic influences in relation to callous-unemotional traits in youths is still sparse and considerable replication and extension studies are required before any policy recommendations can be reliably based on the findings.

Conclusions

Several important findings were highlighted in this chapter: 1) callous-unemotional traits show heritable and non-shared environmental influences in youths; 2) the same genetic and environmental influences are accounting for individual differences in callous-unemotional traits for both males and females (although the magnitude of their influence may vary between sexes); 3) genetic factors account for stability of callous-unemotional traits across development; 4) genetic factors are important in explaining the covariance between callous-unemotional traits and antisocial behavior; 5) negative parental practices constitute a non-shared environmental risk factor for antisocial behavior, but maybe not for callous-unemotional traits; 6) different heritability estimates account for antisocial behavior with or without callous-unemotional traits; 7) research on molecular genetics in relation to callous-unemotional traits is limited, and although new technologies can help, challenges are likely to be encountered; 8) studies investigating gene-environment interplay with respect to callous-unemotional/psychopathic traits are needed; and 9) youths with antisocial behavior and callous-unemotional traits could respond to interventions in a different way than youths with antisocial behavior without callous-unemotional traits given distinct patterns of etiological vulnerability – more research is needed to identify the environmental components that may lead to substantial change in youth callous-unemotional traits.

Genetic research on callous-unemotional traits is promising, with several research groups in different countries focusing on this area. Many important questions remain, and addressing these questions effectively represents a challenge. Further advances in this field will help to understand better how early risk factors can be associated with the development of callous-unemotional traits in youths and psychopathy in adulthood. A better delineation of the specific mechanistic pathways from genetic vulnerability to behavioral outcome (both maladaptive and resilient) could inform interventions for at-risk youths and therefore inform policy making.

Notes

1 See http://www.teds.ac.uk/research.html.
2 There is growing empirical support for the presence of heterogeneous groups of individuals with callous-unemotional traits, more specifically primary callous-unemotional traits and secondary callous-unemotional traits (see Poythress & Skeem, 2006). Primary callous-unemotional traits are hypothesized to be associated with an inherent deficit that is expressed by an absence of conscience, lack of guilt, and no feeling or regard for others, whereas secondary callous-unemotional traits could develop as a result of childhood maltreatment, inconsistent and harsh discipline, family conflicts, and rejection. Data have provided evidence for the distinction between primary and secondary callous-unemotional traits in youth samples on the basis of anxiety, trauma, and other psychological difficulties (e.g., Fanti, Demetriou, & Kimonis, 2013; Kahn et al., 2013). Specific investigations with measured environmental factors (e.g., childhood maltreatment) within twin designs would be needed to explore further the potential distinct etiology of primary versus secondary callous-unemotional traits.

Recommended Reading

Blair, R. J. R, Peschardt, K. S., Budhani, S., Mitchell, D. G. V., & Pine, D. S. (2006). The development of psychopathy. *Journal of Child Psychology and Psychiatry, 47,* 262–275. *This review provides an account of the development of psychopathy at multiple levels, including molecular, neural, cognitive, and behavioral levels.*

Fontaine, N. M. G., Rijsdijk, F. V., McCrory, E. J. P., & Viding, E. (2010). Etiology of different developmental trajectories of callous-unemotional traits. *Journal of the American Academy of Child and Adolescent Psychiatry, 49,* 656–664. *This article, which relies on the analysis of twin data, suggests that the etiology of stable and high levels of callous-unemotional traits in childhood is under strong heritability in males, but is mainly driven by shared environmental contributions in females.*

Frick, P. J., & Viding, E. (2009). Antisocial behavior from a developmental psychopathology perspective. *Development and Psychopathology, 21,* 1111–1131. *This article provides an overview of research on different pathways through which youth can develop severe antisocial behavior, notably the group of youth displaying callous-unemotional traits.*

Moffitt, T. E. (2005). The new look of behavioral genetics in developmental psychopathology: Gene-environment interplay in antisocial behaviors. *Psychological Bulletin, 131,* 533–554. *This article reviews research on behavioral genetics and provides good illustrations on gene–environment interplay in the development of antisocial behavior, such as findings on genes and environments interaction.*

References

American Psychiatric Association. (2013). *Diagnostic and statistical manual of mental disorders* (5th ed.). Washington, DC: American Psychiatric Association.

Beitchman, J. H., Zai, C. C., Muir, K., Berall, L., Nowrouzi, B., Choi, E., & Kennedy, J. L. (2012). Childhood aggression, callous-unemotional traits and oxytocin genes. *European Child and Adolescent Psychiatry, 21,* 125–132.

Bezdjian, S., Raine, A., Baker, L. A., & Lynam, D. R. (2011). Psychopathic personality in children: Genetic and environmental contributions. *Psychological Medicine, 41,* 589–600.

Bezdjian, S., Tuvblad, C., Raine, A., Baker, L. A. (2011). The genetic and environmental covariation among psychopathic personality traits, and reaction and proactive aggression in childhood. *Child Development, 82*, 1267–1281.

Blair, R. J. R, Peschardt, K. S., Budhani, S., Mitchell, D. G. V., & Pine, D. S. (2006). The development of psychopathy. *Journal of Child Psychology and Psychiatry, 47*, 262–275.

Blonigen, D. M., Carlson, S. R., Krueger, R. F., & Patrick, C. J. (2003). A twin study of self-reported personality traits. *Personality and Individual Differences, 35*, 179–197.

Blonigen, D. M., Hicks, B. M., Krueger, R. F., Patrick, C. J., & Iacono, W. G. (2005). Psychopathic personality traits: Heritability and genetic overlap with internalizing and externalizing psychopathology. *Psychological Medicine, 35*, 637–648.

Blonigen, D. M., Hicks, B. M., Krueger, R. F., Patrick, C. J., & Iacono, W. G. (2006). Continuity and change in psychopathic traits as measured via normal-range personality: A longitudinal-biometric study. *Journal of Abnormal Psychology, 115*, 85–95.

Caldwell, M., Skeem, J., Salekin, R., & Van Ryoboek, G. (2006). Treatment response of adolescent offenders with psychopathy features: A two-year follow-up. *Criminal Justice and Behavior, 33*, 571–596.

Cleckley, H. (1976). *The mask of sanity: An attempt to clarify some issues about the so-called psychopathic personality* (5th ed.). St. Louis, MO: Mosby.

Cooke, D. J., Michie, C., & Hart, S. D. (2006). Facets of clinical psychopathy: Toward clearer measurement. In C. J. Christopher (Ed.), *Handbook of psychopathy* (pp. 91–106). New York, NY: Guilford Press.

Dadds, M. R., Cauchi, A. J., Wimalaweera, S., Hawes, D. J., & Brennan, J. (2012). Outcomes, moderators, and mediators of emphatic-emotion recognition training for complex conduct problems in childhood. *Psychiatric Research, 30*, 201–207.

Fanti, K. A., Demetriou, C. A., & Kimonis, E. R. (2013). Variants of callous-unemotional conduct problems in a community sample of adolescents. *Journal of Youth and Adolescence, 42*, 964–979.

Fontaine, N. M. G., McCrory, E. J. P., Boivin, M., Moffitt, T. E., & Viding, E. (2011). Predictors and outcomes of joint trajectories of callous-unemotional traits and conduct problems in childhood. *Journal of Abnormal Psychology, 120*, 730–742.

Fontaine, N. M. G., Rijsdijk, F. V., McCrory, E. J. P., & Viding, E. (2010). Etiology of different developmental trajectories of callous-unemotional traits. *Journal of the American Academy of Child and Adolescent Psychiatry, 49*, 656-664.

Forsman M., Larsson H., Andershed H., & Lichtenstein P. (2007). Persistent disruptive childhood behavior and psychopathic personality in adolescence: A twin study. *British Journal of Developmental Psychology, 25*, 383–398.

Forsman, M., Lichtenstein, P., Andershed, H., & Larsson, H. (2008). Genetic effects explain the stability of psychopathic personality from mid- to late adolescence. *Journal of Abnormal Psychology, 117*, 606–617.

Forsman, M., Lichtenstein, P., Andershed, H., & Larsson, H. (2010). A longitudinal twin study of the direction of effects between psychopathic personality and antisocial behaviour. *Journal of Child Psychology and Psychiatry, 51*, 39–47.

Fowler, T., Langley, K., Rice, F., van den Bree, M. B., Ross, K., Wilkinson, L. S., ... Thapar, A. (2009). Psychopathy trait scores in adolescents with childhood ADHD: The contribution of genotypes affecting MAOA, 5HTT and COMT activity. *Psychiatric Genetics, 19*, 312–319.

Frick, P. J., & Viding, E. (2009). Antisocial behavior from a developmental psychopathology perspective. *Development and Psychopathology, 21*, 1111–1131.

Hart, S. D., & Hare, R. D. (1997). Psychopathy: Assessment and association with criminal conduct. In D. M. Stoff, J. Breiling, & J. D. Maser (Eds.), *Handbook of antisocial behavior* (pp. 22–35). Hoboken, NJ: John Wiley & Sons.

Hawes, D. J., & Dadds, M. R. (2005). The treatment of conduct problems in children with callous-unemotional traits. *Journal of Consulting and Clinical Psychology, 73*, 737–741.

Jones, A. P., Happé, F. G., Gilbert, F., Burnett, S., & Viding, E. (2010). Feeling, caring, knowing: Different types of empathy deficit in boys with psychopathic tendencies and autism spectrum disorder. *Journal of Child Psychology and Psychiatry, 51*, 1188–1197.

Jones, A. P., Laurens, K. R., Herba, C. M., Barker, G. J., & Viding, E. (2009). Amygdala hypoactivity to fearful faces in boys with conduct problems and callous-unemotional traits. *American Journal of Psychiatry, 166*, 95–102.

Kahn, R. E., Frick, P. J., Youngstrom, E. A., Youngstrom, J. K., Feeny, N. C., & Findling, R. L. (2013). Distinguishing primary and secondary variants of callous-unemotional traits among adolescents in a clinic-referred sample. *Psychological Assessment, 25*, 966–978.

Kolko, D. J., & Pardini, D. A. (2010). ODD dimensions, ADHD, and callous-unemotional traits as predictors of treatment response in children with disruptive behavior disorders. *Journal of Abnormal Psychology, 119*, 713–725.

Larsson, H., Andershed, H., & Lichtenstein, P. (2006). A genetic factor explains most of the variation in the psychopathic personality. *Journal of Abnormal Psychology, 115*, 221–230.

Larsson, H., Tuvblad, C., Rijsdijk, F., Andershed, H., Grann, M., & Lichtenstein, P. (2007). A common genetic factor explains the association between psychopathic personality and antisocial behaviour. *Psychological Medicine, 37*, 15–26.

Larsson, H., Viding, E., & Plomin, R. (2008). Callous-unemotional traits and antisocial behavior. *Criminal Justice and Behavior, 35*, 197–211.

Lynam, D. R., Caspi, A., Moffitt, T. E., Loeber, R., & Stouthamer-Loeber, M. (2007). Longitudinal evidence that psychopathy scores in early adolescence predict adult psychopathy. *Journal of Abnormal Psychology, 116*, 155–165.

Malik, A. I., Zai, C. C., Abu, Z., Nowrouzi, B., & Beitchman, J. H. (2012). The role of oxytocin and oxytocin receptor gene variants in childhood-onset aggression. *Genes, Brain and Behavior, 11*, 545–551.

Marsee, M. A., Silverthorn, P., & Frick, P. J. (2005). The association of psychopathic traits with aggression and delinquency in non-referred boys and girls. *Behavioral Sciences and the Law, 23*, 803–817.

Marsh, A. A., Finger, E. C., Mitchell, D. G., Reid, M. E., Sims, C., Kosson, D. S., … Blair, R. J. (2008). Reduced amygdala response to fearful expressions in children and adolescents with callous-unemotional traits and disruptive behavior disorders. *American Journal of Psychiatry, 165*, 712–720.

Moffitt, T. E. (2005). The new look of behavioral genetics in developmental psychopathology: Gene–environment interplay in antisocial behaviors. *Psychological Bulletin, 131*, 533–554.

Moul, C., Dobson-Stone, C., Brennan, J., Hawes, D., & Dadds, M. (2013). An exploration of the serotonin system in antisocial boys with high levels of callous-unemotional traits. *PLoS ONE, 8*, 1–10.

Odgers, C. L., Reppucci, N. D., & Moretti, M. M. (2005). Nipping psychopathy in the bud: An examination of the convergent, predictive, and theoretical utility of the PCL-YV among adolescent girls. *Behavioral Sciences and the Law, 23*, 743–763.

Pasalich, D. S., Dadds, M. R., Hawes, D. I., & Brennan, J. (2011). Do callous-unemotional traits moderate the relative importance of parental coercion versus warmth in child conduct problems? An observational study. *Journal of Child Psychology and Psychiatry, 52*, 1308–1315.

Poythress, N. G., & Skeem, J. L. (2006). Disaggregating psychopathy: Where and how to look for subtypes. In C. J. Christopher (Ed.), *Handbook of psychopathy* (pp. 172–192). New York, NY: The Guilford Press.

Sadeh, N., Javdani, S., Jackson, J. J., Reynolds, E. K., Potenza, M. N., Gelernter, J., ... Verona, E. (2010). Serotonin transporter gene associations with psychopathic traits in youth vary as a function of socioeconomic resources. *Journal of Abnormal Psychology*, *119*, 604–609.

Salekin, R. T. (2006). Psychopathy in children and adolescents: Key issues in conceptualization and assessment. In C. J. Christopher (Ed.), *Handbook of psychopathy* (pp. 389–414). New York, NY: The Guilford Press.

Schwenck, C., Mergenthaler, J., Keller, K., Zech, J., Salehi, S., Taurines, R., ... Freitag, C. M. (2012). Empathy in children with autism and conduct disorder: Group-specific profiles and developmental aspects. *Journal of Child Psychology and Psychiatry*, *53*, 651–659.

Sebastian, C. L., McCrory, E. J. P., Cecil, C. A. M., Lockwood, P. L., De Brito, S. A., Fontaine, N. M. G., & Viding, E. (2012). Neural responses to affective and cognitive Theory of Mind in children with conduct problems and varying levels of callous-unemotional traits. *Archives of General Psychiatry*, *69*, 814–822.

Singh, I., & Rose, N. (2009). Biomarkers in psychiatry. *Nature*, *460*, 202–207.

Taylor, J., Loney, B. R., Bobadilla, L., Iacono, W. G., & McGue, M. (2003). Genetic and environmental influences on psychopathy trait dimensions in a community sample of male twins. *Journal of Abnormal Child Psychology*, *31*, 633–645.

Viding, E., Blair, R. J. R., Moffitt, T. E., & Plomin, R. (2005). Evidence for substantial genetic risk for psychopathy in 7-years-olds. *Journal of Child Psychology and Psychiatry*, *46*, 592–597.

Viding, E., Fontaine, N. M. G., & McCrory, E. J. (2012). Antisocial behaviour in children with and without callous-unemotional traits. *Journal of the Royal Society of Medicine*, *105*, 195–200.

Viding, E., Fontaine, N. M. G., Oliver, B. R., & Plomin, R. (2009). Negative parental discipline, conduct problems and callous-unemotional traits: Monozygotic twin differences study. *The British Journal of Psychiatry*, *195*, 414–419.

Viding, E., Frick, P. J., & Plomin, R. (2007). Aetiology of the relationship between callous-unemotional traits and conduct problems in childhood. *British Journal of Psychiatry*, *49*, 33–38.

Viding, E., Hanscombe, K. B., Curtis, C. J. C., Davis, O. S. P., Meaburn, E. L., & Plomin, R. (2010). In search of genes associated with risk for psychopathic tendencies in children: A two-stage genome-wide association study of pooled DNA. *Journal of Child Psychology and Psychiatry*, *7*, 780–788.

Viding, E., Jones, A. P., Frick, P. J., Moffitt, T. E., & Plomin, R. (2008). Heritability of antisocial behaviour at 9: Do callous-unemotional traits matter? *Developmental Science*, *11*, 17–22.

Viding, E., Price, T. S., Jaffee, S. R., Trzaskowski, M., Davis, O. S. P., Meaburn, E. L., ... Plomin, R. (2013). Genetics of callous-unemotional behavior in children. *PLoS ONE*, *8*, 1–9.

Viding, E., Sebastian, C. L., Dadds, M. R., Lockwood, P. L., Cecil, C. A. M., DeBrito, S., & McCrory, E. J. (2012) Amygdala response to pre-attentive masked fear is associated with callous-unemotional traits in children with conduct problems. *American Journal of Psychiatry*, *169*, 1109–1116.

Visscher, P. M., Brown, M. A., McCarthy, M. I., & Yang, J. (2012). Five years of GWAS discovery. *American Journal of Human Genetics*, *90*, 7–24.

Waller, R., Gardner, F., & Hyde, L. W. (2013). What are the associations between parenting, callous-unemotional traits, and antisocial behavior in youth? A systematic review of evidence. *Clinical Psychology Review*, *33*, 593–608.

White, S. F., Frick, P. J., Lawing, K., & Bauer, D. (2013). Callous-unemotional traits and response to functional family therapy in adolescent offenders. *Behavioral Sciences & the Law*, *31*, 271–285.

19

Developmental Risk Factors

Anthony R. Beech, Ben Nordstrom, and Adrian Raine

Key points

- The brain is organized and sculpted by a lifetime of experiences, these being especially important pre/perinatally, and in infancy and adolescence.
- Therefore, brain development is an extremely long and complex process.
- Evidence would suggest that early adverse experiences, in an interaction with genetic and biological factors, can adversely affect brain development.
- The ensuing atypical morphological organization could result in social with-drawal, pathological shyness, explosive and inappropriate emotionality, and an inability to form normal emotional attachments – and this sets the scene for later criminality.
- Evidence for this is that a number of pre/peri/postnatal risk factors have been identified in offenders.
- It is argued in the chapter that understanding how these risk factors affect the brain is the first step in being able to ameliorate such risk factors, by the use of appropriate brain-based interventions.
- Interventions addressing these problems are outlined in Part V of this book.

Terminology Explained

Adverse life experiences (ACEs) cover everything from physical and sexual abuse experiences to parental separation and divorce.

An **Apgar** score (developed by Virginia Apgar, 1953) is a measure of the physical condition of a newborn infant. It is obtained by adding points (0, 1, 2) for: (a) heart rate, (b) respiratory effort, (c) muscle tone, (d) response to stimulation, and (e) skin coloration. A score of 10 represents the best possible condition of the infant.

Attachment can be broadly defined as the process by which an infant has an inborn biological need to maintain close contact with his or her main caretaker/s, and

---

The Wiley Blackwell Handbook of Forensic Neuroscience, First Edition. Edited by Anthony R. Beech, Adam J. Carter, Ruth E. Mann and Pia Rotshtein.
© 2018 John Wiley & Sons Ltd. Published 2018 by John Wiley & Sons Ltd.

hence create experiences of safeness that impacts the self-soothing systems within the brain.

Conduct disorder (CD) is defined as a repetitive, and persistent, pattern of behavior in childhood in which the basic rights of others, or societal conventions, are flouted, and is often seen as precursor of later antisocial behaviors. Many individuals with CD show little empathy and concern for others, and may frequently misperceive the intentions of others as being more hostile and threatening than is actually the case. Avoidant attachment has often been identified in young people with CD.

The **corpus callosum** is a brain tract consisting of about 200,000,000 axons that interconnect the two cerebral hemispheres. Its primary function is to integrate motor, sensory, and cognitive performances between one side of the cerebral cortex to the same cortical region on the other side.

Externalizing behaviors include disobeying rules, physical aggression, and threatening others.

Fetal alcohol syndrome (FAS) is evidenced by physical birth defects including: a small head and eyes, a very thin upper lip, or other abnormal facial features; deformed limbs or fingers; a smooth ridge between the upper lip and nose; below average height and weight; heart and/or kidney defects and other abnormalities; movement problems, such as poor motor skills, coordination, and balance anomalies, which may give rise to excessive clumsiness.

The **limbic system** is a complex system of nerves and networks in the brain, including the hypothalamus, the hippocampus, and the amygdala. It controls the basic emotions (fear, pleasure, anger) and drives (hunger, sex, dominance, care of offspring). Other areas such as the cingulate gyrus, the ventral tegmental area, the basal ganglia, and the prefrontal cortex are closely connected with the limbic system.

Minor physical anomalies (MPAs) of the individual may have a genetic basis, they might also be caused by factors in the fetal environment, such as anoxia, bleeding, or infection. MPAs have been linked to disorders of pregnancy and are thought by some to be a marker for insults to the fetal neural development towards the end of the first trimester. Thus, they are seen as indirect indications of inferences in brain development.

Pre-eclampsia is a disorder of pregnancy characterized by high blood pressure and a large amount of protein in the urine. The disorder usually occurs in the third trimester of pregnancy and gets worse over time. Pre-eclampsia increases the risk of poor outcomes for both the mother and the baby.

Telomeres are an essential part of human cells that affect how our cells age, and are the caps at the end of each strand of DNA that protect chromosomes, rather like the plastic tips at the end of shoelaces.

The term **teratogen** describes any agent that disturbs the development of an embryo or fetus. Teratogens may cause a birth defect in the child. Teratogens include maternal infections, chemicals, alcohol, tobacco, and illegal drugs.

> The **warrior gene** comprises particular variations in the X chromosome gene that produces monoamine oxidase A (MAO-A), an enzyme that affects the neurotransmitters dopamine, norepinephrine, and serotonin.

Introduction

Brain development and organization is an extremely long and complex process, given that it contains approximately 86 billion neurons, and has around 100 trillion synaptic connections. Brain development through the formation of neurons (brain cells) begins shortly after conception, continues throughout a person's life, and is subject to specific developmental milestones. Once formed, these neurons begin to migrate to the correct location in the brain, and some synapses (connections) begin forming. Prenatal conditions, such as temperature, pressure, and fetal movement, stimulate the development of these connections. By five weeks after conception, the cells in the developing brain begin dividing rapidly to form the neurons that an individual will have for the rest of their life. Processes such as **myelination** (the process of forming a coating or sheath of fatty substances on the axon of a neuron, which allows faster transmission of nerve impulses) and **synaptogenesis** (the formation of synapses between neurons in the nervous system) are well underway. At birth, there is a rapid increase in the growth in the brain, and connectivity with neurons in all parts of the brain making trillions of connections (known as **exuberant synaptogenesis**). Myelination continues in most parts of the brain and is the major cause of the increase in brain size.

Early childhood years contain a period of rapid increases/changes in connectivity in the brain, in fact, in the first four years the brain increases to 80% of its adult size. The process of changes in connectivity is both genetically and experience driven, with the brain producing many more synapses than it will ultimately contain. In order to counter this over-connection, **synaptic pruning** occurs where connections are refined based on sensory, motor, language, and cognitive experience, and parent–child interactions. Connections that are used regularly become stronger and more complex, while those that are not used are lost. The pruning process enables the brain to operate more efficiently and provides room for networks of essential connections to expand.

The brain continues to change and mature throughout adolescence, through myelination and synaptic pruning (most of which occurs between the ages of 10 and 16). This is when adolescents become (if brain development goes well) capable of insight, judgment, inhibition, reasoning, and social conscience. Increased activity in the frontal lobes (the part of the brain that regulates decision making, problem solving, control of purposeful behaviors, consciousness, and emotions) enables the young person to make more sense of the world at both cognitive and emotional levels. This development increases into adulthood, with frontal-lobe development (an area of the brain responsible for judgment, planning, assessing risks, and decision making) being the last area to develop. This development continues until the individual is at least 25 years old, by which time individuals are generally less risky. For example, the UK Automobile Association reports that 26% of car user deaths, and 12% of all road deaths, are young people between 17 and 24 travelling in cars in the UK.[1]

The aim of this chapter is to examine the risk factors that can impact upon the developing brain. Evidence would suggest that early adverse experiences, in an interaction with genetic and biological factors, can adversely affect brain development. The ensuing atypical morphological organization can often result in social withdrawal, pathological shyness, explosive and inappropriate emotionality, and an inability to form normal emotional attachments, setting the scene for later criminality (Joseph, 2003). Evidence for this is that a number of pre/peri/postnatal risk factors have been identified in offenders. It is argued in this chapter that understanding how these risk factors affect the brain is the first step in being able to ameliorate such risk factors, by the use of appropriate brain-based interventions, which are outlined in Part V of this volume.

Developmental Risk Factors and Offending

Social/antisocial behaviors are underpinned by neurobiological action. Probably the most important areas, as regards this chapter are: the **orbital prefrontal cortex (OPFC)**, situated at the very front of the brain, which is considered as the apex of the neural networks of the social brain, and is critical to the adaptation of behavior in terms of controlling intense emotions and impulses; and the **amygdala**, found deep within the temporal lobe, this area's functions are related to arousal and the control of responses associated with fear, emotion, and memory. Other important areas are: (i) the **anterior cingulate cortex (ACC)** situated below the cerebral cortices. This first appeared in animals demonstrating maternal behavior, and provides the basic circuitry for communication, cooperation, and empathy. Damage to this area can include decreased empathy, and emotional stability and inappropriate social behaviors (Brothers, 1996); (ii) the **insular cortex**, a portion of the cerebral cortex, which is a crucial area for understanding what it feels like to be human and is the source of social emotions such as lust, disgust, pride and humiliation, guilt and shame. Together with the premotor cortex, the insular is part of the circuitry that allows individuals to vicariously share the emotions of others; and (iii) the **basal ganglia**, situated in the forebrain, and associated with a variety of functions including cognitions and emotions. Box 19.1 outlines the factors that can affect brain development, particularly in the crucial areas outlined above.

Box 19.1   Factors that can Lead to Problematic Brain Development

1 Abnormalities in fetal development.
2 Prenatal factors (i.e., smoking in pregnancy, maternal alcohol consumption during pregnancy leading to fetal alcohol syndrome/fetal alcohol spectrum disorder).
3 Perinatal risk factors (birth complications, maternal rejection).
4 Postnatal risk factors (adverse childhood experiences, poor nutrition, head injury).
5 Parent–child relationships (attachment experiences).
6 Substance abuse in adolescence and adulthood (alcohol covered in Chapter 17).

Developmental Risk Factors

Such pre, post, and perinatal risk factors, as outlined in Box 19.1, are often caused by problematic development, and this can create disturbances in the neurobiological processes of the brain, sometimes in combination with *genetic* factors. Examples of these interactions will be considered later in the chapter, but we will now examine in more detail the effect on the brain of the risk factors listed in Box 19.1.

Prenatal factors

Abnormalities in fetal development These are subtle minor physical anomalies (MPAs) in individuals, such as having a curved fifth finger, a single palmar crease, low-seated ears, or a furrowed tongue, which are thought to arise from abnormalities in fetal development. These may have a genetic basis, but they might also be due to anoxia, bleeding, or infection (Guy, Majorski, Wallace, & Guy, 1983). Studies have indicated that there is a correlation between MPAs and aggressive behaviors in children as young as three years of age (e.g., Waldrop, Bell, McLauglin, & Halverson, 1978). There is an increased prevalence of MPAs in school-aged boys exhibiting behavioral problems (e.g., Halverson & Victor, 1976). Specifically, MPAs identified at age 14 predict violence at age 17 (Arsenault, Tremblay, Boulerice, & Saucier, 2002). Pine, Shaffer, Schonfield, & Davies (1997) found that the presence of MPAs significantly interacted with other adverse life experiences (see Box 19.2), such as marital conflict and poverty leading to physical neglect, to predict conduct problems in adolescence. As for the relationship with adult offending, Brennan, Mednick, and Raine (1997), in a study of 72 male offspring of psychiatrically ill parents, found that those with both MPAs and family adversity had especially high rates of adult violent offending.

Maternal alcohol, tobacco and drug use The estimated rate of drug use for pregnant women in the US is 13.8% for alcohol, 17.7% for tobacco, and 3.4% for illegal drugs (Lester, Andreozzi, & Appiah, 2004). We will now examine the effects of these teratogens on the fetal brain, and the research that suggests a link with these perinatal risk factors and offending sequalae.

Fetal alcohol syndrome (FAS) and fetal alcohol spectrum disorder (FASD) FAS can arise due to excessive alcohol use in pregnancy, as alcohol is clearly a teratogen. Full blown FAS does not occur in all children exposed in utero, but children who do not display the full FAS syndrome can still have some of the functional deficits characteristic of the syndrome (Schonfeld, Mattson, & Riley, 2005), and there are a range of problems. FASD is the umbrella term used to describe this spectrum of abnormalities, with FAS lying at the most severely affected end of the spectrum. FASD arises because the developing fetus does not process alcohol the same way as an adult, and hence it is more concentrated in the fetus. This concentration of alcohol can prevent enough nutrition and oxygen from getting to the fetus' vital organs, particularly the brain (**fetal hypoxia-ischemia and malnutrition**). Particular areas that are the most vulnerable include the hippocampus, basal ganglia, and corpus callosum (the band of fibers that connect the two cerebral hemispheres) (Swayze et al., 1997). Alcohol appears to be most harmful to the fetus during the first trimester, when a woman might not yet know that she is pregnant. The risk increases if the mother is a heavy drinker, in fact, binge drinking (six or more units of alcohol, which equates to two glasses of wine, is defined as binge drinking) is a particular risk factor. However, consumption of alcohol at any time during pregnancy can be harmful.

FASD, as well as having physical effects, also produces major psychological problems such as: behavioral and emotional regulation problems (outbursts, rigidity, defiance, depression, anxiety, attachment issues, and generally being difficult); attentional problems (i.e., inattention, hyperactivity, and poor impulse control); intellectual disability (ranging from mild to severe); immaturity (here overall performance can be equivalent to children of half the individual's age); language delays (e.g., poor receptive language, slowness of processing verbal instructions); memory issues; and executive functioning issues (i.e., a lack of abstract reasoning and linking actions to consequences, poor problem-solving skills).

There is a great deal of evidence that FASD predisposes individuals to antisocial behavior (e.g., Olson et al., 1997; Roebuck, Mattson, & Riley, 1999). For example, Streissguth, Barr, Kogan, and Bookstein (1996), in a study of 400 adolescents and adults with FASD, found that: 60% had been in trouble with the law, 50% exhibited (unwanted) sexual behavior, while 30% reported alcohol/drug problems. Other evidence suggests that individuals with FASD are at high risk of coming into repeated contact with the criminal justice system, both as victims and offenders (e.g., Boland, Chudley, & Grant, 2002; Chartrand & Forbes-Chilibeck, 2003; Streissguth & Kanter, 1997). As for the prevalence of these problems in forensic populations, the lifetime prevalence of FASD in incarcerated populations was 32% for adolescents and 42% for adults (Streissguth & Kanter, 1997) in the USA. Interestingly, the prevalence of FASD among a sample of adult male offenders entering a federal correctional facility in Canada was 10% in a study reported by MacPherson and Chudley (2007).

Maternal smoking Extensive human and animal studies have noted that the 7,000+ chemicals contained in cigarettes can easily cross the placental barrier and hence have a harmful effect upon the fetal brain (e.g., British Medical Association, 2004; Rogers, 2009). Specifically, Hackshaw, Rodeck, and Boniface (2011) note that in the UK 3,759 babies were born with non-chromosomal congenital abnormalities associated with smoking in 2008. Maternal smoking is also an established risk factor for miscarriages, perinatal mortality, low birth weight, and premature birth (Hackshaw et al., 2011). The specific mechanisms are that cigarette smoke interferes with normal placental function, acting as a vasoconstrictor to reduce uterine blood flow. Hence, the fetus is deprived of oxygen and nutrients (fetal hypoxia-ischemia and malnutrition) (Ganapathy, Prasad, Ganapathy, & Leibach, 2000). Cigarette smoke also acts as *a neuroteratogen* (i.e., specifically affecting the nervous system). Nicotine targets the nicotinic acetylcholine receptors in the fetus's brain to change the pattern of cell proliferation and differentiation (synaptogenesis/synaptic pruning), and causes abnormalities in the development of synaptic activity. Additionally, the by-products of smoking (such as hydrogen cyanide and carbon monoxide) may affect the brain's dopaminergic and noradrenergic systems (Muneoka et al., 1997), as well as glucose metabolism (Eckstein, Shibley, Pennington, Carver, & Pennington, 1997). Maternal smoking can also have an effect upon various brain structures including the cerebral cortices (Olds, 1997; Raine, 2002).

There is a significant body of evidence that demonstrates that maternal smoking predisposes children toward developing antisocial behavior (Wakschlag, Pickett, Cook, Benowitz, & Leventhal, 2002). For example, prenatal smoking predicts externalizing behaviors in childhood, and criminal behavior in adolescence (Fergusson, Woodward, & Horwood, 1998; Orlebeke, Knol, & Verhulst, 1997; Wakschlag et al., 1997). Researchers have also identified a clear dose-dependent relationship between smoking and later criminal behavior, in that a high level of smoking during pregnancy, predicts higher risk of criminality in later life for the child (Brennan, Grekin, & Mednick, 1999; Maughan, Taylor, Caspi, & Moffitt, 2004).

Use of illicit drugs in pregnancy   There is an overlap between the use of licit and illicit drugs during pregnancy, with Wenzel, Kosofsky, Harvey, and Iguchi (2001) reporting that approximately 32% of women who use illicit drugs also consume cigarettes and alcohol during pregnancy. Therefore, it is difficult to tease out the effects of illegal drugs. However, there is some evidence that cocaine-exposed children in utero are more likely to have poor sustained attention, more disorganization, and less abstract thinking than their peers (Lester et al., 2004). Hence, these factors could be seen as potentially setting the scene for impulsive, ill thought-through actions that, in extremis, can result in offending. The use of marijuana in pregnancy is also not risk free to the fetus. An Australian study of almost 420,000 live births (Jacques et al., 2014) reports a higher risk for neonatal intensive care admission for newborns exposed prenatally. Also, there are reports of abnormal responses or behaviors in the newborn, which suggests a toxicity effect – associated symptoms can include exaggerated and prolonged startle reflexes (sleep cycle disturbances with high-pitched crying). However, there have been, to date, no reported follow-up studies as regards subsequent antisocial behaviors. Methamphetamine use is less well studied than those other substances, but women who use methamphetamine frequently also use tobacco, alcohol, and other drugs, which may confound the results of negative birth outcomes (Lester et al., 2004).

Prenatal malnutrition   Although most studies have focused on nutrition in the postnatal period, one study investigated the role of malnutrition in the prenatal period (Neugebauer, Hoek, & Susser, 1999). Neugebauer et al., for example, examined the children of women who were pregnant during the German food blockade of Dutch cities in World War II. The blockade produced near starvation and severe food shortages at the time. The researchers found that the male offspring of women who were in the first and second trimesters of pregnancy during this time had 2.5 times the rate of antisocial personality disorder than the offspring of women who were not affected by food shortages. Another study of prenatal nutrition, reported by Hibbeln et al. (2007), who examined a sample of 11,875 pregnant women and their consumption of fatty acids. Adequate intake of omega-3 fatty acids, such as eicosapentaenoic acid (EPA) and docosahexaenoic acid (DHA), and vitamin D are important for cognitive functioning (Perica & Delas, 2011; Przybelski & Binkley, 2007). Pregnant women who ate food less rich in omega-3 fatty acids (i.e., less than 340 grams a week), had offspring that demonstrated significantly lower scores on a number of neurodevelopmental outcomes, including more antisocial behavior, than the offspring of mothers who consumed more omega-3 rich food.

Perinatal risk factors

There are a number of risk factors that can happen around the period of childbirth, these include: maternal pre-eclampsia (a medical condition in which hypertension arises in pregnancy); premature birth; low birth weight: use of forceps in delivery leading to anoxia (absence of oxygen to the brain) and hence transfer to a neonatal intensive care unit; and low Apgar scores. Such maternal complications have been shown to have deleterious effects on neonatal brain function in that newborn babies who suffer obstetrical complications are also more likely to exhibit externalizing behaviors at age 11 than those without complications (Liu 2004; Liu & Wuerker, 2005). Obstetric complications were found to mediate the relationship between low IQ and externalizing behaviors (Liu, Raine, Wuerker, Venables, & Mednick, 2009). For example, Raine, Brennan, and Mednick (1994) investigated a cohort 4,269 Danish men and found that obstetrical complications significantly interacted with severe maternal rejection (such as efforts to terminate the pregnancy, reporting the pregnancy as unwanted, or attempting to give up custody of the baby) to predict violent crime in adolescence. These findings have since been replicated in the USA, Sweden, Finland, and Canada, where it has been also been found that birth complications interact with a number of psychosocial risk factors, and are related to later antisocial behaviors (e.g., Hodgins, Kratzer, & McNeil, 2001; Kemppainen Jokelainen, Jarvelin, Isohanni, & Rasanen, 2001; Tibbetts & Piquero, 1999).

Attachment styles *Attachment styles describe the way individuals form relationships with others. It is hypothesized that we have an internal working model of relationships, which was developed in early childhood through interaction with the main caregivers. Attentive, respective, caring, and consistent relationships with carers will result in forming a secure attachment style, while violation of these conditions will lead to different types of insecure attachment. For example, conduct disorder is often associated with an avoidant attachment style (Finzi, Ram, Har-Even, Shnitt, & Weizman, 2001).*

Source: © PublicDomainPictures. Used under license from 699pic.

Postnatal/childhood risk factors

These risk factors can include a high level of adverse childhood experiences, poor nutrition, and traumatic brain injury (therapies for which are discussed in Chapter 24).

Poor nutrition   Poor nutrition has been investigated as a risk factor for criminal behavior (Breakey, 1997; Werbach, 1995). The exact mechanism by which malnutrition later affects antisocial behavior is not well understood. It is hypothesized that proteins, or minerals, may either regulate neurotransmitters and hormones or ameliorate neurotoxins (Coccaro, Kavoussi, Kavoussi, & Seroczynski, 1997; Liu & Raine, 2006). Studies have also shown that deficiencies in nutrients such as proteins, zinc, iron, and docosahexaenoic acid (a component of omega-3 fatty acid) can lead to impaired brain functioning and a predisposition to antisocial behavior in childhood and adolescence (Arnold, Pinkham, & Votolato, 2000; Lister et al., 2005; Rosen et al., 1985). Liu and Raine (2006), found that children with protein, iron, or zinc deficiencies at age three had significantly more aggressive and hyperactive behavior at the age of eight, more antisocial behavior at age 11, and more excessive motor activity and conduct disorder (CD) at age 17, compared to controls. Significantly, this study also found a dose-dependent relationship between the extent of malnutrition and the extent of later behavior problems. Longitudinal studies have also shown that malnutrition in infancy is associated with aggressive behavior and attentional deficits in childhood (e.g., Galler & Ramsey, 1989; Galler, Ramsey, Solimano, & Lowell, 1983).

Adverse childhood experiences (ACEs)   Ten ACEs have been formally defined by Felitti et al. (1998) as being predictive of chronic disease/s in adulthood, and in offenders. These are shown in Box 19.2.

Box 19.2   Adverse Childhood Experiences (ACEs)

1   Recurrent physical abuse.
2   Recurrent emotional abuse.
3   Contact sexual abuse.
4   Substance abuse taking place within the home.
5   A household member is in prison.
6   Household mental illness.
7   Family violence (typically to the mother from a partner).
8   Parental separation/divorce.
9   Physical neglect.
10   Emotional neglect.

As for an ACE score, a score of 1 is given if the ACE is present, and zero for its absence, therefore a maximum ACE score will be 10. Having an ACE score of 4 increases the risk of emphysema or chronic bronchitis by a factor of four, and suicide by factor of 12. People with high ACE scores are more likely to be violent, to have more marriages, more broken bones, more drug prescriptions, more depression, and more autoimmune diseases. People with an ACE score of 6 or higher are at risk of their lifespan being shortened by 20 years.[2] High ACE scores have also been linked with risky sexual behaviors, such as engaging in sexual activity prior to the age of 15, teenage pregnancy, and/or having 50 or more sexual partners (Hillis et al., 2004).

Being subject to a number of ACEs has also been identified with immediate negative consequences such as structural and functional changes in the developing brain. Structural changes can include reduced size of the mid-portions of the corpus callosum and attenuated development of the left neocortex, hippocampus, and amygdala (Teicher et al., 2003). While, functional consequences include increased "electrical irritability" in the limbic structures of the brain (Teicher et al., 2003). Other evidence suggests that chromosomal damage can also occur due to the effects of ACEs, such as telemore erosion (associated with cellular aging, disease and morality in later life) (Shalev et al., 2013).

Even though the prevalence of ACEs has shown to be high in the normal population (Hillis et al., 2004), it has been found to be even higher in special populations, for example, the children of alcoholic parents (Dube et al., 2001). As for the incidence of ACEs in offender populations, recent data from the Ministry of Justice in England and Wales (Williams, Papadopoulou, & Booth, 2012), based on 1,435 newly sentenced prisoners (in the years 2005 and 2006) are shown in Box 19.3, together with ACE indications.

Box 19.3   Offenders' Problematic Childhoods

- Nearly a third of all prisoners (29%) reported that they had experienced some form of abuse or neglect in childhood (ACE 1, 2, 9, 10).
- A number had observed violence in the home (41%) as a child – particularly those who stated that they had a family member with an alcohol or drug problem (ACE 7).
- 18% stated that as a child they had a family member with an alcohol problem (ACE 4).
- 14% said that as a child they had a family member with a drug problem (ACE 4).
- Over a third (37%) reported having family members who had been convicted of a serious crime, of whom 84% had been in prison or a young offenders' institution (ACE 5).
- 24% said that they had been in care at some point during their childhood (aspect of ACE 8).

It can be seen from Box 19.3, that the majority of the ACEs (apart from a family member being chronically depressed and being subject to contact sexual abuse) can be seen in this sample. Specifically, we would note that: nearly a third of the sample reporting having experienced some sort of abuse in childhood; almost half had observed violence in the home where they were brought up; 20% had a family member with an alcohol problem; while 14% had a family member with a drug problem. Similar results have been found in a study of 64,329 juvenile offenders in Florida, USA by Baglivio, Swartz, Huq, Sheer, & Hardt (2014). They found that two thirds of the sample reported family violence, parental separation, and household member incarceration (ACEs 1, 5, 8). There was also a clear relationship with the number of ACEs and the number of negative outcomes, in terms of level of offending.

A recent study of 679 male sexual offenders (Levenson, Willis, & Prescott, 2014) found that this group were more than three times more likely to have suffered from sexual abuse (ACE 3) compared to the general population, had twice the odds of having suffered physical abuse (ACE 1), 13 times the odds of verbal abuse (ACE 2), and four times the odds of emotional neglect (ACE 10) and coming from a "broken home" as a child (ACE 8). Such early trauma produces neuronal changes (Solomon & Heide, 2005). Case Study 19.1 provides an example of a young man who committed a homicide in the US whose background clearly shows evidence of many of the ACEs outlined in Box 19.2.

Case Study 19.1 DP

A young woman was murdered in her own home, after a brutal physical assault. The murderer was identified as DP, a 24-year old man with a prior history of violent crime. His defense team did not deny that he had committed the murder, but argued that the crime was impulsive and opportunistic. After the jury found DP guilty of first-degree murder, information was provided at the sentencing portion of his hearing to try to mitigate the sentence in order to avoid execution by lethal injection. Information from DP's history reported at least six adverse childhood risk factors (ACEs):

1 He was born to a single, teenage mother **(ACE 8: one parent)**.
2 He was admitted five times in the first two years of his life to hospital for injuries related to having been shaken violently for crying too much **(ACE 1: recurrent physical abuse)**.
3 He was noted to have eaten paint chips as a baby **(ACE 9: physical neglect)**.
4 His later childhood medical history revealed treatment for severe physical and sexual abuse **(ACEs 2, 3: recurrent physical/contact sexual abuse)**.
5 Social services records reported that his mother was frequently absent **(ACE 10: emotional neglect)**.
6 He often slept in abandoned buildings in a dangerous, inner-city environment as a child **(ACE 9: physical neglect)**.

As for the consequences of these ACEs, neuropsychological testing revealed that he had notable executive functioning deficiencies, due to dramatic reductions in activity in his bilateral prefrontal cortices. Due to the combined influence of these biopsychosocial risk factors, DP was spared the death sentence and was instead given a life-sentence.

Problematic parent-child interactions (attachment)

An individual's attachment style can also be seen as a set of enduring characteristics for making sense of one's life experiences and interactions (Mitchell & Beech, 2011). This model is maintained irrespective of whether the relationship between the individual and their primary caregiver in childhood was positive or negative, and hence is a model for individual's future social interactions, and whether these are broadly negative or positive throughout their lifespan. *Secure* attachments give rise to internal working models of others as safe, helpful, and supportive (Baldwin, 2005), while an *insecure* attachment style causes the individual to become focused on the power of others to control or reject them (Gilbert, 2005). See Box 19.4 for an outline of the four attachment styles – one secure and the other three insecure styles (dismissive, preoccupied, disorganized) – identified in childhood and adulthood. It is of note here that the three insecure attachment styles are more likely to predispose some individuals to offend in certain circumstances. Craissati (2009), for example, notes that violent criminals' lives are associated with extremely disturbed attachment representations. While, a number of other authors have noted the role of coercive parent–child interactions, the absence of a positive and affectionate bond between parent and child, neglect, inconsistent parenting, and severity of punishments (e.g., Frodi, Dernevik, Sepa, Philison, & Bragesjö, 2001; Greenberg, Speltz, & DeKlyen, 1993; Sampson & Laub, 1990).

Box 19.4   Attachment Styles in Childhood

(Adult attachment styles in brackets)

Secure (autonomous) attachment is characterized by objective evaluations of attachment-related experiences, whether these are good or bad. This pattern is associated with sensitive and responsive parenting in childhood. Individuals with a secure attachment style, in childhood and adulthood, have been found to have high levels of self-esteem, viewing others as warm and accepting, and reporting being able to achieve high levels of intimacy in close adult relationships.

Avoidant (dismissive) attachment is characterized by an emphasis on achievement and self-reliance at the expense of intimacy. This pattern is associated with a rejecting or interfering parenting style, in that the parent has behaved in a remote, cold, and controlling way. Hence, if parents are emotionally unavailable the child will tend to pull away from them and so develop a way of operating that minimizes reliance on others for support, as a child, and later in life. This leads to deactivation of *attachment mechanisms*, ultimately resulting in an adult who is emotionally autonomous and only ready to express self-preservative behaviors, at the expense of any warm, interpersonal interactions with others. By definition, such a person would be expected to show some antisocial characteristics from time-to-time, as they are often self-absorbed, and unwilling to approach others for help and emotional support.

Ambivalent (preoccupied) attachment is characterized as the individual being enmeshed in past (typically childhood) attachment experiences, and having an inability to report a coherent view of interactions with others. This style has been found to be associated with an individual experiencing an inconsistent parenting style in childhood, where the parent/s behave in ways that interfere with the child's autonomy or exploration, leading the individual to be uncertain of the quality of relationships, and living in fear of rejection in later life. Hence, the person has a sense of confusion, especially when it comes to relational issues. This style is associated with a heightened sense of rejection, feelings of general incompetence and inadequacy, and in extremis social withdrawal. This style can be often observed in those who sexually abuse children.

Disorganized/disoriented (disorganized) attachment is the style most often associated with parental maltreatment, or where the primary caregivers have experienced an unresolved loss or trauma of their own. Here a parenting style that is frightening (or frightened), leads to the situation where the child is caught in a conflict where what should be their source of security becomes a source of fear. Individuals with this style may not be actively hostile in their interactions with others, but may behave in a *passive-aggressive* manner. This attachment style is common in individuals with psychiatric disorders and in some cases can lead individuals to act out in an aggressive manner.

With regard to specific types of insecure attachment and their relationship to offending patterns, Weinfield, Sroufe, Egeland, and Carlson (2008) note that children with *avoidant* or *disorganized* attachment styles were likely to show angry, aggressive behaviors with parents and peers, perhaps in response to rejection and insensitivity by the caregivers, or because they have a caregiver who is frightening or frightened. Saltaris (2002) found that a history of abuse, and extremely disturbed attachment representations, led to a marked lack of empathy towards others and was associated with subsequent violent criminality. Lyons-Ruth, Alpern, and Repacholi (1993) note that *disorganized* attachment and maternal psychosocial problems were highly predictive of hostile behaviors in young children. Finzi, Ram, Har-Even, Shnitt, and Weizman (2001) found that physically abused children were characterized by an *avoidant* attachment style, and were aggressive and suspicious of others.

Traumatic brain injury (TBI)

Traumatic brain injury (TBI) has also been implicated as a precursor of antisocial behavior (therapy for which is examined in depth in Chapter 24). But with regard to brain injury, it can predispose to violent criminal behavior in later life (e.g., Hughes et al., 2015; Leon-Carrion & Ramos, 2003). A number of other large, longitudinal studies have repeatedly shown an increased incidence of delinquent behavior among youth with a history of TBI (Asarnow, Satz, Light, & Neumann, 1991; McAllister, 1992; Rivera et al., 1994). A further study, which used more severe criteria in the definition of TBI than the previous ones, found that 27.7% of the delinquents in their sample had a history of TBI (Carswell, Maughan, Davis, Davenport, & Goddard, 2004). As Aguilar (2016) notes, the reasons for this are that TBI can affect particular parts of the brain, such as the OPFC, which underpins executive function. The reason for the damage to the OPFC is that it is situated at the very front of the brain, and can be easily damaged by falls, car accidents, assaults, and so on. Such executive function problems can lead to a lack of interpersonal sensitivity, and in extremis impulsive reactive aggression. Evidence from a meta-analysis of 39 studies incorporating data from 4,589 individuals examining the relationship between executive dysfunction and antisocial behavior has been reported by Morgan & Lilienfeld (2000). They found significant effect sizes for juvenile delinquency ($d = .86$) and for CD ($d = .46$). Hux, Bond, Skinner, Belau, and Sanger (1998) found that half of the juvenile delinquents in their sample had a history of TBI, and a third of the delinquents with TBI were thought by their parents to have neuropsychological sequelae from their injuries.

We will now briefly examine some interventions that would appear to be useful in modifying the environmental risk factors outlined above.

Influence of food shortage *The male offspring of women who experienced famine (within the first six months of pregnancy) had 2.5 times the rate of antisocial personality disorder than the offspring of women who were not affected by food shortages.*

Source: © TawnyNina. Used under license from 699pic.

Modifying Environmental Risk Factors

Obviously, not all risk factors for criminal behavior (e.g., male gender, having a biological parent with a history of criminal behavior) are modifiable. However, there are some risk factors (e.g., smoking, nutrition) that potentially can be modified – some of these interventions are outlined in Box 19.5.

Developmental Risk Factors

> ## Box 19.5 Interventions to Modify Environmental Risk Factors
>
> - Successful interventions have been developed to reduce prenatal alcohol exposure (Chang, Wilkins-Haug, Berman, & Goerz, 1999; Chang, McNamara, Orav, & Wilkins-Haug, 2005).
> - Interventions have been designed to reduce smoking in pregnancy, but these have been less effective (Ershoff, Ashford, & Goldenberg, 2004).
> - Other studies have sought to correct nutritional deficits. One randomized, double- blind, placebo-controlled study was performed in a sample of 486 state schoolchildren to see if a daily multivitamin and mineral supplement could reduce antisocial behavior (Schoenthaler & Bier, 2000). The treatment group had a 47% reduction in antisocial behavior after four months, compared to controls.
> - A randomized, double-blind, placebo-controlled trial of omega-3 fatty acid supplementation was carried out in a sample of 50 children. The intervention group had a 42.7% reduction in CD problems (Stevens et al., 2003), compared to controls.
> - Other interventions address more than one risk factor at a time. For example, one highly successful intervention for prevention of later criminal and antisocial behavior involved home nursing visits for pregnant and new mothers. Parenting, health, and nutritional guidance were provided in the sessions (Olds et al., 1998).
> - Prenatal education on nutrition, health, and parenting has been found to lead to reductions in juvenile delinquency at age 15 (Lally, Mangione, & Honig, 1988).
> - A multidimensional intervention was tested in a randomized control trial, involving physical exercise alongside nutritional and educational enrichment in a sample of children aged three to five. The intervention was found to significantly reduce antisocial behavior at age 17, and criminal behavior at age 23, and was especially effective for the subgroup of children who displayed signs of malnutrition at age three. This suggest that the nutritional aspect of the treatment was particularly beneficial (Raine et al., 2003).
> - As for interventions in adulthood, Hansen et al. (2015) found that a long-term fatty fish intervention improved executive function in inpatients with antisocial traits and a history of alcohol and drug abuse.

Conclusions

The brain itself is organized by a lifetime of experience. If the process goes well, then an individual become a well-adjusted child, adolescent, and adult. The speed at which the matured social brain comes on line is biased by early experiences. For some people, it never really takes place because they are subject to adverse developmental courses, early deprivation and other suboptimal rearing conditions, poor attachment experience, and in a number of cases TBI. These risk factors can have very real effects upon the brain, and hence individuals are operating at a suboptimal level, in terms of having poor emotional recognition skills, behaving impulsively – in some cases aggressively – and committing crimes associated with such problems.

The good news is that even in adulthood, the brain is continuously remodeling itself. However, the rate of synaptic formation is much slower in adulthood with synapses generally being formed based only on specific experiences in the adult's life. For example, it has been found that there is an increase in the size of the hippocampus, an area of the brain associated with memory, in those learning to be black cab London taxi drivers (e.g., Maguire, Woollett, & Spiers, 2006). Meanwhile, Lazar et al. (2005) found that the thickness of middle prefrontal OPFC and the insula (areas associated with empathy, controlling intense emotions, and impulses) correlated with time spent in mindful meditation. This suggests that, even where individuals have been subject to the level of problems that have been discussed in this chapter, there is a possibility of rewiring/remodeling the brain. The chapters in Part V of the book outline the types of approaches that can be taken in the forensic field, that have been suggested as useful in such reconfigurations of the problematic brain function outlined in this chapter.

It is probably true to say that the science of epigenetics will become increasingly important in understanding crime. Just because an individual has a genetic make-up that may predispose to crime in certain circumstances it is the environmental factors that will trigger such tendencies. Evidence would suggest that there is a number of situations where there are genetic-environmental interactions. For example, the development of problematic attachment patterns outlined in Box 19.3 are shaped by a combination of genetic factors and social experiences (Fonagy, 2001). Molecular genetic studies have suggested that different attachment styles may reflect variations in the genes for the neurotransmitters dopamine and serotonin (Gillath, McCall, Shaver, Baek, & Chun, 2008). Hence, a particular form (polymorphism) of the DRD2 dopamine receptor gene is associated with an insecure style of attachment characterized by preoccupied/anxious attachment, while a polymorphism of the serotonin 5HT2A receptor gene is associated with an avoidant style of attachment (Gillath et al., 2008). However, even though these candidate genes predispose a person to a certain style of social interactions, the predisposed style can either emerge or be modified by early social experience, and can either act as protective factors or can potentiate antisocial behaviors.

Another example, of gene–environment interaction is work that has found a connection between a version of the monoamine oxidase A (MAO-A) gene (3R) (commonly known as the "warrior gene") and several types of antisocial behavior. Although overall MAO-A has been found to have no overall effect on antisocial behavior, low MAO-A activity in combination with abuse experienced during childhood results in an increased risk of aggressive behavior as an adult (Frazzetto et al., 2007). Caspi et al. (2002), in a large study of gene–environment interaction, identified people with high or low MAO-A activity and also whether or not the individual had been abused as a child. They found evidence of a strong interaction between low MAO-A activity and childhood maltreatment in terms of the likelihood of developing CD. Developmental risk factors such as maternal smoking during pregnancy, poor material living standards, dropping out of school, as well as low IQ were found to be associated with violent behavior in men with the low-activity alleles (which are overwhelmingly the 3R allele) (Fergusson, Boden, Horwood, Miller, & Kennedy, 2012).

Finally, adoption studies are another mechanism for studying genetic and environmental interactions in antisocial behavior (e.g., Rhee & Waldman, 2002). In a study of 862 Swedish male adoptees by Cloninger, Sigvardsson, Bohman, and von Knorring (1982), it was found that if a person had both a biological parent and an adoptive parent who were criminals, the person's likelihood of criminal behavior was greater than the sum of the individual risks. In other words, there was a multiplicative effect of having a biological predisposition to crime and then being raised in a criminogenic environment. Therefore, we would argue for the importance of individuals being both brought up in a caring, nurturing environment and not subject to any of the prenatal, perinatal, or postnatal risk factors outlined in this chapter, which may make them more at risk of committing crime.

Notes

1 See https://www.theaa.com/resources/Documents/pdf/young-drivers-at-risk.pdf.
2 See http://acestoohigh.com/resources/.

Recommended Reading

Cacioppo, J. T., & Bernston, G. G. (Eds.) (2005). *Social neuroscience: Key readings.* Hove, East Sussex: Psychology Press. *This collected volume of essays provides some key readings in understanding how the brain determines social behavior.*

Carey, N. (2012). The epigenetic revolution. London: Icon Books. *An easy to read introduction into the burgeoning science of epigenetics.*

Cassady, J., & Shaver, P. R. (Eds.). (2008). *Handbook of attachment; theory research and clinical applications, second edition.* New York: The Guilford Press. *This provides a good background to the concept of attachment.*

Hodgins, S., Viding, E., & Plodowski, A. (2009). *The neurobiological basis of violence: Science and rehabilitation.* Oxford: Oxford University Press. *A good overview of the neurobiology of violence by leading reserachers in the area.*

Raine, A. (1993). *The psychopathology of crime: Criminal behavior as a mental disorder.* London: Academic Press. *Even though it was published over 20 years ago, this book still provides a nice concise review of genetics, neurochemistry, neuropsychology, psychophysiology, cognitive deficits, and other biological factors and crime.*

Walsh, A., & Beaver, K. M. (Eds.) (2009). *Biosocial criminology: New directions in theory and research.* New York, NY: Routldege. *This provides excellent reviews of the evidence regarding biosocial effects on criminality by a number of authors.*

References

Aguilar, R. (2016). Brain injury and crime. *The Psychologist, 29,* 452–454.

Apgar, V. (1953). A proposal for a new method of evaluation of the newborn infant. *Current Research in Anesthesia and Analgesia, 32,* 260–267.

Arnold, L. E., Pinkham, S. M., & Votolato, N. (2000). Does zinc moderate essential fatty acid and amphetamine treatment of attention-deficit/hyperactivity disorder? *Journal of Child and Adolescent Psychopharmacology, 10,* 111–117.

Arsenault, L., Tremblay, R. E., Boulerice, B., & Saucier, J. F. (2002). Obstetrical complications and violent delinquency: Testing two developmental pathways. *Child Development, 73*, 496–508

Asarnow, R., Satz, P., Light, R., & Neumann, E. (1991). Behavior problems and adaptive functioning in children with mild and severe closed head injury. *Journal of Pediatric Psychology, 16*, 543–555.

Baglivio, M. T., Swartz, K., Huq, M. S., Sheer, A., & Hardt, N. S. (2014). The prevalence of adverse childhood experiences (ACEs) in the lives of juvenile offenders. *OJJDP Journal of Juvenile Justice, 3*, 1–23.

Baldwin, M. W. (2005). *Interpersonal cognition*. New York, NY: Guilford Press.

Boland, F. J., Chudley, A. E., & Grant, B. A. (2002). The challenge of fetal alcohol syndrome in adult offender populations. *Forum on Corrections Research 14*. Accessed November 20, 2007 Retrieved from http://www.csc-scc.gc.ca/text/pblct/forum/e143/143s_e.pdf.

Breakey, J. (1997). The role of diet and behavior in childhood. *Journal of Paediatrics and Child Health, 33*, 190–194.

Brennan, P. A., Grekin, E. R., & Mednick, S. A. (1999). Maternal smoking during pregnancy and adult male criminal outcomes. *Archives of General Psychiatry, 56*, 215–219.

Brennan, P. A., Mednick, S. A., & Raine, A. (1997). Biosocial interactions and violence: A focus on perinatal factors. In A. Raine, P. Brennan, D. Farrington, & S. A. Mednick (Eds.), *Biosocial basis of violence* (pp. 163–174). New York, NY: Plenum Press.

British Medical Association, Board of Science, Education and Tobacco Control Resource Centre (2004). *Smoking and reproductive life. The impact of smoking on sexual, reproductive and child health*. London: author.

Brothers, L. (1996). Brain mechanisms of social cognition. *Journal of Psychopharmacology, 10*, 2–8.

Carswell, K., Maughan, B., Davis, H., Davenport, F., & Goddard, N. (2004). The psychosocial needs of young offenders and adolescents from an inner city area. *Journal of Adolescence, 27*, 415–428.

Caspi, A., McClay, J., Moffitt, T. E., Mill, J., Martin, J., Craig, I. W.,... Pulton, R. (2002). Role of genotype in the cycle of violence in maltreated children. *Science, 297*, 851–854.

Chang, G., McNamara, T. K., Orav, E. J., & Wilkins-Haug, L. (2005). Brief intervention for prenatal alcohol use:. A randomized trial. *Obstetrics and Gynecology, 10*, 991–998.

Chang, G., Wilkins-Haug, L., Berman, S., & Goerz, M. A. (1999). Brief intervention for alcohol use in pregnancy: A randomized trial. *Addiction, 94*, 1499–1508.

Chartrand, L. N., & Forbes-Chilibeck, E. M. (2003). The sentencing of offenders with Fetal Alcohol Syndrome. *Health Law Journal, 11*, 35–91.

Cloninger, C. R., Sigvardsson, S., Bohman, M., & von Knorring, A. (1982). Predisposition to petty criminality in Swedish adoptees. II. Cross-fostering analysis of gene-environment interaction. *Archives of General Psychiatry, 39*, 1242–1247.

Coccaro, E. F., Bergeman, C. S., Kavoussi, R. J., & Seroczynski, A. D. (1997). Heritability of aggression and irritability: A twin study of the Buss-Durkee aggression scales in adult male subjects. *Biological Psychiatry, 41*, 273–284.

Craissati, J. (2009). Attachment problems and sex offending. In A. R. Beech, L. E. Craig, & K. D. Browne (Eds.), *Handbook of assessment and treatment of sexual offenders* (pp. 13–38). Chichester: John Wiley & Sons.

Della Grotta, S., LaGasse, L. L., Arria, A. M., Derauf, C., Grant, P., Smith, L. M., ... Lester, B. M. (2010). Patterns of methamphetamine use during pregnancy: Results from the Infant Development, Environment, and Lifestyle (IDEAL) Study. *Maternal Child Health Journal, 14*, 519–527.

Dube, S. R., Anda, R. F., Felitti, V. J., Croft, J. B., Edwards, V. J., & Giles, W. H. (2001). Growing up with parental alcohol abuse: Exposure to childhood abuse, neglect and household dysfunction. *Child Abuse and Neglect, 25*, 1627–1640.

Eckstein, L. W., Shibley, I. J., Pennington, J. S., Carver, F. M., & Pennington, S. N. (1997). Changes in brain glucose levels and glucose transporter protein isoforms in alcohol- or nicotine-treated chick embryos. *Brain Research and Developmental Brain Research, 15*, 383–402.

Ershoff, D. H., Ashford, T. H., & Goldenberg, R. L. (2004). Helping pregnant women quit smoking. An overview. *Nicotine and Tobacco Research, 6,* S101–S105.

Felitti, V. J., Anda, R. F., Nordenberg, D., Williamson, D. F., Spitz, A. M., Edwards, V., & Marks, J. S. (1998). Relationship of childhood abuse and household dysfunction to many of the leading causes of death in adults: The Adverse Childhood Experiences (ACE) Study. *American Journal of Preventive Medicine, 14,* 245–258.

Fergusson, D. M., Boden, J. M., Horwood, L. J., Miller, A., & Kennedy, M. A. (2012). Moderating role of the MAOA genotype in antisocial behaviour. *The British Journal of Psychiatry, 200,* 116–123.

Fergusson, D. M., Woodward, L. J., & Horwood, L. J. (1998). Maternal smoking during pregnancy and psychiatric adjustment in late adolescence. *Archives of General Psychiatry, 55,* 721–727.

Finzi, R., Ram, A., Har-Even D., Shnitt, D., & Weizman, A. (2001). Attachment styles and aggression in physically abused and neglected children. *Journal of Youth and Adolescence, 30,* 769–786.

Fonagy, P. (2001). The human genome and the representational world: The role of early mother-infant interaction in creating an interpersonal interpretive mechanism. *Bulletin of the Menninger Clinic, 65,* 427–448.

Frazzetto, G., Di Lorenzo, G., Carola, V., Proietti, L., Sokolowska, E., Siracusano, A., … Troisi, A. (2007). Early trauma and increased risk for physical aggression during adulthood: The moderating role of MAOA genotype. *PloS ONE, 2:* e486. doi:10.1371/journal.pone.0000486.

Frodi, A., Dernevik, M., Sepa, A., Philison, J., & Bragesjö, M. (2001). Current attachment representations of incarcerated offenders varying in degree of psychopathy. *Attachment and Human Development, 3,* 269–283.

Galler, J. R., & Ramsey, F. (1989). A follow-up study of the influence of early malnutrition on development. *Journal of the American Academy of Child and Adolescent Psychiatry, 26,* 254–261.

Galler, J. R., Ramsey, F., Solimano, G., & Lowell, W. E. (1983). The influence of early malnutrition on subsequent behavioral development. II. Classroom behavior. *Journal of the American Academy of Child and Adolescent Psychiatry, 22,* 16–22.

Ganapathy, V., Prasad, P. D., Ganapathy, M. E., & Leibach, F. H. (2000). Placental transporters relevant to drug distribution across the maternal – fetal interface. *Journal of Pharmacology and Experimental Therapeutics, 294,* 413–420.

Gilbert, P. (2005). Compassion and cruelty: A biopsychosocial approach. In P. Gilbert (Ed.), *Compassion: Conceptualisations, research and use in psychotherapy* (pp. 9–74). London: Routledge.

Gillath, O., McCall, C., Shaver, P. Baek, J. M., & Chun, D. S. (2008) Genetic correlates of adult attachment style. *Personality and Social Psychology Bulletin, 34,* 1396–1405.

Greenberg, M. T., Speltz, M. L., & DeKlyen, M. (1993). The role of attachment in the early development of disruptive behavior problems. *Development and Psychopathology, 5,* 191–213.

Guy, J. D., Majorski, L. V., Wallace, C. J., & Guy, M. P. (1983). The incidence of minor physical anomalies in adult male schizophrenics. *Schizophrenia Bulletin, 9,* 571–582.

Hackshaw, A., Rodeck, C., & Boniface, S. (2011). Maternal smoking in pregnancy and birth defects: A systematic review based on 173, 687 malformed cases and 11.7 million controls. *Human Reproductive Update, 17,* 589–604.

Halverson, C. F., & Victor, J. B. (1976). Minor physical anomalies and problem behavior in elementary schoolchildren. *Child Development, 47,* 281–285.

Hansen, A., Dahl, L., Olson, G., Thornton, D., Grung, B., & Thayer, F. (2015). A long-term fatty fish intervention improved executive function in inpatients with antisocial traits and a history of alcohol and drug abuse. *Scandinavian Journal of Psychology, 56,* 467–474.

Hibbeln, J. R., Davis, J. M., Steer, C., Emmett, P., Rogers, I., Williams, C., & Golding, J. (2007). Maternal seafood consumption in pregancy and neurodevelopmental outcomes in childhood (ALSPAC study): An observational cohort study. *Lancet, 369,* 578–585.

Hillis, S. D., Anda, R. F., Dube, S. R., Felitti, V. J., Marchbanks, P. A., & Marks, J. S. (2004). The association between adverse childhood experiences and adolescent pregnancy, long-term psychosocial outcomes, and fetal death. *Pediatrics, 113,* 320–327.

Hodgins, S., Kratzer, L., & McNeil, T. F. (2001). Obstetric complications, parenting, and risk of criminal behavior. *Archives of General Psychiatry, 58,* 746–752.

Hughes, N., Williams, W. H., Chitsabesan, P., Walesby, R. C., Mounce, L. T. A., & Clasby, B. (2015). The prevalence of traumatic brain injury among young offenders in custody: A systematic review, *Journal Of Head Trauma Rehabilitation, 30,* 94–105.

Hux, K., Bond, V., Skinner, S., Belau, D., & Sanger, D. (1998). Parental report of occurences and consequences of traumatic brain injury among delinquent and non-delinquent youth. *Brain Injury, 12,* 667–681.

Jacques S. C., Kingsbury, A., Henshcke, P., Chomchai, C., Clews, S., Falconer, J., Abdel-Latif, M. E., Feller, J. M., & Oei, J. L. (2014). Cannabis, the pregnant woman and her child: Weeding out the myths. *Journal of Perinatology, 34,* 417–424.

Joseph, R. (2003). Environmental influences on neural plasticity, the limbic system, emotional development and attachment: A review. *Child Psychiatry and Human Development, 29,* 189–208.

Kemppainen, L., Jokelainen, J., Jarvelin, M. R., Isohanni, M., & Rasanen, P. (2001). The one-child family and violent criminality: A 31-year follow-up study of the Northern Finland 1966 birth cohort. *American Journal of Psychiatry, 158,* 960–962.

Lally, J. R., Mangione, P. L., & Honig, A. S. (1988). Long-range impact of an early intervention with low income children and their families. In D. R. Powell (Ed.), *Parent education as early childhood intervention* (pp. 79–104). Norwood, NJ: Ablex.

Lazar, S. W., Kerr, C. E., Wasserman, R. H., Gray, J. R., Greve, D. N., Treadway, M. T.,... Fischl, B. (2005). Meditation experience is associated with increased cortical thickness. *Neuroreport, 16,* 1893–1897.

Leon-Carrion, J., & Ramos, F. J. C. (2003). Blows to the head during development can predispose to violent cranial behaviour. Rehabilitation of consequences of head injury is a measure for crime prevention. *Brain Injury, 17,* 207–216.

Lester, B. M., Andreozzi, L., & Appiah, L. (2004). Substance use during pregnancy: Time for policy to catch up with research. *Harm Reduction Journal, 1,* 5–49.

Levenson, J. S., Willis, G. M., & Prescott, D. S. (2014). Adverse childhood experiences in the lives of female sex offenders. *Sexual Abuse: A Journal of Research and Treatment, 24,* 64–101.

Lister, J. P., Blatt, G. J., DeBassio, W. A., Kemper, T. L., Tonkiss, J., Galler, J. R., & Rosene, D. L. (2005). Effect of prenatal protein malnutrition on numbers of neurons in the principal cell layers of the adult rat hippocampal formation. *Hippocampus, 15,* 393–403.

Liu, J. (2004). Childhood externalizing behavior. Theory and implications. *Journal of Child and Adolescent Psychiatric Nursing, 17,* 93–103.

Liu, J., & Raine, A. (2006). The effect of childhood malnutrition on externalizing behaviors. *Current Opinion in Pediatrics, 18,* 565–570.

Liu, J., Raine, A., Wuerker, A., Venables, P. H., & Mednick, S. A. (2009). The association of birth complications and externalizing behavior in early adolescents. *Journal of Research on Adolescence, 19,* 93–111.

Liu, J., & Wuerker, A. (2005). Biosocial bases of aggressive and violent behavior- implications for nursing studies. *International Journal of Nursing Studies, 42*, 229–241.

Lyons-Ruth, K., Alpern, L., & Repacholi, B. (1993). Disorganized infant attachment classification and maternal psychosocial problems as predictors of hostile aggressive behavior in the preschool classroom. *Child Development, 64*, 572–585.

MacPherson, P., & Chudley, A. E. (2007). Fetal Alcohol Spectrum Disorder (FASD): Screening and estimating incidence in an adult correctional population. Second International Conference on Fetal Alcohol Spectrum Disorder: Research, Policy, and Practice Around the World, Victoria, British Columbia.

Maguire, E. A., Woollett, K., & Spiers, H. J. (2006). London taxi drivers and bus drivers: A structural MRI and neuropsychological analysis. *Hippocampus, 16*, 1091–1101.

Maughan, B., Taylor, A., Caspi, A., & Moffitt, T. E. (2004). Prenatal smoking and early childhood conduct problems. *Archives of General Psychiatry, 61*, 836–843.

McAllister, T. (1992). Neuropsychiatric sequelae of head injuries. *Psychiatric Clinics of North America, 15*, 661–665.

Mitchell, I. J., & Beech, A. R. (2011). Towards an attachment related neurobiological model of offending. *Clinical Psychology Review, 31*, 872–882.

Morgan, A. B., & Lilienfeld, S. O. (2000). A meta-analytic review of the relationship between antisocial behavior and neuropsychological measures of executive function. *Clinical Psychology Review, 20*, 113–136.

Muneoka, K., Ogawa, T., Kamei, K., Muraoka, S., Tomiyoshi, R., Mimura, Y., … Takigawa, M. (1997). Prenatal nicotine exposure affects the development of the central serotonergic system as well as the dopaminergic system in rat offspring: Involvement of route of drug administrations. *Brain Research and Developmental Brain Research, 102*, 117–126.

Neugebauer, R., Hoek, H. W., & Susser, E. (1999). Prenatal exposure to wartime famine and development of antisocial personality disorder in early adulthood. *Journal of the American Medical Association, 4*, 479–481.

Olds, D. (1997). Tobacco exposure and impaired development: A review of the evidence. *Mental Retardation and Developmental Disabilities Research Reviews, 3*, 257–269.

Olds, D., Henderson, C. R. J., Cole, R., Eckenrode, J., Kitzman, H., Luckey, D., … Powers, J. (1998). Long-term effects of nurse home visition on children's criminal and antisocial behavior: 15-year follow-up of a randomized controlled trial. *Journal of the American Medical Association, 280*, 1238–1244.

Olson, H. C., Streissguth, A. P., Sampson, P. D., Barr, H. M., Bookstein, F. L., & Thiede, K. (1997). Association of prenatal alcohol exposure with behavioral and learning problems in early adolescence. *Journal of the American Academy of Child and Adolescent Psychiatry, 36*, 1187–1194.

Orlebeke, J. F., D. L. Knol, & Verhulst, F. C. (1997). Increase in child behavior problems resulting from maternal smoking during pregnancy. *Archives of Environmental Health, 52*, 317–321.

Perica, M. M., & Delas, I. (2011). Essential fatty acids and psychiatric disorders. Nutrition in clinical practice. *Official Publication of the American Society for Parenteral and Enteral Nutrition, 26*, 409–425.

Pine, D. S., Shaffer, D., Schonfield, I. S., & Davies, M. (1997). Minor physical anomolies. Modifiers of environmental risks for psychiatric impairment? *Journal of the American Academy of Child and Adolescent Psychiatry, 36*, 395–403.

Przybelski, R. J., & Binkley, N. C. (2007). Is vitamin D important for preserving cognition? A positive correlation of serum 25-hydroxyvitamin D concentration with cognitive function. *Archives of Biochemistry Biophysics, 460*, 202–205.

Raine, A. (2002). Biosocial studies of antisocial and violent behavior in children and adults: A review. *Journal of Abnormal Child Psychology, 304*, 311–326.

Raine, A., Brennan, P., & Mednick, S. A. (1994). Birth complications combined with early maternal rejection at age 1 year predispose to violent crime at age 18 years. *Archives of General Psychiatry, 51*, 984–988.

Raine, A., Mellingen, K., Liu, J., Venables, P., Sarno A., & Mednick, S. A. (2003). Effects of environmental enrichment at ages 3–5 years on schizotypal personality and antisocial behavior at ages 17 and 23 years. *American Journal of Psychiatry, 160*, 1627–1635.

Rhee, S. H., & Waldman, I. D. (2002). Genetic and environmental influences on antisocial behavior: A meta-analysis of twin and adoption studies. *Psychological Bulletin, 128*, 490–529.

Rivera, J., Jaffee, K., Polissar, N. L., Fay, G. C., Martin, K. M., Shurtleff, H. A., & Liao, S. (1994). Family functioning and children's academic performance and behavior problems in the year following brain injury. *Archives of Physical Medicine and Rehabilitation, 75*, 369–379.

Roebuck, T. M., Mattson, S. N., & Riley, E.P. (1999). Behavioral and psychosocial profiles of alcohol-exposed children. *Alcoholism. Clinical and Experimental Research, 23*, 1070–1076.

Rogers, J. M. (2009). Tobacco and pregnancy. *Reproductive Toxicology, 28*, 152–160.

Rosen, G. M., Deinard, Schwartz, C., Smith, B., Stephenson, B., & Grabenstein, B. (1985). Iron deficiency among incarcerated juvenile delinquents. *Journal of Adolescent Health Care, 6*, 419–423.

Saltaris, C. (2002). Psychopathy in juvenile offenders: Can temperament and attachment be considered as robust developmental precursors. *Clinical Psychology Review, 22*, 729–752.

Sampson, R. J., & Laub, J. H. (1990). Crime and deviance over the life course: The salience of adult social bonds. *American Sociological Review, 55*, 609–627.

Schoenthaler, S. J., & Bier, I. D. (2000). The effect of vitamin-mineral supplementation on juvenile delinquency among American schoolchildren: A randomized double blind placebo-controlled trial. *Journal of Alternative and Complementary Medicine, 6*, 19–29.

Schonfeld, A. M., Mattson, S. N., & Riley, E. P. (2005). Moral maturity and delinquency after prenatal alcohol exposure. *Journal of Studies on Alcohol, 6*, 19–29.

Shalev, I., Moffitt, T., Sugden, K., Williams, B., Houts, R. M., Danese, A., ... Caspi, A. (2013). Exposure to violence during childhood is associated with telomere erosion from 5 to 10 years of age: A longitudinal study. *Molecular Psychiatry, 18*, 576–581.

Solomon, E. P., & Heide, K. M. (2005). The biology of trauma. *Journal of Interpersonal Violence, 20*, 51–60.

Stevens, L., Zhang, W., Peck., L., Kuczek, Y., Grevstad, N., & Mahon, A. (2003). EFA supplementation in children with inattention, hyperactivity, and other disruptive behaviors. *Lipids, 38*, 1007–1021.

Streissguth, A. P., Barr, H. M., Kogan, J., & Bookstein, F. L. (1996). *Understanding the occurrence of secondary disabilities in clients with fetal alcohol syndrome (FAS) and fetal alcohol effects (FAE).* Technical Report No. 96–06. Seattle, WA: University of Washington, Fetal Alcohol and Drug Unit.

Streissguth, A. P., & Kanter, J. (Eds.) (1997). *The challenge of fetal alcohol syndrome: Overcoming secondary disabilities.* Seattle, WA: University of Washington Press.

Swayze, V. W., Johnson, V. P., Hanson, J. W., Piven, J., Sato, Y., Giedd, J. N., Mosnik D., & Andreasen, N. C. (1997). Magnetic resonance imaging of brain anomalies in fetal alcohol syndrome. *Pediatrics, 99*, 232–240.

Teicher, M. H., Andersen, S. L., Polcari, A., Anderson, C. M., Navalta, C. P., & Kim, D. M. (2003). The neurobiological consequences of early stress and childhood maltreatment. *Neuroscience and Biobehavioral Reviews, 27*, 33–44.

Tibbetts, S. G., & Piquero, A. R. (1999). The influence of gender, low birth weight, and disadvantaged environment in predicting early onset of offending. A test of Moffitt's interactional hypothesis. *Criminology, 37*, 843–878.

Wakschlag, L. S., Lahey, B. B., Loeber, R., Green, S. M., Gordon, R. A., & Leventhal, B. L. (1997). Maternal smoking during pregnancy and the risk of conduct disorder in boys. *Archives of General Psychiatry, 54,* 670–676.

Wakschlag, L. S., Pickett, K. E., Cook, E., Benowitz, N. L. & Leventhal, B. L. (2002). Maternal smoking during pregnancy and severe antisocial behavior in offspring: A review. *American Journal of Public Health, 92,* 966–974.

Waldrop, M. F., Bell, R. Q., McLauglin, B., & Halverson, C. F. (1978). Newborn minor physical anomalies predict short attention span, peer aggression, and impulsivity at age 3. *Science, 199,* 563–564.

Weinfield, N. S., Sroufe, A., Egeland, B., & Carlson, E. (2008). Individual differences in infant-caregiver attachment: Conceptual and empirical aspects of security. In J. Cassidy & P. R. Shaver, *Handbook of attachment: Theory, research, and clinical applications, second edition* (pp. 78–101). New York, NY: Guilford Press.

Wenzel, S. L., Kosofsky, B. E., Harvey, J. A., & Iguchi, M. Y. (2001). Perinatal cocaine exposure: Scientific considerations and policy implications. RAND Monograph report, 1–33. Retrieved from http://www.rand.org/pubs/monograph_reports/MR1347.html.

Werbach, M. (1995). Nutritional influences on aggressive behavior. *Journal of Orthomolecular Medicine, 7,* 45–51.

Williams, K., Papadopoulou, V., & Booth, N. (2012). Prisoners' childhood and family backgrounds. Results from the Surveying Prisoner Crime Reduction (SPCR) longitudinal cohort study of prisoners. *Ministry of Justice Research Series 4/12.* Retrieved from https://www.gov.uk/government/uploads/system/uploads/attachment_data/file/278837/prisoners-childhood-family-backgrounds.pdf.

20

Mental Illness as a Putative Risk Factor for Violence and Aggression

Ahmad Abu-Akel and Sune Bo

> ### Key points
>
> - In this chapter, brief definitions of aggression and violence and their subtypes are outlined.
> - Conceptions and misconceptions regarding the association of mental illness with aggression and violence are considered in three major mental illnesses:
>   - schizophrenia;
>   - personality disorders (including psychopathy) (see also Chapters 9 and 10); and
>   - autism (see also Chapter 11).
> - For each of these, key neurobiological features that are putatively linked with the propensity to commit acts of violence and aggression are discussed.
> - In addition, the presence of additional, comorbid disorders that may aggravate the risk for violence and aggression are also reviewed.
> - Finally, some common underlying psychological and neurobiological causes, highlighting the social brain network as a possible neurobiological framework to understanding violence and aggression in these disorders, are described.

Terminology Explained

Aggression is a ubiquitous phenomenon in humans and its underpinnings are considered to be multifactorial, including socioeconomic, psychological, and neurobiological factors.

Asperger syndrome is mostly a "hidden disability." This means that it is difficult to tell that someone has the condition from their outward presentation. People with the condition have difficulties in three main areas: social communication, social interaction, and social imagination.

The Wiley Blackwell Handbook of Forensic Neuroscience, First Edition. Edited by Anthony R. Beech, Adam J. Carter, Ruth E. Mann and Pia Rotshtein.
© 2018 John Wiley & Sons Ltd. Published 2018 by John Wiley & Sons Ltd.

Autism spectrum disorders (ASD) are a spectrum of psychological conditions characterized by widespread abnormalities of social interactions and communication as well as restricted interests and repetitive behavior. More boys are diagnosed with the condition than girls. There's no cure for ASD, but speech and language therapy, occupational therapy, educational support, plus a number of other interventions are available to support children and parents.

Axis I and **Axis II** disorders were part of the Multiaxial Assessment System of the fourth edition of the *Diagnostic and Statistical Manual (DSM)* (American Psychiatric Association, 2000). Axis I referred to all the major clinical disorders such as schizophrenia, autism, bipolar disorder, and anxiety disorders. Axis II included all personality disorders and intellectual disability. The current *DSM-5* (American Psychiatric Association, 2013) has collapsed Axis I, Axis II, and Axis III (which included general medical conditions) into one axis, thus encompassing all psychiatric and general medical diagnoses.

Mentalizing is the process by which we make sense of each other and ourselves, implicitly and explicitly, in terms of subjective states and mental processes. It is a profoundly social construct in the sense that we are attentive to the mental states of those we are with, physically or psychologically.

Nucleus accumbens is a region in the basal forebrain near to the preoptic area of the hypothalamus. This area plays a central role in the reward circuit. Its operation is based chiefly on two essential neurotransmitters: *dopamine*, which promotes desire, and *serotonin*, whose effects include satiety and inhibition. The nucleus accumbens and the olfactory tubercle collectively form the ventral striatum, which is part of the basal ganglia.

Personality disorders in some individuals are due to a biological propensity to develop personality disorders. In others they appear to be caused by adverse life events. Hence, when an individual is considered to be "personality disordered" the normal developmental process has been derailed in some way.

Positron emission tomography (PET) is a nuclear imaging technique that produces three-dimensional images of functional processes in the living organism. These images rely on the detection of gamma rays that are emitted indirectly by a positron-emitting radionuclide (also called a tracer) that has been introduced to the body (usually into the blood circulation).

Schizophrenia is the most common diagnosis within forensic mental health settings. It is a severe and chronic illness that is characterized by episodes of significant perceptual disturbance: the *positive* symptoms of hallucinations, delusions, and thought disorder – which may/may not, be accompanied by *negative symptoms* (including flattened affect, avolition, anhedonia, etc.) – that result in major changes in an individual's thinking, emotions and behaviors. None of these specific symptoms are exclusive to schizophrenia, or are essential for diagnosis.

Schizophrenia spectrum disorders are a spectrum of psychotic disorders that include: schizophrenia, schizoaffective disorder, delusional disorder, schizotypal personality disorder, schizophreniform disorder, brief psychotic disorder, and psychosis associated with substance use/medical conditions.

> **Violence** is any intentional behavior that involves verbal threats or assaults, or physicality.

Introduction

Precipitated by public misperceptions and stigma, having a mental illness has exaggeratingly been associated with aggressive and violent behavior. In fact, most researchers are in agreement that individuals with mental illness are responsible for only a fraction of violence committed in the society as a whole (van Dorn, Volavka, & Johnson, 2012; Walsh, Buchanan, & Fahy, 2002). At the same time, research points out that a modest, but significant, association exists between mental illness and violence (Fazel & Grann 2006; Joyal, Dubreucq, Grendon, &, 2007; van Dorn et al., 2012). However, the extent to which the presence of a mental illness per se increases the propensity to engage in delinquent and antisocial behavior continues to be a topic of controversy. Equally controversial are delineating factors that may precipitate, or even augment, this association. Refining this association is thus critical for tailoring specific treatment approaches of pathological aggression.

A basic limiting-step of research addressing aggression and violence is the lack of a unifying definition for these general concepts (Alexander, Crouch, Halstead, & Piachaud, 2006; Bo, Abu-Akel, Kongerslev, Haahr, & Simonsen, 2011; Douglas & Ogloff, 2003). Studies have variably defined violence as *behaviors* that include verbal threats or assaults, or as behaviors that necessarily involve physicality. Damaging property and self-harming, including self-mutilation and suicide attempts, have also been considered acts of violence (for a recent review see Bo et al., 2011). While it is conceivable to assume that these varying definitions stem from the different types of information and the sources used to classify violence (Mulvey, 1994), there is a need to agree on a universal definition of what represents violent behavior. The definition used in the Macarthur studies (Steadman et al., 1998) and the growing number of studies that provide detailed accounts of the nature of the violence committed or the aggression displayed (Bo, Abu-Akel, Bertelsen, Kongerslev, M., & Helt Haahr, 2013; Kockler, Stanford, Nelson, Meloy, & Sanford, 2006) could provide the bases for a dialogue that would lead to the formulation of a universally accepted definition of violence and aggression (see Box 20.1).

Box 20.1 Definitions of aggression and violence

Aggression is any behavior that is hostile, injurious, or destructive and has the *potential* to inflict injury or damage to persons or objects. It encompasses both nonviolent aggression, such as harassment and verbal assaults toward others, and violent aggression that entails the use of physical force or power that results in injury or harm.

Violence is any intentional behavior that involves verbal threats or assaults, or physicality. Damaging property and self-harming, including self-mutilation and suicide attempts, have been considered acts of violence as well.

In an attempt to clarify the differences and overlaps between aggression and violence, a useful distinction to make is that between premeditated and impulsive aggression (Barratt & Felthous, 2003; Meloy, 2006; Siever, 2008). Premeditated aggression – also termed instrumental, proactive, or predatory aggression – is a violent act that is planned and deliberately conceived. In contrast, impulsive aggression – also termed reactive or affective aggression – is affectively driven, and is accompanied by high levels of autonomic arousal. Evidence suggests that premeditated aggression is linked to aggressive recidivism, and is a more pathological form of aggression compared to impulsive aggression (Cornell et al., 1996). Importantly, not all acts of aggression (both violent and nonviolent aggression) are criminal or pathological as aggression can be adaptive, occurring in the context of dangerous and imminent threat (Siever, 2008).

In this chapter, we will use the terms violence and aggression interchangeably since the studies we include use very dissimilar definitions of the concepts. However, we stress that future empirical studies should work toward a clearer definition and operationalization of the concepts. In what follows, we evaluate the association between mental illness and violence by examining three major mental illnesses, which include schizophrenia, autism, and personality disorders (including psychopathy). For each of these illnesses, we highlight key neurobiological features that are putatively linked with the propensity to commit acts of violence and aggression. In addition, we examine whether the presence of additional, comorbid disorders aggravates the risk for violence and aggression. Finally, we discuss some common underlying psychological

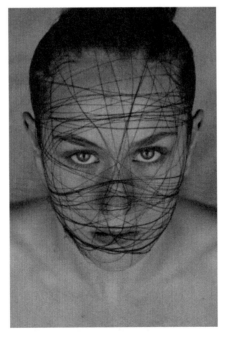

The association of mental illness with violence *Schizophrenia, autism, and personality disorders are conceptualized as separate illnesses, but they are variably associated with increased risk for violence. This risk is exacerbated in the presence of various co-morbid conditions such as substance abuse.*

Source: © Shanon. Used under license from 699pic.

Evaluating The Association Between Mental Illness And Violence

and neurobiological causes, highlighting the social brain network as a possible neurobiological framework to understanding violence and aggression in these disorders.

Schizophrenia

Schizophrenia affects approximately 1% of individuals during the course of their lifetime (McGrath, Saha, Chant, & Welham, 2008), inflicting a broad range of cognitive and psychosocial abnormalities, including interpersonal and social behaviors (van Os & Kapur, 2009). Difficulties in these areas may increase the risk of these patients to engage in aggressive and various delinquent behaviors. While it should be noted that individuals with schizophrenia are more likely to be victims of violence and aggression themselves (Pirarba et al., 2010; Taylor, 2008), epidemiological, prospective, cohort, and cross-sectional studies confirm that they have an enhanced tendency to commit acts of violence and aggression compared to the general population (Fazel, Gulati et al., 2009; Joyal, Dubreucq et al., 2007; Rasanen et al., 1998; Swanson et al., 2006; Walsh, Buchanan, & Fahy, 2002). The prevalence of any violence in patients with schizophrenia has been estimated to be between 15% and 19% (Swanson et al., 2004; Swanson et al., 2006). Furthermore, a meta-analysis has found that men and women with schizophrenia are respectively four and eight times more likely to commit an act of violence compared to men and women from the general population (Fazel, Gulati et al., 2009), albeit that this risk appears to be associated with alcohol abuse.

Research has shown that patients with schizophrenia engage in various acts of aggressive and violent behaviors, including, but not limited to, damaging property, arson, common assault, and homicide, as well as harmful self-mutilation and suicide (Bo et al., 2011). Of these, arson and homicide have been shown to have the strongest associations. Specifically, male arson offenders are 23 times more likely to be diagnosed with schizophrenia, and women 39 times (Anwar et al., 2011). Patients with schizophrenia are 20 times more likely to have comitted a murder (Fazel, Gulati et al., 2009). While these studies confirm that there is some relationship between schizophrenia and violence, explaining this link remains a major challenge.

Understanding the link is often confounded by the heterogenic nature of the illness, which is characterized by the presence of various symptoms. Such symptoms include: hallucinations, delusions, and thought disorders (*positive symptoms*); avolition (lack of drive/motivation), lack of emotions, asociality, and poverty of speech (*negative symptoms*), as well as bizarre behaviors arising from these belief systems and affect. Due to this heterogeneity, researchers have adopted several approaches in an effort to understand the risk for violence in this population. This extensive body of literature can be divided into six main areas: (1) symptomatology, (2) substance abuse, (3) demographic and environmental factors, (4) personality disorders (including psychopathy), (5) socio-cognitive abilities, and (6) neurobiological abnormalities.

Schizophrenic symptomatology

Integral to the diagnosis of schizophrenia is the presence of psychotic symptoms, and so understanding their role in the occurrence of violence is a natural starting point.

Research suggests that there is a relationship between active psychotic symptoms and violence (Fazel, Gulati et al., 2009; Tiihonen et al., 1997; Volavka & Citrome, 2008), and that this relationship, both in frequency and severity, seems to be most pronounced during first-episode psychosis (Large & Nielssen, 2011). However, the relationship between the presence of active psychotic symptoms and violence appears non-random and is primarily linked to the presence of positive symptoms. These include delusional symptoms such as persecutory ideations, persecutory delusions in combination with emotional distress, threat/control-override symptoms (TCO), command hallucinations, and hallucinations of threatening content (Bo et al., 2011).

On the other hand, research shows that the presence of negative symptoms has an attenuating effect on the likelihood of committing serious acts of violence (Swanson et al., 2006), suggesting that clusters of symptoms and the degree of their relative prominence may influence the risk of engagement in violent and aggressive behavior. Importantly, research also suggests that deterioration in these symptoms may not necessarily signal imminent violence (Skeem et al., 2006); and that the amelioration of these symptoms may not necessarily materialize in reduced risk for violence (Abushua'leh & Abu-Akel, 2006). This suggests that other factors beyond symptomatology must be brought to bear in understanding the occurrence of violence in this population.

Comorbidity of schizophrenia and substance abuse

A prominent comorbid condition among patients with schizophrenia is substance abuse. Reports indicate that patients with schizophrenia are three times more likely to have substance abuse problems, and nearly 50% of patients have a diagnosis of substance abuse (Dixon, 1999; Green et al., 2007). The most frequently associated substances are alcohol and cannabis. Older studies have already shown that the risk for violence is significantly enhanced in the presence of alcohol-induced psychoses and in patients with dual diagnosis (Swanson et al., 1990; Tiihonen et al., 1997), a finding that has been confirmed in later studies and meta-analyses (Fazel, Gulati et al., 2009; Fazel, Långström et al., 2009; Short et al., 2013; van Dorn, Volavka, & Johnson, 2012). There is also strong evidence linking cannabis abuse and violence even after controlling for the consumption of alcohol and other substances, albeit to a lesser degree when compared to alcohol or cocaine related violence (see Pickard & Fazel, 2013).

Given the elevated levels of substance abuse comorbidity in schizophrenia (dual diagnosis), it is important to contrast the relative risk for violence in schizophrenic individuals with, and without, substance abuse compared with non-schizophrenic individuals with, and without, substance abuse. In this regard, Fazel, Gulati et al. (2009) concluded from their longitudinal study that there is only a modest association between schizophrenia and violence, and that much of the increased risk can be accounted for by substance abuse comorbidity. These researchers also found that the risk for violence in patients with dual diagnosis is similar to individuals with substance abuse without psychosis.

However, we should be cautious in the extent to which we can attribute the risk for violence in schizophrenic individuals to substance abuse. First, not all patients have access to alcohol, or illicit drugs, and studies suggest that violence can be driven by factors other than psychotic symptoms or substance abuse (Rasanen et al., 1998). Second, environmental and demographic factors may be important determinants of substance abuse among patients with schizophrenia. In this regard, studies have shown that violent individuals with schizophrenia tend to be, among other factors, young, male, and of low socioeconomic status (Elbogen & Johnson, 2009; Swanson et al., 1990), which are factors known to be associated with increased risk for both schizophrenia and substance abuse. Third, it is not entirely clear that substance abuse is independent of schizophrenic pathogenesis (Green et al., 2007), and there are several disease-related theories that can provide explanation for the link between schizophrenia and substance abuse. Here, we highlight two of these models.

The first is the neural diathesis-stress model (Fowles, 1992), and the second is the reward circuitry dysfunction model (Chambers, Krystal, & Self, 2001; Roth, Brunette, & Green, 2005). The *diathesis-stress model* assumes that schizophrenia is associated with both genetic and neurobiological vulnerabilities that are exacerbated by environmental stressors such as substance abuse. Green et al. (2007) summarize three lines of evidence in support of this model: (1) substance abuse is associated with earlier age of onset; (2) adolescent cannabis users who are also carriers of the val/val catechol O-methyl-transferase polymorphism tend to develop psychosis very early in adulthood; and (3) substance abuse in even small quantities markedly increases the risk of relapse. The *reward circuitry dysfunction model* is based on evidence suggesting that dysfunctional brain areas in schizophrenic individuals overlap with the dopamine-mediated reward circuitry. The elevated levels of substance abuse in schizophrenia can thus be seen as compensation for suboptimal levels of experiencing reward. Together, these findings suggest that patients with schizophrenia are especially susceptible to substance abuse and that the link between substance abuse and violence should be viewed in the context of the pathogenesis of schizophrenia.

Comorbidity of schizophrenia and personality disorder

We would note that Chapters 9 and 10 in this volume provide a more in-depth discussion of both psychopathy and personality disorder, so this section is by necessity brief. But, as Hippocrates' famous phrase notes, "it is far more important to know what person the disease has than what disease the person has". This places the concept of personality as an important feature in the general understanding of psychopathology and associated behavioral outcomes. Axis I and Axis II disorders co-occur at particularly high rates in schizophrenia (McMillan et al., 2009). For example, in one study 33% of 549 patients with schizophrenia screened positive for all personality disorder clusters (Moore, Green, & Carr, 2012). Psychopathy also co-occurs in schizophrenia at elevated rates compared to the general population, and ranges from 4% to 8% (Abushua'leh & Abu-Akel, 2006).

Such elevated rates of co-occurrence underscore the pertinent role these disorders have in understanding the psychopathology and behavior of patients with schizophrenia. Studies investigating the augmentative effect of these comorbidities on the occurrence of violence in schizophrenia reveal substantial increases in the risk for violence. Specifically, studies show that patients with comorbid substance abuse (Elbogen & Johnson, 2009; Van Dorn, Volavka, & Johnson, 2012) and/or severe mental disorders (i.e., bipolar and major depressive disorders) (van Dorn et al., 2012) had the highest risk for violence. Elevated risk for violence in schizophrenia has also been linked to the comorbidity of borderline and antisocial personality disorders (Bo, Abu-Akel, Kongerslev et al., 2013), and severe forms of violence including homicide have been associated with comorbid psychopathy (Laajasalo et al., 2011). The probability of violence in schizophrenia has also been linked to the relative dominance of psychopathic tendencies in such a way that the amelioration of symptoms did not reduce the likelihood for violence in patients with high or comorbid psychopathy (Abushua'leh & Abu-Akel, 2006). Collectively, these findings suggest that comorbidity of personality disorders is potentially a significant predictive factor of violence in patients with schizophrenia.

Schizophrenia *Schizophrenia is a severe and chronic illness that is characterized by episodes of significant perceptual disturbance that results in major changes in an individual's thinking, emotions, and behaviors. It is characterized by positive symptoms such as hallucinations, delusions, and thought disorder; and may be accompanied by negative symptoms such as flattened affect and volition.*

Source: Karel Miragaya. Used under license from 123RF.

The association between socio-cognitive abilities and violence in schizophrenia

Violence has also been linked to impairments in socio-cognitive abilities such as theory of mind (or *mentalizing*) and empathy (Abu-Akel & Abushua'leh, 2004; Keenan & Ward, 2000; Miller & Eisenberg, 1988), which broadly refer to understanding the cognitive (i.e., reasoning about knowledge, intentions, and beliefs) and affective (i.e., reasoning about emotions) mental states of oneself and others. Being unable to understand the minds of others, such as their intentional states, may lead to misunderstandings and, in some cases, the erroneous perceptions of these intentions as threatening or hostile, which may in turn lead the individual to respond violently. In this regard, research has shown that an understanding of emotional mental states can reduce the propensity to engage in violence (Tangney, 1991) and function as a potent inhibitor of aggression (Fullam & Dolan, 2006). Lack of this understanding can be a risk factor for violence (Keenan & Ward, 2000).

Given the centrality of socio-cognitive impairments in schizophrenia and their role in social functioning, researchers have recently begun to examine their association with the occurrence of violence in this population (Abu-Akel & Abushua'leh, 2004; Bo, Abu-Akel, Bertelsen et al., 2013; Majorek et al., 2009). Two major findings emerge from this limited body of research. First, the ability to make empathic inferences is associated with a decrease in the likelihood of violence engagement. Second, cognitive mental-state understanding, in the absence of affective mentalizing, increases the possibility for violence. In this regard, Bo, Abu-Akel, Bertelsen et al. (2013) found that having relatively intact cognitive, but deficient affective, mental-state understanding is characteristic of patients with schizophrenia who predominantly commit premeditated aggression; while patients who predominantly commit impulsive aggression suffered from diminished overall mentalizing abilities. The association of intact cognitive mental-state understanding with increased risk for violence may appear paradoxical. However, this seeming contradiction is not illogical given that premeditated aggression involves planning, deception, and manipulation that inherently require functioning mentalizing abilities.

Neurochemical and neurobiological abnormalities in schizophrenia

It is clear that violence in schizophrenia is etiologically heterogeneous. Coupled with our relatively poor understanding of the neurobiology of schizophrenia, it is not surprising that the pathophysiological bases of violent behavior in schizophrenics are poorly understood. This is further complicated by research implicating various genetic, neurochemical, and neuroanatomical factors in the occurrence of violence. Here, we highlight some of the most consistent findings. First, research has consistently demonstrated a link between the neurotransmitter serotonin and aggressive behavior, and particularly impulsive aggression (Davidson, Putnam, & Larson, 2000; Seo, Patrick, & Kennealy, 2008). A similar link has also been made between dopamine and aggression (Siever, 2008). However, it has been suggested that the association of these two transmitters with aggression is better understood in the context of their interaction (Seo, Patrick, & Kennealy, 2008), where serotonin generally has an inhibitory effect over dopamine neurons and signaling (Abi-Dargham, 2007) (see Box 20.2).

> ## Box 20.2   Neuromodulators: dopamine, serotonin, catechol *O*-methyl-transferase
>
> **Dopamine** is a neuromodulator mainly originating from two nuclei known as the *substania nigra* and the *ventral tegmental area*. Dopamine is distributed in the brain through three major pathways: the nigrostriatal, the mesolimbic, and the mesocortical pathways. Dopamine functioning has been linked to hedonic responses, prediction of rewarding and aversive events, and the assignment of incentive/motivational salience to both external and internal stimuli.
>
> **Serotonin** (5-hydroxytriptamine, or 5-HT) is a neuromodulator that virtually innervates all parts of the central nervous system. The primary mode of action of 5-HT is through serotonergic receptors. 5-HT is associated with the regulation of mood, aggression, and cognitive functions including memory and learning, as well as with the modulation of social reward and punishment. Another central function of 5-HT is the *modulation* of dopamine release.
>
> The **Catechol *O*-methyl-transferase (COMT)** enzyme is coded by the COMT gene and has a predominant role in the termination of dopamine activity in the prefrontal cortex.

Here, the association of dopamine with aggression is attributed, in part, to the diminished inhibitory activity of serotonin (Ryding, Lindstrom, & Traskman-Bendz, 2008). A chief support for this connection comes from psychopharmacological studies showing that neuroleptics with potent affinity to receptors of both neurotransmitters (Remington, 2008), such as clozapine, are effective in reducing aggression in patients with schizophrenia (Volavka, 2012). Interestingly, both serotonin and dopamine are also considered chief modulators of the reward circuitry, which includes the ventral striatum, the amygdala, and the orbitofrontal cortex. The hyper-responsivity of this circuitry to the release of dopamine in schizophrenia has been related to positive symptoms, excessive pleasure seeking, substance abuse, and impulsivity, aspects that are known be involved with increased risk for violence.

Moreover, the association of an over-active dopaminergic system with violence has been linked to the role of the catechol *O*-methyl-transferase (COMT) enzyme in the termination of dopamine activity in the prefrontal cortex (Strous et al., 1997). The rate of dopamine termination, and thus its availability in the synaptic space, is variably associated with three Val^{158}Met allelic variants of the COMT gene localized to chromosome 22q11.1–q11.2 (Lachman et al., 1996). The Met/Met variant is associated with the slowest termination, the Met/Val variant is associated with an intermediate speed of termination, and the Val/Val variant is associated with the fastest termination (Akil et al., 2003). Consistent with the association of over-active dopaminergic activity and aggression, a recent meta-analysis has shown that the risk for violence increased by approximately 50% in patients who carry at least one Met allele (coding for slow or intermediate enzymes) compared to patients carrying the Val/Val variant, coding for the fast enzyme (Singh et al., 2012).

In addition to these neurochemical and genetic factors, neuroimaging studies provide additional insights into the correlates of aggression in schizophrenia. Most consistently, these studies point to a dysfunction in the fronto-temporal circuitry, which chiefly involves the orbital and ventral prefrontal cortex, the amygdala and the striatum (Hoptman & Antonius, 2011; Soyka, 2011). These findings are consistent with models attributing general aggression to a disconnection between the frontal (cognitive) regions and the limbic-paralimbic (affective) regions of the brain (Siever, 2008). However, these findings are confounded by any number of factors, such as the comorbidity of substance abuse and various personality disorders. Taking into account such confounds, Joyal, Putkonen et al. (2007) compared violent offenders diagnosed with schizophrenia comorbid with antisocial and substance abuse disorders to offenders with schizophrenia-only diagnosis while performing an executive functioning task. In this study, the patients with comorbid antisocial and substance abuse disorders showed significantly lower activation in the orbital and the ventral prefrontal cortex as well as higher activation in other frontal regions including the interior cingulate. This finding suggests that investigating the neurobiology of offenders with, and without, co-comorbid conditions can provide an important contribution to understanding the neural bases of aggression in mental illness independent of substance abuse.

At present, we lack a unifying theory that can explain the occurrence of aggression in schizophrenia, although some have proposed preliminary models. For example, Schug and Raine (2009) have suggested that patients with schizophrenia can be classified based on whether they are antisocial and appear to differ on the functioning pattern of the dorsolateral region of the prefrontal cortex. Ultimately, understanding the root causes of violence and aggression in schizophrenia requires a multifactorial approach, and the key points identified in the above discussion delineate some of the main areas that future research would need to address.

Autism

Autism spectrum disorders (ASDs) occur in approximately 1% of individuals (Baron-Cohen et al., 2009). Bjorn Hofvander, in Chapter 11, provides an in-depth description of this disorder, hence the discussion here is very brief. ASD is defined by impairment in social communication and social interaction, and by repetitive behavior and restricted interests and activities. Aggressive behavior is a common phenomenon in ASD individuals. Surprisingly, however, there is very little empirical work that systematically examines this phenomenon or assesses its prevalence. Available research suggests that aggression is evident from the early years of development, and is displayed by over 50% of children and adolescents with ASD (Kanne & Mazurek, 2011; Mazurek, Kanne, & Wodka, 2013). Excessive aggression in ASD has been attributed to faulty development of cognitive and emotional faculties, which children use as early as three years of age to regulate their emotion and tame their behavior (Kaartinen et al., 2012). It also appears to be strongly associated with self-injury, sleep problems, and sensory problems (Mazurek et al., 2013), as well as with lower nonverbal IQ and expressive language, severe social deficits, and more repetitive behavior (Dominick et al., 2007).

Less still is known about violent offending in individuals with ASD. However, the existing limited literature reveals that violent offending in individuals with ASD is exacerbated by co-occurring factors commonly found in other pathologies that are associated with increased risk for violence such as in schizophrenics. In this regard, a longitudinal study that followed the offending pattern of individuals with autistic disorders or Asperger syndrome for 12 years, reported that the offenders (7% in total) were primarily males and with Asperger rather than autistic diagnosis, and had comorbid psychotic and/or substance use disorders (Långström et al., 2009). While this study does not answer the question of relative levels of offending in ASD compared to the general populations, a recent study reports that over 4% of incarcerated individuals met a conservative ASD criteria (Fazio, Pietz, & Denney, 2012), which is four times the prevalence rate of ASD in the general population. Given that Asperger syndrome is considered to be a milder form of autism with relatively spared socio-cognitive abilities (Senju et al., 2009), it would be interesting to investigate if these individuals have a specific socio-cognitive profile that predisposes them to offending, similar to that found in patients with schizophrenia (Bo, Abu-Akel, Bertelsen et al., 2013).

Our knowledge of the neurobiological underpinnings of aggression in ASD primarily relies on indirect evidence, and is centered around two main dysregulatory systems. The first is associated with serotonergic-dopaminergic abnormalities, the second is associated with a dysfunctional amygdala. The main insight regarding the association of serotonin and dopamine with aggression in ASD comes from pharmacological studies showing that treatment with neuroleptics that bind to both transmitters has resulted in reduced aggression (Sharma & Shaw, 2012). However, while a recent positron emission tomography (PET) study confirms the association of ASD with disruptions in the functionality of both transmitters (Nakamura et al., 2010), it failed to find significant associations between these neurochemical abnormalities and aggression as evaluated by the Aggression Questionnaire (Buss & Perry, 1992). The authors explain that this negative finding is likely due to a bias in the selection of cooperative high-functioning participants for the PET procedure.

The amygdala is known to play a major role in modulating aggression in healthy individuals (Matthies et al., 2012), which is likely to be serotonin dependent (Passamonti et al., 2012). Given that both the amygdala and the serotonergic systems are severely disrupted in ASD (Nakamura et al., 2010; Morgan, Nordahl, and Schumann 2012), it is feasible to assume that aggression in this population is associated with serotonin-mediated amygdala functioning. However, the exact role of the amygdala in aggression is far from conclusive and it needs to be investigated in the context of its circuitry (i.e., the frontal-limbic circuitry) and the neurotransmitters/modulators that regulate its activity.

Drawing any conclusions regarding the association of ASD with the risk for violence and offending behavior is premature at this stage. Therefore, much research is needed to gain more informed conclusions, and in particular research that addresses the role of co-occurring conditions such as psychosis and intellectual disabilities (Wachtel & Shorter, 2013) as well as comorbid personality disorders (Lugnegard, Hallerback, & Gillberg, 2012). Research addressing the neurobiology of aggression in ASD is very limited, and research investigating neurobiological differences between violent and nonviolent individuals with ASD is virtually absent.

Personality Disorders

Personality pathology is comprised of enduring traits that adversely affect the wellbeing of oneself or others (see Section II of the *DSM-5*: Schizophrenia Spectrum and

Borderline personality disorder *Borderline personality disorder, sometimes referred to as emotional unstable personality, is characterized by extreme mood fluctuations and weak sense of self. When an individual suffers from both schizophrenia and borderline personality disorder the risk of them exhibiting or engaging in criminal behavior and violent acts is magnified.*

Source: © cocoparisienne. Used under license from 699pic.

Other Psychotic Disorders) (American Psychiatric Association, 2013, p. 647). The prevalence rate of personality disorders (see Chapter 10 for a review of different personality disorders) in the general population is estimated to be at about 15% (Grant et al., 2004), and it seems to be cumulative over one's lifetime (Johnson et al., 2008). Research has shown that personality disorders can explain much of the variance in violent and delinquent behavior (Fountoulakis, Leucht, & Kaprinis, 2008; Johnson et al., 2000). For example, Johnson et al. have shown that paranoid, narcissistic, and passive-aggressive personality disorder symptoms were independently associated with risk for violent acts and criminal behavior during adolescence and early adulthood even when controlling for demographic variables and the presence of comorbid substance abuse and psychotic disorders (Johnson et al., 2000). Moreover, personality disorders are highly associated with criminal recidivism even in individuals without substance use disorder (Walter et al., 2011).

Although not an official diagnosis in the current diagnostic system of the *DSM-5* (American Psychiatric Association, 2013), psychopathy (see Chapter 9) is perhaps the most recognized of all the personality disorders (Trull & Durrett, 2005). This severe mental disorder is characterized by interpersonal and affective deficits and is associated with traits such as egocentricity, callousness, emotional dysfunction, manipulativeness, and impulsivity. It shares behavioral overlaps with antisocial personality disorder (ASPD), and is considered by some as the more severe form of the disorder (Coid & Ullrich, 2010). As currently defined, psychopathy has emerged as a reliable and valid construct in predicting violent and aggressive recidivism, the occurrence of severe forms of aggression (Hare & Neumann, 2009), and particularly premeditated aggression (Walsh, Swogger, & Kosson, 2009; Woodworth & Porter, 2002).

Considerable attention has been paid to understanding the neurobiology of individuals with ASPD, and particularly those with psychopathy. An emerging consensus suggests that psychopathy is most commonly associated with abnormalities in the frontal and temporal regions (Anderson & Kiehl, 2012, 2013). Other regions such as the anterior cingulate cortex and the insula have also been implicated in individuals with psychopathy (Decety, Skelly, & Kiehl, 2013). Antisocial behavior results not only from brain abnormalities that are disorder-specific, but also from brain injury. Indeed, lesion studies have shown that damage to the amygdala and the ventromedial prefrontal cortex produce antisocial behavior similar to those found in antisocial disorders (Sinclair & Gansler, 2006). Differential activations in individuals at risk for reactive aggression versus in those at risk for proactive aggression have also been observed. Specifically, individuals at risk for impulsive aggressions showed heightened amygdala activations, whereas psychopaths showed decreased amygdala and orbitofrontal activity in response to emotionally provocative stimuli (Blair, 2010). However, psychopaths are not merely incapable of understanding emotions, but they appear to process them along alternative cognitive pathways in the prefrontal cortex rather than in traditional limbic areas (Anderson & Kiehl, 2012). Accordingly, the apparent lack of emotional awareness in individuals with psychopathy may not be a deficiency, but instead an adaptation which enhances predatory success by keeping higher cognitive levels such as mentalizing abilities (used to deceit and manipulate victims) unaffected by emotionality (Meloy, 2006). In addition to these neurobiological abnormalities, genetic influences explain more than 50% of the variance in antisocial personality and behavior (Ferguson, 2010). Several genes have been implicated in antisocial behaviors that include the COMT gene, the MAOA gene, and the serotonin transporter promoter gene (5-HTT). It is important to emphasize that these genes are not causative but denote a vulnerability factor that in interaction with environmental factors such as family violence may lead to the development of antisocial behavior (Tuvblad et al., 2011).

A major challenge for understanding the neurobiology of aggression in individuals with personality disorders is reconciling the heterogeneous symptoms with which they are associated. These can be divided into implicit personality characteristics such as lacking empathy and egocentricity, and explicit behaviors such as impulsivity and poor behavior controls. The former is associated with affective deficits such as understanding emotions and the mental state of others, while the latter is associated with cognitive deficits such executive functioning and inhibition (Sinclair & Gansler, 2006). This distinction can provide future research an important conceptual framework to understanding aggression patterns within and across personality disorders as well as the strength of the association of specific brain abnormalities with the risk for violent and aggressive behavior.

Conclusions

While schizophrenia, autism, and personality disorders are conceptualized as separate illnesses, they are variably associated with increased risk for violence. This risk is exacerbated in the presence of various comorbid conditions such as psychosis, personality disorders, and substance abuse. Brain abnormalities at the regional, neurochemical, and genetic levels have been associated with the risk for violence and antisocial behavior. In addition to these brain abnormalities, these disorders variably compromise socio-cognitive abilities such as mentalizing and empathy, which are important in regulating social functioning and distress that often arise during interpersonal interactions. The overlap between brain networks implicated in aggression and the processing of socio-cognitive abilities suggest that pathological aggression can be conceptualized as a disorder of the social brain, which chiefly includes the amygdala, the orbitofrontal cortex, and the temporal cortex.

Although the mechanism of aggression underlying specific disorders may vary, aggression seems to result from an imbalance in cortical–subcortical regulation and their associated neuromodulators. According to one model, aggression is regulated by a striatal-frontal network that is modulated by opponent interaction between serotonin and dopamine (Ryding, Lindstrom, & Traskman-Bendz, 2008). Within this network, dopamine augments activation of the nucleus accumbens in aggression, and serotonin decreases aggression through stimulation of prefrontal cortical regions that send inhibitory projections to the nucleus accumbens, which in aggression has been activated from the amygdala. Indispensable to this network is the activity of the COMT enzyme and the serotonin transporter (SERT), which regulate the availability of these transmitters. An extension of this model would be to account for premeditated and impulsive aggression. In this respect, premeditated aggression might be associated with processing emotional information along alternative cognitive pathways in the prefrontal cortex rather than in the limbic-paralimbic regions of the network (Anderson & Kiehl, 2012). Conversely, impulsive aggression might be associated over-engaging the limbic structures of the network at the expense of a more rational and conscious prefrontal activity (Siever, 2008).

Aggression and antisocial behavior are a likely consequence of mental illnesses affecting the social brain. While a unifying network such as this runs the risk of oversimplifying the complexity of aggression and its specific expression within the various disorders, it nonetheless offers a framework that can be useful for research concerned with the development of therapeutic interventions for aggression at both the pharmacological level (by regulating transmission activity within the network) and the behavioral level (by introducing psychotherapeutic interventions aimed at improving socio-cognitive abilities).

Implications for Forensic Practice and Policy

Not long ago, incarceration was the main approach to dealing with antisocial behavior committed by individuals with mental illness. In many instances, jails have inappropriately become surrogate hospitals, a stance that is further complicated by the fact that personnel in these institutions possess limited understanding of the behavioral and neurobiological origins of violence in these individuals. While we still have a long way to go before the field reaches maturity, we are at a point where sufficient evidence has accumulated that warrants policy makers to adopt an alternate approach to dealing with risk for violence in mentally ill people. This approach requires the establishment of therapeutic institutions that are informed by current research and that employ personalized pharmacological and behavioral interventions, specifically tailored to reducing recidivism and the risk for violence. Such investment will lead to significant economic savings given the enormous economic costs of violence and criminal activity related to mental illness (Royal College of Psychiatrists, 2010).

Recommended Reading

Fazel, S., Gulati, G., Linsell, L., Geddes, J. R., & Grann, M. (2009). Schizophrenia and violence: Systematic review and meta-analysis. *PLoS Medicine, 6*(8):e1000120. doi: 10.1371/journal.pmed.1000120. *This paper reports a meta-analysis on data from 18,423 patients with schizophrenia and other psychoses. The link of schizophrenia and other psychoses with violence and offending may be mediated by subtance abuse comorbidity.*

Kanne, S. M., & Mazurek, M. O. (2011). Aggression in children and adolescents with ASD: Prevalence and risk factors. *Journal of Autism and Developmental Disorders, 41*(7), 926–937. doi: 10.1007/s10803-010-1118-4. *This paper assesses risk factors and aggression in 1380 children and adolescents with ASD. Parents reports suggest that the prevalance of aggression in this population to either caregivers and non-caregivers is high. Clinical severity, intellectual abilties, or gender do not seem to explain the occurrence of aggression. Younger children, however, tend to demonstrate greater aggression.*

Siever, L. J. (2008). Neurobiology of aggression and violence. *American Journal of Psychiatry, 165*(4), 429–442. doi: 10.1176/appi.ajp.2008.07111774. *This paper presents a model positing that pathological aggression may be precipitated by a disconnect between the frontal (cognitive) regions and the limbic-paralimbic (affective) regions of the brain.*

Van Dorn, R., Volavka, J., & Johnson, N. (2012). Mental disorder and violence: Is there a relationship beyond substance use? *Social Psychiatry and Psychiatric Epidemiology, 47*(3), 487–503. doi: 10.1007/s00127-011-0356-x. *This paper reports that there is a statiscally significant association between severe mental illness and violence, irrespective of substance abuse status. However, substance abuse comorbidity increases the risk for violence considerably.*

References

Abi-Dargham, A. (2007). Alterations of serotonin transmission in schizophrenia. *International Review of Neurobiology, 78*, 133–164. doi: 10.1016/S0074-7742(06)78005-9.

Abu-Akel, A., & Abushua'leh, K. (2004). "Theory of mind" in violent and nonviolent patients with paranoid schizophrenia. *Schizophrenia Research, 69*(1), 45–53. doi: 10.1016/S0920-9964(03)00049-5.

Abushua'leh, K., & Abu-Akel, A. (2006). Association of psychopathic traits and symptomatology with violence in patients with schizophrenia. *Psychiatry Research, 143*(2–3), 205–211. doi: 10.1016/j.psychres.2005.05.017.

Akil, M., Kolachana, B. S., Rothmond, D. A., Hyde, T. M., Weinberger, D. R., & Kleinman, J. E. (2003). Catechol-O-methyltransferase genotype and dopamine regulation in the human brain. *Journal of Neuroscience, 23*(6), 2008–2013.

Alexander, R. T., Crouch, K., Halstead, S., & J. Piachaud, J. (2006). Long-term outcome from a medium secure service for people with intellectual disability. *Journal of Intellectual Disabiity Research, 50*(4), 305–315. doi: 10.1111/j.1365-2788.2006.00806.x.

American Psychiatric Association (2000). *Diagnostic and statistical manual of mental disorders* (4th ed., text revision) *(DSM-IV-TR)*. Washington, DC: American Psychiatric Association.

American Psychological Association (2013). *Diagnostic and statistical manual of mental disorders* (5th ed.) *(DSM-5)*. Washington, DC: American Psychiatric Association.

Anderson, N. E., & Kiehl, K. A. (2012). The psychopath magnetized: Insights from brain imaging. *Trends in Cognitive Science, 16*(1), 52–60. doi: 10.1016/j.tics.2011.11.008.

Anderson, N. E., & Kiehl, K. A. (2013). Psychopathy: Developmental perspectives and their implications for treatment. *Restorative Neurology and Neuroscience, 32*(1), 103–117. doi: 10.3233/RNN-139001.

Anwar, S., Långström, N., Grann, M., & Fazel, S. (2011). Is arson the crime most strongly associated with psychosis? A national case-control study of arson risk in schizophrenia and other psychoses. *Schizophrenia Bulletin*, *37*(3), 580–586. doi: 10.1093/schbul/sbp098.

Baron-Cohen, S., Scott, F. J., Allison, C., Williams, J., Bolton, P., Matthews, F. E., & Brayne, C. (2009). Prevalence of autism-spectrum conditions: A UK school-based population study. *British Journal of Psychiatry*, *194*(6), 500–509. doi: 10.1192/bjp.bp.108.059345.

Barratt, E. S., & Felthous, A. R. (2003). Impulsive versus premeditated aggression: Implications for mens rea decisions. *Behavioral Sciences and the Law*, *21*(5), 619–630. doi: 10.1002/bsl.555.

Blair, R. J. (2010). Neuroimaging of psychopathy and antisocial behavior: A targeted review. *Current Psychiatry Reports*, *12*(1), 76–82. doi: 10.1007/s11920-009-0086-x.

Bo, S., Abu-Akel, A., Bertelsen, P., Kongerslev, M., & Haahr, U. H. (2013). Attachment, mentalizing and personality pathology severity in premeditated and impulsive aggression in schizophrenia. *International Journal of Forensic Mental Health*, *12*(2), 126–138. doi: 10.1080/14999013.2013.787562.

Bo, S., Abu-Akel, A., Kongerslev, M., Haahr, U. H., & Simonsen, E. (2011). Risk factors for violence among patients with schizophrenia. *Clinical Psychology Review*, *31*(5), 711–726. doi: 10.1016/j.cpr.2011.03.002.

Bo, S., Abu-Akel, A., Kongerslev, M., Haahr, U. H., & Simonsen, E. (2013). The role of co-morbid personality pathology in predicting self-reported aggression in patients with schizophrenia. *Comprehensive Psychiatry*, *54*(5), 423–431. doi: 10.1016/j.comppsych.2012.12.004.

Buss, A. H., & Perry, M. (1992). The Aggression Questionnaire. *Journal of Personality and Social Psychology*, *63*(3), 452–459. doi: 10.1037/0022-3514.63.3.452.

Chambers, R. A., Krystal, J. H., & Self, D. W. (2001). A neurobiological basis for substance abuse comorbidity in schizophrenia. *Biological Psychiatry*, *50*(2), 71–83.

Coid, J., & Ullrich, S. (2010). Antisocial Personality Disorder is on a continuum with psychopathy. *Comprehensive Psychiatry*, *51*(4), 426–433. doi: 10.1016/j.comppsych.2009.09.006.

Cornell, D. G., Warren, J., Hawk, G., Stafford, E., Oram, G., & Pine, D. (1996). Psychopathy in instrumental and reactive violent offenders. *Journal of Consulting and Clinical Psychology*, *64*(4), 783–790. doi: 10.1037/0022-006X.64.4.783.

Davidson, R. J., Putnam, K. M., & Larson, C. L. (2000). Dysfunction in the neural circuitry of emotion regulation – a possible prelude to violence. *Science*, *289*(5479), 591–594. doi: 10.1126/science.289.5479.591.

Decety, J., Skelly, L. R., & Kiehl, K. A. (2013). Brain response to empathy-eliciting scenarios involving pain in incarcerated individuals with psychopathy. *JAMA Psychiatry*, *70*(6), 638–645. doi: 10.1001/jamapsychiatry.2013.27.

Dixon, L. (1999). Dual diagnosis of substance abuse in schizophrenia: Prevalence and impact on outcomes. *Schizophenia Research*, *35*(Suppl), S93–100. doi: 10.1016/S0920-9964(98)00161-3.

Dominick, K. C., Davis, N. O., Lainhart, J., Tager-Flusberg, H., & Folstein, S. (2007). Atypical behaviors in children with autism and children with a history of language impairment. *Research in Developmental Disability*, *28*(2), 145–62. doi: 10.1016/j.ridd.2006.02.003.

Douglas, K. S., & Ogloff, J. R. (2003). Violence by psychiatric patients: The impact of archival measurement source on violence base rates and risk assessment accuracy. *Canadian Journal of Psychiatry*, *48*(11), 734–740.

Elbogen, E. B., & Johnson, S. C. (2009). The intricate link between violence and mental disorder: Results from the National Epidemiologic Survey on Alcohol and Related Conditions. *Archives of General Psychiatry*, *66*(2), 152–161. doi: 10.1001/archgenpsychiatry.2008.537.

Fazel, S., & Grann, M. (2006). The population impact of severe mental illness on violent crime. *American Journal of Psychiatry*, *163*(8), 1397–1403. doi: 10.1176/appi.ajp.163.8.1397.

Fazel, S., Gulati, G., Linsell, L., Geddes, J. R., & Grann, M. (2009). Schizophrenia and violence: Systematic review and meta-analysis. *PLoS Medicine, 6*(8), e1000120. doi: 10.1371/journal.pmed.1000120.

Fazel, S., Långström, N., Hjern, A., Grann, M., & Lichtenstein, P. (2009). Schizophrenia, substance abuse, and violent crime. *Journal of the American Medical Association, 301*(19), 2016–2023. doi: 10.1001/jama.2009.675.

Fazio, R. L., Pietz, C. A., & Denney, R. L. (2012). An estimate of the prevalence of autism-spectrum disorders in an incarcerated population. *Open Access Journal of Forensic Psychology, 4,* 69–80. Retrieved from http://www.forensicpsychologyunbound.ws/OAJFP/Volume_4__2012_files/Fazio%202012.pdf.

Ferguson, C. J. (2010). Genetic contributions to antisocial personality and behavior: A meta-analytic review from an evolutionary perspective. *Journal of Social Psychology, 150*(2), 160–180. doi: 10.1080/00224540903366503.

Fountoulakis, K. N., Leucht, S., & Kaprinis, G. S. (2008). Personality disorders and violence. *Current Opinion in Psychiatry, 21*(1), 84–92. doi: 10.1097/YCO.0b013e3282f31137.

Fowles, D. C. (1992). Schizophrenia: Diathesis-stress revisited. *Annual Review Psychology, 43,* 303–336. doi: 10.1146/annurev.ps.43.020192.001511.

Fullam, R., & Dolan, M. (2006). Emotional information processing in violent patients with schizophrenia: Association with psychopathy and symptomatology. *Psychiatry Research, 141*(1), 29-37. doi: 10.1016/j.psychres.2005.07.013.

Grant, B. F., Hasin, D. S., Stinson, F. S., Dawson, D. A., Chou, S. P., Ruan, W. J., & Pickering, R. P. (2004). Prevalence, correlates, and disability of personality disorders in the United States: Results from the national epidemiologic survey on alcohol and related conditions. *Journal of Clinical Psychiatry, 65*(7), 948–958.

Green, A. I., Drake, R. E., Brunette, M. F., & Noordsy, D. L. (2007). Schizophrenia and co-occurring substance use disorder. *American Journal of Psychiatry, 164*(3), 402–408. doi: 10.1176/appi.ajp.164.3.402.

Hare, R. D., & Neumann, C. S. (2009). Psychopathy: assessment and forensic implications. *Canadian Journal of Psychiatry, 54*(12), 791–802.

Hoptman, M. J., & Antonius, D. (2011). Neuroimaging correlates of aggression in schizophrenia: An update. *Current Opinion in Psychiatry, 24*(2), 100–106. doi: 10.1097/YCO.0b013e328342c8e0.

Johnson, J. G., Cohen, P., Kasen, S., Skodol, A. E., & Oldham, J. M. (2008). Cumulative prevalence of personality disorders between adolescence and adulthood. *Acta Psychiatrica Scandinavica, 118*(5), 410–413. doi: 10.1111/j.1600-0447.2008.01231.x.

Johnson, J. G., Cohen, P., Smailes, E., Kasen, S., Oldham, J. M., Skodol, A. E., & Brook, J. S. (2000). Adolescent personality disorders associated with violence and criminal behavior during adolescence and early adulthood. *American Journal of Psychiatry, 157*(9): 1406–1412. doi: 10.1176/appi.ajp.157.9.1406.

Joyal, C. C., Dubreucq, J-L., Grendon, C., & Millaud, F. (2007). Major mental disorders and violence: A critical update. *Current Psychiatry Reviews, 3*(1), 33–50. doi: 10.2174/157340007779815628.

Joyal, C. C., Putkonen, A., Mancini-Marie, A., Hodgins, S., Kononen, M., Boulay, L., Aronen, H. J. (2007). Violent persons with schizophrenia and comorbid disorders: A functional magnetic resonance imaging study. *Schizophrenia Research, 91*(1–3), 97–102. doi: 10.1016/j.schres.2006.12.014.

Kaartinen, M., Puura, K., Helminen, M., Salmelin, R., Pelkonen, E., & Juujarvi, P. (2012). Reactive aggression among children with and without autism spectrum disorder. *Journal of Autism and Developmental Disorders, 44*(10), 2383–2391. doi: 10.1007/s10803-012-1743-1.

Kanne, S. M., & Mazurek, M. O. (2011). Aggression in children and adolescents with ASD: Prevalence and risk factors. *Journal of Autism and Developmental Disorders, 41*(7), 926–937. doi: 10.1007/s10803-010-1118-4.

Keenan, T., & Ward, T. (2000). A theory of mind perspective on cognitive, affective, and intimacy deficits in child sexual offenders. *Sexual Abuse: A Journal of Rsearch and Treatment, 12*(1), 49–60. doi: 10.1177/107906320001200106.

Kockler, T. R., Stanford, M. S., Nelson, C. E., Meloy, J. R., & Sanford, K. (2006). Characterizing aggressive behavior in a forensic population. *American Journal of Psychiatry, 76*(1), 80–85. doi: 10.1037/0002-9432.76.1.80.

Laajasalo, T., Salenius, T. S., Lindberg, N., Repo-Tiihonen, E., & Hakkanen-Nyholm, H. (2011). Psychopathic traits in Finnish homicide offenders with schizophrenia. *International Journal of Law and Psychiatry, 34*(5), 324–330. doi: 10.1016/j.ijlp.2011.08.004.

Lachman, H. M., Papolos, D. F., Saito, T., Yu, Y. M., Szumlanski, C. L., & Weinshilboum, R.M. (1996). Human catechol-O-methyltransferase pharmacogenetics: Description of a functional polymorphism and its potential application to neuropsychiatric disorders. *Pharmacogenetics, 6*(3), 243–250. doi: 10.1097/00008571-199606000-00007.

Långström, N., Grann, M., Ruchkin, V., Sjostedt, G., & Fazel, S. (2009). Risk factors for violent offending in autism spectrum disorder: A national study of hospitalized individuals. *Journal of Interpersonal Violence, 24*(8), 1358–1370. doi: 10.1177/0886260508322195.

Large, M. M., & Nielssen, O. (2011). Violence in first-episode psychosis: A systematic review and meta-analysis. *Schizophrenia Research, 125*(2–3), 209–220. doi: 10.1016/j.schres.2010.11.026.

Lugnegard, T., Hallerback, M. U., & Gillberg, C. (2012). Personality disorders and autism spectrum disorders: What are the connections? *Comprehensive Psychiatry, 53*(4), 333–430. doi: 10.1016/j.comppsych.2011.05.014.

Majorek, K., Wolfkuhler, W., Kuper, C., Saimeh, N., Juckel, G., & Brune, M. (2009). "Theory of mind" and executive functioning in forensic patients with schizophrenia. *Journal of Forensic Sciences, 54*(2), 469–473. doi: 10.1111/j.1556-4029.2008.00966.x.

Matthies, S., Rusch, N., Weber, M., Lieb, K., Philipsen, A., Tuescher van Elst, L. T. (2012). Small amygdala-high aggression? The role of the amygdala in modulating aggression in healthy subjects. *World Journal of Biological Psychiatry, 13*(1), 75–81. doi: 10.3109/15622975.2010.541282.

Mazurek, M. O., Kanne, S. M., & Wodka, E. L. (2013). Physical aggression in children and adolescents with autism spectrum disorders. *Research in Autism Spectrum Disorders, 7*(3), 455–465. doi: 10.1016/j.rasd.2012.11.004.

McGrath, J., Saha, S., Chant, D., & Welham, J. (2008). Schizophrenia: A concise overview of incidence, prevalence, and mortality. *Epidemiological Review, 30*(1), 67–76. doi: 10.1093/epirev/mxn001.

McMillan, K. A., Enns, M. W., Cox, B. J., & Sareen, J. (2009). Comorbidity of Axis I and II mental disorders with schizophrenia and psychotic disorders: Findings from the National Epidemiological Survey on Alcohol and Related Conditions. *Canadian Journal of Psychiatry, 54*(7), 477–486.

Meloy, J. R. (2006). Empirical basis and forensic application of affective and predatory violence. *Australian and New Zealand Journal of Psychiatry, 40*(6–7), 539–547. doi: 10.1111/j.1440-1614.2006.01837.x.

Miller, P. A., & Eisenberg, N. (1988). The relation of empathy to aggressive and externalizing/antisocial behavior. *Psychological Bulletin, 103*(3), 324–344.

Moore, E. A., Green, M. J., & Carr, V. J. (2012). Comorbid personality traits in schizophrenia: Prevalence and clinical characteristics. *Journal of Psychiatric Research, 46*(3), 353–359. doi: 10.1016/j.jpsychires.2011.11.012.

Morgan, J. T., Nordahl, C. W., & Schumann C. M. (2012). The amygdala in Autism Spectrum Disorders. In T. J. D. Bauxbaum & P. Hof (Eds.), *The neuroscience of Autism Spectrum Disorders* (pp. 297–312). Oxford: Academic Press.

Mulvey, E. P. (1994). Assessing the evidence of a link between mental illness and violence. *Psychiatric Services, 45*(7), 663–668. doi: 10.1176/ps.45.7.663.

Nakamura, K., Sekine, Y., Ouchi, Y., Tsujii, M., Yoshikawa, E., Futatsubashi, M., Mori, N. (2010). Brain serotonin and dopamine transporter bindings in adults with high-functioning autism. *Archives of General Psychiatry, 67*(1), 59–68. doi: 10.1001/archgenpsychiatry.2009.137.

Passamonti, L., Crockett, M. J., Apergis-Schoute, A. M., Clark, L., Rowe, J. B., Calder, A. J., & Robbins, T. W. (2012). Effects of acute tryptophan depletion on prefrontal-amygdala connectivity while viewing facial signals of aggression. *Biological Psychiatry, 71*(1), 36–43. doi: 10.1016/j.biopsych.2011.07.033.

Pickard, H., & Fazel, S. (2013). Substance abuse as a risk factor for violence in mental illness: Some implications for forensic psychiatric practice and clinical ethics. *Current Opinion in Psychiatry, 26*(4), 349–354. doi: 10.1097/YCO.0b013e328361e798

Pirarba, S., Aru, D., Lai, L., Pinna, F., & Carpiniello, B. (2010). Victimization and mental disorders: Results of a case-control study. *Rivista di Psichiatria, 45*(6), 382–392.

Rasanen, P., Tiihonen, J., Isohanni, M., Rantakallio, P., Lehtonen, J., & Moring, J. (1998). Schizophrenia, alcohol abuse, and violent behavior: A 26-year followup study of an unselected birth cohort. *Schizophrenia Bulletin, 24*(3), 437–441.

Remington, G. (2008). Alterations of dopamine and serotonin transmission in schizophrenia. *Progress in Brain Research, 172*, 117–140. doi: 10.1016/S0079-6123(08)00906-0.

Roth, R. M., Brunette, M. F., & Green, A. I. (2005). Treatment of substance use disorders in schizophrenia: A unifying neurobiological mechanism? *Current Psychiatry Reports, 7*(4), 283–291. doi: 10.1007/s11920-005-0082-8.

Royal College of Psychiatrists (2010). *No health without public mental health: The case for action.* Royal College of Psyciatrists, London.

Ryding, E., Lindstrom, E. M., & Traskman-Bendz, L. (2008). The role of dopamine and serotonin in suicidal behavior and aggression. *Progress in Brain Research, 172*, 307–315. doi: 10.1016/S0079-6123(08)00915-1.

Schug, R., & Raine, A. (2009). Comparative meta-analysis of neuropsychological functioning in antisocial schizophrenic persons. *Clinical Psychology Review, 29*(3), 230–242. doi: 10.1016/j.cpr.2009.01.004.

Senju, A., Southgate, V., White, S., & Frith, U. (2009). Mindblind eyes: An absence of spontaneous theory of mind in Asperger syndrome. *Science, 325*(5942), 883–885. doi: 10.1126/science.1176170.

Seo, D., Patrick, C. J., & Kennealy, P. J. (2008). Role of serotonin and dopamine system interactions in the neurobiology of impulsive aggression and its comorbidity with other clinical disorders. *Aggression and Violent Behavior, 13*(5), 383–395. doi: 10.1016/j.avb.2008.06.003.

Sharma, A., & Shaw, S. R. (2012). Efficacy of risperidone in managing maladaptive behaviors for children with autistic spectrum disorder: A meta-analysis. *Journal of Pediatric Health Care, 26*(4), 291–299. doi: 10.1016/j.pedhc.2011.02.008.

Short, T., Thomas, S., Mullen, P., & Ogloff, J. R. (2013). Comparing violence in schizophrenia patients with and without comorbid substance-use disorders to community controls. *Acta Psychiatrica Scandinavica, 128*(4), 306–313. doi: 10.1111/acps.12066.

Siever, L. J. (2008). Neurobiology of aggression and violence. *American Journal of Psychiatry, 165*(4), 429–442. doi: 10.1176/appi.ajp.2008.07111774.

Sinclair, S. J., & Gansler, D. A. (2006). Integrating the somatic marker and social cognition theories to explain different manifestations of Antisocial Personality Disorder. *The New School Psychology Bulletin, 4*(2), 25–47.

Singh, J. P., Volavka, J., Czobor, P., & Van Dorn, R. A. (2012). A meta-analysis of the Val158Met COMT polymorphism and violent behavior in schizophrenia. *PLoS One, 7*(8), e43423. doi: 10.1371/journal.pone.0043423.

Skeem, J. L., Schubert, C., Odgers, C., Mulvey, E. P., Gardner, W., & Lidz, C. (2006). Psychiatric symptoms and community violence among high-risk patients: A test of the relationship at the weekly level. *Journal of Consulting and Clinical Psychology, 74*(5), 967–979. doi: 10.1037/0022-006X.74.5.967.

Soyka, M. (2011). Neurobiology of aggression and violence in schizophrenia. *Schizophrenia Bulletin, 37*(5), 913–920. doi: 10.1093/schbul/sbr103.

Steadman, H. J., Mulvey, E. P., Monahan, J., Robbins, P. C., Appelbaum, P. S., Grisso, T., Silver, E. (1998). Violence by people discharged from acute psychiatric inpatient facilities and by others in the same neighborhoods. *Archives of General Psychiatry, 55*(5), 393–401. doi: 10.1001/archpsyc.55.5.393.

Strous, R. D., Bark, N., Parsia, S. S., Volavka, J., & Lachman, H. M. (1997). Analysis of a functional catechol-O-methyltransferase gene polymorphism in schizophrenia: Evidence for association with aggressive and antisocial behavior. *Psychiatry Research, 69*(2–3), 71–77. doi: 10.1016/S0165-1781(96)03111-3.

Swanson, J. W., Holzer, 3rd, C. E., Ganju, V. K., & Jono, R. T. (1990). Violence and psychiatric disorder in the community: Evidence from the Epidemiologic Catchment Area Surveys. *Hospital and Community Psychiatry, 41*(7), 761–770. doi: 10.1176/ps.41.7.761.

Swanson, J. W., Swartz, M. S., & Elbogen, E. B. (2004). Effectiveness of atypical antipsychotic medications in reducing violent behavior among persons with schizophrenia in community-based treatment. *Schizophrenia Bulletin, 30*(1), 3–20. doi: 10.1093/oxfordjournals.schbul.a007065.

Swanson, J. W., Swartz, M. S., Van Dorn, R. A., Elbogen, E. B., Wagner, H. R., Rosenheck, R. A., Lieberman, J. A. (2006). A national study of violent behavior in persons with schizophrenia. *Archives of General Psychiatry, 63*(5), 490–499. doi: 10.1001/archpsyc. 63.5.490.

Tangney, J. P. (1991). Moral affect: The good, the bad, and the ugly. *Journal of Personal and Social Psychology, 61*(4), 598–607. doi: 10.1037/0022-3514.61.4.598.

Taylor, P. J. (2008). Psychosis and violence: Stories, fears, and reality. *Canadian Journal of Psychiatry, 53*(10), 647–659. doi

Tiihonen, J., Isohanni, M., Rasanen, P., Koiranen, M., & J. Moring, J. (1997). Specific major mental disorders and criminality: A 26-year prospective study of the 1966 northern Finland birth cohort. *American Journal of Psychiatry, 154*(6), 840–845. doi: 10.1176/ajp/154.6.840.

Trull, T. J., & Durrett, C. A. (2005). Categorical and dimensional models of personality disorder. *Annual Review of Clinical Psychology, 1*, 355–380. doi: 10.1146/annurev.clinpsy.1.102803.144009.

Tuvblad, C., Narusyte, J., Grann, M., Sarnecki, J., & Lichtenstein, P. (2011). The genetic and environmental etiology of antisocial behavior from childhood to emerging adulthood. *Behavorial Genetics, 41*(5), 629–640. doi: 10.1007/s10519-011-9463-4.

van Dorn, R., Volavka, J., & Johnson, N. (2012). Mental disorder and violence: Is there a relationship beyond substance use? *Social Psychiatry and Psychiatric Epidemiology, 47*(3), 487–503. doi: 10.1007/s00127-011-0356-x.

van Os, J., & Kapur, S. (2009). Schizophrenia. *Lancet, 374*(9690), 635–645. doi: 10.1016/S0140-6736(09)60995-8.

Volavka, J. (2012). Clozapine is gold standard, but questions remain. *International Journal of Neuropsychopharmacology, 15*(9), 1201–1204. doi: 10.1017/S1461145712000284.

Volavka, J., & Citrome, L. (2008). Heterogeneity of violence in schizophrenia and implications for long-term treatment. *Inernational Journal of Clinical Practice, 62*(8), 1237–1245. doi: 10.1111/j.1742-1241.2008.01797.x.

Wachtel, L. E., & Shorter, E. (2013). Autism plus psychosis: A "one-two punch" risk for tragic violence? *Medical Hypotheses, 81*(3), 404–409. doi: 10.1016/j.mehy.2013.05.032.

Walsh, E., Buchanan, A., & Fahy, T. (2002). Violence and schizophrenia: Examining the evidence. *British Journal of Psychiatry, 180*, 490–495. doi: 10.1192/bjp.180.6.490.

Walsh, Z., Swogger, M. T., & Kosson, D. S. (2009). Psychopathy and instrumental violence: Facet level relationships. *Journal of Personality Disorders, 23*(4), 416–424. doi: 10.1521/pedi.2009.23.4.416.

Walter, M., Wiesbeck, G. A., Dittmann, V., & Graf, M. (2011). Criminal recidivism in offenders with personality disorders and substance use disorders over 8 years of time at risk. *Psychiatry Research, 186*(2–3), 443–445. doi: 10.1016/j.psychres.2010.08.009.

Witt, K., van Dorn, R., & Fazel. S. (2013). Risk factors for violence in psychosis: Systematic review and meta-regression analysis of 110 studies. *PLoS ONE, 8*(2), e55942. doi: 10.1371/journal.pone.0055942.

Woodworth, M., & Porter, S. (2002). In cold blood: Characteristics of criminal homicides as a function of psychopathy. *Journal of Abnormal Psychology, 111*(3), 436–445. doi: 10.1037/0021-843X.111.3.436.

21

Modifying Risk Factors
Building Strengths
Corine de Ruiter

Key points

- Treatment and risk management of forensic populations has traditionally focused on decreasing risk factors for antisocial and aggressive behavior, without paying much attention to increasing positive, strength-based factors. The same is true for research into the neurobiological correlates of mental disorders that are highly prevalent in forensic settings, such as psychopathy and pedophilia.
- Neuroscientific research has uncovered that impulsivity, deficient aggression regulation, and lack of empathy (see Part II of this volume for reviews) in offender samples are related to functional and structural brain abnormalities in the amygdala, dorsolateral prefrontal cortex (dlPFC), and orbitofrontal cortex.
- In this chapter, a positive approach to risk management is proposed.
- Strengths-based approaches, such as mindfulness meditation (see Chapter 26 for more detail) and aerobic exercise (see Chapter 25), reveal a positive effect on prefrontal and limbic structure and functioning, accompanied by improved executive functioning, including better emotion regulation, impulse control, and memory performance.
- It is argued that rehabilitative efforts in forensic populations are still largely risk focused; they could benefit from adjunctive treatments derived from the positive psychology tradition.
- Hence, in the chapter it is proposed that positive forensic neuroscience has the potential to further our insight into neurocognitive processes relevant to rehabilitation of forensic populations.

The Wiley Blackwell Handbook of Forensic Neuroscience, First Edition. Edited by Anthony R. Beech, Adam J. Carter, Ruth E. Mann and Pia Rotshtein.
© 2018 John Wiley & Sons Ltd. Published 2018 by John Wiley & Sons Ltd.

Terminology Explained

Alexithymia refers to a dimensional personality trait defined by trouble identifying and describing emotional experience and an external focus of attention. Typical deficiencies may include problems identifying, describing, and working with one's own feelings, often accompanied by a lack of understanding of the feelings of others; difficulty distinguishing between feelings and the bodily sensations of emotional arousal; restricted imagination; and concrete thinking.

BDNF refers to brain-derived neurotrophic factor, a protein that belongs to the neurotrophin family of growth factors, found in the central and peripheral nervous system. BDNF acts on certain neurons that support the survival of existing neurons and encourage the growth and differentiation of new neurons and synapses. BDNF is active in the hippocampus, cortex, and basal forebrain – areas vital to learning, memory, and complex thought processes.

Eriksen flanker task is a response inhibition test used to assess the ability to suppress responses that are inappropriate in a particular context. The target is flanked by non-target stimuli, which correspond to the same directional response as the target (congruent flankers), to the opposite response (incongruent flankers), or to neither (neutral flankers). For instance, when "F" was the target stimulus, participants had to respond with their left index finger. When "X" was the target stimulus, a right index finger response was required. The incompatible condition had the target response flanked by the opposing target stimulus (i.e., FXF or XFX). The neutral target response was flanked by letters with no response assignment (e.g., LFL or LXL).

Hippocampal volume refers to the magnitude of the hippocampus, a major structure of the brain. Humans and other mammals have two hippocampi, one in each side of the brain. It belongs to the limbic system and plays an important role in the consolidation of information from short-term memory to long-term memory and in spatial navigation.

Mindfulness is a construct derived from Buddhism that is hard to define. It consists of two components: a deliberate intention to attend to momentary experience and an attitude of openness, acceptance, kindness, curiosity, and patience. Mindfulness-based therapies developed in the West are associated with positive effects for improving anxiety and mood symptoms in patients with anxiety and mood disorders.

Neurotrophic factors are a family of molecules – nearly all proteins – that support the growth, survival, and differentiation of both developing and mature neurons. In the mature nervous system, they promote neuronal survival, induce synaptic plasticity, and modulate the formation of long-term memories.

P3 (or P300) amplitude refers to the magnitude of an event-related potential (ERP), the measured brain response that is the direct result of a specific sensory, cognitive, or motor event. ERPs are measured by means of electroencephalography (EEG). Contemporary theories of P3 suggest that the amplitude of this component reflects allocation of attention and executive functioning.

Positive neuroscience focuses on valued cognitive qualities that serve to enrich personal life and/or society. Topics studied in positive neuroscience overlap with those of positive psychology, but use neuroimaging techniques to extend beyond the behavioral observation level and explain the neurobiology that underpins "positive" psychological phenomena such as creativity, optimism, discipline, compassion, and curiosity. In 2009, the Positive Neuroscience Project was started at the University of Pennsylvania.[1]

Protective factor is any characteristic of an individual, their environment, or situation which reduces the risk of future adverse outcomes. In forensic mental health, the adverse outcome of interest is often (re)offending. Protective factors moderate or buffer the impact of exposure to risk factors, thus lowering reoffending risk.

Risk factor is a term used in forensic mental health science to refer to characteristics of an individual or his/her context that increase the risk of (re)offending. Some risk factors are historical and unchangeable, such as a young age at first criminal conviction; some are dynamic and changeable, for instance, by treatment and rehabilitation efforts, such as aggression regulation.

Vipassana is a meditation practice in the Theravada tradition of Buddhism, which is very close to Zen in Mahayana Buddhism. Vipassana uses mindfulness of breathing, while observing all phenomena of the mind, to gain insight into the impermanence of all phenomena, striving for permanent liberation.

Zen Buddhism is a school of Mahayana Buddhism that originated in China as Chan Buddhism. The Chinese Chan is in turn derived from the Sanskrit word Dhyāna. From China, Chan Buddhism spread to Vietnam, Korea, and Japan, where it became known as Japanese Zen. Zen emphasizes meditation practice. During sitting meditation (*zazen* in Japanese), practitioners direct their attention toward counting or watching the breath. The meditator is instructed to be aware of the stream of thoughts, allowing them to pass without interference, thus striving to enter a state of serenity and pure awareness.

Introduction

During the past decades, offender treatment research has made significant progress, leading to an increased use of evidence-based practices in risk assessment and risk management (see, for instance, Logan & Johnstone, 2012). At the same time, our knowledge of the etiology (both in terms of nature and nurture) and the brain correlates of mental disorders often found in individuals in forensic settings (e.g., psychopathy, pedophilia, paranoid schizophrenia) has grown substantially (for an elegant example, see the work of James Cantor outlined in Box 21.1). A strong focus on psychopathology and its risk factors has advanced the field of forensic mental health, but it also is an inherently one-sided approach. This chapter proposes that offender treatment and rehabilitation may benefit from including concepts from positive psychology. A so-called "positive neuroscience" has recently emerged and we will demonstrate with pertinent examples what a positive forensic neuroscience might have to offer treatment and rehabilitation in forensic settings.

Box 21.1 James Cantor's work on brain imaging sexual offenders

Dr. Cantor has been using magnetic resonance imaging (MRI) and other techniques to study the role of the brain in pedophilia and other atypical sexual interests. He is an associate professor of psychiatry at the University of Toronto and the head of research for the Law and Mental Health Program of the Centre for Addiction and Mental Health. Dr. Cantor's team has identified multiple biomarkers associated with pedophilia, including poorer scores on certain neuropsychological tests, more frequent childhood head injuries, lower physical height, elevated rates of school-grade failures, and triple normal rates of non-right-handedness. His 2008 MRI finding of significantly lower white matter density in wide-spread regions of the brain in men with pedophilia (compared to men who committed nonsexual offenses) was published in the *Journal of Psychiatric Research* and was featured by the BBC, *Daily Mail,* and *New Scientist.*

Risk assessment and management

A comprehensive risk assessment and management model that is based on theoretical principles is the risk-needs-responsivity model (RNR) (Andrews, Bonta, & Hoge, 1990; Andrews, Bonta, & Wormith, 2006; Bonta & Andrews, 2007). In the RNR model, the risk principle asserts that criminal behavior can be accurately predicted and that risk management strategies should focus on the higher risk offenders. The need principle highlights the importance of criminogenic needs, also termed dynamic risk factors, because these are the factors amenable to change by risk management strategies; and the responsivity principle describes how treatment should be tailored to the individual offender (Bonta & Andrews, 2007). Structured risk assessment tools have been developed to aid forensic mental health clinicians in their daily practice, and have led to an increase in the level of transparency, compared to former unstructured clinical risk judgments (Monahan, 1981). Research has also shown that offender rehabilitation programs that adhere to RNR principles are more effective than those that do not (Andrews & Bonta, 2010a, 2010b).

This so-called "culture of risk" in forensic psychology and psychiatry has also been met with criticism. Already in the year 2000, Dr. Richard Rogers warned scholars in the risk assessment field that the "overfocus on risk factors is likely to contribute to professional negativism and result in client stigmatization" (p. 598). When structured risk assessment tools such as the Historical Clinical Risk management-20 (HCR-20) (Webster, Douglas, Eaves, & Hart, 1997) and Sexual Violence Risk-20 (SVR-20) (Boer, Hart, Kropp, & Webster, 1997) were introduced in the Dutch forensic mental health system around the year 2000, it was believed that this would be an improvement over the unstructured clinical approach to risk assessment, which was common practice at the time. This was also demonstrated in a study conducted at the Pompe forensic hospital (Philipse, Koeter, van der Staak, & van den Brink, 2006). By 2005, the

Dutch Ministry of Justice had commissioned policy changes that required all forensic psychiatric hospitals to rate their patients' risk level on a structured risk assessment instrument every 12 months by means of consensus ratings between at least two different professionals. Also, structured risk judgments were required when the hospital applied for increased liberties (e.g., supervised or unsupervised leave) for their patients. It is noteworthy that, from 1990 to 2008, the average duration of forensic psychiatric treatment under a judicial mandate increased from a mean of 4.2 years to a mean of 8.4 years at the time of release (Nagtegaal, van der Horst, & Schönberger, 2011). Although it obviously cannot be proven that structured risk assessment tools "caused" this dramatic increase in mandated treatment duration, it is quite plausible that the use of structured risk assessment tools led to a "bias" in the direction of false positives.

Recent research has demonstrated that the manner in which the risk assessment outcome is framed largely determines the release decision that is made on the basis of it. Scurich and John (2011) showed, in a study with 303 university students who acted as mock judges, that risk framed as a 26% probability of violence generally led subjects to authorize civil commitment, whereas the same risk framed in the numerical complement, a 74% probability of no violence, generally led decision makers to decide to release. Thus, subtle manipulation in the framing of risk estimates is a powerful way to affect commitment or release decisions. The general tendency in violence risk assessment practice to frame estimates in terms of the risk of violence, will skew decision makers toward false positives. Consistent with several scholars' calls (e.g., Hart, 2008; Rogers, 2000) for a consideration of protective factors in risk assessments, Webster, Martin, Brink, Nicholls, and Desmarais (2009) asserted that a risk assessment that considers only risk factors or that fails to allow "high scorers" on protective factors may inadvertently bias assessors.

Beyond RNR: Including strengths-based and protective factors

The development of structured tools for the assessment of protective factors for violence risk, such as the Structured Assessment of Protective Factors for violence risk (SAPROF) (de Vogel, de Ruiter, Bouman, & de Vries Robbé, 2009; de Vogel, de Vries Robbé, de Ruiter, & Bouman, 2011; see Table 21.1) and the Short-Term Assessment

Table 21.1 Protective factors in the SAPROF

1. Intelligence	10. Attitudes toward authority
2. Secure attachment in childhood	11. Life goals
3. Empathy	12. Medication (if applicable)
4. Coping	13. Social network
5. Self-control	14. Intimate relationship
6. Work	15. Professional care (if applicable)
7. Leisure activities	16. Living circumstances
8. Financial management	17. External control
9. Motivation for treatment	

Source: de Vogel, de Ruiter, Bouman, & de Vries Robbé (2011).

of Risk and Treatability (START) (Webster, Martin, Brink, Nicholls, & Desmarais, 2009) has recently facilitated research on protective factors.

Several studies found protective factors that provided incremental predictive validity over the use of risk factors alone (Ullrich & Coid, 2011; de Vries Robbé, de Vogel, & Douglas, 2013). Furthermore, evidence was found for a buffering effect of protective factors on risk factors: individuals with moderate to high risk levels, who also possessed high levels of protective factors, showed significantly lower recidivism rates than high and moderate risk cases without protective factors (Lodewijks, de Ruiter, & Doreleijers, 2010; de Vries Robbé et al., 2013). In individuals with moderate and high risk levels, protective factors such as commitment to structured leisure activities (Bouman, de Ruiter, & Schene, 2010) and commitment to school (Lodewijks et al., 2010) served as buffers to mitigate risk of criminal recidivism. Although research on protective factors in forensic mental health is still in its infancy (de Ruiter & Nicholls, 2011), it should alert forensic mental health professionals to the importance of taking protective factors into consideration when performing risk assessments and when implementing risk management and rehabilitation interventions.

In an elaboration on the RNR model, Ward, Melser, and Yates (2007) stated that a reduction of dynamic risk is "a necessary but not sufficient condition for effective treatment" (p. 210). Promotion of human goods, which "are experiences and activities that are likely to result in enhanced levels of wellbeing" (Ward, Mann, & Gannon, 2007, p. 90), should be included when formulating plans for treatment and risk management. This culminated in the development of the good lives model (GLM), which is a strengths-based approach and offers forensic clinicians guidelines to target human goods (i.e., "valued aspects of human functioning and living"; Ward & Brown, 2004, p. 246). The developers of the GLM proposed "that the best way to lower offending recidivism rates is to equip individuals with the tools to live more fulfilling lives rather than to simply develop increasingly sophisticated risk management measures and strategies" (Ward & Brown 2004, p. 244).

The evidence base for the effectiveness of treatment programs designed according to the GLM is still limited. Preliminary studies demonstrate beneficial effects of treatments based on GLM principles. For instance, Mann, Webster, Schofield, and Marshall (2004) compared treatments that included positive approach goals with a more traditional risk management and avoidance goals approach. The offenders in the approach-focused intervention condition showed higher treatment engagement and clinicians rated these offenders as being more genuinely motivated to stop their offending lifestyle (Mann et al., 2004). Several correlational studies have found support for an association between positive goods and desistance from reoffending. For instance, Bouman, Schene, & de Ruiter (2008) found that subjectively experienced higher quality of life was associated with lower recidivism rates in male forensic outpatients, both in the short term (three months) and long term (three years).

The GLM fits within a more general trend in psychology, termed the positive psychology movement (Donaldson, 2011). Positive psychology was the overarching theme of the 1998 Convention of the American Psychological Association, and the first international conference on positive psychology was held in 2002. Furthermore, in January 2000, the *American Psychologist* published a special issue on positive psychology, edited by Martin Seligman and Mihaly Csikszentmihalyi, with papers on issues such as happiness, excellence, and optimal human functioning. In subsequent years, a science of positive psychology developed, including university courses on positive psychology and the scholarly *Journal of Positive Psychology*.

Positive psychology has drawn attention to the study of good character, also termed positive traits, strengths, or virtues (Peterson & Park, 2011). Park and Peterson (2003) proposed that positive traits link the other central issues of positive psychology together, because positive traits facilitate positive experiences, positive social bonds, and positive institutions. Good character is not equivalent to the absence of deficits and problems, but a category of positive traits in its own right (Peterson & Park, 2011). These character strengths help persons flourish, and they are associated with academic success, effective leadership, tolerance for diversity, kindness, frustration tolerance, and altruism (see Park, 2004, for a review). In order to study positive traits, a vocabulary of strengths and tools to measure them is needed. This was the goal of the Values in Action (VIA) project (Peterson & Seligman, 2004).

The VIA project aimed at an aspirational classification of mutually exclusive and exhaustive categories of strengths without claiming finality or hypothesizing a particular background theory (Peterson, 2011). Literature review (Dalsgaard, Peterson, & Seligman, 2005) and field research (Biswas-Diener, 2006) resulted in a list of six core virtues, under which belong 24 positive traits or strengths (see Table 21.2).

The self-report measures of the VIA strengths opened the way for a systematic study of positive traits. Research to date has shown that virtually everyone has some notable strengths, typically between three and seven (Peterson & Park, 2011). VIA strengths are showing robust relations with life satisfaction and psychological wellbeing: love, gratitude, hope, curiosity, and zest (Peterson, Park, & Seligman, 2004). The origins of strengths have not been studied well. A twin study in identical versus fraternal twins found that strengths are moderately heritable, as are many other personality traits (Steger, Hicks, Kashdan, Krueger, & Bouchard, 2007). This study also showed that shared family environment impacted on some of the strengths, for instance, the love of learning. For almost all VIA strengths, non-shared family environment, such as teachers and peers, proved to be a very important influence.

An interesting line of research examines the role of strengths in dealing with adversity. Peterson and Seligman (2003) showed that in the six months after the 9/11 attacks on the World Trade Center, faith, hope, and love were elevated among US respondents but not among Europeans. Successful recovery from a serious somatic disease is associated with modest increases in the strengths of bravery, kindness, and humor, whereas successful recovery from mental health problems is associated with modest increases in appreciation of beauty and love of learning (Peterson, Park, & Seligman, 2006). These were large-scale survey studies, so the processes by which strengths of character develop is still unknown. Peterson (2006) sees strengths as habits, expressed in thoughts, feelings, and actions. The fact that strengths are moderately heritable does not mean they are unchangeable, because habits are built by practice, by reinforcement and by social modeling. Obviously, the situation one is in also matters, not only in the acquisition of strengths, but also in their maintenance. It is easier to apply certain strengths in some situations than in others (Peterson, 2011). Forensic psychiatric hospitals, because of their closed nature, may provide unique opportunities to foster strengths building, because the quality of this social environment can be relatively well managed. A number of the SAPROF items (for instance, empathy, life goals, and self-control) are similar to some of the VIA strengths, and it will be interesting to study these in relation to each other. In the following section, we

560 C. de Ruiter

Table 21.2 The VIA classification of strengths

1. Wisdom and knowledge	• Creativity: thinking of novel and productive ways to do things • Curiosity: taking an interest in all of ongoing experience • Open-mindedness: thinking things through and examining them from all sides • Love of learning: mastering new skills, topics and bodies of knowledge • Perspective: being able to provide wise counsel to others
2. Courage	• Honesty: speaking the truth and presenting oneself in a genuine way • Bravery: *not* shrinking from threat, challenge, difficulty, or pain • Persistence: finishing what one starts • Zest: approaching life with excitement and energy
3. Humanity	• Kindness: doing favors and good deeds for others • Love: valuing close relations with others • Social intelligence: being aware of the motives and feelings of self and others
4. Justice	• Fairness: treating all people the same according to notions of fairness and justice • Leadership: organizing group activities and seeing that they happen • Teamwork: working well as a member of a group or team
5. Temperance	• Forgiveness: forgiving those who have done wrong • Modesty: letting one's accomplishments speak for themselves • Prudence: being careful about one's choices: *not* saying or doing things that might later be regretted • Self-regulation: regulating what one feels and does
6. Transcendence	• Appreciation of beauty and excellence: noticing and appreciating beauty, excellence, and/or skilled performance in all domains of life • Gratitude: being aware of and thankful for the good things that happen • Hope: expecting the best and working to achieve it • Humor: liking to laugh and joke; bringing smiles to other people • Religiousness: having coherent beliefs about the higher purpose and meaning of life

Source: Reprinted with permission from Peterson & Park (2011), p. 53.

Strengths-Based Neuroscience

will examine whether positive, strengths-based approaches to psychological treatment can affect brain functioning.

Strengths-Based Neuroscience

During the past decades, research groups across the world have started to study the structure and functioning of the brain in forensic samples, including individuals with antisocial personality disorder (ASPD) and psychopathy by means of neuroimaging techniques. The most robust findings from these studies point to a reduction in prefrontal grey matter (Raine, Lencz, Bihrle, LaCasse, & Colletti, 2000; Yang et al., 2005), especially in the dorsolateral prefrontal cortex (dlPFC) and the orbitofrontal cortex (Yang & Raine, 2009). Functional neuroimaging studies with response inhibition and fear conditioning tasks have also found reduced brain activity in the dlPFC (Schneider et al., 2000; Völlm et al., 2007), orbitofrontal cortex (Birbaumer et al., 2005; Horn, Dolan, Elliott, Deakin, & Woodruff, 2003; Marsh et al., 2011), and amygdala (Birbaumer et al., 2005; Marsh et al., 2011; Müller et al., 2003; Raine & Yang, 2006). These prefrontal structures in combination with the amygdala form an essential part of several neurocognitive models of aggressive and antisocial behavior (Blair, 2007; Kiehl, 2006; Raine & Yang, 2006). This relatively new knowledge about the antisocial brain has been considered "risky," because it may lead to premature labeling of "at risk" children (Walsh, 2014) and preventive detention of individuals with antisocial and psychopathic personality disorders (Campbell & Eastman, 2014). The actual utility of this knowledge within the legal and correctional context will likely depend on the ability of professionals within these fields to strike a balance between risk- and strengths-based approaches, just as is the case in the practice of violence risk assessment.

Box 21.2   The positive neuroscience project

In 2009, the University of Pennsylvania and the John Templeton Foundation started the Positive Neuroscience Project,[2] which awarded 15 researchers grants to study the intersection between positive psychology and neuroscience, including the neuroscientific study of altruism, empathy, social support, and human touch.

The human brain has considerable plasticity and capacity for resilience (Karatsoreos & McEwen, 2013). For instance, Taren et al. (2014) found that mindfulness training reduced functional connectivity of the right amygdala with the anterior cingulate cortex, implicating that mindfulness training may reduce the strength of the connections among brain areas that drive stress reactivity. The following subsections will elaborate on recent findings from research on structural and functional changes in the brain, as a result of two examples of strengths-based treatment approaches: mindfulness training and physical exercise.

Mindfulness training

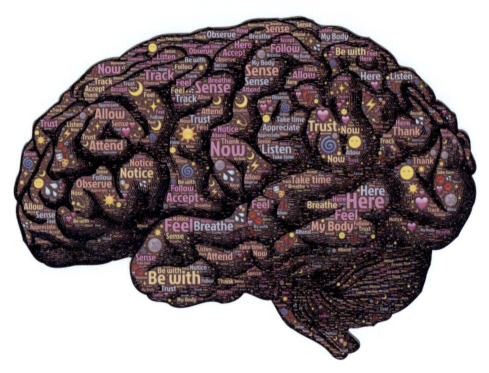

Mindfulness *Mindfulness is a construct derived from Buddhism that is hard to define. It consists of two components: a deliberate intention to attend to momentary experience and an attitude of openness, acceptance, kindness, curiosity, and patience. Mindfulness-based therapies developed in the West are associated with positive effects for improving anxiety and mood symptoms in patients with anxiety and mood disorders.*

Source: Pixabay. https://pixabay.com/en/meditation-mindfulness-1000061/.

Mindfulness training has its roots in Eastern meditation traditions, such as Zen Buddhism and Vipassana, where one practices attending to the breath in a nonjudgmental way. It has also become very popular in Western society. A major aim of mindfulness meditation is to raise awareness of the present moment, characterized by curiosity, openness, and acceptance (Bishop et al., 2004). A literature review that included 39 studies and 1,140 participants receiving mindfulness training reported strong effects for improving a range of psychiatric and medical conditions, such as depression, generalized anxiety disorder, and cancer (Hofmann et al., 2010). Mindfulness impacts attention and emotion regulation, among other neurocognitive effects (Marchand, 2014). In this section, we will provide examples of studies that provide support for the positive effects of mindfulness techniques on brain functioning. These studies can be roughly divided into neuroscientific studies of advanced practitioners of mindfulness, compared to non-practitioners, and studies of the neuroscientific effects of mindfulness training as an intervention on non-experienced healthy subjects. We will begin with a review of a number of studies of the first type.

Reva, Pavlov Loktev, Korenyok, and Aftanas (2014) examined event-related potentials (ERPs) by means of EEG in 20 experienced Sahaja Yoga meditators (mean meditation experience 11.45 years) during an emotional face recognition task and compared them to 20 age-matched healthy volunteers with no meditation experience. The authors found that meditators showed attenuated mid-latency ERPs to both positive and negatively valenced pictures, and this effect was strongest over the right hemisphere (Reva et al., 2014). This finding implies that meditation improves attention and emotion regulation via frontal and prefrontal regions, a finding that is also documented in neuroimaging research during meditative states (Cahn & Polich, 2006). Kozasa et al. (2012) studied the performance of meditators and non-meditators during a functional MRI (fMRI) Stroop Task, which demands attention and impulse control. Non-meditators showed increased activity compared to meditators in the middle temporal, medial frontal, precentral and postcentral gyri, and basal ganglia during the color–word incongruent conditions. These findings are interpreted as suggesting that meditators possess an enhanced ability to sustain attention and control impulses (Kozasa et al., 2012). Luders, Clark, Narr, and Toga (2011) conducted an interesting study into structural brain connectivity (i.e., white matter fiber tract characteristics), comparing 27 experienced meditators (who practiced Zazen, Vipassana, or Shamata; mean meditation practice 23.3 years) to 27 sex- and age-matched controls. Findings demonstrated that structural connectivity was significantly larger in meditators than controls throughout the entire brain, including the frontal, temporal, parietal, occipital lobes, as well as the limbic system and brain stem. The exact mechanisms by which meditation might affect brain connectivity are unknown, but the authors suggest meditation may slow down age-related brain atrophy, perhaps as a result of altering autonomic regulation and immune activity (Cyrasz & Bussing, 2005; Davidson et al., 2003; Kubota et al., 2001).

Besides studies that compared meditators to non-meditators, there also exists a line of research that examines the correlates of mindfulness measured as a personality trait, that is, as the tendency to be mindful in daily life. Trait mindfulness has been linked with higher levels of subjective wellbeing (Brown & Ryan, 2003), empathy (Dekeyzer et al., 2008), and agreeableness (Thompson & Waltz, 2007). Mindfulness as a trait is also related to reduced bilateral amygdala activation and larger prefrontal activation during an affect labeling task (Creswell, Way, Eisenberger, & Lieberman, 2007). These findings suggest that individuals who are mindful may be better able to regulate emotional responses via prefrontal inhibition of amygdala activation (Keng, Smoski, & Robins, 2011). This neuroscientific finding is in line with research results that documented a link between mindfulness and greater ability to let go of negative thoughts about the self (Frewen et al., 2008).

The second type of studies investigated neurocognitive changes in response to mindfulness training. Examples of these research paradigms will also be provided. Santarnecchi et al. (2014) studied the neurocognitive and psychological effects of brief (eight weeks) mindfulness training in 23 meditation-naive subjects and 23 age- and gender-matched control subjects. Structural MRI revealed a significant increase in cortical density in the right insula and the somatosensory cortex, paralleled by significant decreases in state anxiety, alexithymia, and depression in the mindfulness group; no changes were found in the control group. Interestingly, a high and significant negative correlation ($r = -0.72$) was found between alexithymia and insula thickness level in the mindfulness group. The right insula is an important structure for awareness of the interoceptive, somatosensory inputs and emotional awareness.

A study by Allen et al. (2012) expands on these findings. These authors recruited and scanned meditation-naive subjects and randomly assigned them to either a six-week mindfulness training or an active control condition, that is, shared reading and listening of narratives. Compared to the control condition, mindfulness training resulted in greater dorsolateral prefrontal responding during an experimental task that required executive processing. Participants with the greatest amount of self-reported mindfulness training practice showed improvements in response inhibition during processing of negatively valenced emotional stimuli, also shown in increased BOLD (blood-oxygen-level dependent) signals in right anterior insula, left superior frontal gyrus, dorsal cingulate, and bilateral frontal superior medial lobule. The authors conclude that short-term mindfulness training is an effective attention training intervention, but that changes in affective processing require a larger investment of practice time. A recent study found compelling evidence that even a brief mindfulness instruction prior to entry in the MRI scanner affected performance during an emotional expectation paradigm (Lutz et al., 2014). Twenty-four healthy controls received the mindfulness instruction, which emphasized conscious awareness of the self in a non-judgmental way, focusing on thoughts, feelings, or bodily sensations. The written instructions were: "Try to consciously be aware of yourself, of what happens to you at this moment. Do this while expecting the picture and while looking at it. Do not judge; remain conscious and attentive to your present state. You may focus on thoughts, on emotions or on bodily sensations" (p. 778). The control group (N = 22) was instructed to expect and perceive the emotional stimuli. The groups were assigned pseudo randomly (matched for age and gender). Compared to the control condition, the mindfulness intervention was associated with increased activation in prefrontal regions during the expectation of negative and potentially negative pictures. Also, during perception of negative stimuli, reduced activation (effect size $d = 0.71$) was observed in the amygdala, an area reflecting general emotional arousal. Hence, even a brief mindfulness instruction has emotion-regulatory effects at the neural level.

Aerobic exercise

"*Mens sana in corpore sano*" is a phrase, originally from *Satire X* by the Roman poet Juvenalis, who lived in the first century AD. In this work, Roman citizens are warned they should pray for a healthy mind and a healthy body (*orandum est ut sit mens sana in corpore sano*). Over time and separated from its original context, the phrase has become a motto for many athletic societies, suggesting that only a healthy body can produce or sustain a healthy mind. Interestingly, during the past decades numerous studies using neuropsychological tasks and neuroimaging techniques found evidence that a healthy body (mostly defined as increased aerobic fitness) has a positive impact on neurocognitive functioning and brain metabolism. Similar to the earlier review of mindfulness research, a complete review of research on exercise and brain functioning will not be provided here, but a number of interesting findings will be highlighted that may point a way toward a strengths-based approach to rehabilitation of forensic patient and offender populations, and a role for physical exercise therein.

Healthy body *During the past decades numerous studies using neuropsychological tasks and neuroimaging techniques found evidence that a healthy body (mostly defined as increased aerobic fitness, running) has a positive impact on neurocognitive functioning and brain metabolism. These findings point a way towards a strengths-based approach to rehabilitation of forensic patient and offender populations, and a role for physical exercise therein.*

Source: Pixabay. https://pixabay.com/en/runners-silhouettes-athletes-635906/.

It is well known that cognitive functioning deteriorates with increasing age, particularly executive control processes involving the prefrontal and frontal brain areas, including planning, scheduling, inhibition, and working memory (Azari et al., 1992; West, 1996). Thus, it comes as no surprise that a lot of research on exercise and the brain has focused on elderly people. For instance, Kramer et al. (1999) randomly assigned 124 sedentary adults aged 60 to 75 years old, to either aerobic (walking) or anaerobic (stretching) exercise over a six-month period. They found that those who received aerobic training showed substantial improvements in performance on three tasks (e.g., a stop signal task) requiring executive control compared with anaerobically trained subjects. Physical exercise may also delay the onset of dementia and other neurodegenerative diseases (Kramer & Erickson, 2007; Ravaglia et al., 2008; Rolland et al., 2007).

The acute effects of exercise on executive functioning have also been documented. For example, Hillman, Snook, and Jerome (2003) found in an ERP study with 20 undergraduate students that a 30-minute acute bout of exercise on a treadmill followed by the Eriksen flanker task (an executive control task), resulted in larger P3 amplitudes following acute exercise compared to baseline measurements on the flanker task in the same subjects. The P3 component is related to the allocation of attentional and working memory resources to a task and hence facilitates executive control processes. A subsequent study with 20 preadolescent participants (mean age 9.5 years) corroborated and extended these findings (Hillman et al., 2009). Using the same experimental paradigm with the treadmill exercise, Hillman et al. (2009) found an improvement in response accuracy and larger P3 amplitude on a modified flanker task that assessed inhibitory control as well as better performance on an academic achievement test (i.e., the Wide Range Achievement Test, 3rd edition, that assesses academic achievement in the areas of reading, spelling, and arithmetic), following aerobic exercise relative to the resting session. In another study, the same research group examined cardio-respiratory fitness as a "trait" variable in 72 healthy adults (between 18 and 25 years of age) in relation to performance on the flanker task (Themanson, Pontifex, & Hillman, 2008). Again, higher fitness was associated with increased cognitive flexibility, evidenced through greater change in action monitoring and post-error corrections in behavior, and also supported in EEG findings. On the basis of recent meta-analyses (Colcombe & Kramer, 2003; Etnier et al., 2006) it is fair to conclude that although cognitive performance declines in a global fashion with age, physical activity and aerobic fitness may serve to protect against age-related loss of cognitive function, with the greatest benefits for processes requiring executive control (Meeuwsen, 2014).

Exercise has also been related to structural brain changes. Hippocampal and medial temporal lobe volumes are larger in highly fit adults, and physical activity training increases hippocampal volume and memory performance (Chaddock, Erickson, & Prakash, 2010). Erickson et al. (2011) showed, in a one-year randomized controlled trial with 120 older adults (aged 55 to 80 years), that aerobic exercise training increased the size of the anterior hippocampus, leading to improvements in spatial memory. Exercise training increased hippocampal volume by 2%, effectively reversing age-related losses in volume by one to two years. Hippocampal volume declined in the control group. Caudate nucleus and thalamus volumes were unaffected by exercise.

The exact causal mechanisms that drive these findings are still to be determined. A variety of mechanisms have been proposed, such as exercise-induced increase in biochemicals known to increase neuronal proliferation and survival (e.g., BDNF, insulin like growth factor 1, serotonin) (Brezun & Daszuta, 2000; Russo-Neustadt et al., 2001; van Praag et al., 1999; Vaynman & Gomez-Pinilla, 2005). Acute exercise has also been found to increase cerebral blood flow due to increases in brain metabolism, which alters the regulation of oxygen, carbon dioxide, glucose, and lactate to neural tissue (Jorgensen et al., 2000). Research on BDNF in relation to acute and chronic exercise has proliferated in the past years. BDNF plays an important role in various aspects of developmental and adult brain plasticity, including proliferation, differentiation, and survival of neurons, neurogenesis, synaptic plasticity, and cognitive function (Hofer & Barde, 1988; Monteggia et al., 2004; Poo, 2001). Huang et al. (2014) provide a review of 32 studies that examined the effect of acute aerobic exercise, chronic aerobic exercise, and strength training on peripheral BDNF. Evidence from several experimental studies suggests that BDNF concentrations were raised by acute and chronic aerobic exercise. The majority of the studies suggested that strength training had no influence on peripheral BDNF.

Conclusions and Recommendations

The study of brain processes in offenders with psychopathy and ASPD has uncovered a number of quite robust findings demonstrating reduced response inhibition and emotional processing (i.e., deficient empathy), with concomitant neuroimaging findings.

Interestingly, neuroscientific research has shown that mindfulness training has positive effects on exactly these types of neurocognitive processes and brain structures. Experienced practitioners of mindfulness show greater emotional awareness and better emotion regulation and impulse control, and even short-term mindfulness instructions reveal these effects. Thus, adding mindfulness training to standard forensic treatments might result in increased effectiveness in the long term, as a recent study with patients with substance use disorder demonstrated (Bowen et al., 2014). At a 12-month follow up, mindfulness-based relapse prevention offered added benefit in terms of significantly fewer days of substance abuse, compared to standard relapse prevention. Physical exercise, particularly aerobic fitness, also benefits brain functioning in the frontal and prefrontal areas, resulting in improved executive functioning.

Thus, mindfulness training and a physical exercise regime may be good ways to boost the effectiveness of forensic treatments, but of course this needs to be put to empirical test. Still, many unanswered questions remain. Is there a central psychophysiological construct underlying the effectiveness of both mindfulness training and physical exercise? Could will power and discipline (Baumeister & Tierney, 2011) be the key? Does it make a difference whether one practices mindfulness, aerobic exercise, or piano playing regularly? How do these strengths-based approaches interact with the use of psychotropic medication? These are just a few of the highly relevant research issues that need to be addressed by positive forensic neuroscience.

At present, there are already a number of initiatives to use the knowledge from positive neuroscience and positive psychology in the practice of forensic rehabilitation. One of these is the Prison Yoga Project.[3] In this project, yoga is used as a mindfulness practice tool for developing the whole person, increasing sensitivity toward oneself and empathy for others.

> By putting the men and women in correctional settings back in touch with their bodies, they begin to care more about themselves and understand the harm they have caused. Our objective is to provide prisoners with a mindfulness tool to draw on their yoga practice when they're not doing yoga. If they're tangled in a confrontation on the yard, or upon release, or tempted to go back to using, they can draw on what they have learned from yoga for practical solutions. That's the transformational, rehabilitative value of yoga.
> (James Fox, Founder and Director of Prison Yoga Project)

The Prison Yoga Project is a private endeavor that started in the US, expanding to Norway, Germany, and the Netherlands in helping to establish programs in European prisons with affiliate organizations. Strengths-based approaches to forensic rehabilitation, including yoga, mindfulness meditation, aerobic exercise, and other methods, albeit lacking empirical grounding at this moment, appear at least a welcome, positive adjunctive treatment to present risk-focused approaches.

Notes

1 See http://www.posneuroscience.org.
2 Ibid.
3 See http://prisonyoga.org.

Recommended Reading

Bowen, S., Witkiewitz, K., Clifasefi, S. L., Grow, J., Chawla, N., Hsu, S. H., ... Larimer, M. E. (2014). Relative efficacy of mindfulness-based relapse prevention, standard relapse prevention, and treatment as usual for substance use disorders: A randomized clinical trial. *JAMA Psychiatry, 71*, 547–556. doi:10.1001/jamapsychiatry.2013.4546. *This well-designed randomized controlled trial (RCT) demonstrated the incremental value of mindfulness-based relapse prevention over relapse prevention and treatment as usual (12-step program and psychoeducation) for substance abusers, particularly at 12-months follow up. Mindfulness practices may support long-term outcomes by strengthening the ability to monitor and skillfully cope with discomfort associated with craving or negative affect. This study could serve as a model for similar RCTs in forensic populations.*

Keng, S.-L., Smoski, M. J., & Robins, C. J. (2011). Effects of mindfulness on psychological health: A review of empirical studies. *Clinical Psychology Review, 31*, 1041–1056. doi:10.1016/j.cpr.2011.04.006. *This publication provides a nice systematic review of empirical literature across multiple methodologies (correlational studies and intervention studies). It concludes that mindfulness and its cultivation facilitates adaptive psychological functioning.*

Meeusen, R. (2014). Exercise, nutrition and the brain. *Sports Medicine, 44*(Suppl 1), S47–S56. doi: 10.1007/s40279-014-0150-5. *This brief review paper provides a nice summary of recent studies in the burgeoning research into the health enhancing effects of aerobic exercise on the brain. In addition, it focuses on the effects of nutrition on brain functioning, explaining why certain fruits and veggies are essential foods for thought.*

Puddicombe, A. (2012) 10 mindful minutes (TEDx Talk). Retrieved from https://www.ted.com/talks/andy_puddicombe_all_it_takes_is_10_mindful_minutes. *A 10-minute TEDxTalk by Andy Puddicombe on mindfulness and the need to take good care of our most precious possession, our brain/mind. He explains the concept of mindfulness in a very playful manner.*

References

Allen, M., Dietz, M., Blair, K. S., van Beek, M., Rees, G., Vestergaard-Poulsen, P., ... Roepstorff, A. (2012). Cognitive-affective neural plasticity following active-controlled mindfulness intervention. *The Journal of Neuroscience, 32*, 15601–15610. doi:10.1523/JNEUROSCI.2957-12.2012.

Andrews, D. A., & Bonta, J. (2010a). *The psychology of criminal conduct* (5th ed.). New Providence, NJ: LexisNexis.

Andrews, D. A., and Bonta, J. (2010b). Rehabilitating criminal justice policy and practice. *Psychology, Public Policy and Law, 16*, 39–55. doi:10.1037/a0018362.

Andrews, D. A., Bonta, J., & Hoge, R. D. (1990). Classification for effective rehabilitation: Rediscovering psychology. *Criminal Justice and Behavior, 17*, 19–52.

Andrews, D. A., Bonta, J., & Wormith, S. J. (2006). The recent past and near future of risk/need assessment. *Crime & Delinquency, 52*, 7–27. doi:10.1177/0011128705281756.

Azari, N. P., Rapoport, S. I., Salerno, J. A., Grady, C. L., Gonzalez-Aviles, A., Schapiro, M. B., & Horwitz, B. (1992). Interregional correlations of resting cerebral metabolism in old and young women. *Brain Research, 589*, 279–290. doi:10.1016/0006-8993(92)91288-P.

Baumeister, R. F., & Tierney, J. (2011). *Willpower: Rediscovering the greatest human strength.* New York, NY: Penguin Press.

Birbaumer, N., Veit, R., Lotze, M., Erb, M., Hermann, C., Grodd, C., & Flor, H. (2005). Deficient fear conditioning in psychopathy: A functional magnetic resonance imaging study. *Archives of General Psychiatry, 62*, 799–805. doi:10.1001/archpsyc.62.7.799.

Bishop, M., Lau, S., Shapiro, L., Carlson, N. D., Anderson, J., Carmody Segal, Z. V., ... Devins, G. (2004). Mindfulness: A proposed operational definition. *Clinical Psychology: Science and Practice, 11*, 230–241.

Biswas-Diener, R. (2006). From the equator to the north pole: A study of character strengths. *Journal of Happiness Studies, 7*, 273–310.

Blair, R. J. R. (2007). The amygdala and ventromedial prefrontal cortex in morality and psychopathy. *Trends in Cognitive Sciences, 11*, 387–392.

Boer, D. P., Hart, S. D., Kropp, P. R., & Webster, C. D. (1997). *Manual for the Sexual Violence Risk – 20: Professional guidelines for assessing risk of sexual violence.* Burnaby, Canada: Mental Health, Law, & Policy Institute, Simon Fraser University.

Bonta, J., & Andrews, D. A. 2007. *Risk-need-responsivity model for offender assessment and treatment* (User Report No. 2007-06). Ottawa, Ontario: Public Safety Canada.

Bouman, Y. H. A., Schene, A. H., & de Ruiter, C. (2009). Subjective well-being and recidivism in forensic psychiatric outpatients. *International Journal of Forensic Mental Health, 8*, 225–234. doi:10.1080/14999011003635647.

Bouman, Y.H.A., de Ruiter, C., & Schene, A. H. (2010). Social ties and short-term self-reported delinquent behaviour of personality disordered forensic outpatients. *Legal and Criminological Psychology, 15*, 357–372. doi:10.1348/135532509X444528.

Bowen, S., Witkiewitz, K., Clifasefi, S. L., Grow, J., Chawla, N., Hsu, S. H., ... Larimer, M. E. (2014). Relative efficacy of mindfulness-based relapse prevention, standard relapse prevention, and treatment as usual for substance use disorders: A randomized clinical trial. *JAMA Psychiatry, 71*, 547–556. doi:10.1001/jamapsychiatry.2013.4546.

Brezun, J. M., & Daszuta, A. (2000). Serotonin may stimulate granule cell proliferation in the adult hippocampus, as observed in rats grafted with foetal raphe neurons. *European Journal of Neuroscience, 12*, 391–396.

Cahn, B. R., & Polich, J. (2006). Meditation states and traits: EEG, ERP, and neuroimaging studies. *Psychological Bulletin, 132*, 190–211.

Campbell, C., & Eastman, N. (2014). The limits of legal use of neuroscience. In I. Singh, W. P. Sinnott-Armstrong, & J. Savulescu (Eds.), *Bioprediction, biomarkers, and bad behavior: Scientific, legal, and ethical challenges* (pp. 91–117). New York, NY: Oxford University Press.

Chaddock, L., Erickson, K. I., & Prakash, R. S. (2010). A neuroimaging investigation of the association between aerobic fitness, hippocampal volume, and memory performance in preadolescent children. *Brain Research, 1358*, 172–183.

Colcombe, S., & Kramer, A. F. (2003). Fitness effects on the cognitive function of older adults: A meta-analytic study. *Psychological Science, 14*, 125–30.

Creswell, J. D., Way, B. M., Eisenberger, N. I., & Lieberman, M. D. (2007). Neural correlates of dispositional mindfulness during affect labeling. *Psychosomatic Medicine, 69*, 560–565.

Cysarz, D., & Bussing, A. (2005). Cardiorespiratory synchronization during Zen meditation. *European Journal of Applied Physiology, 95*, 88–95.

Dalsgaard, K., Peterson, C., & Seligman, M. E. P. (2005). Shared virtue: The convergence of valued human strengths across culture and history. *Review of General Psychology, 9*, 209–213.

Davidson, R.J., Kabat-Zinn, J., Schumacher, J., Rosenkranz, M., Muller, D., Santorelli, S. F., ... Sheridan, J. F. (2003). Alterations in brain and immune function produced by mindfulness meditation. *Psychosomatic Medicine, 65*, 564–570.

Dekeyser, M., Raes, F., Leijssen, M., Leysen, S., & Dewulf, D. (2008). Mindfulness skills and interpersonal behaviour. *Personality and Individual Differences, 44*, 1235–1245.

De Ruiter, C., & Nicholls, T. L. (2011). Protective factors in forensic mental health: A new frontier. *International Journal of Forensic Mental Health*, *10*, 160–170. doi:10.1080/14999013.2011.600602.

De Vogel, V., de Ruiter, C., Bouman, Y., & de Vries Robbé, M. (2009). SAPROF: *Guidelines for the assessment of protective factors for violence risk* [English version of the Dutch original]. Utrecht, The Netherlands: Forum Educatief.

De Vogel, V., de Vries Robbé, M., de Ruiter, C., & Bouman, Y. (2011). Assessing protective factors in forensic psychiatric practice: Introducing the SAPROF. *International Journal of Forensic Mental Health*, *10*, 171–177. doi: 10.1080/14999013.2011.600230.

De Vries Robbé, M., de Vogel, V., & Douglas, K. S. (2013). Risk factors and protective factors: A two-sided dynamic approach to violence risk assessment. *The Journal of Forensic Psychiatry & Psychology*, *24*, 440–457. doi:10.1080/14789949.2013.818162.

Donaldson, S. I. (2011). Determining what works, if anything, in positive psychology. In S. I. Donaldson, M. Csikszentmihalyi, & J. Nakamura (Eds.), *Applied positive psychology: Improving everyday life, health, schools, work, and society* (pp. 3–11). New York, NY: Routledge.

Erickson, K., Voss, M., Prakash, R., Basak, C., Szabo, A., Chaddock, L., ... Kramer, A. F. (2011). Exercise training increases the size of hippocampus and improves memory. *PNAS*, *7*, 3017–3022.

Etnier, J. L., Nowell, P. M., Landers, D. M., & Sibley, B. A. (2006). A meta-regression to examine the relationship between aerobic fitness and cognitive performance. *Brain Research Reviews*, *52*, 119–30.

Frewen, P. A., Evans, E. M., Maraj, N., Dozois, D. J. A., & Partridge, K. (2008). Letting go: Mindfulness and negative automatic thinking. *Cognitive Therapy and Research*, *32*, 758–774.

Hart, S. D. (2008). Preventing violence: The role of risk assessment and management. In A. C. Baldry, and F. W. Winkel (Eds.), *Intimate partner violence prevention and intervention* (pp. 7–18). Hauppage, NY: Nova Science.

Hillman, C. H., Snook, E. M., & Jerome, G. J. (2003). Acute cardiovascular exercise and executive control function. *International Journal of Psychophysiology*, *48*, 307–314. doi:10.1016/S0167-8760(03)00080-1.

Hillman, C. H., Pontifex, M. B., Raine, L. B., Castelli, D. M., Hall, E. E., & Kramer, A. F. (2009). The effect of acute treadmill walking on cognitive control and academic achievement in preadolescent children. *Neuroscience*, *159*, 1044–1054. doi:10.1016/j.neuroscience.2009.01.057

Hofer, M. M., & Barde, Y. A. (1988). Brain-derived neurotrophic factor prevents neuronal death in vivo. *Nature*, *331*, 261–262.

Hofmann, S. G., Sawyer, A. T., Witt, A., & Oh, D. (2010). The effect of mindfulness-based therapy on anxiety and depression: A meta-analytic review. *Journal of Consulting and Clinical Psychology*, *78*, 169–183.

Horn, N. R., Dolan, M., Elliott, R., Deakin, J. F. W, & Woodruff, P. W. R. (2003). Response inhibition and impulsivity: An fMRI study. *Neuropsychologia*, *41*, 1959–1966. doi:10.1016/S0028-3932(03)00077-0.

Huang, T., Larsen, K. T., Ried-Larsen, M., Møller, N. C., & Andersen, L. B. (2014). The effects of physical activity and exercise on brain-derived neurotrophic factor in healthy humans: A review. *Scandinavian Journal of Medicine and Science in Sports*, *24*, 1–10. doi:10.1111/sms.12069.

Jorgensen, L. G., Nowak, M., Ide, K., & Secher, N. H. (2000). Cerebral blood flow and metabolism. In B. Saltin, R. Boushel, N. Secher, & J. Mitchell(Eds.), *Exercise and circulation in health and disease* (pp. 113–236). Champaign, IL: Human Kinetics Publishers.

Karatsoreos, I. N., & McEwen, B. S. (2013). Annual Research Review: The neurobiology and physiology of resilience and adaptation across the life course. *Journal of Child Psychology and Psychiatry*, *54*, 337–347. doi:10.1111/jcpp.12054.

Keng, S.-L., Smoski, M. J., & Robins, C. J. (2011). Effects of mindfulness on psychological health: A review of empirical studies. *Clinical Psychology Review*, *31*, 1041–1056. doi:10.1016/j.cpr.2011.04.006.

Kiehl, K. A. (2006). A cognitive neuroscience perspective on psychopathy: evidence for paralimbic system dysfunction. *Psychiatry Research*, *142*, 107–128.

Kozasa, E. H., Sato, J. R., Lacerda, S. S., Barreiros, M. A., Radvany, J., Russell, T. A., ... Amaro, E. Jr. (2012). Meditation training increases brain efficiency in an attention task. *Neuroimage*, *59*, 745–749.

Kramer, A. F., & Erickson, K. I. (2007). Capitalizing on cortical plasticity: Influence of physical activity on cognition and brain function. *Trends in Cognitive Science*, *11*, 342–348.

Kramer, A. F., Hahn, S., Cohen, N. J., Banich, M. T., McAuley, E., Harrison, C. R., ... Colcombe, A. (1999). Ageing, fitness and neurocognitive function. *Nature*, *400*, 418–419.

Logan, C., & Johnstone, L. (Eds.) (2012). *Managing clinical risk: A guide to effective practice*. London: Routledge.

Lodewijks, H. P. B., de Ruiter, C., & Doreleijers, T. A. H. (2010). The impact of protective factors in desistance from violent reoffending: A study in three samples of adolescent offenders. *Journal of Interpersonal Violence*, *25*, 56–587. doi: 10.1177/0886260509334403.

Luders, E., Clark, K., Narr, L., & Toga, A. W. (2011). Enhanced brain connectivity in long-term meditation practitioners. *NeuroImage*, *57*, 1308–1316. doi:10.1016/j.neuroimage.2011.05.075.

Lutz, J., Herwig, U., Opialla, S., Hittmeyer, A., Jäncke, L., Rufer, M., ... Brühl, A. B. (2014). Mindfulness and emotion regulation: An fMRI study. *SCAN*, *9*, 776–785. doi:10.1093/scan/nst043.

Mann, R. E., Webster, S. D., Schofield, C., & Marshall, W. L. (2004). Approach versus avoidance goals in relapse prevention with sexual offenders. *Sexual Abuse: Journal of Research and Treatment*, *16*, 65–75. doi: 10.1023/B:SEBU.0000006285.73534.57.

Marchand, W. R. (2014). Neural mechanisms of mindfulness and meditation: Evidence from neuroimaging studies. *World Journal of Radiology*, *6*, 471–479. doi: 10.4329/wjr.v6.i7.471.

Marsh, A. A., Finger, E. C., Fowler, K. A., Jurkowitz, I. T. N., Schechter, J. C., Yu, H. H., ... Blair, R. J. R. (2011). Reduced amygdala–orbitofrontal connectivity during moral judgments in youths with disruptive behavior disorders and psychopathic traits. *Psychiatry Research: Neuroimaging*, *194*, 279–286. doi:10.1016/j.pscychresns.2011.07.008.

Meeusen, R. (2014). Exercise, nutrition and the brain. *Sports Medicine*, *44* (Suppl 1), S47–S56. doi: 10.1007/s40279-014-0150-5.

Monahan, J. (1981). *The clinical prediction of violent behavior*. Rockville, MD: National Institute of Mental Health.

Monteggia, L. M., Barrot, M., Powell, C. M., Berton, O., Galanis, V., Gemelli, T., ... Nestler, E. J. (2004). Essential role of brain-derived neurotrophic factor in adult hippocampal function. *Proceedings of the National Academy of Sciences*, *101*, 10827–10832.

Müller, J., Sommer, M., Wagner, V., Lange, K., Taschler, H., Röder, C. H., ... Hajak, G. (2003). Abnormalities in emotion processing within cortical and subcortical regions in criminal psychopaths: Evidence from a functional magnetic resonance imaging study using pictures with emotional content. *Biological Psychiatry*, *54*, 152–162. doi:10.1016/S0002-3223(03)01749-3.

Nagtegaal, M. H., van der Horst, R. P., & Schönberger, H. J. M. (2011). *Inzicht in de verblijfsduur van tbs- gestelden: Cijfers en mogelijke verklaringen*. [Insight into treatment duration of individuals under the TBS order: Numbers and possible explanations] Meppel, the Netherlands: Boom Juridische Uitgevers.

Park, N., & Peterson, C. (2003). Virtues and organizations. In K. S. Cameron, J. E. Dutton, & R. E. Quinn (Eds.), *Positive organizational scholarship: Foundations of a new discipline* (pp. 33–47). San Francisco, CA: Berrett-Koehler.

Peterson, C. (2006). *A primer in positive psychology.* New York, NY: Oxford University Press.

Peterson, C., & Park, N. (2011). Character strengths and virtues: Their role in well-being. In S. I. Donaldson, M. Csikszentmihalyi, & J. Nakamura (Eds.), *Applied positive psychology: Improving everyday life, health, schools, work, and society* (pp. 49–62). New York, NY: Routledge.

Peterson, C., &. Seligman, M. E. P. (2003). Character strengths before and after September 11. *Psychological Science, 14,* 381–384.

Peterson, C., Park, N., & Seligman, M. E. P. (2006). Greater strengths of character and recovery from illness. *Journal of Positive Psychology, 1,* 17–26.

Philipse, M. W. G., Koeter, M. W. J., van der Staak, C. P. F., & van den Brink, W. (2006). Static and dynamic patient characteristics as predictors of criminal recidivism: A prospective study in a Dutch forensic psychiatric sample. *Law and Human Behavior, 30,* 309–327. doi: 10.1007/s10979-006-9013-4.

Poo, M. M. (2001). Neurotrophins as synaptic modulators. *Nature Reviews Neuroscience, 2,* 24–32.

Raine, A., Lencz, T., Bihrle, S., LaCasse, L., & Colletti, P. (2000). Reduced prefrontal gray matter volume and reduced autonomic activity in antisocial personality disorder. *Archives of General Psychiatry, 57,* 119–127. doi:10.1001/archpsyc.57.2.119.

Raine, A., & Yang, Y. (2006). Neural foundations to moral reasoning and antisocial behavior. *Social Cognitive and Affective Neuroscience, 1,* 203–213. doi:10.1093/scan/nsl033.

Ravaglia, G., Forti, P., Lucicesare, A., Pisacane, N., Rietti, E., Bianchin, M., & Dalmonte, E. (2008). Physical activity and dementia risk in the elderly: Findings from a prospective Italian study. *Neurology, 70,* 1786–1794.

Reva, N. V., Pavlov, S. V., Loktev, K. V., Korenyok, V. V., & Aftanas, L. I. (2014). Influence of long-term Sahaja yoga meditation practice on emotional processing in the brain: An ERP study. *Neuroscience, 281,* 195–201. doi:10.1016/j.neuroscience.2014.09.053.

Rogers, R. (2000). The uncritical acceptance of risk assessment in forensic practice. *Law and Human Behavior, 24,* 595–605.

Rolland, Y., Pillard, F., Klapouszczak, A., Reynish, E., Thomas, D., Andrieu, S., ... & Vellas, B. (2007). Exercise program for nursing home residents with Alzheimer's disease: A 1-year randomized, controlled trial. *Journal of the American Geriatric Society, 55,* 158–165.

Russo-Neustadt, A., Ha, T., Ramirez, R., & Kesslak, J. P. (2001). Physical activity-antidepressant treatment combination: Impact on brain derived neurotrophic factor and behavior in an animal model. *Behavioral and Brain Research, 120,* 87–95.

Santarnecchi, E., D'Arista, S., Egiziano, E., Gardi, C., Petrosino, R., Vatti, G., ... Rossi, A. (2014). Interaction between neuroanatomical and psychological changes after mindfulness-based training. *PloS ONE, 10*(6), e0129754. doi: org/10.1371/journal .pone.0108359.

Schneider, F., Habela, U., Kessler, C., Posse, S., Grodd, W., & Müller-Gärtner, H-W. (2000). Functional imaging of conditioned aversive emotional responses in antisocial personality disorder. *Neuropsychobiology, 42,* 192–201.

Scurich, N., & John, R. S. (2011). The effect of framing actuarial risk probabilities on involuntary commitment decisions. *Law and Human Behavior, 35,* 83–91. doi: 10.1007/s10979-010-9218-4.

Seligman, M. E. P., & Csikszentmihalyi, M. (2000). Positive psychology: An introduction. *American Psychologist, 55,* 5–14.

Steger, M. F., Hicks, B. M., Kashdan, T. B., Krueger, R. F., & Bouchard, T. J. (2007). Genetic and environmental influences on the positive traits of the Values in Action classification, and biometric covariance with normal personality. *Journal of Research in Personality, 41,* 524–539.

Taren, A. A, Giaranos, P. J., Greco, C. M., Lindsay, E. K., Fairgrieve, A., Brown, K. W., … Cresswell, J. D. (2015). Mindfulness meditation training alters stress-related amygdala resting state functional connectivity: A randomized controlled trial. *Social Cognitive Neuroscience, 10,* 1758–1768.

Themanson, J. R., Pontifex, M. B., & Hillman, C. H. (2008). Fitness and action monitoring: Evidence for improved cognitive flexibility in young adults. *Neuroscience, 157,* 319–328. doi:10.1016/j.neuroscience.2008.09.014.

Thompson, B. L., & Waltz, J. (2007). Everyday mindfulness and mindfulness meditation: Overlapping constructs or not? *Personality and Individual Differences, 43,* 1875–1885.

Ullrich, S., & Coid, J. (2011). Protective factors for violence among released prisoners: Effects over time and interactions with static risk. *Journal of Consulting and Clinical Psychology, 79,* 381–390. doi: 10.1037/a0023613.

Van Praag, H., Kempermann, G., & Gage, F. H. (1999). Running increases cell proliferation and neurogenesis in the adult mouse dentate gyrus. *Nature Neuroscience, 2,* 266–270.

Vaynman, S., & Gomez-Pinilla, F. (2005). License to run: Exercise impacts functional plasticity in the intact ad injured central nervous system by using neurotrophins. *Neurorehabilitation and Neural Repair, 19,* 283–295.

Völlm, B., Richardson, P., McKie, P., Elliott, R., Dolan, M., & Deakin, B. (2007). Neuronal correlates of reward and loss in Cluster B personality disorders: A functional magnetic resonance imaging study. *Psychiatry Research: Neuroimaging, 156,* 151–167. doi:10.1016/j.pscychresns.2007.04.008.

Walsh, C. K. (2014). Bioprediction in youth justice. In I. Singh, W. P. Sinnott-Armstrong, and J. Savulescu (Eds.), *Bioprediction, biomarkers, and bad behavior: Scientific, legal, and ethical challenges* (pp. 42–56). New York, NY: Oxford University Press.

Ward, T., & Brown, M. (2004). The good lives model and conceptual issues in offender rehabilitation. *Psychology, Crime & Law, 10,* 243–257.

Ward, T., Mann, R. E., & Gannon, T. A. (2007). The good lives model of offender rehabilitation: Clinical implications. *Aggression and Violent Behavior, 12,* 87–107.

Ward, T., Melser, J., & Yates, P. M. (2007). Reconstructing the risk-need-responsivity model: A theoretical elaboration and evaluation. *Aggression and Violent Behavior, 12,* 208–228. doi:10.1016/j.avb.2006.07.001.

Webster, C. D., Douglas, K. S., Eaves, D., & Hart, S. D. (1997). *HCR-20: Assessing the risk of violence. Version 2.* Vancouver, Canada: Simon Fraser University and BC Forensic Psychiatric Services Commission.

Webster, C. D., Martin, M. L., Brink, J., Nicholls, T. L., & Desmarais, S. (2009). *Manual for the Short-Term Assessment of Risk and Treatability (START) (Version 1.1).* Port Coquitlam, BC: Forensic Psychiatric Services Commission and St. Joseph's Healthcare.

West, R. L. (1996). An application of prefrontal cortex function theory to cognitive aging. *Psychological Bulletin, 120,* 272–292. doi:10.1037/0033-2909.120.2.272.

Yang, Y., & Raine, A. (2009). Prefrontal structural and functional brain imaging findings in antisocial, violent, and psychopathic individuals: A meta-analysis. *Psychiatry Research: Neuroimaging, 174,* 81–88. doi:10.1016/j.pscychresns.2009.03.012.

Yang, Y., Raine, A., Lencz, T., Bihrle, S., LaCasse, L., & Colletti, P. (2005). Prefrontal white matter in pathological liars. *British Journal of Psychiatry, 187,* 320-325. doi: 10.1192/bjp.187.4.320.

Part V
Rehabilitation

Part V

Rehabilitation

22

Engaging with Forensic Populations

A Biologically Informed Approach

Fiona Williams and Adam J. Carter

Key points

- Neurological research has impacted on policy in educational settings, yet the transfer of knowledge has been slow to reach forensic practitioners.
- Forensic populations often have histories which feature abuse, neglect, poor diet, and violence. There are high rates of acquired brain injury.
- Rehabilitation work has recognized the need for treatment approaches to address psychological and sociological factors. There is an emerging literature around the importance of biological factors. We argue that forensic practitioners need to have an awareness of how the brain operates so that they understand the possible impacts that trauma, abuse, or neglect can bring.
- It is likely that forensic clients face a number of neuroprocessing obstacles (Creeden, 2004, 2009), which will need to be accommodated for by rehabilitation services. It is important that treatment approaches are adapted to ensure that delivery is responsive to individual need. At present, this chapter argues, there is insufficient recognition of their likely neuroprocessing deficits.
- Cognitive behavioral approaches should be adapted to ensure that they are accessible to individuals who have acquired brain injury. We recommend that practitioners utilize "brain friendly" treatment techniques to enable responsive delivery.
- Two examples of brain friendly approaches are provided. Readers are introduced to VAK (visual, auditory, and kinesthetic) (a mnemonic which helps practitioners to facilitate in a creative way) and "the great eight" (a set of coping skills that can help to support executive functioning deficits).

The Wiley Blackwell Handbook of Forensic Neuroscience, First Edition. Edited by Anthony R. Beech, Adam J. Carter, Ruth E. Mann and Pia Rotshtein.
© 2018 John Wiley & Sons Ltd. Published 2018 by John Wiley & Sons Ltd.

Terminology Explained

Brain friendly treatment approaches are adaptations to treatment delivery/approach which enable practitioners to be responsive to individual differences and help practitioners to work with neurologically or cognitively impaired individuals.

Executive functioning is generally controlled by the frontal lobes. It relates to a variety of functions that support effective learning and problem solving, including attention, concentration, anticipation, planning, abstract reasoning and concept formation, cognitive flexibility, and the ability to control impulsive, unsuccessful, and inappropriate behavior.

Neuroplasticity refers to the physiological changes in the brain that happen as a result of our interactions with the environment. This process means that we continue to learn and adapt. Individuals who have suffered brain trauma can learn and adapt too.

Traumatic brain injury (TBI) is an acquired damage to the brain that is caused by a violent injury or jolt to the head. This can be a result of a number of different incidents such as a car accident, assault, falling, and so on. There are three levels of TBI severity: mild – loss of consciousness for less than 30 minutes; moderate – loss of consciousness for between 30 minutes to six hours; severe – loss of consciousness for longer than six hours. TBI can have a local effect on the head/brain structure and/or a diffuse effect. Diffuse effects are much more difficult to detect with conventional clinical neuroimaging methods. The heterogeneity of TBI means that its impact on behavior, cognition, and emotion varies between individuals.

Introduction

Our understanding about the development and function of the brain has advanced over recent years (see Chapter 1). This research has started to influence policy and practice in a number of different fields, notably in schools and adult learning (Boyd, 2004; Rose & Nicholl, 1997; Ruston & Larkin, 2001; Ruston, Ruston, & Larkin, 2010), although there is much debate about how well the research has been applied (e.g., Dekker, Lee, Howard-Jones, & Jolles, 2012). Neurological research has also been applied to help us understand what makes people vulnerable to offending (e.g., Williams & Chitsabesan, 2015), but, surprisingly, there have been few attempts to articulate how we should use this research to inform forensic practice.

In this chapter, we attempt to articulate how research concerning brain development and brain trauma can help practitioners engage individuals in forensic work. A range of factors are important in shaping the structure and functioning of the brain – these include biological factors, genetics, and hormones. We also know that experiences such as neglect, trauma, and abuse can have a detrimental impact on brain development and there would appear to be critical periods in the trajectory of brain development. Problems resulting from traumatic brain injury (TBI) or substance misuse can also occur later in life and affect brain development. We argue that treatment approaches with forensic populations should be informed by an understanding of how neurological problems can arise and affect cognitive functioning. It is important that in developing and delivering interventions to forensic clients, we take into account that a range of biological problems alongside difficulties caused by TBI, substance abuse, and so forth could all lead to maladaptive or immature cognitive functioning. Although recognizing that our understanding of how we generalize learning is still in its infancy, we need to make adaptations to programs to accommodate these needs when addressing violent and antisocial behavior. We describe some of the deficits that are common within our client group, and consider the ramifications for treatment. The last part of this chapter is devoted to practical ideas to help practitioners work with individuals who have been affected by neurological damage.

The reader should note that neither of the authors are neuroscientists. Rather, we are forensic psychologists who are keen to learn from the neuroscience literature to improve practice and enhance engagement in therapeutic work. This chapter therefore aims to provide a practical resource using accessible language, which will help practitioners work with forensic clients.

Brief Overview of How the Brain Develops and Functions

Simplified models of the brain divide it into three main functions; the brain stem, the limbic system, and the cortex (e.g., Creeden, 2009). Prenatally, by week 32 the brain has developed most of its structure and generated the majority of its neurons, the building material of the brain. The brain stem, which sits at the top of the spinal cord, is responsible for a number of essential cardiovascular functions to sustain life, including heartbeat and respiration which start to operate immediately at birth (Siegel, 2007). However, the brain keeps developing after the baby is born until the individual is in their mid-20s (Sowell, Peterson, Thompson, Welcome, & Henkenius, 2003).

The limbic system contains the basal ganglia and the amygdala, both critical in screening for threats and generating emotional responses, including the fight, flight, or freeze response and storing information about potential threats for future reference. At the top of the brain is the cerebral cortex, which is the most advanced and developed part of the brain. The frontal lobes are where human "higher functions" take place, located at the very forefront of the brain. The frontal lobes have evolved to also house the prefrontal cortex where executive functioning is carried out. Executive functioning covers a number of significant cognitive skills that enable us to manage our day-to-day activities including choosing between right and wrong, mediation of conflicts, planning, organizing, selective attention, problem solving, impulse control, and social and sexual behavior. There are close links between executive functioning and attention. Posner, Petersen, and Petersen (1990) suggested that executive function ensures that attention is mediated, monitored, and focused.

Trauma and the Brain

Research on the brain suggests that genetic predisposition and experience both work in combination to develop the brain. Early experiences shape the design of the brain and how it functions (Arden & Linford, 2009). Arden and Linford (2009) described how synaptic connections that represent a skill are strengthened when they are used, but, if not used, the connection is weakened. This "use it or lose it" is essential to brain growth. "Brain development, or learning, is actually the process of creating, strengthening, and discarding connections among the neurons; these connections are called synapses. Synapses organize the brain by forming pathways that connect the parts of the brain governing everything we do – from breathing and sleeping to thinking and feeling" (Understanding the Effects of Maltreatment on Brain Development, Child Welfare Information Gateway, 2009, p. 3).

The environment in which a child grows up can affect the way the brain develops. Being subjected to physical abuse and neglect are among the experiences that can affect both the way connections are made, and overall brain functioning. With optimal experiences, the brain develops healthy, flexible, and diverse capabilities. However, if there is disruption to these optimal experiences, there may be significant and lasting consequences (e.g., Creeden, 2009). Neglect can result in difficulties with attention, language and increased impulsivity (e.g., Norman et al., 2012).

> Our brains are sculpted by our early experiences. Maltreatment is a chisel that shapes a brain to contend with strife, but at the cost of deep, enduring wounds.
>
> Teicher (2000, p. 67).

In summary, the neuro-developmental organization of the brain in response to threat or trauma can create ongoing difficulties with the processing of new information. Over attention to threats can also lead to an overactive amygdala and with it raised levels of the stress hormone cortisol, which can impact on the ability for the hippocampus to grow and leave it underdeveloped. The hippocampus is also involved in verbal learning and learning in context (Creeden, 2009). There is, of course, also the physical damage to the brain that abuse brings such as the damage that accompanies shaken baby syndrome, as well as the effect of malnutrition and lack of stimulation (see Chapter 1).

What is the Extent of Neurological Problems within Forensic Populations?

It is important that practitioners working with forensic clients understand how neurological deficits can impact on behavior, and there is a recognized need for neuroscience research to inform practice and policy within forensic settings (Lowings & Wicks, 2012). Lowings and Wicks (2012) reported that between 46% and 86% of the prisoner population in the UK is likely to have a neurological disorder that would interfere with their ability to learn new information and apply existing learning. It has been proposed that there are significant numbers of adult prisoners and young adult offenders in both custody and community who have attention deficit hyperactivity disorder (ADHD) (Young & Goodwin, 2010). This indicates a significant figure of individuals in forensic settings who will have a disorder that could affect their ability to engage with traditional rehabilitative approaches such as cognitive-behavioral group therapies. Language and communication deficits are also common. For example, Bryan, Freer, and Furlong (2007) identified language skills as being below average between 66% and 90% of a sample of 58 juvenile offenders aged 15 to 17 years from a secure college in England. Therefore, interventions that rely heavily upon language and communication may not be appropriate for individuals with deficits in these areas.

Research reveals that the prevalence of TBI is three to eight times higher in those who are in custody than those who are not (Colantonio, Stamenova, Abramowitz, Clarke, & Christensen, 2007; Davies, Williams, Hinder, Burgess, & Mounce, 2012; Hux, Bond, Skinner, Belau, & Sanger, 1998; Moore, Indig, & Haysom, 2014). A systematic review of ten studies (four of which included control groups) revealed that the prevalence rates of TBI among young people in custody ranged from 16.5% to 72.1% (Hughes et al., 2015). In the largest UK TBI study, Pitman, Haddlesley, da Silva Ramos, Oddy, and Fortescue (2012) found that almost half of the men screened on admission into HM Prison Leeds self-reported a history of TBI. Those who reported a TBI were more likely to have committed a violent offence. TBI has also been associated with higher rates of rule-breaking while in custody (Williams & Chitsabesan, 2015). With rising levels of violence in prisons, managing prisoner behavior in custody has become a pressing concern for managers (Williams, 2015). It is important therefore that practitioners working with forensic clients understand how neurological deficits can impact on behavior, and there is a recognized need for neuroscience research to inform practice and policy within forensic settings (Lowings & Wicks, 2016).

What are the Implications for Treatment?

The reoffending literature tells us that impulsivity, poor self-management, and anti-social attitudes are linked to reoffending. As such, forensic practitioners working with this population strive to make improvements in relation to many of these higher order functions. It is vital therefore that we consider impairments to executive functioning and other higher order impairments within our work. In order to ensure that our treatment approach is responsive to individual needs, we must ensure that adjustments to our approach are made.

We propose that forensic treatment approaches should not exclusively focus on psychological or sociological factors. We argue that the impact of biological factors, including an understanding of brain development and function, must be understood and planned for within treatment delivery (Carter & Mann, 2016). It is important to understand how the brain functions, to enable an appreciation of how it can be damaged. If we are to maximize opportunities for learning, it is important that adjustments are made to accommodate for any long-lasting impact from trauma. Within the field of rehabilitation, there are a number of authors who have also advocated this approach and are helping to bridge the gap between neuroscientific study and rehabilitative practice (e.g., see Chapters 24, 30, and 31 in this volume).

Her Majesty's Prison and Probation Service (HMPPS), which oversees rehabilitative programs in custody and community in England and Wales, has been employing flexible and creative delivery methods for some time within its Adapted Sexual Offending Treatment approaches (treatment programs which have been specifically designed for learning-disabled men who have sexually offended; see Williams & Mann, 2010). More recently we have adopted the same methods into our practice with non-learning-disabled individuals, and across all of HMPPS accredited programs. As such, although the techniques described in this chapter were primarily designed to enable responsive delivery to individuals with a learning disability, it is now recognized that these approaches are more responsive with the wider forensic population, particularly those with neurological impairments but also people who are deaf, individuals with autism, and those who have dementia. Creeden (2004, 2009, 2013) has described how adaptations to practice should be made based on an understanding of brain trauma. He described how, in forensic populations, a number of "neuro processing obstacles" can impact on treatment (Creeden, 2004). These neuro processing obstacles affect day-to-day functioning and, as such, can present as various behaviors, which interfere with treatment. Further, it is acknowledged that these neuroprocessing obstacles are often misinterpreted by practitioners. Commonly, those who are not progressing in treatment, have their lack of success attributed to poor motivation, or disruptive behavior. In some cases, these decisions can lead to deselection from treatment or individuals being classified as "in denial." Therefore, there are serious implications for progression through sentence and, in turn, longer imprisonment. In essence, treatment providers tend to quickly attribute problems to "the client as opposed to being a problem with how we understood the behavior or how we were making interventions" (Creeden, 2004, p. 232). It is important that we consider alternative explanations to lack of progression in treatment. Creeden articulated the importance of considering the neuroprocessing obstacles, or biological vulnerabilities, which might impact on treatment success and the need to develop some techniques for managing these.

Brain Adaptation

Although the brain can be damaged by a range of early experiences, it continues to develop new neural connections throughout life. From a rehabilitative point of view, this is promising. Other organs cope with injury by generating new cells to replace the damaged ones; the brain copes with lesions by generating alternative processing routes to compensate for those lost through trauma. New skills can apparently be developed later in life. This process is referred to as "neuroplasticity," and this phenomenon allows the neurons in the brain to compensate for injury, disease, and trauma. For example, if one hemisphere of the brain is damaged, the intact hemisphere may take over some of its functions. The brain compensates for damage in effect by reorganizing and forming new connections between intact neurons. There are a number of examples that illustrate functional and structural changes following training or experiences. For example, Maguire, Woollett, and Spiers (2006) researched the brains of London taxi drivers and compared these to a group of bus drivers. A taxi driver's hippocampus is measurably larger than that of a bus driver. By driving the same route every day, the bus drivers don't need to exercise this part of the brain as much. The taxi drivers, on the other hand, rely on it constantly for navigation.

Neural Plasticity Mechanisms in Non-Forensic Clients

There are some promising indications, but not yet compelling evidence, that certain kinds of training can cause neural plasticity, resulting in changes to brain structure and neural functioning, with improved cognitive ability. Thomas and Baker (2013), in their review of evidence for training-dependent structural plasticity in humans, found only one study from 20 considered that provided "strong evidence for effects that are specific both to the training and to particular regions" (p. 233). This single study, by Erickson et al. (2011), used a randomized control trial with older adults to demonstrate that hippocampus volume could be increased, and with it cognitive performance, as a result of aerobic training. However, we need to understand the specific processes of neural plasticity and to understand the mechanism of neural change and the components of training that bring this change to ensure, for example, that people can generalize learning from training specific tasks. For example, Takeuchi and Kawashima (2012) noted that while factors such as motivation and using a variety of training methods can both enhance training outcomes and help the goals to be met more quickly, we are not yet at the point where people are able to generalize learning from training specific tasks.

Takeuchi and Kawashima reviewed studies that aimed to improve processing speed (the measurement of how quickly an individual carries out fundamental cognitive functions). Processing speed training tasks are generally computer based and invole a subject being given a task to be "performed in an adaptive manner, which means that the difficulties of the task are modulated based on the subject's performance (Takeuchi & Kawashima, 2012, p. 290). While processing speed training varies considerably, it has been shown to transfer benefits to similar tasks, so Takeuchi and Kawashima were interested in seeing how training can be generalized. They concluded that cognitive performance could possibly be improved by using "adaptive procedures to modulate difficulties of training tasks" (p. 298). To conclude, brains impacted by trauma have the ability to develop and modify. We are starting to understand those components that may increase learning, including motivation and feedback during the task (Takeuchi & Kawashima, 2012) and the experiences that lead to generalized effects (Green & Bavelier, 2008). As practitioners working with forensic clients, we must be mindful of the need to design and deliver learning experiences that maximize opportunities to stimulate the brain and activate learning.

Brain Friendly Treatment Approaches

Cognitive behavioral therapy (CBT) approaches typically place a strong emphasis on cognitive ability, requiring individuals to make links in learning quickly. Simple adaptations to CBT can make it accessible to individuals who have impairments and there is a growing literature which supports the use of accessible CBT for individuals who have learning disabilities and neurological impairments. The research shows that CBT is effective with learning disabled individuals (Dodd et al., 2013; Lindsay, Neilson, & Lawrenson, 1997; Stenfert-Kroese et al., 1997; Willner, 2007;) and people with acquired brain injury (Arundine et al., 2012). Ramsay (2010) described the need to make CBT "sticky" so that techniques can be remembered more easily. In HMPPS, we have developed a range of "brain friendly" techniques, which help to make the learning sticky so that opportunities for learning are maximized. These adaptations do no harm to non-impaired individuals and as such they are now advocated for all. Indeed, Roy (2015) described how all newly designed products should be developed not only for learning disabled individuals given that there are generally benefits for all users, not just those for whom the product is designed.

Biologically Informed Approach *An effective rehabilitation relies on the ability to form good communication between the therapist and the offenders. Offenders often have many neuro-cognitive barriers which hinder an effective communication between them and the therapist. Therefore it is essential to consider neuro-biological based strategies to help individuals engage and benefit from rehabilitative programs.*

Source: © Dmaneu. Used under license from Pixabay.

Using brain friendly approaches to overcome language deficits

Research suggests that individuals with neurological deficits may find it more difficult to engage with treatment because of difficulties processing information, which will include communication difficulties as a result of speech and language problems (Williams et al., 2010). A range of language deficits have been associated with trauma and delinquent youth. Language delays and language processing difficulties have been identified as a result of child maltreatment (Culp et al., 1991; Fox, Long, & Langlois, 1988; Rogeness et al., 1986). Verbal abilities appear to be affected in adolescents identified as antisocial or delinquent (Teicher, Andersen, Polcari, Andersen, & Navalta, 2002). Neuro processing obstacles that result in language problems tend to impact on an individual's life in all areas of their day-to-day functioning. Further, this will manifest in treatment and may lead to difficulties in both receptive and expressive skills.

Given that we know that language deficits are common among forensic populations, it is surprising that, to date, there is relatively little description in the literature about how these needs can best be accommodated for in treatment. Indeed, most treatment approaches are "primarily presented in a language based modality (which) largely ignores the type of neuro-processing obstacles that might make it difficult for many of our clients to learn, remember, and retrieve useful information and skills necessary to avoid or prevent further abusive behavior" (Creeden, 2004, p. 234). Traditional assessment and treatment methods are typified by extensive abstract verbal discussion, introspection, and written forms of communication. Sessions are often delivered in a static way with the individuals seated and generally required to listen and add verbal contributions as required. Essentially, only a certain type of learner is likely to benefit from this approach (those who enjoy the cognitive challenge of discussion and engage best when sitting down for two hours). Bearing in mind that this is not the typical profile of most of the forensic population, it is not hard to see why this approach may not be meeting the needs of many individuals. Creeden (2013) advocated that a "body based or sensory-based treatment interventions" should be implemented instead of cognitive-based interventions. Further, he cites Teicher et al's (2002) research on the impact of trauma, which indicated that one consequence of childhood trauma can be a lack of left hemisphere development and deficits in left–right hemisphere integration. Creeden hypothesizes that, as a consequence, individuals affected by trauma are likely to be better at visual learning and kinesthetic or experiential learning than they are at verbal learning. He says "relying exclusively or heavily on "talk therapy" may, in fact, limit treatment progress for many clients" (p. 15). We advocate that practitioners incorporate multiple communication methods in their approach. The brain processes on many levels, using different paths and modalities. It is designed to process many inputs at once and prefers multi-processing (Caine & Caine, 1997). In order to aid learning it is therefore important that we present information in multi-modal ways.

To help practitioners remember to incorporate different techniques into their approach, we encourage them to think of the mnemonic VAK to help them remember to be creative when delivering new information to clients. We know that individuals learn through their senses, and that the human brain is well adapted to processing information from everything that a person sees, hears and does (Sharp, Bowker, & Byrne, 2008). As such, practitioners should work in a way that targets each of the senses. We do not advocate that practitioners identify an individual's preferred learning style, or only use one modality. It is arguably difficult to identify an individual's preferred method of learning and therefore the possible advantages to using different communication routes. Reviews of educational literature and controlled laboratory studies fail to support this approach (Coffield, Moseley, Hall, & Ecclestopne, 2004; Geake, 2008; Kratzig & Arbuthnott, 2006). We appreciate that individuals will vary in relation to their preferred modality depending on the material, their mood, or the situation they are in. As such, it is important that material is presented across the different modalities (Kratzig & Arbuthnott, 2006). Presenting information in multiple sensory modes can support learning (Najjar, 1998). We advocate a strengths-based treatment approach which plays to an individual's strengths. Individuals who have experienced trauma will have a number of strengths; it is the practitioner's role to identify and work with these strengths.

We will now describe some of the techniques that can be used within a brain friendly approach. These techniques have been tried and tested by practitioners who work in forensic settings. They are described under the VAK headings, but it should be noted that some of the ideas span more than one modality. We advocate that practitioners work creatively to "VAK up" their delivery approach, so that it is responsive to individual need and provides an engaging and positive environment for learning.

Using visual methods

A variety of visual prompts can be used to present and discuss information with individuals. Practitioners should work collaboratively with individuals to identify what is most useful to the individual. Rossiter and Holmes (2013) describe how the use of "visual and concrete media can assist communication, comprehension and containment of complex and/or distressing psychological phenomena" (p. 11). Drawn approaches can be helpful when working with individuals who struggle to present themselves verbally. Simple line drawings or representations of information can often help make sense of information. Practitioners should also try to present difficult concepts visually, for example, when talking about time a clock face could be used. A time line can also be used in different ways to help represent time or a series of events. This can be used for isolated events or to represent time over an entire lifetime. Similarly, a drawing of a thermometer can be used to represent feelings. A bank of pictures can be collected from newspaper and magazines to help discussions about issues. Prompts can often help to uncover thoughts that are difficult to access, or thoughts around issues that are difficult for individuals to discuss (e.g., sexual matters). To help individuals make links in learning, present new ideas in relation to areas of interest for the individual. Ireland and Rogers (2004) describe the importance of making exercises "interest- laden" to engage individuals and maintain their attention. Haaven (2006) noted that adults, in general, learn best when the information being taught is clearly relevant to their lives. This can be done in a visual way by using pictures or photographs that are meaningful and relevant to the individual. To help individuals describe the intensity or strength of a feeling a visual representation can be used, for example, a five-point "feelings scale" where 1 is a low intensity feeling and 5 is a very strong feeling. A similar technique using strength of color can also be used. Finally, the use of emojis can also be helpful to aid discussions about feelings.

Memory prompts are commonly needed when working with this client group as neurological damage commonly leaves individuals with encoding, storage, and retrieval difficulties. Practitioners should group information into meaningful chunks to help individuals who have working memory deficits Hurley, Tomasulo, and Pfadt (1998). Prompts can also be used to help support individuals. These could be drawn or written representations such as sticky note reminders, a written list, and so on (in the community, technology –such as text prompts can be useful). It could be presented in various ways (e.g., fridge magnet, key ring fob, etc.). Using a diary can also be a good way of remembering activities, thoughts, and feelings. Further, given that self-monitoring is an issue for many individuals with neurological/cognitive impairment, it is useful to encourage this activity. Diaries can be drawn or written.

Recording individuals in the session undertaking skills practice work can also be a useful way to generate discussion and allow the individual to see themselves/their behavior. This can be a good way of encouraging reflection on non-verbal behavior. Practitioners in HMPPS have recently developed a series of electronic cartoon animations to help convey learning points and reinforce messages.

In order to enable learning, it is important to consider the wider visual environment. Given that therapeutic work with forensic populations generally takes place in prisons or probation offices, which are often bleak environments, it is important to try to make the room where any therapeutic work takes place welcoming, inviting and comfortable. Try to keep the layout of the room the same as changes can be difficult for individuals with attention deficits. It is advised that practitioners manage the visual load of information on display. Distractibility is often an issue in this group and it is important that the number of visual aids is not overwhelming (Ireland & Rogers, 2004). It is also suggested that practitioners consider any windows, which might have interesting views, and so on. Noise can also be very distracting, giving individuals the opportunity to think requires some quiet time.

Using auditory methods

In order to help manage general attention difficulties it is recommended that practitioners consider their use of language, tone, and expression. The simplification of treatment concepts is fundamental when working with those who have learning disability and much of our experience in this area is drawn from our adapted programs, which were specifically designed for this group (Williams & Mann, 2010). Hernadez-Halton et al. (2000) described simplifying verbal communication used to enable discussion about thoughts and feelings. Haaven and Coleman (2000) noted that teaching learning disabled sexual offenders requires more than just breaking skills down into small steps and rewards. Lindsay et al. (1997) described how language needs to be broken down and simplified to enable understanding. Beail (1998, 2001) described the importance of ensuring patient understanding by using simple language structures. Keeling and Rose (2006) outlined a need to simplify and restructure complex concepts to enable understanding. They also noted that in some cases concepts were withdrawn to maximize the potential for learning.

Practitioners should give thought to how they simplify their verbal interactions with individuals. Try to avoid abstract/hypothetical discussions. Abstract concepts are of limited use to persons with brain impairment in the frontal lobes (Stone & Thompson, 2001). Encourage individuals to give concrete examples, which demonstrate the concept that is being discussed. Using examples helps to ensure that the discussion is concrete. Story telling can also be a useful technique to help individuals. Create a scenario or tell a story that highlights the learning point. Make this relevant to group or individual interests if possible, so that it is meaningful to them. Use this technique with the client to encourage/prompt discussion.

Individuals with neurological impairments can often struggle with vocabulary and labeling. This can be particularly pertinent when labeling emotions. Patience and a sensitive method of enquiry is often required to help individuals explain what they are meaning. Rossiter and Holmes (2013) describe the need for an "open-minded, non-judgmental stance and working with a person's belief system" (p. 11).

It is recommended when questioning individuals to ask one clear and unambiguous question at a time, giving time for a response before pursuing. Individuals who struggle to process information will need time to respond. Use simple short sentences, and summarize regularly (using different modalities if possible) so that information is repeated in different ways. Varying tone and pace of language will help to add interest and engage individuals. Consider using rhythm, raps, or music in treatment. Music can have a powerful effect on learning and has been used to good effect in treatment approaches with individuals who have neurological impairments (see Rossiter & Holmes, 2013). Well-chosen music can be used to energize a session and lift the mood. It can recharge individuals and help them to prepare for learning, or relax them so that they feel better able to manage stress or anxiety, or accept and be mindful of their circumstances/situation. It is important that music is chosen carefully and that copyright issues are adhered to.

Re-capping on the key elements of therapy goals is important (Ireland & Rogers, 2004). This should not simply be a recall exercise of "so tell me what you have learnt", but some clarification that there is a genuine understanding of the desired concepts. Check and double-check understanding. Do not accept what is said without checking it out. Are you completely confident that you understand what the individual meant? Do not rely on individuals honestly telling you when they do/do not understand. One of the questions we try to stop practitioners using is "do you understand?" Individuals who struggle with self-esteem issues and have a history of feeling that they are different to others will not want to admit that they don't understand for fear of looking like a failure. Practitioners must learn to use a variety of methods to check this out; for example, asking individuals to draw or show their understanding. Turn the focus of understanding back on yourself – "I'm not sure I did a very good job of explaining that today, can you help me?"

Using kinesthetic methods

A Chinese proverb says: "Tell me, and I'll forget. Show me, and I may remember. Involve me, and I'll understand." In order to enable effective learning, it is important that individuals are involved in the treatment process. In this section, we explore a range of kinesthetic techniques that can be used to good effect with individuals who have neurological impairments.

The use of drama therapy techniques is described in the literature with learning disabled individuals (Chesner, 1995; Sprague, 1991). Drama enables access to learning; visually, auditory, and kinesthetically. HMPPS have developed a range of psychodrama techniques to help individuals show their understanding and demonstrate their learning (Daniels, 2008). Of particular use is the "show me" technique, which enables an individual to show how they would behave or how they did behave in a given situation. The practice scenarios can then be used to enable discussion, and to highlight learning points. Other techniques can also be used including "frozen picture", where practitioners can set up a specific scenario and ask individuals to hold their position (like a photograph). The individual can then step out of the scene to enable reflection on what they can see. Another approach is to encourage the individual to direct you in a scenario – as if they were a director in a film. "Tell me what I should do…" These techniques (when applied safely and correctly) can be very powerful.

Certainly, in our experience, many of the individuals we work with do not respond well to "chalk and talk" style treatment approaches, which remind them of school. For many, their school years were not associated with experiences of success. As such, it is important that we ensure our approach does not remind them of school. Stachen and Shevich (1999) noted that practitioners and clients often sit down when doing treatment work. Attention spans can be more easily maintained if practitioners take opportunities to move in the room; stand up, walk around, write/draw, point at relevant visual cues, and so on. Further, requiring individuals to move by standing, pacing, walking, sitting on the floor, and so on empowers them to become more actively involved in the process. Experience suggests that, in a group setting, individuals become more verbally involved once they have moved about a bit. Practitioners should also use different techniques to make their approach more engaging. For example, using hand gestures to accompany speech aids thought processes. Wagner, Nusbaum, and Glodin-Meadow (2004) found that when gestures were accompanied with verbal presentation, more material was remembered. Using their hands while explaining concepts to students allowed them to concentrate more. This is particularly true if the gestures used matched what was being said (e.g., pointing to a person who was being referred to). The authors suggest that hand gestures "provide a framework that complements and organizes speech and thus lightens the burden on working memory." In our programs, we encourage practitioners to make appropriate use of gestures to support a verbal message. For example, thumbs up/down for OK or not OK.

Another technique that we have incorporated into our treatment approaches is the use of "brain breaks." This term describes a physical activity that is deliberate, involves slow and considered movement, and requires thought. Brain breaks are a feature of accelerated learning programs (Smith, 2002) and are best used to complement learning. They can be used before, during, and after formal learning, and can be part of helping the learner understand and recall concepts and content. The exercises are fun and memorable in themselves. Brain breaks can also be used to alter the mood in the room and create a positive, enthusiastic atmosphere at times when concentration may be slumping,

Thinking of ways to enable movement in treatment can often be difficult for practitioners. One way might be to encourage individuals who are struggling to describe the strength or intensity of their feeling or thought to show it. They can do this in a number of ways – for example, by encouraging the individual to stand on the number on the floor that represents the strength of his/her feeling. The strength of a relationship can also be explored by playing a game of tug of war using a piece of string or a rolled-up piece of paper – for example, who would win the tug of war? Who is the boss in this relationship? Another idea is to use stepping stones across the floor to help individuals describe a sequence of events. A series of feet on the floor will help individuals to talk through the stages. This can also be used to help individuals understand the steps involved in a teaching point, for example, problem-solving steps. Encourage individuals to show what they would or should do by walking through the steps.

Interactive exercises based around the idea of a game can work really well with individuals. We have seen some great creative ideas for games to teach and reinforce learning messages. New technologies should also be considered to enhance learning opportunities. Digital game-based learning has also received widespread interest in relation to health interventions. For example, Nintendo Wii® has been used to help patients with wrist injuries (Decker et al., 2009). There are also some examples of games that have been developed to improve psychological functioning. One example is SPARX, which was developed to help individuals with depression. This is a CBT-based game in which the user choses an avatar to complete a number of challenges. The aim of the game is to rid the fantasy world of "gloomy negative automatic thoughts." Merry et al. (2012) describe promising results with significant decreases of depression scores compared to a waiting-list control group. Recently developed health-related games have been shown to effectively facilitate behaviors, such as healthy lifestyle habits, self-management of illnesses and chronic conditions, and physical activity (Ferguson, 2012). The effectiveness of digital game-based learning has also been seen to improve the motivation of students with learning disabilities (Ke & Abras, 2012), the attention of children with cognitive disabilities (Rezaiyan, Mohammadi, & Fallah, 2007), the psychomotor skills of slightly mentally disabled children (Karal, Kokoç, & Ayyıldız, 2010), and the social problem-solving skills of students with ADHD (Goldsworthy, Barab, & Goldsworthy, 2000). This is an area of potential interest to practitioners working with forensic populations.

Brain Friendly Approaches that Help Individuals Who Have Executive Functioning Deficits

The second area of neuroprocessing obstacles that are common among forensic client groups are executive functioning deficits. Executive functioning refers to the specific cognitive abilities required for the successful execution of purposeful behavior including goal formation, planning, attentional control, and the self-regulation of behavior (Kosaka, 2002). Impairment of these functions has been associated with changes in personality including decreased cooperativeness and self-directiveness (Bergvall, Nilsson, & Hansen, 2003) and increased impulsivity and aggression (Dolan & Anderson, 2002).

Executive functioning is thought to span several brain regions, most notably the prefrontal cortex (Paschall & Fishbein, 2002), and several sub-cortical pathways (Koechlin, Corrado, Pietrini, & Grafman 2000; Monchi, Petrides, Strafella, Worsley, & Doyon 2006). As such, any damage to these areas can lead to difficulties. Individuals with lesions to the prefrontal cortex often have difficulties with planning and decision making, impulsivity, and emotional dysregulation (Masterman & Cummings, 1997; Tateno, Jorge, & Robinson, 2003). A link between aggression and frontal lobe dysfunction (Brower & Price, 2001) has also been observed. Morgan and Lilienfeld (2000) reported on the link between antisocial behavior and deficits in executive functioning. In studies that look at the prevalence of various forensic populations, executive functioning deficits have been reported in populations of male and female incarcerated young adults (Enns, Reddon, Das, & Boukos, 2007; Olvera et al., 2005), as well as non-incarcerated aggressive adolescents (Giancola, Mezzich, & Tarter, 1998; Séguin, Boulerice, Harden, Tremblay, & Pihl, 1999), and aggressive children (Raaijmakers et al., 2008). Two systematic reviews (Vanderploeg, Belanger, & Curtiss, 2009; Kennedy et al., 2008) and two subsequent randomized control trials (Spikman, Boelen, Lamberts, Brouwer, & Fasotti, 2010; Vas, Chapman, Cook, Elliott, & Keebler, 2011) have looked at the impact of interventions for executive functioning deficits. All four studies show that treatment approaches which provide skills training (e.g., problem solving, goal management, and reasoning) are effective at improving performance. As such, it is important that treatment approaches cover these areas.

One of the ways that we do this is by teaching coping skills or "tactics." These skills are taught and rehearsed in treatment via skills practice. These are referred to in treatment as "the great eight" and depicted visually in Figure 22.1.

The great eight tactics help individuals to self-manage and thereby strengthen their ability to be successful and live a life free from offending. The eight coping skills are taught to individuals who are encouraged to practice, monitor, and evaluate their success in their day-to-day lives. Each coping skill is described in Table 22.1.

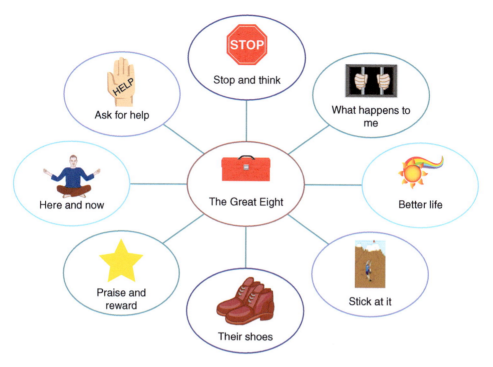

Figure 22.1 The great eight coping skills.

A variety of VAK techniques are used to introduce the tactics to individuals. Practitioners use modelling and role play sketches to help individuals understand the concepts. Individuals are encouraged to personalize the tactics so that they are meaningful to them. They create a visual representation of each tactic, which can be kept in their "toolbox" (the tactics are described as tools that they can use to help them in the future). The language used is tailored so that it is relevant for the individual. As Rossiter and Holmes (2013) describe, it is important that individuals find personal relevance in the concepts they are taught. The tactics need to be introduced at the start of treatment, so that there are plenty of opportunities for repetition and overlearning (Ireland & Rogers, 2004). Practitioners should encourage individuals to choose which tactics they want to practice in any skills practice scenario. Opportunities for practicing are encouraged throughout the treatment and more widely. Individuals are encouraged to self-monitor outside of the treatment sessions. They are asked to record (draw or write) how they have dealt with a situation and which of the tactics they used. In this way, individuals are encouraged to generalize their learning into their day-to-day activities.

It's up to You! The Biggest Obstacle to Accessible Delivery is Us

If we accept that there are a large proportion of forensic individuals who have trauma histories, then we need also to accept that accommodations will need to be made in

Table 22.1 The great eight tactics

"Tactic"	Description
Stop and think	Individuals are encouraged to use "stop and think" as a first stage tactic, so that they give themselves space and time to think and process the situation. They are encouraged to stop and think and then reflect on how they should deal with the situation. This technique encourages individuals to self-monitor, it creates the opportunity to reflect on their thoughts, feelings, and behaviors in a situation. This tactic is especially good for those who have emotional regulation deficits.
What happens to me	The "what happens to me" tactic serves to remind the individual of the consequences of unwanted behavior. Practitioners are encouraged to develop the impact of this tactic by encouraging individuals to focus on all of the senses. For example, if prison is suggested as a consequence of unwanted behavior, individuals are encouraged to describe fully what prison is like for them. They are asked to think about the smell of prison, the sounds of prison, the feelings they have in prison. Strong negative images of the things they hate about prison are focused on. This tactic encourages individuals to think about the consequences to their behavior, which helps to strengthen their problem-solving skills.
Sticking at it	The "sticking at it" tactic encourages persistence and strengthens resilience; a central tenet of risk. As practitioners when working with individuals who have impairments, it is important to be aware of their ability to stick at it and not give up: "I just gave up," "I couldn't do it." Increasing someone's ability to stick at it and be persistent can be a way of validating one's new identity.
Better life	This tactic is about the gains that are aligned with not offending. It represents the individual's idea of a "better life", a successful life. It represents the goals they have for their future life and encourages hope (an important factor in the desistance literature; Maruna, 2001).
Their shoes	This tactic encourages individuals to perspective take. Stepping into someone else's shoes can give us some insight into how the other person might be feeling or thinking. Considering another person's perspective can be important when problem solving.
Praise and reward	This tactic encourages individuals to use self-praise and to reward themselves as they monitor their progress. The "role of "praise and reward" in shaping and maintaining behavior needs to be discussed in treatment so that practitioners can ensure that their approach is meaningful and personal to each individual.
Here and now	The "here and now" tactic is about being completely in touch with the present moment and being open to experiences as they come. It will help individuals to pay more attention to what they are thinking and feeling about things happening currently and to accept this openly without any judgement. This tactic stems from the mindfulness literature (Kabat-Zinn, 2001) and aims to help individuals manage impulsive feelings by encouraging individuals to practice attending to and concentrating on the present moment.
Asking for help	This tactic encourages individuals to practice "asking for help" and seeking support from others. It helps to build and strengthen social capital (McNeil, Farrall, Lightwler, & Maruna. 2012) and develop problem-solving skills.

assessment and treatment to enable effective learning. The delivery of brain friendly techniques is dependent on the skills, ability, and willingness of the practitioners working with this population.

In relation to intellectually disabled individuals, Coleman and Haaven (2001) noted that treatment is often hampered by "old fashioned and inept teaching methods." They observed that practitioners tend to teach in the way they were taught, usually in large rooms, with the teacher at some distance from the class using didactic methods and abstract formal lectures. Practitioners working with forensic clients (usually psychologists and probation officers) have often been trained extensively in talking therapies and, as such, they often feel most comfortable within verbal treatment modalities. They make good use of various different questioning techniques and styles, but are less confident and reluctant to consider other communication methods. An exclusive focus on verbally-based intervention approaches which ignore "neuro processing obstacles ... might make it difficult for our clients to learn, remember and retrieve useful information ..." (Creeden, 2004, p. 234). Traditional CBT treatment methods, which rely on cognitive ability and psychological flexibility and are presented using verbal and written modalities only, are unlikely to be fully accessible for a significant number of individuals who have experienced trauma in their lives. This need for adapted CBT approaches is now being more widely recognized in the literature (Rossiter & Holmes, 2013; Westbrook, Muella, Kennereley, & McManus, 2010). We therefore advocate that all practitioners working with forensic populations are trained in brain friendly treatment methods.

But working in a brain friendly way requires more than just skill and ability, it requires willingness and confidence to work in a different way – ultimately it is down to the practitioner to approach treatment in a different way.

Conclusions

In conclusion, a biologically informed approach encourages practitioners to use brain friendly strategies to help individuals engage and benefit from rehabilitative programs.

> The most effective adult educators may be unwitting neuroscientists who use their interpersonal skills to tailor enriched environments that enhance brain development.
> Cozolino and Sprokay (2006, p. 11).

The growing neuroscientific literature offers insights that help us understand how trauma can impact on the brain. The prevalence of neurological impairments within the forensic population is high and, as such, it is important that we consider the impact of these deficits in all of the work that we do. It is important that as practitioners we work flexibly to ensure that treatment messages are delivered in accessible ways. We advocate that practitioners should think "VAK" when they are planning and delivering an assessment or a treatment intervention. Practitioners should consider how well they have made adaptations to their approach to accommodate an individual's particular needs before problematic behaviors are attributed to an individual, or before a deselection decision is made because of poor compliance with the material and so on. Think carefully before a decision is made that an individual has not made sufficient progress in treatment, ask yourself if the individual was given every opportunity

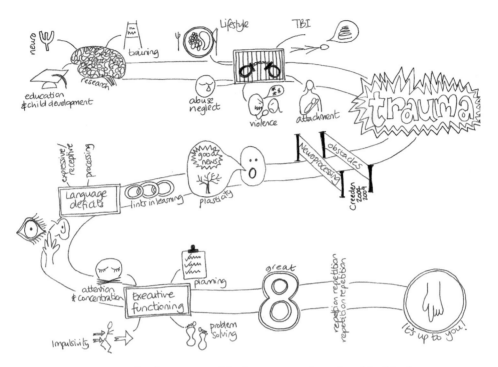

Figure 22.2 Visual summary of the key concepts introduced in this chapter.

to progress? We should also accept that executive functioning difficulties are commonplace within forensic populations. We have found that helping individuals to use the great eight coping tactics (in addition to other more traditional approaches, e.g., problem solving, relationship skills, etc.) also helps with self-management. In keeping with the techniques introduced in this chapter, a visual summary of the key concepts introduced is provided in Figure 22.2.

Recommended Reading

Creeden, K. (2013). Taking a developmental approach to treating juvenile sexual behavior problems. *International Journal of Behavioral Consultation and Therapy, l*, 3–4. *A concise paper with practical suggestions on how to consider developmental factors, including neurodevelopmental issues, and how to incorporate them into the provision of treatment with adolescents displaying sexual behavior problems.*

Gibb, B. (2007). *The rough guide to the brain.* London: Rough Guides Ltd. *A very accessible and illustrated introduction to understanding how the brain has evolved and how it functions.*

Lowings, G. R., & Wicks, B. (2016). *Effective learning after acquired brain injury: A practical guide to support adults with neurological conditions.* Oxford: Routledge. *Contains lot of useful ideas for working with people with brain injury.*

Van der Kolk, B. (2014). The body keeps the score: brain, mind and body in the healing of trauma. New York: Viking. *A fascinating and authoritative book on the effects of trauma and how to heal it drawing on evidence informed therapeutic approaches.*

References

Arden, J. B., & Linford, L. (2009). *Brain-based therapy with adults; Evidence based treatment for everyday practice*, Hoboken, NJ: John Wiley & Sons.

Beail, N. (1998). What works for people with mental retardation? A critical commentary on cognitive–behavioral and psychodynamic psychotherapy research. *Journal: Mental Retardation, 41*, 468–472.

Beail, N. (2001). Recidivism following psychodynamic psychotherapy amongst offenders with intellectual disabilities. *British Journal of Forensic Practice, 3*, 33–37.

Bergvall, A. H., Nilsson, T., & Hansen, S. (2003). Exploring the link between character, personality disorder, and neuropsychological function. *European Psychiatry, 18*, 334–344.

Boyd, D. (2004). Effective teaching in accelerated learning programs. *Adult Learning, 15*, 1–2.

Brower, M. C., & Price, B. H. (2001). Neuropsychiatry of frontal lobe dysfunction in violent and criminal behavior: A critical review. *Journal of Neurology, Neurosurgery and Psychiatry, 71*, 720–726.

Bryan, K., Freer, J., & Furlong, C. (2007), Language and communication difficulties in juvenile offenders. *International Journal of Language and Communication Disorders, 42*, 505–520.

Caine, R. N., & Caine, G. (1997). *Education on the edge of possibility*. Alexandria, VA: Association for Supervision and Curriculum Development. Retrieved from http://www.sedl.org/cgi-bin/mysql/picbib-output.cgi?searchuniqueid=32.

Carter, A. J., & Mann, R. E. (2016). Organizing principles for an integrated model of change for the treatment of sexual offending. In D. P. Boer (Ed.), *The Wiley handbook on the theories, assessment and treatment of sexual offending* (pp. 359–382). Oxford: Wiley-Blackwell.

Chesner, A. (1995). *Dramatherapy for people with learning disabilities*. London: Jessica Kingsley.

Coffield, F., Moseley, D., Hall, E., & Ecclestone, K. Report No. 041543 (2004). Learning styles and pedagogy in post-16 learning: a systematic and critical review. (Learning and Skills Research Centre, 2004). Retrieved from https://elearningindustry.com/critical-analysis-of-learning-styles-pedagogy-post-16-learning.

Colantonio, A., Stamenova, V., Abramowitz, C., Clarke, D., & Christensen, B. (2007). Brain injury in a forensic psychiatry population. *Brain Injury, 21*, 1353–1360.

Coleman, E. and Haaven, J. (2001). Treatment of the intellectually disabled sex offender. In D. R. Laws, S. M. Hudson, & T. Ward (Eds.), *Remaking relapse prevention with sex offenders: A sourcebook* (pp. 27–38). Newbury Park, CA: Sage Publications.

Cozolino, L., & Sprokay, S. (2006). Neuroscience and adult learning. *New Directions for Adult and Continuing Education, Summer 2006*, 11–19.

Creeden, K. (2004). Integrating trauma and attachment research into the treatment of sexually abusive youth. In M. C. Calder (Ed.), *Children and young people who sexually abuse: New theory, research, and practice developments* (pp. 202–216). Lyme Regis, Dorset: Russell House Publishing.

Creeden, K. (2009). How trauma and attachment can impact neurodevelopment: Informing our understanding and treatment of sexual behavior problems. *Journal of Sexual Aggression, 15*, 261–273.

Creeden, K. (2013). Taking a developmental approach to treating juvenile sexual behavior problems. *International Journal of Behavioral Consultation and Therapy, 1*, 3–4.

Culp, R. E., Watkins, R. V., Lawrence, H., Letts, D., Kelly, D. J., & Rice, M. L. (1991). Maltreated children's language and speech development: Abused, neglected, and abused and neglected. *First Language, 11*(33, Pt 3), 377–389.

Daniels, M. (2008). The use of psychodrama in an adapted sex offender treatment programme. *The British Journal of Psychodrama and Sociodrama, 23*, 39–44.

Davies R. C., Williams W., Hinder D., Burgess C. N., & Mounce, L. T. (2012). Self-reported traumatic brain injury and postconcussion symptoms in incarcerated youth. *The Journal of head trauma rehabilitation, 27,* E21–E27.

Decker, J., Li, H., Losowyj, D., & Prakash, V (2009). *Wiihabilitation: Rehabilitation of Wrist Flexion and Extension Using a Wiimote-Based Game System.* Rutgers University. Retrieved from http://citeseerx.ist.psu.edu/viewdoc/download?doi=10.1.1.541.5861&rep=rep1&type=pdf.

Dekker, S., Lee, N. C., Howard-Jones, P., & Jolles, J. (2012). Neuromyths in education. *Frontiers in Psychology, 3,* 429.

Dolan, M., & Anderson, I. M. (2002). Executive and memory function and its relationship to trait impulsivity and aggression in personality disordered offenders. *Journal of Forensic Psychiatry, 13,* 503–527.

Enns, R. A., Reddon, J. R., Das, J. P., & Boukos, H. (2007). Measuring executive function deficits in male delinquents using the cognitive assessment system. *Journal of Offender Rehabilitation, 44,* 43–63.

Erickson, K. I., Voss, M. W., Prakash, R. S., Basak, C., Szabo, A., Chaddocl, L., ... White, S. M. (2011). Exercise training increases the size of hippocampus and improves memory. *Proceedings of the National Academy of Sciences, 108,* 3017–3022.

Ferguson, B. (2012). The emergence of games for health. *Games for Health Journal, 1,* 1–2.

Fox, L., Long, S. H., & Langlois, A. (1988). Patterns of language comprehension deficit in abused and neglected children. *Journal of Speech and Hearing Disorders, 53,* 239–244.

Geake, J. G. (2008). Neuromythologies in education. *Education Research, 50,* 123–133.

Giancola, P. R., Mezzich, A. C., Clark, D. B., & Tarter, R. E. (1999). Cognitive distortions, aggressive behavior, and drug use in adolescent boys with and without a family history of a substance use disorder. *Psychology of Addictive Behaviors, 13,* 22–32.

Goldsworthy, R. C., Barab, S. A., & Goldsworthy, E. L. (2000). The STAR project: Enhancing adolescents' social understanding through video-based, multimedia scenarios. *Journal of Special Education Technology, 15,* 13–26.

Green, C. S., & Bavelier, D. (2008). Exercising your brain: a review of human brain plasticity and training-induced learning. *Psychology of Aging, 23,* 692–701.

Haaven, J. (2006). The evolution of the Old Me/New Me Model. In G. Blasingame (Ed.), *Practical treatment strategies for persons with intellectual disabilities.* Oklahoma City, OK: Wood 'n' Barnes.

Haaven, J., & Coleman, E. M. (2000). Treatment of the developmentally disabled sex offender. In D. R. Laws, S. M. Hudson, & T. Ward (Eds.). *Remaking relapse prevention with sex offenders: A sourcebook* (pp. 369–388). London: Sage Publications.

Hughes, N., Williams, W., Chitsabesan, P., Walesby, R. C., Mounce, L. T., & Clasby, B. (2015). The prevalence of traumatic brain injury among young offenders in custody: a systematic review. *The Journal of Head Trauma Rehabilitation, 30,* 94–105.

Hurley, A. D., Tomasulo, D. J., & Pfadt, A. G. (1998). Individual and group psychotherapy approaches for persons with mental retardation and developmental disabilities. *Journal of Developmental and Physical Disabilities, 10,* 365–386.

Hux, K., Bond V., Skinner, S., Belau D., & Sanger, D. (1998). Parental report of occurrences and consequences of traumatic brain injury among delinquent and non-delinquent youth. *Brain Injury, 12,* 667–681.

Ireland, C.A., & Rogers, J. (2004). ASOTP: Responsivity factors. *Forensic Update British Psychological Society, 78,* 15–20.

Kabat-Zinn, J. (2001). *Full catastrophe living: How to cope with stress, pain and illness using mindfulness meditation.* London: Piatkus.

Karal, H., Kokoç, M., & Ayyıldız, U. (2010). Educational computer games for developing psychomotor ability in children with mild mental impairment. *Procedia- Social and Behavioral Sciences, 9,* 966–1000.

Ke, F., & Abras, T. (2012). Games for engaged learning of middle school children with special learning need. *British Journal of Educational Technology, 44,* 225–242.

Keeling, J., & Rose, J. (2006). The adaptation of a cognitive behavioral treatment programme for special needs sexual offenders relapse prevention with intellectually disabled sexual offenders. *British Journal of Learning Disabilities, 34,* 110–116.

Kennedy, M. R. T., Coelho, C., Turkstra, L., Ylvisaker, M., Moore Sohlberg, M., Yorkston, K., ... Kan, P. F. (2008). Intervention for executive functions after traumatic brain injury: A systematic review, meta-analysis and clinical recommendations. *Neuropsychological Rehabilitation, 18,* 257–299.

Koechlin, E., Corrado, G., Pietrini, P., & Grafman, J. (2000). Dissociating the role of the medial and lateral anterior prefrontal cortex in human planning. *Proceedings of the National Academy of Services, 97,* 7651–7656.

Kosaka, B. (2002). Frontiers in frontal lobe functioning. *Canadian Psychiatric Bulletin, 34,* 7–8.

Lee, N., & Horsfall, B. (2010). Accelerated learning: a study of faculty and student experiences. *Innovative Higher Education, 35,* 191–202.

Lindsay, W. R., Neilson, C., & Lawrenson, H. (1997). Cognitive-behavior therapy for anxiety in people with learning disabilities. In B. Stenfert Kroese, D. Dagnan, & K. Loumidis (Eds.), *Cognitive-behavior therapy for people with learning disabilities* (pp. 124–140). London: Routledge.

Lowings, G. R., & Wicks, B. (2012). The need for cognitive profiles based on neuropsychological assessments to drive individual education plans (IEPs) in forensic settings. *The Journal of Mental Health Training, Education and Practice, 7,* 180–188.

Lowings, G. R., & Wicks, B. (2016). *Effective learning after acquired brain injury: A practical guide to support adults with neurological conditions.* Routledge: Oxford.

Maguire, E. A., Woollett, K., & Spiers, H. J. (2006). London taxi drivers and bus drivers: a structural MRI and neuropsychological analysis. *Hippocampus, 16,* 1091–1101.

Maruna, S. (2001). *Making Good: How ex-convicts reform and rebuild their lives.* Washington, DC: American Psychological Association.

Masterman, D. L., & Cummings, J. L. (1997). Frontal subcortical circuits: The anatomical basis of executive, social and motivated behaviors. *Journal of Psychopharmacology, 11,* 107–114.

McNeill, F., Farrall, S., Lightowler, C., & Maruna, S. (2012). How and why people stop offending: Discovering desistance IRISS Insights, No. 15. Retrieved from http://www.iriss .org.uk/resources/how-and-why-people-stop-offending-discovering-desistance.

Meier, D. (2000). *The accelerated learning handbook.* New York: McGraw-Hill.

Merry, S. N., Stasiak K., Shepherd M., Frampton C., Fleming T., & Lucassen, M. F. G. (2012). The effectiveness of SPARX, a computerised self help intervention for adolescents seeking help for depression: randomised controlled non-inferiority trial. *The British Medical Journal, 344,* e2598.

Monchi, O., Petrides, M., Strafella, A. P., Worsley, K. J., & Doyon, J. (2006). Functional Role of the Basal Ganglia in the Planning and Execution of Actions. *Annals of Neurology, 59,* 257–264.

Moore, E., Indig, D., & Haysom, L. (2014). Traumatic brain injury, mental health, substance use, and offending among incarcerated young people. *The Journal of Head Trauma Rehabilitation, 29,* 239–247.

Morgan, A. B., & Lilienfeld, S. O. (2000) A meta-analytical review of the relationship between antisocial behavior and neuropsychological measures of executive function. *Clinical Psychology Review, 20,* 113–136.

Najjar, L. J. (1998). Principles of educational multimedia user interface design. *Human Factors, 40,* 311–323.

Norman, R. E., Byambaa, M., De, R., Butchart, A., Scott, J., & Vos, T. (2012). The Long-term health consequences of child physical abuse, emotional abuse, and neglect: A systematic review and meta-analysis. *PLoS Med* 9(11), e1001349. doi:10.1371/journal.pmed.1001349.

Olvera, R. L., Semrud-Clikeman, M., Pliszka, S., & O'Donnell, L. (2005). Neuropsychological deficits in adolescents with conduct disorder and comorbid bipolar disorder: A pilot study. *Bipolar Disorders, 1*, 57–67.

Paschall, M. J., & Fishbein, D. H. (2002). Executive cognitive functioning and aggression: A public health perspective. *Aggression and Violent Behavior, 7*, 215–235.

Pitman, I., Haddlesey, C., de Silva Ramos, S., Oddy, M., & Fortescue, D. (2012). The association between neuropsychological performance and self-reported traumatic brain injury in a sample of adult male prisoners in the UK. The Disability Trust Foundation Briefing. Retrieved from http://www.thedtgroup.org/media/4061/prison_research_briefing_paper_16022015.pdf.

Pivec, M. (2007). Editorial: Play and learn: Potentials of game-based learning. *British Journal of Educational Technology, 38*(3), 387–554.

Perry, B. D. Maltreatment and the developing child: How early childhood experience shapes child and culture. The Margaret McCain lecture series. Retrieved from http://www.lfcc.on.ca/mccain/perry.pdf.

Posner, M. I., Petersen, S., & Petersen, E. (1990). The attention system of the human brain. *Annual Review Neuroscience, 13*, 25–42.

Raaijmakers, M. A. J., Smidts, D. P., Sergeant, J. A., Maassen, G., Post-Humus, J. A., van Engeland, H., & Matthys, W. (2008). Executive functions in preschool children with aggressive behavior: Impairments in inhibitory control. *Journal of Abnormal Child Psychology, 36*, 1097–1107.

Rezaiyan, A., Mohammadi, E., & Fallah, P. A. (2007). Effect of computer game intervention on the attention capacity of mentally retarded children. *International Journal of Nursing Practice, 13*, 284–288.

Rogeness, G. A., Hernandez, J. M., Macedo, C. A., Amrung, S. A., & Hoppe, S. K. (1986). Near zero plasma dopamine B hydroxylase and conduct disorder in emotionally disturbed boys. *Journal of American Academy Child Psychiatry, 25*, 251–527.

Rose, C., & Nicholl, M. J. (1997). *Accelerated learning for the 21st Century*. New York: Delacorte.

Rossiter, R., & Holmes, S. (2013). Access all areas: Creative adaptations for CBT with people with cognitive impairments – illustrations and issues. *The Cognitive Behavioral Therapist, 6*, 1–16.

Roy, E. (2015). When we design for disability, we all benefit. TED talk. Retrieved from https://www.ted.com/speakers/elise_roy.

Rushton, S., & Larkin, E. (2001). Shaping the learning environment: Connecting developmentally appropriate practices to brain research. *Early Childhood Education Journal, 29*, 25–33.

Séguin, J. R., Boulerice, B., Harden, P. W., Tremblay, R. E., & Pihl, R. O. (1999). Executive functions and physical aggression after controlling for attention deficit hyperactivity disorder, general memory and IQ. *Journal of Child Psychology and Psychiatry, 40*, 1197–1208.

Sharp, J. G., Bowker, R., & Byrne, J. (2008). VAK or vak-ous? Towards the trivialisation of learning and the death of scholarship. *Research Papers in Education, 23*, 361–384.

Siegel, D. (1999). *The developing mind: Toward a neurobiology of interpersonal experience*. New York, NY: Guilford Press.

Smith, A. (2002). *Move it: Physical movement and learning*. Bodmin, Cornwall: MPG Books Ltd.

Sowell, E. R., Peterson, B. S., Thompson, P. M., Welcome, S. E., & Henkenius, A. L. (2003). Mapping cortical change across the human life span. *Nature Neuroscience, 6*, 309–315.

Spikman, J. M., Boelen, D. H., Lamberts, K. F., Brouwer, W. H., & Fasotti, L. (2010). Effects of a multifaceted treatment program for executive dysfunction after acquired brain injury on indications of executive functioning in daily life. *Journal of International Neuropsychological Society, 16*, 118–129.

Sprague, K. (1991). Everybody's a somebody: Action methods for young people with severe learning difficulties. In Holmes, P., Karp, M., & Sprague, K. (Eds.), *Psychodrama: Inspiration and technique* (pp. 33–51). New York, NY: Tavistock/Routledge.

Stachen, N. M., & Shevich, J. (1999). Working with the intellectually disabled/socially inadequate sex offender in a prison setting. In B. Schwarts (Ed.) *The sex offender: Theoretical advances, treating special populations, and legal developments*. Kingston, NJ: Civic research Institute.

Stone, M. H., & Thompson, E. H. (2001). Executive function impairment in sexual offenders. *Journal of Individual Psychology, 57*, 51–59.

Takeuchi, H., & Kawashima, R. (2012). Effects of processing speed training on cognitive functions and neural systems. *Journal of Neuroscience, 31*, 12139–12148.

Tateno, A., Jorge, R. E., & Robinson, R. G. (2003). Clinical correlates of aggressive behavior after traumatic brain injury. *The Journal of Neuropsychiatry and Clinical Neurosciences, 15*, 155–160.

Teicher, M. D. (2000). Wounds that time won't heal: The neurobiology of child abuse. *Cerebrum: The Dana Forum on Brain Science, 2*, 50–67.

Teicher, M., Andersen, S., Polcari, A., Andersen, C., & Navalta, C. (2002). Developmental neurobiology of childhood stress and trauma. *Psychiatric Clinics of North America, 25*, 397–426.

The British Psychological Society (2015). Children and young people with neuro-disabilities in the criminal justice system. Leicester: The British Psychological Society. Retrieved from www.bps.org.uk/system/files/Public%20files/cyp_with_neurodisabilities_in_the_cjs.pdf.

Thomas, C., & Baker, C. I. (2013). Teaching an adult brain new tricks: A critical review of evidence for training-dependent structural plasticity in humans. *Neuroimage, 73*, 225–236.

Vanderploeg, R. D., Belanger, H. G., & Curtiss, G. (2009). Mild traumatic brain injury and posttraumatic stress disorder and their associations with health symptoms. *Archives of Physical Medicine and Rehabilitation, 90*, 1084–1093.

Vas, A. K., Chapman, S. B., Cook, L. G., Elliott, A. C., & Keebler, M. (2011). Higher order reasoning training years after traumatic brain injury in adults. *Journal of Head Trauma Rehabilitation, 26*, 224–239.

Wagner, S. M., Nusbaum, H., & Goldin-Meadow, S. (2004). Probing the mental representation of gesture: is handwaving spatial? *Journal of Memory and Language, 50*, 395–407.

Westbrook, D., Muella, M., Kennerley, H., McManus, F. (2010). Common problems in therapy. In M. Mueller, H. Kennerley, F. McManus, & D. Westbrook (Eds.), *The Oxford guide to surviving as a CBT therapist*. Oxford: Oxford University Press.

Williams, F. (2015). Reducing prison violence: The role of programmes. *Prison Service Journal. Special Edition. Reducing prison violence*. Retrieved from https://www.crimeandjustice.org.uk/sites/crimeandjustice.org.uk/files/PSJ%20221%20September%202015.pdf accessed 21.7.16.

Williams, F., & Mann, R. E. (2010). The treatment of intellectually disabled sexual offenders in the national offender management service: the adapted sex offender treatment programmes. In L. A. Craig, W. R. Lindsay, & K. D. Browne (Eds.), *Assessment and treatment of sexual offenders with intellectual disabilities: A Handbook*. Chichester: John Wiley & Sons.

Williams, W. H., & Chitsabesan, P. (2015). Young people with traumatic brain injury in custody: An evaluation of a Linkworker Service for Barrow Cadbury Trust and the Disabilities Trust. Retrieved from http://www.barrowcadbury.org.uk/wp-content/uploads/2016/07/Disability_Trust_linkworker_2016Lores.pdf.

Williams, W. H., Mewse, A. J., Tonks, J., Mills, S., Burgesss, C. N., & Cordan, G. (2010). Traumatic brain injury in a prison population: Prevalence and risk for re-offending. *Brain Injury, 24*, 1184–1188.

23

Brain Scanning and Therapeutics

How Do You Know Unless You Look?
Neuroimaging Guided Treatment in
Forensic Settings

Daniel G. Amen and Kristen Willeumier

Key points

- Single photon emission computed tomography (SPECT) is a recognized functional imaging technique that has a number of established clinical indications.
- Knowledge gained in diagnosis and treatment of psychiatry and neurology conditions can be translated to the forensic population.
- Functional imaging of the brain using SPECT highlights similarities between psychiatry/neurological conditions and an offender's behavior.
- SPECT can support diagnosis and point to effective treatment procedures.
- Seven brain functional patterns at the global and local levels are identified with SPECT imaging. They demonstrate potential parallels between forensic behavior and psychiatry/neurology symptoms.
- Abnormal functions of the frontal and temporal lobes are most relevant to forensic behaviors.

Terminology Explained

Attention deficit hyperactivity disorder (ADHD) describes a set of symptoms related to deficits in the ability to control behavior, attention, hyperactivity, and impulsivity.

Alzheimer's disease is the most common form of dementia and is a progressive mental deterioration that can occur in middle or old age. Symptoms tend to begin with memory loss and progress to more generalized confusion about time and

---

The Wiley Blackwell Handbook of Forensic Neuroscience, First Edition. Edited by Anthony R. Beech, Adam J. Carter, Ruth E. Mann and Pia Rotshtein.
© 2018 John Wiley & Sons Ltd. Published 2018 by John Wiley & Sons Ltd.

place, problems with speech, language and mood, and personality changes. All parts of the brain are affected.

Computed tomography (CT) is a three-dimensional X-ray camera that measures the density of brain tissue.

The *Diagnostic and Statistical Manual of Mental Disorders* (**DSM**) (American Psychiatric Association) has been the primary system for classifying mental disorders in the USA for more than 60 years.

Functional magnetic resonance imaging (fMRI) is an imaging method used in an MRI scanner to measure local brain function. This method capitalizes on the different magnetization properties of oxygenated and deoxygenated blood. It uses the **BOLD** (blood oxygenated level dependent) contrast to assess changes in neural activity.

Hyperfrontality (measured by SPECT) describes increased blood flow in frontal cortex, indicative of increased neural activation.

Magnetic resonance imaging (MRI) uses natural magnetic properties of protons within water molecules. MRI measures how these protons "behave" following a radio frequency pulse. Their behavior is affected by their immediate surroundings (e.g., water in grey matter display different magnetic properties than those in white matter). It can be used to measure structural or functional aspects of the brain.

Obsessive compulsive disorder (OCD) involves a group of symptoms in which individuals have a repeated unpleasant and intrusive thought. Relief from the thought is gained by repeating routine behaviors, which may or may not be related to the thought. For example, a person who is afraid of contamination may repeatedly wash their hands.

Perfusion (as measured by SPECT) is blood flow to the brain. **Hyperfusion** occurs when there is an overall increased blood flow in the brain beyond normal healthy levels. **Hypoperfusion** occurs when there is reduced blood flow in the brain, indicating lack of neural activation and responses. Either form of abnormal perfusion can lead to unbalanced behavior.

Photon emission tomography (PET) is an imaging method that uses the distribution of radioactive tracers in the brain. In comparison to SPECT, PET has higher temporal and spatial resolution and is more expensive.

Single photon emission computed tomography (SPECT) is an imaging method that uses a radioactive tracer to provide a three-dimensional representation of the tissue. Typically, in the context of brain imaging, SPECT measures the level of perfusion, which provides an estimation of neural activity.

Traumatic brain injury (TBI) occurs when the brain is violently hit or penetrated, causing damage to brain tissues. Symptoms can vary from mild to severe.

Vascular dementia is a form of dementia caused by a problem with the supply of blood to the brain, often through a series of strokes. Symptoms can include memory loss and difficulties with thinking, problem solving, or language.

Introduction

A strong relationship between violent offenders and various psychiatric and neurological conditions has been well established. These relations are manifested through overlap of seven functional brain patterns found in single photon emission computed tomography (SPECT) of offenders and complex psychiatric and neurological cases. The functional networks are clinically associated with impulsivity, aggression, violence, and psychopathic behavior. Dysregulation of these networks is associated with impaired empathy, moral judgment, reasoning, fear response, and appropriate social behavior. Based on our experience of over 22 years with greater than 83,000 brain SPECT scans, this review describes in detail evidence supporting the involvement of each of these networks in offenders and known psychiatric and neurological conditions. This neural overlap offers promising avenues for capitalizing on knowledge gained in psychiatry and neurology for treating offenders. It is demonstrated that SPECT imaging (see Box 23.1) is a useful tool at identifying functional dysregulation even at the individual level, leading to more accurate diagnosis and effective treatment. This is shown through description of single cases.

Neuroimaging has been widely used in the psychiatric setting for the past 20 years and is emerging as a diagnostic tool in complex psychiatric cases for disorders defined in the fifth edition of the *Diagnostic and Statistical Manual of Mental Disorders (DSM-V5)* (American Psychiatric Association, 2013) including anxiety, depression, attention deficit disorder, substance abuse, and toxicity (Amen et al., 2012). As brain SPECT imaging is becoming more extensively used in psychiatric settings, the underlying neurophysiology of behaviors commonly associated with criminal acts including aggression, impulsiveness, and violence can help inform assessments. While it is understood that the correlation of neural activity in specific brain regions does not imply causation, if the information from neuroimaging is combined with a detailed medical history (family history, substance abuse history, legal history, sexual abuse), neuropsychological assessments, and cognitive tests, then the ability to adequately assess the condition of the subject with regards to rehabilitation and treatment is strengthened.

Box 23.1 SPECT in clinical settings

Neuroimaging can demonstrate both structural and functional deficits in the brain. Structural neuroimaging modalities include magnetic resonance imaging (MRI) and computerized tomography (CT), while functional neuroimaging modalities include SPECT, photon emission tomography (PET), and functional MRI (fMRI). Here, we will focus on SPECT imaging. Where it is relevant we may add additional neuroimaging data from PET or MRI, but the aim of this work is to highlight our experience with SPECT. SPECT is a functional imaging technique that measures cerebral blood flow and metabolic activity patterns in the brain. It uses a radioactive tracer injected into the blood and measures their absorption in the brain tissue using gamma ray cameras. This provides an estimate of cerebral blood flow in three-dimensional space. Blood flow in the brain is tightly coupled with neural activity and local brain metabolism. Hence, SPECT images provide an average map of the way the brain has functioned in the

> past hours (the time between injection and scan). The image resolution is in the order of centimeters. PET is based on similar imaging principles, but provides higher spatial and temporal resolution. fMRI measures changes in oxygen level in the blood, it also has higher spatial and temporal resolution. However, both PET and MRI are much more expensive imaging modalities. SPECT highlights brain functional abnormality in two forms: **hypoperfusion**, indicating reduced blood flow indicative of localized reduced brain activity; and **hyperperfusion**, indicating increased blood flow which suggests abnormal increases in localized brain activation.

Over the past 20 years brain SPECT imaging has developed a substantial, evidence-based foundation and is now recommended by professional societies for numerous indications relevant to psychiatric practice. To date, there are over 31,266 articles on brain SPECT imaging with 2,032 articles related to psychiatry, demonstrating its emergence as a clinically relevant tool in the diagnostic process. SPECT's prolific use in peer-reviewed research supports that it is a well-established and reliable measure of brain function (regional cerebral blood flow – rCBF).[1] Both the American College of Radiology (2007) and the European Society of Nuclear Medicine (ESNM) (Kapucu, Nobili et al., 2009) have published similar evidence-based guidelines for using SPECT to enhance patient care. Commonly accepted clinical indications for SPECT include the following:

1 Evaluating people for cerebrovascular disease.
2 Evaluating patients with suspected dementia including early detection, differential diagnosis, and in the pre-dementia phase.
3 Pre-surgical localization of epileptic foci.
4 Evaluation of traumatic brain injury (TBI), especially in the absence of CT and/or MRI findings.
5 Evaluation of suspected inflammation to provide helpful information in pro-gressive inflammatory disorders including viral encephalitis, vasculitis, and HIV-encephalopathy.
6 Assessing brain death.

Seven neural and clinical patterns have emerged from SPECT research:

1 Overall decreased perfusion due to toxicity, illness or substance abuse.
2 TBI patterns.
3 Cognitive decline and neural degeneration (dementia).
4 Hyperfrontality and negative emotionality.
5 Hypofrontality and behavioral problems.
6 Mood instability, memory problems, and temporal lobe abnormalities.
7 Subtyping dimensional behavior to predict treatment response (aggression and depression).

These observed patterns are not mutually exclusive and can also present overlap symp-toms and neurological profiles. The distinctions are made based on typical observed neuroclinical profiles in order to facilitate the description of underlying causes, diagnosis, treatment, and prognosis. We will now examine each of these in direct application to day-to-day clinical practice with clients and potential forensic implications.

Overall Decreased Perfusion Due to Toxicity, Illness, or Substance Abuse

It is assumed that reduced perfusion at multiple brain regions leads to a decrease in brain functionality, given the known coupling between blood flow and neural activation. This pattern is often associated with toxicity (see Case Study 23.1), illness, or insult to the brain. It is frequently seen in drug and alcohol abuse (see Case Study 23.2), abuse of prescription medications such as benzodiazepines, environmental toxins, such as carbon monoxide poisoning, infectious disease, such as meningitis, anoxic states, significant hypothyroidism, anemia, chemotherapy, and severe dehydration. Seeing this pattern does not give the etiology, but alerts clinicians to search for causes, which will allow them to understand it. However, a specific interest to criminal behavior is the case of substance abuse and its association to overall reduced perfusion.

Case Study 23.1 Overall reduced perfusion due to toxicity

A couple came for evaluation after their marital therapist told them she thought they should get divorced. They had been treated for three years and had spent nearly $20,000 on care. The husband's diagnosis was mixed personality disorder with narcissistic and antisocial features. The couple's family physician recommended another opinion that included SPECT scans. The husband's scan showed overall decreased perfusion (see Figure 23.1). The husband reported

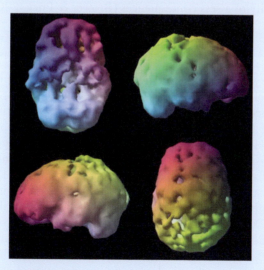

Figure 23.1 Toxic surface scan.

Note: Notice the "Swiss cheese," shriveled appearance, indicating areas of decreased perfusion.

that he did not drink alcohol and had never used drugs, which his wife confirmed. The scan results caused his physician to think through a completely different differential diagnosis beyond personality disorder. It turned out that the husband worked in a furniture factory, finishing cabinets. The inhalants found in finishing products may have compromised brain functioning and showed a toxic pattern on scans (Kucuk et al., 2000). The marital therapy was destined to fail until the husband was removed from the toxic environment. This information significantly changed the treatment plan and was instrumental in helping the couple's marriage.

Substance abuse and violence

Substance abuse in violent offenders often goes undiagnosed. Evidence of a causal relationship between psychiatric disorders, substance abuse (Kertesz, Madan, Wallace, Schumacher, & Milby, 2006), and criminal behavior has been established (Rueve & Welton, 2008). A history of drug and alcohol abuse is highly predictive of criminal behavior and violence (Lindqvist, 1986; Buss, Abdu, & Walker, 1995; Dukarm, Byrd, Auinger, & Weitzman, 1996; Lee &Weinstein, 1997; Schafer & Fals-Stewart, 1997; Amen, 1999) and SPECT imaging can be useful in studying the pathophysiology of alcohol-associated violence. In a SPECT imaging study of 40 alcoholic patients, Kuruoglu et al. (1996) found significant deficits in frontal lobe function, which was pronounced in a subset of the patients who were diagnosed with antisocial personality disorder. Deficits in frontal lobe function may increase the likelihood of an impulsive aggression as the frontal lobes are important in judgment, socially appropriate conduct, and capacity to assess consequences (Brower & Price, 2001).

Case Study 23.2 Alcohol abuse leading to hypoperfusion

SPECT imaging was utilized to illustrate how alcohol can alter brain chemistry and illicit alcohol-induced violence (Amen, 1999). A 20-year-old man came to see us who became violent on many occasions after ingesting alcohol. He had a history of being hyperactive, hyperverbal, impulsive, oppositional, and argumentative. He had been arrested ten times for violent, aggressive behavior, all while intoxicated. Two SPECT brain images were acquired, one when he was alcohol free, the other after he had ingested alcohol. The alcohol-free study revealed marked hyperactivity in the cingulate gyrus, right and left lateral frontal lobes, right and left parietal lobes, and the right lateral temporal lobe (see Figure 23.2). The alcohol intoxication study showed an overall dampening effect on the hyperactive areas of the brain, with only the anterior cingulate gyrus showing excess activity (see Figure 23.3). In addition, the right and left frontal lobes were hypoperfused, decreasing impulse control and judgment, as were the right and left temporal lobes, increasing the likelihood for aggression. These findings show that in an alcohol-free state, this individual has regions of

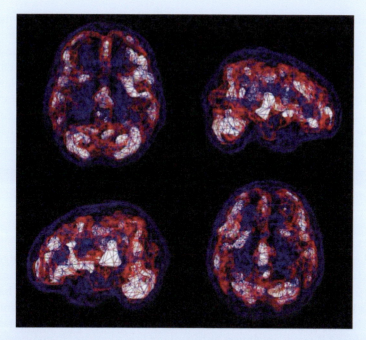

Figure 23.2 No alcohol.
Note: Top down active view. Marked overall increased activity.

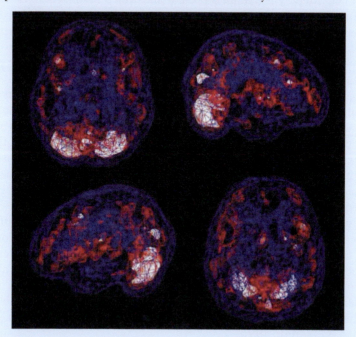

Figure 23.3 Alcohol Induced State.
Note: Top down active view. Overall dampening effect on the brain.

> hyperactivity, which can induce anxiety, cyclic mood tendencies, and irritability (Amen, 1997a, b). He felt more relaxed when he drank, but, by self-medicating, he induced a "violent pattern" in his brain, which resulted in increased cingulate activity, abnormal temporal lobe activity, and hypoperfusion of the prefrontal cortex, a pattern that has been found in violent patients (Amen, Stubblefield, Carmichael, & Thisted, 1996). This case clearly demonstrates the changes that occur in the neural activity with substance abuse and how SPECT imaging can be useful in understanding the pathophysiology of alcohol-related behavioral problems.

TBI Patterns

TBI is a major public health concern. TBI survivors commonly face a range of psychiatric and neurological disorders, affecting functional status, cognition, and mood (Jean-Bay, 2000). Of course, not everyone with a significant brain injury has lasting symptoms. Those who do, however, present daunting problems of differential diagnosis. But how does a psychiatrist know about individual patients and brain injury unless they look? Relying on clinical history alone is inadequate. Even upon extensive questioning, many patients forget that they have sustained a significant brain injury. SPECT can help identify if trauma is present and which brain system or systems are affected. Common findings in head trauma on SPECT include: focal decreased near sight of injury and/or opposite side (contra coup); asymmetrical hypoperfusion in the prefrontal, temporal, parietal, or occipital lobes; flattening of the prefrontal pole; decreased anterior temporal poles; and decreased contralateral cerebellar perfusion. See Case Study 23.3 for an example of missed TBI diagnosis.

SPECT aids in understanding TBI patients' symptomatology and assists clinicians in developing targeted treatment strategies (Jacobs, Put, Ingels, & Bossuyt, 1994) (Baulieu et al., 2001). For example, decreased prefrontal cortex perfusion is often associated with executive dysfunction and may be helped with psychostimulants or other strategies to enhance frontal lobe function. Decreased temporal lobe perfusion, however, is often associated with irritability and mood instability and may be helped with anticonvulsant medication. Evidence in the literature indicates that SPECT helps evaluate perfusion abnormalities not only in blunt brain trauma, but also in cases of postconcussive syndrome and whiplash (Kant, Smith-Seemiller, Isaac, & Duffy, 1997). Brain injured patients with normal EEG, CT, and/or MRI scans often complain of headaches, memory loss, concentration difficulties, dizziness, perceptual sensitivities, and emotional lability. Such patients may be labeled as malingering, when there are significant and demonstrable functional abnormalities present. Researchers investigating the differences between functional and structural imaging techniques have found SPECT to be more sensitive for patients with varying degrees of head trauma (Goshen, Zwas, Shahar, & Tadmor, 1996).

Researchers have also compared the differences between functional and structural imaging in relation to clinical outcome and prognosis. Jacobs et al. (1994) used SPECT to prospectively evaluate 67 mild-to-moderate brain-injured patients. Each

> **Case Study 23.3 Missed TBI diagnosis**
>
> A 26-year-old male patient with severe impulsivity and depression in a drug treatment program was asked ten times, with extensive examples, whether or not he had a brain injury. He said no each time. His SPECT scan (see Figure 23.4), however, showed evidence of substantial hypoperfusion, consistent with trauma in the left frontal-temporal lobe region. When asked again, he then remembered a motorcycle accident where he broke his left jaw, near the site of the SPECT deficit.
>
>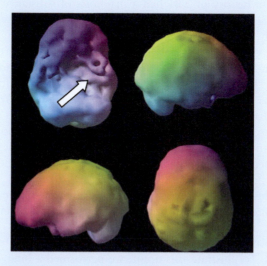
>
> **Figure 23.4** Trauma.
> *Note*: Asymmetrical decreased perfusion left frontal temporal lobe.

patient had a clinical evaluation and SPECT scan within four weeks of the initial injury and three months after the first scan. Of the 33 patients who showed no significant abnormalities on their initial scan, 97% resolved their clinical symptoms within three months. By contrast, in the 34 patients with abnormal initial SPECT scans, 59% continued to experience significant clinical symptoms three months later. The positive predictive value of an abnormal initial scan was only 20/34 (59%), but if the second scan 12 months later was also abnormal the sensitivity for the repeat SPECT was 19/20 (95%). These authors suggest that negative initial SPECT studies are a reliable predictor of a favorable clinical outcome.

SPECT assists in the diagnosis, prognosis, and treatment of TBI patients. SPECT may also help uncover brain trauma in clinically confusing or complex cases because patients often fail to report or forget about significant brain injuries, perhaps due to peritraumatic amnesia. A limitation for SPECT's use in brain trauma is that typically no prior SPECT study is available for comparison. Therefore, it is often not possible to date the trauma with neuroimaging. Remote trauma from childhood often presents neuroimaging findings similar to those seen in more recent trauma.

TBI in forensic populations[2]

SPECT imaging is often used to measure brain deficits as a result of TBI and TBI has been associated with criminal behavior, with prevalence rates as high as 23% (Martell 1992; Colantonio, Stamenova, Abramowitz, Clarke, & Christensen, 2007). Colantonio et al. (2007) studied the incidence of TBI in a forensic population and found that 23% ($n = 394$) had a history of TBI, with the most common injuries resulting from falls (30.8%) and motor vehicle accidents (29.5%) while less than 15% occurred due to assault, blows to the head, non-motorized vehicle, gunshot wounds, and sports-related injury (Colantonio et al., 2007). They report that a larger number of individuals with a history of TBI had a diagnosis of substance abuse than those without, which indicates that those with substance abuse issues may be more prone to TBI or, alternatively, that TBI may increase self-medicating through alcohol or drug abuse. Brain injury or insult increases the risk of cognitive impairment (McDonald, 2002; Salmond & Sahakian, 2005), affective disorder (Hibbard, Uysal, Kepler, Bogdany, & Silver, 1998; Rogers & Read, 2007), executive dysfunction (Marsh & Martinovich, 2006), verbal and physical aggression (James & Young, 2013), and substance abuse (Horner et al., 2005).

In many instances, brain trauma goes undetected and has the potential to result in acts of post-traumatic aggression and violence (Wortzel & Arciniegas, 2013), which demonstrates the necessity of evaluating TBI in order to determine the extent of the trauma and to properly treat the individual. In a previous study we performed on measuring how often SPECT neuroimaging adds relevant information to the diagnosis and treatment of clinical cases, we found that traumatic brain injury (or a toxic brain pattern) went undiagnosed or untreated in 22.9% (25/109) of the cases (Amen et al., 2012), demonstrating the link between undetected brain trauma and psychiatric comorbidities. To illustrate this point, we performed a brain imaging study on 100 professional football players, where we found that TBI from repetitive subconcussive impacts yields global perfusion deficits, resulting in significant hypoperfusion of the frontal and temporal lobes, areas critical in regulating executive function and mood stability (Amen, Newberg et al., 2011). This level of brain injury resulted in neuropsychological and neurocognitive impairments including attentional issues (81%), depression (28%), memory deficits, and dementia (19%) (Amen, Wu et al., 2011). Taken together, SPECT imaging can be useful in the forensic setting to evaluate the organic brain dysfunction as a result of TBI and routine screening for TBI in these populations should be considered. Given the fact that in many instances TBI is ascertained through self-report, and most underreport their TBI history (due to inability to recall the event or their inaccurate definition of a head injury – i.e., thinking it is only a loss of consciousness event and not accounting for impacts to the head without a loss of consciousness), it is important to do the appropriate neuropsychological tests and use neuroimaging if TBI is suspected.

Cognitive decline and Neural Degeneration (Dementia)

To date, autopsy reports have been the "gold standard" for an Alzheimer's disease diagnosis. However, research suggests that SPECT, when used in conjunction with clinical history and other diagnostic tests, is helpful when evaluating patients who are experiencing cognitive decline (Newberg, Alavi, & Payer, 1995) and should be used to help differentiate Alzheimer's disease, vascular dementia (VaD), frontotemporal lobe dementia (FTD), suspected Lewy body Dementia (LBD), normal pressure hydrocephalus, and pseudodementia (PSD) if the diagnosis is in doubt (Pimlott & Ebmeier, 2007).

The functional brain imaging patterns associated with Alzheimer's disease include decreases in the posterior cingulate gyrus, parietal, and medial temporal lobes; FTD include frontal and temporal lobe deficits; VaD, a vascular pattern of decreased activity in multiple areas; LBD often shows decreased occipital lobe perfusion; normal pressure hydrocephalus (NPH) is associated with enlarged ventricles out of proportion to cortical atrophy; and PSD often shows an absence of dementia patterns with increased limbic activity (Alexander, Prohovnik, Sackeim, Steern, & Mayeux, 1995). This differential is critical because the use of high potency antipsychotics in patients with LBD, which often affects the occipital lobes on SPECT (Goto et al., 2010), can cause severe and sometimes irreversible deterioration. Patients diagnosed with different dementia disorders often present with similar symptomatology (e.g., social withdrawal and behavioral disinhibition). Because treatments for these disorders vary, differential diagnosis is critical, particularly since some dementia patients will have a reversible cause, such as depression, NPH (see Case Study 23.4), or VaD, which can be stabilized with intervention.

Case Study 23.4 Cognitive impairment unrelated to dementia

L, a 73-year-old male, suffered with persistent memory problems. His neurologist, without the benefit of imaging, diagnosed him with Alzheimer's disease. Memantine and donezepil (drugs commonly used for the control of Alzheimer's) had no effect. Two years later, his family brought him for further evaluation. His SPECT scan showed significantly enlarged ventricles, without concomitant cortical atrophy (see Figure 23.5). His scan did not show the

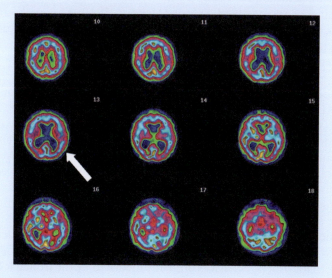

Figure 23.5 Transaxial slices.

Note: Slices 12 and 13 show inverted lobster pattern, associated with ventricular enlargement.

> typical low posterior cingulate and bilateral temporal-parietal hypoperfusion, consistent with Alzheimer's. Given the pattern, and subsequent MRI, he was diagnosed with NPH. After a shunt, his memory markedly improved.

Some would argue that an MRI would be a more appropriate study in evaluating NPH (and the authors of this chapter agree). Yet, functional imaging studies like SPECT provide a wealth of other data, such as giving information on areas of increased and decreased perfusion, in addition to enlarged ventricles, making it a useful screening tool. For example, Bonte, Weiner, Bigio, and White (1997) performed SPECT studies in patients with possible dementia and compared them to images of an elderly healthy control group. Histopathologic correlation was available in 54 patients (from autopsy in 51, from biopsy in three). The results of the study showed SPECT diagnoses were true-positive in 37 patients, true-negative in eight, false-positive in three, and false-negative in six. Sensitivity was 86%, specificity was 73%, and the positive predictive value was 92%, with an accuracy of 83%. The authors concluded that SPECT assists in the early and late diagnoses of Alzheimer's disease and in the differential diagnosis of the dementias when there is a complicated or confusing clinical picture.

Alzheimer's disease and frontotemporal dementia in forensic populations

Aggression has been correlated with Alzheimer's disease and FTD (Mendez, Shapira et al. 2011; Zahodne, Ornstein et al. 2013). Cortical degeneration can also be associated with psychosis, agitation, and depression, and cognitive decline that characterizes this spectrum of neurological disorders may result in individuals who are predisposed to criminal or sociopathic behavior (Mendez, 2010; Kim et al., 2011; Diehl-Schmid, Perneczky, Koch, Nedopil, & Kurz, 2013). Frontotemporal degeneration has been associated with criminal conduct (Diehl-Schmid et al., 2013) and sociopathy (Mendez, Chen, Shapira, & Miller, 2005; Mendez, 2010), and deficits in frontal lobe function have been linked to an impulsive type of aggression (Brower & Price, 2001) and disinhibited, compulsive behavior (Mendez, Lauterbach, & Sampson, 2008).

Using SPECT imaging, Hirono, Mega, Dinov, Mishkin, & Cummings (2000) studied 10 patients who had dementia with and without aggression and found that patients with increased aggression reveal significant hypoperfusion in the left anterior temporal cortex and bilateral dorsofrontal cortex (Hirono et al., 2000). Mendez et al. (2005) studied the sociopathic behavior of a group of FTD patients as compared to Alzheimer's disease patients using brain SPECT imaging and neuropsychological tests. They found that 16 (57%) of the FTD had sociopathic behavior compared to 2 (7%) of the Alzheimer's disease patients, which was correlated with decreased right frontotemporal lobe function (Mendez et al., 2005). The authors propose that the sociopathic behavior was correlated with altered emotional morality including loss of empathy or a lack of concern for others, behaviors primarily mediated by the frontal lobes. Lesions in the prefrontal cortex impair judgment (Bechara, Damasio, & Anderson, 1994) and lesions early on in life lead to impaired social and moral behavior (Anderson, Bechara, Damasio, & Tranel, 1999).

Individuals who suffer from dementia with a psychiatric comorbidity and substance abuse are a high-risk group for violence (Palijan, Radeljak, Kovac, & Kovacević, 2010). A study on 7 dementia patients, all of whom had dementia with loss of frontal lobe function (as observed with MRI), in a forensic hospital revealed that those with alcohol-related problems committed violent crimes (murder, attempted murder, arson, assault) while those without committed nonviolent crimes (Kim et al., 2011). This suggests that a decline in executive function combined with the potential for increased aggressiveness, lack of empathy, and disinhibited, compulsive behavior may be predictive of violent criminal acts in those with dementia.

Hyperfrontality and Negative Emotionality

Hyperfrontality, or increased perfusion in the prefrontal cortex and anterior cingulate gyrus, is associated with a number of different psychiatric illnesses that have a common theme of cognitive inflexibility or getting stuck on negative thoughts or negative behaviors, such as in obsessive compulsive disorder (OCD) (Alptekin et al., 2001; Lacerda et al., 2003), autism, post-traumatic stress disorder, and certain types of anxiety and mood disorders (Hollander, 1996; Carey et al., 2004). This pattern is often seen in patients who are rigid, inflexible, and oppositional (Amen, 1997a), and crosses several different diagnostic groups.

When SPECT scans detect the hyperfrontality pattern, new avenues for intervention are opened up, since this finding has been associated with predicting a positive treatment response for depression using: 1) serotonergic medication in depression (Mayberg et al., 1997; Mayberg et al., 2000; Hoehn-Saric et al., 2001; Seminowicz et al., 2004; Brockmann et al., 2009); 2) sleep deprivation (Wu, Buchsbaum et al. 1999; Wu, Gillin et al. 2008); and 3) repetitive transcranial magnetic stimulation (Langguth et al., 2007). In OCD patients, hyperfrontality can be used in distinguishing them from those with attention deficit hyperactivity disorder (ADHD) (Oner, Oner et al. 2008), while serotonergic medication intervention (Diler, Kibar, & Avci, 2004; Saxena, Brody, Maidment, & Smith, 2004) and cingulotomy (Dougherty et al., 2003) are shown to have positive treatment responses (see Case Study 23.5). Hyperfrontality typically is not associated with a classic *DSM* diagnosis per se, but rather it indicates new directions for treatment by providing a picture of the brain physiology underlying the clinical presentation.

Case Study 23.5 Hyperfrontality in SPECT

V, a 17-year-old male, had severe temporal lobe epilepsy. He also had aggression that was non-responsive to behavioral interventions. His SPECT scan showed severely decreased perfusion in his left temporal lobe (Figure 23.6) consistent with epilepsy, and he showed severely increased perfusion in the anterior cingulate gyrus and lateral frontal lobes (Figure 23.7), a pattern consistent with OCD. Even though V did not have clear OCD symptoms, he was rigid, inflexible, and easily upset when something did not go his way. With the addition of sertraline, an antidepressant that tends to lower rCBF in this brain region (Hoehn-Saric et al., 2001), his behavior significantly improved. Managing V without the benefit of scans handicapped the doctor, patient and family.

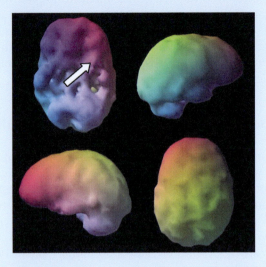

Figure 23.6 Outside surface scan.
Note: Severe left temporal lobe hypoperfusion (arrow).

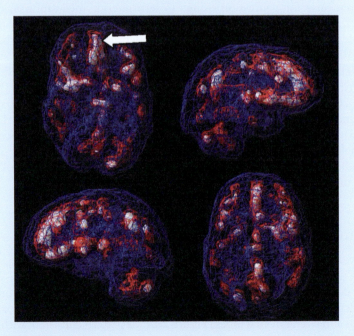

Figure 23.7 Active scan.
Note: Severe hyperfrontality (arrow).

Hypofrontality and Behavioral Problems

Hypofrontality, decreased perfusion or activity in the prefrontal cortex, is another important SPECT finding that is often helpful in understanding and targeting treatment in individual patients. Hypofrontality is associated with a negative response to serotonergic medication in depression (Brockmann et al., 2009) and clozapine in schizophrenia (Molina Rodriguez et al., 1996) as well as with predicting relapse in alcoholics (Noel et al., 2002), improved response to acetylcholine-esterase inhibitors for memory and behavior in Alzheimer's disease (Mega et al., 2000; Kanetaka et al., 2008), predicting a poor response to ketamine in fibromyalgia patients (Guedj et al., 2007), and improved response to stimulants in patients with ADHD symptoms during a concentration challenge (Amen, Hanks, & Prunella, 2008).

Hypofrontality is also associated with antisocial symptoms, impulsive behaviors, and murder (Goethals et al., 2005; Amen, Hanks, Prunella, & Aisa Grenn, 2007) as well as with suicide, which is often an impulsive act (Amen, Prunella, Fallon, Amen, & Hanks, 2009). This is because the prefrontal cortex is involved in higher order functioning, including consciousness, and when there is low perfusion to this area it could result in an individual being unable to comprehend thoughts or to discern right from wrong.

An unregulated prefrontal cortex can result in outbursts of rage or an inability to control acts of aggression. When hypofrontality is present in depressed patients, it is important to be vigilant in their care, as well as involve family support, as they may be less likely to respond to typical antidepressant medications and they may not have the cognitive resources to follow through with recommendations. Given its broad range of involvement in different types of psychiatric illness hypofrontality, like other findings, will not give a specific psychiatric diagnosis, but it allows the clinician to know the underlying pathophysiology of the patient's presenting problem, and can help explain issues with cognitive impairment or behavioral problems.

Links between hypofrontality and aggression/violence in forensic populations

Lesion studies of the frontal lobes result in impulsive aggressive behavior and defects in social and moral reasoning (Grafman, Schwab, Warden, & Pridgen, 1996; Anderson et al., 1999). There is a significant amount of neuroimaging research (SPECT and PET) that demonstrates frontal lobe dysfunction correlates with violent and criminal behavior (Volkow & Tancredi, 1987; Raine et al., 1994; Volkow et al., 1995; Amen et al., 1996; Raine, Buchsbaum, & LaCasse, 1997; Raine et al., 1998; Soderstrom, Tullberg, Wikkelsö, Ekholm, & Forsman, 2000; Soderstrom et al., 2002; Amen et al., 2007).

Using PET, Raine et al. (1994) studied 22 subjects accused of murder compared to age- and gender-matched controls and found decreased glucose metabolism in the lateral and medial prefrontal cortex (Raine et al., 1994). Raine et al. (1997) performed a second study on 41 murderers (who pled not guilty by reasons of insanity) compared to 41 age- and gender-matched controls and found metabolic deficits in the prefrontal cortex, superior parietal gyrus, left angular gyrus, and corpus callosum, with asymmetries in the amygdala, thalamus, and medial temporal lobe (Raine et al., 1997). They next looked at the difference in brain function in 24 accused murderers pleading not guilty by reason of insanity. This group was divided into those who were classified as affective, impulsive, violent offenders ($n = 9$) versus predatory violent offenders ($n = 15$), with each group being compared to matched controls ($n = 41$). Their data demonstrate that affective offenders have lower prefrontal cortex functioning and higher right subcortical functioning. In contrast, they found that the predatory violent offenders demonstrated prefrontal functioning that was equivalent to the controls, suggesting that they have the ability to control their aggressive impulses as compared to the affective murderers (Raine et al., 1998).

In our research on SPECT and aggression, we compared 40 psychiatric patients who had physically attacked another person or destroyed property to a group of matched, non-aggressive psychiatric patient controls and found significant decreased prefrontal cortex activity (Amen et al., 1996). This group also had increases in the basal ganglia/limbic system and left temporal lobe abnormalities that correlate with aggression.

Furthermore, in our imaging research on violence, we studied 30 male murderers who committed impulsive, non-predatory acts of violence (Amen et al., 2007). All of the subjects were scanned while at rest and again while performing a concentration task prior to their sentencing. When comparing this group to healthy, age-matched males, the murderers demonstrated no differences while at rest, but when given a concentration task (which is designed to measure inattentiveness, impulsivity, and reaction time) significant regions of decreased perfusion were found in areas that regulate impulse control, specifically the orbital cortices and the anterior cingulate gyrus.

When these areas have low perfusion, subjects will have challenges managing inhibition, self-censorship, and planning, and give limited thought to the future consequences of their poor behavior. Soderstrom et al. (2000) studied 21 subjects convicted of impulsive violent crimes (unrelated to psychosis, substance abuse, or medication) and found hypoperfusion in the frontal and temporal lobes. When compared to healthy controls, they reported reduced blood flow in the right angular gyrus and right medial temporal gyrus, bilaterally in the hippocampus and left white frontal matter (Soderstrom et al., 2000). Increased rCBF was observed in the parietal association cortex bilaterally. Next, Soderstrom et al. (2002) studied a group of 32 violent offenders who were categorized as psychopathic according to the Psychopathy Checklist-Revised (PCL-R) (Hare, 2003), and demonstrated hypoperfusion in the frontal and temporal lobes (Soderstrom et al., 2002). Taken together, these neuroimaging studies on murderers demonstrate that aggression is correlated with decreased functioning in the prefrontal cortex indicative of an inability to regulate behavior, and may result in impulsive acts of violence.

Mood Instability, Memory Problems and Temporal Lobe Abnormalities

Evaluating temporal lobe function is important in psychiatric medicine, especially as it relates to the evaluation of patients with memory problems, mood instability, aggression, and receptive and expressive language (Hales &Yudofsky, 2007). As described above, the temporal lobes are commonly affected in brain injury. Their function, however, cannot be evaluated simply by clinical phenomenology. SPECT offers a reliable tool to evaluate temporal lobe function. According to Devous, Leroy, and Horman (1990), "Both SPECT and PET have localizing power approaching that of combined scalp and depth EEG."

Patients with epilepsy have high psychiatric comorbidity (Titlic, Basic, Hajnsek, & Lusic, 2009), and psychiatrists increasingly rely on the use of anticonvulsants as "mood stabilizers," which are shown to stabilize or calm overall brain activity and perfusion, especially in the temporal lobes (Leiderman, Balish, Bromfield, & Theordore, 1991; Joo et al., 2006). Temporal lobe epilepsy (TLE) is one of the most frequently encountered chronic epileptic disorders and is associated with numerous psychiatric symptoms, such as depressed mood, anergia, irritability, euphoric mood, atypical pain, insomnia, fear, and anxiety (Blumer, 1995). The medial temporal lobes are frequently involved in TLE and, because they are difficult to evaluate with routine EEG studies, they may be missed. SPECT findings in epilepsy most often reveal focal decreased perfusion in the interictal phase and focal increased perfusion in the seizure's ictal phase. SPECT adds to the clinical evaluation of temporal lobe function by identifying area(s) of abnormality and showing deficits not seen by EEG.

Based on the authors' clinical experience, when abnormalities in the temporal lobes are seen (either low or high perfusion) and mood instability or temper problems are present, anticonvulsants provide a rational treatment option (Gescher & Malevani, 2009; see Case Study 23.6). If there are memory or learning issues (and low temporal lobe perfusion), acetylcholine-esterase inhibitors may be helpful (Freo, Pizzolato, Dam, Ori, & Battistim, 2002), always taking into consideration the clinical picture.

Case Study 23.6 Abnormal temporal lobe perfusion and aggression

C, age 12, was hospitalized for attacking another child at school. This was his third psychiatric hospitalization. C had been diagnosed with ADHD at the age of six, but stimulants caused him to hallucinate. At the age of nine he was hospitalized for an aggressive episode, diagnosed with a mood disorder, and placed on an antidepressant without benefit. By age 12 he had been in psychotherapy for three years, also without benefit. Given his resistant illness, and the tens of thousands of dollars spent on his care, a brain SPECT study was ordered, which showed severe left temporal lobe hypoperfusion (see Figure 23.8). Unilateral

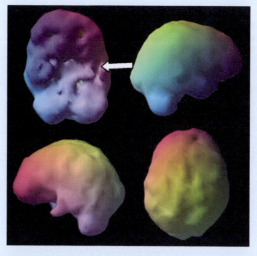

Figure 23.8 C's brain SPECT study.
Note: Severe hypoperfusion left temporal lobe (arrow).

> temporal lobe hypoperfusion is often seen with epileptic phenomena (Devous et al., 1990). On an anticonvulsant C's behavior normalized and he has maintained his progress for over ten years.

Temporal lobe abnormalities within a forensic population

Animal studies implicate the temporal lobes in controlling aggression as lesions in this region may reduce aggressive behaviors (Devinsky & Schachter, 2009). Abnormal firing patterns in the temporal lobes result in an increase in aggressive behaviors and rage as observed in individuals with TLE (Devinsky & Bear, 1984). The temporal lobes are responsible for the generation of affect and emotions. They can be responsible for random outbursts of violence and an inability to control emotions. Therefore, when the temporal lobe regions are functioning abnormally, it can result in criminal behavior or uncontrolled violence.

Neuroimaging studies on violent offenders and psychiatric patients demonstrate reduced blood flow and metabolism in the temporal lobes (Volkow & Tancredi, 1987; Volkow et al., 1995; Amen et al., 1996; Hirono et al., 2000; Soderstrom et al., 2000; Soderstrom et al., 2002; Bufkin & Luttrell, 2005; Anckarsater et al., 2007). Using SPECT, Anckarsater et al. (2007) performed a study on 9 violent offenders who were convicted of lethal or near-lethal violence and found frontotemporal hypoperfusion, a result which remained present in a follow-up examination four years later (Anckarsater et al., 2007). Perfusion deficits in the right medial temporal gyrus were demonstrated in 21 subjects convicted of impulsive violent crimes (Soderstrom et al., 2000) and in the temporal lobes of 32 violent psychopaths (Soderstrom et al., 2002). Hirono et al. (2000) have shown left anterior temporal lobe deficits in aggressive patients with dementia as compared to non-aggressive patients with dementia.

Our group demonstrated left temporal lobe deficits in 40 psychiatric patients with aggression (Amen al. 1996). Finally, using PET, hypoperfusion of the left temporal lobe was demonstrated in four forensic patients with repetitive violence (Volkow & Tancredi, 1987) and hypoperfusion of the left and right temporal medial cortex in 8 psychiatric patients who performed acts of repetitive violence (Volkow et al. 1995). Taken together, these lines of evidence support that dysfunction of the temporal lobes can lead to violent behavior.

Subtyping Dimensional Behavior to Predict Treatment Response: Aggression and Depression

SPECT's use in clinical practice dovetails closely with the spirit of the National Institute of Mental Health (NIMH) research domain criteria (RDoC) initiative, which looks to develop new ways of classifying psychopathology based on observable behavior and neurobiological measures (Insel et al., 2010). In order to construct such a system, it is necessary to obtain accurate measures of the functioning of the brain systems that support various normal and abnormal emotions, undergird critical functions such as attention and memory, and modulate functions such as aggression. SPECT scans have the possibility of facilitating the subtyping of mental illnesses, such as depression, ADHD, OCD, and aggression based on brain system pathophysiology.

Subtyping aggression

The role of brain function in aggression is one of NIMH's five major domains of interest and an area where SPECT imaging may provide immediate clinical help. From our work with 75 murderers, and hundreds of patients who have exhibited serious aggressive behavior ranging from assault, robbery, rape, kidnapping, arson, and bombings, to road rage and stalking, we have seen that aggressive behavior is not defined by one single brain finding, but rather clusters in at least three different patterns (see Box 23.2). The first is impulsive aggression, associated with hypofrontality (as already discussed), a finding reported in antisocial personality disorder (Kuruoglu et al., 1996; Raine, Lencz, Bihrle, LaCasse, & Colletti, 2000). Patients with a compromised prefrontal cortex are frequently unable to regulate aggressive impulses and are at higher risk for exhibiting violent activity than other patients. The second cluster we have labeled "compulsive aggression," often associated with hyperfrontality, where people act out because they cannot get negative thoughts out of their minds, or because they are extremely rigid and inflexible. The third cluster of aggressive patients we've seen have SPECT findings of temporal lobe abnormalities (as discussed earlier). Knowing a violent patient's underlying brain pattern may be helpful to getting them the right help. In the authors' experience, we have often seen multiple patterns associated with violence, such as low prefrontal cortex and temporal lobe perfusion.

Box 23.2 Subtyping aggression

Let's look at two examples of 15-year-old male multiple murderers (KK and PP) with significantly different SPECT patterns. These differences in SPECT patterns would lead to different clinical management decisions. KK was diagnosed with ADHD, dyslexia, and depression. He had been evaluated by two psychiatrists and placed on a psychostimulant and selective serotonin reuptake inhibitors (SSRIs) without benefit. He was arrested after bringing weapons to his high school. After he was released from jail he murdered his mother and father and then went back to his high school the next morning and shot 24 people, killing two more. As part of his pre-trial evaluation, a SPECT scan was performed and showed severe overall decreased perfusion, especially in the area of the left medial temporal lobe and inferior orbital prefrontal cortex. The scan was consistent with prior toxic exposure, anoxia, or infection. The SPECT scan and history raised the possibility that an anticonvulsant (given the severe decreased left temporal lobe perfusion) followed by a psychostimulant (to enhance his low prefrontal cortex perfusion) was worth considering to help modulate his aggressive impulses.

PP had been diagnosed with ADHD and dyslexia. In a rage, he murdered his mother and eight-year-old sister. PP's SPECT scan showed significant hyperfrontality, especially in the anterior cingulate gyrus. As noted above, this

> presentation is more likely to respond to a selective re-uptake inhibitor. The same symptom presentation of multiple murder in both cases, but with very different brain patterns. The differences in the scan patterns give suggestions for different treatment regimens.

Subtyping depression

Anxiety and depressive disorders are two of the most common psychiatric problems worldwide and subtyping these disorders using brain system pathology is an important step in improving treatment outcomes (Phillips, 2007). Functional imaging, including SPECT, helps to elucidate this process in individual patients. As noted, hyperfrontality is associated with a positive response to SSRIs in depressed and anxious patients, while hypofrontality is associated with a negative response, and has been reported in completed suicides. Little et al. (2005), on the other hand, found that lower prefrontal activity prior to treatment was associated with a positive response to buproprion and venlafaxine (Little et al., 2005). These medications involve enhancing dopamine and norepinephrine, which in our experience tends to enhance prefrontal cortex activity, while SSRIs tend to be calming (Hoehn-Saric et al., 2001). Up to 50% or 60% of patients with chronic epilepsy have various mood disorders including depression and anxiety (Beyenburg, Mitchell, Schmidt, Elger, & Reuber, 2005; Jones et al., 2005). Using SPECT gives the clinician a more rational reason to use anticonvulsants when focal areas of increased or decreased perfusion are seen, especially in the temporal regions. Likewise, if overall decreased perfusion is present, it alerts the clinician to look for toxic or metabolic causes of the problem; or, if a brain trauma pattern is seen, commonly associated with anxiety and mood disorders, this can be investigated further as well.

Conclusions: SPECT imaging in forensic populations

Several neuroimaging studies have been performed on murderers and psychiatric patients who have committed violent acts (Bufkin & Luttrell, 2005). Results using HMPAO-SPECT measuring regional cerebral blood flow demonstrate dysfunction in the neural circuitry that regulates emotion, which includes the frontal lobes, amygdala, the limbic system and temporal lobe (Amen et al., 1996; Hirono et al., 2000). Behavioral traits frequently expressed by those who commit criminal acts (psychopaths, sociopaths, murderers, violent offenders), including impulsivity, aggression, and violence, are localized within these neural circuits. For example, the neurobiological correlates of impulsivity are located in the prefrontal cortex or frontal lobes, specifically in the dorsolateral cortex and orbitofrontal cortex. When there is dysfunction in these brain regions, typically observed as reduced metabolic activity or hypoperfusion on a SPECT scan, an individual will have executive function deficits and impulse control challenges, which may increase the likelihood of aggression. Dysfunction of the frontal lobes is exacerbated by comorbid substance abuse and TBI, increasing the risk of violence (Palijan et al., 2010). The neural control of aggression is found within structures located in the temporal lobes, including the amygdala, hippocampus, parahippocampus, and auditory and visual cortices. These regions are critical in the regulation of mood, the encoding and storage of emotional memories, and visual and auditory processing. The amygdala is a region within the temporal lobes that is critical to the processing of emotions and behavior. Aberrant functioning of the amygdala results in a lack of empathy, remorse, moral reasoning, and an inability to properly process emotions. In most criminal cases, it is the inability to feel remorse for their actions or victims that is one of the common traits among those who murder or harm others. The hippocampus and parahippocampus are involved in the storage and retrieval of memories and when these areas are damaged through toxicity, TBI, or substance abuse it can result in significant cognitive dysfunction. Damage to the auditory or visual centers could manifest as visual or auditory hallucinations, which may be attributable to a personality disorder. There are clear neurobiological circuits that are implicated in regulating impulsivity, negative emotion, insensitivity to consequences, emotional detachment, aggression, and violent behavior. SPECT can illuminate the functional deficits in brain regions critical in modulating these behaviors and can aid in guiding the clinician in how to better treat and manage these individuals.

Implications for Practice

There are a number of important areas where SPECT has the potential to provide relevant information to help personalize treatment to patients' specific brain system pathophysiology rather than rely solely on general diagnostic and/or therapeutic categories. We described seven such areas in this chapter. Furthermore, in the authors' experience, another immediate benefit of using brain SPECT imaging is that the patient's and family's guilt, shame, and stigma are significantly reduced as they see the illness as being medical rather than moral, with concurrent improvements in treatment compliance. In the authors' opinion, brain SPECT or any other neuroimaging modality should always occur in conjunction with clinical assessment since it is not the isolated diagnostic accuracy that has greatest importance but rather the value added to routine clinical assessment.

Over the last quarter century, there has been much discussion of the "future of psychiatry" (Reynolds, Lewis, Detre, Schatzberg, & Kupfer, 2009) as we move into a more biologically based paradigm. How would we maintain our subjective patient focus within this new framework? Reynolds et al. have weighed in on this work in progress. One thing that is becoming very clear is that our resident trainees may require more exposure to translational neuroscience during their early years of residency and neuroimaging needs to be an important component of this curriculum (Downar, Krizova Ghaffar, & Zaretsky, 2010). A recent report demonstrated that the integration of a neuroimaging module within a residency program had wide approval by residents. Other programs have experimented with variations but within the neurology rotation of the PGY-1 year. The Psychiatry RRC of the Accreditation Council for Graduate Medical Education will need to take this on in earnest for the development of the field.

This is an exciting time in the history of psychiatry, as the field will likely significantly change over the next 30 years to incorporate functional neuroimaging in clinical practice. Among other techniques, fMRI is often seen as proving the future of neuroimaging. Yet these techniques are much more expensive and are more technically difficult to administer. The authors' hope is that SPECT does not get left out because of a lack of understanding or training in the use of this valuable tool.

Notes

1 See http://www.amenclinics.com/brain-science/spect-research/spect-abstracts.
2 See also Chapter 24.

Recommended Reading

Raine, A., Buchsbaum, M. S., Stanley, J., Lottenberg, S., Abel, L., & Stoddard, J. (1994). Selective reductions in prefrontal glucose metabolism in murderers. *Biological Psychiatry, 36*(6), 365–373. *Raine et al. perform a neuroimaging study measuring glucose uptake using PET in a population of 22 subjects charged with murder who pled not guilty by reason of insanity (NGRI) versus normal, age- and gender-matched controls. Results demonstrate that defendants pleading NGRI are characterized by prefrontal cortex deficits when performing a neuropsychological performance task (continuous performance task). The greatest regional difference between groups was localized to the anterior medial prefrontal cortex. No deficits were observed in temporal or parietal brain regions. Interestingly, the murders were broken down into several subgroups (relationship of offender to victim, planned vs impulsive murder, instrumental vs affective murder, sexual involvement vs non-sexual involvement, sex of victim and age of victim) and there were no differences between the subgroups, suggesting a general predisposition for violence in those with prefrontal cortex deficits. The implications of this work provide the foundation for future research on the neurobiological correlates of violence.*

Mendez, M. F. (2010). The unique predisposition to criminal violations in frontotemporal dementia. *Journal of the American Academy of Psychiatry, 38*(3), 318–323. *Mendez provides case reviews of four FTD patients who committed acts of criminal violence who were of clear consciousness with intact cognition. FTD is a progressive degenerative disorder affecting the ventromedial prefrontal cortex, orbitofrontal cortex, and anterior temporal lobes, which regulate decision making, moral judgment, empathy, and impulsivity. FTD is often associated with sociopathic behavior and can manifest in progressive personality changes, compulsivity, impairment in the regulation of personal conduct, loss of insight, decreased moral empathy, and emotional detachment. Each case illustrates the capacity of individuals with FTD to discern right from wrong but demonstrate the loss of a sense of morality. The applications of understanding FTD and its implications on the criminal justice system are discussed.*

Colantonio, A., Stamenova, V., Colantonio, A., Stamenova, V., Abramowitz, C., Clarke, D., & Christensen, B. (2007). Brain injury in a forensic psychiatry population. *Brain Injury, 21*(13–14), 1353–1360. *Colantonio et al. perform a retrospective chart review of all consecutive admissions within a one-year period to a forensic psychiatry program in Canada, which included minimum and medium security facilities as well as an outpatient unit. Of 394 eligible patient records, 23% had a history of TBI. The importance of patient population studied, how TBI diagnosis was ascertained, and types of TBI is discussed in relation to previous studies. Results from this work emphasize the importance of screening for TBI in forensic prisons in terms of case management and treatment as TBI is often comorbid with substance use, personality disorders, homelessness, attention disorder, and learning disorders. Having a TBI resulted in a higher incidence of aggravated assault, escape, and theft as compared to the non-TBI population. Based on these results, routine neurological screening during admission is recommended.*

Bufkin, J. L., & Luttrell, V. R. (2005). Neuroimaging studies of aggressive and violent behavior: current findings and implications for criminology and criminal justice. *Trauma Violence Abuse, 6*(2), 176–191. *Bufkin and Luttrell provide a review of 17 neuroimaging studies utilizing SPECT, PET, MRI, and fMRI to examine regional brain dysfunction of aggressive and violent offenders. The results reveal individuals who commit impulsive acts have dysfunction in the prefrontal cortex and medial temporal lobes. The prefrontal cortex is involved in decision making, mediating behavior based on social context, perception of social signals, and proper regulation of negative emotion. The amygdala, a subcortical structure of the temporal lobes, is involved in extracting emotional content from the environment and the processing of information that suggests threat, fear, or anger. Dysfunction of these neural circuits or their connectivity may result in the misinterpretation of situations (as dangerous) and increases the probability of an individual committing a violent, impulsive act. The addition of neuroimaging to biological, psychological, and social knowledge provides a more comprehensive understanding of criminal behavior and has implications on policy making and the criminal justice system.*

References

Alexander, G. E., Prohovnik, I., Sackeim, H. A., Steern, Y., & Mayeux, R. (1995). Cortical perfusion and gray matter weight in frontal lobe dementia. *The Journal of Neuropsychiatry and Clinical Neurosciences, 7*(2), 188–196.

Alptekin, K., Degirmenci, B., Kivircik, B., Durak, H., Yemez, B, Derebek, E., & Tunca, Z. (2001). Tc-99m HMPAO brain perfusion SPECT in drug-free obsessive-compulsive patients without depression. *Psychiatry Research, 107*(1), 51–56.

Amen, D. G. (1997a). *Images into the mind.* Fairfield, CA: Mind Works Press.

Amen, D. G. (1997b). Oppositional children similar to OCD on SPECT: Implications for treatment. *Journal of Neurotherapy (August)*, 1–8.

Amen, D. G. (1999). Regional cerebral blood flow in alcohol-induced violence: A case study. *Journal of Psychoactive Drugs, 31*(4), 389–393.

Amen, D. G., Hanks, C., & Prunella, J. (2008). Predicting positive and negative treatment responses to stimulants with brain SPECT imaging. *Journal of Psychoactive Drugs, 40*(2), 131–138.

Amen, D. G., Hanks, C., Prunella, J. R., & Aisa Grenn, B. A. (2007). An analysis of regional cerebral blood flow in impulsive murderers using single photon emission computed tomography. *The Journal of Neuropsychiatry and Clinical Neurosciences, 19*(3), 304–309.

Amen, D. G., Highum, D., Licata, R., Annibali, J. A., Somner, L., & Pigott, H. E. (2012). Specific ways brain SPECT imaging enhances clinical psychiatric practice. *Journal of Psychoactive Drugs, 44*(2), 96–106.

Amen, D. G., Newberg, A., Thatcher, R., Jin, Y., Wu, J., Keator, D., & Willeumier, K. (2011). Impact of playing American professional football on long-term brain function. *The Journal of Neuropsychiatry and Clinical Neurosciences, 23*(1), 98–106.

Amen, D. G., Prunella, J. R., Fallon, J. H., Amen, B., & Hanks, C. (2009). A comparative analysis of completed suicide using high resolution brain SPECT imaging. *The Journal of Neuropsychiatry and Clinical Neurosciences, 21*(4), 430–439.

Amen, D. G., Stubblefield, M., Carmichael, B., & Thisted, R. (1996). Brain SPECT findings and aggressiveness. *Annals of Clinical Psychiatry, 8*(3), 129–137.

Amen, D. G., Wu, J. C., Taylor, D., & Willeumier, K. (2011). Reversing brain damage in former NFL players: implications for traumatic brain injury and substance abuse rehabilitation. *Journal of Psychoactive Drugs, 43*(1), 1–5.

American College of Radiology. (2007). American College of Radiology Practice Guideline for the Performance of Single Photon Emission Computed Tomography (SPECT) Brain Perfusion and Brain Death Studies.

American Psychiatric Association (2013). *Diagnostic and Statistical Manual of Mental Disorders* (5th ed.). Washington, DC: American Psychiatric Association.

Anckarsater, H., Piechnik, S., Tullberg, M., Zuegelitz, D., Sörman, M., Bjellvi, J., ... & Forsman, A. (2007). Persistent regional frontotemporal hypoactivity in violent offenders at follow-up. *Psychiatry Research, 156*(1), 87–90.

Anderson, S. W., Bechara, A., Damasio, H., & Tranel, D. (1999). Impairment of social and moral behavior related to early damage in human prefrontal cortex. *Nature Neuroscience, 2*(11), 1032–1037.

Baulieu, F., Fournier, P., Baulieu, J. L., Dalonneau, M., Chiaroni, P., Eder, V., Legros, B. (2001). Technetium-99m ECD single photon emission computed tomography in brain trauma: comparison of early scintigraphic findings with long-term neuropsychological outcome. *Journal of Neuroimaging, 11*(2), 112–120.

Bechara, A., Damasio, A. R., & Anderson, S. W. (1994). Insensitivity to future consequences following damage to human prefrontal cortex. *Cognition, 50*(1–3), 7–15.

Beyenburg, S., Mitchell, A. J., Schmidt, D., Elger, C. E., & Reuber, M. (2005). Anxiety in patients with epilepsy: systematic review and suggestions for clinical management. *Epilepsy & Behavior, 7*(2), 161–171.

Blumer, D. (1995). *Neuropsychaitry of personality disorders.* Cambridge, MA: Blackwell Science.

Bonte, F. J., Weiner, E. H., Bigio, E. H., & White, C. L. III. (1997). Brain blood flow in the dementias: SPECT with histopathologic correlation in 54 patients. *Radiology, 202*(3), 793–797.

Brockmann, H., Zobel, A., Joe, A., Biermann, K., Scheef, L., Schumacher, A., ... & Boecker, H. (2009). The value of HMPAO SPECT in predicting treatment response to citalopram in patients with major depression. *Psychiatry Research, 173*(2), 107–112.

Brower, M. C., & Price, B. H. (2001). Neuropsychiatry of frontal lobe dysfunction in violent and criminal behaviour: A critical review. *Journal of Neurology, Neurosurgery, and Psychiatry, 71*(6), 720–726.

Bufkin, J. L., & Luttrell, V. R. (2005). Neuroimaging studies of aggressive and violent behavior: Current findings and implications for criminology and criminal justice. *Trauma Violence & Abuse, 6*(2), 176–191.

Buss, T. F., Abdu, R., & Walker, J. R. (1995). Alcohol, drugs, and urban violence in a small city trauma center. *The Journal of Substance Abuse Treatment, 12*(2), 75–83.

Carey, P. D., Warwick, J., Niehaus, D. J. H., van der Linden, G., van Heerden, B. B., Harvey, B. H., ... & Stein, D. J. (2004). Single photon emission computed tomography (SPECT) of anxiety disorders before and after treatment with citalopram. *BMC Psychiatry, 4*, 30.

Colantonio, A., Stamenova, V., Abramowitz, C., Clarke, D., & Christensen, B. (2007). Brain injury in a forensic psychiatry population. *Brain Injury, 21*(13–14), 1353–1360.

Devinsky, J., & Schachter, S. (2009). Norman Geschwinds contribution to the understanding of behavioral changes in temporal lobe epilepsy: The February 1974 lecture. *Epilepsy & Behavior, 15*(4), 417–424.

Devinsky, O., & Bear, D. (1984). Varieties of aggressive behavior in temporal lobe epilepsy. *American Journal of Psychiatry, 141*(5), 651–656.

Devous, M. D., Sr., Leroy, R. F., & Horman, R. W. (1990). Single photon emission computed tomography in epilepsy. *Seminars in Nuclear Medicine, 20*(4), 325–341.

Diehl-Schmid, J., Perneczky, R., Koch, J., Nedopil, N., & Kurz, A. (2013). Guilty by suspicion? Criminal behavior in frontotemporal lobar degeneration. *Cognitive and Behavioral Neurology, 26*(2), 73–77.

Diler, R. S., Kibar, M., & Avci, A. (2004). Pharmacotherapy and regional cerebral blood flow in children with obsessive compulsive disorder. *Yonsei Medical Journal, 45*(1), 90–99.

Dougherty, D. D., Weiss, A. P., Cosgrove, G.R., Alpert, N. M., Cassem, E. H., Nierenberg, A. A., ... Rauch, S. L. (2003). Cerebral metabolic correlates as potential predictors of response to anterior cingulotomy for treatment of major depression. *Journal of Neurosurgery, 99*(6), 1010–1017.

Downar, J., Krizova, A., Ghaffar, O., & Zaretsky, A. (2010). Neuroimaging week: A novel, engaging, and effective curriculum for teaching neuroimaging to junior psychiatric residents. *Academic Psychiatry, 34*(2), 119–124.

Dukarm, C. P., Byrd, R. S., Auinger, P., & Weitzman, M. (1996). Illicit substance use, gender, and the risk of violent behavior among adolescents. *Archives of Pediatrics and Adolescent Medicine, 150*(8), 797–801.

Freo, U., Pizzolato, G., Dam, M., Ori, C., & Battistim, L. (2002). A short review of cognitive and functional neuroimaging studies of cholinergic drugs: Implications for therapeutic potentials. *Journal of Neural Transmission, 109*(5–6), 857–870.

Gescher, D. M., & Malevani, J. (2009). [Mood stabilizer in the psychopharmacotherapy of borderline personality disorder]. *Fortschritte Der Neurologie-Psychiatrie, 77*(7), 389–398.

Goethals, I., Audenaert, K., Jacobs, F., van den Eynde, F., Bernargie, K., Kolindou, A., … van Heeringen, C. (2005). Brain perfusion SPECT in impulsivity-related personality disorders. *Behavioural Brain Research, 157*(1), 187–192.

Goshen, E., Zwas, S. T., Shahar, E., & Tadmor, R. (1996). The role of 99Tcm-HMPAO brain SPET in paediatric traumatic brain injury. *Nuclear Medicine Communications, 17*(5), 418–422.

Goto, H., Ishii, K., Uemura, T., Miyamoto, N., Yoshikawa, T., Shimada, K., & Ohkawa, S. (2010). Differential diagnosis of dementia with Lewy Bodies and Alzheimer Disease using combined MR imaging and brain perfusion single-photon emission tomography. *American Journal of Neuroradiology, 31*(4), 720–725.

Grafman, J., Schwab, K., Warden, D. L., & Pridgen, A. (1996). Frontal lobe injuries, violence, and aggression: a report of the Vietnam Head Injury Study. *Neurology, 46*(5), 1231–1238.

Guedj, E., Cammilleri, S., Colavolpe, C., Taieb, D., de Laforte, C., Niboyet, J., & Mundler, O. (2007). Predictive value of brain perfusion SPECT for ketamine response in hyperalgesic fibromyalgia. *European Journal of Nuclear Medicine and Molecular Imaging, 34*(8), 1274–1279.

Hales, R. E., & Yudofsky, S. C. (2007). *Textbook of neuropsychiatry and behavioral neurosciences* (5th ed.). Arlington, VA: American Psychiatric Publishing.

Hare, R. D. (2003). *Manual for the revised psychopathy checklist* (2nd ed.). Toronto, ON: Multi-Health Systems.

Hibbard, M. R., Uysal, S., Kepler, K., Bogdany, J., & Silver, J. (1998). Axis I psychopathology in individuals with traumatic brain injury. *Journal of Head Trauma Rehabilitation, 13*(4), 24–39.

Hirono, N., Mega, M. S., Dinov, I. D., Mishkin, F., & Cummings, J. L. (2000). Left frontotemporal hypoperfusion is associated with aggression in patients with dementia. *Archives of Neurology, 57*(6), 861–866.

Hoehn-Saric, R., Schlaepfer, T. E., Greenberg, B. D., McLeod, D. R., Pearlson, G. D., & Wong, S. H. (2001). Cerebral blood flow in obsessive-compulsive patients with major depression: Effect of treatment with sertraline or desipramine on treatment responders and non-responders. *Psychiatry Research, 108*(2), 89–100.

Hollander, E. (1996). Obsessive-compulsive disorder-related disorders: The role of selective serotonergic reuptake inhibitors. *International Clinical Psychopharmacology, 11*(Suppl 5), 75–87.

Horner, M. D., Ferguson, P. L., Selassie, A. W., Labbate, L. A., Kniele, K., & Corrigan, J. D. (2005). Patterns of alcohol use 1 year after traumatic brain injury: A population-based, epidemiological study. *Journal of the International Neuropsychological Society, 11*(3), 322–330.

Insel, T., Cuthbert, B., Garvey, M., Heinssen, R., Pine, D. S., Quinn, K., ... Wang, P. (2010). Research domain criteria (RDoC): Toward a new classification framework for research on mental disorders. *American Journal of Psychiatry, 167*(7), 748–751.

Jacobs, A., Put, E., Ingels, M., & Bossuyt, A. (1994). Prospective evaluation of technetium-99m-HMPAO SPECT in mild and moderate traumatic brain injury. *The Journal of Nuclear Medicine, 35*(6), 942–947.

James, A. I., & Young, A. W. (2013). Clinical correlates of verbal aggression, physical aggression and inappropriate sexual behaviour after brain injury. *Brain Injury27*(10), 1162–1172.

Jean-Bay, E. (2000). The biobehavioral correlates of post-traumatic brain injury depression. *The Journal of Neuroscience Nursing, 32*(3), 169–176.

Jones, J. E., Hermann, B. P., Barry, J. J., Gilliam, F., Kanner, A. M., & Meador, K. T. (2005). Clinical assessment of Axis I psychiatric morbidity in chronic epilepsy: A multicenter investigation. *The Journal of Neuropsychiatry and Clinical Neurosciences, 17*(2), 172–179.

Joo, E. Y., Hong, S. B., Tae, W. S., Han, S. J., Seo, D. W., Lee, K., & Lee, M. H. (2006). Effect of lamotrigine on cerebral blood flow in patients with idiopathic generalised epilepsy. *European Journal of Nuclear Medicine and Molecular Imaging, 33*(6), 724–729.

Kanetaka, H., Hanyu, H., Hirao, K., Shimizu, S., Sato, T., Akai, T., ... & Koizumi, K. (2008). Prediction of response to donepezil in Alzheimers disease: Combined MRI analysis of the substantia innominata and SPECT measurement of cerebral perfusion. *Nuclear Medicine Communications, 29*(6), 568–573.

Kant, R., Smith-Seemiller, L., Isaac, G., & Duffy, J. (1997). Tc-HMPAO SPECT in persistent post-concussion syndrome after mild head injury: Comparison with MRI/CT. *Brain Injury, 11*(2), 115–124.

Kapucu, O. L., Nobili, F., Varrone, A., Booik, J., Borght, T. J., Någren, K., ... van Laere, K. J. (2009). EANM procedure guideline for brain perfusion SPECT using (99m)Tc-labelled radiopharmaceuticals, version 2. *European Journal of Nuclear Medicine and Molecular Imaging, 36*(12), 2093–2102.

Kertesz, S. G., Madan, A., Wallace, D., Schumacher, J. E., & Milby, J. B. (2006). Substance abuse treatment and psychiatric comorbidity: Do benefits spill over? Analysis of data from a prospective trial among cocaine-dependent homeless persons. *Substance Abuse Treatment, Prevention, and Policy, 1*, 27.

Kim, J. M., Chu, K., Jung, K. H., Lee, S. T., Choi, S. S., & Lee, S. K. (2011). Criminal manifestations of dementia patients: report from the national forensic hospital. *Dementia and Geriatric Cognitive Disorders Extra, 1*, 433–438.

Kucuk, N. O., Kilic, E. O., Ibis, E., Aysev, A., Gencoglu, E. A., Aras, G.... Erbay, G. (2000). Brain SPECT findings in long-term inhalant abuse. *Nuclear Medicine Communications, 21*(8), 769–773.

Kuruoglu, A. C., Arikan, Z., Vural, G., Karatas, M., Arac, M., & Isik, E. (1996). Single photon emission computerised tomography in chronic alcoholism. Antisocial personality disorder may be associated with decreased frontal perfusion. *British Journal of Psychiatry, 169*(3), 348–354.

Lacerda, A. L., Dalgalarrondo, P., Caetano, D., Camargo, E. E., Etchebehere, E. C. S. C., & Soares, J. C. (2003). Elevated thalamic and prefrontal regional cerebral blood flow in obsessive-compulsive disorder: a SPECT study. *Psychiatry Research, 123*(2), 125–134.

Langguth, B., Wiegand, R., Kharraz, A., Landgrebe, M., Marienhagen, J., Frick, U., ... Eichhammer, P. (2007). Pre-treatment anterior cingulate activity as a predictor of antidepressant response to repetitive transcranial magnetic stimulation (rTMS). *Neuro Endocrinology Letters, 28*(5), 633–638.

Lee, W. V., & Weinstein, S. P. (1997). How far have we come? A critical review of the research on men who batter. *Recent Developments in Alcoholism, 13*, 337–356.

Leiderman, D. B., Balish, M., Bromfield, E. B., & Theordore, W. H. (1991). Effect of valproate on human cerebral glucose metabolism. *Epilepsia, 32*(3), 417–422.

Lindqvist, P. (1986). Criminal homicide in northern Sweden 1970–1981: Alcohol intoxication, alcohol abuse and mental disease. *The International Journal of Law and Psychiatry, 8*(1), 19–37.

Little, J. T., Ketter, T. A., Kimbrell, T. A., Dunn, R. T., Benson, B. E., Willis, M. W., ...Post, R. M. (2005). Bupropion and venlafaxine responders differ in pretreatment regional cerebral metabolism in unipolar depression. *Biological Psychiatry, 57*(3), 220–228.

Marsh, N. V., & Martinovich, W. M. (2006). Executive dysfunction and domestic violence. *Brain Injury, 20*(1), 61–66.

Martell, D. A. (1992). Estimating the prevalence of organic brain dysfunction in maximum-security forensic psychiatric patients. *Journal of Forensic Science, 37*(3), 878–893.

Mayberg, H. S., Brannan, S. K., Mahurin, R. K., Jerabek, P. A., Brickman, J. S., Tekell, J. L., ... Fox, P. T. (1997). Cingulate function in depression: A potential predictor of treatment response. *Neuroreport, 8*(4), 1057–1061.

Mayberg, H. S., Brannan, S. K., Tekell, J. L., Silva, J. A., Mahurin, R. K., McGinnis, S., & Jerabek, P. A. (2000). Regional metabolic effects of fluoxetine in major depression: serial changes and relationship to clinical response. *Biological Psychiatry, 48*(8), 830–843.

McDonald, R. J. (2002). Multiple combinations of co-factors produce variants of age-related cognitive decline: A theory. *Canadian Journal of Experimental Psychology, 56*(3), 221–239.

Mega, M. S., Dinov, I. D., Lee, L., O'Connor, S. M., Masterman, D. M., Wilen, B., ... Cummings, J. L. (2000). Orbital and dorsolateral frontal perfusion defect associated with behavioral response to cholinesterase inhibitor therapy in Alzheimers disease. *The Journal of Neuropsychiatry and Clinical Neurosciences, 12*(2), 209–218.

Mendez, M. F. (2010). The unique predisposition to criminal violations in frontotemporal dementia. *Journal of the American Academy of Psychiatry, 38*(3), 318–323.

Mendez, M. F., Chen, A. K., Shapira, A. K., & Miller, B. L. (2005). Acquired sociopathy and frontotemporal dementia. *Dementia and Geriatric Cognitive Disorders, 20*(2–3), 99–104.

Mendez, M. F., Lauterbach, E. C., & Sampson, S. M. (2008). An evidence-based review of the psychopathology of frontotemporal dementia: A report of the ANPA Committee on Research. *The Journal of Neuropsychiatry and Clinical Neurosciences, 20*(2), 130–149.

Mendez, M. F., Shapira, J. S., & Saul, R. E. (2011). The spectrum of sociopathy in dementia. *The Journal of Neuropsychiatry and Clinical Neurosciences, 23*(2), 132–140.

Molina Rodriguez, V., Montz Andree, R., Pérez Castejón, M. J., Capdevila García, E., Carreras Delgado, J. L, & Rubia Vila, F. J. (1996). SPECT study of regional cerebral perfusion in neuroleptic-resistant schizophrenic patients who responded or did not respond to clozapine. *American Journal of Psychiatry, 153*(10), 1343–1346.

Newberg, A. B., Alavi, A., & Payer, F. (1995). Single photon emission computed tomography in Alzheimers disease and related disorders. *Neuroimaging Clinics of North America, 5*(1), 103–123.

Noel, X., Sferrazza, R., van der Linden, M., Paternot, J., Verhas, M., Hanak, C., ... Verbanck, P. (2002). Contribution of frontal cerebral blood flow measured by (99m)Tc-Bicisate spect and executive function deficits to predicting treatment outcome in alcohol-dependent patients. *Alcohol and Alcoholism, 37*(4), 347–354.

Öner, P., Öner, Ö., Aysen, A., Kücük, Ö., & Ibis, E. (2008). [Comparison of cerebral blood flow in children with obsessive compulsive disorder and attention deficit hyperactivity disorder]. *Turk Psikiyatri Dergisi, 19*(1), 13–18.

Palijan, T. Z., Radeljak, S., Kovac, M., & Kovacević, D. (2010). Relationship between comorbidity and violence risk assessment in forensic psychiatry – the implication of neuroimaging studies. *Psychiatr Danubina, 22*(2), 253–256.

Phillips, M. L. (2007). The emerging role of neuroimaging in psychiatry: Characterizing treatment-relevant endophenotypes. *American Journal of Psychiatry, 164*(5), 697–699.

Pimlott, S. L., & Ebmeier, K. P. (2007). SPECT imaging in dementia. *The British Journal of Radiology, 80 Spec No 2*, S153–159.

Raine, A., Buchsbaum, M. S., & LaCasse, L. (1997). Brain abnormalities in murderers indicated by positron emission tomography. *Biological Psychiatry, 42*(6), 495–508.

Raine, A., Buchsbaum, M. S., Stanley, J., Lottenberg, S., Abel, L., & Stoddard, J. (1994). Selective reductions in prefrontal glucose metabolism in murderers. *Biological Psychiatry, 36*(6), 365–373.

Raine, A., Lencz, T., Bihrle, S., LaCasse, L., & Colletti, P. (2000). Reduced prefrontal gray matter volume and reduced autonomic activity in antisocial personality disorder. *Archives of General Psychiatry, 57*(2), 119–127; discussion 128–119.

Raine, A., Meloy, J. R., Bihrle, S., Stoddard, J., LaCasse, L., & Buchsbaum, M. S. (1998). Reduced prefrontal and increased subcortical brain functioning assessed using positron emission tomography in predatory and affective murderers. *Behavioral Sciences & the Law, 16*(3), 319–332.

Reynolds, C. F., 3rd, Lewis, D. A., Detre, T., Schatzberg, A. F., & Kupfer, D. J. (2009). The future of psychiatry as clinical neuroscience. *Academic Medicine, 84*(4), 446–450.

Rogers, J. M., & Read, C. A. (2007). Psychiatric comorbidity following traumatic brain injury. *Brain Injury, 21*(13–14), 1321–1333.

Rueve, M. E., & Welton, R. S. (2008). Violence and mental illness. *Psychiatry (Edgmont), 5*(5), 34–48.

Salmond, C. H., & Sahakian, B. J. (2005). Cognitive outcome in traumatic brain injury survivors. *Current Opinion in Critical Care, 11*(2), 111–116.

Saxena, S., Brody, A. L., Maidment, K. M., & Smith, E. (2004). Cerebral glucose metabolism in obsessive-compulsive hoarding. *American Journal of Psychiatry, 161*(6), 1038–1048.

Schafer, J., & Fals-Stewart, W. (1997). Spousal violence and cognitive functioning among men recovering from multiple substance abuse. *Addictive Behaviors, 22*(1), 127–130.

Seminowicz, D. A., Mayberg, H. S., McIntosh, A. R., Goldapple, K., Kennedy, S., Segal, Z., & Rafi-Tari, S. (2004). Limbic-frontal circuitry in major depression: a path modeling metanalysis. *Neuroimage, 22*(1), 409–418.

Soderstrom, H., Hultin, L., Tullberg, M., Wikkelso, C., Ekholms, S., & Forsman, A. (2002). Reduced frontotemporal perfusion in psychopathic personality. *Psychiatry Research, 114*(2), 81–94.

Soderstrom, H., Tullberg, M., Wikkelso, C., Ekholm, S., & Forsman, A. (2000). Reduced regional cerebral blood flow in non-psychotic violent offenders. *Psychiatry Research, 98*(1), 29–41.

SPECT Abstracts. Retrieved from http://www.amenclinics.com/brain-science/spect-research/spect-abstracts, R. A. f. U.

Titlic, M., Basic, S., Hajnsek, S., & Lusic, I. (2009). Comorbidity psychiatric disorders in epilepsy: A review of literature. *Bratislavské lekárske listy, 110*(2), 105–109.

Volkow, N. D., & Tancredi, L. R. (1987). Neural substrates of violent behaviour. A preliminary study with positron emission tomography. *British Journal of Psychiatry, 151*, 668–673.

Volkow, N. D., Tancredi, L. R., Grant, C., Gillespie, H., Valentine, A., Mullani, N., … Hollister, L. (1995). Brain glucose metabolism in violent psychiatric patients: A preliminary study. *Psychiatry Research, 61*(4), 243–253.

Wortzel, H. S., & Arciniegas, D. B. (2013). A forensic neuropsychiatric approach to traumatic brain injury, aggression, and suicide. *Journal of the American Academy of Psychiatry, 41*(2), 274–286.

Wu, J., Buchsbaum, M. S., Gillin, J. C., Tang, C., Cadwell, S., Wiegland, M., … Bunney, W. E. (1999). Prediction of antidepressant effects of sleep deprivation by metabolic rates in the ventral anterior cingulate and medial prefrontal cortex. *American Journal of Psychiatry, 156*(8), 1149–1158.

Wu, J. C., Gillin, J. C., Buchsbaum, M. S., Schachat, C., Darnall, L. A., Keator, D. B., … Bunney, W. E. (2008). Sleep deprivation PET correlations of Hamilton symptom improvement ratings with changes in relative glucose metabolism in patients with depression. *Journal of Affective Disorders, 107*(1–3), 181–186.

Zahodne, L. B., Ornstein, K., Consentino, S., Devanand, D. P. & Stern, Y. (2015). Longitudinal relationships between Alzheimer disease progression and psychosis, depressed mood, and agitation/aggression. *The American Journal of Geriatric Psychiatry, 23* (2), 130–140.

24

Therapy for Acquired Brain Injury

Nick Alderman, Caroline Knight, and Jennifer Brooks

Key points

- It is noted in the chapter that despite the proven success of psychologically driven rehabilitation programs in reducing challenging behavior, people with acquired brain injury (ABI) who are predominantly managed through forensic and prison services are not typically in receipt of such programs, yet are the group that are most at risk of recidivism.
- Some ABI survivors acquire an offender "label" entirely as a consequence of which external agency manages the consequences of behavior change following injury; while others will have particular needs that predate this, requiring inputs traditionally provided by forensic psychologists.
- Hence, in this chapter, the following will be covered:
  - the causal influence of ABI on offending behavior, especially with regard to violence and aggression;
  - the benefits of providing neurobehavioral rehabilitation to ABI offenders, as well as those survivors who do not have a forensic history;
  - a conceptual model of psychological therapy; and
  - psychological approaches to managing post-ABI aggression and ways clinical and forensic approaches might be combined within a neurobehavioral rehabilitation framework.
- Finally, a case study will be outlined illustrating the various issues related to ABI.

Terminology Explained

Acquired brain injury (ABI) occurs after birth and is not a consequence of a genetic or congenital disorder. ABI has a sudden outset and is not progressive. Causes include lack of oxygen to the brain, stroke, hemorrhage, tumors, and infections, such as encephalitis or meningitis.

The Wiley Blackwell Handbook of Forensic Neuroscience, First Edition. Edited by Anthony R. Beech, Adam J. Carter, Ruth E. Mann and Pia Rotshtein.
© 2018 John Wiley & Sons Ltd. Published 2018 by John Wiley & Sons Ltd.

Aggression refers to behavior intended to harm oneself or another individual. Impulsive aggression refers to aggression that occurs with little or no amount of forethought or intent: this is what most characterizes this behavior when it occurs as a consequence of ABI. In contrast, instrumental aggression is intentional and planned: it is less characteristic of ABI. Aggressive behavior is manifested as verbal aggression, or physical aggression against objects, self or another person.

The **Overt Aggression Scale-Modified for Neurorehabilitation (OAS-MNR)** uses an operant conceptual framework that enables detailed and reliable examination of the role environmental factors have in mediating ABI aggressive behavior disorders. Using OAS-MNR allows for a set of codes, which provides a shorthand method of capturing complex behavior sequences.

Neurobehavioral rehabilitation A neuropsychological model of rehabilitation conceived for ABI in which neurobehavioral disability and social handicap arising from this are understood in the context of damaged neural systems. The role of the environment is also acknowledged as potentially reinforcing and sustaining behaviors. Consequently, environmental manipulation is utilized to maximize rehabilitation outcomes. Neurobehavioral rehabilitation (NbR) services are distinguishable from psychiatric services in a number of important ways, including: occurring post-acutely; not a medical model, but a psychosocial form of rehabilitation, which draws heavily from learning theory; usually led by neuropsychologists; being community rather than hospital based; delivered by a transdisciplinary team (TDT), which through role release provides optimum conditions for new learning, habit formation, and generalization of skills. Since its inception in 1978, a compelling and robust evidence base regarding the clinical efficacy and cost effectiveness of neurobehavioral rehabilitation has continued to be compiled.

Traumatic brain injury (TBI) is a subset of ABI and may be closed or open. A closed TBI does not expose the brain and is most often a consequence of road traffic collision, fall, or assault. An open TBI results in exposure of brain matter, for example, as a result of penetration from a gunshot wound. Although by no means limited to TBI, this category of ABI is most often associated with offending behavior and aggression.

Introduction

Preceding chapters have highlighted ways that neurobiological factors influence behavior and the relationships these have with criminality. Lack of synchronicity in maturation rate of various systems in the developing brain creates particular vulnerabilities among young people. Reasoning ability appears to be well formed by age 16 years. However, the brain system related to rewards in the mesolimbic area (see Box 24.1) tends to develop more rapidly than related systems, which can result in a disproportionate surge of dopaminergic activity and subsequent heightened increase in reward-seeking behavior. In contrast, the ability to make judgments about longer-term consequences of behavior, and inhibit it, lag behind in development, resulting in poor decisions and risky actions. The ability to arrive at reasoned decisions is further liable to interference from emotion for similar reasons (Tonks et al., 2009).

Box 24.1 Experiencing reward and the meso-limbic area

The mesolimbic dopaminergic (ML-DA) pathway allows for dopamine to be transported from one area of the brain to another. Within the ML-DA pathway dopamine is released from the ventral tegmental area (VTA) to the nucleus accumbens. When pleasure is experienced, dopamine neurons in the VTA are activated, and project through the ML-DA pathway resulting in increased dopamine levels in the nucleus accumbens (an area associated with motivation and reward). The ML-DA system has a fundamental role in the neurobiology of addiction as well as a range of psychiatric disorders such as schizophrenia and depression. Its role in personality traits such as impulsivity and extraversion has also been documented in the literature.

In the UK, ABI impacts on around 8.5% of the population but peaks in childhood and adolescence. Traumatic brain injury (TBI), is most prevalent, typically resulting from road traffic accidents, falls, sporting injuries, and physical assaults (Williams, 2012). While most are categorized as mild in severity, effects of ABI can be catastrophic and pervasive. In young people, ABI can interfere with the maturation process in the developing brain to the extent that neurological inhibitory systems that mediate the potentially detrimental effects of emotion and the need for short-term reward fail to emerge. In such cases, there is an increase in the likelihood of offending as a consequence of impairments in making reasoned judgments.

ABI is also associated with a frequently reported range of neurocognitive impairments including difficulties with attention, memory, information processing, and the executive functions (including poor judgment). An obvious consequence of what is often permanent neurocognitive impairment is further interference in how the person with ABI perceives and interacts with the environment and those in it. For example, decreased awareness of emotional state, both one's own and others, is associated with a reduction in empathy, which can further alienate the person from the consequences of their behavior. The ability to inhibit behavior for immediate reward constitutes a significant risk factor for offending, as does poor social judgment.

Neurocognitive impairment also interacts with other adverse outcomes from ABI to further increase offending risk. Neurobehavioral disability (NBD) is particularly important, comprising elements of executive and attentional dysfunction, poor insight, problems of awareness and social judgment, labile mood, altered emotional expression, poor impulse control, and a range of personality changes. This complex pattern of disability is the product of interactions between damaged neural systems, neurocognitive impairment, and environmental factors, further influenced by premorbid personality traits and post-injury learning through environmental influences (Wood, 2001).

NBD imposes serious long-term social impairment and poor psychosocial outcomes (Kreutzer, Marwitz, Seel, & Serio, 1996), undermining the capacity for independent social behavior, compromising employment opportunities, and acting as a barrier to making and sustaining relationships, resulting in poor quality of life. NBD substantially increases likelihood of offending and contact with forensic services, especially when it primarily manifests as challenging behavior, comprising labile mood, impulsivity, low tolerance, misattribution, irritability, and poor temper control (Wood, 2001). Behavioral disorders are enduring and create severe difficulties for families (Winkler, Unsworth, & Sloan, 2006). Aggression is arguably the most overt and debilitating feature of NBD (Fleminger, Greenwood, & Oliver, 2006). It creates special challenges in rehabilitation units and imposes constraints upon rehabilitation potential (Burke, Wesolowski, & Lane, 1988), persists for many years after injury (Kelly, Brown, Todd, & Kremer, 2008), and tends to get worse over time (Brooks et al., 1987).

Prevalence of ABI Among Offenders

Recent reviews (e.g., Shiroma, Ferguson, & Pickelsimer, 2010; Williams, 2012) highlight that ABI is over represented among offender populations, with ABI, rates among offender groups typically occurring in between 50% and 80% of cases. Results from two recent UK studies are especially informative. Williams et al. (2010), for example, investigated 200 prison inmates finding that 60% self-reported at least one TBI, where 6.6% was rated "moderate" or "severe." Violence was the principal cause. Differences between prisoners who did/did not self-report TBI were evident. Those with self-reported TBI received their first custodial sentence on average five years earlier, and had more prison sentences, compared to those who did not self-report TBI. Pitman, Haddlesey, and Fortescue (2013) screened 613 inmates for TBI. Responses suggested that nearly half (47%) sustained TBI with 8% potentially having incurred "severe" injury. Two or more TBI's were reported by 71%, with the average age at first injury being 18 years. Most (73%) incurred injury prior to their first offence, suggesting a link between TBI and offending. Nearly half of the sample (43%) had been in prison five times or more. While respondents in the TBI group performed significantly worse on measures of cognitive function than the non-TBI group. Anxiety and depression in the TBI group was three times higher, and members of this group were more likely to have been unemployed, to have been sent to prison more frequently, and to have spent more years in prison than non-TBI prisoners.

Studies suggest TBI is characteristic of offender groups: mental health problems and drug and alcohol misuse are also highly prevalent. For example, a meta-analysis by Fazel and Danesh (2002) demonstrated that psychosis and major depression were seven times more likely in TBI offenders, and antisocial personality disorder ten times more likely, than the general population. While increased prevalence of mental health and addiction problems cannot conclusively be attributed to ABI, a proportion certainly can be attributed to TBI (Williams & Evans, 2003). However, regardless of causation, drug and alcohol abuse and mental health problems are more evident among offender groups who have sustained TBI than those that have not (Walker, Hiller, M., Staton, & Leukefeld, 2003).

Aggression as a consequence of ABI is frequent and pervasive. In a review of the literature, Tateno, Jage, and Robinson (2003) found aggression following TBI varied from 11% to 96%. In their own study, Tateno et al. found that a third of their sample had engaged in significant aggressive behavior within six months of injury. Baguley,

Cooper, and Felmingham (2006) investigated outcome among TBI survivors at six months, two years, and five years post-injury. At each follow-up period, 25% met the authors' criteria for "significant" aggressive behavior, and they concluded it was a frequent and long-term sequela of TBI. Kelly et al. (2008) investigated challenging behavior profiles of people with ABI in the community. Aggression was prolific in that nearly 86% had been verbally aggressive, 41.1% had assaulted other people, and 35.3% had been physically aggressive. This study also highlighted longevity of aggression, as mean time since injury was 8.7 years at the time of investigation and as long as 41.3 years.

Associations between ABI, aggression and offending have also been demonstrated. In large scale population studies in Sweden, it has been demonstrated that TBI was a moderate risk factor for violence (Fazel et al., 2009), and that violent crime was over-represented among people with TBI compared to the general population (8.8% versus 3%) (Fazel et al., 2011). Aggression is the most frequent form of challenging behavior requiring admission to services organized specifically to manage severe NBD. For example, Alderman (2007) reported 5,548 incidents of aggression by 108 participants in one such program over a 14-day period, including 729 physical assaults.

The Neurobiology of Impulsivity and Aggression

In order to effectively manage behavior, it is essential to understand its origins to determine if psychological interventions are appropriate and will be effective. As briefly outlined earlier (and more fully discussed in Chapter 4) immature brain systems promote novelty-seeking behavior, increase risk of impulsive action, and, as a consequence, ABI. Anterior brain lesions are strongly implicated in offending, especially violent criminal behavior characterized by impulsive aggression (Brower & Price, 2001).

Neuroanatomical correlates of impulsivity and aggression include the orbitofrontal cortex and its connections with other brain structures. Damage to the orbitotemporal–limbic feedback loop is particularly implicated, in which the inhibitory function of the cortex over the amygdala is disrupted, depriving the cognitive functions of any ability to suppress instinctive emotional reactions (Starkstein & Robinson, 1991). Aggression with this etiology has clear antecedents (Medd & Tate, 2000). Reduction in inhibitory control probably accounts for increased aggressive behavior in people with a premorbid history of violence (Dyer, Bell, McCann, & Rauch, 2006). A recent review highlighted that in addition to neuroanatomical drivers of post-ABI aggression, origins of this behavior are complex and multivariate and include neurocognitive impairment, premorbid personality traits, and post-injury learning (see Alderman, Knight, & Brooks, 2013).

The diverse, complex etiology of behavior change has resulted in numerous attempts to produce taxonomies of factors that underpin ABI aggression, distinguishing explanations that have a predominantly neurological basis from those attributable to neurocognitive impairment (Wood, 2001). For example, violent behavior attributable to reduced inhibitory control has different origins and characteristics to aggression that is a behavioral sequela of electrophysiological disturbance known as the episodic dyscontrol syndrome (EDS) (see Box 24.2), which is one of the post-traumatic temporo-limbic disorders, where aggression is seen as "out of character," occurring in the absence of obvious provoking antecedents.

> **Box 24.2** Episodic dyscontrol syndrome (EDS)
>
> A manifestation of neurologically mediated aggression, EDS comprises one of the posttraumatic temporo-limbic disorders characterized by paroxysmal changes that reflect behavioral sequelae of electrophysiological disturbance in the brain. EDS aggression tends to be brief, clear-cut, and "out of character," without obvious triggers or proceeded by minor frustration to which the magnitude of the behavioral response is grossly out of proportion. The individual, often exhausted after an episode of aggression, will characteristically sleep, and on awakening exhibit great remorse for their behavior. Depressed mood post-incident is common.

Aggression is also highly influenced by neurocognitive impairment, especially executive function disorders, which also have strong neuroanatomical correlates with anterior brain structures. Difficulties are most pronounced when confronted with novel situations requiring application of problem-solving skills; in at least one study, patients with decision-making impairments were found to be more aggressive when compared to other groups (Fellows & Farah, 2007). Reduced ability to initiate use of preserved abilities, monitor performance, and utilize feedback effectively to regulate behavior results in lack of "error awareness," observed as disinhibition, impulsiveness, and poor response to cues. Poor coping can result in frustration and aggression through concurrent difficulties with response inhibition (Alderman, 2003).

Another enduring characteristic of NBD (i.e., reduced ability to empathize with victims of violent behavior), also contributes to aggression and criminality. Increased egocentricity is also frequently reported by relatives of people with ABI and is further enhanced when injury predated development of complex neural networks involving a number of brain areas that underpin empathic function (Shamay-Tsoory, 2004). Diminished empathy is a frequent legacy of ABI and hence underpins many neurobehavioral disorders. It is also associated with lack of tact and social discretion, poor awareness of others' emotional needs and sensitivities, and development of egocentric, self-centered attitudes (Wood & Williams, 2008). People with poor empathic skills encounter many difficulties in their daily lives, particularly in social relationships. Lack of empathy results in difficulties anticipating others feelings and reactions, and reduced awareness of how they come across to others, which further undermine relationships. Potential offenders are less likely to take into account the impact of their behavior on others, especially when immediate needs can be met through impulsive aggression. It is interesting to note that persistent offenders are often described as impulsive and lacking empathy (Williams, 2012), leading to speculation that behavior is attributable to ABI. The effect of the environment is also vitally important, including interaction with carers and clinicians. Post-injury learning is significant, especially when aggression serves an avoidance/escape function (Alderman, 2001). We will now examine the assessment of ABI.

Assessment of ABI

The presence of NBD renders the ABI population inherently "risky." At one extreme, disorders of drive and motivation result in self-neglect; at the other, very challenging behavior, especially violence, results in multiple risks. Safely managing this risk is a key priority. This need is further highlighted as there is evidence the frequency of violence is much higher than is generally reported in forensic mental illness studies. For example, in a sample of 30 patients in a forensic psychiatric hospital, most of whom had a diagnosis of a schizophrenic related disorder, Wilson, Desmarais, Nicholls, and Brink (2010) reported half engaged in at least one episode of challenging behavior over the course of 12 months and, of the 33 incidents recorded, most comprised aggression. Similarly, mean frequency of physical assaults and verbal aggression found in 44 patients in a forensic hospital over 6 months was 0.93 and 3.79 respectively (Grey et al., 2011). In marked contrast, almost 75% of the ABI sample studied by Alderman (2007) had been aggressive at least once in just 14 days. These data further talk up the potential value of utilizing formal risk assessment procedures with ABI offenders. Therefore, in the rest of this section approaches to the assessment of neurocognitive impairment, challenging behaviors, and risk assessment for harmful behaviors will be described.

Assessment of neurocognitive impairment

Understanding neurocognitive impairment is essential in planning how ABI violence can be effectively managed. Cognitive systems form an interface with the world, interpreting experience and managing behavioral output. Deficits in attention, memory, and the executive functions have potentially catastrophic impact. For example, lack of inhibitory control has been attributed to inadequate self-monitoring because of underlying difficulties in maintaining attention, resulting in impulsive, inappropriate social behavior (Alderman, 1996). Similarly, severe memory impairment and executive dysfunction can further degrade ability to attend effectively to environmental stimuli, undermining social cognition, imposing constraints on responding adaptively to change in the social environment. Lack of insight underpins poor motivation to change. Both inefficient processing of cues and reduced awareness regarding consequences of behavior may result from monitoring impairment. A point made earlier regarding deficits to higher level executive functions are also strongly implicated in difficulties with problem solving, which is also associated with violent behavior in offenders with ABI.

Because neurocognitive impairment is strongly associated with challenging behavior, detailed neuropsychological examination is essential to completely inform formulation and treatment. It is beyond the scope of this chapter to attempt any more than to highlight this point and refer the reader to Goldstein and McNeil (2013) (see Recommended Reading section) for a comprehensive introduction to this area.

However, a note of caution is worthy regarding the fundamental need to utilize procedures and tests that actually measure what is intended on the part of the examiner. Performance on some tests administered in the traditional context of the consulting room has not been shown to be representative of how the abilities measured map onto performance in everyday life. Ecological validity is especially important, as neuropsychologists need to be certain that assessment procedures tap into the contexts they are interested in predicting ("representativeness"), and that scores arising from procedures accurately reflect performance of the variables of interest in those situations ("generalizability"). See Burgess et al. (2006) for an overview of this important issue. Practically, the requirement to demonstrate ecological validity has resulted in development of different approaches to neuropsychological examination, including assessment procedures conducted directly in situations of interest, for example, regarding higher level executive function deficits, the Multiple Errands Test and its variants (Dawson et al., 2009).

Further, ways of increasing appropriate service provision to ABI offenders is probably a far more difficult set of problems to manage than knowing what such a service should comprise. The most obvious starting point is to consider ways neurobehavioral rehabilitation can be further developed to take into account particular forensic needs, when these apply. As noted earlier, in addition to ABI, aggression and other challenging behavior may also be the product of a wider set of variables including pre-trauma history, poor mental health, and substance/alcohol misuse. For these patients, problems such as lack of ability to empathize with victims, problem-solving difficulties, and lifestyle choices may be especially pertinent in maintaining offending behavior and require additional inputs to address. Provision to meet these additional needs is required in existing neurobehavioral programs. Potential inputs from forensic psychology to further enhance effectiveness of neurobehavioral rehabilitation for ABI offenders includes "risk" assessment as well as treatment approaches used in forensic services. We will now examine these approaches in more detail.

Assessment of challenging behaviors

The operant model is a core component of neurobehavioral rehabilitation as post-injury learning has been found to be a significant contributor to ABI challenging behavior; in addition, as discussed above, neurocognitive impairment may result in reduced cue saliency in the environment, which may benefit from amplification to circumvent aggression. Detailed functional analysis of behavior, in conjunction with neuropsychological assessment, is a further key to unlocking understanding of behavior and delivering effective interventions. An operant theory of learning conceptualizes behavior as *operating* on the environment and being maintained by its consequences. An operant model therefore provides a conceptual framework and toolkit that enables a detailed analysis of behavior to help understand the function it serves, and how antecedents and contingencies in the environment contribute to its development and maintenance. Detailed analysis results in a formulation about behavior that has a direct link with devising effective interventions, thereby creating continuity between assessment and treatment. Knowledge regarding ABI and the complex origins of NBD further enhance understanding of how neurocognitive impairment and other factors contribute to maintaining violence and other challenging behavior.

Regarding assessment, the Overt Aggression Scale-Modified for Neurorehabilitation (OAS-MNR) (Alderman, Knight, & Morgan, 1997) was specifically developed for ABI using an operant conceptual framework to create a standardized method of reporting aggression that is both valid and reliable. It captures information regarding four types and four levels of severity of individual episodes of aggression, along with associated settings events, antecedents, and interventions. It has good inter-rater reliability and has been successfully employed in clinical work, research, outcome measurement, and service evaluation (Alderman, 2003; Alderman et al., 1999; Watson et al., 2001). While there are many measures of aggression, only the OAS-MNR, and an extended version of this (Giles & Mohr, 2007), have been specifically validated for use in neurorehabilitation. Employing the OAS-MNR, allows for a set of codes, which provides a shorthand means of capturing complex behavior sequences.

While "focal" measures such as the OAS-MNR yield the best quality and most sensitive information, in some settings it is not possible to capture every incident. Use of "global" assessment tools that provide an overview of behavior still make a useful contribution to assessment. The Overt Behavior Scale (OBS) (Kelly et al., 2006) was developed to record challenging behaviors displayed by people with ABI in community settings, including aggression. The St Andrew's-Swansea Neurobehavioral Scale (SASNOS) (Alderman, Wood, & Williams, 2011) consists of 49 items measuring five principal domains and 12 subdomains of NBD, differentiating between provocative behavior, irritability, and overt aggression. Both the OBS and SASNOS were conceptualized for ABI. Straightforward to administer and score, they provide a profile of strengths and weaknesses that aid rehabilitation planning, and have known psychometric properties that enable them to make valuable contributions to assessment, formulation, and determining outcome.

Risk assessment for harmful behaviors

The gold standard method of assessing risk of physical and sexual violence is through the use of actuarial and structured professional judgment (SPJ) tools, see Box 24.3 for a brief description of SPJ tools.

Box 24.3   Types of risk assessment

Predicting future occurrence of risk behaviors on the basis of unstructured clinical decision making relies entirely on the expertise, knowledge, and experience of clinicians. While being eminently flexible, this approach has been criticized because is not standardized and therefore vulnerable to important factors being missed. Actuarial risk assessments claim to predict the probability of future risk behaviors by statistically weighting risk variables using follow up data of recidivistic and non-recidivistic offenders and patients. Consequently, calculated risk scores are related to statistical reference data. This is a similar approach to how insurance companies use statistical data to appraise relevant future risk. However, this approach has been criticized on the basis of lack of practical utility, as it does not inform risk reduction strategies. Finally, tools created to enable the (SPJ approach were introduced to address the perceived limitations with both the previous approaches. SPJ tools are grounded in the theoretical, clinical, and empirical knowledge about violence. Items in SPJ tools prompt clinicians to consider how they contribute to risk, along with their experience and knowledge of the patient, and how risk can be managed.

Actuarial assessments provide an objective and algorithmic approach. In this type of assessment, a score is generated from answers to a number of questions. The score and subsequent likelihood of risk rating is based on data from known groups of recidivistic and non-recidivistic violent offenders. Additional items may also be selected rationally. In contrast, SPJ assessments are more individualized and guided by empirical, clinical, and legal factors through use of structured tools such as the Historical Clinical Risk-20 (HCR-20) (Douglas, Hart, Webster, & Belfrage, 2013). In this type of assessment, information gathering is guided by defined risk factors, as well as the assessor's knowledge. The HCR-20 was developed for use with individuals with mental illness or personality disorder. Consequently, research exploring the psychometric properties of the HCR-20 has been primarily undertaken in correctional, forensic, and civil psychiatric settings (Webster et al., 1997).

As highlighted here, there is plenty of evidence that confirms people with ABI are inherently "risky" and a little that clinicians underestimate this. Despite the growing popularity of SPJ tools in forensic and psychiatric settings, existing tools have not been validated with people with ABI. To begin to address this gap Alderman, Major, and Brooks (2016) evaluated the predictive validity of another well-known SPJ, the Short-Term Assessment of Risk and Treatability (START) (Webster et al., 2009) regarding aggressive behavior. Previous research has underpinned high associations between aggression and a range of variables; these are routinely captured using specific ABI outcome measures in neurobehavioral services and have been previously demonstrated to

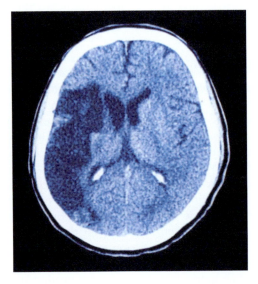

Acquired brain injury *Acquired brain injury occurs after birth and is not a consequence of a genetic or congenital disorder that had a sudden outset and is not progressive. Between 50% and 80% of offenders suffer from acquired brain injuries, a much higher prevalence than expected in the age-matched non-offending population. This is an example of a CT scan (i.e., three-dimensional X-ray) of a stroke patient. The white surrounding is an image of the bone: skull). The dark area on the left side of the image, the lesion, represents the area that was affected by the stroke (lack of fresh blood supply), which led to the death of brain cells. Based on the location of the lesion, this patient is likely to experience language and attention deficit, and be paralyzed on their right side.*

Source: © Puwadol Jaturawutthichai. Used under license from 123RF.

correlate highly with OAS-MNR recordings (Alderman, Wood, & Williams 2011). Alderman et al. sought to determine if START ratings were any more predictive of violence than those variables that are already known to underpin it. Results of hierarchical regression analysis suggested the START did not contribute any unique variance to prediction of OAS-MNR and that the best model was made from a combination of two existing ABI outcome measures, which included a proxy measure of aggression. The authors concluded that, while risk assessment in ABI would undoubtedly benefit from inclusion of SPJ tools, these need to be conceptualized for ABI, rather than imported from forensic psychiatry, in order to take into account fully the diverse and unique range of contributing factors to NBD. In the next section, we will describe approaches to rehabilitation for ABI.

Hence, the remainder of this chapter will consider how the different psychological conceptual frameworks, used in both neurorehabilitation and forensic settings, might be usefully bought together, we also discuss specific neurobiological therapies, and the potential benefits of theese are illustrated through a case study. For the sake of clarity, and given its high prevalence after ABI and dominance as a finding among offenders with ABI, the focus will be on aggression. However, issues highlighted will be equally applicable across the range of neurobehavioral disorders seen after ABI.

A Neurobehavioral Framework for Rehabilitation

A already noted there are clear links between ABI, violent behavior, and offending, especially when brain development is arrested at an early stage. It is also apparent that aggressive behavior disorders have complex origins, including neurocognitive impairment, reduced empathic function, environmental influences, mental health problems, and drug and alcohol abuse. Consequently, combinations of psychological interventions may be required to address different etiologies.

In a recent review by the current authors (Alderman, Knight, & Brooks, 2013) a pragmatic approach is promoted which illustrates the benefits of utilizing an appropriate conceptual framework to provide an overall understanding of violence. This further utilizes an assessment of behavior, devising a formulation to explain it, driving treatment plans, and determining efficacy. In this formulation, reference to "offending" is not made. While this may seem odd given its links with ABI, there is lack of consistency in how the "offender" label is applied to people who engage in violence post-ABI. In part, this further reflects the complex, multivariate causes of aggression. For example, some people acquire a violent history in the absence of ABI, which results in contact with forensic services and subsequently builds their profile as an "offender." This premorbid characteristic may lead to an increase in aggressive behavior following ABI as a consequence of reduced ability to tolerate frustration; while the pre-existing presence of an offender history may be more likely to lead to disposal of subsequent offences through the courts. Alternatively, people with no history of violence who are aggressive post-ABI may be more likely to be managed through psychiatric services. Of course, these two scenarios do not represent all the permutations in how violence is managed but do illustrate how classification as an "offender" can lead to underestimation of prevalence in the "non-offender" ABI population.

Alderman and Burgess (2003) illustrated this by showing where referrals to a specialized neurobehavioral program come from. The tendency was that up to three years after injury, the largest proportion came from physical rehabilitation units (41%). However, after three years this fell dramatically to less than 10%, as behavior was too difficult to be managed in placements ill equipped to manage NBD including aggression. While 9% were resident in forensic settings (prison, high secure hospital, regional secure unit), a third were admitted from a psychiatric facility. The point is that these patients all ended up being referred to specialized services for behavioral management, yet only a minority were categorized as offenders. This also infers that, while ABI is over represented in offender populations, the number of people with ABI who engage in violence is likely to be much higher than the former figures suggest, and indeed more consistent with the very high rates of aggression found as a general outcome of ABI highlighted earlier.

Greater numbers of people with ABI who are not badged as offenders may suggest why there is lack of evidence that existing brain injury rehabilitation programs utilize conceptual models that talk up "forensic" psychology approaches. It may also explain why ABI offenders do not benefit from rehabilitation programs designed for offending behavior, as illustrated by higher recidivism within this group. ABI as a mediator in offence behavior is not routinely considered in such programs; in addition, neurocognitive impairment, lack of insight and awareness, motivational disorders, and other aspects of NBD may in any case work to exclude prisoners with ABI, in much the same way as they do regarding other types of talking therapy (Alderman, 2003).

Of course, this is not to say that conceptual models of offending from forensic psychology have little to offer ABI therapies for aggression and other behaviors symptomatic of NBD; equally, established programs in forensic settings may well benefit from considering ABI issues, both in content and through how users engage meaningfully in such work.

Risk of violence associated with ABI in offender populations is especially associated with concurrent mental health problems, and substance and alcohol abuse problems. Psychological interventions necessarily target these, in conjunction with appropriate neuropsychiatric input if neurological causes are implicated. While violence reduction programs are employed in forensic settings (Wong & Gordon, 2013), evidence for interventions specifically designed to meet the needs of aggressive offenders with ABI are conspicuously absent. In contrast, the evidence base regarding psychological approaches to the management of NBD, including aggression, is comprehensive. Much is derived from highly specialized neurobehavioral programs, not forensic or prison settings. Interventions are primarily aimed at managing factors that maintain NBD in which no specific "forensic" variables are described. However, high numbers of violent offenders with ABI who are subject to repeated custodial sentences suggests there is an acute need for provision of rehabilitation programs that address not only neurobehavioral origins of aggression, but also a wider set of forensic drivers that maintain high risk of violence. To date, such programs have received little attention, perhaps not surprisingly given that recognition of ABI as a prolific characteristic of offender populations has only been relatively recently acknowledged (Williams, 2012).

Box 24.4 Neurocognitive constraints on talking therapies

Evidence highlights a clear need to develop rehabilitation programs that specifically address the needs of offenders with ABI, but what would these look like?

A starting point is to utilize existing psychological programmes employed in forensic services, which typically take the form of talking therapies.

However, in practice, neurocognitive impairments can considerably blunt the benefits typically associated with these including difficulties with: language, especially comprehension; attention, retention, and recall of new information; and executive function, particularly monitoring and problem solving. These result in variable, slow learning, requiring considerable modification of programmes and provision of additional support. Even then, poor generalization of programme benefits because of problems in independently recognizing when to apply new strategies undermines ability to effectively modify behavior.

Talking therapies (see Box 24.4 for neurocognitive constraints on these), particularly cognitive behavior therapy (CBT), have a proven evidence base in the management of violence (e.g., see Haddock, Barrowclough, Shaw, Dunn, Navaco, & Tarrier, 2009; Smeets, Leeijen, van der Molen, & Rommelse, 2014). CBT draws on an information processing model (Hawton, Salkovskis, Kirk, & Clark, 1989), which suggests how people perceive and interpret their experience alters and shapes their behavior. Bias or faulty processing of information may result in disorders of mood and behavior, including aggression. CBT attempts to help recipients understand links between beliefs, thinking, and behavior, identify thinking distortions, and help them generate rational interpretations of events. The "hypothesis testing" approach to therapy ideally results in a shift in how experience is perceived and with this replacement of distorted cognitive schema used to process information and change in belief systems. CBT is successfully employed with many clinical populations, covering a broad range of disorders (see Scott, 1997). CBT has been successfully applied to the management of anger in users of mental health services (Bradbury & Clarke, 2007) and has high face validity for treatment of similar difficulties in ABI, with "how to" manuals being available (O'Neill, 2006). While successful outcomes have been demonstrated regarding mood disorders (Arundine et al., 2012), the CBT evidence base for ABI challenging behavior is lacking. In that there are few case reports conducted with appropriate scientific rigor, and those that are report programs that required heavy modification and implementation over much longer periods than standard CBT treatments.

Challenges to implementing CBT include neurocognitive impairment, disorders of self-awareness, and severity of challenging behavior (Alderman, 2003). Accounts of group delivered CBT for managing aggression among people with ABI are more prolific (Walker, Nott, Doyle, Onus, McCarthy, & Baguley, 2010). Group treatment has obvious benefits for resource allocation, costs, and mutual support, so using this platform has appeal (Psalia & Gracey, 2009). However, inclusion criteria can be highly selective, including the need to be fully oriented, have good communication skills, have preserved ability to learn, be capable of attaining goals, cooperate with requests, have no drug/alcohol dependency, and no premorbid psychiatric history. Consequently, many people with ABI are excluded from such programs.

Multiple drivers of violence as a consequence of ABI also means interventions are necessarily tailored to meet individual needs. Aggression with primarily neurological underpinnings is unlikely to be amenable to management using CBT. For example, lesions to the orbitofrontal cortex and its rich network of connections with other brain structures have been implicated with aggressive behavior. The inhibitory function of the orbitotemporal–limbic feedback loop has previously been described. While it may prove possible to modify underlying belief systems using CBT and other talking therapies, damage to this structure may render expression of instinctive emotion beyond any suppressing control of willed intent. Likewise, other taxonomies of ABI aggression that have a neurological basis for aggression, including the aforementioned post-traumatic temporo-limbic disorders, are also unlikely to respond to psychological interventions. In these cases, neuropharmacological approaches, especially when used in conjunction with behavior modification interventions, have been promoted as the optimum strategies for violence reduction (Wood, 1987).

As a response to these constraints to participation in psychological therapies, as well as inadequate service provision for people with ABI and challenging behavior, specialist neurobehavioral rehabilitation provision became available in the UK in the latter part of the 20th century in which a behavioral management approach, based on operant learning theory, provided the main framework for intervention. The "organic" basis of many forms of challenging behavior, including aggression, was recognized. However, over time, the conceptual basis of neurobehavioral interventions evolved to incorporate constructs, theories, and procedures from cognitive, behavioral, and social psychology employed to promote acquisition and spontaneous use of functional and social skills to reduce social handicap. From a single unit, which comprised 16 beds, neurobehavioral services in the UK have evolved to provide several hundred beds through multiple care pathways defined by age, gender, and level of security (Alderman & Wood, 2013).

The conceptual underpinnings of neurobehavioral rehabilitation comprise a learning process that equips the person, as far as possible, with functional skills, cognitive abilities, and social behaviors lost through ABI, to maximize personal autonomy through enhancing the ability to apply skills spontaneously and adaptively (Wood & Worthington, 2001a; Wood & Worthington, 2001b). Structure is sustained through the physical environment, daily routine, input of a transdisciplinary team, and implementation of methods derived from learning theory. These create a prosthetic environment that increases awareness, improves motivation, shapes behavioral responses into acceptable forms, and optimizes capacity for social learning.

Neurobehavioral rehabilitation has characteristics that distinguish it from other forms of neurorehabilitation:

- It addresses problems that emerge at a post-acute stage of recovery
- While some services are hospital based they are also evident in community settings
- It is not a medical but a psychosocial (or neuropsychological) form of intervention
- Rehabilitation is delivered using a transdisciplinary team (TDT) approach in which goals are social, functional, and client centered

The way the clinical team is organized is especially important. Traditionally, rehabilitation is delivered by an interdisciplinary or multidisciplinary team. However, a TDT approach is ideally suited for optimizing service delivery to the complex, heterogeneous needs of people with ABI where input is provided from multiple disciplines working together, rather than separately. A TDT shares roles across disciplinary boundaries so that communication, interaction, and cooperation are maximized among team members. It is characterized by the commitment of its members to teach, learn, and work together to implement coordinated services. A key outcome of transdisciplinary working is the development of a mutual vision or "shared meaning" among the team. This results in a process of: 1) shared assessment and goal selection; 2) ongoing interaction enabling the entire team to pool and exchange information, knowledge, and skills, and work together cooperatively; and 3) role release, characterized by intervention strategies traditionally being delivered by specific disciplines instead being implemented by the entire team, under supervision of team members whose disciplines are normally accountable for those practices (King, Strachan, Tucker, Duwyn, Desserud, & Shillington, 2009).

Consequently, all team members are responsible for the attainment of all rehabilitation goals by delivering a consistent treatment program, which is not "session bound," providing multiple opportunities to encourage and reinforce new skills and abilities. The aim of rehabilitation is not simply to achieve socially functional behaviors but to help these behaviors become established as social habit patterns that increase their likelihood generalizing to other environments and improve potential for social independence. Regarding violence and ABI, Alderman and Wood (2013) confirmed that aggression is the most frequent form of challenging behavior likely to require admission to neurobehavioral services.

Individual interventions implemented within the therapeutic milieu provided through neurobehavioral rehabilitation rely heavily on methods derived from learning theory, especially operant conditioning, in the form of multicomponent programs utilizing both contingency management and positive behavior support (Alderman, Knight, & Brooks, 2013; Alderman & Wood, 2013). Behavioral methodologies are especially relevant in the management of post-ABI behavior disorders as they are able to create prosthetic structures that circumvent two major contributing factors, neurocognitive impairment and the environment (including acquisition of avoidance and escape behaviors).

Psychoeducational groups to aid understanding of brain injury, its impact, and outcomes are fundamental. Similarly, groups concerned with cognitive rehabilitation are essential to identify coping strategies to circumvent difficulties with problem solving, memory, and attention (Wilson, Gracey, Evans, & Bateman, 2009).

The combination of methods utilized within neurobehavioral rehabilitation is ideally suited to meeting complex needs by creating a therapeutic milieu generating a social climate that increases awareness, improves motivation, and establishes conditions that encourage success. The evidence base for neurobehavioral rehabilitation is principally drawn from single case studies, including reduction of aggression and risk of violence (Alderman et al., 2013; Alderman & Wood, 2013). Studies of group cohorts further support the longer-term benefits of neurobehavioral rehabilitation, including savings in care costs (Oddy & Ramos, 2013). Despite its efficacy it is recognized in the UK that there are not enough services to meet the need, and that the majority of offenders with ABI continue to receive custodial sentences instead of specialist neurorehabilitation that may drive down recidivism (Williams, 2012). UK Government statistics have confirmed a steady increase in the prison population in England and Wales since World War II, and in July 2016 the number was in excess of 85,000; the offence accounting for the largest proportion of prisoners (27%) was violence against the person (Allen & Dempsey, 2016). It is a sobering thought that projecting the prevalence rates of prisoners with ABI of 50% to 80% as summarized by Williams (2012) suggests that a significant proportion of offenders, especially those with a high risk of violence, may benefit from neurobehavioral rehabilitation but are not in receipt of this. Mapping of provision in the UK suggests the current establishment of approximately 400 beds, with the majority in the non-public sector, clearly implies existing provision is inadequate.

Treatment Approaches for ABI

It is beyond the scope of this chapter to describe in detail a complete range of forensic treatment approaches that could usefully contribute to the content of neurobehavioral rehabilitation programs. However, brief notes on several that have particular relevance will be mentioned. The first is relapse prevention (RP), which has historically served as the dominant approach in managing risk of repeat violence. RP is mainly concerned with identifying and then planning management of high-risk situations. RP can also include supporting the individual to gain insight into their own offence chain, with the goal of future successful management of high-risk scenarios. The second approach is the risk-need-responsivity (RNR) model (Andrews & Bonta, 1995), which outlines treatment need according to therapeutic principles. This includes the risk principle (the higher the risk, the more intensive the treatment), the need principle (targeting criminogenic needs), and the responsivity need (ensuing that the intervention is accessible). The RP/RNR approach has been challenged within the literature. Ward, Mann, and Gannon (2007) criticized the RP/RNR model because of concerns regarding lack of guidance on engagement and motivation. The good lives model (GLM) (Ward & Stewart, 2003) was originally formulated as a positive psychological rehabilitation approach for sexual offenders and subsequently utilized in the treatment of a range of offending behaviors. GLM focuses on the individual's strengths and goals as a way of reducing risk. In summary, GLM assumes that individuals seek "goods" (e.g., excellence in agency or excellence in work and play) and offending occurs when internal or external resources are not available to meet these in adaptive ways.

More recently, the Violence Reduction Program (VRP) has been advocated as an approach that focuses on individual strengths and concurrent risk reduction work, which together build a profile of pro-social behaviors (Wong & Gordon, 2013). This model recognizes that drivers of violence are non-homogenous and that a "one size fits all" approach is inadequate. It incorporates key principles of offender rehabilitation from a number of theoretical and evidence-based approaches including multi-systemic therapy, aggression replacement therapy, RP, the transtheoretical model of change, and motivational interviewing. The program is delivered through groups and individual work, at a rate based on client responsivity. Like neurobehavioral rehabilitation, VRP provides a therapeutic milieu that promotes a positive social climate and thus a vehicle for change. VRP utilizes both social learning principles and CBT approaches. Its effectiveness with ABI offenders has not been reported but incorporation of CBT probably places some limitations on its potential. The authors acknowledge that individuals with cognitive problems may require shorter but more frequent sessions, but this remains untested. Nevertheless, the holistic approach, similarities with neurobehavioral rehabilitation, and provision of a forensic toolkit of different approaches suggest VRP may have some potential in the management of post-ABI violence. As suggested, supplementing neurobehavioral rehabilitation with ideas and methods derived from conceptual frameworks drawn from forensic psychology provides a promising starting point for reducing risk and recidivism for violent ABI offenders. This will now be illustrated by Case Study 24.1.

Case Study 24.1 Reducing risk and recidivism for violent ABI offenders

Background

BD sustained a TBI at age nine as a result of a road traffic accident. His score on the Initial Glasgow Coma Scale (Teasdale & Jennett, 1974) (3/15) categorized TBI as "severe." Neuroimaging revealed evidence of focal damage to anterior brain structures, notably the prefrontal cortex and anterior temporal lobe. BD required neurosurgical intervention and a portion of the left frontal lobe was excised. He remained in hospital for one month. As for BD's early years (prior to the age of nine), all developmental milestones were met on time, and he attended mainstream school. Academic performance was "average" and there were no concerns with his ability to make and sustain friendships with peers.

After his accident, BD returned to mainstream education, but he was reported as having difficulty keeping up with peers, both socially and academically. At the age of 14, BD began to use illegal substances and alcohol to cope with low mood associated with peer rejection. He engaged in petty crime, including shoplifting, to fund his habit and, although he was never charged, he did receive multiple police cautions. BD's family reported he was verbally and physically aggressive to his siblings and parents. At the age of 15, BD physically assaulted a male pupil at school. There appeared to be no obvious trigger to this incident, but BD later reported that his peer had looked at him in the "wrong" way. Similar incidents of physical aggression towards other pupils followed, resulting in BD being expelled from school.

At the age of 16 BD physically assaulted a male guest at a family wedding. He stated this guest had been served before him at the bar and that he was "annoyed" as he believed he was next in the queue. He was arrested, charged with grievous bodily harm, and received a 12-month community rehabilitation order. At 18 years of age, BD was physically aggressive to a male neighbor who had complained to the authorities about noise from the family home. BD punched his neighbor in the head when passing him in the street, for which he was arrested, charged, and received a supervision order. He breached his conditions on several occasions and served two short prison sentences. At aged 21, while serving a third custodial term following further breach of his supervision order, concerns were raised regarding verbal aggression towards prison officers and physical assaults on prisoners. He was subsequently referred to a neurobehavioral rehabilitation service.

Assessment

Following admission, BD's aggressive behavior was monitored using the OAS-MNR. Frequency of aggression during the first four weeks was erratic. Behaviors ranged from shouting and swearing at staff, to threats of violence and incidents of physical aggression towards staff and patients. These behaviors were not associated with formal therapy sessions and occurred in the absence of any obvious antecedents. Formal tests administered as part of a neuropsychological assessment suggested his general level of cognitive functioning fell within the "average" range: there were no relative strengths or weaknesses in his profile. Performance on tests of memory was unremarkable, with scores falling within "average" limits. Assessment of executive functions in the context of the consulting room also proved unexceptional.

In contrast, other measures of executive skills were indicative of impairment. BD and clinicians working closely with him completed the Dysexecutive Questionnaire (DEX) (Burgess, Alderman, Emslie, Evans, & Wilson, 1996). This scale consists of 20 items that reflect characteristics of impaired executive functioning, rated on a four-point scale for prevalence/severity, with separate versions for both the person with ABI (self) and others who know them well (Burgess et al., 1996). Comparison of "self" and "other" ratings can help determine difficulties with insight. Clinicians' ratings of BD highlighted observed difficulties with inhibition, impulsivity, and problem solving. BD did not rate himself as having any of these difficulties, suggesting limited insight. Further investigation of BD's problems was undertaken through neuropsychological assessment, in which his performance on tests of executive function fell well below the range expected from neurologically healthy controls.

The SASNOS was completed by the TDT to measure symptoms of NBD and associated social difficulties. As shown in Figure 24.1, clinicians' ratings of BD fell below the "normal" range (less than 40) for the domains of interpersonal behavior, aggression, and inhibition. BD rated him in the expected range for neurologically healthy controls across all five neurobehavioral disability domains on the SASNOS, providing further evidence of limited insight.

Formulation

As BD's ABI resulted in catastrophic damage to anterior brain structures at the age of nine, it was hypothesized that trauma at this age had inevitably disrupted neurodevelopmental maturation of frontal brain systems. While results of cognitive tests administered in the context of the consulting room were unremarkable, other assessment measures reflected executive function impairments consistent with the damage sustained. It was further hypothesized that neurodevelopmental disruption underpinned observed difficulties with expression of emotion, social perception/attribution, and tolerance. Observational recording measures

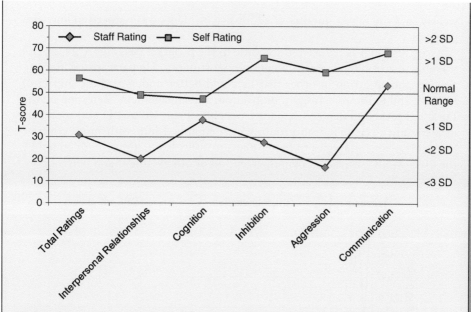

Figure 24.1 Overall and principal domain T-scores from SANOS, reflecting perceived levels of neurobehavioral disability as rated separately by BD and the TDT.

captured the detail of BD's aggressive behavior. Typically, there was no observed escalation when such aggressive behaviors occurred, with incidents being short lived and BD calming down quickly. Aggression was more likely to occur in low-demand situations, where little was expected of him, in the absence of staff prompting him to undertake specific tasks. Instead, his behavior appeared to be stimulus bound, dependent on external cues (such as his immediate environment and staff), and misperception of others intent and actions.

Intervention

BD's lack of insight, neurocognitive impairment, and unwillingness to engage when first admitted to the unit, constrained his engagement in talking therapies. Consequently, neurobehavioral rehabilitation emphasized environmental controls and social learning principles. Using information collected during his assessment, and a subsequent formulation, led to the implementation of an individual needs-led neurobehavioral program to reduce BD's aggression. This comprised of a structured timetable of therapeutic and leisure activity, including taking part in a "Differential reinforcement of low rates of behavior" program (Alderman & Knight, 1997). BD received structured feedback throughout the day, and had the opportunity to earn a daily reinforcer of his choice if his number of aggressive incidents did not exceed a predefined target. This target was initially calibrated by reviewing the OAS-MNR recordings, and was set at a level that ensured success when the program began. It was subsequently reviewed weekly, and the target number of aggressive incidents was reduced in line with progress.

As aggression was reduced in response to the program (see Figure 24.2), BD was able to access further rehabilitation opportunities. He participated in a psychoeducational group in order that he could better understand the impact of his ABI, and to improve insight, motivation, and engagement. Retesting on the DEX and SASNOS demonstrated the benefits of this work. BD also took part in a cognitive rehabilitation group, which equipped him with more effective problem-solving strategies to better manage difficult situations (highlighted by the OAS-MNR), mediated by misperception of others' intent and behavior.

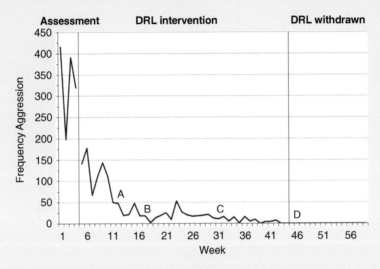

Figure 24.2 Reduction in frequency of aggression as measured using the OAS-MNR
Note: "A" – psychoeducational and cognitive rehabilitation groups commenced; "B" – individual GLM assessment and goals initiated; "C" – moved into transitional living flat and began community work; "D" – discharged into own flat.

BD also completed a GLM assessment. Consequently, he reflected on how he had sought to achieve GLM "goods" around the time of his index offence, and he was able to set goals on how to achieve these needs in the future in more adaptive ways. Goal setting was supported by TDT working. These goals included securing a voluntary work placement and engagement in individual substance misuse work. As further progress was made, BD utilized unescorted leave in the community and secured a voluntary work placement in a local café. His independence and autonomy further increased as he took the opportunity to live in a transitional apartment within the neurobehavioral unit. Eighteen months after admission, BD was discharged to an apartment in the community. At a 12-month follow up, he was successfully maintained in his apartment and he was working in a part-time non-skilled job, with minimal support. No contact with police or aggressive behavior had taken place since discharge.

Case Study 24.1 illustrates how a history of offending behavior typically develops following ABI. There was no evidence to suggest criminality would have evolved if it had not been for the massive disruption to neurobehavioral development, neurocognitive impairment, and subsequent emergence of severe NBD attributable to brain trauma. The case also illustrates how a neurobehavioral approach to managing aggression is applied and how additional inputs from forensic psychology can potentially complement this. While the benefits of using the HCR-20 as a guide to rehabilitation in an ABI population are unknown, GLM seems useful.

Conclusions

It has been noted that ABI is very characteristic of offender populations. It is associated with earlier onset of offending; more frequent use of custodial sentences compared to non-ABI offenders suggests that offence behaviors are not only persistent but more serious too. These are further compounded by mental health and drug and alcohol misuse issues, which themselves are inflamed by the consequences of ABI. Violence and aggression are especially prevalent among offenders with ABI.

Psychological therapies for the management of post-ABI aggression, as part of a wider constellation of pervasive and disabling neurobehavioral disorders have been discussed. To date, such programs have received little attention, perhaps not surprisingly given that recognition of ABI as a prolific characteristic of offender populations has only been recently acknowledged (Williams, 2012).While neurobehavioral rehabilitation, a psychosocial model of intervention, has a proven evidence base in the management of NBD, it has been argued that this form of therapy is not routinely available to offenders with ABI, yet it is this group who have the highest rate of recidivism and spend the longest time in prison. There is no evidence base regarding efficacy of violence reduction and other programs conceptualized for use in forensic and psychiatric settings with ABI offenders, but given the tendency for this group to reoffend outcomes appear to be poor. Neurocognitive impairment and other aspects of NBD, including poor insight, compromise the integrity of CBT approaches, which may be one reason why the evidence base is lacking.

It has also been that argued existing therapies addressing traditional "forensic issues" are not universally applicable for all ABI "offenders," as acquiring this label can be a matter of luck regarding which agency picks up their management. Alternatively, a forensic history can predate and indeed predispose ABI, in which case identifying and modifying frameworks, tools, and methods from forensic psychology, and integrating these within neurobehavioral rehabilitation, is highly desirable. More research is required to fully understand the needs of ABI offenders and what psychological therapies are required. In the meantime, what follows are some potentially key messages for consideration.

Implications for practice

Offending behavior needs to be conceptualized as being symptomatic of wider neurobehavioral disability acquired as a result of brain trauma and, in the case of young people, arrested neurodevelopment.

ABI does not discriminate, while having an offending history may increase risk of injury, this will not apply to all. There is currently inadequate screening for ABI among offender populations and needs arising from this are not being adequately addressed, resulting in repeat offending. It is also important to be wary of the implications of the "offender" and "forensic" labels when applied to people with ABI – there is a lack of consistency in how they are "earned."

We should not rely solely on psychiatric diagnoses, tools, and measures when working with people with ABI – consider assets developed specifically for this population, such as the OAS-MNR, OBS, and SASNOS. Don't assume current SPJ tools work well or add anything new to predicting risk of violence in ABI – bespoke measures conceptualized for this population are required. Also, don't assume that existing offender programs for violence reduction and management of other risks work well for people with ABI – the increased probability of repeat offending suggests the opposite.

People with ABI can be inherently "risky" as a result of neurobehavioral disability, the origins of which are often permanent – these include neurocognitive impairment, poor insight, variable motivation, diminished empathy, labile mood, impulsivity, low tolerance, misattribution, irritability, and poor temper control.

A pragmatic approach to psychological intervention conducted within an appropriate conceptual framework used to underpin treatment is recommended that pursues a structured approach emphasizing the clear but overlapping stages of assessment, formulation, intervention, and outcome measurement. Do make sure neuropsychological procedures and tests actually measure what you think they do. Psychological "talking therapies," such as CBT, require substantial modification when applied to ABI – neurocognitive and neurological underpinnings of violence may greatly undermine efficacy.

Neurobehavioral rehabilitation has a proven evidence base, resulting in good clinical outcomes and reduced care costs – but this needs to be further evolved to include forensic predictors of offence behavior when this is indicated. Neuropsychological interventions to circumvent or limit neurocognitive predictors of offending behavior should be made available (e.g., problem-solving group). Operant learning approaches, including contingency management and positive behavior support methods, are effective in reducing ABI challenging behavior, including risk of violence and aggression.

There needs to be greater collaboration between neurobehavioral rehabilitation and offender/forensic services to develop inclusive conceptual models and effective treatment programs for ABI offenders. Provision for neurobehavioral rehabilitation is insufficient to meet the need – offenders are typically sentenced to custodial sentences and are the most likely group to offend again.

Recommended Reading

Alderman, N., Davies, J. A., Jones, C., & McDonnell, P. (1999). Reduction of severe aggressive behavior in acquired brain injury: Case studies illustrating clinical use of the OAS-MNR in the management of challenging behaviors. *Brain Injury, 13*, 669–704. *This paper presents three case studies to illustrate how the OAS-MNR is used in the assessment of aggression following ABI, in the formulation process, and in tracking efficacy of the interventions subsequently employed to manage behavior. Furthermore, the case studies demonstrate how neurocognitive impairments are considered in the assessment and formulation stages and the role they play in the maintenance of aggressive behavior disorders after ABI. These cases also demonstrate the efficacy of neurobehavioral rehabilitation, the importance given in this process to learning theory, and the person-centered nature of intervention design and implementation.*

Alderman, N., Knight, C., & Brooks, J. (2013). Rehabilitation approaches to the management of aggressive behavior disorders after acquired brain injury. *Brain Impairment, Special Issue: State of the art reviews on mental health in traumatic brain injury, 14,* 5–20. *This review provides a complete explanation of the pragmatic approach taken regarding management of NBD, and aggression in particular. This utilizes the stages of: 1) assessment, where information concerning behavior of interest is collected; 2) formulation, where this information is interpreted using an appropriate conceptual framework for the purpose of understanding and deriving hypotheses about behavior; 3) intervention, where treatment plans are compiled driven by the formulation and informed by the conceptual framework employed; and 4) evaluation, where effectiveness of intervention is determined, and decisions made regarding changing, maintaining, or withdrawing treatment.*

Alderman, N., Knight, C., & Morgan, C. (1997). Use of a modified version of the Overt Aggression Scale in the measurement and assessment of aggressive behaviors following brain injury. *Brain Injury, 11,* 503–523. *This paper describes the OAS-MNR, an observational recording measure that enables objective assessment of the frequency and severity of verbal aggression, and physical aggression towards objects, self or others. The OAS-MNR provides a consistent and reliable shorthand means of capturing complex behaviors, including setting events and antecedents of aggression, and interventions used to manage it. Data contribute to functional analysis, tracking of interventions, and monitoring long-term outcome. The OAS-MNR has excellent psychometric properties for use with an ABI population and continues to be cited in publications regarding clinical interventions, research, and audit.*

Williams, H. (2012). *Repairing shattered lives: Brain injury and its implications for criminal justice.* Report published by the Barrow Cadbury Trust on behalf of the Transition to Adulthood Alliance. Retrieved from http://yss.org.uk/wp-content/uploads/2012/10/Repairing-Shattered-Lives_Report.pdf. *This paper provides compelling reading that presents a comprehensive review of the international literature and considers the implications of the role played by ABI in both offending behavior and its rehabilitation. Regardless of country, the message is clear that ABI has assumed almost epidemic levels within prison settings and yet remains a "silent epidemic" as screening programs are almost non-existent. Current rehabilitation programs fail to consider ABI and rates of recidivism within this group remain high. The messages from this publication are clear: screening for ABI among offenders in prison is a priority, prison staff need training regarding the condition and its consequences, and rehabilitation programs need to be put into place that take into account neurocognitive impairment and other chronic outcomes associated with ABI.*

References

Alderman, N. (1996). Central executive deficit and response to operant conditioning methods. *Neuropsychological Rehabilitation, 6,* 161–186.

Alderman, N. (2001). Management of challenging behavior. In R. L l. Wood, & T. McMillan (Eds.), *Neurobehavioral disability and social handicap following traumatic brain injury* (pp. 175–207). Hove: Psychology Press.

Alderman, N. (2003). Contemporary approaches to the management of irritability and aggression following traumatic brain injury. *Neuropsychological Rehabilitation, 13,* 211–240.

Alderman, N. (2007). Prevalence, characteristics and causes of aggressive behavior observed within a neurobehavioral rehabilitation service: Predictors and implications for management. *Brain Injury, 21,* 891–911.

Alderman, N., & Burgess, P. W. (2003). Assessment and rehabilitation of the dysexecutive syndrome. In R. Greenwood, M. P. Barns, T. McMillan, & T. Ward (Eds.). *Neurological Rehabilitation* (pp. 387–402). Hove: Psychology Press.

Alderman, N., Davies, J. A., Jones, C., & McDonnell, P. (1999). Reduction of severe aggressive behavior in acquired brain injury: Case studies illustrating clinical use of the OAS-MNR in the management of challenging behaviors. *Brain Injury, 13*, 669–704.

Alderman, N., & Knight, C. (1997). The effectiveness of DRL in the management and treatment of severe behavior disorders following brain injury. *Brain Injury, 11*, 79–101.

Alderman, N., Knight, C., & Brooks, J. (2013). Rehabilitation approaches to the management of aggressive behavior disorders after acquired brain injury. *Brain Impairment, Special Issue: State of the art reviews on mental health in traumatic brain injury, 14*, 5–20.

Alderman, N., Knight, C., & Morgan, C. (1997). Use of a modified version of the Overt Aggression Scale in the measurement and assessment of aggressive behaviors following brain injury. *Brain Injury, 11*, 503–523.

Alderman, N., Major, G., & Brooks, J. (2016). What can structured professional judgment tools contribute to management of neurobehavioral disability? Predictive validity of the Short-Term Assessment of Risk and Treatability (START) in acquired brain injury. *Neuropsychological Rehabilitation (March)*, 1–18. doi.org/10.1080/09602011.2016.1158115.

Alderman, N., & Wood, R. Ll. (2013). Neurobehavioral approaches to the rehabilitation of challenging behavior. *NeuroRehabilitation, 32*, 761–770.

Alderman, N., Wood, R. Ll., & Williams, C. (2011). The development of the St Andrew's-Swansea Neurobehavioral Outcome Scale: Validity and reliability of a new measure of neurobehavioral disability and social handicap. *Brain Injury, 25*, 83–100.

Allen, G., & Dempsey, N. (2016). *Prison population statistics* (standard note SN/SG/4334, last updated 4 July 2016). London: House of Commons.

Andrews, D. A., & Bonta, J. (1995). *The level of service inventory-revised*. Toronto: Multi-Health Systems.

Arundine, A., Bradbury, C. L., Dupuis, K., Dawson, D. R., Ruttan, L. A., & Green, R. E. (2012). Cognitive behavior therapy after acquired brain injury: Maintenance of therapeutic benefits at 6 months post-treatment. *Journal of Head Trauma Rehabilitation, 27*, 104–112.

Baguley, I. J., Cooper, J., & Felmingham, K. (2006). Aggressive behavior following traumatic brain injury: how common is common? *Journal of Head Trauma Rehabilitation, 21*, 45–56.

Bradbury, K. E., & Clarke, I. (2007). Cognitive behavioral therapy for anger management: Effectiveness in adult mental health services. *Behavioral and Cognitive Psychotherapy, 35*, 201–208.

Brooks, D. N., McKinlay, W., Symington, C., Beattie, A., & Campsie, L. (1987). The effects of severe head injury upon patient and relative within seven years of injury. *Journal of Head Trauma Rehabilitation, 2*, 1–13.

Brower, M. C., & Price, B. H. (2001). Neuropsychiatry of frontal lobe dysfunction in violent and criminal behavior: a critical review. *Journal of Neurology, Neurosurgery and Psychiatry, 71*, 720–726.

Burgess, P. W., Alderman, N., Emslie, H., Evans, J. J., & Wilson, B. A. (1996). *The Dysexecutive Questionnaire*. In B. A. Wilson, N. Alderman, P. W. Burgess, H. Emslie, & J. J. Evans (Eds.), *Behavioral assessment of the dysexecutive syndrome* (p. 7). Bury St Edmunds: Thames Valley Test Company.

Burgess, P. W., Alderman, N., Forbes, C., Costello, A., Coates, L. M-A., Dawson, D. R., ... Channon, S. (2006). The case for the development and use of "ecologically valid" measures of executive function in experimental and clinical neuropsychology. *Journal of the International Neuropsychological Society, 12*, 194–209.

Burke, H. H., Wesolowski, M. D., & Lane, I. (1988). A positive approach to the treatment of aggressive brain injured clients. *International Journal of Rehabilitation Research, 11*, 235–241.

Dawson, D. R., Anderson, N. D., Burgess, P., Cooper, E., Krpan, K. M., & Stuss, D. T. (2009). Further development of the Multiple Errands Test: Standardized scoring, reliability, and ecological validity for the Baycrest version. *Archives of Physical Medicine and Rehabilitation, 90* (11 Suppl 1), 41–51.

Dolan, M., & Doyle, M. (2000). Violence risk prediction. *British Journal of Psychiatry, 177*, 303–311.

Douglas, K. S., Hart, S. D., Webster, C. D., & Belfrage, H. (2013). *HCR-20V3: Assessing risk of violence – user guide*. Burnaby, Canada: Mental Health, Law, and Policy Institute, Simon Fraser University.

Dyer, K. F. W., Bell, R., McCann, J., & Rauch, R. (2006). Aggression after traumatic brain injury: Analysing socially desirable responses and the nature of aggressive traits. *Brain Injury, 20*, 1163–1173.

Fazel, S., & J. Danesh. (2002). Serious mental disorder in 23,000 prisoners: A systematic review of 62 surveys. *The Lancet, 359*, 545–550.

Fazel, S., Philipson, J., Gardiner, L., Merritt, R. K., & Grann, M. (2009). Neurological disorders and violence: A systematic review and meta-analysis with a focus on epilepsy and traumatic brain injury. *Journal of Neurology, 256*, 1591–1602.

Fazel, S., Lichtenstein, P., Grann, M., & Langstrom, N. (2011). Risk of violent crime in individuals with epilepsy and traumatic brain injury: A 35-year Swedish population study. *PLoS Medicine, 8*, e1001150. http://journals.plos.org/plosmedicine/article?id=10.1371/journal.pmed.1001150

Fellows, L. K., & Farah, M. J. (2007). The role of ventromedial prefrontal cortex in decision making: Judgment under uncertainty or judgment per se? *Cerebral Cortex, 17*, 2669–2674.

Fleminger, S., Greenwood, R. J., & Oliver, D. L. (2006). Pharmacological management for agitation and aggression in people with acquired brain injury. *Cochrane Database Systematic Review, 4*, CD003299.

Giles, G. M., & Mohr, J. D. (2007). Overview and interrater reliability of an incident-based rating scale for aggressive behavior following traumatic brain injury: The Overt Aggression Scale-Modified for Neurorehabiltation-Extended (OAS-MNR-E). *Brain Injury, 21*, 505–511.

Goldstein, L. H., & McNeil, J. E. (Eds.) 2013. *Clinical neuropsychology: A practical guide to assessment and management for clinicians, second edition*. Chichester: Wiley-Blackwell.

Grey, N., Benson, R., Craig, R., Davies, H., Fitzgerald, S., Huckle, P., ... Snowden, R. J. (2011). The Short-Term Assessment of Risk and Treatability (START): A prospective study of inpatient behavior. *International Journal of Forensic Mental Health, 10*, 305–313.

Haddock, G., Barrowclough, C., Shaw, J. J., Dunn, G., Navaco, R. W., & Tarrier, N. (2009). Cognitive-behavioral therapy *v.* social activity therapy for people with psychosis and history of violence: Randomised controlled trial. *The British Journal of Psychiatry, 194*, 152–157.

Hawton, K., Salkovskis, P. M., Kirk, J., & Clark, D. M. (Eds.) (1989). *Cognitive behavior therapy for psychiatric problems: a practical guide*. Oxford: Oxford University Press.

Kelly, G., Brown, S., Todd, J., & Kremer P. (2008). Challenging behavior profiles of people with acquired brain injury living in community settings. *Brain Injury, 22*, 457–470.

Kelly, G., Todd, J., Simpson, G., Kremer, P., & Martin, C. (2006). The Overt Behavior Scale (OBS): A tool for measuring challenging behaviors following ABI in community settings. *Brain Injury, 20*, 307–319.

King, G., Strachan, D., Tucker, M., Duwyn, B., Desserud, S., & Shillington, M. (2009). The application of a transdisciplinary model for early intervention services. *Infants and Young Children, 22*, 211–223.

Kreutzer, J. S., Marwitz, J. H., Seel, R., & Serio, C. D. (1996). Validation of a neurobehavioral functioning inventory for adults with traumatic brain injury. *Archives of Physical Medicine and Rehabilitation, 77*, 116–124.

Medd, J., & Tate, R. (2000). Evaluation of an anger management therapy programme following acquired brain injury: A preliminary study. *Neuropsychological Rehabilitation, 10*, 185–201.

O'Neill, H. (2006). *Managing anger* (2nd ed.). London: Whurr.

Oddy, M., & Ramos, S. S. (2013). The clinical and cost-benefits of investing in neurobehavioral rehabilitation: a multi-centre study. *Brain Injury, 27*, 1500–1507.

Pitman, I., Haddlesey, C., & Fortescue, D. (2013). The prevalence of traumatic brain injury among adult male offenders in the UK. Briefing Paper by the Disabilities Trust. Retrieved from http://www.thedtgroup.org/media/338403/Prison%20Research%20Briefing.pdf.

Psalia, K., & Gracey, F. (2009). The mood management group. In B. A.Wilson, F. Gracey, J. J.Evans, & A. Bateman (Eds.), *Neuropsychological rehabilitation: Theory, models, therapy and outcome* (pp. 112–122). Cambridge: Cambridge University Press.

Scott, J. (1997). Advances in cognitive therapy. *Current Opinion in Psychiatry, 10*, 256–260.

Shamay-Tsoory, S. G. (2004). Impairment in cognitive and affective empathy in patients with brain lesions: Anatomical and cognitive correlates. *Journal of Clinical and Experimental Neuropsychology, 26*, 1113–1127.

Shiroma, E. J., Ferguson, P. L., & Pickelsimer, E. E. (2010). Prevalence of traumatic brain injury in an offender population: A meta-analysis. *Journal of Correctional Health Care, 16*, 147–159.

Smeets, K. C., Leeijen, A. A. M., van der Molen, M., & Rommelse, N. N. J. (2014). Treatment moderators of cognitive behavior therapy to reduce aggressive behavior: a meta-analysis. *European Child and Adolescent Psychiatry, 24*, 1–10.

Starkstein, S. E., & Robinson, R. G. (1991). The role of the human lobes in affective disorder following stroke. In H. S. Levin, H. M. Eisenberg, & A. L. Benton (Eds.), *Frontal lobe function and dysfunction* (pp. 288–303). Oxford: Oxford University Press.

Tateno, A., Jage, R. E., & Robinson, R. G. (2003). Clinical correlates of aggressive behavior after traumatic brain injury. *Journal of Neuropsychiatry and Clinical Neurosciences, 15*, 155–160.

Teasdale, G., & Jennett, B. (1974). Assessment of coma and impaired consciousness. A practical scale. *Lancet, 2*, 81–84.

Tonks, J., Slater, A., Frampton, I., Wall, S. E., Yates, P., & Williams, W. H. (2009). The development of emotion and empathy skills after childhood brain injury. *Developmental Medicine and Child Neurology, 51*, 8–16.

Walker, A. J., Nott, M. T., Doyle, M., Onus, M., McCarthy, K., & Baguley, I. J. (2010). Effectiveness of a group anger management program after severe traumatic brain injury. *Brain Injury, 24*, 517–524.

Walker, R., Hiller, M., Staton, M., & Leukefeld, C. G. (2003). Head injury among drug abusers: An indicator of co-occurring problems. *Journal of Psychoactive Drugs, 35*, 343–353.

Ward, T., Mann, R. & Gannon, T. (2007). The good lives model of offender rehabilitation: clinical implications. *Aggression and Violent Behavior, 12*(1), pp 87–107

Ward, T., & Stewart, C. (2003). Criminogenic needs and human needs: A theoretical model. *Psychology, Crime and Law, 9*, 125–143.

Watson, C., Rutterford, N., Shortland, D., Williamson, N., & Alderman, N. (2001). Reduction of chronic aggressive behavior ten years after brain injury. *Brain Injury, 15*, 1003–1015.

Webster, C. D., Martin, M., Brink, J., Nicholls, T. L., & Desmarais, S. L. (2009). *Manual for the Short Term Assessment of Risk and Treatability (START) (Version 1.1)* Coquitlam, Canada: British Columbia Mental Health & Addiction Services.

Williams, H. (2012). *Repairing shattered lives: Brain injury and its implications for criminal justice.* Report published by the Barrow Cadbury Trust on behalf of the Transition to

Adulthood Alliance. Retrieved from http://yss.org.uk/wp-content/uploads/2012/10/Repairing-Shattered-Lives_Report.pdf.

Williams, W. H., & Evans, J. J. (2003). Brain injury and emotion: An overview to a special issue on biopsychosocial approaches in neurorehabilitation. *Neuropsychological Rehabilitation, 13*, 1–11.

Williams, W. H., Mewse, A. J., Tonks, J., Mills, S., Burgess, C. N. W., & Cordan, G. (2010). Traumatic brain injury in a prison population: Prevalence, and risk for reoffending. *Brain Injury, 24*, 1184–1188.

Wilson, B. A., Gracey, F., Evans, J. J., & Bateman, A. (Eds.) (2009). *Neuropsychological rehabilitation: Theory, models, therapy and outcome.* Cambridge: Cambridge University Press.

Wilson, C. M., Desmarais, S. L., Nicholls, T. L., & Brink, J. (2010). The role of client strengths in assessments of violence risk using the Short-Term Assessment of Risk and Treatability (START). *International Journal of Forensic Mental Health, 9*, 282–293.

Winkler, D., Unsworth, C., & Sloan, S. (2006). Factors that lead to successful community integration following severe traumatic brain injury. *Journal of Head Trauma Rehabilitation, 21*, 8–21.

Wong, S. C. P., & Gordon, A. (2013). The Violence Reduction Program: A treatment program for violence prone forensic clients. *Psychology, Crime and Law, 19*, 461–465.

Wood, R. Ll. (1987). *Brain injury rehabilitation: A neurobehavioral approach.* London: CroomHelm.

Wood, R. Ll. (2001). Understanding neurobehavioral disability. In R. Ll. Wood & T. McMillan (Eds.), *Neurobehavioral disability and social handicap following traumatic brain injury* (pp. 3–27). Hove: Psychology Press.

Wood, R. Ll., & Worthington, A. D. (2001a). Neurobehavioral rehabilitation: A conceptual paradigm. In R. Ll. Wood & T. McMillan (Eds.), *Neurobehavioral disability and social handicap following traumatic brain injury* (pp. 107–131). Hove: Psychology Press.

Wood, R. Ll., & Worthington, A. D. (2001b). Neurobehavioral rehabilitation in practice. In R. Ll. Wood & T. McMillan (Eds.), *Neurobehavioral disability and social handicap following traumatic brain injury* (pp. 133–155). Hove: Psychology Press.

Wood, R. Ll., & Williams, C. (2008). Inability to empathize following traumatic brain injury. *Journal of the International Neuropsychological Society, 14*, 289–296.

25

The Impact of Physical Exercise on Antisocial Behavior

A Neurocognitive Perspective

Dylan B. Jackson and Kevin M. Beaver

Key points

- There has been a great deal of debate over the effectiveness of treatment programs aimed at reducing antisocial and criminal behaviors.
- Recent research has suggested that interventions targeting brain structure and functioning are promising for the treatment of antisocial behavior.
- One avenue of treatment that benefits brain health and could also reduce antisocial behavior is regular physical exercise.
- The current chapter reviews the body of research indicating that physical exercise induces neurocognitive benefits that could counteract the neurocognitive deficits that characterize a number of offenders.
- Suggestions for future research are also discussed.

Terminology Explained

Attention deficit hyperactivity disorder (ADHD) describes a set of symptoms related to deficits in the ability to control behavior, attention, hyperactivity, and impulsivity.

Brain-derived neurotrophic factor (BDNF) is a key protein that promotes the brain's ability to change in terms of neuronal growth and connectivity.

CA1 and CA3 neurons can be found on particular regions of the hippocampus (a part of the brain associated with memory, and other functions).

Monoamines refer to the neurotransmitters dopamine, noradrenaline, and serotonin.

A **neurocognitive** deficit is a reduction or impairment of cognitive function usually after illness, substance abuse, and/or brain injury.

The Wiley Blackwell Handbook of Forensic Neuroscience, First Edition. Edited by Anthony R. Beech, Adam J. Carter, Ruth E. Mann and Pia Rotshtein.
© 2018 John Wiley & Sons Ltd. Published 2018 by John Wiley & Sons Ltd.

Neurotrophins induce the development, growth, and functionality of nerve cells.

Risk-need-responsivity (RNR)is an approach where treatment service is delivered to higher risk, as opposed to lower risk, cases (the **risk** principle); criminogenic needs are targeted for change (the **need** principle); styles and approaches to treatment are designed to have the most effect upon criminogenic needs, that is, delivering treatment that is the most engaging and understandable (the **responsivity** principle).

Introduction

An emerging line of research has begun to examine the possibility that neurocognitive impairment might play a key role in explaining why individuals engage in disruptive and antisocial behaviors, including delinquency and crime. Findings generated from these studies have indicated that such deficits significantly influence misconduct as well as the development of criminogenic traits, such as low self-control (Beaver, Wright, & DeLisi, 2007). The growing support for specific neurocognitive impairments as key predictors of antisocial traits and behaviors has important implications for the treatment of such traits and behaviors. Despite Martinson's (1974) claim that "nothing works" when it comes to offender rehabilitation, recent research suggests that the treatment of offenders is indeed a worthwhile endeavor (see Cullen & Jonson, 2011), and that such treatment appears to be most effective when it appropriately targets cognitive behavioral elements and learning based on risk-need-responsivity (RNR) (Pearson, Lipton, Cleland, & Yee, 2002). Even so, newer programs that are based on the findings from empirical studies should be further developed to improve the effectiveness of treatment programs. One type of intervention that has the potential to increase program effectiveness and reduce recidivism is physical exercise.

It is important to point out that research examining the link between physical exercise and antisocial behaviors is sparse and inconclusive (Faulkner et al., 2007; Tkacz, Young-Hyman, Boyle, & Davis, 2008; Wiles et al., 2008). Nevertheless, a number of recent, rigorous studies have demonstrated that participation in regular physical exercise significantly reduces the symptoms of attention deficit hyperactivity disorder (ADHD) (Archer & Kostrzewa, 2012; Chang, Liu, Yu, & Lee, 2012), symptoms that have repeatedly been found to predict crime and delinquency (Pratt, Cullen, Blevins, Daigle, & Unnever, 2002). Physical exercise also optimizes brain health in a number of ways. Participation in physical exercise has been shown to improve executive functioning (Best, 2010; Diamond & Lee, 2011; Spitzer & Hollmann, 2013), induce hippocampal growth, blood flow and neurogenesis (Burdette et al., 2010; Cotman, Berchtold, & Christie, 2007), enhance brain plasticity through elevated production of neurotrophic factors (Colcombe et al., 2004), and alter the level and functioning of key monoamines, such as serotonin (or 5-HT) and dopamine, in several brain structures (Dishman et al., 2006; Meeusen & de Meirleir, 1995). A number of the neurocognitive changes that unfold as a result of regular physical exercise overlap significantly with the neurocognitive features that protect against antisocial behaviors and criminogenic traits. As a result, it is reasonable to suggest that a program including a component of regular physical exercise be considered as a viable option for treating antisocial behavior.

The purpose of this chapter is to examine some of the literature that has explored the links among physical exercise, brain structure and functioning, and antisocial phenotypes. Toward this end, the current chapter will be divided into four sections. First, the relationship between executive dysfunction and antisocial behavior will be assessed in conjunction with the benefits of physical exercise on executive functioning. Second, hippocampal abnormalities and dysfunction as an explanation of offending will be reviewed, together with research demonstrating the structural and functional improvements to the hippocampus that can result from exercise. Third, the role of monoamines (e.g., serotonin and dopamine) in the production of antisocial behavior will be outlined along with the effect of exercise on the production and synthesis of monoamines. Fourth, the relationship between diminished brain-derived neurotrophic factor (BDNF) and criminogenic traits will be discussed, as will the ability of exercise to increase BDNF levels in the brain. Finally, the feasibility of physical exercise as a core feature of offender treatment will be discussed.

The Link between Cognitive Deficits and Antisocial Behavior

A body of research has examined brain-based correlates of antisocial behavior, with variations in brain structure and functioning being linked to antisocial traits and behaviors (Beaver et al., 2007; Blair, 2004). In a review of the literature, for example, Raine (2008) argued that abnormalities in the structure and function of several brain areas have been linked to aggressive, antisocial conduct, including, but not limited to, the angular gyrus, the anterior cingulate, the posterior cingulate, and the amygdala. While abnormalities in all of these regions have the potential to influence misconduct, perhaps no brain structure has been studied as thoroughly as the prefrontal cortex. The prefrontal cortex is responsible for executive functions, which consist of planning, paying attention, delaying gratification, understanding abstractions, and inhibiting inappropriate behaviors (Ishikawa & Raine, 2003; Raine, 2002).

Recent research highlights the importance of neurocognitive functioning in producing antisocial phenotypes and, at the same time, protecting individuals from patterns of behavior in which they continually make poor decisions, act impulsively, and seek immediate reward (Raine, Lencz, Bihrle, LaCasse, & Colletti, 2000). For example, Cauffman, Steinberg, and Piquero (2005) conducted a case-control study where they compared a sample of incarcerated youth to a sample of youth enrolled in California high schools. Their results revealed that, relative to non-incarcerated youth, incarcerated youth exhibit poorer performance on tasks that activate cognitive functions mediated by the prefrontal cortex. Such findings suggest that those with functional and structural impairment to the prefrontal cortex are at risk for criminal involvement.

Physical Exercise Enhances Various Aspects of Cognitive Functioning

In recent years, research has indicated that engaging in a physical exercise program enhances executive functions (Archer & Kostrzewa, 2012; Chang et al., 2012). Whether participants are children (Best, 2010; Diamond & Lee, 2011; Hillman et al., 2009), adolescents (Spitzer & Hollmann, 2013), or adults (Colcombe et al., 2004;

Hillman, Snook, & Jerome, 2003), it appears that engaging in moderate levels of physical exercise (including aerobic games and sports) enhances several prefrontal capacities, including goal-directed thinking and planning (Best, 2010), sustained attention (Diamond & Lee, 2011; Hillman et al., 2009), concentration (Spitzer & Hollmann, 2013), working memory (Diamond & Lee, 2011), cognitive flexibility (Chang et al., 2012; Hillman et al., 2009), improved stimulus classification (Hillman et al., 2003), social competency (Kang, Choi, Kang, & Han, 2011), response inhibition (Smith et al., 2013), and impulse control (Archer & Kostrzewa, 2012).

The impact of physical exercise *If regular physical exercise improves significantly the neurocognitive features that protect against antisocial behaviors and criminogenic traits, it is reasonable to suggest that a program including a component of physical exercise be considered as a viable option for treating antisocial behavior.*
Source: © Dolgachov. Used under license from 123RF.

Improvements in many of these outcomes are particularly salient for children diagnosed with ADHD, an important risk factor for future misbehavior and delinquency (Pratt et al., 2002). A recent study by Smith et al. (2013) enrolled a sample of young children with ADHD symptoms in an eight-week moderate-to-vigorous physical activity program. The participants demonstrated significant improvement in response inhibition and impulsivity following the eight-week period. Similarly, a study by Verrett, Guay, Berthiaume, Gardiner, and Béliveau (2012) found that when slightly older children (ages 7 to 12) with ADHD participated in a ten-week physical activity program, their attention, information processing, and social interaction skills improved relative to controls. While the mechanisms linking physical exercise to a reduction in several ADHD symptoms are not entirely clear, increased activation of the dorsolateral prefrontal cortex (dlPFC) as a result of exercise-induced dopamine release may partially explain the effect (Chang et al., 2012). Research also indicates that antisocial individuals are more likely to show significant impairment and reduced activity in the left dlPFC, which is implicated in planning, organizing, operant conditioning, and perceptions of others' intentions and behavior (Raine, 2008; Yang & Raine, 2009).

The Impact of Physical Exercise on Antisocial Behavior 663

To summarize, findings from existing studies have provided some evidence indicating that physical exercise strengthens cognitive performance and reinforces the functions of the prefrontal cortex (Diamond & Lee, 2011; Hillman et al., 2003; Spitzer & Hollmann, 2013). A high-functioning prefrontal cortex, in turn, enables social competency and minimizes the likelihood of misbehaviors, as it facilitates planning, impulse control, delayed gratification, concentration, and elements of moral judgment and empathy (Damasio, 1994; Raine, 2008). In light of the research to date linking poor executive functioning to antisocial behavior (Beaver et al., 2007), it is reasonable to suggest that involvement in regular physical activity might reduce the likelihood of offending behaviors by improving executive functioning.

Hippocampal Abnormalities and Antisocial Behavior

Box 25.1   The role of the hippocampus in behavior

In addition to the prefrontal cortex, other neurocognitive structures and systems are also relevant to the development of antisocial behaviors. One of these is the hippocampus, a limbic structure which is largely responsible for converting short-term memory into long-term memory (Raine, 2008). In conjunction with the prefrontal cortex and the amygdala, the hippocampus regulates affect, fear conditioning, and sensitivity to social cues (see Raine, 2008; Raine et al., 2004). The hippocampus also plays a vital role in memory consolidation and has important implications for proper social learning and judgment. The memory functions of the hippocampus provide information about the learning context, including the relationship between the various social cues that constitute the learning experience (Olsson & Phelps, 2007).

If the functions of the hippocampus are defective, then proper social judgments and contextual learning may become impaired (see Box 25.1). Research has indicated that when such impairments occur, the risk of antisocial behaviors increases (Marsh & Blair, 2008). It is not surprising, therefore, that structural and functional abnormalities in the hippocampus have been empirically linked to antisocial propensity and criminal conduct as well (Kiehl et al., 2001; Raine & Yang, 2006).

Ultimately, abnormalities in hippocampal structure and functioning appear to place individuals at greater risk for antisocial behavior, in part by impairing memory consolidation, social information processing, and proper fear conditioning. To the extent that the defects in the hippocampus are rectified, misbehaviors characterized by fearlessness and a disregard for future consequences (e.g., crime) may be ameliorated. One method of enhancing the structural and functional properties of the hippocampus is through regular participation in physical exercise.

Enhanced hippocampal features due to physical exercise

A number of studies have indicated that physical exercise results in neurocognitive benefits to the hippocampus (Cotman et al., 2007; Olson, Eadie, Ernst, & Christie, 2006).

Some of these benefits include increased hippocampal blood flow (Burdette et al., 2010), enlargement of the hippocampal structure (Erickson et al., 2011), enhanced genetic transcription and availability of hippocampal growth factors (Cotman et al., 2007), elevations in hippocampal synaptic plasticity (Cotman et al., 2007), and heightened hippocampal neurogenesis (Olson et al., 2006). A recent study by Burdette et al. (2010) found that adults who engaged in a four-month exercise training program showed greater blood flow and connectivity in the hippocampus as well as enhanced connectivity between the hippocampus and the anterior cingulate cortex (ACC). These findings seem to suggest that the increased blood flow may be a result of exercise-induced neurogenesis and synaptogenesis in the hippocampus, and as such would increase the demand for blood. Moreover, the enhanced communication between the hippocampus and the ACC likely improves a number of cognitive functions, including reward-based learning and the processing of emotion.

Apart from functional changes to the hippocampus, a recent study by Erickson et al. (2011) provides evidence that exercise can also lead to structural improvements in the hippocampus. Analyzing data from a sample of 120 adults, a randomized controlled trial revealed that adults assigned to exercise training experienced a 2% growth in hippocampal volume (relative to controls), resulting in enhanced memory functioning. The findings imply that exercise can benefit individuals by improving memory and object recognition and preventing their deterioration as individuals get older (see Cotman et al., 2007; Erickson et al., 2011).

The structural and functional changes in the hippocampus that result from exercise can also lead to a number of adaptive changes in cognition and behavior in younger age groups. In one study, preadolescent children who engaged in regular fitness activities evinced greater bilateral hippocampal volume relative to their less active counterparts (see Chaddock et al., 2010). Other research has shown that exercise during the adolescent period increases the hippocampal neurogenesis of CA1 and CA3 neurons (Uysal et al., 2005). While exercise-induced changes in hippocampal structure and function have often been associated with heightened spatial and relational memory (see Chaddock et al., 2010), some studies have linked them to behavioral improvements as well (Naylor et al., 2008).

It is highly plausible, then, that regular physical exercise might reduce the risk of antisocial traits and behaviors in part by enhancing hippocampal structure and function (Chaddock et al., 2010; Erickson et al., 2011; Naylor et al., 2008), particularly since antisocial populations are more likely to be characterized by irregularities in the hippocampus (Kiehl et al., 2001; Raine et al., 2004; Raine & Yang, 2006). To our knowledge, however, no research has explicitly tested the role of exercise in reducing antisocial behavior through enhanced hippocampal features. Whether exercise has such an effect will need to be addressed directly in future research.

Role of Monoamines in Antisocial Behavior

In addition to exploring the effect of specific brain structures on offending, a number of researchers have also examined the influence of neurotransmitters on risky and aggressive behaviors (Moore, Scarpa, & Raine, 2002; van Goozen, Fairchild, Snoek, & Harold, 2007). Much of this research has focused on a subgroup of neurotransmitters called monoamines and whether they are implicated in various antisocial behaviors, including misconduct. The results from these studies provide some evidence suggesting that variation in both the levels and processing of the monoamines dopamine and serotonin are linked to various criminogenic traits and behaviors, such as impulsivity, risk seeking, and various forms of delinquency (Moore et al., 2002; Peterson et al., 2010).

Dopamine, an excitatory neurotransmitter, plays a vital role in the reinforcement of habits, the facilitation of learning and memory, and the conditioning of preferences through inducing feelings of pleasure and reward (Wise, 2008). The processing of dopamine in the brain also has important implications for reward seeking and impulsive behaviors, such as misconduct. To illustrate, Hommer, Bjork, and Gillman (2011) recently found that dopamine modulated individual differences in reward seeking and addiction. Their results suggest that individuals with compulsive and addictive tendencies tend to respond minimally to ordinary, socially acceptable rewards, yet respond vigorously to inherently rewarding substances (e.g., drugs or alcohol). The differential response seems to be a partial function of the lower dopamine receptor availability on post-synaptic neurons among pathologically impulsive individuals (see Peterson et al., 2010).

This line of research implies that high-risk individuals tend to experience maladaptive rewards as more salient and thus may have additional motivation to seek them out. For some individuals, aggression and violence may constitute a particularly salient reward. A study by van Erp & Miczek (2000) revealed that aggressive and violent subjects tend to undergo increases in dopamine levels in both the nucleus accumbens and the prefrontal cortex for 60 minutes following their violent outburst. The findings intimate that the aggressive and violent behaviors of antisocial individuals may be partially explained by the dopaminergic reward that such behaviors engender.

Apart from exploring the link between antisocial behaviors and dopaminergic responsivity to reward, scholars have also examined the relationship between baseline dopamine synaptic levels and a penchant for misconduct. Studies of risk-seeking adolescents have shown a diminished basal rate of available dopamine in the synaptic clefts of neurons in the ventral striatum (see Laviola, Macrì, Morley-Fletcher, & Adriani, 2003). Similar deficiencies in synaptic dopamine have been proposed for individuals with ADHD (Swanson et al., 2007). This type of neurochemical profile of at-risk individuals may contribute to baseline boredom and dissatisfaction (i.e., reward deficiency), which appears to compel dopamine-deficient individuals to seek increasingly risky stimuli to raise the levels of dopamine found in the synapses of the ventral striatum.

In addition to dopamine, the inhibitory neurotransmitter serotonin has also been linked to antisocial outcomes (Berman, McCloskey, Fanning, Schumacher, & Coccaro,2009; Moore et al., 2002). While typically associated with depression and schizophrenia (López-Figueroa et al., 2004; Meltzer, Li, Kaneda, & Ichikawa, 2003), a number of studies have revealed that a decrease in serotonin availability and/or turnover increases the likelihood of aggression, violence, and negative emotionality (for a recent review, see Lesch, Araragi, Waider, van den Hove, & Gutknecht, 2012). Conversely, experimental enhancement of serotonin levels has been shown to reduce the odds of responding to provocation with aggression (Berman et al., 2009) and to increase moral objection to harmful acts (Crockett, Clark, Hauser, & Robbins, 2010).

In sum, the available research provides some evidence – though it is far from definitive – that dopamine and serotonin may be involved in antisocial behaviors, particularly through their influence on mood, judgment, and perceived reward. What is essential to point out, however, is that variation in levels of neurotransmitters changes in response to certain environmental stimuli. This has important implications for prevention and intervention programs because changes in the environment may actually be able to produce changes in neurotransmitter levels. One environmental mechanism that has been found to affect neurotransmitters, including dopamine and serotonin, is physical exercise.

Beneficial changes in monoamine synthesis in response to physical exercise

Physical exercise has been shown to result in heightened neurological activity, including enhanced synthesis of monoamines such as dopamine and serotonin. For example, regular treadmill running appears to increase basal levels of serotonin in the dorsal raphe nucleus and leads to increased turnover and availability of serotonin in the cortical structures of the brain (see Dishman et al., 2006). Endogenous opioids, particularly beta-endorphins, are typically enhanced following physical exercise as well, which may improve mood and reduce stress (Dishman & O'Connor, 2009). These opioids interact with monoamines, particularly dopamine, to reduce pain and psychological stress and to increase the reward associated with the exercise experience. Running in particular has been found to increase both dopamine release (Meeusen, Piacentini, & de Meirleir, 2001) and turnover (Hattori, Naoi, & Nishino, 1994). This increase in dopamine production and turnover has been found to promote neuronal plasticity and improve mood, cognitive functioning, and learning capacity (Dishman et al., 2006).

A review by Meeusen and de Meirleir (1995) provides evidence for increases in dopamine activity in the hypothalamus, midbrain, prefrontal cortex, hippocampus, and striatum in response to exercise. The review suggests that these elevations in dopamine activity in select brain regions seem to occur in response to both acute and chronic cardiovascular exercise. A more recent study by Kim et al. (2011) sheds some light on the link between physical exercise and traits and behaviors symptomatic of ADHD. In this study, their analysis revealed that impulsivity and inattention were ameliorated in response to a 28-day exercise program, primarily due to a significant enhancement in the synthesis of dopamine in both the prefrontal cortex and the nucleus accumbens.

It should be noted that a number of the brain regions where dopamine increases as a result of exercise are the same regions that are implicated in misbehaviors when dopamine availability is insufficient. Therefore, it is reasonable to suggest that physical exercise might serve as a useful intervention to counteract antisocial traits and behaviors. Exercise is likely to improve neurological health in relevant brain regions by increasing the synthesis of dopamine, serotonin, norepinephrine, and beta-endorphins (see Dishman et al., 2006; Dishman & O'Connor, 2009). While regular, aerobic exercise tends to result in an "exercise high" (Dishman & O'Connor, 2009), it also appears to facilitate additional monoamine activity and turnover, which could be useful in reducing the negative symptomology of antisocial individuals. Consequently, it is entirely plausible that a program of regular physical exercise could help to compensate for the suboptimal neurotransmission of monoamines like dopamine and serotonin that can place individuals on an antisocial path.

Insufficient BDNF and Criminogenic Traits

Apart from monoamine neurotransmitters, there are other chemicals in the brain called neurotrophins, or growth factors, which are involved in the development and maintenance of neurons. Neurotrophins are a group of proteins that aid the process of neurogenesis (i.e., the growth of new neurons from neuronal stem cells) and, more broadly, are essential in the facilitation of brain plasticity, particularly use-dependent plasticity (see Cotman & Berchtold, 2002). One of the more commonly studied neurotrophins is BDNF, which is the most abundant neurotrophin in the human brain (Hong, Liou, & Tsai, 2011) and the most broadly abundant neurotrophin in the adult forebrain and the hippocampus (Spitzer & Hollmann, 2013). BDNF is manufactured and released by glutamatergic neurons and has a number of functions, with one of the most important being the survival, proliferation, and plasticity of the dopaminergic and serotonergic systems (see Berton et al., 2006). In short, BDNF is essential to neurocognitive health and maturation, as it is partially responsible for producing and differentiating dendrites and synapses throughout the brain.

A dysfunctional BDNF system has the potential to result in a number of neuropsychiatric disadvantages, including reduced cognitive abilities (Yamada, Mizuno, & Nabeshima, 2002) and problems with executive functioning (Rybakowski, Borkowska, Czerski, Skibińska, & Hauser, 2003). Although BDNF activity can be stimulated or suppressed by various environmental factors, genetic mechanisms also play an important role in the manufacture of BDNF proteins (Hong et al., 2011). Because the impact of BDNF is relevant to numerous brain structures and neurotransmitter systems, a deficiency in BDNF has the potential to lead to conduct problems through a variety of neurological pathways (see Archer & Kostrzewa, 2012).

Recent research has indicated that the risk of ADHD increases when BDNF activity is diminished (see Tsankova et al., 2006). The link between lower BDNF availability and impulsive, reward-seeking behavior might be partially explained by the intricate relationship between BDNF and dopamine. For instance, research has revealed that dopaminergic pathways in the brain are partly modulated by BDNF, since BDNF seems to be implicated in the responsiveness of dopamine receptors on target neurons (see Guillin et al., 2001). BDNF also appears to differentiate and aid the survival of dopaminergic neurons in the midbrain (e.g., the ventral striatum). Some scholars have posited that the likely result of BDNF deficits in the ventral striatum are symptoms of reward deficiency (see Hong et al., 2011). Such deficiencies would be expected to incite stimulation-seeking behaviors and ADHD-like symptoms, which would in turn increase the risk of delinquent behavior (see Pratt et al., 2002).

Research has also revealed that BDNF is intimately related to serotonin levels in the brain. BDNF appears to modulate the outflow of serotonin, since an infusion of BDNF increases serotonin turnover and availability. A high-functioning BDNF system also buttresses the survival and the differentiation of serotonergic neurons (Martinowich & Lu, 2007). Interestingly, drugs used to treat psychopathologies of mood (e.g., selective serotonin reuptake inhibitors – SSRIs) work in part by increasing BDNF availability and synthesis (Martinowich & Lu, 2007). Since antisocial behavior has been associated with lower serotonin availability and turnover (see Moore et al., 2002; Virkkunen, Goldman, Nielsen, & Linnoila, 1995), it is plausible that an increase in BDNF activity in the brain might reduce the risk of antisocial behaviors by increasing the synthesis of serotonin.

In sum, BDNF seems to play a crucial role in the modulation of key systems of neurotransmission, in part because BDNF increases the number of neurotransmitter vesicles that reside closer to the synaptic gap (Spitzer & Hollmann, 2013). BDNF also facilitates the proper maturation and plasticity of brain structures implicated in various dimensions of healthy cognition, including learning, memory, and self-regulation (Berchtold, Chinn, Chou, Kesslak, & Cotman, 2005; Spitzer & Hollmann, 2013). It is reasonable, therefore, to suggest that BDNF availability in the brain may be an important predictor of criminal traits and behaviors, since low levels can produce abnormalities and stunted maturation in relevant brain structures as well as dysfunctional dopaminergic and serotonergic systems that increase the odds of antisocial behaviors.

Anaerobic exercise *Regular exercise, particularly aerobic exercise rather than strength building, can reduce antisocial propensity.*
Source: © Wavebreak Media Ltd. Used under license from 123RF.

Increased BDNF availability as a result of physical exercise

A number of recent studies have indicated that physical exercise significantly increases BDNF activity (Cotman & Berchtold, 2002; Hötting & Röder, 2013; Vaynman, Ying, & Gomez-Pinilla, 2004). One study by Ploughman (2008) revealed that elevated BDNF levels are sustained for several days after exercise has ceased. The findings intimate that even somewhat regular participation in physical exercise is beneficial. Berchtold et al. (2005) found similar increases in BDNF for subjects who engaged in physical exercise every day and those who did so every other day. A review of the literature suggests that sustained increases in BDNF levels are most likely to occur with prolonged low-to-moderate intensity exercise (see Ploughman, 2008).

Due to the increases in BDNF, participation in moderate physical exercise on a fairly regular basis is accompanied by a host of neurological shifts, including neurogenesis in the hippocampus (Thomas, Sather, & Whinery, 2008), enhanced neuroprotection and synaptic plasticity in the cerebellum and frontal cortex (Bixby et al., 2007), as well as the proliferation of neuronal tissues, synapses, and dendritic spines in various brain areas (Hötting & Röder, 2013; Vaynman et al., 2004). As a result of these neurological shifts, exercise-induced changes in BDNF are likely to result in enhanced general cognitive ability (Thomas et al., 2008), heightened memory and learning capacity (Ploughman, 2008; Vaynman et al., 2004), a reduction in negative emotions (e.g., anxiety) (Cotman et al., 2007), and potential improvement in executive functions (Bixby et al., 2007). Thus, increased BDNF expression appears to be a key mechanism through which exercise improves neurocognitive health (see Berchtold et al., 2005).

Exercise-induced enhancement of BDNF in the brain also has the potential to reduce the expression of antisocial traits and propensities. Adequate BDNF might counteract the risk of antisocial behavior indirectly by stimulating heightened levels of serotonin and dopamine in relevant brain structures, such as the hippocampus and the prefrontal cortex. Dysfunction in these brain areas has been linked to antisocial personality as well as misconduct (see Raine, 2008). Researchers have discovered that impairment in the hippocampus can interfere with proper fear of punishment, whereas deficits in the prefrontal cortex can lead to impulsive and callous behavior (Raine & Yang, 2006). Taken together, the findings suggest that synaptic growth and maturity in these structures, which are partially a product of adequate BDNF availability, might reduce the risk of misconduct.

Enhanced BDNF activity also has the potential to improve the functioning of dopaminergic and serotonergic systems, which can play a key role in the development of antisocial propensity (see Berman et al., 2009; Comings et al., 2000). Although dopaminergic/reward deficiency and low serotonin availability may increase the odds of risky and illegal behaviors, BDNF may counteract this risk by increasing dopaminergic and serotonergic synthesis in relevant brain structures. While research has not empirically examined a link between exercise, BDNF, and antisocial behavior, the ability of exercise to compensate for any genetically-induced deficit in BDNF availability is quite plausible, since the manufacture of BDNF is notably sensitive to environmental enrichments and extra-cellular stimuli (Pham, Winblad, Granholm, & Mohammed, 2002). Hence, any suboptimal neurotransmitter activity, inadequate neuronal plasticity, or diminished neuroprotection that may be induced by a naturally low-functioning BDNF system has the potential to be counteracted by the heightened BDNF activity that is sustained by regular, physical exercise. Because of its role in promoting these neurocognitive benefits, physical exercise should be given proper consideration as a potential treatment of antisocial tendencies.

Conclusions and Implications for Practice

This chapter has postulated that an exercise training program can serve as a potential option to reduce antisocial phenotypes. Although exercise training has not yet been widely implemented, the available evidence is consistent with the argument that regular exercise (particularly aerobic exercise) can reduce antisocial propensity and behavior by enhancing a variety of neurocognitive features, including executive functioning (Best, 2010; Diamond & Lee, 2011; Hillman et al., 2009), hippocampal structure and functioning (Burdette et al., 2010; Naylor et al., 2008), monoamine synthesis (Dishman et al., 2006; Meeusen & de Meirleir, 1995), and BDNF-induced plasticity

(Berchtold et al., 2005; Hötting & Röder, 2013). The potential neurocognitive mechanisms by which physical exercise can minimize antisocial involvement are numerous, and may work together in ways not yet anticipated or empirically explored.

Nevertheless, the state of the current literature suggests that a number of the neurocognitive changes that result from consistent, physical exercise are precisely the changes that are needed to counteract the structural and functional brain deficits that seem to characterize a number of antisocial individuals. Explicit tests of whether exercise training reduces misconduct by improving specific dimensions of neurocognitive functioning, however, are virtually non-existent (for an exception, see Raine et al., 2001). Future research on the benefits of exercise for behavioral outcomes should seek to incorporate a broader spectrum of neurocognitive features in order to further validate the use of exercise training in treating antisocial individuals.

It should be noted that basic exercise training constitutes a rehabilitation effort that is cost-effective and easy to implement. If future research corroborates the present argument that exercise minimizes antisocial outcomes by reducing associated neurocognitive risk, then implementation of such programs in the curriculum of schools, treatment facilities, and prisons would likely be desirable and feasible, both logistically and economically. Despite growing optimism concerning the prospect of offender rehabilitation (see Cullen & Jonson, 2011), programs that effectively prevent and/or treat criminal and antisocial conduct are still in demand. Historically, the inability of criminologists to construct knowledge and determine which interventions actually work has led to an overreliance on incarceration as a way to manage criminal populations (Cullen, 2011). The growing number of studies that place the roots of antisocial behaviors partially in the brain may represent a new opportunity to offer evidence-based treatment.

Recommended Reading

Beaver, K. M., Wright, J. P., & Delisi, M. (2007). Self-control as an executive function: Reformulating Gottfredson and Hirschi's parental socialization thesis. *Criminal Justice and Behavior, 34*, 1345–1361. *An important study highlighting the relevance of functioning in the prefrontal cortex and individual levels of impulsivity and low self-control. This study was pivotal in revealing the clear relevance of neuropsychological functioning in the development of antisocial traits.*

Cauffman, E., Steinberg, L., & Piquero, A. R. (2005). Psychological, neuropsychological and physiological correlates of serious antisocial behavior in adolescence: The role of self-control. *Criminology, 43*, 133–176. *A valuable case-control study demonstrating a robust association between neuropsychological functioning and serious antisocial behavior in adolescents. The study compares a host of cognitive functions in detained adolescent populations to adolescents in a number of California high schools.*

Pratt, T. C., Cullen, F. T., Blevins, K. R., Daigle, L., & Unnever, J. D. (2002). The relationship of attention deficit hyperactivity disorder to crime and delinquency: A meta-analysis. *International Journal of Police Science & Management, 4*, 344–360. *A seminal meta-analysis demonstrating the robust association between ADHD symptomatology and criminal outcomes. Importantly, ADHD may be an important mechanism that links early health behaviors, like exercise, to subsequent antisocial behavior.*

Raine, A. (2002). Annotation: The role of prefrontal deficits, low autonomic arousal, and early health factors in the development of antisocial and aggressive behavior in children. *Journal of Child Psychology and Psychiatry, 43*, 417–434. *An important discussion of the link between prefrontal functioning and autonomic arousal to various antisocial and aggressive behaviors. These links are particularly relevant in light of early diet and exercise intervention programs that improve autonomic functioning in children.*

Raine, A., Venables, P. H., Dalais, C., Mellingen, K., Reynolds, C., & Mednick, S. A. (2001). Early educational and health enrichment at age 3–5 years is associated with increased autonomic and central nervous system arousal and orienting at age 11 years: Evidence from the Mauritius Child Health Project. *Psychophysiology, 38,* 254–266. *A pivotal prospective study linking early diet and exercise enrichment programs in children to improved nervous system and cognitive functions later in childhood.*

References

Archer, T., & Kostrzewa, R. M. (2012). Physical exercise alleviates ADHD symptoms: Regional deficits and development trajectory. *Neurotoxicity Research, 21*(2), 195–209.

Beaver, K. M., Wright, J. P., & Delisi, M. (2007). Self-control as an executive function: Reformulating Gottfredson and Hirschi's parental socialization thesis. *Criminal Justice and Behavior, 34*(10), 1345–1361.

Berchtold, N. C., Chinn, G., Chou, M., Kesslak, J. P., & Cotman, C. W. (2005). Exercise primes a molecular memory for brain-derived neurotrophic factor protein induction in the rat hippocampus. *Neuroscience, 133*(3), 853–861.

Berman, M. E., McCloskey, M. S., Fanning, J. R., Schumacher, J. A., & Coccaro, E. F. (2009). Serotonin augmentation reduces response to attack in aggressive individuals. *Psychological Science, 20*(6), 714–720.

Berton, O., McClung, C. A., DiLeone, R. J., Krishnan, V., Renthal, W., Russo, S. J., ... & Nestler, E. J. (2006). Essential role of BDNF in the mesolimbic dopamine pathway in social defeat stress. *Science, 311*(5762), 864–868.

Best, J. R. (2010). Effects of physical activity on children's executive function: Contributions of experimental research on aerobic exercise. *Developmental Review, 30*(4), 331–351.

Bixby, W. R., Spalding, T. W., Haufler, A. J., Deeny, S. P., Mahlow, P. T., Zimmerman, J. B., & Hatfield, B. D. (2007). The unique relation of physical activity to executive function in older men and women. *Medicine and Science in Sports and Exercise, 39*(8), 1408.

Blair, R. J. R. (2004). The roles of orbital frontal cortex in the modulation of antisocial behavior. *Brain and Cognition, 55*(1), 198–208.

Burdette, J. H., Laurienti, P. J., Espeland, M. A., Morgan, A., Telesford, Q., Vechlekar, C. D., ... Rejeski, W. J. (2010). Using network science to evaluate exercise-associated brain changes in older adults. *Frontiers in Aging Neuroscience, 2,* 23.

Cauffman, E., Steinberg, L., & Piquero, A. R. (2005). Psychological, neuropsychological and physiological correlates of serious antisocial behavior in adolescence: The role of self- control. *Criminology, 43,* 133–176.

Chaddock, L., Erickson, K. I., Prakash, R. S., Kim, J. S., Voss, M. W., VanPatter, M., ... & Kramer, A. F. (2010). A neuroimaging investigation of the association between aerobic fitness, hippocampal volume, and memory performance in preadolescent children. *Brain Research, 1358,* 172–183.

Chang, Y. K., Liu, S., Yu, H. H., & Lee, Y. H. (2012). Effect of acute exercise on executive function in children with attention deficit hyperactivity disorder. *Archives of Clinical Neuropsychology, 27*(2), 225–237.

Colcombe, S. J., Kramer, A. F., Erickson, K. I., Scalf, P., McAuley, E., Cohen, N. J., ... & Elavsky, S. (2004). Cardiovascular fitness, cortical plasticity, and aging. *Proceedings of the National Academy of Sciences of the United States of America, 101*(9), 3316–3321.

Comings, D. E., Gade-Andavolu, R., Gonzalez, N., Wu, S., Muhleman, D., Blake, H., ... P MacMurray, J. (2000). Comparison of the role of dopamine, serotonin, and noradrenaline genes in ADHD, ODD and conduct disorder: multivariate regression analysis of 20 genes. *Clinical Genetics, 57*(3), 178–196.

Cotman, C. W., & Berchtold, N. C. (2002). Exercise: A behavioral intervention to enhance brain health and plasticity. *Trends in Neurosciences, 25*(6), 295–301.

Cotman, C. W., Berchtold, N. C., & Christie, L. A. (2007). Exercise builds brain health: Key roles of growth factor cascades and inflammation. *Trends in neurosciences, 30*(9), 464–472.

Crockett, M. J., Clark, L., Hauser, M. D., & Robbins, T. W. (2010). Serotonin selectively influences moral judgment and behavior through effects on harm aversion. *Proceedings of the National Academy of Sciences, 107*(40), 17433–17438.

Cullen, F. T. (2011). Beyond adolescence-limited criminology: Choosing our future – the American Society of Criminology 2010 Sutherland address. *Criminology, 49*(2), 287–330.

Cullen, F. T., & Jonson, C. L. (2011). Rehabilitation and treatment programs. *Crime and Public Policy,* 293–344.

Damasio, A. R. (1994). *Descartes' error: Emotion, rationality and the human brain.* New York, NY: Putnam.

Diamond, A., & Lee, K. (2011). Interventions shown to aid executive function development in children 4 to 12 years old. *Science, 333*(6045), 959–964.

Dishman, R. K., Berthoud, H. R., Booth, F. W., Cotman, C. W., Edgerton, V. R., Fleshner, M. R., … Zigmond, M. J. (2006). Neurobiology of exercise. *Obesity, 14*(3), 345–356.

Dishman, R. K., & O'Connor, P. J. (2009). Lessons in exercise neurobiology: The case of endorphins. *Mental Health and Physical Activity, 2*(1), 4–9.

Erickson, K. I., Voss, M. W., Prakash, R. S., Basak, C., Szabo, A., Chaddock, L., … Kramer, A. F. (2011). Exercise training increases size of hippocampus and improves memory. *Proceedings of the National Academy of Sciences, 108*(7), 3017–3022.

Faulkner, G. E., Adlaf, E. M., Irving, H. M., Allison, K. R., Dwyer, J. J., & Goodman, J. (2007). The relationship between vigorous physical activity and juvenile delinquency: A mediating role for self-esteem? *Journal of Behavioral Medicine, 30*(2), 155–163.

Guillin, O., Diaz, J., Carroll, P., Griffon, N., Schwartz, J. C., & Sokoloff, P. (2001). BDNF controls dopamine D3 receptor expression and triggers behavioural sensitization. *Nature, 411*(6833), 86–89.

Hattori, S., Naoi, M., & Nishino, H. (1994). Striatal dopamine turnover during treadmill running in the rat: Relation to the speed of running. *Brain research bulletin, 35*(1), 41–49.

Hillman, C. H., Pontifex, M. B., Raine, L. B., Castelli, D. M., Hall, E. E., & Kramer, A. F. (2009). The effect of acute treadmill walking on cognitive control and academic achievement in preadolescent children. *Neuroscience, 159*(3), 1044–1054.

Hillman, C. H., Snook, E. M., & Jerome, G. J. (2003). Acute cardiovascular exercise and executive control function. *International Journal of Psychophysiology, 48*(3), 307–314.

Hommer, D. W., Bjork, J. M., & Gilman, J. M. (2011). Imaging brain response to reward in addictive disorders. *Annals of the New York Academy of Sciences, 1216*(1), 50–61.

Hong, C. J., Liou, Y. J., & Tsai, S. J. (2011). Effects of BDNF polymorphisms on brain function and behavior in health and disease. *Brain Research Bulletin, 86*(5), 287–297.

Hötting, K., & Röder, B. (2013). Beneficial effects of physical exercise on neuroplasticity and cognition. *Neuroscience & Biobehavioral Reviews, 37*(9 Pt B), 2243–2257.

Ishikawa, S. S., & Raine, A. (2003). Prefrontal deficits and antisocial behavior: A causal model. In B. B. Lahey, T. E. Moffitt, & A. Caspi (Eds.), *Causes of Conduct Disorder and Juvenile Delinquency* (pp. 277–304). Newe York, NY: Guilford Press.

Kang, K. D., Choi, J. W., Kang, S. G., & Han, D. H. (2011). Sports therapy for attention, cognitions and sociality. *International Journal of Sports Medicine, 32*(12), 953–959.

Kiehl, K. A., Smith, A. M., Hare, R. D., Mendrek, A., Forster, B. B., Brink, J., & Liddle, P. F. (2001). Limbic abnormalities in affective processing by criminal psychopaths as revealed by functional magnetic resonance imaging. *Biological Psychiatry, 50*(9), 677–684.

Kim, H., Heo, H. I., Kim, D. H., Ko, I. G., Lee, S. S., Kim, S. E., ... Kim, C. J. (2011). Treadmill exercise and methylphenidate ameliorate symptoms of attention deficit/hyperactivity disorder through enhancing dopamine synthesis and brain-derived neurotrophic factor expression in spontaneous hypertensive rats. *Neuroscience Letters, 504*(1), 35–39.

Laviola, G., Macrì, S., Morley-Fletcher, S., & Adriani, W. (2003). Risk-taking behavior in adolescent mice: Psychobiological determinants and early epigenetic influence. *Neuroscience & Biobehavioral Reviews, 27*(1), 19–31.

Lesch, K. P., Araragi, N., Waider, J., van den Hove, D., & Gutknecht, L. (2012). Targeting brain serotonin synthesis: Insights into neurodevelopmental disorders with long-term outcomes related to negative emotionality, aggression and antisocial behaviour. *Philosophical Transactions of the Royal Society B: Biological Sciences, 367*(1601), 2426–2443.

López-Figueroa, A. L., Norton, C. S., López-Figueroa, M. O., Armellini-Dodel, D., Burke, S., Akil, H., ... Watson, S. J. (2004). Serotonin 5-HT1A, 5-HT1B, and 5-HT2A receptor mRNA expression in subjects with major depression, bipolar disorder, and schizophrenia. *Biological Psychiatry, 55*(3), 225–233.

Marsh, A. A., & Blair, R. J. R. (2008). Deficits in facial affect recognition among antisocial populations: a meta-analysis. *Neuroscience & Biobehavioral Reviews, 32*(3), 454–465.

Martinowich, K., & Lu, B. (2007). Interaction between BDNF and serotonin: Role in mood disorders. *Neuropsychopharmacology, 33*(1), 73–83.

Martinson, R. (1974). What works? – Questions and answers about prison reform. *The Public Interest, 35*, 22–54.

Meeusen, R., & de Meirleir, K. (1995). Exercise and brain neurotransmission. *Sports Medicine, 20*(3), 160–188.

Meeusen, R., Piacentini, M. F., & de Meirleir, K. (2001). Brain microdialysis in exercise research. *Sports Medicine, 31*(14), 965–983.

Meltzer, H. Y., Li, Z., Kaneda, Y., & Ichikawa, J. (2003). Serotonin receptors: Their key role in drugs to treat schizophrenia. *Progress in Neuro-Psychopharmacology and Biological Psychiatry, 27*(7), 1159–1172.

Moore, T. M., Scarpa, A., & Raine, A. (2002). A meta-analysis of serotonin metabolite 5-HIAA and antisocial behavior. *Aggressive Behavior, 28*(4), 299–316.

Naylor, A. S., Bull, C., Nilsson, M. K., Zhu, C., Björk-Eriksson, T., Eriksson, P. S., ... Kuhn, H. G. (2008). Voluntary running rescues adult hippocampal neurogenesis after irradiation of the young mouse brain. *Proceedings of the National Academy of Sciences, 105*(38), 14632–14637.

Olson, A. K., Eadie, B. D., Ernst, C., & Christie, B. R. (2006). Environmental enrichment and voluntary exercise massively increase neurogenesis in the adult hippocampus via dissociable pathways. *Hippocampus, 16*(3), 250–260.

Olsson, A., & Phelps, E. A. (2007). Social learning of fear. *Nature neuroscience, 10*(9), 1095–1102.

Pearson, F. S., Lipton, D. S., Cleland, C. M., & Yee, D. S. (2002). The effects of behavioral/cognitive-behavioral programs on recidivism. *Crime & Delinquency, 48*(3), 476–496.

Peterson, E., Møller, A., Doudet, D. J., Bailey, C. J., Hansen, K. V., Rodell, A., ... Gjedde, A. (2010). Pathological gambling: Relation of skin conductance response to dopaminergic neurotransmission and sensation-seeking. *European Neuropsychopharmacology, 20*(11), 766–775.

Pham, T. M., Winblad, B., Granholm, A. C., & Mohammed, A. H. (2002). Environmental influences on brain neurotrophins in rats. *Pharmacology Biochemistry and Behavior, 73*(1), 167–175.

Ploughman, M. (2008). Exercise is brain food: the effects of physical activity on cognitive function. *Developmental Neurorehabilitation, 11*(3), 236–240.

Pratt, T. C., Cullen, F. T., Blevins, K. R., Daigle, L., & Unnever, J. D. (2002). The relationship of attention deficit hyperactivity disorder to crime and delinquency: A meta- analysis. *International Journal of Police Science & Management, 4*(4), 344–360.

Raine, A. (2002). Annotation: The role of prefrontal deficits, low autonomic arousal, and early health factors in the development of antisocial and aggressive behavior in children. *Journal of Child Psychology and Psychiatry, 43*(4), 417–434.

Raine, A. (2008). From genes to brain to antisocial behavior. *Current Directions in Psychological Science, 17*(5), 323–328.

Raine, A., Ishikawa, S. S., Arce, E., Lencz, T., Knuth, K. H., Bihrle, S., ... Colletti, P. (2004). Hippocampal structural asymmetry in unsuccessful psychopaths. *Biological Psychiatry, 55*(2), 185–191.

Raine, A., Lencz, T., Bihrle, S., LaCasse, L., & Colletti, P. (2000). Reduced prefrontal gray matter volume and reduced autonomic activity in antisocial personality disorder. *Archives of General Psychiatry, 57*(2), 119.

Raine, A., Venables, P. H., Dalais, C., Mellingen, K., Reynolds, C., & Mednick, S. A. (2001). Early educational and health enrichment at age 3–5 years is associated with increased autonomic and central nervous system arousal and orienting at age 11 years: Evidence from the Mauritius Child Health Project. *Psychophysiology, 38*(2), 254–266.

Raine, A., & Yang, Y. (2006). Neural foundations to moral reasoning and antisocial behavior. *Social Cognitive and Affective Neuroscience, 1*(3), 203–213.

Rybakowski, J. K., Borkowska, A., Czerski, P. M., Skibińska, M., & Hauser, J. (2003). Polymorphism of the brain-derived neurotrophic factor gene and performance on a cognitive prefrontal test in bipolar patients. *Bipolar disorders, 5*(6), 468–472.

Smith, A. L., Hoza, B., Linnea, K., McQuade, J. D., Tomb, M., Vaughn, A. J., ... Hook, H. (2013). Pilot physical activity intervention reduces severity of ADHD symptoms in young children. *Journal of Attention Disorders, 17*(1), 70–82.

Spitzer, U. S., & Hollmann, W. (2013). Experimental observations of the effects of physical exercise on attention, academic and prosocial performance in school settings. *Trends in Neuroscience and Education, 2*, 1–6.

Swanson, J. M., Kinsbourne, M., Nigg, J., Lanphear, B., Stefanatos, G. A., Volkow, N., ... & Wadhwa, P. D. (2007). Etiologic subtypes of attention-deficit/hyperactivity disorder: Brain imaging, molecular genetic and environmental factors and the dopamine hypothesis. *Neuropsychology Review, 17*(1), 39–59.

Thomas, J. D., Sather, T. M., & Whinery, L. A. (2008). Voluntary exercise influences behavioral development in rats exposed to alcohol during the neonatal brain growth spurt. *Behavioral Neuroscience, 122*(6), 1264.

Tkacz, J., Young-Hyman, D., Boyle, C. A., & Davis, C. L. (2008). Aerobic exercise program reduces anger expression among overweight children. *Pediatric Exercise Science, 20*(4), 390.

Tsankova, N. M., Berton, O., Renthal, W., Kumar, A., Neve, R. L., & Nestler, E. J. (2006). Sustained hippocampal chromatin regulation in a mouse model of depression and antidepressant action. *Nature Neuroscience, 9*(4), 519–525.

Uysal, N., Tugyan, K., Kayatekin, B. M., Acikgoz, O., Bagriyanik, H. A., Gonenc, S., ... & Semin, I. (2005). The effects of regular aerobic exercise in adolescent period on hippocampal neuron density, apoptosis and spatial memory. *Neuroscience Letters, 383*(3), 241–245.

Van Erp, A. M., & Miczek, K. A. (2000). Aggressive behavior, increased accumbal dopamine, and decreased cortical serotonin in rats. *The Journal of Neuroscience, 20*(24), 9320–9325.

Van Goozen, S. H., Fairchild, G., Snoek, H., & Harold, G. T. (2007). The evidence for a neurobiological model of childhood antisocial behavior. *Psychological bulletin, 133*(1), 149.

Vaynman, S., Ying, Z., & Gomez-Pinilla, F. (2004). Hippocampal BDNF mediates the efficacy of exercise on synaptic plasticity and cognition. *European Journal of Neuroscience, 20*(10), 2580–2590.

Verret, C., Guay, M. C., Berthiaume, C., Gardiner, P., & Béliveau, L. (2012). A physical activity program improves behavior and cognitive functions in children with ADHD: An exploratory study. *Journal of Attention Disorders, 16*(1), 71–80.

Virkkunen, M., Goldman, D., Nielsen, D. A., & Linnoila, M. (1995). Low brain serotonin turnover rate (low CSF 5-HIAA) and impulsive violence. *Journal of Psychiatry and Neuroscience, 20*(4), 271.

Wiles, N. J., Jones, G. T., Haase, A. M., Lawlor, D. A., Macfarlane, G. J., & Lewis, G. (2008). Physical activity and emotional problems amongst adolescents. *Social Psychiatry and Psychiatric Epidemiology, 43*(10), 765–772.

Wise, R. A. (2008). Dopamine and reward: The anhedonia hypothesis 30 years on. *Neurotoxicity Research, 14*(2–3), 169–183.

Yamada, K., Mizuno, M., & Nabeshima, T. (2002). Role for brain-derived neurotrophic factor in learning and memory. *Life Sciences, 70*(7), 735–744.

Yang, Y., & Raine, A. (2009). Prefrontal structural and functional brain imaging findings in antisocial, violent, and psychopathic individuals: A meta-analysis. *Psychiatry Research: Neuroimaging, 174*(2), 81–88.

26
Treating Emotion Dysregulation in Antisocial Behavior
A Neuroscientific Perspective
Steven M. Gillespie and Anthony R. Beech

Key points

- The aim of the present chapter is to discuss the potential applications of mindfulness and heart rate variability (HRV) biofeedback techniques for improving emotion regulation among antisocial populations.
- It begins by outlining a body of research that highlights problems in affective functioning and emotion regulation in relation to antisocial behavior, as well as findings of structural and functional abnormalities in the neural circuitry underlying emotion regulation.
- It then describes the neurobiological underpinnings of emotion regulation as highlighted through the use functional brain imaging procedures.
- Finally, it is argued that the functioning of these neural circuits can be affected by the meditative practice of mindfulness and the use of HRV biofeedback training.
- Here it is maintained that the results of clinical research and a limited number of studies conducted in a forensic context suggest that such techniques may hold therapeutic utility in the treatment of emotion regulation difficulties in antisocial populations.

Terminology Explained

Autonomic functioning refers to the functioning of the autonomic nervous system (ANS), a part of the peripheral nervous system that controls functions including breathing, heart rate, and respiratory rate. Divisions of the ANS include the

---

The Wiley Blackwell Handbook of Forensic Neuroscience, First Edition. Edited by Anthony R. Beech,
Adam J. Carter, Ruth E. Mann and Pia Rotshtein.
© 2018 John Wiley & Sons Ltd. Published 2018 by John Wiley & Sons Ltd.

sympathetic division, responsible for increases in heart rate and respiratory rate, and the parasympathetic division, responsible for reductions in heart rate and respiratory rate.

Cognitive behavioral therapy (CBT) is a form of psychotherapy whereby negative and/or irrational thoughts are challenged with the aim of altering unwanted behavior patterns. Commonly used in the treatment of anxiety and mood disorders.

Diurnal patterns of salivary cortisol secretion are patterns in the release of the stress hormone cortisol, as measured in the saliva of participants, occurring over the course of a day.

Emotion regulation is the conscious control of emotion. Emotions can be up-regulated (made stronger/more intense) or down-regulated (felt less strongly/intensely) using a number of emotion regulation strategies.

Heart rate variability (HRV) biofeedback is a form of therapy that aims to maximize fluctuations in the inter-beat interval of the heart via changes in respiration. Participants are provided with heart rate biofeedback typically via a computerized display.

Mindfulness is a form of acceptance-based meditation with a focus on maintaining attention in a non-judgmental manner in the present moment. Shown to be successful in the treatment of anxiety and mood disorders.

Spatial resolution refers to the accuracy or detail of a graphic display. The ability to distinguish the fine details of the brain is an important consideration in brain imaging.

Introduction

We have previously considered problems in emotion control specifically in relation to sexual offending (Gillespie, Mitchell, Fisher, & Beech, 2012). However, emotion control is of interest beyond sexual offenders, with impaired regulation of emotion also linked with generally antisocial behavior and violence. The current chapter will therefore aim to discuss these problems in a much broader context, widening the relevance of this chapter.

An *emotion* can be seen as a mental state that arises spontaneously rather than through conscious effort and which is often accompanied by distinct physiological changes (Gross & Thompson, 2007). *Affect* can be defined as the conscious experience of such emotions. Emotions are directly linked to the goals of the individual; they are multi-faceted and involve multi-system changes, such as changes in behavior, autonomic functioning, or physiology (Gross & Thompson, 2007); they can be experienced as positive or negative, fleeting or more prolonged, and at various levels of intensity, from the very weak to the very strong. The process by which emotions are generated in response to a given situation can be understood in terms of the four steps or events that make up the *modal model of emotion*: (1) situation, (2) attention, (3) appraisal, and (4) response.

According to the modal model, a psychologically relevant situation attracts our attention and begins a process of situation appraisal. This appraisal can occur across a number of dimensions (Ellsworth & Scherer, 2003), including the novelty of the situation, the extent to which the situation is interpreted as positive or negative, and the extent to which the situation is relevant to our individual goals or needs. Following situation appraisal an emotional response may be generated. However, emotions are constantly moderating both internal and external situations, causing us to reappraise and respond to the situation as it develops (Gross & Thompson, 2007). Thus, the generation of an emotional response may cause changes to the internal or external situation that first captured our attention, and so the modal model of emotion may be thought of as a feedback loop whereby the output (the generation of an emotion) causes changes at the input level (the situation in which we find ourselves).

Gross (1998a) suggests that differing strategies for emotion regulation can take place at five points along the chain of events constituting the modal model of emotion. These strategies can be classified as *antecedent focused* or *response focused*. Antecedent-focused strategies include *situation selection, situation modification, attentional deployment*, and *cognitive change*, and these strategies have greatest impact prior to emotional response generation. In contrast, response-focused strategies such as *response modulation* are of greatest use following the generation of an emotional response (Gross & Munoz, 1995). For more detail on antecedent-focused and response-focused strategies for emotion regulation, see Box 26.1.

Box 26.1 Strategies for Emotion Regulation

Antecedent-focused Strategies

Situation selection. Situation selection strategies involve actively avoiding or seeking out particular situations that lead to the generation of a particular wanted or unwanted emotional response. Situation selection is therefore reliant on past experience and forethought. ***Example***: one may avoid the fear precipitated by social situations by avoiding interactions with strangers.

Situation modification. Situation modification strategies refer to attempts to modify an external, physical situation such that the outcome becomes more or less desirable. ***Example***: one may modify the situation of an uncomfortable date with a stranger by joining friends in a bar, reducing the need for continued interaction.

Attentional deployment. Emotions can be regulated without the need to change or modify the external, physical situation. For example, *concentration* involves directing attention toward the emotional aspects of the situation, while *distraction* involves directing attention away from emotional aspects of a situation (Gross & Thompson, 2007). Alternatively, attention deployment may refer to physical efforts such as covering one's own eyes (e.g., during a scary film).

Cognitive change. The ability to change the ways in which emotional situations are appraised. Ochsner and Gross (2007) note that the reappraisal of an emotional situation, for example, as threatening or rewarding, represents one form of cognitive change. Through the use of reappraisal, emotional responses to the same situation may vary as a product of circumstance, goals, and motivations. The process of reappraisal is dependent upon higher-order cognitive processes (Ochsner & Gross, 2005).

Response-focused Strategies

Response modulation. This can be used to modulate or change our response following emotion generation. Response modulation involves direct influences on physiology, experience, or behavior (Gross & Thompson, 2007). Drugs, exercise, cigarettes, and alcohol may all act to modulate particular aspects of our emotional response. A common form of response modulation whereby emotionally expressive behaviors are inhibited is referred to as *suppression* (Gross & Levenson, 1993). Suppression can have effects on both expressive behavior and physiology while inhibiting emotional states (Gross & Levenson, 1997; Gross, 1998b).

Antisocial Behavior and Impaired Emotion Regulation

In this section we will consider the findings on anxiety and negative emotionality in relation to generally antisocial behavior, drawing upon research findings that suggest particular problems in emotion regulation among a subgroup of people with convictions and a diagnosis of antisocial personality disorder (ASPD), as defined in the *Diagnostic and Statistical Manual of Mental Disorders*, Version 5 (DSM-5; American Psychiatric Association (APA), 2013).

A growing body of research now suggests a link between antisocial behavior and anxiety, with many individuals with ASPD presenting with lifetime anxiety disorder (AD) (DSM-5) (Goodwin & Hamilton, 2003; Lenzenweger, Lane, Loranger, & Kessler, 2007; Sareen, Stein, Cox, & Hassard, 2004). For example, it has been proposed that ASPD co-morbid with AD (ASPD+AD) may represent a diagnostic variant to ASPD alone (Coid & Ullrich, 2010). The findings of Coid and Ullrich (2010) showed that individuals with ASPD and a diagnosis of AD showed an increased failure to conform to social norms, and higher levels of deceitfulness, impulsivity, and irritability/aggressiveness (Coid & Ullrich, 2010). Thus, heightened levels of anxiety among individuals with ASPD may have implications for the types of antisocial behavior observed.

However, evidence that anxiety can protect against antisocial behavior has also been presented. For example, among detained children who showed conduct problems and other mental disorders, it was found that those with a diagnosis of generalized AD had a significantly decreased chance of developing a modified version of ASPD in emerging adulthood, even after accounting for symptoms and diagnosis of conduct problems and conduct disorder (CD) (Washburn et al., 2007). Furthermore, Moffitt et al. identified elevated levels of anxiety and depression, indicative of impaired regulation of emotion, among males who showed a less severe pattern of low-level, chronic offending, relative to those with life-course persistent or adolescence-limited antisocial behavior (Moffitt, Caspi, Harrington, & Milne, 2002).

Despite inconsistencies in findings of a relationship between anxiety and antisocial behavior, further support for a positive relationship between these two constructs has also been noted by Vassileva, Kosson, Abramowitz, and Conrod (2005). These authors found evidence for a cluster of individuals with convictions who showed elevated anxiety scores as well as severe drug and alcohol problems. Furthermore, positive correlations between antisocial and lifestyle features of psychopathic personality have also been observed with stress reaction, aggression, and overall negative emotionality (Verona, Patrick, & Joiner, 2001), with trait anxiety and social anxiety (Gillespie, Mitchell, Satherley, Beech, & Rotshtein, 2015), and with emotional distress, fearfulness, and anger hostility in a sample of individuals with convictions (Hicks & Patrick, 2006). Thus, several lines of evidence including lifetime rates of AD in those with ASPD, and the relationship of antisocial and lifestyle psychopathic tendencies with anxiety and negative emotionality, are consistent in the finding that anxiety and antisocial behavior are positively correlated. We would suggest therefore that therapies that aim to improve emotion regulation may help to reduce anxiety and negative emotionality in offenders who present with extreme levels of antisocial behavior, especially where antisocial behavior is not otherwise accounted for by the presence of the core callous-unemotional and affective features of psychopathy.

Traumatic Early Experiences and Antisocial Behavior

Findings on the relationship between antisocial behavior, anxiety, and negative affectivity may be in part due to traumatic early experiences. Such traumatic experiences may include severe neglect, physical and sexual abuse, as well as problematic attachment formation. Creeden (2004) (see Chapter 30) suggests that early traumatic experiences may confer neurodevelopmental perturbations of anatomical regions involved in emotion generation and emotion regulation. For example, it has been shown that early experience may have implications for the structural and functional development of the amygdala (Mehta et al., 2009; Tottenham et al., 2010; Tottenham et al., 2011), the functions of which include the control of autonomic responses associated with fear, hormonal secretions, arousal, and emotional memory. Thus, adverse early experiences may affect the neurodevelopment and functioning of the amygdala in such a way that the individual appears to be hyper-responsive to threats in the environment. Additional research on the neurodevelopmental effects of early traumatic experiences suggest perturbed development of the prefrontal cortex, including an increase in grey matter volume in ventral regions (Carrion et al., 2009; Richert, Carrion, Karchemskiy, & Reiss, 2006), altered orbital prefrontal cortex structure (Hanson et al., 2010), and abnormal recruitment of the prefrontal cortex in response to negative affective stimuli. Taken together, these findings support the hypothesis that early trauma may lead to structural and functional abnormalities in regions that are critically involved in emotion response generation and regulation. In the following section, we will review in greater detail the specific structures involved in the cortical control of emotion.

Neural Circuits Underlying Emotion Regulation

In order to gain a finer understanding of the neural processes underlying the conscious control of emotion, researchers have used a variety of brain imaging techniques in order to better understand the contributions of various anatomical structures to emotion regulation (see Boxes 26.2 and 26.3). For example, early work form Jackson et al. (2003) used electrophysiological methods to measure the functioning of frontal neural territories in the regulation of negative affective states (Jackson et al., 2003). Findings from Jackson et al. indicated that participants with greater left anterior electroencephalogram (EEG) activity showed faster recovery times following an aversive event. These findings indicate a role of left prefrontal areas in the regulation of emotional states.

Box 26.2 Neural Structures Involved in Emotion Regulation: The Amygdala

The amygdala's functions are largely related to vigilance, the control of behavioral, autonomic and endocrine responses associated with fear, the control of reproductive behaviors, reward, and aversive conditioning (Cozolino, 2008). The amygdala has also been strongly implicated in negative affective states, particularly the processing of fear-inducing stimuli and in the generation of fear responses. The link between the amygdala and the processing of fear is supported by the results of neuropsychological (Adolphs, Tranel, Damasio, & Damasio, 1994; Broks et al., 1998) and brain imaging research (Breiter et al., 1996a; Morris et al., 1996; Whalen et al., 2001), which implicate the amygdala in the recognition of fearful facial affect. Abnormal functioning of the amygdala has also been implicated in numerous ADs including post-traumatic stress disorder (PTSD) (Liberzon et al., 1999; Rauch et al., 2000), obsessive compulsive disorder (OCD) (Breiter et al., 1996b), and social phobia (Birbaumer et al., 1998). The association of emotion regulation with anxiety and mood disorders is also evident in neuroimaging research. For example, activation levels in a neural circuit comprising the orbital prefrontal cortex (OPFC) and amygdala has been linked with an increased propensity to experience anxiety (Davidson, 2002). Also, Hahn et al. (2011) have observed disconnection between areas of the prefrontal cortex and amygdala in patients presenting with social AD, while reduced recruitment of prefrontal cortex and a failure to attenuate amygdala outputs has also been noted as a possible prelude to violence (Davidson, Putnam, & Larson, 2000).

Box 26.3 Neural Structures Involved in Emotion Regulation: The Orbitofrontal Cortex

The orbitofrontal cortex represents a core region of the social brain and is critical to the adaptation of behavior in response to predicted changes in reinforcement (Rushworth, Behrens, Rudebeck, & Walton, 2007). Connections of the orbitofrontal cortex with the hypothalamus allow for the integration of internal information with external information from the surrounding environment. Thus, the orbitofrontal cortex bridges the cognitive analysis of social events taking place within the cerebral cortex, and emotional reactions mediated by the amygdala and the autonomic nervous system (Hariri, Bookheimer, & Mazziotta, 2000; Mah, Arnold, & Grafman, 2004). An inhibitory role of the orbitofrontal cortex in autonomic functioning, via the amygdala and other subcortical regions, means that this area is also critically involved in emotional regulation (Fuster, 1985; Shore, 2004). The involvement of the orbitofrontal cortex in processes such as generating an expectation of the reaction of others that can be used to direct behavior (Blair & Cipolotti, 2000), calculations of the magnitude of reward or punishment value, the representation of preferences, or using others in soothing interactions further add to the role of the orbitofrontal cortex in emotion regulation (Damasio, 1994; O'Doherty, Kringelbach, Rolls, Hornak, & Andrews, 2001; Rushworth et al., 2007). Regions of the orbitofrontal cortex have also been strongly linked to the experience of affective states, including anxiety (Rauch, Savage, Alpert, Fischman, & Jenike, 1997; Milad & Rauch, 2007) and anger. In relation to anger, damage to the orbitofrontal cortex has been found to result in heightened levels of anger and impulsive, aggressive, and violent behavior (Anderson, Bechara, Damasio, Tranel, & Damasio, 1999; Blair & Cipolotti, 2000). The relationship between the orbitofrontal cortex and the experience of anger is also supported by the findings of increased orbitofrontal cortex activation in response to angry emotional expressions (Blair, Morris, Frith, Perrett, & Dolan, 1999). It is suggested by Davidson et al. (2000) that these regional activations may be indicative of an automatic response to regulate the expression of anger.

Although findings from EEG research have confirmed a role of prefrontal areas in emotion regulation, these methods are constrained by poor spatial resolution in electrophysiological methods. Thus, others have used techniques that offer finer spatial resolution, including functional magnetic resonance imaging (fMRI). In one of the earliest of these fMRI studies, Schaefer et al. (2002) investigated the effects of conscious emotion regulation on neural activity within the amygdala. In this study, participants were presented with a negative emotional stimulus and were asked to either "maintain" their emotional response or "passively view" the stimulus. Findings indicated a more prolonged increase in amygdala activity among participants who were asked to maintain their emotional response. These findings provided early evidence that conscious regulation of emotion may be driven by alterations in amygdala activation.

As well as revealing activation levels of the amygdala during passive and directed viewing, researchers have also used fMRI to shed light upon the functional relationship between the amygdala and prefrontal cortex during the reappraisal of negative emotions. For example, Ochsner et al. found that the reappraisal of a negative emotional response was associated with reductions in negative affect and increased activation of regions of the prefrontal cortex (Ochsner, Bunge, Gross, & Gabrieli, 2002). Furthermore, the authors also found a reduction in the amygdala response during reappraisal, showing an inverse relationship between ventrolateral prefrontal cortex (vlPFC) and amygdala activity. Thus, areas of the prefrontal cortex, including most notably the vlPFC, may exert control over the amygdala response during the cognitive reappraisal of negative emotions. These findings were extended in later research by Ochsner et al. (2004), who showed that the direction of the amygdala response is consistent with the direction of emotional regulation, with increased neural activity within the amygdala during the up-regulation of a negative emotional response, compared with reductions in amygdala activation during the down-regulation of emotion.

The relationship between the prefrontal cortex and amygdala activation in emotion regulation may also have an impact upon levels of secretion of the "stress hormone" cortisol. Urry et al. (2006) used fMRI to measure activity in ventromedial prefrontal cortex (vmPFC) and amygdaloid circuitry during the suppression of negative affect and also measured diurnal patterns of salivary cortisol secretion. Analyses of imaging data revealed that increasing negative affect was associated with altered activation in regions of the prefrontal cortex and amygdala, while participants who demonstrated increased vmPFC and reduced amygdala responding also showed steeper declines in cortisol levels through the course of the day (Urry et al., 2006). The effective regulation of emotional states may therefore be related to adaptive functioning of the hypothalamic-pituitary-adrenal axis (HPA) system that is involved in the release of hypothalamic and adrenocortical hormones including cortisol.

Although the research findings described above have been derived from studies of the conscious regulation of negative emotions, parallels can be noted in relation to findings on the regulation of more positive emotional states, including the conscious regulation of sexual arousal. Beauregard, Lévesque, and Bourgouin (2001) used fMRI to investigate conscious regulation of sexual arousal while viewing erotic film excerpts. Participants were instructed to either attempt to inhibit their sexual arousal or respond in a normal manner. Normal viewing of sexually arousing film excerpts was associated with increased activity in limbic structures, including the amygdala, as well as activation in paralimbic regions. However, although the authors failed to observe any activity in limbic structures during the attempted inhibition condition, significant regions of activation were identified in frontal regions, including the dorsolateral prefrontal cortex, with reduced loci of activity also noted in the amygdala, hypothalamus, and anterior temporal pole (Beauregard et al., 2001). It is concluded that prefrontal attenuation of the amygdala response and outputs to the hypothalamus and temporal pole, involved in endocrine and autonomic responding during sexual arousal, may underlie the conscious inhibition of sexual arousal. In the main section of the chapter we will discuss research findings, which indicate that the use of two particular therapeutic techniques, namely mindfulness meditation and heart rate variability (HRV) biofeedback, may alter the functioning of those neural circuits involved in emotion regulation. The use of such techniques may represent a useful adjunct to traditional therapies for improving emotion regulation in antisocial populations.

Mindfulness

Mindfulness *Mindfulness can be defined as the ability to attend to stimuli, as they are experienced, in a non-judgmental and accepting manner.*
Source: © Antonio Guillem. Used under license from 123RF.

Kabat-Zinn (1990) described mindfulness as a process of sustained attention to experience in the current moment. In an operational definition of mindfulness, Bishop et al. (2004) propose a two component model. The first component, the self-regulation of attention in the present moment, refers to focusing attention for sustained periods of time and without allowing the mind to wander. When the mind does wander, attention should be refocused. The second component emphasizes the orientation of experience, or maintaining of a curious attitude of openness toward thoughts, feelings, and sensations and acknowledging and accepting their presence. Mindfulness therefore may be defined as the ability to attend to stimuli, as they are experienced, in a non-judgmental and accepting manner (Bishop et al., 2004; Kabat-Zinn, 2003; Martin, 1997; Takahashi et al., 2005).

Teasdale and colleagues (Teasdale, Segal, Williams, & Mark, 1995; Teasdale, Segal, & Williams, 2003) suggested that such an "acceptance-based" approach to mindfulness may allow individuals to escape from rumination on unpleasant thoughts and feelings. This is consistent with results showing that more mindful individuals demonstrate a less ruminative pattern of thinking (Borders, Earleywine, & Jajodia, 2010), are less reactive in coping with emotional experience (Shapiro, Carlson, Astin, & Freedman, 2006), and show greater acceptance of negative emotions (Arch & Craske, 2006). Furthermore, programs of mindfulness-based stress reduction (MBSR; Grossman, Niemann, Schmidt, & Walach, 2004) can lead to reductions in emotional reactivity and lesser tendency to engage in ruminative thinking (Ramel, Goldin, Carmona, & McQuaid, 2004; Teasdale et al., 2000).

Howells (2010) discussed the need for forensic practice to develop with advances in the broader clinical field. Day (2009) suggested that one of the aims of therapy in a forensic context should be to aid offenders in bringing to awareness those processes involved in the onset of negative affective states (Day, 2009). For example, many offenders show problems in describing and identifying emotional states, particularly following exposure to trauma (Day et al., 2008). Furthermore, adolescent offenders often present with difficulties in labeling the emotional states of themselves and others (Savitsky & Czyzewski, 1978) and in reflecting upon and managing emotions (Moriarty, Stough, Tidmarsh, Eger, & Dennison, 2001). Thus, one of the aims of mindfulness may be to aid offenders in recognizing and dealing with the emotions of themselves and others. The results of Creswell, Way, Eisenberger, and Lieberman (2007) are therefore particularly noteworthy. These authors found that mindfulness is associated with more success in an affect labeling task, coupled with greater activation in areas of prefrontal cortex and attenuation of the amygdala response. Thus, more mindful participants may show greater abilities in affect labeling coupled with reduced reactivity to these emotions.

The findings of Creswell et al. (2007) are consistent with results of later research, which investigated the effects of trait mindfulness on neural activity in circuits recruited during emotion regulation. In this study, Modinos, Ormel, and Aleman (2010) used fMRI to scan 18 healthy participants during the reappraisal of negative emotion. Results showed that reappraisal elicited neural activation in regions including the dorsal prefrontal cortex. Furthermore, trait mindfulness was predictive of reappraisal related activity, with a positive association observed between mindfulness and activation of the dorsomedial prefrontal cortex. Here, the degree of prefrontal activity was inversely related to activation of the amygdala, consistent with a role in the down-regulation of negative emotional experience. Thus, individual differences in mindfulness predict activity in neural circuits involved in the cognitive control of emotion.

The finding of increased prefrontal activation in association with mindfulness is consistent with findings from a review of the neurobiological and clinical features of mindfulness (Chiesa & Serretti, 2010). Findings from this systematic review showed that mindfulness practice causes activation of the prefrontal and the anterior cingulate cortices. Furthermore, long-term meditation was found to be associated with enhanced activity in areas of the prefrontal cortex involved in attention (Chiesa & Serretti, 2010). These findings are consistent with the results of Frewen et al. (2010) who showed that mindfulness was associated with the degree of prefrontal activity in participants while watching relaxing imagery. Other results show that mindfulness is linked with a pattern of cerebral activation that is associated with positive affect in meditators compared with non-meditators and that these differences were positively related to markers of immune functioning (Davidson et al., 2003).

Mindfulness in forensic settings

Although the use of mindfulness programs in forensic settings is still in its infancy, some studies have found benefits of such meditational programs among offending participants. For example, Fix and Fix (2013) reviewed the usefulness of mindfulness-based treatments in reducing aggression. Although some studies showed methodological flaws, the results in general were supportive of the use of mindfulness for reducing aggressiveness. Furthermore, Samuelson, Carmody, Kabat-Zinn, and Bratt (2007) report that between 1992 and 1996, approximately 2,000 individuals in Massachusetts correctional institutions took part in a MBSR program, with 12–20 participants attending each course. Although the report does not provide extensive detail of the activities performed during mindfulness sessions, MBSR typically consists of body scan meditation, where attention is focused in turn on different parts of the body, mindful stretching exercises, and sitting mindfulness meditation (Samuelson et al., 2007). Participants would also typically take part in discussions on the integration of mindfulness in to everyday life. Samuelson et al. report that sessions lasted for 60–90 minutes, and courses were typically of six to eight weeks in duration. They report that although benefits were recorded across measures of hostility, self-esteem, and mood states, changes were typically greater for females compared to males. However, the authors do not report the effects of MBSR on aggressive or other behaviors of interest within the facility. The results of Samuelson et al. do however suggest that mindfulness may be an effective intervention for individuals with convictions, helping them to handle the stress of incarceration and to better deal with emotional challenges.

The effects of mindfulness meditation have also been examined by Singh and colleagues who evaluated the benefits of mindfulness programs with in a sample of psychiatric patients with a history of mental illness and hospitalization (Singh et al., 2007a) and a sample of three adolescents with a diagnosis of conduct disorder (CD) (Singh et al., 2007b). In their study with adolescents, Singh et al. (2007b) asked participants to take part in a mindfulness meditation known as "meditation on the soles of the feet," that requires participants to focus attention in the present moment on a neutral part of the body. This technique, and other similar techniques, allows the participant to focus attention away from an anxiety provoking or emotionally challenging thought or situation. Participants arranged to meet with a therapist three days per week for four weeks for mindfulness training, and follow up was conducted over one school year. In this study, the authors observed reductions in cruelty and non-compliance over a one-year follow up period, while Singh and colleagues (2007a) observed reduced signs of verbal and physical aggression among three individuals with a history of mental illness. Singh et al. (2011) have also used meditation on the soles of the feet and an additional "mindful observation of thoughts" technique to reduce deviant sexual arousal in a sample of three adult male sexual offenders with learning disability. Although these results again provide evidence for the usefulness of mindfulness modules, these reports are limited by small sizes. Furthermore, the methodology employed for analysis does not allow for the interpretation of effect sizes and significance levels in these data.

Perhaps most notably, mindfulness modules have also been successfully incorporated into forensic therapeutic programs including dialectical behavior therapy (DBT) (Linehan, 1993), a commonly used program in the treatment of patients with a diagnosis of borderline personality disorder (BPD) (DSM-5, APA, 2013) (Nee & Farman, 2005; Hogue, Jones, Talkes, & Tennant, 2007). DBT seeks to blend traditional cognitive behavioral approaches with acceptance-based approaches, including mindfulness, to help patients to develop skills believed to be theoretically important for the resolution of psychiatric disorder (Welch, Rizvi, & Dimidjian, 2006). The mindfulness component of DBT emphasizes the use of mindful observation, description, and participation; and states that these actions should be performed non-judgmentally, one-mindfully, and effectively (see Welch et al., 2006). However, unlike other mindfulness-based practices, DBT does not require formal mindful meditation, such as sitting meditation. Such meditations do, however, form a common part of other mindfulness courses, including MBCT. As outlined by Welch et al., emerging evidence would suggest that mindfulness forms an effective part of DBT through helping individuals with BPD to develop more acceptance-based techniques for emotion regulation, as opposed to the use of techniques such as suppression and avoidance that are common among BPD sufferers (Rosenthal, Cheavens, Lejuez, & Lynch, 2005). In a test of the therapeutic benefits of DBT for BPD, Verheul et al. (2003) randomly assigned 58 women with BPD to either 12 months of DBT or "treatment as usual," which involved clinical management through not more than two sessions per month with a psychologist or psychiatrist. Results showed that DBT was associated with better retention rates and greater reductions in self-mutilating and self-harming behaviors compared with the treatment as usual control group. Other studies also report successful treatment outcome following DBT for the treatment of BPD, as reviewed by Koerner and Dimeff (2000) and Rizvi and Linehan (2001).

Although the evidence presented here provides a platform for the use of mindfulness in a forensic context, it should be noted that there is currently a lack of empirical research to support a conclusion that mindfulness would reduce recidivism rates and help individuals to desist from criminal behavior. A priority for future research should be to measure treatment outcome following mindfulness among individuals with convictions and to measure recidivism rates following release into the community. Furthermore, we would also note that, as yet, there is a relative lack of studies that employ psychophysiological or other measures of neurobiological outcomes in a forensic setting. Although such measures may not be necessary for participation in mindfulness courses, the use of such measures would provide a means for understanding the mechanism of change among forensic clients following mindfulness-based practice.

Heart Rate Variability Biofeedback Techniques

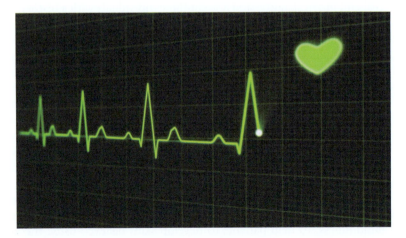

Heart rate variability *High levels of HRV are reflected in good emotion control and a strong physiological ability to recover from stressors. Thus, emotional responses are intimately involved with the functioning of the autonomic nervous system (ANS).*

Source: © PublicDomainPictures. Used under license from 699pic.

It is well established that the act of breathing affects the cardiac cycle (Bernardi et al., 1989). This effect stems from the respiratory sinus arhythmia (RSA) whereby the heart rate is slowed down during expiration (Bernardi, Porta, Gabutti, Spicuzza, & Sleight, 2001). The vagal nerve of the parasympathetic division of the autonomic nervous system (ANS) is critically involved in the slowing of the heart (Levy, 1990; Uijtdehagge & Thayer, 2000). Thayer and Lane (2009) note that as the "braking effect" of the vagus on heart rate increases, so too do fluctuations in the inter-beat interval of the heart. The measurement of these fluctuations in the intervals between beats of the heart is referred to as heart rate variability (HRV) (Thayer & Brosschot, 2005). Increases in HRV can be achieved by manipulating breathing so as to increase vagal output. For example, Bernardi et al. (2001) argued that HRV is maximized when respiration slows to six breaths per minute (0.1 Hz). High levels of HRV are reflected in good emotion control and a strong physiological ability to recover from stressors (Dishmanet al., 2000; Johnsen et al., 2003). Thus, emotional responses are intimately involved with the functioning of the ANS. This relationship has been termed the "heart–brain connection" (Thayer & Lane, 2009). In their model of neurovisceral integration, Thayer and Lane (2009) argue that an organism must be able to respond and adapt to a changing environment, and that these adaptations are shaped by physiology and behavior, as well as cognitive, affective, and social influences. It is proposed that HRV may represent an index of a flexible system; a system that integrates information from various systems and is capable of adapting to environmental demands (Thayer & Sternberg, 2006).

Low levels of HRV have been implicated in various clinical disorders, including those characterized by heightened levels of anxiety and worry (Brosschot, Van Dijk, & Thayer, 2007), stress (Dishman et al., 2000), and panic (Garakani et al., 2009). Results of such studies suggest that cardio-regulatory processes may be used to both predict and distinguish between different clinical symptoms and disorders. For example, patients with generalized anxiety disorder (GAD) (DSM-IV-TR, APA, 2000) tend to show low HRV both at rest and when stressed (Thayer, Friedman, & Borkovec, 1996), while patients with panic disorder (DSM-5, APA, 2013) show increased heart rate and decreased HRV both at rest and during a 30 breaths-per-minute hyperventilation challenge (Garakani et al., 2009). Furthermore, Garakani et al. (2009) showed that cognitive behavioral therapy (CBT) was associated with decreased heart rate and increased HRV, as well as improvements on clinical measures. Thus, the benefits of CBT may be reflected in changes in cardio-regulatory processes, which allow the individual to exert greater vagal control over heart rate.

Neural correlates of HRV

Research evidence from behavioral testing, including tests of executive function and advanced neuroimaging work, indicate a relationship between HRV and the functioning of the prefrontal cortex. This link has been simply demonstrated by Hansen, Johnsen, and Thayer (2003) who found that participants with high levels of HRV also showed better performance on cognitive tests that tap executive function. Similarly, Hansen, Johnsen, Sollers, Stenvik, and Thayer (2004) found that lowering HRV through cessation of aerobic exercises was associated with reduced performance on executive tasks. These findings indicate an important link between HRV and success on tests of executive functioning, which are dependent upon the functioning of the prefrontal cortex.

However, these cognitive tests were carried out under normal experimental conditions. As such it is notable that similar results have been found while participants are in a state of apparent stress. For example, Johnsen et al. (2003), showed that dental phobic subjects with higher HRV, compared to those with low HRV, were better able to inhibit an inappropriate response when confronted with phobia related words. Similar results have also been demonstrated by Bornas et al. (2005) who presented flight related aversive stimuli, including flight images and sounds, to flight fearful participants with low and high HRV. Again, results showed that high HRV was crucial for inhibiting an inappropriate response, with low HRV flight fearful participants reporting more elevated levels of self-report anxiety. High HRV is therefore seemingly related to an ability to inhibit a prepotent emotional response. Such findings could have implications for the treatment of individuals who present with an aggressive or angry response in the face of frustration, stress, or perceived hostility.

These findings are consistent with observations from a review of studies on the relationship between HRV and cognitive, affective, and autonomic function. In reviewing these studies, Thayer, Hansen, Saus-Rose, and Johnsen (2009) suggest that there is evidence for a relationship between HRV, prefrontal neural function, and cognitive performance (Thayer et al., 2009). This link is supported by neuroimaging findings that show a relationship between HRV and activity in the medial prefrontal cortex (Lane et al., 2009). Lane et al. (2009) showed that when participants were presented with emotion inducing film clips, high-frequency HRV correlated with activity in various regions including superior prefrontal cortex, rostral anterior cingulate cortex, and dorsolateral prefrontal cortex (dlPFC). Furthermore, increases in emotional arousal were associated with reductions in HRV. Thayer et al. (2009) suggest that the prefrontal cortex may be taken off-line during emotional experience, such that more prepotent responses may be used to guide behavior. Such behaviors are less deliberately organized, and are guided by subcortical structures, including the amygdala. However, such a pattern of responding prevents adaptive adjustment in modern society, with long-term inactivation of the prefrontal cortex linked with defensive responding and hypervigillance, a characteristic feature of anxiety (Thayer et al., 2009). Thus, the relationship between HRV and improved regulation of affective states may reflect increased prefrontal inhibitory control over the amygdala (Thayer & Sternberg, 2006).

Consistent with the suggestion that physiological parameters may be linked with adaptive responding, research has shown that those with severely antisocial behavior show abnormalities in physiological responding. Although many findings indicate a strong link between a low resting heart rate and antisocial behavior (for a review and meta-analysis see Ortiz & Raine, 2004), alternative findings suggest that vagal modulation may be compromised in antisocial behavior. For example, Mezzacappa et al. (1997) conducted a four-to six-year follow up study of 175 adolescent males taking measures of heart rate and vagally mediated HRV, antisocial behavior, and anxiety. Similar to the findings from Ortiz and Raine's (2004) meta-analysis, results showed that heart rate was inversely related to antisocial behavior, while a positive relationship of HRV and anxiety was also observed (Mezzacappa et al., 1997). However, results also showed that antisocial behavior was linked with a disruption to vagally mediated, phasic respiratory effects on heart rate. Furthermore, Beauchaine, Gatzke-Kopp, and

Mead (2007) observed poor vagal modulation of cardiac output among children with CD aged 4–18. Taken together, these results suggest that while antisocial behavior may be linked with low resting heart rate, such individuals may also show poor vagal modulation of cardiac output. We would suggest therefore that HRV biofeedback training may represent one means of strengthening vagally mediated HRV.

Biofeedback Techniques

Biofeedback refers to the recording of physiological functions so that an individual can gain greater awareness over changes in these systems or functions. Thus, HRV biofeedback refers to the recording of changes in heart rate and HRV, which provide an individual with greater awareness over changes in HRV. Biofeedback devices can be used by therapists to calculate an optimal pattern of breathing for achieving maximal increases in HRV. For example, Lehrer, Vaschillo, and Vaschillo (2000) developed a biofeedback system that could help practitioners to induce a pattern of slow and controlled breathing among patients with the aim of achieving subsequent increases in HRV. Participants using this system are first asked to coordinate their respiratory rate with that of a pacing stimulus, a light displayed on screen moving in vertical lines. This pacing stimulus indicates to the participant when to inhale and when to exhale (breath in and breath out). Over the course of the following week participants are instructed to practice breathing at this rate for 20-minute periods twice weekly. In the next session, participants are taught to manipulate their breathing using biofeedback in such a way that causes maximal fluctuations in heart rate in conjunction with respiration (Lehrer et al., 2000). Lehrer et al. note that this formal biofeedback may have advantages over paced breathing and other techniques that are frequently practiced as part of Eastern meditative practices, including yoga. In contrast to techniques developed during meditation, formal cardiac biofeedback is replicable, standardized, and can be learned quickly and easily by most individuals (Lehrer et al., 2000).

Reiner (2008) successfully integrated the use of HRV biofeedback into treatment for AD patients receiving CBT. Twenty participants were recruited and instructed to use a biofeedback device that operated a point giving system for achieving increased fluctuations in heart rate. Participants were instructed to use the device for 20 minutes throughout the day over a three-week treatment period. Following biofeedback training, participants showed significant reductions in anxiety, anger, and stress, as well as increases in positive affect.

Biofeedback techniques have also been successfully integrated in to treatments for depression. For example, Siepman, Aykac, Unterdörfer, Petrowski, and Mueck-Weymann (2008) observed the effects of six sessions of HRV biofeedback conducted over two weeks among a sample of 14 patients. Participants underwent three sessions of biofeedback training per week for two weeks. Each session lasted for approximately 25 minutes and participants underwent biofeedback with the aim of maximizing HRV. The biofeedback device provided participants with a pacing stimulus matched to the respiratory rate that caused maximal fluctuations in heart rate for each participant. These authors observed reductions in depression and anxiety, as well as decreased heart rate and increased HRV. The results reported by Siepman and colleagues (2008) suggest that maximizing HRV may have therapeutic effects on levels of anxiety and depression in depressed patients. These results likely reflect the functioning of a more flexible cardiac system that is linked with changes in emotion regulatory neural circuits including the prefrontal and the anterior cingulate cortex (Thayer & Lane, 2000). Similar results in the treatment of depression have also been reported by Hassett et al. (2007) and Karavidas et al. (2007), while HRV biofeedback has also been used in the treatment of PTSD (Tan, Dao, Farmer, Sutherland, & Gevirtz, 2011). Although it should be noted that many of these studies share a focus on self-report instruments for the measurement of changes in clinical symptoms, and some fail to include measures of heart rate and HRV, the results of these and other studies are nonetheless consistent in the suggestion that HRV biofeedback represents a clinically useful adjunct to behavioral therapies aimed at reducing anxiety, anger, and autonomic arousal.

Conclusions and Implication for Forensic/Practice, Ethical Implications and Policy

In summary, we have made an argument that some individuals who demonstrate antisocial behavior also show pathological levels of emotion dysregulation. For example, both individuals with ASPD and those with an acquired or "secondary" psychopathy have been found to present with heightened levels of anxiety. These findings go against the previously hypothesized role of anxiety as a protective factor for antisocial behavior. Here we have suggested that therapeutic intervention for people who show antisocial behavior or who have criminal convictions should consider that emotion dysregulation reflects poor prefrontal control over lower level subcortical circuits. This understanding provides a mechanism of change for considering potential therapeutic interventions.

In this chapter we have discussed the use of two therapeutic approaches, mindfulness meditation, and the use of controlled breathing techniques that lead to increases in vagally mediated HRV. Furthermore, we also highlight that these techniques have been shown to strengthen prefrontal functioning. We propose that such approaches may be of benefit as a therapeutic adjunct to traditional behavior therapies for individuals with co-morbid antisocial behavior and emotion dysregulation. Although there are no obvious ethical issues with the use of such interventions, participants should be aware of the aims of the therapy and provided with a basic understanding of the underlying principles. We would recommend that such interventions be provided according to the risk, need, and responsivity principles (Andrews, Bonta, & Hoge, 1990), such that intervention is available most readily for clients who show the highest risk level, who are in greatest need of emotion regulation intervention, and who are most likely to show a therapeutic response.

Although the benefits of mindfulness have been well noted, its potential side effects are less well understood. Indeed, to our knowledge, any adverse side effects of mindfulness meditation are yet to have been reported in the empirical literature. However, caution should be taken when practicing mindfulness with clients who show symptoms of anxiety, depression, or other mental health disorder. In such contexts, mindfulness should be taught by trained professionals who have clinical experience of working with clients affected by these disorders. Similarly, although controlled breathing techniques can be undertaken with the help of cues that signal the beginning and end of expiration and inspiration, any efforts to measure heart rate and/or HRV should be undertaken with equipment that is fit for purpose and interpreted by trained professionals. Individualized HRV biofeedback sessions should also be run by professionals with the requisite training.

While the benefits of mindfulness training are likely to be greatest following intensive training with experienced meditators, it should be noted that changes in emotion regulation have been noted after minimal mindfulness training. For example, beginner meditators showed changes in neural activation in regions involved in emotion regulation following minimal training over a seven-day period involving detailed instruction and recorded guided mindfulness sessions (Taylor et al., 2011). However, the extent to which these changes represent long-term benefits is unknown. We would suggest that mindfulness should be instructed by experienced meditators with a full grasp of the concepts and techniques involved in mindfulness meditation, as well as experience of how to deal with any potential difficulties that may arise as a result of mindfulness practice.

The mechanisms by which mindfulness may exert its benefits have been shown to vary between beginner and experienced meditators. For example, Taylor et al. (2011) found that beginners showed increased down-regulation of the left amygdala, via higher order cortical regions, in response to a range of affective stimuli. This mechanism of action is therefore consistent with that outlined in the earlier section on the neurobiology of emotion regulation. In contrast, mindfulness benefits in more experienced meditators were shown to reflect a more acceptance-based mechanism, with an absence of responding in several regions known to be active during ruminative thinking (Taylor et al., 2011). The authors conclude that these results may reflect the disengagement of appraisal and thought-related process. Finally, beginner and experienced meditators showed no difference in their ratings of affective stimuli, suggesting that despite differential mechanisms, mindfulness was an effective emotion regulation strategy for both groups of participants. Notably, beginners in this study had undergone minimal mindfulness training of 20 minutes per day for seven days prior to testing. However, traditional mindfulness-based programs – including mindfulness-based cognitive therapy for the treatment of recurrent depression – typically involve eight weekly two-hour group training sessions (Teasdale et al., 2000).

It should also be noted that individuals may be differentially sensitive to the benefits of mindfulness training. Studies have indicated that there may be an interaction of serotonin genes with the effectiveness of mindfulness techniques, such that individuals who express a particular serotonin transporter gene polymorphism (a distinct phenotype arising from the expression of different alleles of the same gene) tend to have trouble with emotion regulation but benefit substantially from mindfulness training. While there is limited research on the relation of serotonin transporter gene polymorphisms with aggression and antisocial behavior, it would nonetheless be predicted that individuals with convictions with marked impairments in emotion regulation would benefit from mindfulness-based therapies.

Finally, despite a great deal of evidence for the beneficial outcomes of mindfulness-based meditation in relation to clinical and non-clinical samples, it should be emphasized that evidence for its use in forensic samples remains limited. While we would encourage the use of mindfulness and breathing-based meditations with forensic samples, those introducing such therapies should be committed to rigorously evaluating the benefits of such interventions. A greater understanding of "what works" in relation to mindfulness in forensic settings will pave the way for the introduction of such

694   *S. M. Gillespie and A. R. Beech*

interventions into main stream treatment programs for improving emotion regulation among individuals with convictions.

Recommended Reading

Bishop, S. L., Lau, M., Shapiro, S., Carlson, L., Anderson, N. D., Carmody, J., ... Devins, G. (2004). Mindfulness: A proposed operational definition. *Clinical Psychology: Science and Practice, 11*, 230–241. *This review paper proposes a two component model of mindfulness that includes the self-regulation of attention in the present moment; and the maintaining of a curious attitude of openness toward thoughts, feelings, and sensations. Mindfulness here is defined as the ability to attend to stimuli, as they are experienced, in a non-judgmental and accepting manner.*

Coid, J., & Ullrich, S. (2010). Antisocial personality disorder and anxiety disorder: A diagnostic variant? *Journal of Anxiety Disorders, 24*, 452–460. *In this paper, it was found that individuals with ASPD and a diagnosis of an AD showed an increased failure to conform to social norms, as well as higher levels of deceitfulness, impulsivity, and irritability/aggressiveness. It is proposed that ASPD co-morbid with anxiety disorder (ASPD+AD) may represent a diagnostic variant to ASPD alone. Thus, heightened levels of anxiety among individuals with ASPD may have implications for the types of antisocial behavior observed.*

Davidson, R. J., Putnam, K. M., & Larson, C. L. (2000). Dysfunction in the neural circuitry of emotion regulation – A possible prelude to violence. *Science, 289*, 591–594. *Davidson et al. review the literature on the neural mechanisms of emotion regulation and suggest that impulsive aggression and violence arises as a consequence of dysfunction in neural circuits involving the prefrontal cortex, amygdala, and the anterior cingulate cortex. They suggest that impulsive violence may reflect a greater propensity to experience negative affect, including anger, distress, and agitation, and an impaired ability to respond appropriately to the anticipated negative outcomes associated with violent and aggressive behavior.*

Ochsner, N., Bunge, S. A., Gross, J. J., & Gabrieli, J. D. E. (2002). Rethinking feelings: An fMRI study of the cognitive regulation of emotion. *Journal of Cognitive Neuroscience, 14*, 1215–1229. *These authors used fMRI techniques to investigate the neural bases of emotion regulation. Results showed that reappraisal of negative emotion was associated with reductions in negative affect and increased activation in regions of prefrontal cortex. An inverse relationship of vlPFC activation and amygdala activity was also observed, suggesting that areas of prefrontal cortex may exert control over the amygdala response during the cognitive reappraisal of negative emotion.*

Samuelson, M., Carmody, J., Kabat-Zinn, J., & Bratt, M. A. (2007). Mindfulness-based stress reduction in Massachusetts correctional facilities. *The Prison Journal, 87*, 254–268. *In this paper, the authors evaluate the effectiveness of a mindfulness-based stress reduction program that approximately 2,000 individuals took part in between 1992 and 1996, in Massachusetts correctional institutions. The results showed benefits of the program on hostility, self-esteem, and mood states.*

References

Adolphs, R., Tranel, D., Damasio, H., & Damasio, A. (1994). Impaired recognition of emotion in facial expressions following bilateral damage to the human amygdala. *Nature, 372*, 669–672.

Andrews, D. A., Bonta, J., & Hoge, R. D. (1990). Classification for effective rehabilitation: Rediscovering psychology. *Criminal Justice and Behavior, 17*, 19–52.

American Psychiatric Association (APA) (2000). *Diagnostic and statistical manual of mental disorders* (3rd ed.) (*DSM-5*). Washington, DC: American Psychiatric Association.

Anderson, S. W., Bechara, A., Damasio, H., Tranel, D., & Damasio, A. R. (1999). Impairment of social and moral behavior related to early damage in human prefrontal cortex. *Nature Neuroscience, 2*, 1032–1037.

Arch, J. J., & Craske, M. G. (2006). Mechanisms of mindfulness: Emotion regulation following a focused breathing induction. *Behavior Research and Therapy, 44*, 1849–1858.

Beauchaine, T. P., Gatzke-Kopp, L., & Mead, H. K. (2007). Polyvagal theory and developmental psychopathology: Emotion dysregulation and conduct problems from preschool to adolescence. *Biological Psychology, 74*, 174–184.

Beauregard, M., Lévesque, J., & Bourgouin, P. (2001). Neural correlates of conscious self-regulation of emotion. *Journal of Neuroscience, 21*, RC165.

Bernardi, L., Keller, F., Sanders, M., Reddy, P. S., Griffith, B., Meno F., & Pinsky, M. R. (1989). Respiratory sinus arrhythmia in the denervated human heart. *Journal of Applied Physiology, 67*, 1447–1455.

Bernardi, L., Porta, C., Gabutti, A., Spicuzza, L., & Sleight, P. (2001). Modulatory effects of respiration. *Autonomic Neuroscience: Basic and Clinical, 90*, 47–56.

Birbaumer, N., Grodd, W., Diedrich, O., Klose, U., Erb, M., Schneider, F., … Flor, H. (1998). fMRI reveals amygdala activation to human faces in social phobics. *NeuroReport, 9*, 1223–1226.

Bishop, S. L., Lau, M., Shapiro, S., Carlson, L., Anderson, N. D., Carmody, J., … Devins, G. (2004). Mindfulness: A proposed operational definition. *Clinical Psychology: Science and Practice, 11*, 230–241.

Blair, R. J. R., & Cipolotti, L. (2000). Impaired social response reversal: A case of "acquired sociopathy." *Brain, 123*, 1122–1141.

Blair, R. J. R., Morris, J. S., Frith, C. D., Perrett, D. I., & Dolan, R. (1999). Dissociable neural responses to facial expressions of sadness and anger. *Brain, 122*, 883–893.

Borders, A., Earleywine, M., & Jajodia, A. (2010). Could mindfulness decrease anger, hostility, and aggression by decreasing rumination? *Aggressive Behavior, 36*, 28–44.

Bornas, X., Llabrés, J., Noguera, M., López, A. M., Barceló, F., Tortella-Feliu, M., & Fullana, M. À. (2005). Looking at the heart of low and high heart rate variability fearful flyers: self-reported anxiety when confronting feared stimuli. *Biological Psychology, 70*, 182–187.

Breiter, H. C., Etcoff, N. L., Whalen, P. J., Kennedy, W. A., Rauch, S. L., Buckner, R. L., … Rosen, B. R. (1996a). Response and habituation of the human amygdala during visual processing of facial expression. *Neuron, 17*, 875–888.

Breiter, H. C., Rauch, S.L., Kwong, K. K., Baker, J. R., Weisskoff, R. M., Kennedy, D. N., … Rosen, B.R. (1996b). Functional magnetic resonance imaging of symptom provocation in obsessive compulsive disorder. *Archives of General Psychiatry, 53*, 595–606.

Broks, P., Young, A. W., Maratos, E. J., Coffey, P. J., Calder, A. J., Isaac, C. L., … Hadley, D. (1998). Face processing impairments after encephalitis: amygdala damage and recognition of fear. *Neuropsychologia, 36*, 59–70.

Brosschot, J. F., Van Dijk, E., & Thayer, J. F. (2007). Daily worry is related to low heart rate variability during waking and the subsequent nocturnal sleep period. *International Journal of Psychophysiology, 63*, 39–47.

Carrion, V. G., Weems, C. F., Richert, K., Hoffman, B. C., & Reiss, A. L. (2010). Decreased prefrontal cortical volume associated with increased bedtime cortisol in traumatized youth. *Biological Psychiatry, 68*, 491–493.

Chiesa, A., & Serretti, A. (2010). A systematic review of neurobiological and clinical features of mindfulness meditations. *Psychological Medicine, 40*, 1239–1252.

Coid, J., & Ullrich, S. (2010). Antisocial personality disorder and anxiety disorder: A diagnostic variant? *Journal of Anxiety Disorders, 24*, 452–460.

Cozolino, L. (2008). *The neuroscience of human relationships.* New York: Norton.

Creeden, K. (2004). The neurodevelopmental impact of early trauma and insecure attachment: Re-thinking our understanding and treatment of sexual behavior problems. *Sexual Addiction & Compulsivity, 11*, 223–247.

Creswell, J. D., Way, B. M., Eisenberger, N. I., & Lieberman, M. D. (2007). Neural correlates of dispositional mindfulness during affect labeling. *Psychosomatic Medicine, 69*, 560–565.

Damasio, A. R. (1994). *Descartes' error: Emotion, reason and the human brain.* New York: Puttnam.

Davidson, R. J. (2002). Anxiety and affective style: Role of prefrontal cortex and amygdala. *Biological Psychiatry, 51*, 68–80.

Davidson, R. J., Kabat-Zinn, J., Schumacher, J., Rosenkranz, M., Muller, D., Santorelli, S. F., ... Sheridan, J. F. (2003). Alterations in brain and immune function produced by mindfulness meditation. *Psychosomatic Medicine, 65*, 564–570.

Davidson, R. J., Putnam, K. M., & Larson, C. L. (2000). Dysfunction in the neural circuitry of emotion regulation—A possible prelude to violence. *Science, 289*, 591–594.

Day, A. (2009). Offender emotion and self-regulation: Implications for offender rehabilitation programming. *Psychology, Crime and Law, 15*, 119–130.

Day, A., Davey, L., Wanganeen, R., Casey, S., Howells, K., & Nakata, M. (2008). Symptoms of trauma, perceptions of discrimination, and anger: A comparison between Australian indigenous and nonindigenous prisoners. *Journal of Interpersonal Violence, 23*, 245–258.

Dishman, R. K., Nakamura, Y., Garcia, M. E., Thompson, R. W., Dunn, A. L., & Blair, S. N. (2000). Heart rate variability, trait anxiety, and perceived stress among physically fit men and women. *International Journal of Psychophysiology, 37*, 121–133.

Ellsworth, P. C., & Scherer, K. R. (2003). Appraisal processes in emotion. In R. J. Davidson, K. R., Scherer, & H. Goldsmith (Eds.), *Handbook of affective sciences* (pp. 572–595). New York: Oxford University Press.

Fix, R. L., & Fix, S. T. (2013). The effects of mindfulness-based treatments for aggression: A critical review. *Aggression and Violent Behavior, 18*, 219–227.

Frewen, P. A., Dozois, D. J. A., Neufeld, R. W. J., Lane, R. D., Densmore, M., Stevens, T. K., Lanius, R. A. (2010). Individual differences in trait mindfulness predict dorsomedial prefrontal and amygdala response during emotional imagery: An fMRI study. *Personality and Individual Differences, 49*, 479–484.

Fuster, J. M. (1985). The prefrontal cortex and temporal integration. In A. Peters & E. G. Jones (Eds.), *Cerebral cortex: Volume 4. Association and auditory cortices* (pp. 151–171). New York: Plenum Press.

Garakani, A., Martinez, J. M., Aaronson, C. J., Voustianiouk, A., Kaufmann, H., & Gorman, J. M. (2009). Effect of medication and psychotherapy on heart rate variability in panic disorder. *Depression and Anxiety, 26*, 251–258.

Gillespie, S. M., Mitchell, I. J., Fisher, D., & Beech, A. R. (2012). Treating disturbed emotional regulation in sexual offenders: Potential applications of mindful self-regulation and controlled breathing techniques. *Aggression and Violent Behavior, 17*, 333–343.

Gillespie, S. M., Mitchell, I. J., Satherley, R. M., Beech, A. R., & Rotshtein, P. (2015). Relations of distinct psychopathic personality traits with anxiety and fear: Findings from offenders and non-offenders. *PLoS ONE, 10*(11), e0143120.

Goodwin, R. D., & Hamilton, S. P. (2003). Lifetime comorbidity of antisocial personality disorder and anxiety disorders among adults in the community. *Psychiatry Research, 117*, 159–166.

Gross, J. J. (1998a). The emerging field of emotion regulation: An integrative review. *Review of General Psychology, 2*, 271–299.

Gross, J. J. (1998b). Antecedent- and response-focused emotion regulation: Divergent consequences for experience, expression, and physiology. *Journal of Personality and Social Psychology, 74*, 224–237.

Gross, J. J., & Levenson, R. W. (1993). Emotional suppression: Physiology, self-report, and expressive behavior. *Journal of Personality and Social Psychology, 64,* 970–986.

Gross, J. J., & Levenson, R. W. (1997). Hiding feelings: The acute effects of inhibiting positive and negative emotions. *Journal of Abnormal Psychology, 106,* 95–103.

Gross, J. J., & Munoz, R. F. (1995). Emotion regulation and mental health. *Clinical Psychology: Science and Practice, 2,* 151–164.

Gross, J. J., & Thompson, R. A. (2007). Emotion regulation: Conceptual foundations. In J. J. Gross (Ed.), *Handbook of emotion regulation* (pp. 3–27). New York, NY: Guilford Press.

Grossman, P., Niemann, L., Schmidt, S., & Walach, H. (2004). Mindfulness-based stress reduction and health benefits: A meta-analysis. *Journal of Psychosomatic Research, 57,* 35–43.

Hahn, A., Stein, P., Windischberger, C., Weissenbacher, A., Spindelegger, C., Moser, E., ... Lanzenberger, R. (2011). Reduced resting-state functional connectivity between amygdala and orbitofrontal cortex in social anxiety disorder. *NeuroImage, 56,* 881–889.

Hansen, A. L., Johnsen, B. H., Sollers, J. J., Stenvik, K., & Thayer, J. F. (2004). Heart rate variability and its relation to prefrontal cognitive function: the effects of training and detraining. *European Journal of Applied Physiology, 93,* 263–272.

Hansen, A. L., Johnsen, B. H., & Thayer, J. F. (2003). Vagal influence on working memory and attention. *International Journal of Psychophysiology, 48,* 263–274.

Hanson, J. L., Chung, M. K., Avants, B. B., Shirtcliff, E. A., Gee, J. C., Davidson, R. J., & Pollak, S. D. (2010). Early stress is associated with alterations in the orbitofrontal cortex: A tensor-based morphometry investigation of brain structure and behavioral risk. *The Journal of Neuroscience, 30,* 7466–7472.

Hariri, A., Bookheimer, S. Y., & Mazziotta, J. C. (2000). Modulating emotional responses: Effects of a neocortical network on the limbic system. *NeuroReport, 11,* 43–48.

Hassett, A. L., Radvanski, D. C., Vaschillo, E. G., Vaschillo, B., Sigal, L. H., Karavidas, M. K., ... Lehrer, P. M. (2007). A pilot study of the efficacy of heart rate variability (HRV) biofeedback in patients with fibromyalgia. *Applied Psychophysiology and Biofeedback, 32,* 1–10.

Hicks, B. M., & Patrick, C. J. (2006). Psychopathy and negative emotionality: Analyses of suppressor effects reveal distinct relations with emotional distress, fearfulness, and anger–hostility. *Journal of Abnormal Psychology, 115,* 276–287.

Hogue, T. E., Jones, L., Talkes, K., & Tennant, A. (2007). The Peaks: A clinical service for those with dangerous and severe personality disorders. *Psychology, Crime and Law, 13,* 57–68.

Howells, K. (2010). The 'third wave' of cognitive-behavioral therapy and forensic practise. *Criminal Behavior and Mental Health, 20,* 251–256.

Jackson, D. C., Mueller, C. J., Dolski, I., Dalton, K. M., Nitshke, J. B., Urry, H. L., ... Davidson, R. J. (2003). Now you feel it, now you don't: Frontal brain electrical asymmetry and individual differences in emotion regulation. *Psychological Science, 14,* 612–617.

Johnsen, B. H., Thayer, J. F., Laberg, J. C., Wormnes, B., Raadal, M., Skaret, E., ... Berg, E. (2003). Attentional and physiological characteristics of patients with dental anxiety. *Journal of Anxiety Disorders, 17,* 75–87.

Kabat-Zinn, J. (1990). *Full catastrophe living: Using the wisdom of your mind to face stress, pain and illness.* New York, NY: Dell.

Kabat-Zinn, J. (2003). Mindfulness-based interventions in context: Past, present, and future. *Clinical Psychology: Science and Practice, 10,* 144–156.

Karavidas, M. K., Leherer, P. M., Vaschillo, E., Vaschillo, B., Marin, H., Buyske, S., ... Hassett, A. (2007). Preliminary results of an open label study of heart rate variability biofeedback for the treatment of major depression. *Applied Psychophysiology and Biofeedback, 32,* 19–30.

Koerner, K., & Dimeff, L. A. (2000). Further data on dialectical behavior therapy. *Clinical Psychology: Science and Practice, 7,* 104–112.

Lane, R. D., McRae, K., Reiman, E. M., Chen, K., Ahern, G. L., & Thayer, J. F. (2009). Neural correlates of heart rate variability during emotion. *Neuroimage, 44,* 213–222.

Lehrer, P. M., Vaschillo, E., & Vaschillo, B. (2000). Resonant frequency biofeedback training to increase cardiac variability: Rationale and manual for training. *Applied Psychophysiology and Biofeedback, 25*, 177–191.

Lenzenweger, M. F., Lane, M. C., Loranger, A. W., & Kessler, R. C. (2007). DSM-IV personality disorders in the National Comorbidity Survey Replication. *Biological Psychiatry, 62*, 553–564.

Levy, M. N. (1990). Autonomic interactions in cardiac control. *Annals of the New York Academy of Sciences, 601*, 209–221.

Liberzon, I., Taylor, S. F., Amdur, R., Jung, T. D., Chamberlain, K. R., Minoshima, S., ... Fig, L. M. (1999). Brain activation in PTSD in response to trauma-related stimuli. *Biological Psychiatry, 45*, 817–826.

Linehan, M. M. (1993). *Cognitive behavioral treatment of Borderline Personality Disorder.* New York: Guilford Press.

Mah, L., Arnold, M. C., & Grafman, J. (2004). Impairment of social perception associated with lesions of the prefrontal cortex. *American Journal of Psychiatry, 161*, 1247–1255.

Martin, J. P. (1997). Mindfulness: A proposed common factor. *Journal of Psychotherapy Integration, 7*, 291–312.

Mehta, M. A., Golembo, N. I., Nosarti, C., Colvert, E., Mota, A., Williams, S. C., ... Sonuga-Barke, E. J. (2009). Amygdala, hippocampal and corpus callosum size following severe early institutional deprivation: The English and Romanian Adoptees study pilot. *Journal of Child Psychology and Psychiatry, 50*, 943–951.

Mezzacappa, E., Tremblay, R. E., Kindlon, D., Saul, J. P., Arseneault, L., Seguin, J., ... Earls, F. (1997). Anxiety, antisocial behavior, and heart rate regulation in adolescent males. *Journal of Child Psychology and Psychiatry, 38*, 457–469.

Milad, M. R., & Rauch, S. L. (2007). The role of the orbitofrontal cortex in anxiety disorders. *Annals of the New York Academy of Sciences, 1121*, 546–561.

Modinos, G., Ormel, J., & Aleman, A. (2010). Individual differences in dispositional mindfulness and brain activity involved in reappraisal of emotion. *Social Cognitive and Affective Neuroscience, 5*, 369–377.

Moriarty, N., Stough, C., Tidmarsh, P., Eger, D. E., & Dennison, S. (2001). Deficits in emotional intelligence underlying adolescent sex offending. *Journal of Adolescence, 24*, 743–751.

Morris, J. S., Frith, C. D., Perrett, D. I., Rowland, D., Young, A. W., Calder, A. J., & Dolan, R. J. (1996). A differential neural response in the human amygdala to fearful and happy facial expressions. *Nature, 383*, 812–815.

Murakami, H., Matsunaga, M., & Ohira, H. (2009). Association of serotonin transporter gene polymorphism and emotion regulation. *NeuroReport, 20*, 414–418.

Nee, C., & Farman, S. (2005). Female prisoners with borderline personality disorder: Some promising treatment developments. *Criminal Behavior and Mental Health, 15*, 2–16.

O'Doherty, J., Kringelbach, M. L., Rolls, E. T., Hornak, J., & Andrews, C. (2001). Abstract reward and punishment representations in the human orbitofrontal cortex. *Nature Neuroscience, 4*, 95–102.

Ochsner, K. N. & Gross, J. J. (2005). The cognitive control of emotion. *Trends in Cognitive Sciences, 9*, 242–249.

Ochsner, K. N., & Gross, J. J. (2007). The neural architecture of emotion regulation. In J. J. Gross (Ed.), *Handbook of emotion regulation* (pp. 87–110). New York, NY: Guilford Press.

Ochsner, K. N., Ray, R. D., Cooper, J. C., Robertson, E. R., Chopra, S., Gabrieli, J. D. E., & Gross, J. J. (2004). For better or for worse: Neural systems supporting the cognitive down- and up-regulation of negative emotion. *NeuroImage, 23*, 483–499.

Ochsner, N., Bunge, S. A., Gross, J. J., & Gabrieli, J. D. E. (2002). Rethinking feelings: An fMRI study of the cognitive regulation of emotion. *Journal of Cognitive Neuroscience, 14*, 1215–1229.

Ortiz, J., & Raine, A. (2004). Heart rate level and antisocial behavior in children and adolescents: A meta-analysis. *Journal of the American Academy of Child & Adolescent Psychiatry, 43*, 154–162.

Ramel, W., Goldin, P. R., Carmona, P. E., & McQuaid, J. R. (2004). The effects of mindfulness meditation on cognitive processes and affect in patients with past depression. *Cognitive Therapy and Research, 28*, 433–455.

Rauch, S. L., Savage, C. R., Alpert, N. M., Fischman, A. J., & Jenike, M. A. (1997). The functional neuroanatomy of anxiety: A study of three disorders using positron emission tomography and symptom provocation. *Biological Psychiatry, 42*, 446–452.

Rauch, S. L., Whalen, P. J., Shin, L. M., McInerney, S. C., Macklin, M. L., Lasko, N. B., … Pitman, R. K. (2000). Exaggerated amygdala response to masked facial stimuli in posttraumatic stress disorder: a functional MRI study. *Biological psychiatry, 47*, 769–776.

Reiner, R. (2008). Integrating a portable biofeedback device into clinical practice for patients with anxiety disorders: Results of a pilot study. *Applied Psychophysiology and Biofeedback, 33*, 55–61.

Richert, K. A., Carrion, V. G., Karchemskiy, A., & Reiss, A. L. (2006). Regional differences of the prefrontal cortex in pediatric PTSD: an MRI study. *Depression and Anxiety, 23*, 17–25.

Rizvi, S. L., & Linehan, M. M. (2001). Dialectical behavior therapy for personality disorders. *Current Psychiatry Reports, 3*, 64–69.

Rosenthal, M. Z., Cheavens, J. S., Lejuez, C. W., & Lynch, T. R. (2005). Thought suppression mediates the relationship between negative affect and borderline personality disorder symptoms. *Behavior Research and Therapy, 43*, 1173–1185.

Rushworth, M. F. S., Behrens, T. E. J., Rudebeck, P. H., & Walton, M. E. (2007). Contrasting roles for cingulate and orbitofrontal cortex in decisions and social behavior. *Trends in Cognitive Sciences, 11*, 168–176.

Samuelson, M., Carmody, J., Kabat-Zinn, J., & Bratt, M. A. (2007). Mindfulness-based stress reduction in Massachusetts correctional facilities. *The Prison Journal, 87*, 254–268.

Sareen, J., Stein, M. B., Cox, B. J., & Hassard, S. T. (2004). Understanding comorbidity of anxiety disorders with antisocial behavior: findings from two large community surveys. *The Journal of Nervous and Mental Disease, 192*, 178–186.

Savitsky, J. C., & Czyzewski, D. (1978). The reaction of adolescent offenders and nonoffenders to nonverbal emotion displays. *Journal of Abnormal Child Psychology, 6*, 89–96.

Schaefer, S. M., Jackson, D. C., Davidson, R. J., Aguirre, G. K., Kimberg, D. Y., & Thompson-Schill, S. L. (2002). Modulation of amygdalar activity by the conscious regulation of negative emotion. *Journal of Cognitive Neuroscience, 14*, 913–921.

Shapiro, S. L., Carlson, L. E., Astin, J. A., & Freedman, B. (2006). Mechanisms of mindfulness. *Journal of Clinical Psychology, 62*, 373–386.

Shore, A. N. (2004). *Affect regulation and the original of the self: The neurobiology of emotional development.* Hillsdale, NJ: Lawrence Erlbaum.

Siepman, M., Aykac, V., Unterdörfer, J., Petrowski, K., & Mueck-Weymann, M. (2008). A pilot study on the effects of heart rate variability biofeedback in patients with depression and in healthy subjects. *Applied Psychophysiology and Biofeedback, 33*, 195–201.

Singh, N. N., Lancioni, G. E., Joy, S. D. S., Winton, A. S. W., Sabaawi, M., Wahler, R. G., & Singh, J. (2007a). Adolescents with conduct disorders can be mindful of their aggressive behavior. *Emotional and Behavioral Disorders, 15*, 56–63.

Singh, N. N., Lancioni, G. E., Winton, A. S. W., Adkins, A. D., Wahler, R. G., Sabaawi, M., & Singh, J. (2007b). Individuals with mental illness can control their aggressive behavior through mindfulness training. *Behavior Modification, 31*, 313–328.

Singh, N. N., Lancioni, G. E., Winton, A. S., Singh, A. N., Adkins, A. D., & Singh, J. (2011). Can adult offenders with intellectual disabilities use mindfulness-based procedures to control their deviant sexual arousal? *Psychology, Crime & Law, 17*, 165–179.

Takahashi, T., Murata, T., Hamada, T., Omori, M., Kosaka, H., Kikuchi, M., ... Wada, Y. (2005). Changes in EEG and autonomic nervous activity during meditation and their association with personality traits. *International Journal of Psychophysiology, 55*, 199–207.

Tan, G., Dao, T. K., Farmer, L., Sutherland, R. J., & Gevirtz, R. (2011). Heart rate variability (HRV) and posttraumatic stress disorder (PTSD): A pilot study. *Applied Psychophysiology and Biofeedback, 36*, 27–35.

Taylor, V. A., Grant, J., Daneault, V., Scavone, G., Breton, E., Roffe-Vidal, S., ... Beauregard, M. (2011). Impact of mindfulness on the neural responses to emotional pictures in experienced and beginner meditators. *NeuroImage, 57*, 1524–1533.

Teasdale, J. D., Segal, Z. V., & Williams, J. M. G. (2003). Mindfulness training and problem formulation. *American Clinical Psychology: Science and Practice, 10*, 157–160.

Teasdale, J. D., Segal, Z. V., Williams, J. M. G., & Mark, G. (1995). How does cognitive therapy prevent depressive relapse and why should attentional control (mindfulness) training help? *Behavior Research and Therapy, 33*, 25–39.

Teasdale, J. D., Williams, J. M., Soulsby, J. M., Segal, Z. V., Ridgeway, V. A., & Lau, M. A. (2000). Prevention of relapse/recurrence in major depression by mindfulness-based cognitive therapy. *Journal of Consulting and Clinical Psychology, 68*, 615–623.

Thayer, J. F., & Brosschot, J. F. (2005). Psychosomatics and psychopathology: Looking up and down from the brain. *Psychoneuroendocrinology, 30*, 1050–1058.

Thayer, J. F., Friedman, B. H., & Borkovec, T. D. (1996). Autonomic characteristics of generalized anxiety disorder and worry. *Biological Psychiatry, 39*, 255–266.

Thayer, J. F., Hansen, A. L., Saus-Rose, E., & Johnsen, B. H. (2009). Heart rate variability, prefrontal neural function, and cognitive performance: The neurovisceral integration perspective on self-regulation, adaptation and health. *Annals of Bahvioral Medicine, 37*, 141–153.

Thayer, J. F., & Lane, R. D. (2000). A model of neurovisceral integration in emotion regulation and dysregulation. *Journal of Affective Disorders, 61*, 201–216.

Thayer, J. F., & Lane, R. D. (2009). Claude Bernard and the heart-brain connection: Further elaboration of a model of neurovisceral integration. *Neuroscience and Biobehavioral Reviews, 33*, 81–88.

Thayer, J. F., & Sternberg, E. (2006). Beyond heart rate variability: Vagal regulation of allostatic systems. *Annals of the New York Academy of Sciences, 1088*, 361–372.

Tottenham, N., Hare, T. A., Millner, A., Gilhooly, T., Zevin, J. D., & Casey, B. J. (2011). Elevated amygdala response to faces following early deprivation. *Developmental Science, 14*, 190–204.

Tottenham, N., Hare, T. A., Quinn, B. T., McCarry, T. W., Nurse, M., Gilhooly, T., ... Casey, B. J. (2010). Prolonged institutional rearing is associated with atypically large amygdala volume and difficulties in emotion regulation. *Developmental Science, 13*, 46–61.

Uijtdehagge, S. B. H., & Thayer, J. F. (2000). Accentuated antagonism in the control of human heart rate. *Clinical Autonomic Research, 10*, 107–110.

Urry, H. L., van Reekum, C. M., Johnstone, T., Kalin, N. H., Thurow, M. E., Scaefer, H. S., ... Davidson, R. J. (2006). Amygdala and ventromedial prefrontal cortex are inversely coupled during regulation of negative affect and predict the diurnal pattern of cortisol secretion among older adults. *The Journal of Neuroscience, 26*, 4415–4425.

Vassileva, J., Kosson, D. S., Abramowitz, C., & Conrod, P. (2005). Psychopathy versus psychopathies in classifying criminal offenders. *Legal and Criminological Psychology, 10*, 27–43.

Verheul, R., van den Bosch, L. M. C., Koeter, M. W. J., De Ridder, M. A. J., Stijnen, T., & Van Den Brink, W. (2003). Dialectical behavior therapy for women with borderline personality disorder 12-month, randomised clinical trial in The Netherlands. *The British Journal of Psychiatry, 182*, 135–140.

Verona, E., Patrick, C. J., & Joiner, T. E. (2001). Psychopathy, antisocial personality, and suicide risk. *Journal of Abnormal Psychology, 110,* 462–470.

Whalen, P. J., Shin, L. M., McInerney, S. C., Fischer, H., Wright, C. I., & Rauch, S. L. (2001). A functional MRI study of human amygdala responses to facial expressions of fear versus anger. *Emotion, 1,* 70–83.

Welch, S. S., Rizvi, S., & Dimidjian, S. (2006). Mindfulness in dialectical behavior therapy (DBT) for borderline personality disorder. *Mindfulness-based treatment approaches: Clinician's guide to evidence base and applications* (pp. 117–139).

27

The Pharmacological Treatment of Sex Offenders

Don Grubin

Key points

- It is noted that the weaker a drive, the easier it is to control. In deciding whether this could be of benefit, an understanding of a range of factors concerning how medication affects sex drive and possible side effects need to be taken into account.
- Although not fully understood, enough is known about the biological basis of sexual behavior to inform the appropriate prescription of medication to control sexual arousal.
- A lack of experience and a misunderstanding of the aims of prescribing and where it sits in relation to public protection and patient care have contributed to a failure to utilize medication in helping to manage sexual arousal.
- Diagnostic manuals do not conceptualize problematic sexual behavior in a way that supports medication decisions. Most people convicted of a sexual offence will not receive a medical diagnosis but some might still benefit from medication.
- Although the direction of sex drive and the nature of preferred stimuli, which inform paraphilia diagnoses, and not addressed by medication, the intensity, frequency, and intrusiveness of sexual arousal, as well as factors that influence it are amenable to both psychological and medical interventions.
- Medical interventions that reduce the intrusiveness of sexual fantasy or level of sexual arousal can both improve engagement with other treatment methods and allow for the strengthening of psychological mechanisms to take place.
- A reduction of testosterone levels can weaken the basis upon which sexual offending behavior is initiated.
- The interaction between neurotransmitters and hormones involved in sexual motivation, arousal, and behavior is complex and only partly understood, but enough is known about the interaction between testosterone, dopamine, and

---

The Wiley Blackwell Handbook of Forensic Neuroscience, First Edition. Edited by Anthony R. Beech, Adam J. Carter, Ruth E. Mann and Pia Rotshtein.
© 2018 John Wiley & Sons Ltd. Published 2018 by John Wiley & Sons Ltd.

serotonin to inform the prescribing of medication to help with controlling sexual arousal associated with these neurotransmitters.

- Selective serotonin reuptake inhibitors (SSRIs), as well as anti-androgens, can reduce the frequency and intensity of sexual fantasy, urges, and arousal in a manner that is consistent with current understanding of the underlying neurobiology.
- Where high levels of sexual arousal or preoccupation make the application of psychological techniques difficult, reduction of arousal using medication may have a role. When prescribed, drugs should be for this medical indication rather than pubic protection, although an associated reduction in risk may assist risk management.

Terminology Explained

Androgens are a group of hormones comprised of testosterone and some of its metabolites or breakdown products that modulate male sexual development.

Anti-androgens are a class of drugs that act by reducing the action of the androgen hormone testosterone.

Anti-libidinal is a name for drugs that suppress sex drive.

Castration describes physical removal of the testis in men or the ovaries in women.

Chemical castration is the use of medication to block the production of testosterone by the testis. As a medical procedure, castration, whether physical or "chemical," is used in the treatment of cancers that are sensitive to testosterone, and for some endocrine conditions.

Dopamine is another monoamine neurotransmitter. It is plays a particular role in systems involved in reward, pleasure and addiction. Dopamine systems are also important in the control of movement, with a loss of dopamine containing neurons resulting in Parkinson's disease.

Follicle stimulating hormone (FSH) (like luteinizing hormone – LH) is a gonadotropin hormone released by the pituitary gland. It stimulates sperm production in men and the maturation of eggs in the ovaries of women.

Gonadotropin releasing hormone (GnRH) is a hormone released by cells in the hypothalamus that stimulates the synthesis and release of the gonadotropins (LH and FSH).

GnRH agonists describe a class of drugs that mimic the action of GnRH, but over time result in a cessation of gonadotropin synthesis and release by the pituitary gland, and hence production of testosterone in the testes.

Hormone is a substance produced by cells in the central nervous system or in glands in the body that is secreted into the blood stream and acts at a distance site. Sometimes referred to as a "chemical messenger."

Hypersexuality is a poorly defined term that refers to a high level of sexual drive, either in terms of frequency of sexual urges or their intensity.

Luteinizing hormone (LH) is a gonadotropin hormone, that is, it is a hormone that acts on the testes in men and ovaries in women). It is released by the pituitary gland in the brain and stimulates the production of testosterone by cells in the testes, while in women in stimulates the production of estrogen by the ovaries and also ovulation.

Monoamines are a group of neurotransmitters that have a similar chemical structure, which include dopamine, serotonin, adrenaline (epinephrine), and noradrenaline (nor-epinephrine). They are particularly important in relation to mood states and arousal.

Neurotransmitter is a substance released by a nerve cell (neuron) that acts on a nearby nerve cell, in effect allowing one nerve cell to communicate with another. It may either excite or inhibit the cell it acts upon.

Psychophenomenology is a term that refers to describing the characteristics of a mental state or subjective experience.

Serotonin, also known as 5-hydroxytraptamine (or 5-HT), is a monoamine neurotransmitter associated with a range of functions, including regulation of mood, appetite, sleep, sexual activity, and impulse control.

Selective serotonin reuptake inhibitors (SSRIs) are a class of drugs that inhibit the reuptake of serotonin by neurons in the brain, which has the effect of increasing serotonin levels and activity around its target cells.

Testosterone is the primary androgen hormone, and is necessary for the development of male gender characteristics in utero, the development of male secondary sexual characteristics at puberty, and normal sexual functioning.

Introduction

Problematic sexual behavior and sex offending are dependent on sex drive, sexual arousal, and sexual functioning. Although successful treatment requires psychological change, medication that helps an individual to manage their arousal can be an important adjunct to psychological therapies. An understanding of the neurobiology of sexual arousal is thus useful in understanding how medication affects sexual arousal and drive. Serotonergic and dopaminergic neural systems, interacting with testosterone, are fundamental to sexual behavior, and offer prime targets for medical treatment. Selective serotonin reuptake inhibitors (SSRIs) and anti-androgens are the two classes of drug that appear to be most effective in reducing arousal and sexual interest. Prescribing, however, should be based on medical indications rather than offending risk or notions of social control.

Psychological, social, and cultural factors are important contributors to sex offending behavior and form the targets of most successful treatment programs. Sex offending, however, while firmly rooted in psychosocial earth is also dependent on sex drive, sexual arousal, and sexual functioning. It is difficult, and probably unwise, to separate "sex" from sex offending, even where the primary "pathology" is not biological in nature.

Sexual arousal and sex drive can be influenced by medication, and indeed they are often impacted by unwanted effects of medication prescribed for other reasons. The potential for prescribing medication as an adjunct to sex offender treatment, however, is often overlooked, particularly by the non-medical therapists who typically work with these individuals. There are a number of reasons for this. It is sometimes claimed, for example, that such an explicit medical approach to sex offending suggests that an offender is less responsible for his/her behavior by implying it is caused by mental disorder, and that medication should be reserved only for those in whom there is an overt "medical" cause such as a brain lesion or mental illness (discussed further in Grubin & Mason, 1997), although why this should be different for psychological therapies is unclear. But resistance can also come from physicians themselves. Psychiatrists and general practitioners, the types of doctor usually involved, tend to have limited experience of prescribing in this area and may lack confidence in prescribing for this indication. In addition, doctors sometimes raise concerns that when prescribing for sex offenders the aim is public safety and the social control of an offender rather than for the benefit of the patient, and thus in conflict with their duties as a doctor (Harrison, 2008; Melella, Travin, & Cullen, 1989), although such views reflect a misunderstanding of the role of medication in sex offender treatment.

The correct drug, chosen for the right individual, based on medical indications, can provide a powerful adjunct to psychological therapy while falling well within the bounds of the doctor–patient relationship. Sometimes it is the only viable treatment. In this context, treatment is on a voluntary basis with consent. While public safety may be served, it is as an indirect benefit rather than a primary target. In many ways, this is not dissimilar to psychological therapy – just as offender/patients can decide whether or not to take medication, they can choose when and whether to make use of what they learn from psychological treatment.

The Rationale for Prescribing Medication in Sexual Offenders

Humans are less governed by their drives than most other animals, where external constraints and physical conditions are the primary determiners of whether a drive is acted on. In humans, however, our ability and willingness to control our drives varies not only with environmental circumstances, but with more subtle nuances of psychological state, personality, the use of disinhibitors like alcohol or drugs, and a range of other factors. They can be manipulated (e.g., by conscious avoidance of stimuli), redirected, suppressed, or ignored. The extent to which they are controlled, however, depends on a recognition of a need to do so, but also on the strength of the drive itself. This is true not only for sex drive (or from a more evolutionary perspective the drive to reproduce) but also for other drives such as hunger or sleep.

The weaker a drive the more readily it can be controlled. In terms of appetite and sleep the level of drive is determined through a complex array of sensory receptors, hormones, and neurotransmitters interacting within neurophysiological systems. Although these drives can be controlled to an extent with the use of psychological techniques, these are not always successful. In the case of a poorly regulated drive to eat, for example, physical interventions such as appetite suppressants or gastric banding may be useful adjuncts, enabling psychological mechanisms to be strengthened to improve long-term appetite control. Although this is sometimes seen as providing a medical "excuse" for overeating, it is now well recognized that physical interventions are appropriate and beneficial to health (National Institute of Clinical Excellence (NICE), 2014).

Similarly, the control of both the initiation and maintenance of sexual activity can be improved with the use of medication in cases where individuals find it difficult to do so unaided, for whatever reason. Although the relevant hormonal and neurotransmitter systems, as well as the interaction between the brain centers that govern sexual behavior, are only partially understood, enough is known to allow for prescribing to be rational and effective. However, the distinct ways in which medication affects sex drive, and varying side effect profiles, means that a range of factors need to be taken into account in deciding whether medication is indicated, and if so, what type. This in turn requires not only an understanding of how different medications interact with sex drive and sex functioning, but also an appreciation of just what one is treating.

Sex Offending: Behavior or Pathology?

In order for doctors to prescribe for sex offenders there needs to be clear medical rather than social reasons for initiating the drug treatment. But most sex offenders do not have diagnoses, at least of the kind that would traditionally warrant medical intervention. Even when they fulfill the *International Classification of Diseases*, tenth revision (*ICD-10*) (World Health Organization, 1992) or the *Diagnostic and Statistical Manual of Mental Disorders*, fifth edition (*DSM-5*) (American Psychiatric Association, 2013) criteria for disorders of sexual preference, the way in which problematic sexual behavior is conceptualized in the manuals does not help support medication decisions. This is because the *DSM* and *ICD* definitions are based on notions of "unconventional" arousal, illegality, and harm rather than on the phenomenology associated with the psychological and physical characteristics of the arousal itself. There is no handle medication can grab on to – medication is not typically indicated as a response to moral concerns or the need for social control.

Furthermore, the diagnostic manuals have little to say about non-paraphilic but "hypersexual" or problematic sexual behavior that an individual may find difficult to manage, and is probably more common in sex offenders than paraphilias per se. A "non-paraphilic sexual desire disorder" (also referred to as "paraphilic related disorder") encompassing notions of hypersexuality was proposed as a diagnostic category for *DSM-5* (Kafka, 2010) but was not in the end included, perhaps because of problems in reaching a consensus in what "hypersexual" means (although the converse of this issue does not prevent both male and female *hypoactive* sexual desire disorders from being included in both the *DSM* and *ICD*).

A better conceptualization of the psychopathology of problematic sexual behavior would provide a means to identify potential neuropharmacological interventions and improve knowledge of their mode of action. Towards this end, a range of phenomenologically based models with which to understand problematic sexual behavior have been put forward, relating it to the psychopathology found in other conditions such as obsessive compulsive spectrum, impulsivity, affective, and addiction disorders,

708 *D. Grubin*

as well as a more fundamental dysregulation of sexual desire (hypersexuality by another name), raising the possibility of shared neurobiological mechanisms (for a more thorough review see Kafka, 2010).

A good example of this is the phenomenology seen in the obsessive compulsive disorder (OCD) spectrum (*DSM-5*, 2103). Although there is no direct relationship between OCD and sexually problematic behaviors, the core features of OCD – ruminations (typically but not always unwanted) and compulsions (repetitive behaviors that when resisted result in increasing levels of anxiety) – are reported by some sexual offenders in describing their sexual behavior, whether in association with a paraphilia or not. OCD is known to involve dysfunction in cortico-striato-thalamic pathways (in effect, brain pathways involved in the initiation of behavior), in which serotonin and serotoninergic receptors as well as other neurotransmitters such as dopamine play fundamental roles (Pauls, Abramovitch, Rauch, & Geller, 2014). Other related conditions such as impulse control disorders and possibly addictions appear to have comparable, albeit not identical, clinical features and may be part of a similar neuropathological spectrum (Brewer & Potenza, 2008). Even if it transpires that similarities between these conditions and the behavior seen in sex offending offer no more than a useful analogy, they nevertheless provide a symptom cluster by which a medication protocol can be structured and its effects measured.

Mood provides another potential link between problematic sexual behavior, phenomenology, and neurobiological mechanisms. A number of studies have reported high levels of mood disorders in sex offenders, with depression and dysthymia particularly common (Kafka, 2003; Langström, Sjöstedt, & Grann, 2004). Loss of libido is a common symptom in depression, but it has been suggested that in some offenders the problematic sexual behavior may act as a mood regulator, especially in those who have either inherently low levels of sexual inhibition or high levels of sexual excitation (Bancroft, Graham, Janssen, & Sanders, 2009). In these cases, medication that targeted mood stabilization would provide an indirect means of addressing the sexual psychopathology, although it has also been suggested that there may be a common basis for both in brain monoamine systems (Kafka, 2003).

Another type of mental disorder that has a potential link with problematic sexual behavior is personality disorder. Studies often report a high incidence of personality disorder in sex offender populations (Langström et al., 2004), and while in many cases this is likely to be a reflection of antisocial attitudes, in others personality traits associated with, for example, poor impulse control and emotional dysregulation may be the primary cause of sex offending rather than any form of paraphilia. There is increasing, albeit still limited, evidence of brain abnormalities underlying at least some personality disorders relating to specific brain areas such as the prefrontal cortex and limbic system, and to the way information is communicated between neural systems (Boccardi et al., 2011; Motzkin, Newman, Kiehlm, & Koenigs, 2011; Völlm, et al., 2004). As the neurobiology of personality disorder becomes better understood additional targets for medication may emerge, which again could have an indirect impact on sex offending.

In summary, the direction of sex drive and the types of stimuli an individual finds most preferential – which are the basis for paraphilia diagnoses – are notoriously difficult to address directly, and medication has little role to play in the treatment of paraphilia per se. But the characteristics of the drive in terms of intensity, frequency, and intrusiveness, and other factors that influence its control such as impulsivity and emotional regulation, are more amenable to treatment – both psychological and medical – regardless of whether the problematic sexual behavior is paraphilic or non-paraphilic in nature. As the neurohormonal systems that underlie sex drive and its control become more fully elucidated it will be possible to better focus medical interventions. This will allow prescribing protocols to be more firmly tied to medical indications rather than simply represent a crude attempt to manage the risk posed by an individual.

Neurobiological Targets for Prescribing

Our understanding of the neurobiology of sexual functioning is limited, and much of it is based on animal studies. It is further complicated by cultural, environmental, and psychological factors that can be difficult to disentangle from the hard biology. Because gender differences in sexual response make matters even more complex, and because the majority of sexual offenders are male, the discussion here relates only to men (a more in-depth review of the biology of sexual behavior can be found in Bancroft, 2009).

Sexual behavior is modulated by the interaction between an array of neural and hormonal systems, but monoaminergic systems (i.e., those involving the neurotransmitters serotonin and dopamine) and the steroid hormone testosterone appear to be most central (Bancroft, 2009). In general, testosterone and dopaminergic activity appear to be synergistic in enhancing sexual excitation and arousal, while serotonergic activity is associated with inhibition of the sexual drive; dopamine and serotonin have this type of counterbalancing effect on drives generally. In addition, dopamine inhibits the release of prolactin, a hormone that in females is important for lactation and ovarian function but whose role is unclear in males. However, high levels of dopamine are associated with erectile difficulties and a diminution of libido – drugs that block dopamine activity such as the neuroleptics that are often prescribed in conditions such as schizophrenia. But while neurotransmitters play an important role in modulating sexual behavior, testosterone is fundamental to male sexual development, sex drive, and sexual functioning; in primates and to a lesser extent in humans it is also related to social hierarchy (Mazur & Booth, 1998), aggression, and emotional stability and regulation. It influences sexual behavior relatively slowly through effects that are largely mediated through the genome by which it enhances the processing of relevant sensory stimuli, influences neurotransmitter activity, and increases sexual responsiveness (Hull, Muschamp, & Sato, 2004). Testosterone will now be examined in more detail.

Testosterone

Testosterone is produced primarily by the Leydig cells in the testes, where high local concentrations are necessary for sperm production; about 5% of circulating testosterone is synthesized in the adrenal glands. Testosterone is mainly bound to blood proteins, with only about 2% free and biologically active, although even bound hormone may have some physiological activity. Bound and free testosterone are in equilibrium, with the former in effect acting as a store and thereby dampening the effects of overall changes in blood levels. The amount of circulating testosterone is substantially higher than that required to maintain sexual arousal. This suggests that its "secondary" actions (e.g., the maintenance of male secondary sexual characteristics) require substantially more hormone than what is needed for sexual functioning, which makes sense from an evolutionary perspective. It also means that sexual arousal and functioning are not especially sensitive to changes in testosterone levels within a normal range, although other aspects of functioning that are influenced by testosterone activity such as emotional regulation may be more readily affected.

Testosterone production in the testes is stimulated by luteinizing hormone (LH), a peptide hormone that is synthesized in the anterior pituitary gland. LH release itself is controlled by another peptide hormone, gonadotropin releasing hormone (GnRH), so called because it stimulates the release of both LH and a second hormone that regulates gonadal functioning, follicle stimulation hormone (FSH). GnRH is synthesized by cells in the hypothalamus, a brain center that sits just above the pituitary gland and which performs a central role in modulating biological drives and the hormonal environment of the body. It is released in a pulsatile manner into blood vessels that travel the short distance from the hypothalamus to the anterior pituitary gland. GnRH release is in turn modulated by input from a range of other brain centers, both cortical and subcortical. The testosterone that is produced as the ultimate outcome of this process completes the circle through a feedback loop in which it inhibits the release of both LH and GnRH (see Figure 27.1).

In addition to their input into the pituitary gland, GnRH producing cells also project to the limbic system (in particular the amygdala) as well as a number of other brain areas, and although the direct effects of this are unclear this pathway provides another means for GnRH to influence sexual behavior.

In understanding testosterone's impact on sexual behavior, it is worth noting that it has both organizational and activational effects on the central nervous system (Sisk, 2006). The former refers to its role in shaping the structural design of the male brain and subsequent sexual responsivity, which takes place both in the perinatal period and

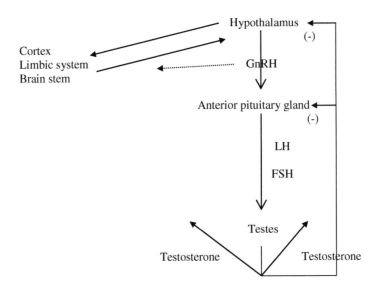

Figure 27.1 The control of testosterone secretion.

during puberty and which is influenced genetically as well as by social experience – this will therefore vary to some extent between individuals. In contrast, activation effects are dynamic, and relate to testosterone's day-to-day impact on post-pubertal functioning in the context of established organizational structures, which means that interventions targeting testosterone levels will not necessarily have the same impact in everyone.

Cells that are sensitive to testosterone are found throughout the body, in tissues as diverse as bone, skin, and muscle, as well as the sexual organs and the brain. Testosterone has both anabolic and adrenergic effects, that is, it stimulates tissue growth and also influences male sexual development, activity, and functioning. Testosterone exerts its effects through receptors that are located inside cells, some of which bind to it while others bind to its active metabolite dihydrotestosterone. In the male brain, testosterone receptors are most dense in hypothalamic nuclei, the amygdala and other areas of the limbic system, the prefrontal cortex, and the temporal cortex, all parts of the brain known to be involved in processing sexual stimuli or initiating and maintaining sexual behavior. Testosterone has also been shown to influence responsiveness to sexual stimuli in areas of the brain where testosterone receptors have not yet been demonstrated, such as the insula and claustrum, both of which are closely connected to limbic system activity, suggesting that it also has more general or indirect activating effects on neural systems (Bancroft, 2009).

Testosterone is required for normal levels of sexual interest and arousal. Although erections and sexual intercourse can still occur in castrated men (bearing in mind that a small amount of the hormone will still be produced by the adrenal gland), or when levels of testosterone are at pre-pubertal levels, there is little in the way of spontaneous sexual interest or behavior. This is also the case when testosterone activity is antagonized by medication. The erectile response becomes strongly stimulus bound, dependent on immediate sexual cues such as erotic imagery, and is lost once the stimulus is removed. Its effect on sexual functioning, however, is not immediate but can take weeks to become fully apparent – although sexual interest is restored somewhat more quickly if testosterone levels are restored, for example, in hypogonadal men receiving testosterone replacement therapy (Bancroft, 2005).

While the relationship between testosterone and sexual behavior is clear, there does not appear to be such a strong association between the hormone and violent sexual behavior per se, with meta-analyses finding only a modest relationship between the two, with co-relation coefficients (r) less than 0.15 (Archer, Birring, & Wu, 1998; Book, Starzyk, & Quinsey, 2001), although the situation may be different when extremely high doses are used, such as those taken by abusers of anabolic steroids. Part of the problem is that testosterone levels are not measured until a good deal of time after offending has taken place, but, in any case, other factors also contribute to aggression, making interpretation difficult. Perry, Kutscher, Lund, Yates, Holman, and Demers (2003), for example, reported that aggression was increased in weight lifters who used anabolic steroids, but this was confounded by the fact that those who were more aggressive also had more antisocial, borderline, and histrionic personality traits. Furthermore, changes in testosterone often follow, rather than precede, relevant behaviors. For instance, testosterone levels have been found to be higher in the members of winning teams in competitive sports, but the rise occurs after, not before, the competition has finished (Mazur & Lamb, 1980).

Thus, sufficient levels of circulating testosterone are necessary for most sex offending to take place (but not all, as in some cases offending may be driven by issues that have little to do with sex), although the relationship seems to be largely permissive rather than causal in nature. In addition to its role in the physical aspects of sexual functioning, testosterone has effects on the responsiveness of both general and specific neurological arousal mechanisms, it influences the processing of sexual sensory stimuli, it impacts on motivation, attention, and mood, and it is associated with aggression and dominance, all of which are potentially relevant to sexually problematic behavior. Therefore, treatments aimed at moderating the activity of testosterone, while not necessarily addressing the "root cause" of sex offending in a psychological sense, can nonetheless weaken the foundation on which sex offending sits. In this respect, it is of interest that one study involving 501 sex offenders found that testosterone levels were positively correlated with sex offence recidivism, but only in those who failed to complete a psychological treatment program (Studer, Aylwin, & Reddon, 2005). The roles of dopamine and serotonin will now be examined.

Dopamine and serotonin

The neurotransmitter dopamine, which is synthesized in the midbrain, is typically associated with "goal directed behaviors" and reward. Dopaminergic systems in the midbrain and limbic system are involved in a number of appetitive drives such as appetite, thirst, and sleep as well as sex; they have a facilitating effect and are "activating" in nature. Separate dopaminergic systems appear to be involved in arousal and the behavioral aspects of sexual performance. As indicated previously, dopamine also has an influence on sexual behavior through its role as an inhibitor of prolactin release from the posterior pituitary gland, thereby suppressing a hormone which dampens sexual arousal and functioning. Testosterone interacts synergistically with dopaminergic systems in the limbic system, facilitating dopamine release and perhaps increasing receptor sensitivity (Hull et al., 2004).

Another separate and distinct midbrain dopamine system plays an important role in movement, and if damaged results in the symptoms of rigidity, tremor, and difficulty initiating movement that are seen in Parkinson's disease. Drugs that block dopaminergic activity and interfere with the functioning of this system have similar effects, which makes the use of dopamine antagonists as a means of lowering sexual drive problematic.

In contrast with dopamine, the neurotransmitter serotonin (the chemical name for which is 5-hydroxytryptamine or 5-HT) has an inhibitory influence on appetitive behaviors, although the situation is complicated by the large number of different serotonin receptors found in the brain and elsewhere in the body (to date, seven main receptor types, and 15 receptor subtypes, have been described, with some receptor subtypes having opposite effects to others). Serotonergic activity inhibits ejaculation, which is why drugs that increase levels of serotonin can cause delayed ejaculation. In addition to its direct effects on neural systems, serotonin has been shown in animal experiments to inhibit dopamine release in the limbic system (Hull et al., 2004). Where testosterone appears to act synergistically with dopaminergic systems, it is antagonistic to serotonergic ones, and in animal experiments has been found to impair the activity of some serotonin receptor types (Simon, Cologer-Clifford, Lu, McKenna, & Hu, 1998). Low levels of serotonin are associated with mood disorders, OCD, panic attacks, and impulsive aggression. This reciprocal relationship between dopamine and serotonin may have had an important evolutionary function in enabling organisms to regulate sexual behavior depending on environmental circumstances (Bancroft, 1999).

Most of the evidence regarding the role of dopamine and serotonin in sexual behavior comes from animal studies or is inferred from the effects of medication in humans. For example, in both rats and primates hypothalamic dopamine activity is associated with male sexual approach and mating behavior, while serotonin activity inhibits sexual behavior (reviewed in Kafka, 2003). In humans, drugs used in Parkinson's disease that enhance dopamine activity can increase libido and sexual behavior. On the other hand, the SSRIs, which increase the amount of serotonin available at receptor sites and are used to treat depression, can cause a range of sexual dysfunctions including a loss of sexual interest, impaired sexual arousal, and sexual anhedonia (reduction in the pleasure associated with orgasm).

The role of other hormones and neurotransmitters

If sexual behavior were simply a matter of interactions between testosterone, dopamine, and serotonin we would have a much better understanding of sexual functioning and its problems. However, many other neurotransmitters and hormones are involved in sexual motivation, arousal, and behavior. For example, the peptide hormone oxytocin is known to play an important role in attachment, social behavior, sexual arousal, orgasm, and sexual satiety (Beech & Mitchell, 2005). Although this has been appreciated for many years, the extent to which oxytocin may be a primary factor in sexually problematic behavior, or can form the basis of putative treatments for it, remains to be elucidated. Uncertainty also surrounds the role of the endorphins, and neurotransmitters such as noradrenaline, acetylcholine, GABA, glutamate, and nitric oxide, to name just a few of the compounds that are known to have some input into the regulation of sex hormone production and sexual behavior. Our limited understanding means that typically the effects of medication on sexual performance when prescribed for other reasons are sometimes unpredicted, usually unwanted, and generally non-specific.

Medications Used in The Management of Sexual Arousal

Given what is known about the neurobiology of sexual drive, the most obvious target for medical intervention intended to reduce the intensity and frequency of sexual arousal and functioning is testosterone. Much of what is known about the effects of lowering testosterone activity in men comes from studies of castrated individuals.

Castration, that is, the removal of the testicles or orchidectomy, takes away the primary source of testosterone production, resulting in a highly predictable reduction in the intensity of sexual drive (or libido) and an impairment in sexual functioning generally. In animal husbandry, it has long been known as a reliable means to produce less sexually active and more docile males. Similar effects are seen in humans when orchidectomy is carried out for medical reasons, such as the treatment of testosterone sensitive prostate cancer. In the early to mid-20th century castration was used in a number of European countries as a means of dealing with supposedly high-risk sex offenders, albeit that in practice many of those castrated do not appear to have been particularly "high risk," including learning disabled individuals, homosexuals, indecent exposers, first time offenders, boys as young as 13, and even some women (presumably charged with prostitution, although this is not clear) (Heim & Hursch, 1979; Sturup, 1968). Reported recidivism rates over long follow-up periods are low, less than 5% (Weinberger, Sreenivasan, Garrick, & Osran, 2005). In terms of sexual functioning, castrated offenders typically report substantial reductions in their sex drives, although many retained some sexual functioning and responsiveness (Heim & Hursch, 1979). The primary impact of castration and its effectiveness in reducing sexually problematic behavior is through a diminution of sexual interest rather than any impairment in sexual functioning.

In addition to its effect on sexual behavior, castration is associated with a range of more general problematic effects on health. The lack of testosterone causes osteoporosis (a reduction in bone density with an associated risk of fracture), elevated cardiovascular risk due to metabolic changes and altered blood lipid levels, troublesome flushes and sweating, and breast growth that is probably the result of an alteration in the ratio of testosterone to estrogen. Depression, fatigue, loss of muscle mass, and weight gain are some of the other not uncommon side effects. Castration, of course, is also physically mutilating, and many surgeons are reluctant to carry out a surgical procedure that is not without risk in order to meet a social rather than a medical need. Thus, while physical castration is still carried out on a voluntary basis on small numbers of men in some countries, it is not an attractive option.

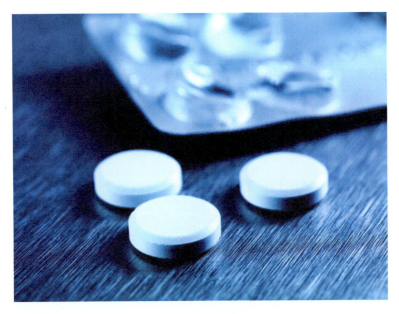

Pharmacological treatment of sex offenders *Reducing sexual interest, arousal, and drive are the main targets of medication for sexual offenders. Selective serotonin reuptake inhibitors (SSRIs) and anti-androgens are the two classes of drug which appear to be most effective in achieving this aim.*
Source: © Kitch Bain. Used under license from 123RF.

Anti-androgen medication

Medications that reduce testosterone levels and activity are referred to as anti-androgens or anti-libidinals. They bring about a reduction in sex drive similar to that seen in physical castration, but their effects are reversible, and depending on the drug the impact on sexual functioning can be titrated to a degree. Their use is sometimes described as "chemical castration." Anti-androgens are often prescribed in the treatment of prostate cancer, and a large amount of experience has been built up in respect of this indication. These drugs lower the biological activity of testosterone in a number of ways: by reducing testosterone synthesis, blocking its access to receptors in its target cells, or by increasing its metabolism and removal from the body.

Estrogens (the primary type of sex hormone found in females), although strictly speaking not an anti-androgen, have anti-androgen effects and were the first of this type of medication prescribed, with their use in sex offenders going back to the late 1940s. They were effective in reducing sexual interest and masturbatory activity to levels found in hypogonadal men (Bancroft et al., 1974). Even though levels of testosterone in blood increased, the proportion of free testosterone – that is, the proportion of hormone not bound to plasma proteins – decreased, thereby lowering testosterone activity. The problem with estrogens is that they increase the risk of cardiovascular and cerebrovascular disease and also some carcinomas. Although prescribed to treat sexually aggressive men into the 1970s, their use is no longer recommended in this setting (Thibaut, et al., 2010).

The two most commonly prescribed anti-androgens are cyproterone acetate in Europe and Canada, and medroxyprogesterone (MPA) in the USA and to a lesser extent in Canada (cyproterone acetate is not available in the USA). They have been in regular use since the 1960s. While there is some overlap, these drugs have somewhat different modes of action. Both reduce the release of GnRH and LH through effects on the hypothalamic-pituitary axis, but MPA also increases testosterone metabolism in the liver, while cyproterone in addition blocks testosterone receptors. This latter effect means that it can retain its efficacy even where an individual takes exogenous testosterone, unlike in physical castration where the effect on sex drive can be ameliorated by the surreptitious use of testosterone.

Cyproterone acetate and MPA have similar side effect profiles in respect of feminization, mood changes, weight gain, and gynecomastia, as well as more serious side effects associated with cardiovascular risk, osteoporosis, and metabolic changes, in particular relating to the adrenal glands and the regulation of blood glucose levels and the risk of diabetes. Cyproterone acetate in addition can be toxic to the liver, and because it can impact on bone maturation and testicular development it should not be prescribed to those under 18 years of age. In view of these factors, patients prescribed either drug require regular monitoring, including the need for periodic blood tests. It is also worth noting that alcohol increases the rate of cyproterone breakdown in the liver, reducing its efficacy in the presence of heavy alcohol use.

In recent years, GnRH agonists such as leuprolide, tryptorelin, and goserelin have become more regularly prescribed. GnRH agonists act by overstimulating hypothalamic release of GnRH, shifting it from pulsatile to continuous in nature. The result is that LH release from the pituitary gland is at first markedly increased with a concomitant rise in blood testosterone levels (because of which testosterone receptor blockers are used in the initial weeks when GnRH agonists are prescribed to treat androgen sensitive prostate tumors), but this is followed by a depletion of pituitary LH and a subsequent marked reduction in testosterone synthesis and release; GnRH receptors also become less sensitive, or "down-regulated." Although costlier than cyproterone acetate and MPA, GnRH agonists appear to have greater efficacy, at least when compared to standard doses of the two drugs. This may in part be because of its effects besides those on pituitary functioning related to GnRH activity in the limbic system, although this is of course speculative given what little is known about the role of GnRH on limbic system functioning. While apparently more potent and having a similar side effect profile to cyproterone and MPA, the incidence of side effects with GnRH agonists may be lower, although bone mineral loss is particularly problematic and requires more regular monitoring (Czerny, Briken, & Berner, 2002; Thibaut et al., 2010).

There are numerous case reports and a number of studies in relation to the use of anti-androgens in sex offenders (reviewed by Briken, Hill, & Berner, 2003; Prentky, 1997; Thibaut et al., 2010). They typically describe marked reductions in sexual interest, fantasy, and behavior, and low recidivism rates of the same order as reported in the follow-up of physically castrated offenders (with some exceptions). Rösler and Witztum (1998), for example, reported that in men who remained on tryptorelin for a year, sexual fantasies and urges disappeared completely, and masturbation frequency dropped to at most twice a fortnight. Consistent with this, a large meta-analysis of treatment outcomes found that pharmacological treatments had a higher effect size on recidivism than did psychological treatments on their own (Lösel & Schmucker, 2005).

Given the nature of the population, however, the robustness of the research into anti-androgen efficacy is limited. Few of the studies involve randomization to treatment or placebo (which in any case is problematic as the side effects of medication make it difficult to mask), and indeed there is usually an absence of comparison groups of any kind. Most of the studies involve small numbers of subjects, they often fail to take into account those who drop out of treatment, and they are reliant on self-report measures of sexual activity. In this respect, it is of interest that one small study in which a placebo was used found that, although both treatment and control groups reported a reduction in sexual arousal and activity, polygraph testing could confirm this only for the treatment group (Schober et al., 2005).

Some reassurance, however, comes from an opportunistic study reported by Maletzky, Tolan, and McFarland (2006), who described outcome in offenders who had had a parole evaluation to determine whether or not they should be prescribed MPA prior to conditional release from prison. In the event, 134 men were recommended for anti-androgen medication (out of 275 prisoners who were evaluated), but only 79 of them actually received the medication following release. None of those on medication committed a new sex offence, just one had a "sexual violation," and none were in prison after a maximum follow-up of four years; of the 55 men who should have received MPA but did not (for a range of reasons), 18% had committed another sex offence, and 16% were "back in prison" for sexual violations. When parole officers were asked about the functioning of these men, 89% of the medication group were said to be "doing well," as opposed to 56% of the comparison group. Although the generalizability of these findings is limited by potential biases, the results are highly suggestive of the potential benefits of anti-androgen medication.

In spite of the difficulties inherent in the research into the use of anti-androgens, they produce repeated and predictable reductions in sexual arousal and sexual behavior in a manner that is consistent with the underlying neurobiology. From a clinical perspective, there is little question that these drugs are effective libido-lowering agents. While it is plausible to conclude that this should be associated with a reduction in sexually problematic behavior, risk, and offending, the research in this respect is more inferential, and has not yet been backed up with cost–benefit type analyses.

SSRIs

Because of serotonin's inhibiting effect on drive that counterbalances the actions of dopamine, and because of its relationship to mood and impulsivity, serotonin systems represent the next most promising target after testosterone for medication aimed at reducing sexual arousal. By delaying the reuptake of serotonin by nerve cells, SSRIs increase serotonergic activity. They are widely used in the treatment of depression and, in higher doses, OCD, as well as some other mental illnesses. By the early 2000s there were over 200 case reports and open studies regarding their use in individuals displaying problematic sexual behavior (Kafka, 2003). Most described reductions in the frequency and intensity of sexual fantasy, urges, and arousal. Fluoxetine and sertraline are the two SSRIs most commonly prescribed and, although one would expect limited differences between the drugs, Kafka (1994) found that some individuals who did not respond to sertraline improved when switched to fluoxetine.

Sexual side effects are a common complaint when SSRIs are used for other conditions (Baldwin & Foong, 2013; Balon, 2006), so it is perhaps not surprising that these can influence sexually problematic behavior. It is not clear, however, whether their efficacy is the result of a reduction in the intensity of sexual rumination and urges, enhancement of mood, decreased impulsivity, lessening of libido, sexual anhedonia, or a combination of these actions. Clinical consensus appears to be coalescing around their use in cases where there is marked sexual rumination or preoccupation, a compulsive aspect to the sexual behavior, or where the sexually problematic behavior is associated with low mood (Thibaut et al., 2010). Compared with the anti-androgens, however, they have a much milder side effect profile (with gastrointestinal symptoms such as nausea and change in bowel habit being most common), and even where the primary issue is high libido a trial of SSRIs may be of benefit, or even the drugs of choice if anti-androgens are contraindicated.

As with the anti-androgens, evidence concerning the use of SSRIs in treating problematic sexual behavior is supportive rather than robust. Again, there are few randomized trials or even comparison studies, most studies involve small numbers of participants with a heavy reliance on self-report, and there is an absence of any analysis of cost-effectiveness. The situation hasn't improved since a systematic review by Adi et al. in 2002 found insufficient data of high enough quality to enable them to reach any firm conclusions regarding clinical effectiveness or cost–benefit. Based on the studies, however, the considered continued use of SSRI medication in sex offenders was thought warranted pending further research.

Anti-psychotic and other medication

For completeness, neuroleptic medication such as benperidol and fluphenazine, used in the treatment of psychotic disorders, should be mentioned. In the past, these drugs were sometimes prescribed with the aim of reducing levels of sexual arousal, based on their blockage of dopamine receptors and also on their ability to lessen arousal more generally (they are also referred to as "major tranquillizers"). Although loss of libido and erectile difficulties are indeed a common side effect of these drugs, their impact on sexual functioning is inconsistent and unreliable. Given their much more predictable association with Parkinson's-type movement related side effects, there is little to recommend these drugs in the treatment of problematic sexual behavior except where it is secondary to psychotic illness.

Mood stabilizers, anxiolytics such as buspirone (which acts at serotonin receptors), and the opioid receptor blocker naltrexone have been said to be effective in a small number of case reports, but there is neither the evidence nor the clinical experience to reach any conclusions about them in treating sexually problematic behavior.

Prescribing Protocols

Decisions about medical treatment can become confused if the focus is on reducing recidivism rather than on assisting individuals to manage sexual arousal. So long as attention is directed to the latter, however, the issues are straightforward. Like any treatment discussion between doctor and patient, benefits and possible side effects are considered, informed consent is required, and medication is taken on a voluntary basis (see Tables 27.1 and 27.2 for treatment algorithms). If the individual is better able to manage his sexual arousal and behavior one would expect recidivism risk to reduce, but that is a secondary outcome. In the end, responsibility for problematic sexual behavior remains with the patient.

Table 27.1 Treatment algorithm based on World Federation of Societies of Biological Psychiatry (WFSBP) Guidelines for the biological treatment of paraphilias.

LEVEL	DESCRIPTION	TREATMENT
1	Paraphilic fantasies, compulsions, and behaviors, aim not to impact on conventional sex activity or desire	Psychotherapy (preferably CBT)
2	"Hands off" paraphilias with low risk of violence	If Level 1 treatment unsatisfactory, SSRIs in OCD doses
3	"Hands on" paraphilias with fondling but without penetration, absence of sexual sadism	If Level 2 treatment unsuccessful after 4–6 weeks, add low dose anti-androgen
4	Moderate or high risk of sexual violence (intrusive fondling), limited number of victims, absence of sexual sadism	If Level 3 treatment unsuccessful, full dose anti-androgen, with possible SSRI adjunct
5	High risk of sexual violence and severe paraphilias, sexual sadism present, or unsatisfactory response to Level 4	Aim to almost completely suppress sex drive and activity with GnRH agonist
6	Most severe paraphilias (catastrophic cases)	Aim to completely suppress sex drive and activity with GnRH agonist plus anti-androgen

Source: The World Journal of Biological Psychiatry (2010), 11, 604–655.

The Pharmacological Treatment of Sex Offenders 719

Table 27.2 Treatment algorithm based on presentation (plus psychological treatment in most cases)

PRESENTATION	TREATMENT
High levels of sexual rumination or preoccupation	SSRI in OCD doses; if unsuccessful then oral anti-androgen
Fantasy or behavior associated with mood dysregulation	If depression, SSRI; if variability in mood, mood stabilizer
Compulsive or impulsive aspect to sexual behavior	SSRI in OCD doses; if unsuccessful then oral anti-androgen
High sex drive	Oral anti-androgen; if unsuccessful then GnRH agonist

If medication appears to be indicated, in most cases the choice is effectively between an anti-androgen and an SSRI. Although there is recognition that these classes of medication target different components of sexual functioning, published guidelines tend to conflate medical indication with risk as referred to above. Protocols suggested in Bradford (2001), Briken et al. (2003), and Thibaut et al. (2010), for example, are similar, and recommend that SSRIs are considered where behavior and risk are less severe, while anti-androgens are reserved for cases where behavior and risk are more worrying, requiring greater reduction in sexual arousal. For instance, Thibaut et al. (2010) suggest an algorithm that is based on six levels of treatment, with lower levels comprising "hands off" paraphilias that can be treated with SSRIs, while anti-androgens are used when the behavior is "hands on" in nature, increasing in dose in line with increases in the degree of sexual violence until GnRH agonists are finally prescribed.

Although this type of approach is understandable, it runs the risk of prescribing for purposes of social control rather than the needs of the individual. It may be, for example, that a "lower level" case might benefit from a GnRH agonist if arousal and distress are high even though offending severity is low, while in some instances SSRI medication may be more appropriate for a sexually violent individual

An alternative is to base treatment decisions primarily on phenomenological presentation, with risk considerations secondary. In this model, individuals who present with high levels of sexual rumination, preoccupation or compulsion, or where problematic sexual fantasy and behavior are associated with low mood, would be prescribed an SSRI in the first instance, regardless of the nature of the fantasy or behavior. Where the primary problem relates to high levels of drive, then an anti-androgen would be indicated, with GnRH agonists used if cyproterone acetate (or MPA) is not fully effective. In this scenario, compliance is not an issue as the recipient is not an offender with license conditions, but a patient who is free to decide whether or not to take medication.

Conclusions and Implications for Practice and Policy

The medical treatment of individuals who engage in sexually problematic behavior is based on a research foundation of neurobiological theory and a weight of clinical studies rather than randomized double blind controlled trials. In other words, the research is supportive, even if its pedigree could be stronger. Nevertheless, both SSRIs and anti-androgens seem to be clinically effective, and there is a reasonable consensus regarding their potential benefit. It is important, however, that medication is used as a treatment rather than a symbolic punishment for sexually offending, or prescribed to reduce risk rather than to treat a medical presentation (Grubin & Beech, 2010). It is not up to doctors to assume primary responsibility for public safety, but they can contribute to it by assisting the individual to address those factors that make him more likely to offend. Risk, however, is best managed by those working in the criminal justice system.

Although psychological approaches are generally the preferred option in sex offender treatment, where high levels of sexual arousal or preoccupation make such techniques difficult the reduction of arousal through pharmacological means may be of benefit, with one complementing the other. Indeed, a large meta-analysis of treatment outcome found that while pharmacological treatment had a higher effect size on recidivism than psychological treatments on their own, medical treatment typically also included a cognitive-behavioral component that had an independent treatment effect (Lösel & Schmucker, 2005). Sexual behavior in human beings is more than a manifestation of testosterone interacting with monoaminergic neurotransmitter systems in the central nervous system. But given the importance of hormones and neurotransmitters to what is in effect a strong biological drive, it makes no sense to ignore the neurobiology. When drugs work, the clinical effect can be dramatic, with offenders reporting great benefit from no longer being preoccupied by sexual thoughts or dominated by sexual drive.

Recommended Reading

Bancroft, J. H. J. (2009). *Human sexuality and its problems* (3rd ed.). London: Churchill Livingstone. *A thorough review of human sexual behavior covering biology, physiology, and psychology.*

Bancroft, J., & Vukadinovic, Z. (2004). Sexual addiction, sexual compulsivity, sexual impulse disorder or what? Towards a theoretical model. *Journal of Sex Research, 41*, 225–234. *A good illustration of the importance of phenomenology in understanding "abnormal" sexual behavior.*

Book, A. S., Starzyk, K. B., & Quinsey, V. L. (2001). The relationship between testosterone and aggression: A meta-analysis. *Aggression and Violent Behavior, 6*, 579–599. *Although a dated review, its general conclusions have not been negated by subsequent studies.*

Heim, N., & Hursch, C. J. (1979). Castration for sex offenders. Treatment or punishment? A review and critique of recent European literature. *Archives of Sexual Behavior, 8*, 281–304. *An old study but the fullest review of the effects of physical castration.*

Kafka, M. P. (2003). The monoamine hypothesis for the pathophysiology of paraphilic disorders: An update. *Annals of the New York Academy of Sciences, 989*, 86–94. *A good review of the role of monoamine neurotransmitters in sexual behavior.*

Kafka, M. P. (2010). Hypersexual disorder: A proposed diagnosis for DSM-V. *Archives of Sexual Behavior, 39*, 377–400. *A good discussion of the issues associated with the concept of "hypersexuality."*

Thibaut, F., De La Barra, F., Gordon, H., Cosysns, P., & Bradford, J. M. W. (2010). The World Federation of Societies of Biological Psychiatry (WFSBP) Guidelines for the biological treatment of paraphilias. *World Journal of Biological Psychiatry, 11*, 604–655.

References

Adi, Y., Ashcroft, D., Browne, K., Beech, A., Fry-Smith, A., & Hyde, C. (2002). Clinical effectiveness and cost-consequences of selective serotonin reuptake inhibitors in the treatment of sex offenders. Health Technology Assessment, 6, No. 28. London: HMSO. Retrieved from http://www.journalslibrary.nihr.ac.uk/__data/assets/pdf_file/0020/65090/FullReport-hta6280.pdf.

American Psychiatric Association (2013). *Diagnostic and statistical manual of mental disorders* (5th ed.) (*DSM-5*). Arlington, VA: American Psychiatric Association.

Archer, J., Birring, S. S., & Wu, F. C. W. (1998). The association between testosterone and aggression among young men: Empirical findings and a meta-analysis. *Aggressive Behavior, 24*, 411–420.

Baldwin, D. S., & Foong, T. (2013). Antidepressant drugs and sexual dysfunction. *British Journal of Psychiatry, 202*, 396–397.

Balon, R. (2006). SSRI-associated sexual dysfunction. *American Journal of Psychiatry, 163*, 1504–1509.

Bancroft, J. (1999). Central inhibition of sexual response in the male: A theoretical perspective. *Neuroscience and Biobehavioral Reviews, 23*, 763–784.

Bancroft, J. (2005). The endocrinology of sexual arousal. *Journal of Endocrinology, 10*, 411–427.

Bancroft, J. (2009). *Human sexuality and its problems* (3rd ed.). Edinburgh: Churchill Livingtone/Elsevier.

Bancroft, J., Graham, C. A., Janssen, E., & Sanders, S. (2009). The dual control model: Current status and future directions. *Journal of Sex Research, 46*, 121–142.

Bancroft, J., Tennent, G., Loucas, K., & Cass, J. (1974). The control of deviant sexual behavior by drugs: 1. Behavioral changes following oestrogens and anti-androgens. *British Journal of Psychiatry, 125*, 310–315.

Beech, A. R., & Mitchell, I. J. (2005). A neurobiological perspective on attachment problems in sexual offenders and the role of selective serotonin re-uptake inhibitors in the treatment of such problems *Clinical Psychology Review, 25*, 153–182.

Boccardi, M., Frisoni, G. B., Hare, R. D., Cavedo, E., Najt, P., Pievani, M., ... Tiihonen, J. (2011). Cortex and amygdala morphology in psychopathy. *Psychiatry Research, 193*, 85–92.

Book, A. S., Starzyk, K. B., & Quinsey, V. L. (2001). The relationship between testosterone and aggression: A meta-analysis. *Aggression and Violent Behavior, 6*, 579–599.

Bradford, J. M. W. (2001). The neurobiology, neuropharmacology, and pharmacological treatment of the paraphilias and compulsive sexual behavior. *Canadian Journal of Psychiatry, 46*, 26–34.

Brewer, J. A., & Potenza, M. N. (2008). The neurobiology and genetics of impulse control disorders: Relationships to drug addictions. *Biochemical Pharmacology, 75*, 63–75.

Briken, P., Hill, A., & Berner, W. (2003). Pharmacotherapy of paraphilias with long-acting agonists of luteinising hormone-releasing hormone: A systematic review. *Journal of Clinical Psychiatry, 64*, 890–897.

Carter, C. S. (1992). Oxytocin and sexual behavior. *Neuroscience and Biobehavioral Reviews, 16*, 131–144.

Czerny, J. P., Briken, P., & Berner W. (2002). Antihormonal treatment of paraphilic patients in German forensic psychiatric clinics. *European Psychiatry, 17*, 104–106.

Grubin, D. & Beech, A. R. (2010). Chemical castration for sex offenders. *British Medical Journal, 340*, 433–434.

Grubin, D., & Mason, D. (1997). Medical models of sexual deviance. In D. R. Laws & W. O'Donohue (Eds.), *Sexual deviance: Theory, assessment, and treatment*. London: Guilford Press.

722 D. Grubin

Harrison, K. (2008). Legal and ethical issues when using antiandrogenic pharmacotherapy with sex offenders. *Sexual Offender Treatment, 3*. Retrieved from www.sexual-offender-treatment.org/2-2008_01.html.

Heim, N., & Hursch, C. J. (1979). Castration for sex offenders: Treatment or punishment? A review and critique of recent European literature. *Archives of Sexual Behavior, 8*, 281–304.

Hull, E. M., Muschamp, J. W., & Sato, S. (2004). Dopamine and serotonin: Influences on male sexual behavior. *Physiology and Behavior, 83*, 291–307.

Kafka, M. P. (1994). Sertraline pharmacotherapy for paraphilias and paraphilia-related disorders: An open trial. *Annals of Clinical Psychiatry, 6*, 189–195.

Kafka, M. P. (2003). The monoamine hypothesis for the pathophysiology of paraphilic disorders: An update. *Annals of the New York Academy of Sciences, 989*, 86–94.

Kafka, M. P. (2010). Hypersexual disorder: A proposed diagnosis for DSM-V. *Archives of Sexual Behavior, 39*, 377–400.

Langström, N., Sjöstedt, G., & Grann, M. (2004). Psychiatric disorders and recidivism in sexual offenders. *Sexual Abuse: A Journal of Research and Treatment, 16*, 139–150.

Lösel, F., & Schmucker, M. (2005). The effectiveness of treatment for sexual offenders: A comprehensive meta-analysis. *Journal of Experimental Criminology, 1*, 1–29.

Maletzky, B. M., Tolan, M., & McFarland, B. (2006). The Oregon depo-Provera program: A five-year follow-up. *Sexual Abuse: A Journal of Research and Treatment 18*, 303–316.

Mazur, A., & Booth, A. (1998). Testosterone and dominance in men. *Behavioral and Brain Sciences, 21*, 353–363.

Mazur, A., & Lamb, T. (1980). Testosterone, status, and mood in human males. *Hormones and Behavior, 14*, 236–246.

Melella, J. T., Travin, S., & Cullen, K. (1989). Legal and ethical issues in the use of antiandrogens in treating sex offenders. *Bulletin of the American Academy of Psychiatry and the Law, 17*, 223–232.

Motzkin, J. C. Newman, J. P., Kiehlm, K. A., & Koenigs, M. (2011). Reduced prefrontal connectivity in psychopathy. *Journal of Neuroscience, 31*, 17348–17357.

NICE (2014). NICE Guidelines: Obesity: identification, assessment and management of overweight and obesity in children, young people and adults. NICE guidelines [CG189]. Retrieved from http://www.nice.org.uk/guidance/cg189.

Pauls, D. L., Abramovitch, A., Rauch, S. L., & Geller, D. A. (2014). Obsessive-compulsive disorder: an integrative genetic and neurobiological perspective. *Nature Reviews Neuroscience, 15*, 410–424.

Perry, P. J., Kutscher, E. C., Lund, B. C., Yates, W. R., Holman, T. L., & Demers, L. (2003). Measures of aggression and mood changes in male weightlifters with and without androgenic anabolic steroid use. *Journal of Forensic Sciences, 48*, 646–651.

Prentky, R. A. (1997). Arousal reduction in sexual offenders: A review of antiandrogen interventions. *Sexual Abuse: A Journal of Research and Treatment, 9*, 335–347.

Rösler, A., & Witztum, E. (1998). Treatment of men with paraphilia with a long-acting analogue of gonadotropin-releasing hormone. *New England Journal of Medicine, 338*, 416–422.

Schober, J. M, Kuhn, P. J., Kovacs, P. G., Earle, J. H., Byrne, P. M., & Fries, R. A. (2005). Leuprolide acetate suppresses pedophilic urges and arousability. *Archives of Sexual Behavior, 34*, 691–705.

Simon, N. G., Cologer-Clifford, A., Lu, S. F., McKenna, S. E., & Hu, S. (1998). Testosterone and its metabolites modulate 5HT1A and 5HT1B agonist effects on intermale aggression. *Neuroscience and Biobehavioral Reviews, 23*, 325–336.

Sisk, C. L. (2006). New insights into the neurobiology of sexual maturation. *Sexual and Relationship Therapy, 21*, 5–14.

Studer, L. H., Aylwin, A. S., & Reddon, J. R. (2005). Testosterone, sexual offense recidivism, and treatment effect among male sex offenders. *Sexual Abuse: A Journal of Research and Treatment, 17*, 171–181.

Sturup, G. K. (1968). Treatment of sexual offenders in Herstedvester Denmark. *Acta Psychiatrica Scandinavica, 44 (Suppl. 204)*, 1–64.

Thibaut, F., de la Barra, F., Gordon, G., Cosyns, P., Bradford, J. M. W., & the WFSBP Task Force on Sexual Disorders. (2010). The World Federation of Societies of Biological Psychiatry (WFSBP) Guidelines for the biological treatment of paraphilias. *World Journal of Biological Psychiatry, 11*, 604–655.

Völlm, B., Richardson, P., Stirling, J., Elliott, R., Dolan, M., Chaudhry, I., … Deakin, B. (2004). Neurobiological substrates of antisocial and borderline personality disorder: Preliminary results of a functional fMRI study. *Criminal Behavior and Mental Health, 14*, 39–54.

Weinberger, L. E., Sreenivasan, S., Garrick T., & Osran, H. (2005). The impact of surgical castration on sexual recidivism risk among sexually violent predatory offenders. *Journal of the American Academy of Psychiatry and Law, 33*, 6–36.

World Health Organization. (1992). *The ICD-10 Classification of Mental and Behavioral Disorders: Clinical Descriptions and Diagnostic Guidelines.* Geneva: World Health Organization.

28

Understanding and Using Compassion-Focused Therapy in Forensic Settings

Russell Kolts and Paul Gilbert

Key points

- Compassion-focused therapy (CFT) is based on the understanding that evolution has shaped the basic potentials for our motives and emotions. These powerfully influence how human beings will develop and are not of our choosing or design. Hence the kind of person we become is the consequence of social shaping acting upon our genetic predispositions.
- CFT recognizes shame – the sense that one is bad, flawed, or is seen as such by others – as a factor that often prompts avoidance, preventing individuals from taking responsibility for their actions and working directly with the sources of suffering in their lives.
- Compassion, and the cultivation of a compassionate version of the self, provide a vehicle for rehabilitation: enabling the individual to turn towards, take responsibility for, and work with the challenging aspects of their lives and their own motives, impulses, and emotions.
- The stage can be set for compassion through the cultivation of wisdom, involving certain realizations:
  - That our brains were built *for* us (by evolution), not *by* us, and that they function in ways that can be tricky and create problems for us.
  - That the interaction between old-brain motive and emotion-centers and new brain capacities for imagery, thinking, and meaning-making can create loops that can keep us trapped in threat-based modes of processing.
  - That we are powerfully shaped by early social forces – such as attachment environments – that we have little power to design or control.
- Key to CFT is the function of three major evolved emotion regulation systems, associated with threat and self-protection, goal-attainment and resource-acquisition, and experiences of safeness, soothing, and contentment. The safeness/soothing system acts through physiological mechanisms

---

The Wiley Blackwell Handbook of Forensic Neuroscience, First Edition. Edited by Anthony R. Beech, Adam J. Carter, Ruth E. Mann and Pia Rotshtein.
© 2018 John Wiley & Sons Ltd. Published 2018 by John Wiley & Sons Ltd.

- to help regulate experiences of threat, and is a target of intervention and training in CFT.
- Emotions and organizing social motives called social mentalities powerfully organize processes of attention, thinking and reasoning, mental imagery, felt emotional experience, motivation, and behavior.
- Key to CFT is the cultivation of compassionate motives and related competencies, organized in the concept of the compassionate self.
- CFT can assist forensic clients to gain mindful insight into the nature of their minds and dispositions, learn new and helpful ways to cope with their often difficult lives, overdependence on threat-based emotions and fear of resistance to social connectedness and compassion. This enables them to be more flexible in their engagement with the world and thereby take greater responsibility for their behavior.
- The process of CFT includes:
  - assessment of the nature, reasons and dispositions towards criminal behavior;
  - psychoeducation about how and why the human brain evolved and what it evolved to do;
  - the problems of allowing one's mind to stay on automatic particularly when regulated via threat processing;
  - clarifying the nature of compassion as building courage and wisdom to engage with unhelpful motives and powerful and problematic emotions;
  - developing the compassionate self and compassionate resources, and understanding how to use compassion motivation and wisdom to address life difficulties and painful states of mind.

Terminology Explained

Alleles are alternative forms of genes caused by mutations.

Compassion-focused therapy (CFT) is rooted in evolutionary, social, and developmental psychology and the neuroscience of affect regulation. CFT therefore helps people recognize that "we have brains built for us not by us." No one chooses to have a brain that is capable of panic or rage, love or grief, compassion or hatred – these are gene-built potentials within and individual.

Evolutionary psychology is a branch of psychology that suggests what makes us human (mental and psychological traits) are the functional products of natural/sexual selection in human evolution.

Oxytocin underpins attachment formation and associated behaviors. Vaginal birth and breast-feeding are associated with increased oxytocin release and are correlated with good attachment formation.

Phenotypes are the observable characteristics of an individual arising from the interaction between the person's genes and the environment.

Introduction

The theoretical and empirical basis for Compassion-focused therapy (CFT) is rooted in evolutionary, social, and developmental psychology and the neuroscience of affect regulation (Gilbert, 2005a, 2010a,b) (see Box 28.1). This approach suggests that human capacity for behaving compassionately and morally, or aggressively and immorally, is related to evolved phenotypes that are shaped and choreographed via the interaction of genetic disposition and environmental priming and shaping (Belsky & Pluess, 2009; Boyce & Ellis, 2005; Boyce, Essex, & Ellis, 2005). We now know, for example, that different alleles of neurotransmitter genes (e.g., short versions) can be associated with increased risk of mental health. However, that risk may only be manifest in certain (e.g., hostile or neglectful) environments. In loving environments, those same alleles may actually convey benefits (Belsky & Pluess, 2009). These insights are central for CFT – for both client and therapists – because they significantly reduce shaming and blaming and set the path for how to take responsibility for cultivating the mind in different ways.

Box 28.1   Compassionate focused therapy background

CFT begins with the premise that humans are created in the evolutionary flow of life – and that the human brain is the product of hundreds of millions of years of evolution, change, and adaptation, and many of our basic emotional and motivational systems can in fact be traced back to reptilian evolution (MacLean, 1990). For example, capacities for fight, flight, submissive behavior, territorial acquisition, and sexual behavior, including fighting over sexual access, are very ancient traits. Like other animals, humans are primed to monitor their relative status (Boksem, Kostermans, Milivojevic, & De Cremer, 2011; Johnson & Leedom, 2012). The same facial expressions, intense eye gazes, postures, and stiff musculature are used in the threat displays of reptiles, primates, and humans (Maclean, 1990). As is the case for other species, triggers for human inter-male violence are often linked to status issues (which for humans can be associated with shame, disrespect, humiliation, and the avoidance of inferiority) (Cohen, Vandello, & Rantilla, 1998; Johnson & Leedom, 2012) and sexual access (Barkow, 1989). Moreover, individual variation in the propensity to engage in status fights and general aggression are noted within members of many different species (Sapolsky, 2004). For example, some baboon (dominant) males are affiliative and cooperative and only fight when provoked (secure dominants), whereas others provoke and pick fights – and are sometimes labeled as insecure dominants (Sapolsky, 2004). So, humans carry forward many motivational processes and potential social strategies from earlier evolutionary adaptations.

While a review of the literature on the complex relationships between inherited biological factors, social shaping, and criminality is beyond the scope of this chapter, there is considerable evidence that a range of different factors predict criminal behavior (Andrews & Bonta, 2010). Antisocial peers and associates are consistently found to be one of the strongest contributors to criminal behavior, with delinquent peers serving to model and reinforce antisocial behavior and actively discourage prosocial behavior (Andrews & Bonta, 2010). Social context, such as growing up in a disadvantaged neighborhood, has a significant impact on risk for criminal behavior (Wikström & Loeber, 2000). Young men who would be considered low risk for antisocial behavior based on various predictors – attitudes, personality, and immediate interpersonal environment – are placed at risk when living in highly disadvantaged neighborhoods (Andrews & Bonta, 2010). In addition to direct social shaping, indirect influences such as low socioeconomic status (Tuvblad, Grann, & Lichenstein, 2006) and family dysfunction (Button, Scourfield, Martin, Purcell, & McGuffin, 2005) are connected with increased risk of antisocial behavior, while a number of studies have linked insecure attachment styles with aggression and antisocial behavior (for reviews of this literature, see van IJzendoorn, 1997; Mitchell & Beech, 2011).

In many cases the criminal behaviors that led to incarceration are just the sort of aggressive, manipulative, rank-focused strategies that are shaped and rewarded by the combination of hostile environments and non-secure attachment histories. Assisting clients in understanding the ways that these environments can serve to shape our phenotypes can both give them a non-shaming perspective on how they got to where they are and help them envision the different choices they could begin to make in order to craft a more promising future.

The Older and Newer Brain – How the Brain Sets Us Up for Difficulties

One of the key concepts of CFT is that the human brain is actually quite "tricky," and carries potentials for both the best (compassion) and worst (cruelty) in us through no fault of our own. In fact, in some Buddhist teachings it is suggested that the unawakened and unenlightened mind is chaotic and potentially dangerous (crazy) to self and others because it will act out in the world whatever desire, passion, anxiety, or anger arises within it (Vessantara, 1993). CFT links this problem to the way in which the brain has evolved (as shown in Figure 28.1) (see Box 28.2).

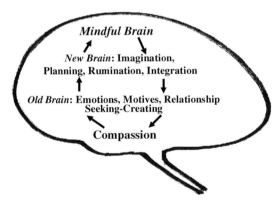

Figure 28.1 Older brain and newer brain.
Source: Gilbert & Choden (2013), *Mindful Compassion*, reprinted with permission from Constable & Robinson Ltd.

Understanding and Using Compassion-Focused Therapy 729

Box 28.2 Human cruelty

CFT invites us to look directly and fairly uncomfortably at the real nature of our minds and to recognize that our intelligent minds, when linked into the motivations of tribal and social or personal dominance psychology, can lead to the most terrible of atrocities. For example, over the last 3,000 years, humans are well noted for the ingenuity of their tortures and methods of killing people (Gilbert, 2005a). When violence, cruelty, and even sadism are used in the service of tribal group conflict and defense it is rarely regarded as immoral (Gay, 1995). Rape, which in civil society is regarded as a crime, is relatively common in certain war zones and women can be left with a terrible legacy of bearing children for which they may often be shamed by their own communities – this was a major problem in the Balkans (Ingnatiff, 1999).

If we first look at what we can call old or older brain functions, many of our basic motivations and emotions – be it for territorial ownership, joining groups, seeking out sexual partners, looking after offspring, forming attachments, responding to threats to status, responding to affection signals – are all trans-species and are shared with many other animals. In terms of strategic behaviors, aggression, stealing, and rape are certainly not confined to humans. Chimpanzees have even been recorded as ganging up on individuals in a split off group, and deliberately murdering them (Goodall, 1990).

However, there are also capacities for affection, and in the case of humanity, major changes in the regulation of motivations and emotions began to arise about two million years ago. From here, pre-humans started to develop increased cognitive competencies, which allow us to think systemically. Unlike other animals, we can imagine and plan, engage in "mental time travel" (think about the past and the future), anticipate, and have a sense of self and imagined self within different scenarios. This new brain makes it possible for us to develop language, symbol use, writing, science, art, and much more besides. But it is also a source of serious difficulty for humans.

One way we explain this to clients (psychoeducation plays a key role in CFT) is to imagine a zebra running away from a lion. Once the zebra gets away, it will quickly calm down and go back to grazing. For humans, however, this is less likely because we may well begin to ruminate and imagine "what could have happened if I had got caught?" We may create fantasies of what it would be like to be eaten alive or "what if there is a lion out tomorrow or maybe two lions?" Ruminating and running "what if" simulations in our minds about the potential issues one can run into can be helpful to anticipate, prevent, and solve problems, but can also be a focus for anxiety and brooding anger.

Humans also have a "sense of self" so we can also run simulations in our minds about what we might do, imagining ourselves doing different things and the outcomes that might result from these actions. Having a sense of self means that we can also imagine ourselves in the minds of others: "what are others thinking about me and how are they going to relate to me?" All of this can cause serious difficulties because our thinking, fantasies, and how we define our sense of self can be a source of continuous stimulation of the sense of threat and hence the threat systems in the body (Sapolsky, 2004). This ability is also the *basis for shame* and sense of humiliation that can be at the root of many mental health and criminality problems (Gilbert, 2007; Reilly, Rochlen, & Awad, 2013).

When working with men in prisons this turns out to be an important issue – men's constant monitoring of their relative status in comparison to other men and whether they are held in esteem and respected or not. To lose respect in a prison (shame) can be a very dangerous position to be in. This is also a key theme (the importance of authority and respect) and this potential threat comes up with staff in relationship to the prisoners too.

As far as we know, the people who dropped the atomic bomb on Nagasaki and Hiroshima were not in any way psychopaths or mentally ill, and that includes all those who actually worked to develop such a weapon, but the suffering that was caused by that act was horrific and impacted on many tens of thousands over generations. CFT makes clear from the outset that the human mind is a set of varied potentials, and much depends on what is activated within us and how we can regulate it. In this way, we move away from thinking about "pathologies" and more toward thinking about the kinds of phenotypes and psychobiological patterns that have been activated within individuals. Moreover, the focus is on the way in which phenotypes are whole-organism responses and adaptations to social contexts (Boyce & Ellis, 2005; Boyce et al., 2005). Indeed, we now know that early life experiences can actually change genetic expression (Belsky & Pluess, 2009) and the structure of the brain itself (Cozolino, 2007, 2013). So, CFT helps people recognize that "we have brains built for us not by us." No one chooses to have a brain that is capable of panic or rage, love or grief, compassion or hatred – these are gene-built potentials within us.

Secondly, we commonly use examples such as "if I (as the therapist) had been kidnapped as a three-day-old baby into a violent drug gang and brought up in that family and culture, how would I be today?" It's very important that clients begin to recognize that much of what they feel they are, their values, and sense of self have been mostly socially created for them *not* by them. Given such backgrounds, it's pretty obvious that the current versions of Russell and Paul, who are now professors writing this book chapter, would simply not exist. We might well be dead, or have committed some atrocities ourselves, or be in prison, and so on.

How Motives Organize the Mind

CFT argues that what organizes our minds is linked to basic motivations and values, which, in turn, become the framework for a sense of identity. For example, looking at the bottom of Figure 28.1, consider what would happen if compassion became the motivation for how we operate in the world. It would influence the way we pay attention to things, how we think, the kinds of feelings that are stimulated in us, and the behaviors that we enact. In contrast, if we were motivated for self-protection, status, and ensuring that other people don't threaten us, our whole way of organizing our minds and indeed brains would be very different (Crocker & Canevello, 2008; Crocker, Canevello, Breines, & Flynn, 2010; Johnson & Leedom, 2012). These motivational systems that link to identity are also highly culturally contextualized. For example, Twenge, Gentile, DeWall, Ma, Lacefield, and Schurtz (2010) have shown that over the last 30 years there seems to have been a rise in narcissistic traits, especially in the young.

In addition, however, repeated emotional experiences can play major roles in the kinds of motives we develop. So, for example, if we repeatedly experience others as hostile to us, we are going to develop very different social motives and a sense of self than if people are repeatedly kind and helpful to us. The brain will basically try to grow and organize itself to fit adaptively into the social niche in which it finds itself. Through a behavioral lens, we can see this process play out in terms of the reinforcement of certain social strategies and the non-reinforcement or even punishment of others. This shaping applies not only to specific behaviors, but also to underlying motives and understandings of the social world and our place within it.

In CFT, social motives are linked to what are called social mentalities (Gilbert, 2005b). Social mentalities are simply motivations that are focused on our interactions with others and are dependent on the actions of others for their fulfillment. So, for example, a competitive mentality orientates an animal to pay attention to others in such a way that they can avoid stimulating more powerful individuals who could hurt them (and show submissive behavior where appropriate) while also challenging those who are weaker (Gilbert, 1992; Johnson & Leedom, 2012). For humans, who may be less focused on aggressive forms of competitiveness, attention is on relative social attractiveness, social standing, and wanting to avoid being seen as inferior (Barkow, 1989; Gilbert, 1992). A care-giving social mentality, on the other hand, pays attention to the needs and distress of others and behaves in a way to try to relieve that distress (Gilbert, 2005). So, a social mentality is always organized around social interactions. Figure 28.2 shows how different social mentalities organize different qualities of mind.

So repeated emotional experiences help to shape our phenotypes, and thus our social mentalities and how they are expressed and developed. To explore this further, and how this can be linked to compassion, we now consider what kinds of emotions can become stimulated in us and how they help to shape our social identities and sense of self.

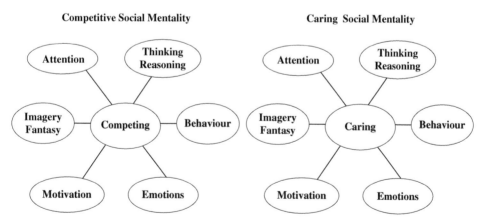

Figure 28.2 Social mentalities of mind.

Source: Gilbert & Choden (2013), *Mindful Compassion*, reprinted with permission from Constable & Robinson Ltd.

Figure 28.3 Three types of emotion regulation system.
Source: Gilbert (2009), *The Compassionate Mind*, reprinted with permission from Constable & Robinson Ltd.

CFT and the Three Systems of Emotion

Another core principle of CFT is to consider the functions of evolved emotional systems, and their developmental trajectories. Key to understanding the link between motivational systems like competitiveness status or attachment and affiliation is to consider how different types of emotion are regulated (Depue & Morrone-Strupinsky, 2005). Panksepp (1998) has outlined a number of different, functional emotion systems. In CFT, however, we focus on three major ones (depicted in Figure 28.3) as follows.

1 *Threat and self-protection focused system*
   This enables detecting, attending and processing, and responding to threats. There is a menu of threat-based emotions such as anger, anxiety, and disgust, and a menu of defensive behaviors such as fight, flight, submission, freeze, and so on. The threat system has been well studied and we now know something of the basic physiological systems involved, such as the amygdala and hypothalamic-pituitary adrenal axis, which is central to the organization of threat (LeDoux, 1998). Threat processing is the most basic form of processing, and can easily turn off positive emotion and dominate our motivations (e.g., to get safe, avoid danger, enact vengeance). Indeed, it is sometimes called the "negativity bias" (Baumeister, Bratslavsky, Finkenauer, & Vohs, 2001).
2 *Drive, seeking and acquisition focused system*
   This enables the paying of attention to advantageous resources, and with some degree of "activation," involving an experience of pleasure in pursuing and

securing resources and goals. This is a basic reward and reinforcing system so that animals will repeat actions that are positively rewarded. It has also been linked to the concept of a behavioral approach system (Depue & Morrone-Strupinsky, 2005), and to the status and dominance-seeking system. Indeed, when individuals feel they are winning or improving their social status, they usually experience positive emotion, whereas losing status is associated with increased threat emotion (Johnson, & Leedom, 2012).

3   *Contentment, soothing, and affiliative-focused system*
This enables a state of peacefulness and openness when individuals are no longer threat focused or seeking resources – but are satisfied. This system is linked to feelings of wellbeing. Over evolutionary time, this system of calming (threat and drive) has been adapted for many functions of attachment and affiliative behavior (Depue & Morrone-Strupinsky, 2005; Porges, 2007). The system is linked to the endorphin-oxytocin systems, which function to promote trust and affiliative behavior (Insel, 2010). Recipients of affiliation experience a calming of the threat system (MacDonald & Macdonald, 2010).

So, briefly then, we have specialized emotions for identifying and responding to threats, for seeking out rewards, and responding to positive events. These tend to involve arousal and activation of the sympathetic nervous system. However, we also have emotions associated with slowing down, feeling content and safe in relationships, which are linked to the parasympathetic nervous system. In fact, CFT focuses on how to help clients stimulate and balance sympathetic and parasympathetic arousal with parasympathetic training such as breathing and mindfulness techniques (discussed further).

The Power of Threat

The human brain is set up to be highly responsive to threats. In fact, it operates on a "better safe than sorry" principle (Gilbert, 1989; Marks, 1987). The reason for this is because failing to notice legitimate threats could result in serious injuries or even death. A simple example we give to clients is to imagine Christmas shopping. You go to ten shops and in nine shops the assistant is really helpful to you, and wishes you a nice day. However, in one shop, the assistant is extremely rude, perhaps even offensive, doesn't try to help you, and gives you the wrong change. Who do you ruminate and think about when you go home and talk to your partner about your trip? Usually it's the rude one. We quickly forget the details of the nine people who were helpful but focus on the details of the one who was rude and maybe what we should do to get our own back – write to the store manager? This is a normal psychology but of course many forensic clients get caught up in this in a very serious way.

Consider also what this attention is doing to the body. Imagine if you were to learn to focus on and remember the nine people who were helpful to you rather than allowing your mind to dwell on the one who was not. Now imagine growing up in a very threatening world. Not only do you have to deal with the natural tendency for your brain to be threat focused, additionally you will be highly orientated to threat because of your social conditioning. Hence a whole set of defensive behaviors, including aggressiveness, are primed in us. Helping clients understand that we have a natural tendency to be biased toward threat sometimes called "the negativity bias" is very important (Baumeister et al., 2001). It provides the basis to help them learn how to work against a normal natural bias in their brains – not as a pathology but as a natural negativity bias.

The power of threat *If nine out of ten people are kind and helpful to us, it is the one antisocial person that sticks in our mind. We focus on the details of this incident rather than the positive ones. This is a normal psychology but many forensic clients get caught up in this in a very serious way.*
Source: Pixabay. https://pixabay.com/en/burmeseboy-emotional-anger-2312416/.

Attachment and Affiliation

One thing all animals have to learn fairly quickly is how to deal with a potentially threatening world. Turtles, for example, have no attachment object to turn to when threatened and therefore have to be mobile and active, able to go it alone, from the day they are born. The evolution of parental investment in mammals, however, meant that the young infant's need for food and warmth could be provided by the parent. This was to have a profound and fundamental influence on subsequent evolution of mind (Cozolino, 2007; Siegel, 2012). In addition, the parent provides stimuli that help to regulate the infant's threat system by calming and soothing them (Bowlby, 1969; Hofer, 1994). So, when the infant is distressed, the physical contact and vocal tones of the mother or father will initiate the release of oxytocin, stimulating the parasympathetic nervous system and producing a calming response (Porges, 2007).

It is now known that these basic systems for being calmed by affection and affiliation with others play very major roles in affect regulation (Cozolinio, 2007; Siegel, 2012). When a child experiences their caregivers as attentive, protective, and caring, they experience the world as safe or easily made safe, and this stimulates socially-focused strategies for affiliative engagement. Over time, this is associated with the development of capacities for trust, taking an interest in others, mentalizing, and empathy. In contrast, when a child experiences their caregivers as empathically mis-attuned, neglectful or abusive they are unable to easily regulate threat through affiliative processes. In consequence, socially-focused strategies develop in a threat-oriented manner – focused on the potential power of others and self-focused defensive strategies centered on protecting the self from others rather than connecting with them (Gilbert, 2005a). It's not surprising, therefore, to find that many individuals who are convicted of rape and aggressive or violent acts in non-war situations come from highly abusive backgrounds.

The essence of Bowlby's (1969) attachment theory was that the relationship between the child and the parent provides a number of core qualities that will serve the child on his/her maturation journey. First, the parent provides a *secure base* that is protective and fulfils the infant's needs and maintains relatively low levels of threats. As the child grows up, this secure base also provides the confidence to go out and explore the world. In addition, the parent is helping the child to understand and regulate their own emotions so that every bump in the road is not a major disaster and they experience others who are willing to validate their emotions. Second, this secure base also becomes the source of *a safe haven* because, when the child moves into the world and becomes stressed or overwhelmed, he/she can return to the secure base where he/she receives calming and soothing. The many and complex relationships between attachment and subsequent offending behavior have been well reviewed by Mitchell and Beech (2011). Central to compassion is that a secure child is able to see others as sources of help and support, which orientates the child to have a more trusting, sharing, open, and compassionate approach to him/herself and others (Gillath, Shaver, & Mikulincer, 2005).

The essence of the argument is that in some forensic populations the affiliative processing systems that regulate threat, and also provide the emotional basis for taking an interest in the welfare of self and others, are insufficiently developed or have become toxic due to inappropriate care-giving. To some extent, then, therapy needs to address this developmental problem by specifically targeting affiliative systems, both to self and others. Building compassionate capacity is one way to do this. Recently, Cozolino (2013) has outlined how schools can also begin to act as a safe base and a haven that provide (distressed) children positive, validating, and encouraging relationships, which enable them to re-orientate themselves to more affiliative strategies. There is much that could be drawn from this understanding of how schools can work with emotionally troubled children that could also be applied in prison settings.

The Nature of Compassion

CFT is contextualized in an understanding of the nature of the human mind, the arbitrariness of genetic endowment and social shaping, along with the three different types of emotion regulation system. Compassion helps us to grapple with these nature-given difficulties or what we call "tricky brain." Compassion can be defined in many ways, but a common way is: "As a sensitivity to suffering, and the causes of suffering, in self and others with a commitment to try to alleviate and prevent it" (Gilbert & Choden, 2013). This is important because one of the common reasons people are imprisoned is that they have caused harm or suffering to others. So, one of the challenges is to not only help people work with their own suffering but also the suffering they have caused others.

Shame and guilt

This raises the question about what it is that normally stops people from harming others in a non-war context. The fear of punishment and retaliation is an obvious reason, as is shame and the fear of being shamed. However, shame is an emotion that is regarded as narcissistic to the extent that it focuses the attention very much on the self, the potential damage to the self in one's own eyes and the eyes of others (Gilbert, 1998, 2007). While long considered a "moral emotion," thought to inhibit bad behavior, research indicates that shame is often *not* helpful.

> Across study after study, the propensity to experience shame has been linked not to fine, upstanding moral character and behavior but rather to evading responsibility, blaming the victim, mismanaging anger, and in the extreme, hostile aggression … When shamed, people feel physically, psychologically, and socially diminished … The knee-jerk response is not to apologize and repair but rather to hide or escape. This is understandable because the pain is great, the self is impaired, and the job (to transform the self from fundamentally flawed to good) is impossibly immense.
>
> (Tangney et al. (2011), pp. 710–711).

The fear of shame by a peer group can also lead youths to actually be complicit in criminal acts. Moreover, punishment from an external authority (getting arrested) is not shameful but can actually be a badge of honor in the peer group (Andrews & Bonta, 2010). So, although undoubtedly the fear of punishment can and does constrain immoral behavior, much depends on who is doing the "shaming." In addition, shame and the defenses to shame include justification, denial, and dissociation from the harm one causes (Baumeister, 1997). Additionally, people who are prone to criminal acts often believe they will not get caught. So, as the behaviorists have pointed out for many years, the fear of punishment (and shame) is always a dubious way of regulating behavior because people will try to avoid punishment but not necessarily engage in the desired prosocial behavior. This is why hiding, concealing, justifying, and denying are common in criminal acts. Shame does not open people to compassion – but guilt does.

As Crook (1986) and Gilbert (1989) point out, the evolution of caring had to have a distress-sensitive and harm avoidance capacity; that is, some kind of negative emotion that arises in the context of harm to others. So, for example, when we see others in distress, this can trigger personal distress and caring behavior. If one is the cause of that harm, there can be personal distress with efforts to repair. The result of this distress – refraining from harm in the future – would be adaptive. For example, in the attachment context, avoiding doing harm to one's offspring (and genetic relatives) will assist them to prosper. Avoiding doing harm to one's potential allies and friends is adaptive, for "injuring" friends will affect their ability to support you, and they may turn against you. This is the basis of guilt, where the attention is external (rather than inward and self-focused), focused on the harm to the other, centered on the "harmful" behavior (rather than a global judgment of self), with some kind of emotional attunement to the harm one has caused, and the primary emotions are ones of sadness and remorse (rather than fear and anger, as in shame) (Gilbert, 2007; Kim et al., 2011). When guilt rather than shame is the core of moral behavior, then one is clearly much more in the territory of compassion. This is because one is not so motivated to protect the self (as in shame), but rather one does *not want to be* a source of suffering for others.

Understanding and Using Compassion-Focused Therapy

There is now considerable evidence that shame and guilt operate in very different ways and from two very different motivational and emotional systems (Gilbert, 1989, 2007; Kim et al., 2011). The recognition that guilt rather than shame is important in helping people become more "moral" and aware of the harm they cause others is evident in the shift from retribution to restorative justice (Shapland, Robinson, & Sorsby, 2011; Zehr, 2002). At its simplest, the former is focused on shaming and punishing whereas the latter is on bringing perpetrators and victims together and processing harm that has been done. In these situations, people who have caused harm may well have their capacity for caring and compassion stimulated – partly because they can't use avoidance (Gilbert, 2010b; Shapland et al., 2011). This can then become the basis of genuine responsibility taking. At deeper levels, these distinctions are related to the way in which society views and treats criminal behavior in general.

Compassion then, as defined as "a sensitivity to suffering, and the causes of suffering, in self and others with a commitment to try to alleviate and prevent it," (Gilbert, 1989, 2010b) is part of the care-giving social mentality that evolved with attachment, alliance formation, and altruism (Warneken & Tomasello, 2009). This definition highlights two very important but different psychologies. The first is the psychology of engagement, the ability to notice, engage with, and tolerate suffering, in contrast to not noticing, turning away from, avoiding, denying, or even enjoying suffering. The second is the psychology of alleviation and prevention. In the CFT model, these two different psychologies are typically represented as two interacting circles that are labeled attributes (the psychology of engagement) and skills (the psychology of alleviation and prevention). This is depicted in Figure 28.4.

Compassion should be seen as "flow" to the extent there is the compassion we experience coming to us *from others*, the compassion we experience *toward others*, and the compassion we can direct toward the self, *self-compassion*. These two circles apply to each of those three dynamics of relating. For example, we can sense that other people care about us, are sensitive to our feelings, and are empathic to us. We can be caring, sensitive, and empathic to others and to ourselves. This is what we mean by flow, and flow is important because the way we experience other people's compassion may have an impact on our capacities to provide compassion. CFT works on each of those three domains – giving to others, receiving from others, and self-compassion. For any individual, the starting point may be somewhat different. While some people find it easier to begin with self-compassion, others need to experience compassion coming into them (being treated with respect and compassion) and yet others find it easier to begin by becoming compassionate to others. We can very briefly look at these different attributes and skills.

Caring The compassion journey can start with an awareness of suffering, which then triggers a motivation to engage rather than disengage. The motivation for caring becomes important because if individuals have no interest in the wellbeing of themselves or others then they are hardly likely to pay attention to suffering. Indeed, recent research suggests that people with psychopathic traits can be empathic but they lack caring motivation – they don't empathize spontaneously (Meffert, Gazzola, den Boer, Bartels, & Keysers, 2013). In compassion, the caring motivational, social mentality organizes what we pay attention to, and is the basis for orientating to suffering.

Compassion: Motive and Competencies

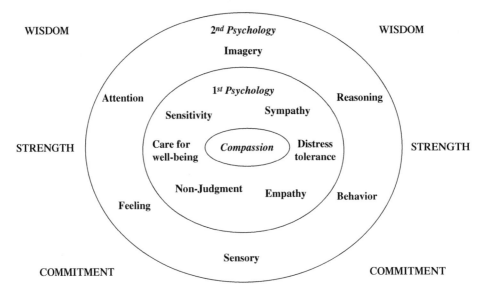

Figure 28.4 Multi-modal compassionate mind training.
Source: Gilbert P. (2010b), *The Compassionate Mind*, reprinted with permission from Constable & Robinson Ltd.

Sensitivity This relates to attention and the way and to what we attend. So, for example, arachnophobic individual (someone with a phobia of spiders) is very sensitive and attentive to the potential presence of spiders. Individuals with caring motivation are attentive to the needs and distress of others and self. Paying attention to a stimulus will then create an emotional reaction to that stimulus; that is to say, we emotionally tune in – which in the case of suffering can give rise to a sympathetic emotional response.

Sympathy There are many debates about the nature of sympathy and empathy, but in this model sympathy refers to our immediate emotional reactions to suffering (Decety & Ickes, 2011). For example, if we see a child fall and hit their head and scream in pain, we can have an automatic bodily reaction. These bodily reactions, however, may well be suppressed in individuals who are vulnerable to engaging in cruelty, that is to say, they don't show certain types of physiological reaction to the scenes of people in pain (Blair, Mitchell, & Blair, 2005).

Distress tolerance In turning toward suffering in oneself or others, and becoming attuned to that pain, there needs to then be an ability to tolerate the pain. Much has been written on the role of distress tolerance in many therapy approaches and how low levels of distress tolerance can result in denial, dissociation, and avoidance. There is now good evidence that unprocessed trauma and difficulties in an individual can lead to poor distress tolerance in themselves or others (van der Hart & Steele, 2013).

Empathy There are many different aspects to empathy (Decety & Ickes, 2011), but one of them is the capacity to understand the motives and intentions of self and others. Empathy includes capacities for mentalizing and theory of mind – both of which can be compromised in some criminal populations, especially if they suffer along the Asperger spectrum (Frith, 2004). Recent research shows that, while those with psychopathic personalities display reduced spontaneous brain activity associated with empathy in comparison to non-psychopathic controls, these differences decrease significantly when the individuals are prompted to engage in empathy (Meffert et al., 2013). It is now well understood that empathy by itself is not necessarily compassionate and can actually be used to harm and exploit others. The worst torturer to have is an empathic one, and the most manipulative marketer will be empathic with his buying customers.

Non-judgment This quality refers to the tendency for us to be able to engage with and accept suffering without condemning or trying to avoid it. It does not mean "no preference." For example, there is a strong preference for people working in prisons to help stop criminal acts. But the issue is that one can feel fully accepted without being shamed or criticized. So, the focus is on being understood rather than judged.

All of these attributes are interdependent. For example, if you lose any one of them then compassion can suffer. A drop in motivation, lack of distress tolerance, or difficulties with empathy can each compromise compassion. Hence, therapists need to be aware of where compassion blocks arise because they may arise in different attributes for different people. For example, some people can be very motivated to be compassionate but lack mentalizing or empathy competencies. Others may be quite empathic but have very little caring motivation.

Skills of Compassion

The skills of compassion unfold from the attributes. Looking around the outer circle, we can see that learning to pay attention to what is helpful is one way to cultivate "the good" and is an essential part of attention training. Compassionate reasoning uses many basic cognitive interventions, as does imagery. Compassionate behavior is an important part of compassion training – particularly for this population – because it often involves courage. Here it is important to help distinguish between different types of courage. There is physical courage of course, and many men and women in forensic settings may well show this to the extent they are prepared to engage in fighting or risking physical harm to defend their reputation or sense of toughness. Emotional courage, however, which is the ability to tolerate emotional pain, may be much less well developed. Understanding the cultivation of compassion as the cultivation of "emotional courage" is often a challenge for people, particularly those with difficult attachment histories who have not learned to soothe themselves in the face of challenging emotions.

Processing pain

CFT suggests that it is very difficult to process the pain we cause others if we haven't processed the pain that has been caused to ourselves (Gilbert & Irons, 2005). If children have had to learn to turn off their own pain, to suppress and dissociate from it, then this is probably one source of the inability to be in touch with the pain they cause others. Indeed, there is increasing evidence that people with borderline difficulties find sadness (e.g., in contrast to anger) a very difficult emotion to process (Lecours & Bouchard, 2011) and, for some people, grieving for their own life losses, tragedies, and harms is very painful (Gilbert & Irons, 2005). Indeed, both of the authors of this chapter have encountered clients who only began to engage with change when they became able to grieve.

Fears of compassion

One of the problems with beginning the process of compassion is that it requires some degree of the affiliative system to come online. When this happens, however, it will open up earlier emotional memories in the caring and attachment systems. For example, a child who is loved in the morning but beaten at night by a drunken parent will have very complicated emotional memories and internal representations of caring others. They will have difficulty in discriminating whether (and when) others will be kind or abusive. These individuals are particularly unlikely to "open up" and process emotional pain because they cannot create a secure base or safe haven in the therapeutic relationship very easily (Liotti, 2009; Nijenhuis & Boer, 2009; van der Hart & Steele, 2013), and because experiences of closeness may be conditioned to evoke feelings of threat.

In these contexts, it is also not uncommon to find that if clients do begin to make definitive connections to the therapist, they also become more frightened of and more hostile to the therapist. This is referred to as attachment phobia and is well articulated in the trauma literature (Nijenhuis & Boer, 2009). This is because the aversive memories are being stimulated along with the memories and desires for connectedness (Liotti, 2009). Therapists need to be wary therefore that in the early stages of developing compassion, which will involve a form of relating to self and others, they may have to first detoxify the attachment and affiliative systems. This can be emotionally difficult for both therapist and client (van der Hart & Steele, 2013). However, simply warning clients of this and explaining how and why this works can be enormously helpful to them.

On a ward for complex cases, a nurse who understood this model might have a "good and reasonably affiliative" session with a client with borderline difficulties but find that two hours later the client is "acting out" and self-harming. Some staff may take this as attention seeking or evidence that the client is beyond help. Rather than being perplexed by this behavior, our insightful nurse is able to begin to explore the feelings that had been aroused after leaving the therapy and in this way the client is able to begin to recognize that they had indeed had good therapy but that leaving the session brought back a feeling of being acutely alone. Leaving the session (so now being on their own) can stimulate memories of aloneness and then feeling completely unloved and vulnerable to abuse, along with a great deal of emotional pain or rage.

So, remembering the definition of compassion (which is sensitivity to the suffering in self and others on the causes of suffering with a commitment to try to alleviate and prevent it), we can see that compassion is a way of engaging with the pain within clients. Moreover, using the two compassion psychologies, it is possible to see where clients get blocked in the compassion process. For example, some people may be blocked because they misunderstand the nature of compassion and the courage involved, others get blocked because as they begin to engage in suffering they have to process their own past suffering and become overwhelmed, yet others run into all kinds of difficulties associated with unprocessed emotional memories. Even for people who have come to hate their parents, it can be very difficult to process the grieving for the parent they actually wanted and the love of a mother and father they actually needed as a child. Blocked off from those feelings, they can remain in states of coldness and even dangerousness.

The Processes of CFT

Flowing from the approach described above, CFT seeks to assist forensic clients to learn new, better ways to cope with their often difficult lives and take greater responsibility for their behavior. The process generally unfolds in the following way:

1 Assessment – which is the normal process of the psychological assessment looking at life history, core experiences, and current issues.
2 Psychoeducation of the evolutionary model.
3 Formulation within the context of the evolutionary model.
4 Clarifying the nature of compassion and dispelling myths – building the therapeutic contract for compassion work.
5 Preparing for compassion work – bodywork including slow and focused breathing.
6 Developing compassionate self and compassion resources (e.g., compassion image).
7 Putting the compassionate self to work, which helps build the moral basis and capabilities for guilt and new compassionate self-identity as the antidote to the offending self.

As this process unfolds in a nonlinear way, the therapist continually models the compassion that he or she seeks to help foster in the client. The day-to-day reality of many incarcerated individuals is one in which almost every aspect of their experience – what they wear, eat, do; who they interact with; and so forth – is all dictated by the worst thing they've done (or, at least, the worst thing they've been caught doing). Almost all aspects of their daily experience can function as constant reminders of a shaming past and of a criminal self-identity. In a vacuum, this experience can serve to reinforce the shame, aggressive, rank-focused social mentalities (and related behavior) that resulted in their incarceration in the first place. Hence, in CFT, the treatment experience is designed to provide new learning experiences, and explore other ways of existing in the world, other versions of themselves, different identities that they can aspire to cultivate. This motivation permeates the therapy – so, for example, in this section, we will use the word "client" rather than "offender" or "inmate."

How the brain sets up for difficulties *Unlike other animals we can imagine and plan, engage in "mental time travel," anticipate, and have a sense of self and imagined self within different scenarios. Imagine a zebra running away from a lion. Once the zebra gets away, it will quickly calm down and go back to grazing. For humans, however, this is less likely because we may well begin to ruminate and imagine "what could have happened if..."*

Source: © Kuloser. Used under license from Pixabay.

Assessment

As in other models of therapy, CFT begins with an initial assessment process. In addition to presenting problems and current symptoms, emphasis is placed upon developing an understanding of the client's attachment history, core experiences including trauma history, sense of self and relating style, current dynamics and contingencies that help to maintain the presenting problems, and potential obstacles to therapeutic work.

Psychoeducation

Forensic clients are helped to understand the evolutionary and environmental forces that have helped to shape the form their lives have taken. This is of particular importance in working with forensic clients, who by the virtue of their interaction with the criminal justice system may simply be surrounded by a system of influences that communicate and reinforce a deviant self-concept (Braithwaite, 1989). In the early stages of CFT, clients are acquainted with the compassionate mind model, helping the forensic client to understand how and why they became the way they are, to understand how their motives and behaviors make sense within their evolutionary-social context, and to engage them in the desires and (compassionate) ways for change.

Formulation within the context of the evolutionary model

From the perspective of CFT, the forensic client presents with a number of often well-entrenched dynamics that function to shape and reinforce undesirable (and, in many cases, illegal) motivations and behavioral strategies that can make rehabilitation very challenging. So, in CFT, time is spent creating an initial formulation of the clients' difficulties within the context of the evolutionary model. This formulation will contain four primary components: 1) innate and historical influences, 2) key internal and external threats and fears, 3) externally focused and internally focused safety strategies, which give rise to 4) unintended consequences – that fuel more distress, safety strategies, and difficulties – including self-criticism (Gilbert, 2010a).

In this way, client difficulties, including their offending, are conceptualized within a context of historical influences, perceived threats, and the often maladaptive threat-based efforts that the individual has developed in response to these threats. In addition, clients can be helped to understand why they might have little interest in the impact of their criminal behavior on others, or justify or deny negative effects. Hence, beginning the process of reflection in a non-judging and compassionate atmosphere can be the start of the development of mentalization and responsibility taking.

Clarifying the nature of compassion and dispelling myths: building the therapeutic contract for compassion work

One potential obstacle to doing compassion work with forensic groups has to do with myths about it. Both authors have had experiences in which clients have eye-rolled at the first mention of compassion, and we regularly hear client perceptions of compassion to mean being weak, effeminate, or simply "giving people everything they want." These perceptions may be particularly pronounced in males holding to traditionally masculine norms; a recent study revealed a significant negative relationship between self-compassion and masculine norm adherence (Reilly, Rochlen, & Awad, 2013). Overcoming this obstacle involves clarifying the nature of compassion and debunking myths about it. This process involves two steps: defining compassion and modeling it in the therapeutic relationship.

Defining compassion as a strength An initial stage in the therapy involves eliciting how the client defines compassion and what they think about it. Via discussion, clients are presented with a definition of compassion that contains the two components discussed earlier: a sensitivity to suffering and a commitment to prevent and alleviate it (Gilbert, 2010a, b). In this way, we begin the process of defining compassion not as a weakness, but as a *strength* – the strength to approach suffering and difficult experiences, and to stay in contact with such experiences while working with them. It can help to contrast compassion with other (often avoidant) responses these clients may have engaged in when faced with difficulties in the past, such as anger and aggression, and to explore the consequences of these actions. In this way, forensic clients can begin to redefine their understanding of what constitutes strength and weakness. For example, forensic clients may feel that to be strong means to maintain an aggressive persona; however, aggression has been linked with the *avoidance* of difficult emotional states (Reddy, Meis, Erbes, Polusny, & Compton, 2011), a relationship that can often be confirmed by the client's discussion of his or her own experiences. Compassion is explored as an alternative that will allow the client to *approach and work with* difficult emotions and situations.

Modeling compassion There are multiple tasks the CFT therapist seeks to accomplish in his or her interactions with the forensic client. The first, and one of the most powerful, is to provide a model of compassion – a warm, kind, empathic, and genuine guide for the therapeutic work – as well as an assertive model of direct, non-deceptive communication and the establishment and maintenance of appropriate boundaries. The importance of this is two-fold. At the behavioral level, the therapist is providing the client with a model of how one can relate to oneself and others in a compassionate manner, using the power of social learning to teach prosocial behavior (Bierhoff, 2005). Additionally, in interacting with the client in this manner, the therapist seeks to create a socially safe experience within the context of the therapeutic relationship. From this perspective, the therapeutic relationship serves as a secure base from which the client can approach, explore, and learn to work with difficult emotions as well as develop new, adaptive capacities and a sense of self-agency (Wallin, 2007; Knox, 2011). This aspect of the therapeutic relationship is particularly important for individuals in correctional settings who may have had both a problematic attachment history and a conditioned threat response to interpersonal closeness and the feelings of vulnerability that come with it. In forensic settings, this can be a slow process. For these clients, the therapeutic relationship itself can feel like an exposure trial in which they gradually (and sometimes very slowly) learn to tolerate increasing levels of closeness and honesty with the therapist and to gradually relinquish dominance-based strategies of relating. As this process progresses, the individual can slowly begin to feel safe within his or her relationship with the therapist (Gilbert, 2010). Finally, in relating to the client compassionately, honestly, assertively, and interestedly, the therapist can begin to help slowly begin to shift their implicit understanding and orientations toward relationships (e.g., from threatening and unpredictable to potentially helpful and safe), other people (e.g., from avoidance and indifference to empathy), and themselves (e.g., from shameful to hopeful and worthy of kindness and compassion). This process unfolds as the therapist provides validation and empathic responses to the client, supports and encourages them in exploring difficult emotions and situations, and through Socratic dialogue helps them to compassionately consider how they got to where they are.

Preparing for compassion work

In preparing the client to do compassion work, CFT emphasizes the development of preliminary skills. Two of the most primary of these are mindfulness and soothing rhythm breathing.

Teaching attention One of the core qualities of training is to teach people about the power of attention, and how to use their own attention effectively. Remember the example of the Christmas shopping assistant and the negativity bias. There are many ways to do this, such as inviting people to focus on their left foot, then switch to the right foot, then their hands. Clients can then realize that when they are focusing on the left foot they become *more aware* of specific sensations and *un*aware of the hands. So, attention becomes like a spotlight or zoom lens. It makes things bigger in our minds when we focus on them but it *also puts things into darkness* (e.g., forgetting the helpful Christmas assistants when we focus on the rude one). Secondly, they learn that attention can be shifted. Third, you can show the physiological power of attention by inviting clients to do the following. First, get them to focus on a happy memory, for a minute or two, maybe one where they were laughing a lot, and ask the client to "notice what happens in your body." Then ask them to focus on an argument or an aggressive incident. Tell them to pay attention to what happens in their body. Help clients notice the change. You can also ask them to remember what happens in the body if they lay in bed and think erotic fantasies! The point is to give very detailed insight into the way in which attention influences not just our behavior but complex bodily processes as well. Although these are simple interventions they can have profound implications and effects on clients who have never really understood how powerful attention is and therefore how important it is to *pay attention to what attention is doing*! This leads to the issue of mindfulness and then on to the deliberate cultivating and focusing of attention on a particular motivational system, which is of course compassion.

Mindfulness In cultivating mindfulness, clients learn to nonjudgmentally accept and observe their experiences, and to relate to thoughts and emotions as mental experiences without identifying or fusing with them. As discussed, forensic clients often live in a mental world defined by a variety of rank-based dominance hierarchies and emotional distance from others. This is basically a world of interpersonal threat in which the attention is focused on sources of threat, producing threat emotions with an accompanying feeling of urgency to action. Mindfulness helps us to recognize and interrupt this process. So, by becoming more mindful of the triggers and feelings of anger, for example, one can begin to choose not to act it out. Without this mindful awareness, emotions are quickly and often mindlessly translated into behavior.

In this way, mindfulness can assist clients in identifying the arising of their threat-based thoughts, motivations, and emotions, so that they can learn to interrupt habitual cycles of rumination and behavior. Once clients are able to notice these processes, they are in the position to begin to shift attention into more compassionate perspectives. A growing body of research supports the use of mindfulness interventions for the treatment of a wide variety of mental health issues, such as anxiety and mood disorders (Hofmann, Sawyer, Witt, & Oh, 2012), and a number of authors have utilized mindfulness approaches in the attempt to treat aggression (Fix & Fix, 2013). Additionally, mindfulness is also included as a component in approaches designed to assist individuals in cultivating compassion for themselves and others (Gilbert & Choden, 2013; Germer, 2009; Neff, 2011).

Bodywork: soothing rhythmic breathing Noting the powerful role of bodily arousal in contributing to feedback loops that help to produce and maintain emotions, CFT makes extensive use of bodywork, particularly working with the breath. One such skill that is taught to all CFT clients is soothing rhythm breathing, which involves slowing down the rate of breathing to around five or six breaths per minute. You want clients to achieve whole lung capacity and must teach them to have even in and out breaths. Many clients have very poor breathing and often collapse the out breath, but the out breath is important for parasympathetic stimulation.[1] Once this breathing technique is achieved, the focus of attention should on the sense of slowing occurring in the body (Gilbert, 2010a, b). In addition to the stress-reducing qualities that have resulted in breathwork, this is also being applied in a wide variety of clinical populations (Brown, Gerbar, & Mench, 2013).

Posture is important in breathwork. If clients are sitting in a chair they need to sit with a straight back, shoulders in line with the head, chest open, and shoulders slightly back rather than pulled in. This maintains an alert posture. It's important to help clients distinguish between creating a point of inner stillness and slowness from relaxation, especially that associated with a more "floppy" muscle tone. CFT slowing is sometimes called "stilling" and can be compared to the diver on the high diving board who tries to find a point of stillness and focus before they dive. So, stillness is a focus on slowness, not relaxation as such, because the body is still alert. We also draw attention to the fact that by slowing down the body will feel slightly heavier and more grounded and learning how to create this sense of "grounded space" is important.

Developing the Compassionate Self

In CFT, a major effort to get the soothing/affiliative emotion regulation system online in an ongoing way takes the form of cultivation of the compassionate self. Using techniques drawn from acting, the client engages in exercises in which they imagine themselves having the various qualities of compassion such as those described previously (empathy, caring, distress tolerance), as well as others such as confidence and wisdom. Clients are prompted to imagine how they would think, feel, behave – even look and sound – as a deeply compassionate being who already possessed the qualities described above.

The idea is to help the individual cultivate a new version of themselves with strong new coping capacities that allow them to work with their challenges from the perspective of the affiliative system rather than threat-focused and rank-based social mentalities. In contrast to the self-critical, hopeless, or hostile, angry "selves" the client may be more familiar with, the cultivation of the compassionate self is designed to help them connect with their underlying capacity to direct warmth and nurturance toward themselves and others, and to help them develop compassionate capacities required to work with life challenges and difficult emotions in ways that don't create problematic unintended consequences (Gilbert, 2010a, b). In the language of attachment, we are helping clients develop the capacity to become secure bases for themselves and others.

Putting the compassionate self to work

For compassionate self work to be effective, it needs to quickly move from the more abstract – generally imagining having the various qualities described above – to a much more concrete consideration of how to apply these qualities in approaching difficult emotions and life situations (Gilbert, 2010a). Once the initial compassionate self imagery work has been introduced, the client is prompted to frequently connect with the perspective of his or her compassionate self, and to consider how this self would approach the difficult emotion, interaction, or life situation that the client is faced with. This can take a number of different forms.

Compassionate motivation A foundation of CFT involves assisting clients to connect with the motivation to change their way of being in the world by cultivating a compassionate identity and sense of self. Particularly with forensic populations, the question of "Why would I want to do that?" must be addressed. In this process, Socratic dialogues and thought experiments are used to help clients explore the costs and benefits of cultivating compassion – very similar to motivational interviewing. The various "myths" about compassion are explored and dealt with. Clients are asked to consider what it would take for them to gradually commit to cultivating compassion and what would block them (Kolts, 2012). Clients are also invited to consider their values – for example, by asking them to think about what they would most like others to say about them at their eulogy – and how compassion could help them pursue these values in their lives (Kolts, 2010). If a client says "I don't care," the therapist invites the thought experiment "Well, just as out of interest, supposing you did care, what would you like them to say?" It is interesting that simply using the "But let's pretend that you do…" can actually produce quite a lot of insight.

Compassionate attention   In CFT, clients learn to focus their attention in ways that help them to explore and bring about more compassionate states of mind and to regulate challenging emotions. As we've mentioned, this process involves bodywork and teaching body awareness – for example, as we mentioned above, using the breath to create a feeling of slowing down and trying to promote parasympathetic arousal (Porges, 2007) and looking at the different body postures of compassion versus aggression. We can explore the different emotions that come when we (deliberately) create neutral or aggressive facial expressions in contrast to a friendly face. We create in our minds friendly voice tones in comparison to aggressive ones. Attention can be directed to different motivations; for example, by inviting the client to imagine an argument and then acting it out with the aggressive self followed by the compassion self. The client is invited to simply be curious and mindfully notice the complex differences – the things they feel comfortable with and uncomfortable with, the distinctions between compassion and submissiveness, and the differences between compassionate assertiveness and aggression.

Compassionate imagery   As discussed in the first half of the chapter, a primary goal of CFT is to facilitate client shifts out of a threat-based mode of processing and into states defined by psychological safeness, soothing, and compassion. We'll briefly describe some of the ways that imagery is used in these efforts.

1   Safe-place meditation – the client is guided through soothing imagery in which they imagine feeling completely safe and at peace, and envision being in a place that helps them feel this way.
2   Ideal compassionate other meditation – the client imagines a completely understanding and kind being who directs acceptance and compassion to them.
3   Compassionate self practice – using techniques drawn from method acting, clients envision themselves as already having compassionate characteristics such as kindness, wisdom, confidence, empathy, and the ability to tolerate distress. They imagine how they would feel, think, look, sound, and behave as this deeply compassionate being. For example, they can imagine experiencing empathy and sympathy for themselves, and for others who are suffering, and to imagine what that experience would be like.

Other imagery exercises used involve compassion flowing into the client from others, as well as compassion flowing out of the client and into others. More Gilbert (detailed descriptions of these and other imagery exercises used in CFT can be found in Gilbert (2010a, b) and Kolts (2012).

Compassionate thinking CFT approaches thought work in a way that falls between mindfulness approaches that seek to nonjudgmentally observe, accept, and release unhelpful thoughts (Segal, Williams, & Teasdale, 2002) and more traditional CBT approaches that seek to replace such thoughts with more adaptive alternatives. In CFT, the client is helped to nonjudgmentally identify particular types of thinking that are problematic for them (self-critical thinking and self-attacking, angry rumination, etc.) and to generate more adaptive ways of thinking from the perspective of the compassionate self (Gilbert, 2010b; Kolts, 2012). The idea is to assist clients in cultivating habits of thought that involve compassion, wisdom, kindness, mentalization, and helpful problem solving.

Let's consider the case of a harsh, self-critical thought. The idea is that the client mindfully observes the thought, compassionately accepts it as understandable mental activity produced by, for example, an activated threat system and historical conditioning, and then considers the situations from the kind, wise, confident perspective of the compassionate self. The nuances here are important: the client is not "arguing with" or "answering back" to the self-critical thought, which can lend validity to the original thought and set the client up to lapse back into it (Segal, Williams, & Teasdale, 2002). Instead, he or she shifts *perspectives* to that of the compassionate self, using techniques such as mentalizing to make helpful, validating observations about the thought *process* (e.g., "I'm being very self-critical. It makes sense that I would do that because I'm not performing as well as I'd like, and my father used to ridicule me in situations like this."), and to soothe the self and get the safeness system online (e.g., "What would help me to feel safe as I struggle with this difficult situation?" "What advice might I give a mate to help him cope?").

Compassionate thinking can also take the form of compassionate reappraisal, which involves considering perceived transgressions that others have committed from a compassionate perspective – as opposed to, for example, ruminating about the perceived offense. Whereas ruminating about offenses has been linked with increased negative self-reports, heightened sympathetic nervous system activity (Witvliet, Ludwig, & Vander Laan, 2001), and impaired heart rate vulnerability (Witvliet, Knoll, Hinman, & DeYoung, 2010; Witvliet, DeYoung, Hofelich, & DeYoung, 2011), thinking compassionately about the perceived offender – such as considering that they are a human being who behaved badly and genuinely wishing for them to undergo a positive change – has been linked with increased forgiveness, calming physiological reactions, reductions in negative emotion ratings, increased positive emotions, and facial EMG results indicative of smiling (Witvliet et al., 2010, 2011). Clinically, this can be facilitated via Socratic dialogue, using mentalizing:

"Can we consider any way that this person's behavior might have made sense?"
"What emotions must they have been experiencing that would have prompted them to act in this hurtful way?"
"Do happy, healthy people act like that?"

Such questions can also assist forensic clients in exploring their own transgressions and the causes and conditions in their own lives that led to them.

CFT also specifically emphasizes the difference between shameful self-attacking and compassionate self-correction. This is particularly relevant for forensic clients, for whom the development of compassion for those they have wronged can easily spiral into self-shaming, which can keep them locked in a threat-based mode of processing or simply prompt them to engage in experiential avoidance. Compassionate self-correction requires people to be able to tolerate guilt, of course, but it is then aimed at helping such clients coach themselves to improve in ways that are focused on the desire to improve (versus on condemning and punishing), which are forward-looking and emphasize improvement (versus focused on past errors), which are given with kindness and encouragement (versus with contempt) and that emphasize building on positives, strengths, and hopes (versus focusing on deficits and failure) (Gilbert, 2010b).

Compassionate behavior   Behavioral strategies are used extensively to facilitate client rehearsal of compassionate coping. For example, clients are asked to monitor their mood episodes (e.g., anger episodes) and to generate compassionate reappraisals and coping strategies to use in such situations (Kolts, 2010). Activity scheduling is used to facilitate compassionate behaviors, which can include both self-compassionate self-care behaviors as well as helping behaviors such as providing social support to others, which has been linked to enhanced longevity (Brown, Nesse, Vinokur, & Smith, 2003) and better mental health functioning (Schwartz, Meisenhelder, Yunsheng, & Reed, 2003).

Conclusions

This chapter has aimed to acquaint the reader with the theoretical model, patient conceptualization, and basic practices of CFT, as it can be applied with forensic populations. In the first section, we introduced and discussed the theoretical underpinnings of CFT in terms of *evolutionary psychology* and the *social shaping of the self*, and explored how these factors can shape phenotypes associated with criminal behavior. We also presented a basic model of how emotions play out in the mind and a discussion of how our evolved brains can present challenges as we work with these emotions. We then introduced the concept of compassion, and explored how the cultivation of various compassionate mental qualities can be beneficial for those who struggle with behavioral and emotional disturbances. The final section of the chapter focused upon the clinical process of CFT, and presented some strategies and techniques that are used.

Implications for Forensic Practice

In this chapter, we have sought to introduce CFT and how it can be applied in order to better understand and treat individuals who criminally offend. We provided an overview of the theory underlying CFT, emphasizing how the interaction of evolved genetic potentials and social shaping can impact the development of offending behavior. We have introduced the three circles model of emotions, and discussed how compassion can be used to assist individuals in working with challenging affective states.

Finally, we presented a general overview of how CFT can be applied to forensic populations, highlighting some key strategies and techniques that can be used to assist forensic populations to cultivate compassionate characteristics and work more adaptively with challenging emotions, situations, and backgrounds.

Note

1 See http://www.coherence.com.

Recommended Reading

Bowlby, J. (1969). *Attachment and loss, vol. 1: Attachment*. London: Hogarth Press. *In this classic text, Bowlby lays out the foundational concepts behind attachment dynamics in human life.*

Cozolino, L. (2007). *The Neuroscience of human relationships: Attachment and the developing brain*. New York, NY: W.W. Norton & Company. *In these two texts, Cozolino has done an excellent job at translating the emerging field of interpersonal neurobiology in well-integrated, understandable ways.*

Cozolino, L. (2013). *The social neuroscience of education*. New York, NY: W.W. Norton & Company.

Depue, R. A., & Morrone-Strupinsky, J. V. (2005). A neurobehavioral model of affiliative bonding. *Behavioral and Brain Sciences, 28*, 313–395. *This foundational paper lays out the neurological basis of soothing and affiliation as it is represented in compassion-focused therapy.*

Wikström, P-O. H., & Loeber, R. (2000). Do disadvantaged neighborhoods cause well-adjusted children to become adolescent delinquents? A study of male juvenile serious offending, individual risk and protective factors, and neighborhood context. *Criminology, 38*, 1109–1142. *This paper provides a poignant example of the power of social shaping and its relationship to antisocial behavior.*

References

Andrews, D. A., & Bonta, J. (2010). *The psychology of criminal conduct*. New York, NY: Anderson.

Barkow, J. H. (1989). *Darwin, sex and status: Biological approaches to mind and culture*. Toronto: University of Toronto Press.

Baumeister, R. F. (1997). *Evil: Inside human cruelty and violence*. New York, NY: Freeman.

Baumeister, R. F., Bratslavsky, E., Finkenauer, C., & Vohs, K. D. (2001). Bad is stronger than good. *Review of General Psychology, 5*, 323–370.

Begley, S. (2007). *Train Your Mind, Change Your Brain*. New York, NY: Ballantine Books.

Belsky, J., & Pluess, M. (2009). Beyond diathesis stress: Differential susceptibility to environmental influences. *Psychological Bulletin, 135*, 885–908. doi:10.1037/a0017376.

Bierhoff, H-W. (2005). The psychology of compassion and prosocial behavior. In P. Gilbert (Ed.), *Compassion: Conceptualisations, research and use in psychotherapy* (pp. 9–74). London: Routledge.

Blair, J., Mitchell, D., & Blair, K. (2005). *The psychopath: Emotion and the brain*. Malden, MA: Blackwell Publishing.

Boksem, M., Kostermans, E., Milivojevic, B., & De Cremer, D. (2011). Social status determines how we monitor and evaluate our performance. *Social, Cognitive and Affective Neuroscience*, Advance Access published March 18, 2011. doi:10.1093/scan/nsr010.

Boyce, W. T., & Ellis, B. J. (2005). Biological sensitively to context 1: An evolutionary-developmental theory of the origins and functions of stress reactivity. *Development and Psychopathology, 17*, 271–302.

Boyce, W. T., Essex, M. J., & Ellis, B. J. (2005). Biological sensitively to context 11: Empirical explorations of an evolutionary-developmental theory. *Development and Psychopathology, 17*, 271–302.

Bowlby, J. (1969). *Attachment and loss, vol. 1: Attachment.* London: Hogarth Press.

Braithwaite, J. (1989). *Crime, shame, and reintegration.* New York, NY: Cambridge University Press.

Brown, R. P., Gerbarg, P. L., & Muench, F. (2013). Breathing practices for treatments of psychiatric and stress-related medical conditions. *Psychiatric Clinics of North America, 36,* 121–140.

Brown, S. L., Nesse, R. M., Vinokur, A. D., & Smith, D. M. (2003). Providing social support may be more beneficial than receiving it: Results from a prospective study of mortality. *Psychological Science, 14,* 320–327.

Button, T. M. M., Scourfield, J., Martin, N., Purcell, S., & McGuffin, P. (2005). Family dysfunction interacts with genes in the causation of antisocial symptoms. *Behavior Genetics, 35,* 115–120.

Cohen, D., Vandello, J., & Rantilla, A. K. (1998). The sacred and the social: Cultures of honor and violence. In P. Gilbert & B. Andrews (Eds.), *Shame: Interpersonal behavior, psychopathology, and culture* (pp. 261–282). New York, NY: Oxford University Press.

Cozolino, L. (2007). *The neuroscience of human relationships: Attachment and the developing brain.* New York, NY: W.W. Norton & Company.

Cozolino, L. (2013). *The social neuroscience of education.* New York, NY: W.W. Norton & Company.

Crocker, J., & Canevello, A. (2008). Creating and undermining social support in communal relationships: The role of compassionate and self-image goals. *Journal of Personality and Social Psychology, 95,* 555–575.

Crocker, J., Canevello, A., Breines, J. G., & Flynn, H. (2010). Interpersonal goals and change in anxiety and dysphoria in first-semester college students. *Journal of Personality and Social Psychology, 98,* 1009–1024.

Crook, J. H. (1986). The evolution of leadership: A preliminary skirmish. *In* C. F. Graumann & S. Moscovici (Eds.), *Changing conceptions of leadership.* New York, NY: Springer Verlag.

Decety, J. & Ickes, W. (2011). *The social neuroscience of empathy.* Boston, MA: MIT Press.

Depue, R. A., & Morrone-Strupinsky, J. V. (2005). A neurobehavioral model of affiliative bonding. *Behavioral and Brain Sciences, 28,* 313–395.

Egan, G. (2013). *The skilled helper* (10th international ed.). New York, NY: Brooks/Cole.

Fix, R. L., & Fix, S. T. (2013). The effects of mindfulness-based treatments for aggression: A critical review. *Aggression and Violent Behavior, 18,* 219–227.

Frith, U. (2004). Emanuel Miller lecture: Confusions and controversies about Asperger syndrome. *Journal of Child Psychology and Psychiatry, 45,* 672–686.

Gay, P. (1995). *The cultivation of hatred.* New York, NY: Norton & Company.

Germer, C. K. (2009). *The mindful path to self-compassion: Freeing yourself from destructive thoughts and emotions.* New York, NY: Guilford Press.

Gilbert, P. (1989). *Human nature and suffering.* Hove: Lawrence Erlbaum Associates, Inc.

Gilbert, P. (1992). *Depression: The evolution of powerlessness.* Hove/New York, NY: Lawrence Erlbaum Associates, Inc./Guilford Press.

Gilbert, P. (1998). The evolved basis and adaptive functions of cognitive distortions. *British Journal of Medical Psychology, 71,* 441–464.

Gilbert, P. (2005a). Compassion and cruelty: A biopsychosocial approach. In P. Gilbert (Ed.), *Compassion: Conceptualisations, research and use in psychotherapy* (pp. 9–74). London: Routledge.

Gilbert, P. (2005b). Social mentalities: A biopsychosocial and evolutionary reflection on social relationships. In M. W. Baldwin (Ed.). *Interpersonal cognition.* (pp. 299–335). New York, NY: Guilford Press.

Gilbert, P. (2007). The evolution of shame as a marker for relationship security. In J. L. Tracy, R. W. Robins, & J. P. Tangney (Eds.), *The self-conscious emotions: Theory and research* (pp. 283–309). New York, NY: Guilford Press.

Gilbert, P. (2010a). *Compassion focused therapy: Distinctive features*. London: Routledge.

Gilbert, P. (2010b). *The compassionate mind*. London: Constable & Robinson.

Gilbert, P., & Choden (2013). *Mindful compassion*. London: Constable & Robinson.

Gilbert, P., & Irons, C. (2005). Focused therapies and compassionate mind training for shame and self-attacking. In P. Gilbert (Ed.), *Compassion: Conceptualisations, research, and use in psychotherapy* (pp. 263–325). London: Routledge.

Gillath, O., Shaver, P. R, & Mikulincer, M. (2005). An attachment-theoretical approach to compassion and altruism. In P. Gilbert (Ed.), *Compassion: Conceptualisations, Research and use in psychotherapy* (pp. 121–147). London: Routledge.

Goodall, J. (1990). *Through a window. Thirty years with the chimpanzees of Gnome*. New York, NY: Penguin.

Hackmann, A., Bennett-Levy, J., & Holmes, E. A. (Eds.) (2011). *Oxford guide to imagery in cognitive therapy* (Oxford Guides to Cognitive Behavioral Therapy). Oxford: Oxford University Press.

Hofer, M. A. (1994). Early relationships as regulators of infant physiology and behavior. *Acta Paediatiricia Supplement, 397*, 9–18.

Hofmann, S. G., Sawyer, A. T., Witt, A. A., & Oh, D. (2010). The effect of mindfulness-based therapy on anxiety and depression: A meta-analytic review. *Journal of Consulting and Clinical Psychology, 78*, 169–183.

Ingnatiff, M. (1999). *The warrior's honor: Ethnic war and modern conscience*. London: Vintage.

Insel, T. R. (2010). The challenge of translation in social neuroscience: A review of oxytocin, vasopressin, and affiliative behavior. *Neuron, 65*, 768–779.

Johnson, S. L., & Leedom, L. J. (2012). The dominance behavioral system and psychopathology: Evidence from self-report, observational, and biological studies. *Psychological Bulletin, 138*, 692–743. doi:10.1037/a0027503.

Kim, S., Thibodeau, R., & Jorgensen, R. S. (2011). Shame, guilt, and depressive symptoms: A Meta-analytic review. *Psychological Bulletin, 137*, 68–96, doi:10.1037/a0021466.

Klimecki, O. M., Leiberg, S., Ricard, M., & Singer, T. (2013). Differential pattern of functional brain plasticity after compassion and empathy training. *Social Cognitive and Affective Neuroscience*. Advance Access published May 9, 2013. doi:10.1093/scan/nst060.

Knox, J. (2011). *Self-agency in psychotherapy: Attachment, autonomy, and intimacy.* (Norton Series on Interpersonal Neurobiology). *New York, NY*: W.W. Norton & Company.

Kolts, R. L. (2010). *True strength: A compassion-focused therapy approach to working with anger*. Unpublished treatment manual.

Kolts, R. L. (2012). *The compassionate mind approach to managing your anger: Using compassion-focused therapy*. London: Constable & Robinson.

Kolts, R. L. (2013). *Applying CFT in working with problematic anger: The "true strength" prison program*. Symposium presented at the 2nd International Conference on Compassion Focused Therapy, London.

Lecours, S., & Bouchard, M. A. (2011). Verbal elaboration of distinct affect categories and BPD symptoms. *Psychology and Psychotherapy, 84*, 26–41. doi:10.1111/j.2044-8341.2010.02006.x.

LeDoux, J. (1998). *The emotional brain*. London: Weidenfeld & Nicolson.

Liotti, G. (2009). Attachment and dissociation. In P. F Dell & J. A O'Neil (Eds.), *Dissociation and the dissociative disorders: DSM-V and beyond* (pp. 53–66). London: Routledge.

MacDonald, K., & MacDonald, T. M. (2010). The peptide that binds: A systematic review of oxytocin and its prosocial effects in humans. *Harvard Review of Psychiatry, 18*, 1–21.

Marks, I. M. (1987). *Fears, phobias, and rituals: Panic, anxiety, and their disorders*. Oxford, UK: Oxford University Press.

Maclean, P. D. (1990). *The triune brain in evolution*. New York, NY: Plenum Press.

Meffert, H., Gazzola, B., den Boer, J. A., Bartels, A. A. J., & Keysers, C. (2013). Reduced spontaneous but relatively normal deliberate vicarious representations in psychopathy. *Brain, 136*, 2550–2563.

Mitchell, I. J., & Beech, A. R (2011). Towards an attachment related neurobiological model of offending. *Clinical Psychology Review, 31,* 872–882.

Neff, K. (2003). Self-compassion: An alternative conceptualization of a healthy attitude toward oneself. *Self and Identity, 2,* 85–101.

Neff, K. (2011). *Self-compassion: Stop beating yourself up and leave insecurity behind.* New York, NY: William Morrow.

Nijenhuis, S., & Boer, J. A. (2009). Psychobiology of traumatisation and trauma-related structural dissociation of the personality. In P. F. Dell & J. A. O'Neil (Eds.), *Dissociation and the dissociative disorders: DSM-V and beyond* (pp. 337–366). London: Routledge.

Panksepp, J. (1998). *Affective neuroscience.* New York, NY: Oxford University Press.

Porges, S. W. (2007). The polyvagal perspective. *Biological Psychology, 74,* 116–143.

Reddy, M. K., Meis, L. A., Erbes, C. R., & Compton, J. S. (2011). Associations among experiential avoidance, couple adjustment, and interpersonal adjustment in returning Iraqi war veterans and their partners. *Journal of Consulting and Clinical Psychology, 79,* 515–520.

Reilly, E. D., Rochlen, A. B., & Awad, G. H. (2013). Men's self-compassion and self- esteem: The moderating roles of shame and masculine norm adherence. *Psychology of Men & Masculinity,* Advance online publication. doi:10.1037/a0031028.

Sapolsky, R. M. (2004). *Why zebras don't get ulcers* (3rd ed.) New York, NY: St. Martin's Press.

Schwartz, C., Meisenhelder, J. B., Yunsheng, M., & Reed, G. (2003). Altruistic social interest behaviors are associated with better mental health. *Psychosomatic Medicine, 65,* 778–785.

Segal, Z. V, Williams, J. M. G., & Teasdale, J. D. (2002). *Mindfulness-based cognitive therapy for depression.* London: Guilford Press.

Shapland, J., Robinson, G., & Sorsby, A. (2011). *Restorative justice in practice: Evaluating what works for victims and offenders.* London: Willan.

Siegel, D. (2012). *The developing mind: How relationships and the brain interact to shape who we are* (2nd ed.). New York, NY: Guilford Press.

Twenge, J. M., Gentile, B., DeWall, C. N., Ma, D., Lacefield, K., & Schurtz, D. R. (2010). Birth cohort increases in psychopathology among young Americans, 1938–2007: A cross-temporal meta-analysis of the MMPI. *Clinical Psychology Review, 30,* 145–154.

Tuvblad, C., Grann., M., & Lichtenstein, P. (2006). Heritability for adolescent antisocial behavior differs with socioeconomic status: Gene-environment interaction. *Journal of Child Psychology and Psychiatry, 47,* 734-743.

van der Hart,O., & Steele, K (2013) Trauma-related dissociation: Theory and treatment of dissociation of the personality. In I. Kennedy, H. Kennerley, & D. Person (Eds.) *Cognitive behavioral approaches to the understanding and treatment of dissociation* (pp. 205–220). London: Routledge.

Van IJzendoorn, M. H. (1997). Attachment, emergent morality, and aggression: Toward a developmental socioemotional model of antisocial behavior. *International Journal of Behavioral Development, 21,* 703-727.

Vessantara. (1993). *Meeting the Buddhas: A guide to Buddhas, Bodhisattvas and Tantric Deities.* New York, NY: Winhorse Publications.

Wallin, D. J. (2007). *Attachment in Psychotherapy.* New York, NY: Guilford Press.

Warneken, F., & Tomasello, M. (2009). The roots of human altruism. *The British Journal of Psychology, 100,* 455–471.

Widom, C. S. (1989). Does violence beget violence? A critical examination of the literature. *Psychological Bulletin, 106,* 3–28.

Wikström, P-O. H., & Loeber, R. (2000). Do disadvantaged neighborhoods cause well-adjusted children to become adolescent delinquents? A study of male juvenile serious offending, individual risk and protective factors, and neighborhood context. *Criminology, 38,* 1109–1142.

Witvliet, C. V. O., DeYoung, N. J., Hofelich, A. J., & DeYoung, P. A. (2011). Compassionate reappraisal and emotion suppression as alternatives to offense-focused rumination:

Implications for forgiveness and psychophysiological well-being. *Journal of Positive Psychology, 6*, 286–299.

Witvliet, C. V. O., Knoll, R. W., Hinman, N. G., & Deyoung, P. A. (2010). Compassion-focused reappraisal, benefit-focused reappraisal, and rumination after an interpersonal offense: Emotion regulation implications for subjective emotion, linguistic responses, and physiology. *The Journal of Positive Psychology, 5*, 226–242.

Witvliet, C. V. O., Ludwig, T., & Vander Laan, K. (2001). Granting forgiveness or harbouring grudges: Implications for emotions, physiology, and health. *Psychological Science, 12*, 117–123.

Zehr, H. (2002) *The little book of restorative justice*. New York, NY: Good Books.

29

The Neurobiology of Eye Movement Desensitization Reprocessing Therapy

Derek Farrell

Key points

- Post-traumatic stress disorder (PTSD) is a disorder of information processing, characterized by hyper-arousal, impaired stimulus differentiation, avoidance, and persistent re-experiencing of the traumatic memory, among other symptoms. PTSD can arise after exposure to a traumatic event or adverse life experience, particularly events that were intentionally caused.
- Eye movement desensitization and reprocessing (EMDR) therapy is an integrative, transdiagnostic psychotherapeutic approach that specifically targets distressing memories of adverse life experiences. The psychological treatment intervention has been recognized by a number of authorities as an evidence-based, empirically supported treatment for PTSD. EMDR therapists also use the psychotherapeutic approach for other clinical conditions – the rationale being that distressing memories are not unique to PTSD. There is ever-increasing promising evidence supporting the wider application of EMDR therapy with other clinical populations including psychosis, depression, phobias, and obsessive compulsive disorder (OCD).
- EMDR therapy involves several therapeutic stages but the most unique is bilateral stimulation (BLS), when the patient recounts a traumatic memory while attending to external visual, acoustic or tactile stimuli.
- The underlying theoretical model for EMDR, the Adaptive Information Processing (AIP) model, is not a neuroscientific model although it uses some of the language of neurobiology. There are several hypotheses about the neuroscientific mechanisms of EMDR, with some evidence to support each. It is probable that there are multiple mechanisms behind its impact.
- EMDR training and research needs to expand and diversify in order to keep up with practice expansion. Many EMDR therapists are interested in seeing more research into the neuroscientific basis for EMDR's efficacy.

The Wiley Blackwell Handbook of Forensic Neuroscience, First Edition. Edited by Anthony R. Beech, Adam J. Carter, Ruth E. Mann and Pia Rotshtein.
© 2018 John Wiley & Sons Ltd. Published 2018 by John Wiley & Sons Ltd.

Terminology Explained

Adaptive Information Processing (AIP) model purports that the primary source of psychopathology is the presence of memories of adverse life experiences that have been inadequately processed. These inappropriately stored memories, which include perceptions, sensations, beliefs, and emotions that occurred at the time of the adverse life event, can be triggered by current internal and external stimuli, contributing to ongoing dysfunction. These dysfunctionally stored memories can be past, present, or future.

Dismantling study – effective treatments are taken apart so as to determine which of the components/ingredients is responsible to account for the treatment effect or outcome.

Rapid eye movement (REM) sleep is a kind of sleep that occurs at intervals during the night and is characterized by rapid eye movements, more dreaming and bodily movement, and faster pulse and breathing.

Slow wave sleep (SWS) is often referred to as deep sleep that is dreamless, occurring regularly during a normal period of sleep with intervening periods of REM sleep. It is characterized by delta waves and lower levels of autonomic psychological activity.

Introduction

Eye movement desensitization and reprocessing (EMDR) therapy is an integrative psychotherapeutic approach that directly addresses the experiential contributors of both health and dysfunction (Shapiro, 2014). It was developed by American psychologist Francine Shapiro in 1989, under what she considers were rather 'serendipitous' circumstances. Here, while giving attention to a particular thought that had been bothering her, Shapiro was aware of her eyes moving back and forth diagonally in a certain way. She then noticed that after a while these thoughts did not bother her anymore. Shapiro was intrigued as to how this happened. Her sense was that she had 'stumbled' upon the brain's natural healing process, a process that also occurs during rapid eye movement (REM) sleep (Shapiro, 2012). EMDR suggests that a trauma memory can be thought of as information about a traumatic event that has become "locked in the nervous system" (Shapiro, 2002) almost in its original form (van der Kolk, 2002). The traumatic memory is manifested and re-experienced in terms of images, thoughts, sounds, smells, emotions, physical sensations, and beliefs (van der Kolk & Fisler, 1995). Shapiro's (2002) overview of EMDR is shown in Box 29.1.

Box 29.1 Shapiro's (2016) overview of EMDR

EMDR therapy is an eight-phase psychotherapeutic approach that emphasizes the physiological information processing system in the origin and treatment of mental health issues (Shapiro, 2001, 2014). Its theoretical basis is the Adaptive Information Processing (AIP) model, which holds that the primary source of psychopathology is the presence of memories of adverse life experiences that have been inadequately processed. These inappropriately stored episodic memories, which include the perceptions, sensations, beliefs, and emotions that occurred at the time of the adverse life event, can be triggered by current internal and external stimuli, contributing to ongoing dysfunction. This model was developed in the early 1990s and since then has been supported by research demonstrating the role played by disturbing life events in the genesis of many forms of psychological and somatic symptomology (e.g., Afifi, Mota, Dasiewicz, MacMillan, & Sareen, 2012; Felitti et al., 1998).

In its inception, EMDR was seen as an original, quite revolutionary, technique in the treatment of post-traumatic stress disorder (PTSD). Box 29.2 sets out the characteristics of PTSD.

Post-traumatic stress disorder *PTSD is a complex, often chronic, and debilitating syndrome that develops in response to a traumatic life events such as combat, sexual assault, natural disasters, and other extreme stressors.*
Source: © Katarzyana Bialasiewicz. Used under license from 123RF.

Box 29.2 PTSD Defined

PTSD is an increasingly recognized and potentially preventable condition (Bisson et al., 2007). It is a complex, often chronic and debilitating syndrome that develops in response to traumatic life events such as combat, sexual assault, natural disasters, and other extreme stressors (Weathers, Keane, & Foa, 2009).

PTSD was first recognized and systematically diagnosed in the aftermath of the US/Vietnam war although nowadays it is recognized with more diverse trauma populations. The majority of research investigations into PTSD relate to clinical samples exposed to specific traumatic events (Hapke et al., 2006). The clinical picture for PTSD trauma survivors is often complicated by features including guilt and shame, dissociation, alterations in personality, affect dysregulation, marked impairment in intimacy and attachment (Farrell et al., 2011; Herman, 1992); comorbidity disorders such as depression, substance misuse, and other anxiety disorders (Weathers et al., 2009). PTSD therefore involves cognitive, affective, behavioral, and physiological elements and effective treatments have to accommodate and address each of these four elements. *DSM-5* (American Psychiatric Association, 2013) stipulates five characteristics in relation to diagnostic criteria for PTSD: (1) the person was exposed to a stressor; (2) the traumatic event is persistently re-experienced as intrusion symptoms; (3) persistent effortful avoidance of distressing trauma-related stimuli after the event; (4) negative alterations in cognitions and mood that began or worsened after the traumatic event; and (5) trauma-related alterations in arousal and reactivity that began or worsened after the traumatic event.

EMDR has been through six significant stages in its development and is a psychotherapy approach that is still evolving (Farrell et al., 2011). The six stages are shown in Box 29.3.

Box 29.3   Six Stages in the Development of EMDR

Stage 1 – Revolutionary (Evangelical)
Stage 2 – Critical review
Stage 3 – Dismantling
Stage 4 – More robust evidence base
Stage 5 – Political acknowledgment – Adoption in both national and international guidelines as an effective evidence-based treatment for PTSD
Stage 6 – Increasing evidence-based practice and practice-based evidence for other mental health conditions

---

Some of the initial claims regarding EMDR therapy were grandiose, even evangelical, and therefore it was inevitable that the approach was going to be subjected to critical consideration. Indeed, some of the early criticisms were extremely hostile and acerbic. However, the process of critical scrutiny of EMDR and of its assertions was justified and necessary, and in fact was fundamental if EMDR was going to be taken seriously. The case in support of EMDR was not helped by the fact that early EMDR research studies were not as methodologically robust as they could have been. As the assertions of EMDR were so unusual, regarding a profoundly sensitive and highly political mental health condition such as PTSD, criticism was always going to focus on its most controversial aspect, that of bilateral stimulation (BLS). What followed were more robust research studies (outlined below) that gave more credibility to the assertion that EMDR proffered something significant for people suffering from PTSD.

The endorsement of EMDR as an empirically supported treatment for PTSD now comes from many sources (e.g., the American Psychiatric Association, 2004; Bisson & Andrew, 2007; California Evidence-Based Clearinghouse for Child Welfare, 2010; Department of Veterans Affairs and Department of Defense, 2004, 2010; International Society of Traumatic Stress Studies, Foa, Keene, Friedman & Cohen, 2008; National Institute of Health and Clinical Excellence, 2005; Pagani et al., 2007; van der Kolk, 2008; World Health Organization (WHO), 2013; WHO & UNHCR, 2015). As Farrell and Keenan (2013) noted, there is now also emerging practice-based evidence relating to the application of EMDR with a myriad of other mental health conditions other than PTSD (Bae, Kim, & Park, 2008; Brown, McGoldrick, & Buchanan, 1997; de Jongh, Ten Broeke & Renssen, 1999; de Roos, Veenstra, de Jongh, den Hollander-Gisman, Van der Wee & Van Rood, 2010; Keenan & Farrell, 2000; Maxfield, 2007; Mevissen & de Jongh, 2010; Ricci, Clayton, & Shapiro, 2006). These include depression, phobias, substance misuse, peak-performance, forensic populations, psychosis, and bi-polar affective disorder to name just a few. EMDR has a strong track record as a humanitarian assistance endeavor, and mental health workers in numerous projects around the world have been trained to provide EMDR in the aftermath of a natural or human disaster.

Brooks-Gordon, Bilby, and Wells (2006) undertook a systematic review of nine randomized controlled trials (RCTs) that explored the use of cognitive behavioral interventions (CBT) with sexual offenders – improving cognitive reasoning and emotional regulation. Their conclusion was that the results were disappointing, highlighting an increase in re-arrest rates. In existing treatment interventions for sex offenders, treatment for trauma is not a typical component, despite the emergence of enhanced understanding of etiological models of offending behavior. Ricci (2006) illustrated how EMDR proved a successful intervention in the treatment of a child molester, as evidenced by increased motivation for treatment and empathic response. Ricci et al. (2006) found that adding EMDR with standard CBT-RP demonstrated improvements on all six subscales of the Sex Offender Treatment Rating Scale [Insight, Deviant Thoughts, Awareness of Situational Risks, Motivation, Victim Empathy, and Offense Disclosure] and that these results were statistically significant. Further findings demonstrated reduction in deviant sexual arousal, measured by penile plethysmograph (PPG).

Payne, Watt, Rogers & McMurran (2008) supported the view that there can be a correlation between offending behavior and trauma with15–32% meeting the criteria for PTSD. This argument is also made by Crisford, Dare & Evangeli (2008), who also purported a positive correlation between offense-related cognitions and higher levels of offense-related trauma.

However, despite the promise of EMDR as an effective intervention with this forensic population, it should only be considered as an experimental application until further research emerges. Early indication shows promise with utilizing EMDR therapy adjunctively. Nonetheless, Clark, Tyler, Gannon, & Kingham (2014) considered that if you return a traumatized violent or sexual offender into the community without treating the trauma symptoms then they are still at risk of re-offending.

Despite the developing evidence-based practice in EMDR, its practice and subsequent application with such diverse mental health issues has progressed at a pace that outstrips empirical research – although this is rapidly changing. The theoretical framework of AIP (see following section) continues to be subjected to critical consideration, because many people feel uncomfortable with a therapy that lacks a coherent theory of change, even in the light of empirical evidence of efficacy. This is despite the fact that other empirically supported therapies which also lack a cogent theory to explain change, for example cognitive behavioral therapy (CBT) and interpersonal therapy (IPT), appear to be subjected to less hostility and critical review than EMDR therapy. And given the net widening of EMDR usage, a second equally important question is not 'how does it work?' but rather 'does it work for conditions other than PTSD?' This is a question that causes considerable debate within the EMDR community itself and to date requires further investigation and research.

The Processes Involved in EMDR

The hallmark of EMDR is the assumption that physiologically stored memories are the primary foundation of pathology; and the primary agent of change in EMDR is specifically targeted information processing. The AIP theoretical framework guides the clinical application of EMDR in a manner that is both explanatory and predictive of positive treatment effects (Shapiro & Laliotis, 2011). What links the diverse clinical populations mentioned above is an experience of 'trauma' and consequent blocked information processing. It is the ubiquitous interpretation of the EMDR AIP theoretical framework that enables EMDR therapists to use this paradigm with wider applications over and above that of PTSD. The AIP model is described in Box 29.4.

Box 29.4   The AIP Model.

The AIP model posits several assumptions:

1   As humans we possess an intrinsic information processing system that has evolved to enable us to reorganize our responses to disturbing events from an initial dysfunctional state of disequilibrium to a state of adaptive resolution.
2   Trauma – as a result of stress hormones, trauma causes an imbalance in the nervous system, thus creating blocked or incomplete information processing.
3   This dysfunctional information is then stored in its unprocessed state.
4   Identifying these dysfunctional information "hotspots" of unprocessed events is central to EMDR treatment.
5   The processing of these dysfunctional memories results in a reconfiguration of the memory of the trauma, with clients often experiencing a sense of emancipation from the disturbance the trauma memory generates similar to post-traumatic growth.

As noted at the beginning of the chapter, EMDR was formulated and introduced to the international mental health community by Francine Shapiro. While its initial core component was eye movement desensitization (EMD), Shapiro subsequently concluded that the process was much more than *desensitization* and that an integral aspect of EMDR involved the *reprocessing* of distressing memories, through eye movements, to a more adaptive and functional resolution (Shapiro, 1995, 2007, 2012, 2016; Shapiro & Forrest, 2001; Solomon & Shapiro, 2008). EMDR incorporates imaginal exposure under conditions of divided attention while experiencing some form of oscillatory BLS (Sack, Lempa, Steinmetz, Lamprecht, & Hofmann, 2008). Using forms of BLS with a specific traumatic memory appears to activate a healing process thought to involve intrinsic information processing which then integrates sensory, emotional, somatic, and cognitive components of an experience into a non-intrusive memory network without residual distress (Shapiro, 2002). The primary target in EMDR processing is traumatic memories. EMDR (Shapiro & Forrest, 2001) contains eight treatment phases and addresses past, present, and future aspects of disturbing memories (see Box 29.5).

Box 29.5 The Eight Phases of EMDR

Phase 1: History Taking
- Review the client's history in detail
- Identify salient issues (past, present, and future)
- Case conceptualization from an AIP perspective
- Develop a target treatment plan

Phase 2: Preparation
- Establish rapport
- Therapeutic relationship and attunement
- Access internal and external resources
- Affect regulation

Phase 3: Assessment
- Identify disturbing target memory
- Identify salient cognition
- Create a positive belief statement
- Link with currently held emotions and body sensations

Phase 4: Desensitization
- Activate target material
- Bilateral stimulation (BLS) and dual attention stimulation (DAS)
- Mindful observation of process, new insights, and associations
- Continue until disturbance is reduced

Phase 5: Installation
- Connection of positive belief statement with target event

Phase 6: Body Scan
- Connection of the target event, positive belief statement, and bodily sensations

> **Phase 7: Closure**
> - Ensuring that the client is re-oriented to the present
>
> **Phase 8: Re-Evaluation**
> - Has the previous target been adequately processed
> - Evidence of impact of levels of functioning
> - Orientation to the overall care plan and target sequence

In the first phase (history taking), the therapist identifies memories of traumatic events that have been inadequately processed. The second phase (preparation) is focused on building a therapeutic alliance and ensuring the client's readiness for treatment. Processing of unresolved memories is conducted during the next four phases (assessment, desensitization, installation, body scan). Phase 7 outlines steps for closure of the session, and Phase 8 (re-evaluation) is conducted at the beginning of each subsequent session.

During the processing phases, the client first identifies the perceptual, cognitive, somatic, and affective components of the target memory, and rates the level of emotional disturbance, using the Subject Units of Disturbance scale (SUD; 0 = no disturbance; 10 = worst possible). Then the client focuses on the memory while simultaneously attending to an external BLS for approximately 25–30 seconds. BLS can be horizontal eye movements, or alternating bilateral tactile or auditory stimulation. After each set of BLS the client is asked what new material was elicited; this new material generally becomes the focus of the next set of BLS. This procedure continues throughout the session, with alternating elicitation of new material, and subsequent focus on that material with BLS. Sometimes, the client's processing may stall, with no new material reported. When this happens, the therapist can suggest a new topic for attention during the next set of BLS. This intervention is called a therapeutic or cognitive interweave (Korn, 2009). As the session continues, the client typically describes the elicitation of more adaptive information and reports a decrease in distress. When the SUD rating becomes 0 or 1, a new positive belief about self is paired with the memory of the targeted incident, using BLS. The memory is considered fully processed when the client reports no distress, and endorses a new adaptive and positive perspective.

In summary, therefore, EMDR is an eight-phase approach that treats the condition by (a) accessing and processing the memories related with the dysfunction, (b) identifying and focalizing the current problems that triggered the problem and (c) incorporating memory templates for appropriate future actions, including those aimed at evolutive deficits, useful skills and necessary behaviors for optimum functioning (Shapiro, 2010).

Evidence for the Impact of EMDR

From the start of the 21st century, EMDR has been adopted in both national and international guidelines as an effective treatment for PTSD. However, this adoption is not universal. For example, the US Institute of Medicine endorses trauma-focused CBT

The function of EMDR *One known symptom of PTSD is that the traumatic event is persistently re-experienced as intrusion symptoms. EMDR is aimed at alleviating these intruding images and thoughts.*
Source: © DasWortgewand. Used under license from Pixabay.

(TF-CBT) and prolonged exposure but not EMDR; whereas the National Institute of Health and Clinical Excellence (NICE) UK, and the WHO endorse TF-CBT and EMDR, but not the use of medication; while the International Society of Traumatic Stress Studies (ISTSS) endorses TF-CBT, EMDR, and medication. What is interesting about these choices is that they are all based on reviews of exactly the same research studies and meta-analyses.

In August 2013, the WHO published 'Guidelines for the management of conditions that are specifically related to stress'. These guidelines were developed in recognition of a gap in evidence-based guidelines for managing problems and disorders related to stress in primary health care and other non-specialized health care settings. The guidelines recommended the following management strategies for problems and disorders that are specifically related to the occurrence of a major stressful event (WHO, 2013, p. 3): Trauma-focused CBT and EMDR therapy for children, adolescents, and adults with PTSD. The guidelines explained the difference between the two therapeutic approaches in the following way: "Like CBT with a trauma focus, EMDR therapy aims to reduce subjective distress and strengthen adaptive cognitions related to the traumatic event. Unlike CBT with a trauma focus, EMDR does not involve (a) detailed descriptions of the event, (b) direct challenging of beliefs, (c) extended exposure, or (d) homework." (p. 1).

Box 29.6 summarizes the research base for EMDR for PTSD, and for mental health issues other than PTSD, but none of these later studies are yet at the level of RCT. Quite rightly, and in accord with all other treatment approaches until randomized studies are carried out and published, then EMDR is always going to be subjected to critical consideration. Using the RCT as a benchmark, therefore, the only disorder for which EMDR has established efficacy is PTSD.

> **Box 29.6 Empirical Evidence for EMDR**
>
> To date, there have been 15 international treatment guidelines (8 meta-analyses, 37 randomized control studies [RCTs], and 22 non-randomized international studies in support of the efficacy of EMDR).
>
> There are also 43 studies examining the theoretical framework underpinning EMDR:
>
> 21 studies exploring the mechanism of action
> 25 studies focusing upon the use of eye movement in EMDR
> 23 studies exploring psychophysiological and neurobiological evaluations

How Trauma Affects the Brain

In order to gain a neuroscientific understanding of the efficacy of EMDR for PTSD, it is important to understand how trauma affects information processing. The impact of trauma on the brain's information processing systems is explained by Leeds (2009, 2016), and can be summarized as follows: hyper-arousal, narrowing of attention, impaired stimulus discrimination, intrusive re-experiencing of state dependent memory, avoidance, numbing, dissociative coping, substance abuse, and loss of meaning.

Shvil, Rusch, Sullivan & Neria (2013) conceptualized PTSD as a disorder of the brain's fear response. This disorder occurs as a consequence of emotional processing dysregulation within the brain's psychophysiological and neurological mechanisms. They consider that the biomarkers outlined in Box 29.7 should be used as objective gold standards as a diagnostic tool for PTSD, thus emphasizing that PTSD is a neuro-psychophysiological condition.

> **Box 29.7 Suggested PTSD Biomarkers for Diagnosis of PTSD**
>
> - Neural activation
>   - Altered emotional neuro-circuitry
>   - Hyper-activation of amygdala, dorsal anterior cingulate cortex, and insula
>   - Hypo-activation of medial prefrontal cortex, anterior cingulate cortex, rostral anterior cingulate cortex, and ventral medial frontal gyrus
>   - Abnormal hippocampal activity
> - Psychophysiology
>   - Heightened resting heart rate, but also peaks faster in individuals with PTSD
>   - Lower heart rate variability
>   - Enhanced startle response

- Behavioral
  - Avoidance
  - Hyper-vigilance
  - Attention bias toward word cues

While *DSM-5* now lists PTSD as a trauma disorder, Stickgold (2002) argued that PTSD is actually a memory disorder. The next section further explores the link between PTSD and memory, and suggests potential neurological underpinnings.

Memory, PTSD, and the Brain

Recent magneto-encephalography (MEG) studies (Georgopoulos et al., 2010) have revealed increased circuit activity in the right hemisphere of the brain in clients diagnosed with PTSD. This is the activity that results in debilitating, involuntary flashbacks. These MEG studies also found differences between signals in the temporal and parieto-occiptal right hemisphere of the brain. The temporal cortex is thought to be responsible for reliving of past experiences. What is interesting about these MEG studies is that previous studies using conventional brain scans (CT and MRI) were not able to identify these aspects of brain activity. As a consequence, Georgopoulos et al. proposed that MEG could be used to diagnose PTSD.

Van der Kolk (2015) considered that most patients with PTSD construct a narrative of their trauma over time. It is characteristic of PTSD that sensory elements of the trauma itself continue to intrude as flashbacks and nightmares, altered states of consciousness in which the trauma is relived, un-integrated with an overall sense of self. Therefore, van der Kolk et al. considered that extreme emotional arousal leads to failure of the central nervous system to synthesize the sensations related to the trauma into an integrated whole. This picks up the early work of Pierre Janet (1889), the first researcher to articulate the difference between ordinary (narrative) and traumatic (episodic) memories. Current understanding of the differences (see van der Kolk & Fisler, 1995) is outlined in Box 29.8.

Box 29.8   Traumatic and Narrative Memory compared (van der Kolk & Fisler, 1995)

Traumatic/Episodic Memory	Ordinary/Narrative memory
• Images, sensations, affective and behavioral states	• Narrative: semantic and symbolic
• Invariable – does not change over time	• Social and adaptive
• Highly state dependent. Cannot be evoked at will	• Evoked at will by the narrator
• Automatically evoked in special circumstances	• Can be condensed or expanded depending on social demands.
• Cannot be condensed in time	

Narrative memory is not like a photograph. It evolves over time, is neither linear nor chronological but instead a representation of past experiences. In contrast, very little of our experience is remembered as episodic memory. Instead, the brain extracts and abstracts the meaning of our experiences. At the age of 40 a person has lived through 250,000 hours of memory, yet only approximately 1,000 hours of episodic memory are available (Stickgold, 2002). In clients with PTSD, the memory of the traumatic event is recorded differently, because the body's natural system is not able to process and understand the event. Van der Kolk (2015) considered, therefore, that individuals are not traumatized by the experience but rather the memory of that experience. These autobiographical trauma memory networks (episodic memory) contain emotionally-laden imagery influenced by the orbital prefrontal cortex, posterior cingulate cortex, amygdala, and hippocampus (Markowitsch, Vandekerckhove, Lanfermann, & Russ, 2003).

EMDR and episodic memory

The demand for effective, empirically supported treatment for psychological trauma that addresses episodic memory brings us back to EMDR. According to the EMDR protocol, the formatting of traumatic memory involves a number of important elements central to this particular psychological treatment approach. EMDR first centers upon the activation of the traumatic memory material, identifying the key attributes of the imagery representing the worst aspect of the memory event, the attribution of meaning of the memory in the form of a negative cognition or maladaptive self-assessment, a preferred positive cognition with a rating around its valence and validity, a subjective evaluation of emotions and associated presently held levels of disturbance, and finally the manifestations of this disturbance in relation to bodily and physical sensations. This activation process which occurs in Phase 3 of EMDR is then followed by Phase 4 to stimulate the memory network to a position of desensitization and reprocessing. The goal of EMDR is to reduce the disturbing valence of the episodic trauma memory by changing the nature of the memory from *re-experiencing* to *remembering*. The basic essence of EMDR therapy is therefore depicted in Figure 29.1 through activating the target memory, stimulating it bilaterally, and then moving the construct of the memory from episodic (traumatic) to narrative memory.

Following are some of the more contemporary theories that hypothesize potential mechanisms for action in accounting for the effectiveness of EMDR. Although these will be explored individually, the strongest likelihood is that there are potentially a multiplicity of factors that contribute to successful outcome from EMDR psychotherapy.

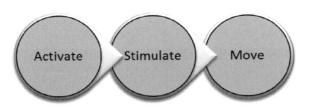

Figure 29.1 How EMDR addresses a target memory.

Mechanisms of Action in EMDR

According to Maxfield (2008), certain requirements must be fulfilled to establish whether a component is a mechanism for change. Currently, most studies that explore the underlying mechanisms of action in EMDR tend to evaluate the role of mediators. In considering the relationship between predictor and outcome, a mediator is a variable that is often continuous and therefore to understand its function and impact, it must be subjected to some form of regression analysis. As Lee & Drummond (2008), and Maxfield, Melnyk, & Hayman (2008) demonstrate, the primary focus of most dismantling studies in EMDR have focused upon eye movements. The problem with this endeavor is that there is much more to EMDR than just eye movements. However, the role of eye movements in EMDR will be explored from the following perspectives:

- Psychophysiology
- Neuroplasticity
- Working memory
- REM sleep
- AIP

Psychophysiology

Sack et al. (2008) demonstrated that EMDR treatment significantly reduced subjective disturbance and psychophysiological reactivity to an individualized traumatic script. Psychophysiological monitoring during EMDR treatment (BLS) highlighted a significant decrease in heart rate, increase in parasympathetic tone and psychophysiological de-arousal. Sack et al. demonstrated a rationale for using BLS for approximately 25–30 seconds. This duration provides EMDR clients with a sufficient amount of time to activate the traumatic memory material. Stickgold (2002) hypothesized that BLS in patients with PTSD reinstates a level of inter-hemispheric interaction that encourages the transformation of episodic information into narrative memory with a concomitant reduction in episodic memories. However, Propper & Christman (2008) considered that we require more investigation into the exact nature of how eye movements affect aspects of inter-hemispheric interaction and activation, from both functional and neurophysiological perspectives, and how those effects influence an individual's memory retrieval ability and emotional states.

Neuroplasticity

Another potential explanation to account for the changes produced by EMDR relates to neuroplasticity. Neuroplasticity is the ability of the brain to change its structure in response to experiences. New experiences can activate neurons, which turn on genes that enable structural changes to be made to strengthen the connections among neurons (Siegel, 2012). The basic principle of neuroplasticity is the brain's ability to effectively rewire itself and forge out new links and connections. Remarkably, a Spanish histologist, physician, and pathologist called Santiago Ramón y Cajal developed the initial concept of neuroplasticity in 1899. His thesis was the following:

- The strength of synaptic connections is not fixed, but plastic and modifiable
- Changes in synaptic strength can be modified by neural activity

- Learning produces prolonged changes in the strength of synaptic connections by causing a growth of new synaptic processes
- The persistence of these synaptic anatomical changes can serve as the mechanism for memory
- Neurons should be able to modulate their ability to communicate with one another
- The persistence of these alterations in basic synaptic communication, a functional property called synaptic plasticity, can provide the elementary mechanisms for memory storage (Bergmann, 2012a, 2012b).

Two great epochs of neuroplasticty are:

- Infancy – a 'critical period' when the brain sets up basic processing machinery
- Adult plasticity – when the brain refines its machinery as it masters a wide repertoire of skills and ability

According to Schwartz, Stapp, & Beauregard (2005), one of the tenets of neuroplasticity is that in order for the brain to form new connections and change, it must be stimulated through activity. Both thoughts and imagination physically change the brain, especially through focused attention, to positively "rewire" it. Billions of learned associations between the "self" and its unique experiences underlie each brain's idiosyncratic genesis, form, and expression. Information is always related to other inputs, because the brain is constantly constructing representations of things that are correlated in little moments of time. Bergmann (2012a) considered that neural firing is associated with mental experience such as perceiving, thinking, feeling, or remembering. In order to remember something, neurons fire in a certain pattern that is shaped by a past experience. There are two ways in which neuroplasticity impacts upon neuronal structure: neurogenesis or epigenesis. *Neurogenesis* is the development of nerve tissue, a process that occurs continuously across our entire life. *Epigenesis* is the process by which experiences impact upon and alter the regulation of our gene experiences. These alterations can be structural. Genes are not changed by experiences; the expression of genes is changed (Siegel, 2012).

Epigenetics

Epigenetics can be significantly affected by the consequences of severe neglect and trauma in childhood. These adverse childhood experiences can alter the expression of genes that are responsible for the circuitry that controls the body's response to stress. Borysenko (2013) suggested that when brains do not grow well as a consequence of neglect or abuse, the individual may have inherited epigenetic compromises in the ability to self-regulate. One of the arguments to support why EMDR and TF-CBT are effective is that they both share the same neurobiological objective which is to down-regulate the amygdala so as to allow the hippocampus and medial prefrontal cortex to come back on line (Bisson, 2008). With EMDR, the explanation would be that processing of trauma memory experiences is literally forging out new connections through modification of that memory experience and integrating it into a construct of an implicit interpretation of that memory and experience. The experience may still be vivid but is instead remembered rather than re-experienced.

The working memory hypothesis

As Stickgold (2008) showed, working memory allows us to access memory files, retrieve related material, compare this with what we have currently perceived, synthesize new material with old, reach new understandings, and decide on appropriate conclusions and/or actions. However, working memory capacity is extremely limited – humans can only hold small amounts of information in their conscious awareness. We live in a vibrant and complex world with lots of information trying to get our attention at any one time; our eyes, for example, receive approximately 1mb of information every second.

Multiple studies demonstrate how, when faced with two competing tasks requiring the same working memory, performance is degraded (Baddeley, 2000; Baddeley & Andrade, 2000; Cocchini et al., 2002; Stickgold, 2008). As a dual attention task becomes more difficult, performance on the primary task diminishes. This is relevant then in considering the effects of eye movements in EMDR. When someone engages in eye movements while simultaneously focusing upon a distressing image within a memory, this taxes the resources of the visuo-spatial sketchpad resulting in deterioration in the quality of the image, and the image becoming less vivid and emotional (Stickgold, 2008; van den Hout, Muris, Salemink, & Kindt, 2001; van den Hout, Engelhard et al., 2011; Kemps & Tiggemann, 2007). Lee and Drummond (2008) found that the greatest improvement with EMDR occurred when clients with PTSD gave distancing responses using a detached or observer perspective from the traumatic memory. Their studies demonstrated that both slow eye movements and fast eye movements decreased ratings of image vividness, thought clarity, and emotional intensity compared with no eye movements; however, fast eye movements produced a larger decrease than slow eye movements.

The problem with the working memory hypothesis is that its primary focus centers upon imagery in relation to vividness, clarity, and emotionality. As indicated earlier, the full EMDR protocol does not focus entirely upon memory image and then subjecting this image to eye movement. Memory imagery is only part of the characteristics of a trauma memory, which also contains cognitive, emotional, and somatosensory components. A second problem with this hypothesis can be explained by considering what happens when you focus on a dot on the wall for 25–30 seconds with the specific instruction to only focus on the dot. What invariably happens is that your brain will automatically 'move on' to something else, creating a natural form of distancing. As such, Lee & Drummond (2008) considered that the working memory hypothesis provides only a 'parsimonious explanation' in relation to EMDR. More research is needed to focus on other forms of BLS used in EMDR and explore their effects on working memory.

REM sleep

In *DSM-IV*, PTSD was classified as an 'anxiety disorder'. However, Stickgold (2002) argued that PTSD is best described as a memory disorder rather than an anxiety disorder, and that there is a link between the way EMDR and sleep both affect memory. Sleep supports learning, reliving emotional distress, and helps separate emotions from their context. During REM sleep, there is a higher susceptibility to emotional processing of material and weakly associated information can become linked together. In relation to memory and PTSD, both slow wave sleep (SWS) and REM are important as SWS puts daily memories through a transformation process which then allows REM to process it in another way. Sleep therefore appears to balance emotional memories. In clients who experience sleep disorder there is an over-activation of the amygdala. Rasch & Born (2007) suggested that reactivation of memories during sleep can enhance the sleep-dependent consolidation of those memories. The hypothesis for EMDR, therefore, is that BLS and EMDR can alter brain states in a manner similar to that seen during REM sleep. More 'dismantling studies' are needed to explore further the connection between REM sleep and EMDR processing of traumatic memory networks.

AIP

In its 25-year history, EMDR has evolved from a simple technique into a distinct, integrative, client-centered psychotherapy approach, whose theoretical underpinning is that of AIP (Shapiro, 2007; Shapiro & Laliotis, 2011; Solomon & Shapiro, 2008). According to Solomon & Shapiro (2008), AIP posits that a particular distressing incident may become stored in its state specific form (episodic memory), frozen in time in its own neural network and unable to connect with other memory networks that contain more adaptive information. AIP is not a neurobiological model in the sense that it can be investigated by CT, fMRI, or MEG. Meusser et al. (1998) considered that the AIP model is actually nothing more than a metaphor, albeit a helpful one at that. However, Shapiro uses the language of neurobiology to guide case conceptualization and to explain treatment effects, and Lansing, Amen, Hanks & Rudy (2005) provided some justification for this, through the use of brain scans exploring before and after effects of EMDR on PTSD sufferers. Their scans revealed high levels of limbic activity and reduced prefrontal cortex activity pre-EMDR intervention, with these levels of activity switching post intervention. That said, testing the predictions of AIP is as yet insufficient, as more component analysis is needed with distinct clinical populations and treatment conditions. Even so, the overwhelming viewpoint of practice-based evidence in support of AIP from EMDR clinicians is that it provides an extremely useful framework that translates well into the clinical environment (Farrell et al., 2013).

Eye Movements in EMDR

Davidson & Parker (2001) reported meta-analyses of the efficacy of EMDR. They concluded that although EMDR was an effective treatment intervention, the eye movements themselves were unnecessary to the overall treatment effect. The Australian Centre for Post Traumatic Stress (Forbes et al., 2007), who concluded that adults with PTSD should be provided with trauma-focused interventions (TF-CBT and EMDR) in addition to exposure therapy, subsequently noted that "available evidence does not support the importance of EMs per se in EMDR." They concluded instead that the treatment gains come from engagement with the traumatic memory, cognitive reprocessing, rehearsal of coping, and a mastery of response. Lee & Cuipers (2012) undertook a re-analysis of the Davidson & Parker data. Davidson & Parker used an analysis that weighted all studies equally, rather than the usual practice of weighting each study in relation to the number of participants involved, and used a fixed effects model rather than a random effects model. Using a different approach to weighting, and including additional studies published since Davidson & Parker's review, Lee et al. demonstrated that eye movements *did* have a significant advantage over no eye movements, an assertion supported further by Schubert, Lee & Drummond (2011).

Lee et al. (2008) determined that the eye movements specifically result in:

- Decreased vividness of memory images and related thoughts
- Decreased emotionality related to memory image
- Physiological changes such as lower heart rate, skin conductance, and increased heart rate variability
- Increased cognitive flexibility
- Increased episodic memory

However, all of these findings were produced under laboratory conditions rather than with clients with a PTSD diagnosis. In fact, more recent meta-analyses also do support the efficacy of the eye movement component in EMDR. These are highlighted in Box 29.9.

Box 29.9 Eye Movement BLS and Meta-Analyses in EMDR

Lee, Taylor & Drummond (2006)
- EMDR with eye movement was found to lead to significantly greater reduction of distress than EMDR without eye movement.

Schubert, Lee & Drummond (2011)
- Eye movement component in EMDR is beneficial, and is coupled with distinct psychophysiological changes that may aid in processing negative memories.

Jeffries & Davis (2012)
- The results suggest support for the contention that EMs are essential to this therapy and that a theoretical rationale exists for their use. It is suggested, however, that EMs may be more effective at reducing distress, and thereby allow other components of treatment to take place.

Lee & Cuipers (2013)
- Eye Movements (EMs) do have an additional value in EMDR treatment … that EMs do alter the processing of emotional memories … the processes involved in EMDR are different from other exposure based therapies.

Nieuwenhuis et al. (2013)
- Increased memory retrieval in two experiments support "the possibility that alternating bilateral activation of the left and right hemispheres exerts its effects on memory by increasing the functional connectivity between the two hemispheres."

772   *D. Farrell*

Despite the continued controversy surrounding the efficacy of eye movements, the evidence currently suggests that it is a significant aspect of EMDR, necessary to its treatment effect.

The Relationship Between EMDR and CBT

In the early days of EMDR, with the focus being on desensitization, the technique was considered to be consistent with that of CBT. As EMD became EMDR, and as Shapiro further developed her ideas and theories by introducing the AIP model as a theoretical construct and the use of bilateral and dual attention stimulation, EMDR has developed into a distinct psychotherapeutic approach. Running parallel to these developments in EMDR has been an increasingly hostile reception from the CBT community, particularly in the USA, with much of this controversy focusing on the significance of the BLS element within EMDR. Despite several meta-analyses supporting the incorporation of BLS, there is still a tendency for this aspect to be seen as superfluous to other factors that create therapeutic change – for example, activation of memory networks, dosed exposure, cognitive restructuring, subjective evaluation, demand characteristics, and the impact of the therapeutic relationship.

O'Donohue & Fisher's textbook on CBT explicitly states that CBT and EMDR are not the same approach:

> Cognitive Behavioral Therapy (CBT) is an important therapeutic paradigm as it has been shown repeatedly to be an efficacious and effective intervention for a variety of psychological problems ... it might be argued, in an important technical sense, that it is the only valid therapeutic paradigm ... the only, or at least the foremost, paradigm in psychotherapy ... it is not a 'one problem therapy' as some interventions are, for example EMDR.
>
> (2000, p. 15)

However, others (e.g., Bannick, 2012) claim that EMDR is a derivative of CBT: "Mindfulness, ACT, and EMDR are considered to be the third wave in CBT." (p. 16).

EMDR Research and Training

In some ways, it could be argued that EMDR contributes to its own criticism. There are potentially two areas of focus: research and training. Some of the earlier research supporting EMDR was not of a standard conducive with scientific rigor, and as a result was subjected to critical consideration and review. EMDR research in the last 20 years has been much more robust. Nonetheless, there are still gaps in the EMDR research repertoire. Many EMDR studies are currently in operation, but until these studies have been independently scrutinized and subjected to external, blind peer review, then EMDR will remain empirically supported only for PTSD. In an ongoing Delphi study, 108 EMDR consultants were asked which areas EMDR research should concentration upon (Farrell et al., 2013). The results strongly favored neurobiology and brain imaging (see Figure 29.2 below). There is also significant interest in the evaluation of EMDR with other clinical populations.

The second issue relates to training in EMDR. In its 30-year history, EMDR has evolved from a simple technique into an integrative psychotherapy approach (Shapiro,

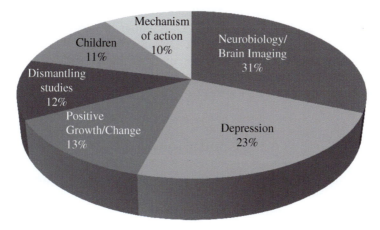

Figure 29.2 The most important issues for EMDR research Farrell et al., 2013.

2007, 2016). However, over this time period the format of training has remained relatively unaltered. This then raises the question as to how EMDR training needs to reflect the development from the original stance of 'EMDR as a technique' to 'EMDR as an integrative psychotherapeutic approach.' EMDR training is relatively short and only trains licensed mental health workers. The shortness of the training is primarily justified by the assumption that EMDR is ostensibly secondary psychotherapy training and therefore builds upon existing skills and knowledge. This was probably a reasonable assumption at the start, but EMDR is now considered an integrated psychotherapeutic approach (Shapiro & Solomon, 1995, Shapiro & Laliotis, 2011) in its own right, which guides case conceptualization and has at its core an idiosyncratic treatment protocol (Farrell, 2013). The format of the teaching and learning of EMDR therapy does not reflect the developments in the psychotherapeutic approach. The major paradigm in the teaching and learning of EMDR is that of an entrepreneurial model. As Carrere (2014) highlighted, in many ways this has been an extremely successful training endeavor in that some 150,000 clinicians have been trained in EMDR worldwide (Carrere, 2014). There are nonetheless different generations of EMDR training – some current and others works in progress. These are shown in Box 29.10.

Box 29.10   Different Generations of EMDR Training

1st Generation   Entrepreneurial model through private training institutes
2nd Generation   EMDR humanitarian training – bono fide
3rd Generation   EMDR in academic institutions – postgraduate activity
4th Generation   EMDR training for future mental health workers: psychologists, psychiatrists, mental health nurses, mental health social workers, psychotherapists, etc., as part of their core training curricula
5th Generation   EMDR training for para-professionals
6th Generation   EMDR for non-mental health workers: UN peace keepers, international and national NGO workers, aid workers, etc.

774   *D. Farrell*

One of the big differences between EMDR and CBT training is that CBT training is frequently taught in academic institutions. Throughout the whole of Europe, there are only two universities that offer academic EMDR training. It is probable that the EMDR evidence base is poorer for not having immersed itself in academic institutions in the past. The EMDR community needs to promote EMDR training into universities if it is to gain the academic credibility its existing empirical research base could be said to deserve.

Conclusions

EMDR is a psychotherapeutic approach that emphasizes the brain's intrinsic information processing system and how memories are stored. Presenting trauma symptoms are viewed as resulting from disturbing experiences that have not been adequately processed and have been encoded in state specific, dysfunctional form (Shapiro, 1995, 2001, 2007). The heart of EMDR involves the transmutation of these dysfunctionally stored experiences into an adaptive resolution that promotes psychological health. For EMDR to be applied effectively, the clinician needs a framework that identifies appropriate target memories and order of processing to obtain optimal treatment effects. The AIP model, which informs EMDR treatment, contains a variety of tenets and predictions that implicate various potential agents of change. It acknowledges that as human beings we possess a physiologically-based information processing system that is responsible for digesting or metabolizing information so that it can be used in a healthy life-enhancing manner. Part of our hard wiring is an innate natural tendency toward mental health, where psychological self-healing is just as purposeful as other physiological processes (Farrell, Keenan, Tareen, & Rana, 2010). While EMDR initially often sounds bizarre to clients (see Case Study 29.1), its evidence base as a treatment for PTSD is robust.

Case Study 29.1 The use of EMDR with someone who had been in a road traffic accident

Sam, a 47-year-old man, was referred for psychological treatment following a road traffic collision, which involved a near death experience, where Sam was the passenger, and the driver was his nephew. The car had been struck by a steel bar, which pierced the windscreen and impacted into the driver's head, resulting in a horrific injury. The referral for treatment was prompted by Sam's solicitor being concerned that a previous psychological intervention had not proved useful. Consequently, Sam was coerced into attending the appointment. During history taking, Sam disclosed persistent intrusive images, hyper-arousal, and avoidance behavior. These symptoms were so significant they were impacting upon his normal occupational and social levels of functioning. Sam met the criteria for PTSD (APA, 2013). Prior to attending this appointment, Sam had previously had six sessions of counseling and ten sessions of TF-CBT. In Sam's opinion he indicated that he'd found these sessions helpful, however he still had PTSD.

It was recommended to Sam that he have EMDR. Sam knew nothing about EMDR and after being provided with a suitable explanation, he retorted: "So what you want me to do is think about that worst memory of holding my nephew's brain, even though that memory makes me feel physically sick and keeps me awake at night. You also want me to think about that negative cognition 'It is my fault', be aware of the emotions it generates and how it makes me feel, and notice where I feel the disturbance in my body? Yeah? And then you are going to wave your hand in front of my face making my eyes move side to side? And that's going to help, yeah? Ok then."

After three years of symptoms, Sam responded to just four sessions of EMDR. He no longer met the criteria for *DSM-5* PTSD and after the second session had gone back to work.

Hearing Sam describe EMDR in this way must surely lead any observer to consider such a psychological treatment intervention to sound strange at the very least. To ask a client to "re-experience" the memory of a traumatic incident and then move their eyes from side to side seems preposterous. To speculate a scientific rationale for this requires a sophisticated review of what EMDR is, consideration of what EMDR's mechanism for action is, and finally an outline of how EMDR has become a truly international, empirically robust, psychological treatment intervention for PTSD.

EMDR, over these last 30 years, has moved from being a simple technique and method to a distinctive psychotherapeutic approach that guides case conceptualization and a protocol treatment intervention (Shapiro, 2007). To date, it is only considered to be an evidence-based therapy for the treatment of PTSD (Maxfield, 2009). The ever-increasing evidence-based practice and practice-based evidence of EMDR suggests its potential effectiveness with other mental health conditions, but more robust empirical evidence is needed in support of these assertions. While the vast majority of EMDR clinicians routinely report success with other mental health conditions, including anxiety and affective disorders, the provision of EMDR for non-PTSD disorders can only still be considered experimental and untested.

The development of EMDR into academic institutions would be a welcome endeavor. The need for further PTSD and EMDR research needs to take account of the following questions:

- Are the changes in brain structure and function found in PTSD a result of the disorder or pre-disposed?
- What is the most appropriate way to respond psychosocially immediately after a traumatic event?
- What are the most effective and efficient treatments for children and adolescents with PTSD and complex trauma?
- What are the more specific EMDR treatment considerations that have to be acknowledged for more complex trauma population?
- Can EMDR treatment as an early intervention prevent the onset of PTSD?
- What are the component elements in EMDR that are more significant than others?

776 D. Farrell

- What are the health economic benefits of EMDR Humanitarian Assistance Programs and Trauma Capacity Building Projects and their subsequent impact on local communities?
- What is EMDR's mechanism of action?

The search for EMDR's mechanism of action will continue. This chapter has outlined some of the central frameworks that currently exist. Robert Stickgold (2008) reminds us of a useful comparison in relation to advancing scientific understanding of mechanisms of action. He recounts Fleming's discovery of penicillin as an antibiotic in 1928, and how it was not until 1965 that its mechanism of action was finally discovered. This comparison serves to reassure that it is not surprising we are still at the early stages of seeking a detailed mechanism of action for EMDR.

Recommended reading

Marich, J. (2011). *EMDR made simple: Four approaches to using EMDR with every client.* Eau Claire, WI: Premier Publishing and Media.

Shapiro, F. (2012). *Getting past your past: Take control of your life with self-help techniques from EMDR therapy.* New York: Rodale.

Shapiro, F., & Forrest, M.S (2016). EMDR: *The breakthrough therapy for overcoming anxiety, stress and trauma.* New York: Basic Books.

Shapiro, F. (2018). *Eye movement desensitization and reprocessing (EMDR) therapy (3rd ed.): Basic principles, protocols, and procedures.* New York: Guilford Press.

Van Der Kolk, B. (2015). *The body keeps the score: Brain, mind, and body in the healing of trauma.* New York: Penguin Books.

References

Afifi, T. O., Mota, N. P., Dasiewicz, P., MacMillan, H. L., & Sareen, J. (2012). Physical punishment and mental disorders: Results from a nationally representative US sample. *Pediatrics, 130*, 184–192.

American Psychiatric Association. (2004). *Practice guidelines for the treatment of patients with acute stress disorder and posttraumatic stress disorder.* Arlington, VA: American Psychiatric Association.

American Psychiatric Association (2013). *Diagnostic and statistical manual of mental disorders* (5th ed.) (*DSM-5*). Washington, DC: American Psychiatric Association.

Baddeley, A. (2000). The episodic buffer: A new component of working memory? *Trends in Cognitive Sciences, 4*(11), 417–423.

Baddeley, A. D., & Andrade, J. (2000). Working memory and the vividness of imagery. *Journal of Experimental Psychology: General, 129*(1), 126–145.

Bae, H., Kim, D., & Park, Y. C. (2008). Eye movement desensitization and reprocessing for adolescent depression. *Psychiatry Investigation, 5*(1), 60–65.

Bannink, F. (2012). *Practicing positive CBT: From reducing distress to building success.* Chichester, UK: John Wiley & Sons.

Bergmann, U. (2012a). *Neurobiological foundations for EMDR practice.* New York: Springer Publishing Company.

Bergmann, U. (2012b). Consciousness examined: An introduction to the foundations of neurobiology for EMDR. *Journal of EMDR Practice and Research, 6*(3), 87–91.

Bisson, J., & Andrew, M. (2007). Psychological treatment of post-traumatic stress disorder (PTSD). *Cochrane Database of Systematic Reviews 2007, Issue 3*: CD003388

Borysenko, J. (2013) Mind-Body Medicine. Plenary Speech at 2013 EMDRIA Conference, Austin, TX.

Brown, K. W., McGoldrick, T., & Buchanan, R. (1997). BDD: Seven cases treated with EMDR. *Journal of Behavioral and Cognitive Psychotherapy, 25*, 203–207.

Bisson, J. I. 2008. Using evidence to inform clinical practice shortly after traumatic events. *Journal of Traumatic Stress 21*(6), 507–512.

Bisson, J., & Andrew, M. (2007). Psychological treatment of post-traumatic stress disorder (PTSD). *Cochrane Database of Systematic Reviews, 3*. Art. No. CD003388.

Bisson, J. I., Ehlers, A., Matthew, R., Pilling, S., Richards, D. A., & Turner, S. W. (2007). Psychological treatments for chronic post-traumatic stress disorder: systematic review and meta-analysis. *British Journal of Psychiatry, 190*(2), 97–104.

Brooks-Gordon, B., Bilby, C., & Wells, H. (2006). A systematic review of psychological interventions for sexual offenders I: Randomized control trials. *The Journal of Forensic Psychiatry and Psychology, 17*(3), 442–466.

California Evidence Based Clearinghouse [CEBC]. (2010). The California Evidence-Based Clearinghouse for Child Welfare. http://www.cebc4cw.org/.

Cajal S. R. (1899). Estudios sobre la corteza cerebral humana I: corteza visual. Rev. Trim. Microgr. 4, 1–63 Translated in: DeFelipe J., Jones E. G., translators. (1988). Cajal on the Cerebral Cortex New York: Oxford University Press.

Carrere, R.C. (2014). Scaling up what works: Using EMDR to help confront the world's burden of traumatic stress. *Journal of EMDR Practice and Research, 8*, 187–195.

Clark, L., Tyler, N., Gannon, T. A., & Kingham, M. (2014). Eye movement desensitisation and reprocessing for offence-related trauma in a mentally disordered sexual offender. *Journal of Sexual Aggression, 20*(2), 240–249.

Cocchini, G., Logie, R. H., Della Sala, S., MacPherson, S. E., & Baddeley, A. D. (2002). Concurrent performance of two memory tasks: Evidence for domain-specific working memory systems. *Memory and Cognition, 30*, 1086–1095.

Crisford, H., Dare, H., & Evangeli, M. (2008). Offence-related posttraumatic stress disorder (PTSD) symptomatology and guilt in mentally disordered violent and sexual offenders. *The Journal of Forensic Psychiatry & Psychology, 19*(1), 86–107.

Davidson, P. R., & Parker, K. C. (2001). Eye movement desensitization and reprocessing (EMDR): a meta-analysis. *Journal of Consulting and Clinical Psychology, 69*(2), 305.

Department of Veterans Affairs and Department of Defense. (2004). *VA/Department of Defense clinical practice guideline for the management of post-traumatic stress*. Washington, DC: Veterans Health Administration, Department of Veterans Affairs and Health Affairs, Department of Defense. Office of Quality and Performance publication 10Q-Clinical Practice Guidelines/PTSD-04.

Department of Veterans Affairs and Department of Defense (2010). *VA/DoD Clinical Practice Guideline for the Management of PTSD and Acute Stress Reaction*. Washington, DC.

De Jongh, A., Ten Broeke, E., & Renssen, M. R. (1999). Treatment of specific phobias with eye movement desensitization and reprocessing (EMDR): Protocol, empirical status, and conceptual issues. *Journal of Anxiety Disorders, 13*(1), 69–85.

De Roos, C. J., Veenstra, A. C., de Jongh, A., den Hollander-Gijsman, M. E., Van der Wee, N. J. A., Zitman, F. G., & Van Rood, Y. R. (2010). Treatment of chronic phantom limb pain using a trauma-focused psychological approach. *Pain Research and Management, 15*(2), 65–71.

Elofsson, U. O., von Schèele, B., Theorell, T., & Söndergaard, H. P. (2008). Physiological correlates of eye movement desensitization and reprocessing. *Journal of Anxiety Disorders, 22*(4), 622–634.

Farrell, D. P., Keenan, P. S., Ali, M. W., Bilal, S., Tareen, S. M., Keenan, L., & Rana, M. H. (2011). Training Pakistani mental health workers in EMDR in the aftermath of the 2005 earthquake in Northern Pakistan. *Counselling Psychology Quarterly, 24*(2), 127–137.

Farrell, D. (2013) *Enhancing competency in EMDR through effective clinical supervision and consultation.* Workshop presented 2013 EMDRIA Conference, September, Austin, TX.

Farrell, D., & Keenan, P. (2013). Participants' experiences of EMDR training in the United Kingdom and Ireland. *Journal of EMDR Practice and Research, 7*(1), 2–16.

Felitti, V. J., Anda, R. F., Nordenberg, D., Williamson, D. F., Spitz, A. M., Edwards, V., ... Marks, J. S. (1998). Relationship of childhood abuse and household dysfunction to many of the leading causes of death in adults: The adverse childhood experiences (ACE) study. *American Journal of Preventive Medicine, 14,* 245–258.

Foa, E. B., Keane, T. M., Friedman, M. J., & Cohen, J. A. (Eds.). (2008). *Effective treatments for PTSD: Practice guidelines from the International Society for Traumatic Stress Studies.* New York: Guilford Press.

Forbes, D., Creamer, M., Phelps, A., Bryant, R., McFarlane, A., Devilly, G. J., ... & Newton, S. (2007). Australian guidelines for the treatment of adults with acute stress disorder and post-traumatic stress disorder. *Australian and New Zealand Journal of Psychiatry, 41*(8), 637–648.

Georgopoulos, A. P., Tan, H. M., Lewis, S. M., Leuthold, A. C., Winskowski, A. M., Lynch, J. K., & Engdahl, B. (2010). The synchronous neural interactions test as a functional neuromarker for post-traumatic stress disorder (PTSD): A robust classification method based on the bootstrap. *Journal of Neural Engineering, 7*(1), 016011.

Hapke, U., Schumann, A., Rumpf, H. J., John, U., & Meyer, C. (2006). Post-traumatic stress disorder. *European Archives of Psychiatry and Clinical Neuroscience, 256*(5), 299–306.

Herman, J. L. (1992). Complex PTSD: A syndrome in survivors of prolonged and repeated trauma. *Journal of Traumatic Stress, 5*(3), 377–391.

Janet, P. (1889). *L'automatisme psychologique: essai de psychologie expérimentale sur les formes inférieures de l'activité humaine* (Vol. 2). impr. Ch. Hérissey.

Jeffries, F. W., & Davis, P. (2013). What is the role of eye movements in eye movement desensitization and reprocessing (EMDR) for post-traumatic stress disorder (PTSD)? A review. *Behavioural and Cognitive Psychotherapy, 41*(03), 290–300.

Keenan, P. S., & Farrell, D. (2000). Treating non-psychotic morbid jealousy with EMDR-A case report. *International Journal of Psychology, 35,* 3–4, 201–211.

Kemps, E., & Tiggemann, M. (2007). Reducing the vividness and emotional impact of distressing autobiographical memories: The importance of modality-specific interference. *Memory, 15*(4), 412–422.

Kim, D., Bae, H., & Chon Park, Y. (2008). Validity of the subjective units of disturbance scale in EMDR. *Journal of EMDR Practice and Research, 2*(1), 57–62.

Korn, D. L. (2009). EMDR and the treatment of complex PTSD: A review. *Journal of EMDR Practice and Research, 3*(4), 264–278.

Lansing, K., Amen, D. G., Hanks, C., & Rudy, L. (2005). High-resolution brain SPECT imaging and eye movement desensitization and reprocessing in police officers with PTSD. *The Journal of Neuropsychiatry and Clinical Neurosciences, 17*(4), 526–532.

Lee, C. W., & Cuijpers, P. (2013). A meta-analysis of the contribution of eye movements in processing emotional memories. *Journal of Behavior Therapy and Experimental Psychiatry, 44*(2), 231–239.

Lee, C. W., & Drummond, P. D. (2008). Effects of eye movement versus therapist instructions on the processing of distressing memories. *Journal of Anxiety Disorders, 22*(5), 801–808.

Lee, C. W., Taylor, G., & Drummond, P. D. (2006). The active ingredient in EMDR: Is it traditional exposure or dual focus of attention? *Clinical Psychology and Psychotherapy, 13*(2), 97–107.

Leeds, A. M. (2009). Resources in EMDR and other trauma-focused psychotherapy: A review. *Journal of EMDR Practice and Research, 3*(3), 152–160.

Leeds, A. M. (2016). *A Guide to the Standard EMDR Therapy Protocols for Clinicians, Supervisors, and Consultants.* Springer Publishing Company.

Markowitsch, H. J., Vandekerckhove, M. M., Lanfermann, H., & Russ, M. O. (2003). Engagement of lateral and medial prefrontal areas in the ecphory of sad and happy autobiographical memories. *Cortex, 39*(4), 643–665.

Maxfield, L. (2007). Current status and future directions for EMDR research. *Journal of EMDR Practice and Research, 1*(1), 6–14.

Maxfield, L. (2008). EMDR treatment of recent events and community disasters. *Journal of EMDR Practice and Research, 2*(2), 74–78.

Maxfield, L. (2009). EMDR milestones: The first 20 years. *Journal of EMDR Practice and Research, 3*(4), 211–216.

Maxfield, L., Melnyk, W. T., & Hayman, G. C. (2008). A working memory explanation for the effects of eye movements in EMDR. *Journal of EMDR Practice and Research, 2*(4), 247–261.

Mevissen, L., & De Jongh, A. (2010). PTSD and its treatment in people with intellectual disabilities: A review of the literature. *Clinical Psychology Review, 30*(3), 308–316.

Mueser, K. T., Goodman, L. A., Trumbetta, S. L., Rosenberg, S.D., Osher, F. C., Vidaver, R., Auciello, P., & Foy, D. W. (1998). Trauma and posttraumatic stress disorder in severe mental illness. *Journal of Consulting and Clinical Psychology, 66,* 493–499.

National Institute for Health and Clinical Excellence. (2005). *Post-traumatic stress disorder.* London: Royal College of Psychiatrists and the British Psychological Society.

Nieuwenhuis, S., Elzinga, B. M., Ras, P. H., Berends, F., Duijs, P., Samara, Z., & Slagter, H. A. (2013). Bilateral saccadic eye movements and tactile stimulation, but not auditory stimulation, enhance memory retrieval. *Brain and Cognition,* 81, 52–56.

O'Donohue, W. T., & Fisher, J. (Eds.) (2012). *Cognitive Behavior Therapy.* Chichester, UK: Wiley.

Pagani, M., Högberg, G., Salmaso, D., Nardo, D., Sundin, Ö., Jonsson, C., ... & Hällström, T. (2007). Effects of EMDR psychotherapy on 99mTc-HMPAO distribution in occupation-related post-traumatic stress disorder. *Nuclear Medicine Communications, 28*(10), 757–765.

Payne, E., Watt, A., Rogers, P., & McMurran, M. (2008). Offence characteristics, trauma histories and post-traumatic stress disorder symptoms in life sentenced prisoners. *The British Journal of Forensic Practice, 10*(1), 17–25.

Perry, B. D., & Pollard, R. (1997, November). Altered brain development following global neglect in early childhood. In *Proceedings from the Society for Neuroscience Annual Meeting (New Orleans).*

Propper, R. E., & Christman, S. D. (2008). Interhemispheric Interaction and Saccadic Horizontal Eye MovementsImplications for Episodic Memory, EMDR, and PTSD. *Journal of EMDR Practice and Research, 2*(4), 269–281.

Rasch, B., & Born, J. (2007). Maintaining memories by reactivation. *Current Opinion in Neurobiology, 17*(6), 698–703.

Ricci, R. J. (2006). Trauma resolution using eye movement desensitization and reprocessing with an incestuous sex offender an instrumental case study. *Clinical Case Studies, 5*(3), 248–265.

Ricci, R. J., Clayton, C. A., & Shapiro, F. (2006). Some effects of EMDR on previously abused child molesters: Theoretical reviews and preliminary findings. *Journal of Forensic Psychiatry and Psychology, 17*(4), 538–562.

Ricci, R. J., & Clayton, C. A. (2008). Trauma resolution treatment as an adjunct to standard treatment for child molesters: A qualitative study. *Journal of EMDR Practice and Research, 2*(1), 41–50.

Sack, M., Lempa, W., Steinmetz, A., Lamprecht, F., & Hofmann, A. (2008). Alterations in autonomic tone during trauma exposure using eye movement desensitization and reprocessing (EMDR) – Results of a preliminary investigation. *Journal of Anxiety Disorders*, 22(7), 1264–1271.

Santiago, P. N., Ursano, R. J., Gray, C. L., Pynoos, R. S., Spiegel, D., Lewis-Fernandez, R., ... & Fullerton, C. S. (2013). A systematic review of PTSD prevalence and trajectories in DSM-5 defined trauma exposed populations: intentional and non-intentional traumatic events. *PloS one*, 8(4), e59236.

Schubert, S. J., Lee, C. W., & Drummond, P. D. (2011). The efficacy and psychophysiological correlates of dual-attention tasks in eye movement desensitization and reprocessing (EMDR). *Journal of Anxiety Disorders*, 25(1), 1–11.

Schwartz, J. M., Stapp, H. P., & Beauregard, M. (2005). Quantum physics in neuroscience and psychology: A neurophysical model of mind–brain interaction. *Philosophical Transactions of the Royal Society of London B: Biological Sciences*, 360(1458), 1309–1327.

Shapiro, F. (1989). Eye movement desensitization: A new treatment for post-traumatic stress disorder. *Journal of Behavior Therapy and Experimental Psychiatry*, 20(3), 211–217.

Shapiro, F. (1995). *Eye movement desensitisation and reprocessing: Basic principles, protocols, and procedures*. Guilford Press, New York & London

Shapiro, F. (2001). *Eye Movement Desensitisation and Reprocessing: Basic Principles, Protocols, and Procedures*. Guilford Press, New York & London

Shapiro, F. (2002). EMDR 12 years after its introduction: past and future research. *Journal of Clinical Psychology*, 58(1), 1–22.

Shapiro, F. (2007). EMDR, adaptive information processing, and case conceptualization. *Journal of EMDR Practice and Research*, 1(2), 68–87.

Shapiro, F. (2012). EMDR therapy: An overview of current and future research. *Revue Européenne de Psychologie Appliquée/European Review of Applied Psychology*, 62(4), 193–195.

Shapiro, F. (2014). The role of eye movement desensitization and reprocessing (EMDR) therapy in medicine: addressing the psychological and physical symptoms stemming from adverse life experiences. *The Permanente Journal*, 18(1), 71.

Shapiro, F. (2016) Clinician's Corner: EMDR Therapy. International Society for Traumatic Stress Studies. 2 April 2016 in Stress Points. http://www.istss.org/education-research/traumatic-stresspoints/2016-april/clinician-s-corner-emdr-therapy.aspx

Shapiro, F., & Forrest, M. S. (2001). *EMDR: Eye movement desensitization and reprocessing*. New York: Guilford.

Shapiro, F., & Laliotis, D. (2011). EMDR and the adaptive information processing model: Integrative treatment and case conceptualization. *Clinical Social Work Journal*, 39(2), 191–200.

Shapiro, F., & Solomon, R. M. (1995). *Eye movement desensitization and reprocessing*. John Wiley & Sons, Inc.

Shvil, E., Rusch, H. L., Sullivan, G. M., & Neria, Y. (2013). Neural, psychophysiological, and behavioral markers of fear processing in PTSD: A review of the literature. *Current Psychiatry Reports*, 15(5), 1–10.

Siegel, D. J. (2012). *Pocket guide to interpersonal neurobiology: An integrative handbook of the mind (Norton Series on Interpersonal Neurobiology)*. New York: WW Norton & Company.

Solomon, R. M., & Shapiro, F. (2008). EMDR and the adaptive information processing model: Potential mechanisms of change. *Journal of EMDR Practice and Research*, 2(4), 315–325.

Stickgold, R. (2002). EMDR: A putative neurobiological mechanism of action. *Journal of Clinical Psychology*, 58(1), 61–75.

Stickgold, R. (2008). Sleep-dependent memory processing and EMDR action. *Journal of EMDR Practice and Research*, 2(4), 289–299.

Van den Hout, M., Muris, P., Salemink, E., & Kindt, M. (2001). Autobiographical memories become less vivid and emotional after eye movements. *British Journal of Clinical Psychology*, *40*, 121–130.

van den Hout, M. A., Engelhard, I. M., Beetsma, D., Slofstra, C., Hornsveld, H., Houtveen, J., & Leer, A. (2011). EMDR and mindfulness. Eye movements and attentional breathing tax working memory and reduce vividness and emotionality of aversive ideation. *Journal of Behavior Therapy and Experimental Psychiatry*, *42*(4), 423–431.

Van der Kolk, B. A. (2002). Beyond the talking cure: Somatic experience and subcortical imprints in the treatment of trauma. *EMDR as an integrative psychotherapy approach: Experts of diverse orientations explore the paradigm prism*, 57–83.

Van Der Kolk, B. (2015). *The body keeps the score: Brain, mind, and body in the healing of trauma*. New York: Penguin Books.

Van der Kolk, B. A., & Fisler, R. (1995). Dissociation and the fragmentary nature of traumatic memory: background and experimental evidence. *Journal of Traumatic Stress*, *9* (5), 505–525.

Van der Kolk, B. A., Spinazzola, J., Blaustein, M. E., Hopper, J. W., Hopper, E. K., Korn, D. L., & Simpson, W. B. (2007). A randomized clinical trial of EMDR, fluoxetine and pill placebo in the treatment of PTSD: Treatment effects and long-term maintenance. *Journal of Clinical Psychiatry*, *68*, 37–46.

Weathers, F. W., Keane, T. M., & Foa, E. B. (2009). Assessment and diagnosis of adults. *Effective treatments for PTSD: Practice guidelines from the international society for traumatic stress studies*, 23–61.

World Health Organization (2013). *Guidelines for the management of conditions specifically related to stress*. http://apps.who.int/iris/bitstream/10665/85119/1/9789241505406_eng.pdf

World Health Organization (WHO) and United Nations High Commissioner for Refugees (UNHCR). mhGAP Humanitarian Intervention Guide (mhGAP-HIG): Clinical management of mental, neurological and substance use conditions in humanitarian emergencies. Geneva: WHO, 2015.

30

Adjusting the Lens
A Developmental Perspective for Treating Youth with Sexual Behavior Problems

Kevin Creeden

Key points

- Interventions and treatment models often fail to draw upon our understanding of developmental and experiential factors, particularly with the treatment of sexual behavior problems in children and adolescents.
- Advances in our understanding of the development of the brain and impact of trauma on neurodevelopment and behavior have not translated into changes in treatment.
- Considered in a framework of optimal child and adolescent functioning, sexual behavior problems can be viewed as indicative of difficulties in child development, and as such are no different than other problematic behavior.
- Developmental difficulties associated with sexual problems may manifest as self-regulation and inhibitory control problems, mental health issues, learning problems, low academic ability, and difficulties in forming and sustaining relationships.
- Rather than seeking only to remove unwanted behavior, a developmental framework helps focus on enhancing growth. Enhancing growth is common to parental approaches with children generally, making it easier to engage them and other family members in the process.
- Sexually abusive behavior in adolescence is largely motivated by a need for attachment, acceptance, nurturance, and competence.
- Focusing on eliminating unwanted behavior as a measure of change may limit treatment providers from addressing issues of broader personal growth necessary to maintain a non-sexually abusive life.
- Clinicians working from a neurodevelopmental perspective should draw upon multi-modal treatment interventions and not rely solely on *talk therapies* that could limit progress of their clients.
- Starting with an assessment of the young person's strengths and skills will help individualize a treatment approach to address deficits and overcome

---

The Wiley Blackwell Handbook of Forensic Neuroscience, First Edition. Edited by Anthony R. Beech, Adam J. Carter, Ruth E. Mann and Pia Rotshtein.
© 2018 John Wiley & Sons Ltd. Published 2018 by John Wiley & Sons Ltd.

- obstacles to positive growth. Family and other social support should be enlisted in the process.
- Risk should be conceptualized as an assessment of strengths, capacities, and limitations in the context of the environmental demands and the support that environment has to offer an individual. This approach makes clear everyone's responsibility in ensuring safety and progress, and is consistent with our understanding of how relational and environmental influences shape adolescent development.

Terminology Explained

Adverse Childhood Experiences (ACE) study is an epidemiological research study conducted by the Kaiser Permanente health care organization and the US Center for Disease Control (CDC) that has demonstrated ACEs with health and social problems as an adult.

Structured assessment guides (e.g., ERASOR – Estimate of Risk for Adolescent Sexual Offender Recidivism); JSOAP-II – Juvenile Sexual Offender Assessment Protocol, 2nd version) are used to aid in the review of risk factors identified as being associated with an individual re-engaging in sexual offending or sexually problematic behavior. To a more limited degree, these protocols also examine dynamic factors associated with adolescent treatment progress and resiliency.

Foundation skills are the basic competencies that need to be taught and developed first and foremost. These skills facilitate our ability to learn and integrate more complex levels of information and successfully manage more complex tasks/demands. Foundation skills include: concentration, visual and auditory processing, sensory motor integration, short- and long-term memory, self-regulation, social attunement, and delaying gratification.

Sensory assessment is usually completed by an occupational therapist to examine how a person discriminates and modulates sensory information and how that sensory processing impacts on foundational mechanisms such as postural-ocular skills, visual perceptual skills, and fine and gross motor skills, as well as the ability of the brain to conceive, organize, and carry out a sequence of actions.

Introduction

Treating juveniles with sexual behavior problems has changed significantly over the last 20 years, with a shift from a reliance on adult treatment approaches to a focus on more developmental, holistic, or strength-based treatment models. This change has been informed by significant advancements in the fields of neuroscience and neurodevelopment, and evolving approaches to the treatment of trauma and attachment problems. However, these treatment approaches have often been presented as a proposed menu of different treatment interventions rather than an integrated model for the assessment and treatment for youth with sexual behavior problems. This chapter seeks to outline a treatment model used at The Whitney Academy, USA, that utilizes current research and thinking from the fields of neurodevelopment, trauma treatment, and attachment theory to address sexual behavior problems in youth where the focus is on the acquisition and demonstration of positive, adaptive developmental skills as a measure of treatment progress and risk reduction.

Theories addressing the etiology of sexual offending and sexually problematic behaviors frequently highlight the importance of a variety of developmental variables and developmental experiences (Barbaree, Marshall, & McCormick, 1998; Marshall & Marshall, 2000; Ward & Stewart, 2003; Knight & Sims-Knight, 2004; Stinson & Becker, 2013), while our treatment of these behaviors often fails to specifically integrate this understanding into our treatment models and interventions. This failure is most noteworthy when it comes to the treatment of children and adolescents with sexual behavior problems, since developmental issues and changes are actively being "played out" during the treatment process.

Despite the fact that our understanding of child and adolescent brain development, adolescent learning styles, and the impact of trauma on neurodevelopment and behavior has advanced dramatically over the past decade, surveys of treatment providers continue to identify cognitive behavioral treatment approaches as the primary treatment model for addressing sexual behavior problems in adolescents (McGrath, Cumming, Burchard, Zeoli, & Ellerby, 2010). Rather than separating our understanding and treatment of adolescent sexual behavior problems from the framework of *normal* or *optimal* child and adolescent development, this author believes that it is more reasonable to view these behaviors as an indication that the adolescent is experiencing obstacles to progressing on a positive developmental trajectory. Treatment can then be framed as a process for identifying the developmental skills or experiences that may be lacking and interventions can be focused on providing these youth with the supports, skills, and resources necessary to foster learning, growth, and resilience.

The Advantages of a Developmental Focus

Developmental perspective for treating *With a developmental framework, the treatment is geared towards enhancing growth and promoting individual and social integration rather than just diminishing risk or eliminating unwanted behavior.*

Source: © OpenClipart-Vectors. Used under license from pixabay.

The most obvious argument for adopting a developmental framework for our understanding and treatment of children and adolescents with sexual behavior problems is that this framework parallels our goals for youth in our society in general. It highlights a focus on adaptive strengths, skill development, and the goal of increased competency rather than focusing on pathology, deviancy, and dangerousness. With a developmental framework, the treatment is geared toward enhancing growth and promoting individual and social integration rather than just diminishing risk or eliminating unwanted behavior. My experience is that this focus on growth and strength is also consistent with the view that most parents take toward their own children and therefore makes it easier to engage parents and other family members in being active participants in the treatment process.

From a systemic perspective, the advantage of utilizing a developmental framework is that it allows for the possibility of describing treatment issues, treatment needs, and treatment interventions in a language that is already familiar and accessible to the other adults who are engaged in this adolescent's life. There is a great deal of theory and research about child development that already directs and informs norms and activities around parenting, education, social interaction, social responsibility, and youth safety. While we should engage in research that expands our understanding of child development and enhance our capacity for promoting optimal development for all children, there may not be a need to create a *specialized* language or set of dynamics that separates or discriminates children and adolescents with sexual behavior problems from other youth who experience serious problems in making or sustaining developmental progress.

A developmental perspective encourages the treatment provider and the broader systems involved with these youth (juvenile justice, education, social welfare) to remember that adolescence is a period of considerable change and fluidity, and that many of the issues that we are prone to identify as risks for juveniles with sexual behavior problems (e.g., self-absorption, limited empathy, high degree of sexual interest, accessing pornography, easily influenced by peers, taking limited responsibility for their behavior) are also difficulties for many other adolescents who do not have serious behavioral difficulties (Scott & Grisso, 1997; Scott & Steinberg, 2008). This is not to suggest that the adolescents we treat do not present with significant risks or serious behavioral and emotional concerns, rather it reminds us that the developmental process and the impetus toward maturity is working in our favor. We should remain aware that some of the issues we pathologize in the adolescents who enter treatment also exist, to a greater or lesser degree, in many adolescents and may diminish or even resolve without significant therapeutic intervention or perhaps largely through support, guidance, and patience.

Finally, a developmental approach to treatment should naturally facilitate a more individualized treatment approach since the developmental experiences, the level of personal skills or deficits, the individual's learning style, and the constellation of family dynamics, social supports, and environmental resources is likely to look different for each adolescent we treat. Although common developmental goals and milestones can be used to frame our understanding, inform our assessments, and direct our treatment, the paths used for each adolescent and their family in achieving those goals can be quite diverse.

Developmental Issues and Sexual Behavior Problems

There are key issues present in much of our treatment population that provide the motivation for engaging in a developmental treatment approach to sexual behavior problems. In particular, many of the children and adolescents we treat have experienced disruptions in attachment relationships resulting in difficulties in self-regulation and ongoing relational problems. In addition, our clients frequently experience *developmental trauma*, which Heller and LaPierre (2012) define as *ongoing experiences* of neglect, abuse, and mis-attunement (see Chapter 31 in this volume). The impact of trauma experiences on neurodevelopment (and therefore child development in general) appears to be a central component in understanding the etiology of sexual behavior problems and therefore is a key area to address in the treatment of these problems. While I am not arguing that every adolescent who engages in problematic or abusive sexual behavior necessarily has a history of abuse, neglect, or attachment difficulties, I would argue that those adolescents who present with the greatest level of treatment challenges and concerns, as well as the greatest risk for engaging in future sexual and non-sexual offenses, are adolescents who present with these life experiences.

The importance of attachment relationships

Attachment can be defined as a construct that includes all the processes used for engaging and maintaining social relationships. These processes can include the needs for warmth, food, protection, and the buffering against stress (Hofer, 2006). Coming from an evolutionary perspective, Bowlby (1969, 1973, 1980) proposed that attachment is an innate biological system that promotes proximity-seeking behavior between an infant and a specific attachment figure in order to increase the likelihood of survival (Sroufe, 2000). Conceptualized in this way, attachment is viewed as the central organizing feature of the infant's early social environment and the outcomes from these experiences provide the basis for personal safety and shape one's capacity to effectively engage in social relationships. The experience of a secure parent–child relationship has been shown to serve as a protective factor that helps ameliorate the impact of both emotional and physical challenges (Porges, 2011; Sachser, Durschlag, & Hirzel, 1998; Sroufe, Duggal, Weinfield, & Carlson, 2000). In contrast, the absence of a secure and attuned child/caregiver relationship is seen as having negative effects on the individual's ability to regulate physical and emotional reactions to stressors and can lead to disturbed social relationships in later life (Bales & Carter, 2009; O'Connor, 2005).

As we learn more about the neurobiological responses to social interactions it would appear that early attachment interactions are the common factor that lie at the intersection of neurodevelopment, emotional and behavioral regulation, reward seeking, traumatic experience, social development, and one's capacity for intimacy (Hart, 2011; Porges, 2011; Mayes, Magidson, Lejuez, & Nicholls, 2009). Attachment theory and an expanding amount of neurological research suggests that the emotion regulation process that results from the interactions of the child and a positively engaged caregiver generates a regulatory system that incorporates both neurobiological and social/emotional responses (Hart, 2011; Mayes et al. 2009; Fonagy, Gergely, Jurist, & Target, 2004; Schore, 2002).

The presence or absence of secure attachment relationships has not been identified through research as directly determining those individuals who will engage in sexually abusive behavior or differentiating individuals who commit sexual offenses from non-sexual offenders. However, Barbaree, Marshall, and McCormick (1998), Marshall and Marshall (2000), and Hudson and Ward (2000) contend that the consequences of poor attachment relationships lead to dynamics and deficits that are at the very core of sexual offending behavior. Specifically, Marsa et al. (2004) found that 93% of the sexual offenders in their study evidenced an insecure attachment style and that secure attachment was less common in the sex offender group than in any other of the three groups studied (violent, non-sex offenders; non-sex offenders; and community controls).

Research from the National Child Traumatic Stress Network (2003) identified the seven most frequent types of developmental insults that contribute to behavioral difficulties in children. These developmental insults are emotional abuse (59%), the loss of important relationships (56%), impaired caregivers (47%), exposure to domestic violence (46%), sexual abuse (41%), neglect (34%), and physical abuse (28%). I would suggest that at least five of these "developmental insults" directly involve disruptions in early attachment relationships and that depending on the circumstances, all seven of these experiences may directly involve the nature of the parent–child interaction and the attachment relationship.

In considering the role that attachment difficulties play in our understanding and treatment of sexually problematic behavior in children and adolescents, it may be more important to appreciate the central neurological role that attachment plays in the development of self-regulation, reward seeking, and adaptive problem solving and how skills and deficits in these areas can lead to sexually problematic behavior, than it is to draw a direct causal connection between insecure attachment relationships and sexual offending behavior (Stinson & Becker, 2013; Ward, Polaschek, & Beech, 2006; Umhau, George, Reed, Petrulis, Rawlings, & Porges, 2002). Furthermore, when considering the research on protective factors that promote resiliency in childhood, it should not be surprising to find that the presence of a long-term caring relationship with at least one other person is often cited, along with a capacity to self-soothe and a sense of personal competence, as the key elements in a protective process (Masten & Coatsworth, 1998; Egeland, Carlson, & Sroufe, 1993; Widom, 1991).

I have previously presented my belief that sexually abusive behavior is in large part motivated by an individual's fundamental need for attachment (safety, attunement, nurturance, acceptance, and care) and that to understand abusive behavior we need to view it in the context of attachment and relationship, while appreciating the anxiety that can be elicited when attachment is either lacking or lost (Creeden, 2006). This need to address attachment issues is especially pertinent to our treatment of sexual behavior problems in children and adolescents, since increasingly the research would suggest that early attachment experiences are the cornerstone to neurological, physiological, and psychological development (Hart, 2011; de Haan & Gunnar, 2009; Porges, 2012; Siegel, 1999).

The impact of trauma on neurodevelopment

Emotional and behavioral regulation, promoted by a sense of safety and parental engagement, are important developmental foundations for pro-social functioning. A number of studies, from a range of professional disciplines, have identified the immediate and long-term effects that a wide variety of adverse experiences, some of which may be viewed as specifically traumatic, can have on child development (de Bellis, Wooley, & Hooper, 2013; de Bellis, Hooper, Spratt, & Wooley, 2009; Middlebrooks & Audage, 2008; American Academy of Pediatrics, 2002; Teicher, Andersen, Polcari, Andersen, & Navalta, 2002; Perry, 2001; Bremner & Vermetten, 2001; Boring, Frustaci, & Ryan, 1999). These adverse experiences may include: pervasive neglect, emotional abuse, physical abuse, exposure to family violence, or the loss of family members through death or abandonment. Some of the developmental problems associated with the child's experience of persistent stressors include: attachment difficulties, significant deficits in self-regulatory functioning and inhibitory control, sensory integration problems, specific learning disabilities, academic problems, poor peer relationships, mental health problems, and involvement in the juvenile justice system (Scheeringa, 2011; de Bellis et al., 2013; de Bellis et al., 2009; Raine, Mellingen, Liu, Venables, & Mednick, 2003; Blair & James, 2001; Aguilar, Sroufe, Egeland, & Carlson, 2000; Lyons-Ruth, Alpern, & Repacholi, 1993; Moffitt, 1993).

Prasad, Kramer, and Ewing-Cobbs (2005) suggested that the social and emotional difficulties seen in abused and neglected children may stem from neuropsychological difficulties that reflect alterations in brain maturation. Brain imaging studies of maltreated children revealed maturational decreases in specific brain regions such as the prefrontal cortex and the right temporal lobe when compared with controls (Tupler & de Bellis, 2006). Utilizing tensor-based morphometry (TBM), Hanson et al. (2010) found significantly smaller brain volumes in the orbitofrontal cortex of abused children when compared to non-abused children. The authors also found that these differences were associated with a wide range of difficulties these abused children experienced in their social lives, including specific problems in parent–child relationships, peer relationships, behavioral difficulties, and academic problems. De Bellis et al. (2009) found evidence that childhood experiences of abuse and neglect can lead to a wide range of learning difficulties, including lower IQ's and specific problems in reading, mathematics, complex visual attention, visual memory, language, verbal memory and learning, planning, and problem solving. Previous research has shown that 30% or more of children who have suffered abuse and neglect develop specific learning difficulties (Streek-Fisher & van der Kolk, 2000). Studies in US correctional facilities have shown that large percentages of the adult prison population have identified learning disabilities, with as many as 80% of the prison population being functionally illiterate and 95% of those under age 22 lacking a high school diploma (Moody, Holzer, & Roman, 2000; Vermont Correctional System, 2000). Given that positive engagement in school and the development of personal competency are among the strongest protective factors for youth at risk, the presence of learning disabilities can present as an important and frequently overlooked obstacle to developmental progress for our treatment population.

In their critical review of neuroimaging studies examining the impact of different types of childhood abuse and neglect on brain structure and function, Hart and Rubia (2012, p. 17) concluded that:

> There is consistent evidence that childhood maltreatment is associated with neuropsychological impairments in academic achievement, IQ, memory, emotion processing, working memory, attention, and response inhibition. There is also evidence for changes in brain structure and function, most consistently in ventromedial and orbitofrontal-limbic regions and networks of affect control, but with emerging evidence for some deficits also in lateral fronto-striatal and parieto-temporal regions that mediate EFs (executive functions), such as response inhibition, attention, and working memory.

The identified functional difficulties of emotion processing, affect control, response inhibition, and working memory, along with other executive functioning skills associated with adaptive problem solving, would appear to be especially pertinent to the problems we regularly see exhibited by youth engaging in sexually problematic behavior. Difficulties stemming from hyper- or hypo-arousal to various types of emotional stimuli associated with different types of abuse and neglect can create significant problems in a range of self-regulatory capacities (Jedd et al., 2015; McLaughlin et al., 2015; Ogden & Fisher, 2015; Pine et al., 2005; Pollak & Kistler, 2002). Identifying and intervening in the neurodevelopmental difficulties associated with childhood trauma and maltreatment can become especially complex and difficult, because many of the adolescents we treat present with multiple types of maltreatment occurring at different developmental stages in their lives.

Through their ongoing ACE (Adverse Childhood Experience) study, the Center for Disease Control (CDC) has shown that beyond the impact that a single, specific, adverse childhood experience can have on development, there is a broader *cumulative harm* that emerges from repeated or pervasive exposure to these experiences (Middlebrooks & Audage, 2008). Along with a range of health-related problems, the risk for specific behaviors that are related to child and adolescent sexual behavior problems, including early initiation of sexual behavior, multiple sexual partners, and risk for intimate partner violence are shown to increase in a "strong and graded fashion" with the addition of each identified ACE (CDC, 2013). Schwartz, Cavanaugh, Prentky, and Pimental (2006) documented the evidence that high levels of neglect, family violence, psychological abuse, physical abuse, and sexual abuse are experienced by large percentages of adolescents identified with serious aggressive and sexual behavior problems.

While new information is now being regularly being published, the current studies would seem to suggest that the neurobiological impact of trauma will not express itself through a fixed set of cognitive, emotional, or behavioral difficulties, but rather along a continuum of structural or functional neurological responses influenced by genetics, the developmental stage at which the child experiences trauma, the persistence of those traumatic experiences, and the availability of supportive resources provided by primary caretakers and the community (Creeden, 2006).

Defining a Developmental Approach

I would suggest that a developmental approach to the treatment of sexual behavior problems can be defined by four basic principles: 1) assessment is focused on identifying the absence or limitations in "foundation skills" that create obstacles to a positive developmental trajectory and personal resiliency; 2) treatment goals and treatment progress are measured by the individual's ability to acquire, integrate, and utilize developmental skills and learning that promote pro-social and adaptive functioning consistent with the adolescent's age and capacities; 3) treatment interventions are prioritized based on developmental needs and are informed by our understanding of what promotes effective and integrated learning in children and adolescents; and 4) the individuals and systems engaged in providing services to these youth understand that a wide range of family, peer, school, and environmental variables influence healthy adolescent development and incorporate that understanding into their determinations regarding the personal restrictions, treatment interventions, treatment plans, and treatment resources needed to effectively intervene with these adolescents and their families.

Assessment

The underlying premise for all developmental theories is that developmental proceeds from the simple to the complex, and that the positive engagement in early developmental experiences and tasks leads to the acquisition of skills and traits. These skills and traits provide the foundation for higher-level skill acquisition and the ability to engage in and carry out more complicated tasks in later development (Creeden, 2013). When we use normal child development as our framework for assessing adolescents with sexual behavior problems, we are looking to identify those early "foundation" skills that may be missing or limited in the adolescent we are evaluating. In some adolescents, experiences in much earlier developmental stages related to attachment disruptions, trauma, and associated neurodevelopmental issues may be identified. In other clients, more immediate obstacles or influences on developmental progress may present as targets for intervention. In either case, the clinician should utilize a clear, working knowledge of developmental theory that can be informed and augmented by a variety of resources that identify specific developmental skills (physical, cognitive, social-emotional) that are generally related to different developmental periods in a child and adolescent's life (e.g., The Institute for Human Services, 2007; McLaughlin et al., 2015).

As in any assessment, it will be important to gain information from a range of sources including direct observation and interaction with the client and family, the use of pertinent assessment instruments, and through information provided by the client, family, school, and other involved parties who have knowledge of the client's developmental competencies. It is important to have a broad source of information in these assessments because it is not unusual for adolescents to present differently in different settings. It may also be the case that when developmental difficulties are present, they are not necessarily *global* in nature. Rather, adolescents may appear developmentally "on track" in several areas of their life (for example athletics or social interests) and yet experience significant, but sometimes less noticeable gaps in other developmental areas (such as language processing or executive functioning). By providing families, schools, and others with information about skills and abilities that might be expected for the child's chronological age and engaging them in identifying those areas where the child may be struggling or facing obstacles, the assessment can serve as a process for education, alliance building, and cooperation. In addition, this process can achieve a variety of goals:

- It places the adolescent's current functioning into context and often informs parents and other involved parties about realistic expectations and typical versus atypical issues that may be present for children at particular developmental stages
- It allows for a more holistic view of the adolescent that identifies strengths as well as weaknesses, and also identifies deficits that may have been ignored, not attended to, or not previously recognized
- It can stimulate discussion with the client and the family regarding events or experiences in the adolescent's life that may have inhibited, enhanced, or influenced development at particular ages
- It helps the evaluator place the adolescent's sexual behaviors and level of sexual knowledge into a developmental context

792   *K. Creeden*

- It helps identify and prioritize the focus of treatment interventions and treatment goals
- It provides an ongoing framework for recognizing and measuring treatment progress (Creeden, 2013)

Assessment instruments

In regard to specific test instruments, there are already a wide variety of assessment instruments utilized in the evaluation of adolescents with sexual behavior problems, including personality inventories (e.g., Millon Adolescent Clinical Inventory, Minnesota Multiphasic, Personality Inventory-A), instruments that target specific symptoms (e.g., Beck Depression Inventory), and assessment tools that focus on risk for violent aggression (e.g., Structured Assessment of Violence Risk in Youth). From my perspective, there is nothing inherent in taking a developmental treatment approach that would preclude the use of these or any other assessment instruments that are typically used with this treatment population. As this writer has noted before (Creeden, 2013), the current instruments designed to structure the clinician's assessment of risk for future sexual offense recidivism such as the ERASOR (Worling & Curwen, 2001) and the JSOAP-II (Prentky & Righthand, 2003) continue to be viewed as useful tools, although arguably they may be inherently limited, because by design, they identify collective risk factors rather than individual dynamics (Latham & Kinscherff, 2012).

Utilizing a developmental treatment approach requires the use of additional tools that provide a framework for assessing the youth's developmental progress when compared to others their age and also examines those areas where research has indicated that the experience of trauma can have a neurodevelopmental impact, resulting in processing difficulties that create significant obstacles to effectively acquiring and utilizing a range of skills. Based on current research, I would argue for the inclusion of specific instruments that: target the presence of trauma symptoms (e.g., The Trauma Checklist for Children); provide information on language-based skills (e.g., Verbal Comprehension Index of the WISC-IV, SCAN-A, The Clinical Evaluation of Language Fundamentals-5); examine a range of executive functioning abilities (e.g., Behavior Rating Inventory of Executive Function, Wisconsin Card Sort, Conner's Continuous Performance Test); examine various types of memory (e.g., Working Memory Index of the WISC-IV, Wechsler Memory Scale, Bender Gestalt Test-II, Rey Complex Figure Test). In addition, instruments that provide a general assessment of adaptive behavior such as the Casey Life Skills Assessment, and provide an assessment of skills associated with increased resiliency, such as the Resiliency Scales for Children and Adolescents, also help facilitate a broad assessment picture.

One area that is frequently overlooked when evaluating children and adolescents with disrupted or dysregulated behavior is the presence of significant sensory processing and/or sensory integration issues. When appropriate, a sensory screening or sensory assessment completed by, or in conjunction with, an occupational therapist can be an important addition to a comprehensive evaluation.

Using the framework of normative child development as the foundation for our evaluations, including our evaluations of risk for sexual recidivism, and consistently informing our assessments with current research on the neurodevelopmental impact of trauma, broadens our perspective and understanding of these adolescents. It assists in insuring that the clinician, as well as the other involved systems, continues to view this adolescent and their behavior in the context of an ongoing developmental process.

The principles of Risk-Needs-Responsivity (Bonta & Andrews, 2010) are increasingly used in the sex offense treatment field as a central component for informing assessment protocols and developing treatment programs. I believe the use of a developmental framework in our assessments can more effectively inform our understanding of dynamic and static *risk* issues in adolescence as they specifically relate to the individual's personal history, family interactions, social relationships, and behavioral decision making. By design, a developmental framework examines developmental *needs* (as opposed to criminogenic needs) and more adaptive pathways to developmental progress. It can directly identify issues and obstacles related to *responsivity* for the individual and the family by incorporating an understanding of the neurological, behavioral, and learning issues associated with trauma, thereby providing a fresh perspective for treatment providers, educators, and others.

Treatment goals and progress

The adolescents we treat are most frequently identified for treatment because they have engaged in a particular, or more frequently a variety of, abusive, illegal, and problematic behaviors. Often, the various social systems involved with these individuals (schools, juvenile justice, child welfare, etc.) are driven by a behavior management approach in identifying treatment interventions, treatment goals, and treatment progress, especially when the presenting issues involve aggressive and/or sexualized behavior. Treatment progress or success is therefore typically measured by the degree to which identified problematic behaviors either diminish or desist. This is perhaps most obvious in situations involving treatment programs and treatment interventions where success is defined solely by their ability to lower recidivism rates for sexually offending behaviors or in some instances by also lowering recidivism rates for general delinquency. While lowering or eliminating the amount of abusive or illegal sexual behavior in which these youths engage is clearly a legitimate and important goal of treatment, we should also acknowledge that it is a very narrow goal, especially when considered in the context of research that indicates already low sexual recidivism rates for most adolescents (Reitzel & Carbonell, 2006). A narrow focus on behavior management in many of our systemic and individual treatment interventions leads to a situation where treatment progress for the adolescent is frequently measured by 'the absence of bad' behavior rather than the acquisition of skills and experiences that provide the foundation for long-term growth and pro-social development. It can also lead to adolescents doing well in highly structured, monitored, and supportive treatment settings only to re-engage in problematic behavior if they return to the community without the structure and support necessary to sustain that progress.

Adopting a developmental treatment model provides a systemic structure that necessitates a 'holistic' approach to treating adolescent sexual behavior problems. It would also mean identifying treatment goals and interventions that:

1   Facilitate stable family relationships.
2   Provide a safe living environment.

794   K. Creeden

3   Increase the adolescent's capacity for self-regulation.
4   Actively teach adaptive problem solving and coping skills.
5   Increase social skills and provide opportunities for pro-social peer interaction.
6   Improve school performance and vocational competency.
7   Enhance the adolescent's capacity for personal intimacy.
8   Provide clear and accurate sex education that promotes healthy sexuality.

Many clinicians and treatment programs would argue that they already address these issues, but too often these are viewed as adjuncts to the goal of behavior management rather than the necessary developmental ingredients that make not only behavior management but also personal competency and growth possible.

In operationalizing the Developmental Treatment Model, we have identified six developmental domains that are necessary for personal growth and development. These domains are labeled as attachment, self-regulation, cognitive skills, social skills, adaptive living skills, and healthy sexuality. While each domain may overlap with one or more domains in several ways, it seemed that each of these domains presented as areas where we could assess skills, target interventions, and measure progress in a manner that focused on and promoted developmental integration and pro-social functioning. Within each domain there are four phases, with each phase identifying evidence of increased levels of learning, integration, and utilization of specific skills associated with the domain (see Table 30.1).

The matrix in Table 30.1 was in no way meant to be all-inclusive or universal in defining developmental treatment goals. As can be seen, many of the goals are specific to functioning within our program or reflective of the individual client's ability to learn and use information provided through different treatment interventions or curriculum that our program utilizes. That being said, we feel that even those developmental markers that are specific to progress in our program are reflective of broader developmental skills involving self-regulation, the development of personal boundaries, social cooperation, individuation, and effective pro-social problem solving. The matrix is used as an initial assessment tool that allows us to identify strengths and deficits in each domain within different settings (education, residential, medical, clinical) in the program and then identify and prioritize treatment goals by targeting the enhancement of skills/experiences in a particular domain phase or by providing the teaching, experience, support, and guidance needed to promote progress to the next phase in a particular developmental domain or domains. Additionally, utilizing the matrix as a *snapshot* of the adolescent's developmental progress also helps identify areas in need of additional intervention and support, along with possible concerns or areas of risk as the adolescent leaves the program and moves into the broader community. While the Developmental Matrix was created within the context of a residential treatment program for adolescents, it can easily be adapted to reflect treatment goals or specific developmental markers identified in community-based treatment settings for children, adolescents, and young adults. In using the Developmental Matrix in this manner, it may actually serve as a tool to negotiate a treatment contract with the adolescent, the family, and other involved systems (school, court, protective services, etc.) so that measures of treatment progress are clearly delineated and understood in the framework of broader developmental growth.

Table 30.1 Developmental Treatment Model: Phase-oriented program goals

	Phase 1	Phase 2	Phase 3	Phase 4
Self-Regulation	1. I can control my feelings and behavior but I need a lot of help so I don't have problems	1. I can manage my emotions and behavior even during exciting or difficult times by getting help from staff and thinking about the consequences	1. I have at least 3 self-calming activities that I use on my own	1. I take time most days to be calm and "mindful"
	2. I can name certain feelings and how they make my body feel	2. I use at least 3 different self-regulation activities and measure their effectiveness with the help of staff	2. I can make plans to deal with difficult situations and use them with adult or peer support	2. I can anticipate likely emotional responses to positive and negative events
	3. My feelings can get out of control all of the sudden	3. I can pay attention in class for at least 30 minutes at a time	3. I usually think before I act and consider the consequences of my actions for myself	3. I can use my plans to deal with difficult situations even without the help of others
	4. A lot of time I need help from someone to figure out how I'm feeling	4. I can play games or do activities without any problem most of the time (even if I lose)	4. I can identify and discuss my emotions after experiencing them	4. I usually think before I act and accurately understands consequences for my behavior and the impact of my behavior on others
	5. I can identify some triggers to problem behaviors but that doesn't help me stop the behavior	5. I made a plan to deal with things that trigger me and use it with adult help	5. I can have difficult feelings (anger, sadness, frustration, disappointment, anxiety) without a major behavior crisis or harming myself, others or destroying property	5. I can talk about my feelings and what caused them even when I'm upset
	6. I can recognize the physical sensations that accompany strong emotions	6. My mood does not change a lot from day to day	6. I have no problem playing a game or doing a task that takes an hour	6. I can work on a task or be part of an activity even when I'm worried about something else or frustrated
	7. I practice self –regulation skills when staff remind me	7. I don't let small disappointments or problems bother me all day	7. My mood can change without having behavior problems	7. Most days I feel my mood is pretty positive

(*continued*)

Table 30.1 (*Continued*)

	Phase 1	Phase 2	Phase 3	Phase 4
Attachment	1. I pay attention to others around me and what they are doing and saying 2. I participate in attunement exercises in group 3. I can share staff attention without getting jealous 4. I can name 3 things I'm good at 5. I can be around others without feeling nervous 6. I usually prefer to do things alone and not with others but will do things with peers if I am asked	1. I can interact with others for short periods during structured activities or games 2. I have relationships with adults who I can trust to take care of me 3. I can share the attention of staff w/other students most of the time without being jealous or bothered 4. I can name positive things about others 5. I can usually ask staff or others for help without misbehaving, being provocative, or being in crisis 6. I like to be helpful to others 7. I usually expect that other people will treat me well and fairly 8. I have peers who I enjoy doings things with	1. I like doing structured activities (group; games, etc.) and I can get along with others while doing them 2. I can tell how others are feeling by their voice, body language, and other non-verbal cues 3. I care about how my behavior affects others and will change my behavior to help them if it's something positive 4. I can name people who I know will help me 5. I can have a long conversation with certain adults and peers about important things 6. I can ask for help when I need it 7. Other people consider me a friend 8. I'd rather do things with others than by myself most of the time	1. I will talk with others and adjust conversations and behavior to different social situations and different relationships 2. I have age appropriate friendships 3. It upsets me when others are sad, worried, or hurt even if I'm doing OK 4. I care about how others feel even when I'm having difficulties 5. I have a best friend who also considers me a best friend 6. I can correctly anticipate how others are going to feel think, and respond about things that I say and do

Adaptive Living Skills

1. I can get through the daily routine & schedule but staff need to give me a lot of help and tell me what to do
2. I complete my hygiene and self-care with staff help.
3. I need rewards in order to complete tasks.
4. I usually need some help or directions from adults when I make choices
5. I need help to complete chores
6. I can do school work but I usually need the teacher to make me finish it all
7. I can put things where they belong after I use them

1. I can follow daily routines and complete tasks with minimal staff directives.
2. I complete hygiene and self-care skills with just a few reminders from staff
3. I complete my chores and tasks without asking for rewards.
4. I can set goals with staff and follow through
5. I can make good choices in relation to what I need but only with staff encouragement and added incentives.
6. I usually complete all of my school work
7. I like looking at vocational/job options and preferences and trying new ideas
8. I have tried to do new activities and develop new interests

1. I can follow a daily schedule and complete tasks on my own.
2. I complete hygiene and self-care independently
3. I can complete community-based tasks (e.g. shopping, appointments, food ordering with some adult help
4. I complete assignments without being told and
5. I ask for help when needed.
6. I can set realistic future goals for myself and make good choices in relation to my own needs with adult help.
7. I am developing job related skills with adult encouragement and direction.
8. I have interests and activities that I pursue on my own and practice regularly

1. I complete daily living tasks without help or reminders and help others with their responsibilities willingly.
2. I can complete most community based tasks and activities independently
3. I can use public transportation to get from one place to another
4. I am motivated to achieve my goals and do things to achieve them without having to be told.
5. I make realistic plans for the future.
6. I can make realistic school or job choices based on preferences and abilities
7. I have at least 3 leisure activities that I enjoy doing regularly. At least 1 involves activities with others

(continued)

Table 30.1 (*Continued*)

	Phase 1	Phase 2	Phase 3	Phase 4
Social	1. I like doing things alone but will play with others if I have to 2. I like taking part in structured activities 3. I will start short conversations about things that I need from others. 4. I can accurately describe appropriate social responses when presented with examples of different social situations even if I can't always do them 5. I keep appropriate physical boundaries most of the time w/direction from adults 6. I can handle community tasks and activities with staff planning, structure, and assistance despite even if I am anxious 7. I follow the rules because it keeps me out of trouble	1. I participate in specific play activity such as board games or athletics with minimal arguing, negative comments, or physical dysregulation 2. I can accurately describe social interactions that occur within the daily setting 3. I keep appropriate physical boundaries most of the time without adult or peers telling me 4. I enjoy community trips and activities when adults are present to help me 5. I think about the needs, feelings, and rights of others to follow program rules or the law 6. I accept responsibility for my behaviors without arguing most of the time 7. I have tried out for or joined an athletic team or social activity group 8. I introduce myself to new adults and peers that I meet 9. I accept feedback from adults without getting mad, embarrassed, or defensive	1. I will initiate play with adults and peers 2. I can have conversations about things other people are interested in 3. I can comfortably do activities in the community with some adult support and direction 4. I regularly maintain good physical boundaries 5. I consider the needs and feelings of others on a regular basis even if that person is not a friend or family 6. I almost always accept responsibility for my behavior without lying or blaming others 7. I try to learn from and change past negative behavior 8. I understand hints or indirect cues to adapt my behavior in different situations 9. I can be part of a group of friends	1. I comfortably take part in a wide variety of activities within the program and broader community 2. I interact comfortably and independently in the community 3. I can adapt my behavior to keep good personal 4. boundaries in different social situations 5. I believe in and apply the "The Golden Rule" in behavioral decision making and judgment. 6. I accept responsibility for my behaviors even when I expect negative consequences to come from that

(*continued*)

Cognitive

1. I understand program rules and restrictions
2. I can complete a single step task with instruction and coaching
3. I can pay attention in class more than 15 minutes at a time
4. I can name one goal for school, clinical, and residential progress
5. I know the difference between similarities & comparisons
6. I know the 10 Wise Ways in BrainWise

1. I make an effort to complete school work even if it's hard for me most of the time
2. I can stay involved in a task or instruction for 30 minutes without getting distracted
3. I can complete a single step task without help
4. I can organize school work, residential tasks, and clinical tasks with adult help
5. I can accurately remember information or use memory guides in school, therapy and social settings
6. I will follow suggestions and reminders to help me learn better and easier in school
7. I can put together a puzzle or model on my own

1. I complete my schoolwork almost all of the time
2. I can pay attentive to school work or an activity without reminders from adults
3. I use information and lessons learned in one setting or school subject and apply to another with adult direction
4. I use ideas from BrainWise to help solve problems and come up with a range of behavioral options
5. I use memory and learning skills that I learned in school to help me in other parts of my life
6. I can put together an item reading the instructions

1. I can think about the ways I make decisions and change things that don't work too well
2. Academic achievement commensurate with intellectual skills
3. I can organize tasks and solve problems on my own in ways that are effective and healthy
4. I use information from a variety of situations and topics and uses this information in school, relationships, social situations, and emotional problems
5. I can organize and complete a task that takes several days with little adult help

Table 30.1 (*Continued*)

	Phase 1	*Phase 2*	*Phase 3*	*Phase 4*
Healthy Sexuality	1. I understand Whitney's "Sexual Behavior Rules" 2. Any type of touch tends to makes me scared or sexually aroused 3. I admit my sexual behavior has hurt myself and others in the past 4. I want help in changing the sexual behavior that got me into trouble. 5. I understand and can describe the difference between abusive and non-abusive behavior 6. I want help in understanding and dealing with how I was hurt in the past 7. I want to learn more about sexual development and non-abusive sexual behavior	1. I understand how things that happened to me effect the way I have behaved sexually 2. I have learned about normal child and adolescent sexual development. 3. I can discuss sexual matters without becoming dysregulated, nervous or sexually pre-occupied 4. I can engage in sexual behavior without causing upset or harm to others physically, emotionally, socially 5. I can concentrate on other things during the day without always thinking about sex 6. I know that pornography does not show accurate or healthy sexual relationships 7. I can avoid using pornography when it is against the rules 8. I pay attention to my body and how it feels	1. I understand and can describe the effect of my abusive behavior on myself and others. 2. I can talk about how I was harmed by others and how it made me feel about myself and others 3. I keep clear, positive personal boundaries (relational/emotional/sexual) with others. 4. My sexual fantasies do not include violence, young children or things that are harmful to me or others 5. I have genuine sexual interest in age appropriate relationships. 6. I can avoid pornography when it is causing me problems 7. I am comfortable with my body and I can enjoy a lot of different physical sensations	1. I avoid mistreatment of others (sexual & otherwise) 2. I understand how to use contraception to prevent pregnancy and STD's. 3. I do not use sex as a way to get others to like me or pay attention to me 4. My history of victimization does not cause me to hurt myself or others in sexual and non-sexual ways 5. I can describe what I want from a healthy sexual relationship. 6. I am able to meet sexual needs in a positive, non-abusive manner. 7. I do not allow others to use me or abuse me sexually

Source: Whitney Academy (2016).

Treatment interventions from a developmental perspective

As noted earlier, while particular milestones, skills, and experiences may be recognized as promoting a positive developmental trajectory, the path to reaching those skills or integrating those experiences will vary greatly depending on the individual child, family, and environmental circumstances. There is no workbook or curriculum to follow when taking a developmental treatment approach, and interventions from a range of disciplines and treatment perspectives are frequently utilized. When developing a treatment plan or considering treatment interventions, we use our understanding of the tasks and skills associated with different stages of child development and our understanding of the process of neurodevelopment as an indication of where to focus treatment priorities and what type of treatment modality might best facilitate interventions.

From a child development perspective, this means attending to the earliest developmental tasks first (e.g., attunement, attachment, body awareness, self-regulation, delaying gratification) before moving to higher-level developmental tasks (e.g., empathy, learning and integrating social rules and skills, moral judgment). Obviously, when working with adolescents who have sexual behavior problems, there is frequently the need to address a variety of these issues simultaneously. However, taking a developmental approach helps the clinician, and the other involved systems, maintain a realistic perspective in terms of treatment progress by recognizing that in order for an adolescent to effectively integrate and utilize higher-level skills they must first build competency in the *foundation skills*.

In following a developmental approach to treatment, we feel the process of brain development, which can be broadly described as *bottom to top* (brain stem to neocortex), *right to left* (right hemisphere to left hemisphere), and *back to front* (occipital lobe to prefrontal cortex), provides something of a template for how developmental tasks and experiences are best learned and integrated. By maintaining a neurodevelopmental perspective, the clinician is encouraged to use multi-modal treatment interventions and guided toward focusing on more *bottom-up* interventions (e.g., body-based, sensory-based, and experiential) before *top-down* interventions (e.g., insight oriented, analytical, language loaded) especially when addressing early developmental deficits or gaps.

This approach also takes into account the ongoing research evidence indicating that one consequence of experiencing childhood trauma may be specific language-based learning deficits, meaning that many of the adolescents with whom we work can have a greater facility for visual learning, kinesthetic learning, and experiential learning than they do for verbal learning (de Bellis et al., 2009; Teicher et al., 2002). This would suggest that relying exclusively on *talk therapy* might actually limit progress for many of the clients and families we treat. Jensen (2005, 2000) also points out that all children and adolescents are likely to be more engaged in the learning process, and better able to integrate information when information is presented in a variety of modalities, and attention is paid to the factors that influence neurological processing.

It is critical to emphasize that the assessment and treatment process described above does not suggest that every adolescent begin treatment with a focus on the same issues and skills or with the same treatment interventions. Instead, treatment starts with an assessment of an adolescent's strengths and skills, while identifying those developmental gaps or deficits that may be creating obstacles to pro-social growth and progress.

As in the developmental process of any child, the progression of skills over a variety of developmental domains may be quite uneven; for example, an adolescent may have significant abilities in adaptive living skills and limited capacities for attachment, or they may have very advanced cognitive skills while having quite poor social skills. It is through engagement with the adolescent, family, school, and other involved systems using a developmental perspective that treatment needs and goals are prioritized. Frequently, the difficult task in this process is creating the proper balance that enables the adolescent to continue to explore and utilize their areas of developmental competency while 'back filling' enough of the foundation skills and experiences necessary for future growth and stability.

Case Study 30.1 Treatment at The Whitney Academy

Mike is a 15-year-old male referred to our treatment program following a failed placement in another residential setting and numerous psychiatric hospitalizations. Previous behavioral problems include physical aggression directed toward adults and peers, oppositional behavior, destruction of property, and self-harming behaviors such as scratching and cutting, without an apparent effort to be specifically suicidal. Mike also has a history of sexually assaulting a younger female cousin on at least two occasions. Mike has acknowledged that the sexual incidents between him and his cousin occurred, but he has at various times described the incidents as consensual. Mike is also reported to have engaged in sexual behavior with his roommate at a prior residential treatment facility and there are concerns that he may have engaged a younger, autistic brother in sexual behavior.

Mike was born one month prematurely to a mother with a history of alcoholism, bi-polar disorder, and numerous suicide attempts. His father was never actively involved in his life and has been absent since age one. His father was physically abusive to Mike's mother and is reportedly incarcerated. It appears that Mike experienced periods of abuse and neglect while in his mother's care. Mike's maternal grandparents have been separately involved in his life and Mike lived with his maternal grandmother for a period of one year and with his maternal grandfather for three years, all before the age of ten.

Mike had a very difficult history in school. He was frequently bullied and isolated. Attention problems and behavioral problems are regularly noted. His most recent intellectual assessment indicated a full-scale IQ of 74 with verbal skills (VCI = 8 9) being higher that his perceptual reasoning (PRI = 75). Matt's processing speed and working memory were also both in the borderline range of functioning.

Mike's maternal grandfather was an alcoholic. Reportedly while he was living with his grandfather, an aunt who was five years older than him sexually abused Mike. Overall, Mike's mother and maternal grandmother have remained involved, but boundaries are poor and the overall family environment is highly dysfunctional. Mike's first psychiatric hospitalization occurred at age ten, for threatening his mother with a knife and engaging in self-injurious behavior. Following hospitalization, he was placed in a residential treatment setting. At this program, Mike was psychiatrically hospitalized several times for brief periods and eventually hospitalized for six months at age 11. Once back at the residential program he was hospitalized several more times, the last time being for 13 months.

During his first two weeks in our program, Mike was broadly compliant with the daily routine. He did evidence occasional panic attacks when he was expected to participate in certain activities throughout the day. In school, verbal power struggles with teachers were not infrequent and these sometimes escalated into Mike becoming oppositional and verbally threatening. Physically, Mike is somewhat short and severely overweight. Generally, Mike walks with his shoulders slumped and his head down, making only occasional eye contact. Mike tried to present to peers as if he were very "street-wise" and gang involved, but rather than increase his status among his peers they would dismiss him as being a fraud.

During his third week in the program, Mike began refusing to take his medication and he started refusing to eat, taking in only small amounts of water. He gouged his leg with a wooden stick and became physically assaultive to staff, including head-butting, punching, and spitting. Mike voiced that we would have to send him to the hospital and that he was going to slowly kill himself by not eating. Mike's not eating lasted three days, the self-harming and physically aggressive behaviors extended over two weeks. Mike was regular monitored by medical staff and was placed on 'one to one' with residential staff during this period. Staff would sometimes need to physically intervene with Mike if he were trying to harm himself or someone else. These physical holds were typically brief and involved two staff simply holding Mike's arms while standing on either side of him. Mike would not struggle during these times and the need for any type of physical intervention with Mike soon diminished.

Our initial assessment of Mike utilizing the Developmental Matrix had placed him on Phase 1 in attachment; Phase 1 in self-regulation; Phase 2 in cognitive skills; Phase 2 in social skills; Phase 2 in adaptive living skills; and Phase 1 in healthy sexuality. Mike had shown some capacity for self-regulation during his first two weeks in the program, but his ongoing anxiety with peers and staff and his general mistrust of others had placed him in a situation where he was not only "defending" himself against anticipated rejection and failure but he was actively trying to leave the program by engaging in behavior that had worked before: aggression, self-harm, and oppositional behavior. The primary focus for treatment interventions was to provide safety by focusing on a consistent predictable schedule, clear (non-crisis driven) behavioral expectations, consistent opportunities for attunement/attachment, and actively teaching Mike ways he could regulate his physiological state and his behavioral responses and while still remaining safe.

Mike was assigned a peer mentor and was roomed with two other adolescents who were behaviorally stable and had developed good relationships with staff. These peers made sure that Mike isolated himself less frequently during activities and they supported him to make better choices regarding his behavior. In group therapy, there was an emphasis on experiential exercises that focused on accurately identifying emotions in oneself and others, psycho-education about how early "bad" experiences impact your body and brain, and how to develop alternative problem solving options when the ones you usually use are not working. These interventions often involved play, charades, role-play, and giving the group outdoor tasks and challenges that they needed to solve as a group. Individually, the focus was on body posture, sensory activities, biofeedback (HRV), and brief mindfulness-based activities to help Mike develop a greater sense of connection and control of his body and his emotions.

Within the first six months, Mike's behavior had stabilized, he was making consistent academic effort and was showing that his academic competencies were significantly better than his prior assessments had indicated. We discovered that once Mike was less hyper-vigilant and hyper-aroused, his concentration and ability to apply himself to tasks and activities significantly improved. Mike had developed some peripheral friendships with other adolescents in his home. He was an active participant in group and individual therapy and he had started family therapy with his mother. Mike became quite good at recognizing the physical cues of his anxiety and had developed active ways to manage these situations, modulating both his physical state and his behavioral responses. Mike is still prone to exaggerating conflicts with peers or staff in an effort to get his therapist or other staff to "pay attention" to him. However, these "crises" are now relayed verbally and do not entail behaviors that harm himself or others. He can speak about how these feelings of being ignored or not attended to arise when he sees staff whom he values attending to other peers. Mike can acknowledge that he will "create a crisis" to reassure himself that staff will respond to his needs. These attachment dynamics remain at the core of Mike's treatment and we regularly work to highlight these patterns when they appear in therapy, family relationships, and peer relationships, with a focus on how you can feel attended to, valued, and cared for without having to be in crisis.

Nine months into treatment, Mike is beginning Phase 3 of self-regulation and healthy sexuality; and is in the midst of working on Phase 3 in adaptive living skills, social skills, and cognitive skills. Mike is actively working on attunement and attachment but this remains an area where there is a great deal of variability in terms of maintaining progress. Mike now exercises more regularly, has lost some weight, and joined the program's basketball team (which he is quite proud of). Academically, he has improved two grade levels and talks about enjoying school. He has also reached a point in his family treatment where he wants to begin talking with his mother about how he wants to maintain a relationship with her but does not think that going back home to live is a good option for him. For her part, Mike's mother has become more positive and supportive of Mike's progress and more open about listening to Mike's concerns and needs regarding his relationship with her and the broader family.

If we were to consider the content of Mike's treatment, we might think that there has been a relatively small level of focus on the specific details of his sexually abusive behavior and his own sexual victimization. Treatment interventions have been more heavily focused on body-based aspects of self-regulation, improving his peer relationships, enhancing his academic functioning, and facilitating a sense of being accepted, connected, valued, and supported by the adults in his immediate environment. Mike has been involved in discussions regarding adolescent sexual development, and positive sexual behavior and sexual relationships without an expectation that he would divulge the specifics of his offenses or the details of his own trauma history. Mike appears to have a greater sense of his own competence, has experienced some success, and has some positive relationships with peers and adults. He has indicated that he is now ready to directly address the behaviors and experiences that precipitated his initial referral to our program.

Mike's path forward is not completely clear and certainly there remains a considerable amount of work to do. He will need to bridge the gains he has made in a residential setting to an increasing level of community-based, independent functioning. Systemically, social service agencies will need to provide the planning, resources, and support necessary to create a structure that enhances Mike's continued progress. Mike may remain with our program anywhere from an additional six to nine months. The focus of treatment during that time will likely be his family relationships, his physically and sexually assaultive behavior, and his own history of trauma. However, all of that will take place in the context of providing continued positive experiences in school, with peers, and with the adults who are responsible for his care and safety on a daily basis.

The role of supportive systems and the environment

The final component of a developmental treatment approach is understanding that child and adolescent development does not occur in a vacuum, and therefore to facilitate optimal development we need to engage, utilize, and assist the family systems, school systems, and other involved social systems in providing the necessary structure, support, resources, and care that enable developmental growth and progress. In some cases, this will mean not only providing treatment, education, and guidance but also providing advocacy for adolescents and their families to receive basic needs and services (Saxe, Ellis, & Kaplow, 2007). Research has already shown that treatment outcomes for youth with sexual behavior problems is enhanced when families are actively engaged in treatment (Borduin, Schaeffer, & Heiblum, 2009; Worling, Litteljohn, & Bookalam, 2010).

However, in a large number of cases we continue to usher young people into group treatment models that do little to involve families in their child's care and even less to address environmental and family system changes that may need to occur in the home (Huey, Henggeler, Brodino, & Pickrel, 2000; Schladale, 2006). Borrowing from the Trauma Systems Therapy Approach outlined by Saxe et al. (2007), our developmental treatment model seeks to assess the family's capacity to meet the adolescent's needs for safety, structure, supervision, and care in the context of the adolescent's current developmental needs. Just as in normal child development, the more limited the developmental capacities of the individual child (regardless of age), the greater the need will be for adult engagement, direction, support, and supervision. Conversely, a higher degree of developmental skills would suggest that families might focus on facilitating later developmental tasks, such as increased personal responsibility, improved independent decision making, pro-social peer affiliation, and a greater degree of moral development.

As noted earlier, our clients frequently experience learning difficulties, some of which may be the result of their own histories of neglect, abuse, and other types of trauma. If we are going to address and support developmental progress, treatment providers need to be actively engaged in educating and supporting schools to be places where our clients experience safety, acceptance, and competence. Too often, adolescents in our care are simply viewed as behavioral management problems with little motivation for or investment in academic progress. My experience is that many of the adolescents I treat have come to see school as places where they regularly experience failure, criticism, rejection, and (at times) threat. Providing schools with information about the learning difficulties associated with trauma and its neurodevelopmental impact, while also assisting them in developing effective teaching and behavior management strategies for these students, can enable schools to become partners in the developmental process rather than obstacles.

Providing judges, probation officers, and social service workers with a view of our clients through a developmental lens in our assessments, case formulations, and treatment plans encourages a coordinated and systemic response to treatment needs and provides for a more accurate understanding of future risk involving sexual offending and general delinquent behaviors (Caldwell, 2007; Reitzel & Carbonell, 2006; Spice, Viljoen, Latzman, Scalora, & Ullman, 2013). There is, I believe, a strong need within the field to stop conceptualizing *risk* as a set of personality dynamics, historical experiences, and set of behaviors encapsulated in the adolescent that results in the individual being labeled as *high*, *medium*, or *low* risk and rather evaluate risk through a perspective that assesses the adolescents strengths, capacities, and limitations in the context of the environmental demands we are expecting them to meet, and the environmental supports and resources the system is capable of providing. This makes for a more realistic assessment and also rightfully identifies the responsibilities of the adolescent, the family, and the supporting systems in ensuring safety and progress.

Conclusions

Sexuality and sexual behavior are basic elements of our human make-up and as such form an integral part of who we are and how we develop. Sexual behavior is also used to meet a wide range of needs beyond our basic biological needs. Connection, acceptance, nurturance, caring, competence, and self-worth are only some of the emotional needs that our sexual interactions with others can sometimes be used to fulfill. In our efforts to alert society at large to the prevalence of sexually abusive behavior and the harm it can cause, we (as a field) have promoted the need for the specialized treatment of sexual behavior problems and the specialized training of the providers of that treatment. In doing so, we have served to raise awareness, support research, and encourage treatment for those individuals who engage in harmful sexual behavior. However, we have also engaged in a process that may have distorted our own perspective on sexual behavior and that tends to isolate research and progress in the field of sexual offender treatment from research and knowledge available from other fields of study. I believe this is especially true when it comes to our treatment of children and adolescents who engage in problematic or harmful sexual behavior.

Adjusting the Lens

807

Research from the fields of neuroscience, education, developmental psychology, sociology, and trauma so obviously overlap with what we are trying to address in our understanding and treatment of sexually abusive behavior that we severely hamper our clients and ourselves if we are not incorporating this information into our practice. More importantly, if we lose sight of the fact that self-regulation, social skills, empathy, personal responsibility, and moral judgment are skills that emerge and develop over time and through a process, then we seriously risk distorting our view of the adolescents we treat and encourage the broader society to do so as well. At present, this distortion has led to social policy and legal system responses that appear to do nothing to promote community safety and even less to support developmental progress in the youth we treat. We have long understood that a variety of developmental variables influence this behavior, we are learning more about how these variables impact neurodevelopment and in turn, learning and behavior. It is important that we directly articulate that understanding in our treatment models and in our systemic responses to children and adolescents with sexual behavior problems.

Recommended Reading

The Adverse Childhood Experiences (ACE) Study. Retrieved from http://www.cdc.gov/violenceprevention/acestudy/. *This is one of the largest investigations ever conducted to assess associations between childhood maltreatment and later life health and wellbeing. The study is a collaboration between the US Center for Disease Control and Kaiser Permanente's Health Appraisal Clinic in San Diego. The sample for the study includes more than 17,000 individuals undergoing a comprehensive physical examination who chose to provide detailed information about their childhood experience of abuse, neglect, and family dysfunction. The study findings suggest that certain experiences are major risk factors for the leading causes of illness and death, as well as poor quality of life. The ACE Study uses the ACE Score, which is a total count of the number of ACEs reported by respondents. The ACE Score is used to assess the total amount of stress during childhood and has demonstrated that as the number of ACE increase, the risk for a range of learning, behavioral, mental, and physical health problems increases in a strong and graded fashion.*

De Bellis, M.D., Woolley, D.P., & Hooper, S. (2013). Neuropsychological findings in pediatric maltreatment: relationship of PTSD, dissociative symptoms, and abuse/neglect indices to neurocognitive outcomes. *Child Maltreatment, 18,* 171–183. *The authors examine the impact of maltreatment on a range of neuropsychological and neurocognitive functions including IQ, attention, visual-spatial skills, memory, language, and academic achievement. The study compares the functioning of maltreated children with a control group, but it also provides a comparison between these groups and a group of maltreated children with PTSD. The two maltreated groups perform significantly lower than the controls on IQ, academic achievement, and almost all of the neurocognitive domains. The authors argue that all children identified by protective services should be assessed for the integrity of their neuropsychological functioning and academic skills.*

De Hann, M., & Gunnar, M. (Eds.) (2009). *Handbook of developmental social neuroscience.* New York, NY: Guilford Press. *De Hann and Gunnar have compiled a volume that explores the dynamic relationship between biology and social behavior from infancy through adolescence. Leading researchers discuss key processes in typical and atypical development. The chapters examine how complex social abilities emerge from basic brain circuits; whether there are elements of social behavior that are "hard wired" in the brain; and how the impact of early experiences can shape neurodevelopment and ongoing social behaviors.*

Hart, S. (2011). *The impact of attachment.* New York, NY: Norton Press. *The author, a Danish psychologist, integrates a discussion of attachment theory with research in neurobiology and behavioral theories to examine normal child development and a range of relational and behavioral problems. What emerges is a useful guide for how to apply neurodevelopmental research from an attachment-based perspective in clinical practice.*

Hart, H., & Rubia, K. (2012). Neuroimaging of child abuse: A critical review. *Frontiers in Human Neuroscience, 6,* 1–24. *The authors, both neuroscientists at King's College in London, summarize the current evidence for the effects of child maltreatment on brain structure, cognition, and behavior in children and adolescents. They identify a wide range of neuropsychological and neuroimaging studies that show an association between child maltreatment and a number of cognitive and structural deficits. However, the authors also note some limitations to these abuse-related studies, most notably accounting for the impact the presence of comorbid psychiatric disorders on these effects. The review highlights what the authors view as the better controlled studies and outlines the neuropsychological and structural effects that appear most clearly supported by the present research.*

References

Aguilar, B., Sroufe, L. A., Egeland, B., & Carlson, E. (2000). Distinguishing the early-onset/persistent and adolescence-onset antisocial behavior types: From birth to 16 years. *Development and Psychopathology, 12,* 109–132.

American Academy of Pediatrics. (2002). *The psychological maltreatment of children – technical report.* Retrieved from http://pediatrics.aapublications.org/content/109/4/e.68.full.html.

Bales, K., & Carter, C.S. (2009). Neuroendocrine mechanisms of social bonds and child-parent attachment, from the child's perspective. In M. DeHann & M. Gunnar (Eds.), *Handbook of developmental social neuroscience* (pp. 246–264). New York, NY: Guilford Press.

Barbaree, H. E., Marshall, W. L., & McCormick, J. (1998). The development of sexually deviant behavior among adolescents and its implications for prevention and treatment. *Irish Journal of Psychology, 19,* 1–31.

Bonta, J., & Andrews, D. A. (2010). Viewing offender assessment and rehabilitation through the lens of the Risk-Need-Responsivity Model. In F. McNeill, P. Raynor, & C. Trotter (Eds.), *Offender supervision: New directions in theory, research and practice* (pp. 19–40). Oxon: Willan Publishing.

Borduin, C. M., Schaeffer, C. M., & Heiblum, N. (2009). A randomized clinical trial of multisystemic therapy with juvenile sexual offenders: Effects on youth social ecology and criminal activity. *Journal of Consulting and Clinical Psychology, 77,* 26–37.

Bowlby, J. (1969). *Attachment and loss. Volume I: Attachment.* New York, NY: Basic Books.

Bowlby, J. (1973). *Attachment and loss. Volume II. Separation, anxiety and anger.* New York, NY: Basic Books.

Bowlby, J. (1980). *Attachment and loss. Volume III. Loss, sadness and depression.* New York, NY: Basic Books.

Center for Disease Control (2013). Adverse childhood experiences study: Major findings. Retrieved from http://www.cdc.gov/ace/findings.htm.

Creeden, K. (2006). Trauma and neurobiology: Considerations for the treatment of sexual behavior problems in children and adolescents. In R. Longo and D. Prescott (Eds.), *Current perspectives: Working with sexually aggressive youth and youth with sexual behavior problems.* Holyoke, MA: NEARI Press.

Creeden, K. (2013). Taking a developmental approach to treating sexual behavior problems. *International Journal of Behavioral Consultation and Therapy, 8,* 12–16.

De Bellis, M. D., Hooper, S., Spratt, E., & Woolley, D. P. (2009). Neuropsychological findings in childhood neglect and their relationships to pediatric PTSD. *Journal of the International Neuropsychological Society, 15*, 868–878.

De Bellis, M. D., Keshavan, M., Clark, D., Casey, B., Giedd, J., Boring, A., ... Ryan, N. (1999). Developmental traumatology. Part II: Brain development. *Biological Psychiatry, 45*, 1271–1284.

Egeland, B., Carlson, E., & Sroufe, L. A. (1993). Resilience as process. *Development and Psychopathology, 5*, 517–528.

Fonagy, P., Gergely, G., Jurist, E., & Target, M. (2004). *Affect regulation, mentalization, and the development of the self.* New York, NY: Other Press.

Hanson, J. L., Chung, M. K., Avants, B. B., Shirtcliff, E. A., Gee, J. C., Davidson, R. J., & Pollak, S. D. (2010). Early stress is associated with alterations in the orbitofrontal cortex: A tensor-based morphometry investigation of brain structure and behavioral risk. *Journal of Neuroscience, 30*, 7466–7472.

Hart, S. (2011). *The impact of attachment.* New York, NY: Norton Press.

Heller, L., & LaPierre, A. (2012). *Healing developmental trauma: How early trauma affects self-regulation, self-image, and the capacity for relationship.* Berkley, CA: North Atlantic Books.

Hofer, M. A. (2006). Psychobiological roots of early attachment. *Current Directions in Psychological Science, 15*, 82–88.

Hudson, S. M., & Ward, T. (2000). Interpersonal competency in sex offenders. *Behavior Modification, 24*, 494–527.

Huey, S., Henggeler, S., Brodino, M., & Pickrel, S. (2000). Mechanisms of change in multi-systemic therapy: Reducing delinquent behavior through therapist adherence and improved family and peer functioning. *Journal of Consulting and Clinical Psychology, 68*, 451–467.

Institute for Human Services (2007). *Developmental milestones chart.* Retrieved from www.rsd.k12.pa.us/Downloads/Development_Chart_for_Booklet.pdf.

Jensen, E. (2000). *Different brains, different learners: How to reach the hard to reach.* San Diego, CA: The Brain Store.

Jedd, K., Hunt, R. H., Cicchetti, D., Hunt, E., Cowell, R. A., Rogosch, F. A., ... Thomas, A. M. (2015). Long-term consequences of childhood maltreatment: Altered amygdala functional connectivity. *Developmental Psychopathology, 27*, 1577–1589.

Knight, R. A., & Sims-Knight, J. E. (2004). Testing an etiological model for male juvenile sexual offending against females. *Journal of Child Sexual Abuse, 13*, 33–55.

Latham, C., & Kinscherff, R. (2012). *A developmental perspective on the meaning of problematic sexual behavior in children and adolescents.* Holyoke, MA: NEARI Press.

Marsa, F., O'Reilly, G., Carr, A., Murphy, P., O'Sullivan, M., Cotter, A., & Hevey, D. (2004). Attachment styles and psychological profiles of child sex offenders in Ireland. *Journal of Interpersonal Violence, 19*, 228–251.

Marshall, W. L., & Marshall, L. E. (2000). The origins of sexual offending. *Trauma, Violence, and Abuse: A Review Journal, 1*, 250–263.

Masten, A., & Coatsworth, J. D. (1998). The development of competence in favorable and unfavorable environments: Lessons from research on successful and unsuccessful children. *American Psychologist, 53*, 205–220.

Mayes, L., Magidson, J., Lejuez, C., & Nicholls, S. (2009). Social Relationships as Primary Rewards: The Neurobiology of Attachment. In M. DeHann & M. Gunnar (Eds.), *Handbook of developmental social neuroscience* (pp. 342–377). New York, NY: Guilford Press.

McGrath, R., Cumming, G., Burchard, B., Zeoli, S., & Ellerby, L. (2010). *Current practices and emerging trends in sexual abuser management: The Safer Society 2009 North American Survey.* Brandon, VT: Safer Society Press.

McLaughlin, K. A., Green, J. G., Gruber, M. J., Sampson, N. A., Zaslavsky, A. M., & Kessler, R. C. (2012). Childhood adversities and first onset of psychiatric disorders in a national sample of US adolescents. *Archives of General Psychiatry, 69*(11), 1151–1160.

Middlebrooks, J. S., & Audage, N. C. (2008). *The effects of childhood stress on health across the lifespan*. Atlanta, GA: Center for Disease Control and Prevention and National Center for Injury Prevention and Control.

Moffitt, T. E., (1993). Adolescence-limited and life-course-persistent antisocial behavior: A developmental taxonomy. *Psychological Review, 4*, 674–701.

Moody, K. C., Holzer, C. E. III, & Roman, M. J. (2000). Prevalence of dyslexia among Texas prison inmates. *Texas Medicine, 96*, 69–75.

National Child Traumatic Stress Network. (2003). *Report of the Complex Trauma Task Force*. Durham, NC and Los Angeles, CA: National Center for Child Traumatic Stress.

O'Connor, T. (2005). Attachment disturbances associated with early severe deprivation. In C. S. Carter, L. Ahnert, K. Grossman, S. Hardy, M. E. Lamb, … N. Sachser (Eds.), *Attachment and bonding: A new synthesis* (pp. 257–267). Cambridge, MA: MIT Press.

Ogden, P., & Fisher, J. (2015). *Sensorimotor psychotherapy: Interventions for trauma and attachment*. New York, NY: W.W. Norton:

Perry, B. (2001). The neurodevelopmental impact of violence in childhood. In D. Schetky & E. Benedek (Eds.), *Textbook of child and adolescent forensic psychiatry* (pp. 221–238). Washington, DC: American Psychiatric Press.

Pine D. S., Mogg K., Bradley B. P., Montgomery L. A., Monk C. S., McClure E., … Kaufman J. (2005). Attention bias to threat in maltreated children: implications for vulnerability to stress-related psychopathology. *American Journal of Psychiatry, 162*, 291–296.

Pollak, S., & Kistler, D. (2002). Early experience is associated with the development of categorical representations for facial expression and emotion. *Proceedings of the National Academy of Sciences, 99*, 9072–9076.

Porges, S. (2011). *The Polyvagal Theory: Neurological foundations of emotion, attachment, communication, and self-regulation*. New York, NY: WW Norton.

Prasad, M., Kramer, L.A., & Ewing-Cobbs, L. (2005). Cognitive and neuro-imaging findings in physically abused pre-schoolers. *Archives of Disease in Childhood, 90*, 82–85.

Prentky, R. A., & Righthand, S. (2003). *Juvenile sex offender assessment protocol: Manual*. Bridgewater, MA: Justice Resource Institute.

Raine, A., Mellingen, K., Liu, J., Venables, P. H., & Mednick, S. A. (2003). Effects of environmental enrichment at 3–5 years on schizotypal personality and antisocial behavior at ages 17 and 23 years. *American Journal of Psychiatry, 160*, 1627–1635.

Reitzel, L. R., & Carbonell, J. L. (2006). The effectiveness of sexual offender treatment for juveniles as measured by recidivism: A meta-analysis. *Sexual Abuse: A Journal of Research and Treatment, 18*, 401–421.

Resnick, M., Harris, D. L., & Blum, R. (1993). The impact of caring and connectedness on adolescent health and well-being. *Journal of Pediatrics and Child Health, 29*, 53–59.

Sachser, N., Durschlag, M., & Hirzel, D. (1998). Social relationships and the management of stress. *Psychoneuroendochrinology, 23*, 891–904.

Saxe, G., Ellis, B. H., & Kaplow, J. (2007). *Collaborative treatment of traumatized children and teens: The trauma systems therapy approach*. New York, NY: Guilford Press.

Scheeringa, M. (2011). PTSD in children younger than the age of 13: Toward developmentally sensitive assessment and management. *Journal of Child and Adolescent Trauma, 4*, 181–197.

Schladale, J. (2006). Family matters: The importance of engaging families in treatment with youth who have caused sexual harm. In R. Longo & D. S. Prescott (Eds.), *Current perspectives: Working with sexually aggressive youth and youth with sexual behavior problems* (pp. 493–514). Holyoke, MA: NEARI Press.

Schore, A. N. (2002). Dysregulation of the right brain: A fundamental mechanism of traumatic attachment and the psychopathogenesis of posttraumatic stress disorder. *Australian and New Zealand Journal of Psychiatry, 36,* 9–30.

Schwartz, B., Cavanaugh, D., Prentky, R., & Pimental, A. (2006). Family violence and severe maltreatment in sexually reactive children and adolescents. In R. Longo and D. S. Prescott (Eds.), *Current perspectives: Working with sexually aggressive youth and youth with sexual behavior problems* (pp. 443–472). Holyoke, MA: NEARI Press.

Scott, E., & Grisso, T. (1997). The evolution of adolescence: A developmental perspective on juvenile justice reform. *Journal of Criminal Law and Criminology, 88,* 137–189.

Scott, E. S., & Steinberg, L. (2008). Adolescent development and the regulation of youth crime. *The Future of Children, 18,* 15–33.

Siegel, D. (1999). *The developing mind: Toward a neurobiology of interpersonal experience.* New York, NY: Guilford Press.

Spice, A., Viljoen, J., Latzman, N., Scalora, M., & Ullman, D. (2013). Risk and protective factors for recidivism among juveniles who have offended sexually. *Sexual Abuse: A Journal of Research and Treatment, 25,* 347–369.

Sroufe, L. A. (2000). Early relationships and the development of children. *Infant Mental Health Journal, 21,* 67–74.

Sroufe, L.A., Duggal, S., Weinfield, N., & Carlson, E. (2000). Relationships, development, and psychopathology. In A. Sameroff, M. Lewis, & S. Miller (Eds.), *Handbook of developmental psychopathology* (2nd ed.). New York, NY: Kluwer Academic/Plenum Publishers,

Stinson, J., & Becker, J. (2013). *Treating sexual offenders: An evidence-based model.* New York: Guilford Press.

Streeck-Fischer, A. & van der Kolk, B. (2000). Down will come baby cradle and all: Diagnostic and therapeutic implications of chronic trauma on child development. *Australian and New Zealand Journal of Psychiatry, 34,* 903–918

Teicher, M., Andersen, S., Polcari, A., Andersen, C., & Navalta, C. (2002). Developmental neurobiology of childhood stress and trauma. *Psychiatric Clinics of North America, 25,* 397–426.

Tupler, L. A., & de Bellis, M.D. (2006). Segmented hippocampal volume in children and adolescents with posttraumatic stress disorder. *Biological Psychiatry, 59,* 523–529.

Umhau, J., George, D., Reed, S., Petrulis, S. G., Rawlings, R., & Porges, S. (2002). Atypical autonomic regulation in perpetrators of violent domestic abuse. *Psychophysiology, 39,* 117–123.

Vermont Department of Corrections (2000). *Facts and Figures: FY 2000.* Retrieved from http://doc.vermont.gov/about/reports/ff-archive/facts-and-figures-2000/view.

Ward, T., & Stewart, C. A. (2003). The treatment of sex offenders: Risk management and good lives. *Professional Psychology: Research and Practice, 34,* 353–360.

Worling, J. R., & Curwen, T. (2001). Estimate of Risk of Adolescent Sexual Offense Recidivism (Version 2.0: The "ERASOR"). In M. C. Calder (Ed.), *Juveniles and children who sexually abuse: Frameworks for assessment* (pp. 372–397). Lyme Regis, Dorset: Russell House Publishing.

Worling, J. R., Litteljohn, A., & Bookalam, D. (2010). 20-year prospective follow-up study of specialized treatment for adolescents who offended sexually. *Behavioral Sciences and The Law, 28,* 46–57.

Part VI

Ethical, Legal, and Political Implications

31

The Impact of Neglect, Trauma, and Maltreatment on Neurodevelopment

Implications for Juvenile Justice Practice, Programs, and Policy

Bruce D. Perry, Gene Griffin, George Davis, Jay A. Perry, and Robert D. Perry

Key points

- Insights from neuroscientific research into brain development, brain functioning, and traumatology should inform juvenile justice practice, programs, and policy.
- Although our knowledge base about the brain is in its infancy, to date it provides valuable insights into the origins of criminal behavior.
- Neurodevelopmental organization of the brain evolves from lower to higher regions of the brain and is shaped by experience.
- If a child experiences adversity, his/her potential is impacted with profound effects on development, which include functioning of the neural networks involved in mediating the stress response.
- The brain and body have widely distributed systems that mediates the stress response and can be impaired by developmental trauma.
- Arousal response and dissociation are the two major and interactive adaptive response patterns to a significant threat. The arousal response prepares the individual to fight or take flight. The dissociative response is engaged when fighting is futile or fleeing not possible, and it is hypothesized that it helps the individual prepare to survive injury.
- Both the arousal and dissociative response can become sensitized so that future stressors activate the most common adaptive response.

The Wiley Blackwell Handbook of Forensic Neuroscience, First Edition. Edited by Anthony R. Beech, Adam J. Carter, Ruth E. Mann and Pia Rotshtein.
© 2018 John Wiley & Sons Ltd. Published 2018 by John Wiley & Sons Ltd.

- If a youth develops sensitized stress reactivity, he/she will be more likely to demonstrate regressed, impulsive, and reactive behaviors, which has important implications for understanding how they will process, learn, and react in a juvenile justice system.
- Individuals with a relational history characterized by abuse and inconsistency will create relational associations that are negative and when interacting with others is likely to be threat inducing and dysregulating where intimacy is associated with threat and loss and where infringement of personal space violations can trigger aggressive and violent behavior.
- Compromised executive functioning in the brains of youth who experienced childhood trauma mean they are more likely to have poor judgment, be impulsive, and engage in high-risk behaviors.
- Implications of a neurodevelopmental perspective for the juvenile justice system comprise:
  - child protection is crime prevention;
  - punitive practices are not rehabilitative and often create new problems;
  - trauma-informed interventions should be favored;
  - relational health should be at the center of interventions with juveniles; and
  - justice models should fully incorporate neurodevelopmentally aware and trauma- informed practice into juvenile justice models.

Terminology Explained

Adverse childhood experiences (ACEs) can lead to greater risk for numerous problems in later life. The original ACE study (Felliti et al., 1998) demonstrated a correlation between childhood adversity and risk for physical health problems. Since that time this set of epidemiological studies has been instrumental in helping shape a broader understanding of the role of developmental trauma in shaping emotional, social, cognitive, and physical health.

The **amygdala** is a complex structure situated deep within the temporal lobe. This area's functions are related to arousal, interpretation of potential threat-related cues, and multiple other sensory-regulatory functions, including mediating responses associated with fear, emotion, and memory. It is *not* the "fear center" – it does, however, play a major role in mediating stress-related and threat-related functioning.

Executive functioning is an umbrella term for the management (regulation, control) of cognitive processes, including working memory, reasoning, flexibility, problem solving, and planning. The development of executive functioning can be profoundly impaired by disorganizing or dysregulating input from sensitized stress response systems.

Neuroplasticity is an umbrella term referring to the capacity of neurons and neural networks to change in response to microenvironmental (e.g., stimulation by

The Impact of Neglect, Trauma, and Maltreatment 817

neurotransmitters, neuromodulators) and macroenvironmental (e.g., complex sensory signals created by human to human interactions) experience. The malleability of neural networks confers remarkable adaptive qualities to human beings, allowing the ongoing capacity for learning and healing from adversity.

The reticular activating system (RAS) is a set of inter-connected nuclei originating in lower areas of the brain (i.e., brainstem and diencephalon) that collectively play a major role in arousal and regulation of transitions (including sleep), and influence "upstream" functioning of many other areas in the brain (including limbic and cortical systems). Dysfunction of subsystems of the RAS are hypothesized to be involved in many neuropsychiatric conditions including post-traumatic stress disorder.

State-dependent functioning refers to the important role that an individual's "state" plays in determining which neural networks in the brain are activated or de-activated. The most obvious example is sleep; key areas in the brain are "shut down" and others are activated. Similarly, activation of the stress response networks in response to threat will activate some areas (e.g., locus coeruleus, amygdala) and shut down others (e.g., various cortical regions). All functioning of the brain – emotional, social, cognitive, and behavioral – is sensitive to "state." The implications for juvenile justice are profound.

Introduction

Over the last 20 years, advances in neuroscience have provided invaluable insights that have implications for understanding human development and behavior. Among these insights is the profound impact that childhood trauma and maltreatment have on the brain; this, in turn, plays a major role in creating complex and multi-dimensional problems that impact every sector of our society including the juvenile justice system. This includes the myriad disciplines involved in family courts, juvenile justice, and the adult criminal justice systems. This chapter will present some key concepts related to brain development, brain functioning, and traumatology that provide invaluable perspective when crafting juvenile justice practice, programs, and policy. Some of the key implications of this neurodevelopmental perspective are summarized in Box 31.1.

Box 31.1 Key implications of a neurodevelopmental perspective for the juvenile justice system

1 Child protection is crime prevention. Early identification of risk and diversion are cost- and person-effective strategies.
2 Punitive practices do not build new skills or promote healthy development; they do not lead to effective remediation or rehabilitation. Punitive practices often create new problems including aggression and make existing issues

worse. Simply stated, punitive practices do not result in the intended decrease in recidivism, and offending, or promote rehabilitation.
3. Respectful, relationally enriched, humane and trauma-informed interventions will have highest probability of success.
4. Promoting relational health by increasing the quality, number, and density of supportive, nurturing and trauma-informed people is the most effective and enduring form of intervention. Connection to family, community, and culture facilitate healthy development, including healing from traumatic experiences, minimizing substance abuse, and developing of new skills.
5. Total systemic exposure to – and adoption of – neurodevelopmentally aware and trauma-informed practices will be essential for juvenile justice models to optimize outcomes for individuals and for society.

Neurosciences are just beginning to unravel the astounding complexity of the human brain (e.g., Johnson, Blum, & Giedd, 2009). For a tiny taste of its structural complexity, consider that there are approximately 86 billion neurons and up to 400 trillion synapses in the human brain (Azevedo et al., 2009; Herculano-Houzel, 2009); add to this the *dynamic* complexity of always active, always changing

Developmental insult types *A wide range of developmental insults contribute to serious emotional, social, and behavioral problems. These include intrauterine insults such as exposure to alcohol or other drugs of abuse; disruptions of attachment that may be caused by various factors such as postpartum depression or domestic violence; and neglect and various forms of trauma such as physical, sexual, and emotional abuse.*

Source: © Lightwise. Used under license from 123RF.

neural networks – there are roughly 2.5 quadrillion neuronal depolarizations per minute (e.g., Whalley, 2013). In a recent interview regarding progress in neuroscience, Dr. Jeff Lichtman stated, "if understanding everything there is to know about the brain is one mile ... we have come about three inches." (*National Geographic: A Voyage into the Brain*).[1]

Despite the infancy of our knowledge base about the functioning of the brain, there are multiple useful concepts and principles that can help us better understand the origins of antisocial, impulsive, and illegal behaviors. These same concepts can help us better craft practices, programs, policy, and law to: 1) minimize the development of maladaptive, antisocial behaviors; and 2) remediate, educate, and heal those who exhibit these behaviors.

We believe that a neurodevelopmental perspective can add to an understanding of antisocial, criminal, and offending behaviors. The purpose of this chapter is to provide an overview of some key principles of neurobiology that can contribute to creating more developmentally-aware and trauma-informed practices within the juvenile justice system.

Key Principles of Neurobiology

Brain development: Timing and process

The brain develops most rapidly in the first five years after conception, but it continues to have important maturational changes through young adult life – primarily increased myelination in pre-existing neural networks (see Geidd et al., 1999). In general, neurodevelopmental organization proceeds from lower, central to higher, outer structures (i.e., brainstem to cortex) and is greatly influenced by experience. A key principle of development and neuroplasticity is use-dependence – neural networks change with activation or lack of activation (for more detailed discussion, see Perry, 2002). While core processes in neurodevelopment are genetically mapped, the final phenotypic expressions of brain-mediated capabilities are very experience dependent. When developing neural networks receive patterns of stimulation during sensitive and critical periods in development, they will organize, modify, and become optimally functional. The actual neural architecture of the brain – and the resulting functional capabilities – mirrors the nature, timing, and pattern of experience. When a child grows up in a family and community enriched in healthy relational interactions that provide (among basic physical needs) cognitive, motor, and social stimulation, he/she will have a higher probability of expressing their potential to become creative, productive, and humane. When a child experiences chaos, neglect, threat, violence, and other developmental adversities, his/her potential is blunted. This disrupted development is often expressed as undeveloped, fragmented, or maladaptive functioning in emotional, cognitive, and behavioral domains.

The long-term consequences of developmental maltreatment and adversity are complex and heterogeneous (see Perry, 2002, 2009). In fact, an in-depth study of the differential effects of the nature, timing, and quantity of adversity, as well as the impact potential of attenuating or resilience-related factors on development has really just begun (see Perry, 2006, 2009). While there is so much more to know, what we do know is that trauma, neglect, and maltreatment during childhood have profound

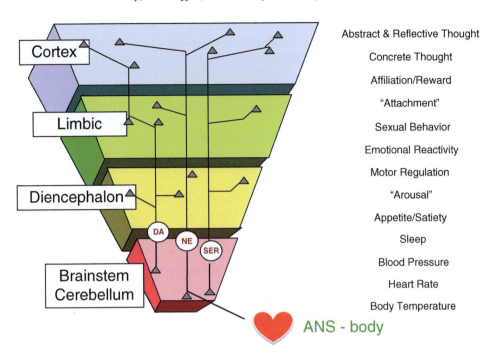

Figure 31.1 Efferent distribution of key regulatory networks.
Source: Bruce D. Perry © 2010–2015.
Note: NA: norepinephrine; DA: dopamine; SER: serotonin; ACH: acetylcholine.

effects on physical, social, emotional, behavioral, and cognitive development (e.g., Anda et al., 2006). Some of the mechanisms related to these developmental adversities are related to the neural networks involved in mediating the stress responses.

The brain is organized in a hierarchy that develops in a sequential manner. Figure 31.1 shows the four developmentally distinct regions (brainstem, diencephalon, limbic, and cortical) are woven together by multiple neural networks. The monoamine and other related systems originate in lower brain areas and have widespread impact on widely distributed upstream systems in the brain and the downstream systems of the body. These regulatory networks play a role in integrating, processing, and acting on incoming patterns of neural activity from the primary sensory networks (such as touch, vision, and sound that monitor the external environment), somatic networks (such as motor-vestibular, cardiovascular, and respiratory that monitor the internal environment) and cerebral networks (such as cortical modulating networks that monitor the brains internal environment). This ongoing, dynamic input from the brain, body, and world is integrated, processed, and acted on to help regulate the individual.

Impact of trauma and neglect on the stress response systems

Some of the primary neural systems impacted by developmental trauma are those involved in the stress response (see Perry, Stolk, Vantini, Guchait, & Prichard, 1983;

Perry & Pollard, 1998). The brain and body have a set of widely distributed systems that mediate the stress response; this involves the neuroendocrine, neuroimmune, central, and autonomic nervous systems (see Figure 31.1). Several important monoamine (adrenergic, noradrenergic, and dopaminergic), cholinergic, and serotonergic neural networks originate in lower areas of the brain (brainstem and diencephalon) and send projections upstream to essentially all other regions of the brain, and downstream to the neuroendocrine and autonomic nervous systems, which communicate with and influence the regulation of the rest of the body (e.g., Dautan et al., 2014; Huang, Ghosh, & van den Pol, 2006; Sara & Bouret, 2012; Schiff et al., 2012).

This complex and diverse distribution gives these centrally located networks a unique role in the stress responses; rapid activations and deactivations of various neural and physiological functions can be coordinated and regulated by these networks. Further, all incoming sensory input from the body and from the outside world directly communicates with these neural networks that are key components of the reticular activation system (RAS) (see Steriade, 1996). The RAS is essential for regulation of multiple arousal-related functions including sleep, attention, vigilance, reward anticipation, reward, and interpretation of threat (Kinomura, Larsson, Gulyas, & Roland, 1996). Through these and related mechanisms, the development and regulation of the monoamine, serotonergic, and cholinergic networks of the lower brain are essential to hundreds of important brain-mediated functions. When these systems develop normally, there can be smooth integrated regulation of cognition, emotional regulation, social interactions, motor movements, and dozens of other functions essential to healthy human development and functioning. When the development or regulation of these systems is altered, a cascade of functional deficits can result.

As already mentioned, neural networks are plastic – they are malleable; neural number, physical structure of the neuron including dendritic and synaptic density, and structure all change with various patterns of activation. One determinant of how the neural networks change is the pattern of activation (see Figure 31.2).

As Figure 31.2 shows, two very different effects on the sensitivity of the stress response systems can be created with different patterns of activation. The tolerance-inducing pattern that leads to resilience involves smaller, predictable doses of challenge or stress and the sensitizing pattern associated with vulnerabilities involves unpredictability and more severe or prolonged activation.

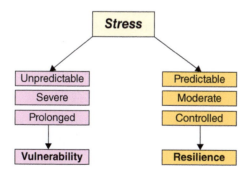

Figure 31.2 Variable effects of stress response activation.
Source: Bruce D. Perry © 2007–2014.

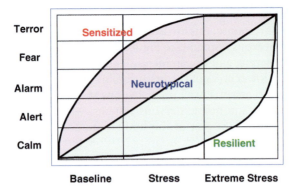

Figure 31.3 Differential stress reactivity.
Source: Bruce D. Perry © 2007–2014.

The variable impact of different patterns of activation on the monoamine and serotonergic networks that are crucial to the stress response has been a focus of research in animal models since the 1980s (e.g., Farfel, Kleven, Woolverton, Seiden, & Perry, 1992; Kalivas & Stewart, 1991; Kleven, Perry, Woolverton, & Seiden, 1990) and in humans over the last 20 years (e.g., Perry & Pollard, 1998; Steketee & Kalivas, 2011). One clinically relevant feature of the stress response systems is their malleability; basically, how reactive and responsive they are to stimulus (stressor) can be modified by activation (see Steketee & Kalivas, 2011). By activating the stress- response systems in moderate, controllable, and predictable doses the sensitivity of these systems decreased; the individual is more capable of tolerating a dose of stressor. This capability is related to the ability to demonstrate resilience in the face of significant or extreme stress (Ungar & Perry, 2012). In turn, the activation of these systems in variable, unpredictable, or extreme patterns will lead to a host of molecular and physiological changes that make these systems sensitized; the baseline level of activity is increased and for any given stimulus (stressor) there will be a more extreme (and disproportional) response. This has profound clinical implications (see Figure 31.3 and Table 31.1).

Figure 31.3 illustrates three stress-reactivity curves; the middle straight line indicates a neurotypical relationship between the level of external challenge, stress, or threat and the appropriate proportional shift in internal state required to adapt, adjust, and cope with the level of stress; with minor stressors, there are minor shifts in the internal state and with major stressors a larger shift in internal state is required. The upper (sensitized) curve illustrates the distorted, sensitized stress-reactivity curve that results from patterns of extreme, unpredictable, or prolonged stress activation such as is seen in many youth and adults in the juvenile and criminal justice systems. In this case, there is a significant overactivity at baseline and an overreaction even in the face of relatively minor challenges. All learning – social, emotional, behavioral, or cognitive – requires exposure to novelty; in turn, novelty will activate the stress response systems. In an individual with neurotypical reactivity this will create a moderate, but manageable, dose of stress. Repetition with novelty (such as in an academic setting – or certain therapeutic situations) will ultimately lead to a tolerance pattern (see Figure 31.2) and the capacity to demonstrate resilience (lower curve). In contrast, a sensitized individual will find the introduction to simple challenges such as transitions, new academic

Table 31.1 State-dependent functioning

Sense of Time	Extended Future	Days Hours	Hours Minutes	Minutes Seconds	No Sense Of Time
Arousal Continuum	REST	FLOCK/VIGILANCE	RESISTANCE Crying	DEFIANCE Tantrums	AGGRESSION
Dissociative Continuum	REST	AVOIDANCE	COMPLIANCE Robotic	DISSOCIATION Fetal Rocking	FAINTING
Regulating Brain Region	NEOCORTEX Cortex	CORTEX Limbic	LIMBIC Diencephalon	DIENCEPHALON Brainstem	BRAINSTEM Autonomic
Cognitive Style	ABSTRACT	CONCRETE	EMOTIONAL	REACTIVE	REFLEXIVE
Internal State	CALM	ALERT	ALARM	FEAR	TERROR

Source: adapted, with permission, from Perry, B. D. (2008).

concepts, and complex or unpredictable social situations overwhelming – even fear inducing, thereby inhibiting opportunities for normal social, emotional, and cognitive development. We hypothesize that this is one of the primary mechanisms underlying many of the emotional, behavioral, and developmental problems seen in the juvenile justice population.

The individual's response to any significant stressor will vary depending upon many factors including pre-existing stress response sensitivity, the presence of relational buffers, and the nature of the stressor (for review, see Perry, 2008). Whether the threat is immobilizing, painful, prolonged, avoidable, interpersonal, a natural disaster, unexpected, or anticipated are among the many features that will determine the specific recruitment of the body's heterogeneous stress response capabilities. There are two major and interactive adaptive response patterns to significant threat: the arousal response and dissociation. The arousal response activates the individual and prepares them to flee or fight (see Perry, Pollard, Blakely, Baker, & Vigilante, 1995; Perry, 2008). Dissociation is less well characterized and is engaged when there is a perception that fighting is futile or fleeing impossible; the dissociative response is more internalizing and is hypothesized to help the individual prepare to survive injury. Peripheral blood flow decreases, heart rate goes down, and the release of endogenous opioids and dissociation at the cognitive and emotional level occurs. In many cases, both of these adaptive responses will be activated during the same complex traumatic experience.

Both response patterns can become sensitized such that future stressors or challenges will activate the most common adaptive pattern used in a similar situation in the individual's past. In combination with state-dependent shifts in cognition and behavior, this can lead to impulsive, aggressive, and maladaptive antisocial behaviors (e.g., a young boy growing up in a domestic violence situation who used a fight or flight response during those traumatic experiences may respond to authoritarian males – even when they are not being threatening – with hostility and aggression).

State-dependent functioning of neural systems

When challenged with a variety of stressors (including perceived threat), the body responds in an adaptive fashion, making changes in the state of arousal (mental state), mode of thinking (cognition), and physiological activation (e.g., increased heart rate, muscle tone, rate of respiration). In response to a challenge, or overt threat, the mental and physical state will move along an arousal continuum – from calm to arousal, then to alarm, fear, and terror (see Table 31.1).

Different individuals may have different styles of adaptation to threat depending upon a wide range of factors, including age, nature of threat, history of previous exposure to trauma, and gender (see Perry et al., 1995; Perry, 2008). Some use a primary hyperarousal response, others a primary dissociative response. Most use some combination of these two adaptive styles in any typical traumatic experience. When an individual grows up in an unpredictable, chaotic, or threatening environment, his/her stress response systems become sensitized (see Figure 31.3).

As this takes place, different networks in the brain will shut down and others will be recruited (Hermans et al., 2011). While clearly over-simplifying the process, the more threatened the individual feels, the more their functioning shifts from higher, more complex, and mature cortical networks to lower and more reactive networks (see Hermans et al., 2011; Perry et al., 1995; Perry & Pollard, 1998). The more threatened, the more primitive (or regressed) thinking and behaving becomes. An individual in a state of alarm will be less capable of concentrating, more anxious, and more attentive to non-verbal cues, such as tone of voice, body posture, and facial expressions. This has important implications for understanding the way the youth in a juvenile justice system will process, learn, and react in a given situation. The sensitized youth will be more likely to demonstrate regressed, impulsive, and reactive behaviors. If the youth was maltreated in the context of their primary caregiving relationships (discussed further in the following section), a neutral or minimally negative relational interaction can be enough to move the individual along this arousal continuum and result in maladaptive social interactions and very impulsive (often aggressive) responses. A simple redirection, reminder of rules, or expressions of frustration can precipitate a major behavioral outburst. This state-dependent functioning of a sensitized stress response that has been associated with previous interpersonal harm is one of the main reasons that contingency-based points/level programs not only do not build skills but tend to escalate youth and make it more likely that they will behave in regressive and aggressive ways (discussed further in the following section; Mohr, Martin, Olson, Pumariega, & Branca, 2009). One key to understanding traumatized youth is to remember that they will often, at baseline, be in a state of low-level fear – responding by using either a hyperarousal or a dissociative adaptation – and that their emotional, behavioral, and cognitive functioning will reflect this regressed state.

Neurosociology: Importance of relational neurobiology

Humans are a social species. The glue of a civil society is the capacity to form and maintain healthy relationships with some empathic perspective for others (see Szalavitz & Perry, 2010). Without this fundamental capacity, human interactions are characterized by selfish, manipulative, and exploiting behaviors. Others are viewed as less valuable or worthy; the result can be antisocial or even abusive, aggressive behaviors to satisfy self-interests. The creation of a core neurobiological capacity for healthy, empathic relationships requires healthy caregiving and parenting. Furthermore, the development of resilient stress and relational neural networks depends upon attentive, attuned, and responsive caregiving (see Beeghly, Perry, & Tronick, 2016). With these early relational experiences, an infant can develop the neurobiological capacity to form and maintain healthy relationships, to share, to become empathic, to love, and to become a productive member of a community (see Szalavitz & Perry, 2010).

The patterned, repetitive bonding interactions of the attentive, attuned, and responsive caregivers creates an internal catalogue of associations with human relational cues (e.g., tone of voice, eye contact, touch) and helps organize key areas of the brain involved in stress reactivity, reward, and relational functioning, including the amygdala. (see Szalavitz & Perry, 2010; Tronick & Perry, 2015). The size of the amygdala (a brain area very involved in interpreting and acting on threat-related cues) in adult life, for example, correlates positively with the size and complexity of social networks (Bickart, Wright, Dautoff, Dickerson, & Barrett, 2011). For individuals with relational histories of inconsistent or abusive care (all too common in youths and adults in the justice system), relational associations will be negative; interacting with others will likely be threat inducing and dysregulating. Intimacy becomes associated with threat and loss, not comfort and safety. This has profound clinical implications; among them is an alteration of the sense of personal space.

Each of us has a sense of physical boundaries; when another person is approximately three meters away this is considered a social space; when someone gets within 1.2 meters (approximately) this is our personal space and within 0.5 meter is intimate space (for more on the study of personal space or proxemics, see Hall, 1966). The closer someone becomes to us, the more vigilant we become, the more the amygdala will activate. We may feel significantly threatened by the proximity if we have not invited the person to be so physically close (see Kennedy, Gläscher, Tyszka, & Adolphs, 2009).

Table 31.1 shows that different individuals may have different styles of adaptation to threat depending upon a wide range of factors, including age, nature of threat, history of previous exposure to trauma, and gender (see Perry et al., 1995; Perry, 2008). Some use a primary hyperarousal response, others a primary dissociative response. Most use some combination of these two adaptive styles in any typical "traumatic" experience. When an individual grows up in an unpredictable, chaotic, or threatening environment, his/her stress response systems become sensitized (see Figure 31.3).

An inter-related concept, the intimacy barrier, focuses on both personal and emotional space boundaries (see Perry, Hambrick, & Perry, 2016). The emotional component of this barrier can include any topics (e.g., sexuality) or personal issues (e.g., weight, cultural or religious beliefs) that you hold as personal and intimate. When the intimacy barrier is crossed without permission (e.g., someone makes a negative comment about race or religion or for a child in the child welfare system someone asks about your family), the individual feels threatened. The stress response systems (including the amygdala) activate (see Kennedy et al., 2009) and the individual will engage in protective behaviors. The nature of these protective behaviors will vary depending upon: 1) the sensitivity of the individual's stress response system (see Figure 31.3); and 2) the adaptive preferences the individual may have developed based upon earlier developmental trauma (see Table 31.1; Perry, et al., 1995; Perry & Pollard, 1998).

If the individual utilizes a freeze/flight/fight response, when someone crosses this barrier, verbalizations (e.g., raised voice, profanity, threats) or behaviors (e.g., pushing, hitting) may be used to attempt to push the offending person back across the intimacy barrier. If the predominant style of adaptation is dissociation, the person will avoid social interactions. If this is not possible, he may passively disengage. It can be very confusing for peers, carers, and educators when their intended nurturing behaviors and words are met with either overt hostile and aggressive behavior or indifferent and dismissive attitudes.

It is important to note that not all people share the same sensitivity or threshold for what is an intimacy barrier violation. Consider what happens if an individual has both early attachment problems and a sensitized stress response system –as do many youths in the juvenile justice system (see Amatya & Barzman, 2012; Kenny, Blacker, & Allerton, 2014; Levy & Orlans, 2000;). In the same way, a combat veteran may be emotionally and behaviorally reactive when re-exposed to cues or triggers associated with combat (e.g., gunfire, the sound and feel of a helicopter), the individual with attachment problems and relationally-mediated abuse will find relational cues (e.g., eye contact, tone of voice, touch, and physical proximity) threatening. A person with a high degree of relational sensitivity will often misinterpret neutral or positive social interactions from peers as threatening and respond by either avoiding or disengaging (which leads to problems with social learning and peer interactions) or, worse, by using aggressive, hostile, or hurtful words or behaviors to push peers, teachers, and parents away. In extreme cases, as the child grows up, this relational sensitivity can result in significant antisocial or even assaultive behaviors. It is no surprise therefore that individuals in prison (90% of whom have histories of interpersonal trauma in child-hood) have a much larger sense of personal space than the average person (Wormith, 1984), and will often respond to personal space violations with aggressive and violent behaviors.

Impaired cortical development and executive functioning

The majority of research in this area suggests that the neuropsychological factors involved in offending behavior include compromised executive functioning (weaker cortically-mediated functions) in combination with an increase in impulsivity and other dysregulated diencephalon/brainstem mediated functions (see Perry, 2009; Piquero, Jennings, & Farrington, 2010). These neuropsychological characteristics are all well-documented sequelae of childhood trauma and maltreatment and the expected result of impaired cortical development in the face of: 1) higher probabilities of chaotic and cognitively impoverished environments; and 2) impaired cognitive stimulation seen with chronic dysregulation and sensitization of the stress response systems (Perry et al., 1995; Perry & Pollard, 1998; Perry, 2009; Perry & Dobson, 2013).

Executive functioning is a rough indicator of the strength of cognitive regulatory capacity relative to the dysregulation (i.e., disorganization, under-development, impairment) of lower networks in the brain; in essence, it is an estimate of how hard it is for an individual to use cortical (top-down, flexible, future-oriented, rational) mechanisms to self-regulate. This capability is related to self-control indicators (Moffit et al., 2011; Piquero et al., 2010) known to be predictive of positive outcomes in high-risk children. In order for an individual to function in any cognitive-predominant activity (i.e., following directions, attend in a classroom) he/she needs the capacity for cortical (top-down) regulation. The older a child gets, the more we expect them to be capable of listening, following directions, sitting for sustained periods of time, and learning. These are all challenging tasks for many severely maltreated children as both youths and adults in the justice systems (Hanson & Morton-Bourgon, 2005; McGarvey, 2012). These youths often think and behave in a much less mature man-ner than their chronological age – the result can be a toxic negative feedback cycle of adults (teacher, staff member, parole officer, judge) getting frustrated, angry, confused, and demoralized while the youth feels stupid, inadequate, misunderstood, rejected, and unloved. All of this just creates more threat, loss, rage, and chaos – reinforcing and adding to their history of developmental adversity and distrust of the adults in the system.

Optimal self-regulation and executive functioning cannot be reached until well past adolescence. Simply stated, the brain of a youth will be more likely to lead to poor judgment and impulsive, high-risk behaviors – and this is under typical developmental conditions. Maltreatment and trauma will predictably delay or interrupt this process and result in emotional, social, cognitive, and behavioral functioning that is well below the chronological age of the youth. The result may be a 15-year-old with the self-control of a two-year old and the reasoning capacity of a six-year old. Unfortunately, while most youths in the juvenile justice system have these splinter developmental capacities, we create expectations, programs, practice, and policy based upon their chronological age; and the outcomes from these efforts predictably fail.

Implications for the juvenile justice system

The principles of neurobiology outlined above are neither comprehensive nor fully elaborated, yet they provide important insights for forensic mental health and the juvenile justice system. Some of the primary policy, program, and practice implications will be outlined here. At the core of these implications is the knowledge that the vast majority of individuals in the juvenile and adult criminal justice system have experienced significant developmental adversity and, often, overt trauma as children (e.g., Abram et al., 2004; Baglivio, Epps, Swartz, Huq, Sheer, & Hardt, 2014; DeLisi et al., 2010; Hawkins et al., 2000; Kerig & Becker, 2010).

Children, youths, and adults are at greater risk for health, behavioral, emotional, and social problems following adverse childhood experiences (ACEs) (see Felliti et al., 1998; Anda et al., 2006) (see Box 31.2). Children, youth, and adults in the criminal justice systems are all too often growing up in these fragmented childhoods with very high rates of exposure to violence, sexual and physical victimization, and other adversities (Abram et al., 2004; Kerig, 2012a, 2012b). A recent study examined the prevalence of ACEs in juvenile offenders in Florida (Baglivio et al., 2014).

Box 31.2   Categories of ACEs

1   *Emotional abuse.*
2   *Physical abuse.*
3   *Sexual abuse.*
4   *Emotional neglect.*
5   *Physical neglect.*
6   *Family violence.*
7   *Household substance abuse.*
8   *Household mental illness.*
9   *Parental separation or divorce.*
10   *Household member incarceration.*

Very high rates of adversity were documented, with fewer than 5% of this population reporting no history of an ACE. Further, Baglivio et al. (2014) found that "Of the 13,692 females with one or more ACE indicators, 92% reported at least two ACEs, 80% reported at least three, 63% reported at least four, and 46% reported five or more. Of the 48,844 males who reported at least one ACE indicator, 89% reported two or more, 71% reported three or more, 48% reported four or more, and 28% reported five or more."

The adversities reported in this population are associated with significant long-term risk for health, mental health, academic, social, and antisocial behaviors (see Anda et al., 2006; Fellitti et al., 1998). These adverse life events would result in sensitization of the stress response system and, often, disruptions of neurotypical development of relational neurobiology as discussed above. Taken together, these developmental adversities are likely to be major factors in the etiology of the dysregulated, impulsive, substance-using, and antisocial behaviors which increase the probability that these children and youth would be involved in the mental health, healthcare, and juvenile justice systems. Earlier in life, the anxiety, depression, hopelessness, and disconnection, which are manifestation of these trauma-related changes in the brain, often can lead to increased risk for school failure, social and behavioral problems, and self-medicating use of alcohol and drugs. This, of course, can cascade into the actions that lead to involvement in the juvenile justice system. Early in life these are treated as mental health and educational problems, but as children get older the very same trauma-related issues enter the arena of truancy, assault, possession, and use of illicit substances, defacing of public property, and so forth.

Prevention, early identification, and diversion

The primary policy implications of a neurodevelopmental perspective are to focus on prevention of the predisposing vulnerabilities associated with impulsive, reactive, aggressive, and antisocial behaviors. A focus on policy and law related to employment, housing, poverty, and a host of contributing factors that put early childhood and young vulnerable families at greater risk seems sensible and just.

Early childhood provides unique opportunities for prevention and diversion due to the increased malleability of the brain during this time in life. By the time a child is four years old, more than 80% of the primary neural architecture has been established. The primary implication of this is that experiences of early childhood – good and bad – will have a disproportionate influence on shaping the individual. Early identification of struggling families, home visitation, economic and housing supports, high-quality early childhood programs, and trauma-informed pre-school programs can all divert young children from trajectories that increase risk for health, academic, emotional, and social problems, including ending up in the juvenile justice system (e.g., Schweinhart and Weikart, 1993; Walker et al., 2011; Campbell et al., 2014).

Sentencing and intervention

What should a society do with children and youth who commit crimes? In the USA, children and youth have always been viewed as different from adults with regard to judgment, reasoning, and culpability under the law (see Griffin & Sallen, 2013; Steinberg & Scott, 2003). And clear cognitive impairment or obvious mental illness – both neurobiological conditions – have always been taken into consideration in sentencing. As we learn more about the brain and its development, the courts in the USA have considered this knowledge. In recent landmark cases, including Supreme Court cases, the neurodevelopmental immaturity of the adolescent cortex plays a role in judgment and impulsivity and has been cited in modifying sentencing guidelines (*Graham v. Florida*, 2011; *Miller v. Alabama*, 2012). There is an increasing awareness by the

Judiciary that developmental trauma is a crucial factor in considering assessment and treatment of the youth in the juvenile justice systems. It remains to be seen how and if the core learnings from this young area of clinical neuroscience will begin to inform case law and the legislation (Arredondo, 2003; National Child Traumatic Stress Network, 2008).

Curiously, despite the well-documented under-development of the adolescent cortex and the knowledge that the most common neuropsychological deficits in the juvenile justice population include executive functioning problems, the majority of treatment approaches and programs are based upon top-down, cortex-dependent therapies and strategies. These include a cognitive focus on changing distortions in thinking to modifying maladaptive behaviors through role-playing and reinforcement to the use of multi-systemic therapy focusing on the offender, their family, and larger community. Cognitive behavioral therapy (CBT) seems to be the most widely used in treatment of offenders, whether juvenile or adult. This effort to use cognitive methods to change thinking and behavior has been shown to have some modest level of success in lowering recidivism rates – from 1.4% to 8.2%, compared to 14% in the larger population of offenders (Hanson & Morton-Bourgon, 2005). However, these treatment programs have been applied to offending populations as if they are a homogeneous group. Considering the complexities of development, the variable nature and timing of adversity and attenuating factors, the population in the juvenile justice system is far from homogeneous.

Fishbein and Sheppard (2006) examined the role of neuropsychological functioning in inmates' response to various forms of treatment. They observed that neuropsychological deficits including impulsivity, difficulties in social-emotional regulation, and attention play an important role in the behavioral outcomes for the inmates studied. With an understanding that there exist identifiable subgroups within inmate populations, they expose a critical need to better assess youth entering the juvenile justice system; they are clearly not a homogeneous group. The ability to identify fundamental differences between offenders who respond to standard correctional therapies and those who do not is of prime importance if more effective treatments are to be designed. Without the ability to understand the underlying strengths and weaknesses of youthful offenders, programs and interventions will continue to be applied in a one-size-fits-all manner and recidivism rates will continue to be high.

In the last decade, trauma-informed programs and practices have been developed and applied in juvenile justice systems (e.g., Ford, Chapman, Hawke, & Albert, 2007; Ford & Blaustein, 2013; Griffin, Germain, & Wilkerson, 2012; Perry & Dobson, 2013). In all of these approaches there is recognition of the need to assess the trauma history, identify the strengths and vulnerabilities of the youth, and target interventions to, initially, address the regulation problems. Further, all of these trauma-informed interventions are moving away from punitive and contingency-based program elements and towards more attachment aware, relational approaches. Considering the neurobiological factors outlined above these are sound strategies.

As we have discussed in earlier sections, many studies have demonstrated that youth in the juvenile justice system have high rates of attachment problems. And the frequency of transgenerational trauma, neglect, substance use and abuse, domestic violence, and other factors that disrupt optimal early bonding experiences is very high in the juvenile justice population. This has a number of primary implications. The stress response systems of these individuals will be more sensitized and overly reactive leading to a host of problems with learning, social development, and self-regulation (e.g., more impulsive reactive and less rational behaviors), and typical relationally-mediated rewards that serve to shape behavior during development will be less effective. Further than just suggesting that respectful, relationally-based approaches will be effective, these neurodevelopmental principles predict that typical contingency-based and punitive interventions will be ineffective and even inappropriate with these individuals (Mohr et al., 2009). This is of utmost importance in the area of rehabilitation and remediation. Currently, in the US and many other countries, points and level systems permeate the juvenile justice programs and rely on a set of practices that will predictably escalate and further dysregulate traumatized or maltreated youth.

Common practices such as mandatory shackling in court or solitary confinement are punitive and potentially destructive (Griffin & Wolff, 2015); they reinforce old maladaptive patterns of coercive and abusive interactions with adults and may create new traumatic experiences further compromising potential for healthy development and functioning. Juvenile justice practice elements that are punitive or operant based: 1) have no capacity to generalize any behavior changes outside of the specific context of the program or setting; 2) do not create internal motivation that will provide the moral and social values to modify self-absorbed, antisocial or illegal behavior; 3) do not teach new skills; and 4) will predictably escalate and further dysregulate a youth who has trauma-related problems, resulting in higher rates of aggression, impulsivity, non-compliance, and learning problems. In other words, practices, policy, and law that are not developmentally respectful and trauma-informed, while well-intended, will not help children and youths in the juvenile justice system and will frequently make their complex problems worse.

Conclusions

Understanding an individual's path to the present will be the best way to create effective approaches, supports, interventions, and resources to help them succeed. This means that a developmentally informed assessment with a focus on trauma and on potential resilience-related factors must be part of an effective juvenile justice program. Any one-size-fits-all intervention or punishment will not be effective. Individualized, humane, and developmentally matched interventions will have a higher probability of success (see Table 31.1). In contrast, developmentally mismatched and non-trauma-informed interventions will have minimal probability of success; they may provide temporary containment, isolation, or retribution but they cannot provide long-term meaningful change that will ultimately enhance or protect the community.

Note

1   See https://www.mcb.harvard.edu/archive/jeff-lichtman/.

Recommended Reading

Steinberg, L., & Scott, E. S. (2003). Less guilty by reason of adolescence: Developmental immaturity, diminished responsibility, and the juvenile death penalty. *American Psychologist, 58,*

1009–1018. *Steinberg looks at issues of normal development as applied to juvenile justice. Recognizing that the adolescent does not yet have fully developed cortical capacity and therefore aspects of cognition including judgment will be relatively "diminished." The authors argue that these factors should be considered in sentencing.*

Anda, R. F., Felitti, V. J., Bremner, J. D., Walker, J. D., Whitfield, C., Perry, B. D., ... Giles, W. H. (2006). The enduring effects of abuse and related adverse and epidemiology. *European Archives of Psychiatry and Clinical Neuroscience, 256*, 174–186. *This is a review of the ACEs studies and an outline of possible mechanisms that may be related to the observed correlations between childhood adversity and emotional, behavioral, social, and physical health problems later in life.*

Perry, B. D., & Dobson, C. (2013). Application of the neurosequential model (NMT) in maltreated children. In J. Ford & C. Courtois (Eds.), *Treating complex traumatic stress disorders in children and adolescents* (pp. 249–260). New York, NY: Guilford Press. *This is an overview and example of how a developmentally informed and trauma sensitive assessment and treatment model can be applied in complex children and youth. This is an example of the kind of assessment that can be used to understand the individual needs and strengths of youth in ways that will allow an individualized treatment approach.*

Griffin, G., & Sallen, S. (2013). Considering child trauma issues in juvenile court sentencing. *Children's Legal Rights Journal, 34*, 1–22. *This is an overview and discussion of the need to incorporate a developmental and trauma-informed approach to youth in the juvenile justice system. Without the trauma "lens" misunderstanding of behavior can lead to ineffective and excessively punitive practices which are unlikely to help the youth or, ultimately, society.*

References

Abram, K. M., Teplin, L. A., Charles, D. R., Longworth, S. L., McClelland, G. M., & Dulcan, M. K. (2004). Posttraumatic stress disorder and trauma in youth in juvenile detention. *Archives of General Psychiatry, 61*, 403–410.

Amatya, P., & Barzman, D. H. (2012). The Missing link between juvenile delinquency and pediatric posttraumatic stress disorder: An attachment theory lens. *International Scholarly Research Network Pediatrics, 2012*, 1–6.

Anda, R. F., Felitti, V. J., Bremner, J. D., Walker, J. D., Whitfield, C., Perry, B. D., ... Giles, W. H. (2006). The enduring effects of abuse and related adverse and epidemiology. *European Archives of Psychiatry and Clinical Neuroscience, 256*, 174–186.

Arredondo, D. E. (2003). Child development, childrens' mental health and the juvenile justice system: Principles for effective decision-making. *Stanford Law and Policy Review, 14*, 13–28.

Azevedo, F. A., Carvalho, L. R., Grinberg, L. T., Farfel, J. M., Ferretti, R. E., Leite, R. E., ... Herculano-Houzel, S. (2009). Equal numbers of neuronal and nonneuronal cells make the human brain an isometrically scaled-up primate brain. *Journal of Comparative Neurology, 513*, 532–541.

Baglivio, M. T., Epps, N., Swartz, K., Huq, M. S., Sheer, A., & Hardt, N. S. (2014). The prevalence of adverse childhood experiences (ACE) in the lives of juvenile offenders. *Journal of Juvenile Justice, 3*, 1–23.

Beeghly, M., Perry, B. D., & Tronick, E. (2016). Self-regulatory processes in early development. *Oxford Handbooks Online*. Oxford: Oxford University Press. Retrieved from http://www.oxfordhandbooks.com/view/10.1093/oxfordhb/9780199739134.001.0 001/oxfordhb-9780199739134-e-3&gt.

Bickart, K. C., Wright, C. I., Dautoff, R. J., Dickerson, B. C., & Barrett, L. F. (2011). Amygdala volume and social network size in humans. *Nature Neuroscience, 14*, 163–164.

Campbell, F., Conti, G., Heckman, J. J., Moon, S. H., Pinto, R., Pungello, E., & Pan, Y. (2014). Early childhood investments substantially boost adult health. *Science, 343,* 1478–1485.

Dautan, D., Huerta-Ocampo, I., Witten, I. B., Delsseroth, K., Bolam, J. P., Gerdjikov, T., & Mena-Segovia, J. (2014). A major source of cholinergic innervation of the striatum and nucleus accumbens originates in the brainstem. *Journal of Neuroscience, 34,* 4509–4518.

DeLisi, M., Drury, A. J., Kosloski, J. E., Caudill, E. W., Conis, P. J., Anderson, C. A., ... Beaver, K. M. (2010). The cycle of violence behind bars: Traumatization and institutional misconduct among juvenile delinquents in confinement. *Youth Violence and Juvenile Justice, 8,* 107–121.

Farfel, G., Kleven, M. S., Woolverton, W. L., Seiden, L. S., & Perry, B. D. (1992). Effects of repeated injections of cocaine on catecholamine receptor binding sites, dopamine transporter binding sites and behavior in *rhesus* monkeys. *Brain Research, 578,* 235–243.

Fellitti, V. J., Anda, R. F., Nordenberg, D., Williamson, D. F., Spitz, A. M., Edwards, V., ... Marks, J. S. (1998). Relationship of childhood abuse and household dysfunction to many of the leading causes of death in adults. The Adverse Childhood Experiences (ACE) study. *American Journal of Preventive Medicine, 14,* 245–258.

Fishbein, D., & Sheppard, M. (2006). Assessing the role of neuropsychological functioning in inmates' treatment response. *National Criminal Justice Reference Services,* No. 216303. Retrieved from https://www.ncjrs.gov/App/abstractdb/Abstract DBDetails.aspx?id=237914.

Ford, J. D., & Blaustein, M. E. (2013). Systemic self-regulation: A framework for trauma informed services in residential juvenile justice programs. *Journal of Family Violence, 24,* 1650–1659.

Ford, J. D., Chapman, J. F., Hawke, J., & Albert, D. (2007). Research and program brief: Trauma among youth in the juvenile justice system. *Critical issues and new directions.* National Center for Mental Health and Juvenile Justice, Delmar, NY. Retrieved from http://www.ncmhjj.com/pdfs/Trauma_and_Youth.pdf.

Graham v. Florida, 130 Supreme Court (2011).

Griffin, G. E., Germain, J., & Wilkerson, R. G. (2012). Using a trauma-informed approach in juvenile justice institutions. *Journal of Child and Adolescent Trauma, 5,* 271–283.

Griffin, G., & Sallen, S. (2013). Considering child trauma issues in juvenile court sentencing. *Children's Legal Rights Journal, 34,* 1–22.

Griffin, G., & Wolff, P. (2015). The Convergence of U.S. Juvenile Justice Policies and the U.N. Convention On The Rights Of The Child. *Boston University International Law Journal: Current Topics in International Law, October.* Retrieved from http://www. bu.edu/ilj/2015/10/29/the-convergence-of-u-s-juvenile-justice-policies-and-the-u-n-convention-on-the-rights-of-the-child/.

Hall, E. T. (1966). *The hidden dimension.* New York, NY: Anchor Books.

Hanson, R. K., & Morton-Bourgon, K. E. (2005). The characteristics of persistent sexual offenders: A meta-analysis of recidivism studies. *Journal of Consulting and Clinical Psychology, 73,* 1154–1163.

Hawkins, J. D., Herrenkohl, T. I., Farrington, D. P., Brewer, D., Catalano, R. F., Harachi, T. W., & Cothern, L. (2000). Predictors of youth violence. *Juvenile Justice Bulletin.* U.S. Department of Justice, Office of Justice Programs, Office of Juvenile Justice and Delinquency Prevention, Washington, DC.

Herculano-Houzel, S. (2009). The human brain in numbers: A linearly scaled-up primate brain. *Frontiers in Human Neuroscience, 3,* 1–11.

Hermans, E. J., van Marle, H. J. F., Ossewaarde, L., Henckens, M. J. A. G., Qin, S., van Kesteren, M T. R., ... Fernandez, G. (2011). Stress-related noradrenergic activity prompts large-scale neural network reconfiguration. *Science, 334,* 1150–1153.

Huang, H., Ghosh, P., & van den Pol, A. N. (2006). Prefrontal cortex-projecting glutamatergic thalamic paraventricular nucleus-excited by hypocretin: A feedforward circuit that may enhance cognitive arousal. *Journal of Neurophysiology, 95,* 1656–1668.

Johnson, S. B., Blum, R. W., & Giedd, J. N. (2009). Adolescent maturity and the brain: The promise and pitfalls of neuroscience research in adolescent health Policy. *Journal of Adolescent Health, 45,* 216–221.

Kalivas, P. W., & Stewart, J. (1991). Dopamine transmission in the initiation and expression of drug- and stress-induced sensitization of motor activity. *Brain Research Reviews, 16,* 223–244.

Kennedy, D. P., Gläscher, J., Tyszka, J. M., & Adolphs, R. (2009). Personal space regulation by the human amygdala. *Natural Neuroscience, 12,* 1226–1227.

Kenny, D. T., Blacker, S., & Allerton, M. (2014). Reculer pour mieux sauter: A review of attachment and other developmental processes inherent in identified risk factors for juvenile delinquency and juvenile offending. *Laws, 3,* 439–468.

Kerig, P. K. (2012a). Introduction to Part I: Trauma and juvenile delinquency: Dynamics and developmental mechanisms. *Journal of Child and Adolescent Trauma, 5,* 83–87.

Kerig, P. K. (2012b). Introduction to Part II: Trauma and juvenile delinquency: New directions in interventions. *Journal of Child and Adolescent Trauma, 5,* 187–190.

Kerig, P. K., & Becker, S. P. (2010). From internalizing to externalizing: Theoretical models of the processes linking PTSD to juvenile delinquency. In S. J. Egan (Ed.), *Posttraumatic stress disorder (PTSD): Causes, symptoms and treatment* (pp. 33–78). Hauppauge, NY: Nova Science Publishers.

Kinomura, S., Larsson, J., Gulyas, B., & Roland, P. E. (1996). Activation by attention of the human reticular formation and thalamic intralaminar nuclei. *Science, 271,* 512–515.

Kleven, M., Perry, B. D., Woolverton, W. L., & Seiden, L. S. (1990). Effects of repeated injections of cocaine on D1 and D2 dopamine receptors in rat brain. *Brain Research, 532,* 265–270.

Levy, T. M., & Orlans, M. (2000). Attachment disorder as an antecedent to violence and anti-social patterns in children. In T. M. Levy (Ed.), *Handbook of attachment interventions* (pp. 1–26). London: Academic Press.

McGarvey, S. C. (2012). Juvenile justice and mental health: Innovation in the laboratory of human behavior. *Jurimetrics, 53,* 97–120.

Miller v. Alabama, 567 U.S. Supreme Court (2012).

Moffitt, T. E., Arsenault, L., Belsky, D., Dickson, D., Hancox, R. J., Harrington, H., ... Caspi, A. (2011). A gradient of childhood self-control predicts health, wealth and public safety. *Proceedings of the National Academy of Sciences Early Edition, 108,* 2693–2698.

Mohr, W. K., Martin, A., Olson, J. N., Pumariega, A. J., & Branca, N. (2009). Beyond point and level systems: Moving toward child-centered programming. *American Journal of Orthopsychiatry, 79,* 8–18.

National Child Traumatic Stress Network. (2008). Judges and child trauma: Findings from the national child traumatic stress network/national council of juvenile and family court judges focus groups. *Service Systems Brief, 2,* 1–4.

Perry, B. D. (2002). Childhood experience and the expression of genetic potential: what childhood neglect tells us about nature and nurture. *Brain and Mind, 3,* 79–100.

Perry, B. D. (2006). The neurosequential model of therapeutics: Applying principles of neuroscience to clinical work with traumatized and maltreated children. In N. B. Webb (Ed.), *Working with traumatized youth in child welfare* (pp. 27–52). New York, NY: Guilford Press.

Perry, B. D. (2008). Child maltreatment: The role of abuse and neglect in developmental psychopathology in In T. P. Beauchaine & S. P. Hinshaw (Eds.), *Textbook of child and adolescent psychopathology,* (pp. 93–128). New York: John Wiley & Sons.

Perry, B. D. (2009). Examining child maltreatment through a neurodevelopmental lens: Clinical applications of the neurosequential model of therapeutics. *Journal of Loss and Trauma, 14*, 240–255.

Perry, B. D., & Dobson, C. (2013). Application of the neurosequential model (NMT) in maltreated children. In J. Ford & C. Courtois (Eds.), *Treating Complex Traumatic Stress Disorders in Children and Adolescents* (pp. 249–260). New York, NY: Guilford Press.

Perry, B. D., Hambrick, E., & Perry, R. D. (2016). Clinical challenges following inter-country adoptions and transracial adoptions: In R. Fong & R. McCoy (Eds.), *Trauma related to inter-country and transracial adoption: A neurodevelopmental perspective* (pp. 126–153). New York, NY: Columbia University Press.

Perry, B. D., & Pollard, R. (1998). Homeostasis, stress, trauma, and adaptation: A neurodevelopmental view of childhood trauma. *Child and Adolescent Psychiatric Clinics of North America, 7*, 33–51.

Perry, B. D., Pollard, R., Blakely, T., Baker, W., & Vigilante, D. (1995). Childhood trauma, the neurobiology of adaptation and use-dependent development of the brain: How states become traits. *Infant Mental Health Journal, 16*, 271–291.

Perry, B. D., Stolk, J. M., Vantini, G., Guchait, R. B., & U'Prichard, D. C. (1983). Strain differences in rat brain epinephrine synthesis and alpha-adrenergic receptor number: Apparent *in vivo* regulation of brain alpha-adrenergic receptors by epinephrine. *Science, 221*, 1297–1299.

Piquero, A. R., Jennings, W. G., & Farrington, D. P. (2010). On the malleability of self-control: Theoretical and policy implications regarding a general theory of crime. *Justice Quarterly, 27*, 803–834.

Roper v. Simmons, 543 U.S. 551 (2005).

Sara, S. J., & Bouret, S. (2012). Orienting and reorienting: The locus coeruleus mediates recognition through arousal. *Neuron, 76*, 130–141.

Schiff, N. D., Shah, S. A., Hudson, A. E., Nauvel, T., Kalik, S. F., & Purpura, K. P. (2012). Gating of attentional effort through the central thalamus. *Journal of Neurophysiology, 109*, 1152–1163.

Schweinhart, L. J., & Weikart, D. P. (1993). Success by empowerment: The high/scope Perry preschool study through age 27. *Young Children, 49*, 54–58.

Steinberg, L., & Scott, E. S. (2003). Less guilty by reason of adolescence: developmental immaturity, diminished responsibility, and the juvenile death penalty. *American Psychologist, 58*, 1009–1018.

Steketee, J. D., & Kalivas, P. W. (2011). Drug wanting: Behavioral sensitization and relapse to drug-seeking behavior. *Pharmacological Reviews, 63*, 348–365.

Steriade, M. (1996). Arousal: Revisiting the reticular activating system. *Science, 272*, 225–226.

Szalavitz, M., & Perry, B. D. 2010. *Born for love: Why empathy is essential and endangered*. New York, NY: Harper Collins.

Tronick, E., & Perry, B. D. (2015) The multiple levels of meaning making: the first principles of changing meanings in development and therapy. In G. Marlock & H. Weiss, with C. Young & M. Soth (Eds.) *Handbook of body therapy and somatic psychology* (pp. 345–355). Berkeley, CA: North Atlantic Books.

Ungar, M., & Perry, B. D. (2012). Trauma and resilience. In R. Alaggia & C. Vine (Eds.) *Cruel but not unusual: Violence in Canadian families* (pp. 119–143). Waterloo, CA: WLU Press.

Walker, S. P., Chang, S. M., Vera-Hernández, M., & Grantham-McGregor, S. (2011). Early childhood stimulation benefits adult competence and reduces violent behavior. *Pediatrics, 127*, 849–857.

Whalley, K. (2013). Balancing firing rates *in vivo*. *Nature Reviews Neuroscience, 14*, 820–821.

Wormith, J. S. (1984). Personal space of incarcerated offenders. *Journal of Clinical Psychology, 40*, 815–827.

32

Forensic Neuropsychology and Violence
Neuroscientific and Legal Implications
John Matthew Fabian

Key points

- This chapter focuses on the burgeoning field of forensic neuropsychology and violence, and, in particular, the literature on neuropsychological and neurological risk factors related to violent and sexually violent offending, especially in its application in legal contexts.
- Empirical evidence is outlined related to violence including neurodevelopmental conditions, prevalence of traumatic brain injury (TBI), and neurocognitive effects of substance abuse and post-traumatic stress disorder (PTSD). Here it is noted that the majority of the research linking neuropsychology and neuroimaging to violence addresses lower levels of intelligence in criminal offender populations as well as the relationship between criminality and frontal lobe dysfunction, namely in executive functioning and in the areas of dorsolateral prefrontal cortex (dlPFC), medial frontal cortex, orbitofrontal cortex, and ventromedial cortex.
- The chapter emphasizes the neuropsychological assessment related to violent and sexually violent offending specifically in areas of attention, executive functioning, and verbal and language deficits.
- In addition to neuropsychological impairments, studies on neuroimaging and violence are explored, as well as recent empirical evidence addressing specific neuroimaging techniques and violence risk assessment. The neuroimaging empirical findings, similar to the neuropsychology literature, emphasize the frontal and limbic systems of the brain when investigating violence and aggression.
- Violence risk assessment methods are also briefly discussed, with the chapter highlighting their questionable application, and the lack of evidence-based

---

The Wiley Blackwell Handbook of Forensic Neuroscience, First Edition. Edited by Anthony R. Beech, Adam J. Carter, Ruth E. Mann and Pia Rotshtein.
© 2018 John Wiley & Sons Ltd. Published 2018 by John Wiley & Sons Ltd.

> research when utilizing these assessment instruments with those offenders with cerebral dysfunction.
>
> - Finally, the chapter explores recent case law considering the application of criminal forensic neuropsychology and neuroscience in the courts.

Terminology Explained

Amicici curiae (friend of the court) is someone who gives advice to a court case but is not acting on behalf of either the defense or the prosecution.

(Capital) mitigation (also referred to as "mitigating factors" or "mitigating evidence") is evidence the defense can present in the sentencing phase of a capital trial to try and get the sentence lessened so that the defendant is not sentenced to death. Mitigation evidence addresses culpability and can include mental illness, brain damage/dysfunction, remorse, youthfulness, childhood abuse and/or neglect, a minor role in the homicide, or the absence of a prior criminal record. The US Supreme Court has ruled that in deciding between the death penalty and life in prison, the jury may consider any mitigating evidence they find relevant.

Conduct disorder (CD) is the term given to a repetitive, and persistent, pattern of behavior in childhood in which the basic rights of others or societal conventions are violated. Children with CD often show antisocial personality disorder (ASPD) as adults.

Executive functioning refers to the quality of cognitive processes such as working memory, reasoning, impulse control, judgment, flexible thinking, problem solving, and planning.

Forensic neuropsychology is a new and rapidly evolving subspecialty of clinical neuropsychology that applies neuropsychological principles and assessment to legal decision making. A forensic neuropsychology expert presents reliable/valid assessment data about the relationship between neurocognitive dysfunction/neuropathology and the behavioral and/or cognitive issues related to criminal behavior and legal proceedings.

Magnetic resonance imaging (MRI) brain scans are created by using powerful magnetic fields to distinguish tissue of differing types, thereby producing high-resolution images of discriminable structures in a completely non-invasive manner. A structural MRI scan can provide information about the thickness, density, and interconnections of differing brain areas.

Miranda rights, also known as the **Miranda warning**, is a right to silence warning given by police in the USA to criminal suspects in police custody (or in a custodial interrogation) before they are interrogated. The suspect is told they have the right to remain silent and that anything they say may be used in evidence against them. If the suspect chooses to remain silent the interrogation must stop. The police can only ask basic factual questions without giving the Miranda warning.

Mens rea ("guilty mind") is the state of mind indicating culpability for crime, meaning that the person knew what they were doing and knew it was wrong.

Photon emission tomography (PET) is a functional imaging technique that relies on injecting subjects with a radioactively labeled substance, such as glucose. Three-dimensional images of the subject's brain can then be obtained, and neural activity will show up as areas of higher radioactive signal due to glucose metabolism, thereby indicating brain function.

Post-traumatic stress disorder (PTSD) is a psychiatric disorder that can develop after a person is exposed to a traumatic event, usually one which felt life threatening, such as sexual assault, warfare, traffic accidents, or terrorism. Diagnostic symptoms include disturbing recurring flashbacks, memories, and nightmares, avoidance or numbing of memories of the event, and hyperarousal (feeling on edge all the time). As most people experience some of these symptoms after a traumatic event, the diagnosis of PTSD is reserved for people for whom these symptoms continue more than a month after the traumatic event(s).

Risk assessment is the assessment, evaluation, and estimation of the level of likelihood of future offending (typically sexual offending or violence).

Single photon emission tomography (SPECT) is another form of functional imaging, which also involves the injection of a radioactive tracer. A scanner detects the amount of radiation coming from different parts of the brain. These differences are due to differences in *regional cerebral blood flow* (rCBF) and reflect different levels of activity in various parts of the brain.

Traumatic brain injury (TBI) occurs when the brain is violently hit or penetrated, causing damage to brain tissues. Symptoms can vary from mild to severe.

Introduction: Violence and Brain Imaging

It has been found that neuropsychological deficits are commonly associated with anti-social outcomes, such as aggression, delinquent behavior, and low self-control (e.g., Cauffman, 2005). For example, recent research with adult offenders and especially violent offenders, has highlighted significant neuropsychological findings. Specifically, deficits in verbal abilities are consistent predictors of antisocial behaviors (e.g., Raine et al., 2005). Similarly, Moffitt and Silva (1988) found that delinquent offenders were at greater high risk of attention deficit hyperactivity disorder (ADHD), as well as verbal, visuospatial, and visual motor integration skill deficits. These studies suggest a neurodevelopmental risk for aggression and violence.

Structural and functional neuroimaging and neuropathology, as noted in previous chapters, inform us that such problems are linked with cerebral dysfunction in the frontal and temporal lobes and limbic system (Fabian, 2010). Brower and Price (2001) reported cumulative evidence from neuroimaging studies outlining aggression, violence, and its link to reduced prefrontal cortical size and reactivity. Evidence is most significant for an association between focal prefrontal damage and an impulsive sub-type of aggressive behavior rather than an association with predatory and planned aggression. For example, Bufkin and Luttrell (2005) found that 100% of single photon emission tomography (SPECT) and photon emission tomography (PET) studies reported deficits in prefrontal functioning with frontal lobe deficits in violent, aggressive, and antisocial groups. Analysis of specific regions of the brain that included the medial prefrontal cortex revealed that individuals who are aggressive and/or violent had significantly lower prefrontal activity in the orbitofrontal (40% of ten studies), anteriomedial cortex (50% of studies), mediofrontal cortex (20% of studies), and/or superior frontal cortex (10% of studies). The magnetic resonance imaging (MRI) studies (50% of four studies) reported less grey matter volume in prefrontal and frontal regions and (one of four studies) nonspecific white matter abnormalities not localized to the frontal cortex.

Two areas of the brain – the ventromedial and orbitofrontal cortexes (comprising the prefrontal cortex) have been associated with both neurological and neuropsychological dysfunction and violence. These areas are associated with understanding and processing information, understanding other's reactions, decision making, controlling impulses, and stopping behavior, emotional regulation, and manipulating learned and stored information while making decisions (Fabian, 2010). Dysfunctions in the orbitomedial region of the prefrontal cortex are related to impulsive aggression (Davidson, Puttnam, & Larson, 2000).

Further research by Wahlund and Kristiansson (2009) analyzed 12 articles relevant to studying aggression, psychopathy, and brain imaging and found a trend of smaller brain tissue and decreased activity of the frontal lobes in individuals with antisocial and violent behavior. They found that in 11 structural studies examined there were noticed differences in brain tissue of the frontal lobes, temporal lobes, corpus callosum, and amygdala in antisocial and psychopathic individuals compared to control subjects.

Studies including PET brain imaging have shown lower glucose metabolism in the frontal lobes and temporal lobes of violent patients, both in the prefrontal and orbitofrontal cortex (Goyer et al., 1994; Volkow et al., 1995). Raine, Buchsbaum, and LaCasse (1997) examined PET scan data with murderer groups and found reduced glucose metabolism in medial and lateral prefrontal cortex areas. When the murderers were subdivided into affective and predatory violence, the latter group showed a pattern in glucose metabolism more similar to the control group, while the impulsive group showed less metabolism in the prefrontal regions but an increased metabolism in subcortical regions.

In contrast, SPECT imaging studies that examined brain activity differences in violent aggressive individuals have consistently revealed evidence of reduced blood flow both in the prefrontal cortex and in the temporal lobes (Flannery, Vazsonyi, & Waldman, 2007). Other studies indicated prisoners with violent offenses assessed with electroencephalograms (EEGs) revealed that more than half of habitually aggressive subjects had EEG abnormalities, usually in the frontal lobe area, compared to only about 10% of other subjects who had committed a single violent act (Williams, 1969).

The other parts of the brain that have been indicated in violence and sexual violence are the temporal lobes. The temporal lobes and limbic system, the amygdala in particular, are structures that when damaged can impact the processing of unprovoked and excessive anger, memory and intellectual impairment, behavioral dyscontrol, receptive language impairment, and the regulation responses that suggest threat (Fabian, 2010). The amygdala, in particular, which is located bilaterally within the temporal lobe, functions as a core of the limbic system. It is responsible for the regulation of emotional impulses and for impulsivity, and it is hypothesized that impairment of these areas is related to violence (Fabian, 2010).

Bufkin and Luttrell (2005) found that 70% of SPECT and PET studies they reviewed included temporal lobe dysfunction in the aggressive and violent groups with reductions in left temporal lobe activity in six of seven studies. Specific areas in the temporal region that were affected included medial/temporal lobe subcortical circuits such as the amygdala, hippocampus and vasoganglia, as well as subcortical dysfunction with excessive subcortical activity specifically on the right side of the brain and reduction of cortical activity in general. Six of six MRI studies reviewed reported temporal irregularities including asymmetrical grey patterns in temporal-parietal region, decrease in anterior/inferior temporal lobe volume including the amygdala-hippocampal region and/or adjacent areas, and increases in left temporal lobe volume or pathology specific to the amygdala. Studies comparing aggressive and non-aggressive individuals using SPECT neuroimaging have found differences in temporal as well as prefrontal cortex functioning (Patrick & Verona, 2007). Further, a number of PET studies have reported differences in the temporal cortex, however, the studies reporting differences in prefrontal cortex regions appear to outnumber the temporal cortex studies.

Volkow and Tancredi (1987) found significantly decreased left temporal blood flow and glucose metabolism in violent patients whom they tested against controls. Volkow and Colleagues (1995) reported significant reduction bilaterally in medial temporal regions as well as the prefrontal cortex in a group of psychiatric patients with histories of repeat violence. Wong et al. (1997) compared brain activity in violent and nonviolent forensic patients against normal controls. Utilizing PET imaging, the subgroup of patients with a history of repetitive violent offending evidenced reduced functioning in both the right and left anterior inferior temporal regions compared with the nonviolent patient group and the control group. Gatzke-Kopp, Raine, Buchsbaum, and LaCasse (2001) examined resting EEG in a subsample of murderers and found abnormalities in the region of the temporal lobes despite PET imaging not revealing dysfunction in that region.

In summary, neuropathology and structural impairment as evidenced in neuroimaging studies as being related to violent offending suggests a connection between the damaged frontal-temporal circuitry with a trend toward frontal lobe structural and functional damage (Blake, Pincus, & Buckner, 1995).

The next section briefly outlines some of the biopsychosocial and neurodevelopmental risk factors (see also Chapter 17) that can lead to these problems, and may be useful to investigation and forensic neuropsychological assessments.

Biopsychosocial and Neurodevelopmental Risk Factors in Violence

Early risk factors leading to neuropsychological impairment are described in Box 32.1.

Box 32.1   Pre-, peri-, and post-risk factors in violence[1]

1   Young age of mother during pregnancy.
2   Maternal alcohol, nicotine, and drug use during pregnancy and during labor.

3 Infant drug positive test at birth.
4 Mother victimized by domestic violence during pregnancy causing prenatal vulnerability to central nervous system dysfunction.
5 Poor maternal diet and medical care during pregnancy.
6 Maternal depression and mental illness during pregnancy.
7 Fetal maldevelopment, minor physical abnormalities, and fetal alcohol syndrome.
8 Low birth weight.
9 Low heart rate at birth.
10 Perinatal birth complications including oxygen deprivation at birth.
11 Parental criminality and substance abuse.
12 Parental mental illness.
13 Exposure to parental physical abuse and emotional neglect.
14 Lack of attachment to primary caregivers.
15 Exposure to parental domestic violence between parents.
16 Exposure to housing instability and deplorable home conditions.
17 Exposure to toxins, lead, parasites, and infection.
18 Poor socioeconomic conditions.
19 Lack of attachment to community resources.
20 Deficient parental and offspring education.
21 Lack of parental involvement with the child.
22 Substance abuse and dependence history (brain dysfunction is more common among individuals with these problems, and are more likely to have preexisting neurological conditions and cope ineffectively with conditions by use of substances).
23 Experience of violent victimization within the community.
24 Exposure of poly-trauma/poly-victimization.
25 Exposure to early head injury and neuropsychological and psychological symptoms of Post-traumatic Stress Disorder (PTSD).
26 History of ADHD.
27 History of language-based learning disorders.

Importantly, there is a cumulative effect of these biopsychosocial risk factors in terms of the likelihood of violence, especially when considering the perfect storm analogy in that these risk factors work in conjunction and place an individual at risk not only to aggression but to cerebral dysfunction and neuropsychological impairments (Fabian, 2009; Freedman & Hemenway, 2000; Loeber et al., 2005; Saner & Ellickson, 1996). These factors will now be examined in slightly more detail in terms of early trauma, brain development, and violence, along with family factors.

Violence and neuropsychological functioning

Similar to neuroimaging data in their connection to violence, functional neuropsychological studies have also emphasized the prefrontal cortex and frontal executive system of the brain including the limbic system and amygdala (Barkataki et al., 2005; Fabian, 2010). Three domains of cognitive impairment have been associated with violent behavior including executive functions, verbal abilities, and abnormalities in cerebral dominance, namely right hemisphere dominance over left-language abilities (Raine & Buchsbaum, 1996; Séguin, Pihl, Harden, Tremblay, & Boulerice, 1995). Various studies inform us of frontal lobe dysfunction in offenders by means of neuropsychological testing.

When considering neuropsychological assessment of offenders, Morgan and Lilienfeld (2000) performed a meta-analytic review of the relationship between antisocial behavior and executive functioning in neuropsychological assessment. Their results inform us that antisocial groups performed 0.62 standard deviations worse on executive functioning tests than comparison groups; however, evidence for the specificity of these deficits relative to impairments on other neuropsychological tasks was inconsistent.

Kuin, Masthoff, Kramer, and Scherder (2015) found evidence across different populations for a significant positive relationship between executive functioning as measured through risk taking with making decisions and higher levels of aggression. This relationship appears to be stronger with respect to reactive than to proactive aggression.

Other studies have suggested a link between neuropsychological impairment and violence. Yeudall and Fromm-Auch (1979) found that on the Halstead-Reitan neuropsychological battery, a violent offender group had significantly more anterior (including frontal lobe) neuropsychological dysfunction than a normal group. Langevin, Wortzman, Dickey, Wright, and Handy (1988) examined neuropsychological functioning between homicidal, violent, and nonviolent male offenders. They found that 33% of the murderers were significantly impaired on sections of the Halstead-Reitan Battery and 21% were significantly impaired on the Luria-Nebraska, whereas the nonviolent samples were not significantly impaired. A study of murderers by Blake et al. (1995) found not only evidence of frontal lobe and temporal lobe dysfunction, but also evidence of neuropsychological abnormalities in all subjects. Taking into account forensic psychiatric patients, Sreenivasan, Kirkish, Shotaw, Welsh, and Ling (2000) administered neuropsychological tests to violent non-criminally responsible offenders and mentally ill prisoners. They found that both groups displayed a pattern of lowered functioning in key cognitive areas. Both groups demonstrated cognitive rigidity, one aspect of orbitofrontal deficit and a potential factor in impulsive aggression.

Some studies on psychopaths pertaining to their neuropsychological functioning have examined deficits in frontal lobe functioning, finding response perseveration deficits (Gorenstein, 1982; Newman, Patterson, & Kosson, 1987). Day and Wong (1996) found psychopaths to display perceptual asymmetries and visuospatial deficits. Other studies suggest prototypal psychopathy is associated with deficits in ventromedial prefrontal function rather than dorsolateral prefrontal impairments. Psychopaths have been found to experience impairment similar to those patients with amygdala lesions, and are deficient in examinations measuring orbitofrontal–ventromedial skills (Lapierre, Braun, & Hodgins, 1995). Similarly, Wahlund and Kristiansson (2009) analyzed 12 articles relevant to studying aggression, psychopathy, and brain imaging and found a trend of smaller brain tissue and decreased activity of the frontal lobes in individuals with antisocial and violent behavior. They found that in 11 structural studies

examined there were noticed differences in brain tissue of the frontal lobes, temporal lobes, corpus callosum, and amygdala in antisocial and psychopathic individuals
compared to control subjects. Psychopaths in particular are prone to lack skills requiring verbal mediation, concept integration, anticipating consequences of actions, and
utilizing feedback from behaviors to modify maladaptive response patterns (Miller,
1987). Dolan and Park (2002) reported that subjects with antisocial personality disorder (ASPD) displayed impairments on dorsolateral frontal executive function tasks
of planning ability and set shifting. They also displayed deficits in dorsolateral prefrontal go/no-go tasks and in visual memory tasks. Fedora and Fedora (1983) found
greater impairment of dominant left hemisphere function among criminal psychopaths
on the Halstead-Reitan Battery. Lapierre et al. (1995) noted that psychopaths were
significantly impaired on all orbitofrontal–ventromedial tasks including go/no-go and
a maze task, but scored similarly to non-psychopaths on tasks related to dorsolateral
frontal cortex functioning.

Research suggests that habitually violent offenders with conduct disorder (CD)
or ASPD exhibit impairments in a broad range of executive and memory functions
(Dolan, 1994; Moffitt & Henry, 1989). While IQ has been suggested to be related
to violence, Moffitt, Lynam, and Silva (1994) assessed whether global neuropsychological performance (IQ, motor coordination, auditory-verbal learning, visuospatial
perception, and executive functioning) was associated with criminality. While they
found that verbal skills and verbal memory abilities were most robustly related to
delinquency, neuropsychological scores at age 13 predicted delinquency at age 18,
suggesting a neurodevelopmental quality to criminality.

Although verbal deficits are significantly related to delinquency, and to some
degree adult criminality, the clinical diagnosis of attention deficit hyperactivity disorder (ADHD), a condition of attentional and prefrontal lobe executive dysfunction,
is also significantly related to delinquency and early aggression (Lilienfeld & Waldman,
1990).

In summary, neuropsychological studies on violence emphasize verbal and language
deficits, attention and executive deficits focusing on impaired decision making, impulsivity, and decision making.

Early trauma, brain development, and violence

There are a number of neurobiological consequences of early stress and childhood
mental treatment on the developing brain (Teicher et al., 2003). Research indicates
that early and severe stress and maltreatment produce a cascade of neurobiological events that may change structural functional brain development (Teicher et al.,
2003). Childhood maltreatment, including neglect and abuse, is an adverse experience associated with heightened potential for psychiatric and mental illness as well
as behavioral dysfunction. Relevant to neurobiological effects of maltreatment, exposure to early stress programs the individual to display enhanced stress responsiveness.
Early abuse and neglect affects important developmental processes including neurogenesis, synaptic overproduction and pruning, and myelination during specific sensitive periods (Teicher et al., 2003). Concerning neurobiological manifestations of
early stress and childhood maltreatment related to violence and the brain, both the

amygdala and prefrontal cortex are susceptible to early damage. Functional manifestations of early stress and childhood maltreatment affect the amygdala, as it appears to play a role in the fear conditioning and controlled aggressive oral and sexual behaviors (Pincus & Tucker, 1978). Early stress, abuse, and neglect may activate the development of the prefrontal cortex changing its development and producing precocious maturation but stunted functional capacity (Teicher, Ito, Glod, Schiffer, & Gelbard, 1996).

Further research has indicated a connection between early trauma and violence. Childhood abuse increases the risk of criminality by at least 50% (Widom, 1997). Severe childhood trauma is common in pre-teen homicide offenders (Shumaker & Prinz, 2000), adolescent homicide offenders (Lewis et al., 1995), death row inmates (Beckman, 2004), and adult homicide offenders (Lewis et al., 1997). Blake et al. (1995) assessed murderers referred by attorneys for neurological examinations as well as neuropsychological testing that revealed abnormalities in all subjects concluding that prolonged and severe abuse likely interacts with neurological brain dysfunction and contributes to violent behavior.

Various studies have shown that infants who suffer birth complications are more likely to develop CD, delinquency, and commit impulsive crime and violence in adulthood when other psychosocial risk factors are present (e.g., Raine, 2002b). Werner (1989) found that birth complications interacted with a negative family environment (paternal separation, illegitimate child, marital discord, parental mental health problems, and paternal absence) in predisposing offspring to delinquency. Other research has revealed that birth complications significantly interact with maternal rejection of a child in predicting violent offending at age 18 (Raine, Brennan, & Mednick, 1994). Birth complications such as anoxia (lack of oxygen), forceps delivery, and preeclampsia (hypertension leading to anoxia) are thought to contribute to brain damage and may be an element of early sources of brain dysfunction observed in child and adult antisocial groups.

In summary, early childhood trauma and abuse and birth complications have detrimental effects on the emotional, psychological, behavioral, and cognitive development of youth. The abuse and early trauma have a connection and accumulative impact with other risk factors such as low socioeconomic status, parental psychopathology, and criminality. Important to the early effects of childhood trauma and abuse are other neurodevelopmental risk factors that require some exploration in this chapter, including ADHD, learning disorder, and early neuropsychological impairments.

While the substance of this chapter is the link between neuropsychology and violence, the role of environmental factors and specifically family factors also impacts one's risk for aggression and also has some relationship with neuropsychological development, which will now be examined.

Family factors and violence

One's family environment shapes and molds a person's interpersonal relationships. Family factors that are correlated with violence include both family interactions and family structure. Negative family interactions include: physical abuse; physical and emotional neglect; parental rejection; sexual abuse; witnessing violence in the family; and the lack positive interaction, bonding attachment, and support from parental figures. Negative family management practices include harsh and early punitive discipline, inconsistent discipline ranging from lax to harsh styles, poor supervision, and low parental confidence (Capaldi & Patterson, 1996; Weeks & Widom, 1998; Widom, 1989). Family structure deficits include parental separation, family disruption, and single parent homes. Family separation and breakup may lead to residential mobility and offspring foster home and group home placement for example. The consequences of overall family dysfunction can lead youth to engage in negative peer relationships and possess a weak commitment to school. Parental psychopathology and mental illness, substance abuse, and criminality are all associated with offspring criminality and violence (Mednick, Gabrielli, & Hutchings, 1984).

Importantly, many of these parental and family risk factors are related to offspring neuropsychological development as well as a risk of future violence. The more types of violence a youth is exposed to within the family – such as parental violence, family attitudes condoning violence, and child abuse – as well as the frequency and severity of violence toward the children, the more likely youth will be violent (Dutton & Hart, 1992). The family risk factors of violence may lead to the development of individual risk factors associated with violence including low self-esteem, social isolation, depression, post-traumatic stress disorder (PTSD), head injury, suicide attempts, and delinquency (Widom, 1993). Family violence, neglect, and abuse ultimately affect an offspring's brain, personality, and emotional development.

In the next section, the brain and its relationship to violence will be examined in specific syndromes, specifically: ADHD, language-based learning disorders, PTSD, substance abuse disorders, and traumatic brain injury (TBI).

Violence and Specific Diagnoses, Conditions, and Neuropsychological Functioning

ADHD

ADHD is one of the most significant mental disorders that is present in criminal defendants and individuals arrested for offenses and/or imprisoned and incarcerated (Barkley, 2008). Symptoms include: deficits in attention, difficulty controlling behaviors, impulsivity, and hyperactivity. Importantly, the disorder lends itself to impairment in delays in the development of inhibition and self-regulation. More specifically, Barkley notes that ADHD: disrupts the capacity for working or representational memory; reduces the power of sensing and accurately conveying information to oneself; creates a delay in the internalization of speech during development; and impairs the development of self-control.

The concept of attention is the base of cognitive activity. Cortical arousal, selective and sustained attention, planning ability, information acquisition, and storage or retrieval of knowledge are all related to functional attention (Fabian, 2010). Low autonomic activity in the brain manifested by stimulation seeking, perceptual motor impairments, restlessness, psychomotor impulsivity, and fearlessness predisposes one to a diagnosis of ADHD, and subsequently to aggressive and criminal behaviors. Related deficits of ADHD are shown in Box 32.2.

Box 32.2   Related deficits of ADHD

1 Sustaining attention and concentration.
2 Planning, organizing, and initiating thoughts and behavior.
3 Controlling/stopping impulses and behavior.
4 Emotional/behavioral modulation and regulation.
5 Inhibiting unsuccessfully inappropriate or impulsive behaviors.
6 Using working memory and knowledge to regulate behavior.
7 Exhibiting behavioral flexibility to changing contingencies and modulating/changing behavior in light of expected consequences.
8 Lacking empathy and appreciation of how one's behavior impacts others.
9 Manipulation of learned and stored information when making decisions.

Moffitt and Silva (1988) found that delinquent offenders were at higher risk of having conditions of ADHD, as well as verbal, visuospatial, and visual motor integration skill deficits on neuropsychological testing. A number of prospective studies that have followed children diagnosed with ADHD in adolescence and adulthood have found significant higher rates of arrests relative to controls (Satterfield, Hoppe, & Schell, 1982). Further, those children with ADHD, as well as conduct problems, are more likely to exhibit a severe and persistent course of antisocial behavior (Hinshaw & Lee, 2003). Research suggests that adults with a childhood history of hyperactivity are more likely to develop personality disorders, alcoholism, and psychopathy compared to comparison groups (Vitelli, 1996).

Vitelli (1996) also examined the prevalence of childhood conduct disorder (CD) and ADHD in adult maximum-security inmates. Based on structured interviews, in a study of inmates 63% of the sample was found to meet the diagnosis of CD in the fifth edition of the *Diagnostic and Statistical Manual of Mental Disorders* (*DSM-IV*) (American Psychiatric Association, 1994). Ninety-two percent of the inmates who received medication therapy for childhood ADHD, or would have been assessed for behavioral problems as children, met *DSM-IV* criteria for childhood CD. Similarly, in another investigation, a 14-year follow-up longitudinal study found that ADHD and antisocial behavior in childhood were among the most important predictors of later offending behavior at age 32 (Farrington, 1990).

It should be highlighted that predisposing factors not only contribute to the development of conduct disorder and ADHD, but also often exist comorbidly with these disorders and the manifestations of juvenile and antisocial behavior. These factors include: family, social, environmental, and biological/genetic factors.

In summary, the presence of ADHD has some connection and correlation with the early onset and persistence of antisocial behavior from youth through adulthood. In the context of correctional setting, ADHD is often measured using the CAARS (Conners, Erhardt, & Sparrow, 2004).

848   *J. M. Fabian*

Autism spectrum disorder

Only recently has autistic spectrum disorder (ASD) gained some recognition and concern as being a neurodevelopmental condition associated with potential for violence and sexual violence (Allely, Minnis, Thompson, Wilson, & Gillberg, 2014; Fabian, 2011). Follow-up studies suggest that people with ASDs are no more likely to commit violent crime than the greater population (Mouridsen, Rich, Isager, & Nedergaard, 2008). In contrast, several studies have addressed the prevalence of ASDs in forensic settings, indicating that they are substantially higher in forensic populations than in general community samples (Murrie, Warren, Kristiansson, & Dietz, 2002; Scragg & Shah, 1994). Violent individuals with ASDs are more likely to be diagnosed with what formerly was called Asperger's syndrome than autistic disorder (Långström, Grann, Ruchkin, Sjostedt, & Fazel, 2009). Hare (1999) screened all patients including those in special forensic hospitals and found that 2.4% had ASD on case reviews and 1.6% of the total sample had Asperger's syndrome. Homicide and other violent index offenses were equally often found among ASD and non-ASD patients, whereas arson was overrepresented and sexual offenses underrepresented. Another study examined detailed developmental histories for presenting evaluations of cohort young adult males with personality disorder with identification of prevalence rates of 15% for definite ASD and an additional 12% for probable ASD (Siponmaa, Kristiansson, Jonson, Nyden, & Gillberg, 2001).

Importantly for the consideration of ASD with criminality and violence, ASD is well known to be prevalent with other types of coexisting psychiatric disorders (Newman & Ghaziuddin, 2008). The literature suggests that ASD diagnoses may be confounded by comorbid conditions including depression, ADHD, learning disorder, epilepsy, Tourette's syndrome, bipolar disorder, obsessive-compulsive disorder (OCD), and ASPD (Fabian, 2011). The comorbidity issue may be in part a reason why ASD might be underdiagnosed in criminal offender populations. Långström et al. (2009) studied Swedish criminal offenders and found that 7% were convicted of violent nonsexual crimes. Violent individuals with ASD were more often male and diagnosed with Asperger's syndrome than autism disorder. Comorbid psychotic and substance use disorders were associated with violent offending, and the authors concluded that violent offending and ASD were related to similar co-occurring psychopathology as found among violent individuals without ASD (Långström et al., 2009).

Where most criminal offenders do not have a history of ASD, certain diagnostic features associated with the disorder may be associated with elevated risk of criminality including:

1 Deficits in theory of mind (the ability to estimate the kind of perceptual affect and emotional life of others as well as self).
2 Deficits in social-emotional reciprocity including abnormal social approach and failure to share common interests, emotions, and affect.
3 Deficits in understanding and appreciating nonverbal communicative behaviors, leading to social isolation.
4 Deficits in developing, maintaining, and understanding relationships.
5 Deficits in intimacy with others.
6 Risk of social rejection and isolation.
7 Poor empathy skills related to theory of mind (ToM).

Perhaps the most consistent evidence of the effect of severe and sustained impairments in social interaction criteria for ASD relates to deficits in empathy. Men with ASD and charged with sexual and violent offenses and murder seem generally unaware of the harm they cause their victims (Murrie et al., 2002). This deficiency in empathy is often misunderstood for psychopathic traits when they are in fact a core component of the theory of mind (ToM). ToM is the ability to attribute mental states such as intents, desires, pretending, and knowledge to oneself and others and to understand that others have these same issues and perspectives yet they are different from one's own. Development of ToM is interconnected with language development in humans (Milligan, Astington, & Dack, 2007). Simon Baron-Cohen (1991) suggested that children with autism do not employ ToM and they have significant difficulties with tasks requiring a child to understand other persons' beliefs. Individuals with autism are likely to show extreme deficits in ToM and initially in pretend and imaginative play with their contemporaries, which leads to them have distortion in understanding and responding to emotions including empathy. The ToM, along with language-based deficits, places an individual with autism at significant emotional and neurocognitive delay.

In addition to ToM factors related to violent offending, the issue of circumscribed interests has also gained concern in the literature. There is an emergent support for the relation between the pursuit of a circumscribed interest and offending (Dein & Woodbury-Smith, 2010). Circumscribed interests that are pursued with abnormal intensity are a major diagnostic feature of ASD. Connection with the criminal justice system can occur as a result of stealing something of interest, and simply because of the antisocial nature of the interest itself. This author has also examined high-functioning autistic juveniles and young adults who not only have emotional deficits related to social reciprocity and empathy, but also restricted obsessive interests in violent video gaming that further nurtures an emotional detachment, insensitivity, and numbness to violence toward others.

Social naiveté and inability to appreciate consequences or appreciate the severity of one's behaviors, and again how they impact others, can be related to ASD and criminal offending. A study by Soderstrom, Nilsson, Sjodin, Carlstedt, and Forsman (2005) found that high psychopathy and unemotionality scores and behavioral dyscontrol factors were significantly correlated with high-functioning autistic traits. In addition to empathy and behavioral dysregulation, individuals with autism or ASD held in secure incarceration units are more susceptible to exploitation, bullying, violence, abuse, and intimidation because of their social naiveté and awkwardness. The risks that arise from these factors are magnified by their inability to articulate their frustrations appropriately.

In addition to emotional and behavioral dysfunction and impairments among those with ASD, the assessment of neuropsychological functioning is also indicated with this population (Fabian, 2011). While those with ASD may exhibit IQs within the normative range, there is likely a verbal versus performance IQ discrepancy favoring greater verbal skills. While those with ASD may have IQ scores in the average range, other neuropsychological assessments should be considered including evaluation of motor skills, visual and motor coordination, visual perceptual skills, visuospatial construction, visual memory, and facial recognition, as well as concept formation and executive functioning (Fabian, 2011). An assessment of ADHD should always be considered due to its high rate of comorbidity with ASD and its connection as a disorder with criminality and violence. A communication assessment may also be indicated in an ASD evaluation. The assessment of adaptive behavioral functioning also may be important to examine both individually and with collateral informants that know the affected individual. Neuropsychological testing including the assessment of emotional intelligence and perception, such as assessing emotional voice tones and facial expressions is also indicated in the neuropsychological assessment (Montgomery, McCrimmon, Schwean, & Saklofske, 2010).

In addition to neuropsychological correlates to autism, structural and functional brain imaging is also indicated in this neurodevelopmental condition. ASD rated patterns of low function and aberrant activation of the brain differ on whether the brain is doing social or nonsocial tasks (Di Martino et al., 2009). A review by Anckarsäter (2006) assessed central nervous changes in social dysfunction related to autism, aggression, and psychopathy. The authors suggested that autism has been linked to abnormal social brain functioning and neurological disorders, with no abnormalities in the perception of human faces and gazes associated with a deficient or abnormal mentalizing ability in subjects with autism. The authors hypothesized that autism is an example of a social interaction disorder, as are other disorders that may be linked to violent offending including schizophrenia and psychopathy, for example. The authors suggest the core abnormalities in the pathogenesis of autism are hypothetically located in the amygdala, adjacent limbic structures, and corpus collosum (Manes et al., 1999). Abnormalities in the brainstem are also proposed to be relevant for autism (Johansson et al., 2001). In addition, the frontal cortex interplays with limbic structures and plays a central role in the deviant processing of mentalizing documented autism (Happe et al., 1996). Overall, the authors suggest that this neuroimaging and neuroanatomical functioning and research establish autism as a social brain disorder.

When returning to the connection between the neurodevelopmental disorder of autism and violence, the disorder affects neuropsychological functioning and neuroanatomical structure of the brain. Neuropsychological and emotional functioning, as well as executive functioning including working memory, planning, cognitive flexibility, and inhibitory control, are said to be impaired in children and adults with autism and are linked to a number of areas of the brain including the prefrontal cortex/paracingulate cortex, temporoparietal junction, temporal pole, amygdala, periamygdaloid cortices, rostral anterior medial prefrontal cortex, adjacent anterior paracingulate cortex, and perigenual anterior cortex (Di Martino et al., 2009).

These neuropsychological functions and neuroanatomical structural and functional brain correlates are very similarly identified in other disorders linked to violence such as psychopathy and ASPD. Interestingly, Allely et al. (2014) conducted a systematic review regarding mass and serial killings, and found that these extreme forms of violence may be a result of a highly complex interaction of biological, psychological, and sociological factors, and a significant proportion of mass or serial killers may have had neurodevelopmental disorders such as ASD and/or head injury. They found that, among 239 eligible killers in their study, 28% had highly probable or possible ASD and, within the ASD group, about 7% also had head injuries. They hypothesized that probably more than 10% of serial/mass killers have ASD and a similar proportion have a history of head injuries.

In summary, the relatively recent research on the neuropsychological and neuroimaging of ASD appears to be somewhat consistent with other disorders linked with criminality and violence. In particular, individuals with ASD are known to have deficits with language and communication delays, and are likely to have difficulties expressing their thoughts and feelings. They tend to then isolate themselves and become emotionally void and withdrawn. This research is similar to the findings related in the chapter relevant to verbal and language deficits with criminal offenders in general. Further, those with ASD have deficits with empathy and ability to appreciate the thoughts and feelings of others, similar to findings with those with ASPD and psychopathy. Finally, neuroimaging studies of ASD also implicate the frontotemporal areas of the brain, especially during tests assessing social and emotional functioning and moral reasoning (Schneider et al., 2013).

TBI

The prevalence of TBI in the general population is about 101 cases per 100,000 individuals with ages of peak incidents among young adults and older adults beyond 80 years of age with a higher prevalence for males than females (Langlois, Rutland-Brown, & Wald, 2006). With staggering increase of rates of incarceration both in state and federal prison systems in the USA, there has also been an increase in prevalence of TBI in criminal offender populations. The risk of not only head injury but violence is profound in younger males (15 to 25 years old). Offender populations with TBI may have an increase in co-occurrence of comorbid conditions including substance abuse, aggression, and learning and neurodevelopmental difficulties. Between 25% and 87% of offenders report having sustained a head injury or a TBI (Blake, Pincus, & Buckner 1995; Barnfield & Leathem, 1998; DelBello et al., 1999). Shiroma, Ferguson, and Pickelsimer (2010) performed a meta-analysis of studies of brain injury in an offender population. They found the prevalence of head injuries with loss of consciousness in these studies was 50.19%. The authors found that without adjusting for different definitions of TBI, methods of determination, proportion of males in the sample, or the similarities of sample populations, the overall estimated prevalence of TBI in the offender population was 60.25% in over 20 studies of 4,865 offenders.

TBI is known to be associated with increased risk of violence and aggression both acutely and over the long term. As many as 50% of patients with moderate to severe TBI display agitation and potentially aggressive behavior during the confusion state and postconcussive syndrome (Sandel & Mysiw, 1996). Other studies have found 20% of severe TBI patients to be physically violent over a five-year follow-up period (Brooks, Campsie, Symington, Beattie, & McKinlay, 1986). In follow-up periods ranging from 1 to 15 years after the injury, aggressive behavior occurred in 31% to 71% of patients who experienced severe TBI (Silver, McAllister, & Yudofsky, 2011).

When considering the structural and functional brain relationships with TBI and violence, abnormal limbic and frontal lobe structure and function are often found to be present in those who exhibit aggression and violent behavior (Filley et al., 2001). Large studies on war veterans with head injuries have also tended to find association between frontal lobe lesions due to head injuries and aggressive or antisocial behavior. The Vietnam Head Injury Study[2] found that subjects with lesions limited to the frontal lobes tended to show more aggressive and violent behaviors compared with patients with non-frontal head injury and controls without head injury (Grafman et al., 1996). The study also found significant correlation between increased aggression and focal mediofrontal and orbitofrontal injury identified in brain computed tomography (CT) scans. TBI, with subsequent frontal dysfunction, whether caused from diffuse or focal damage, may consistently threaten the capacity for inhibition of violent behavior.

Prison systems *With a staggering increase in rates of incarceration both in state and federal prison systems in the USA, there has also been an increase in prevalence of TBI in criminal offender populations.*
Source: © TryJimmy. Used under license from 699pic.

IQ and language-based learning disorders

Language-based deficits are another area of neurodevelopmental disorders related to criminality and violence. Specifically, research has found that the most common characteristic of delinquency and adult criminal behavior is low IQ, especially low verbal IQ, as those with verbal shortage often rely on physical and emotional modes of self-expression (Fabian, 2010). Intelligence and IQ are a measure of neuropsychological fortitude and represent executive functioning including sustained attention, concentration, social judgment, language processing, abstract reasoning, planning, and initiating purposeful behavior (Moffitt & Lynam, 1994). Normal auditory and verbal memory and verbal abstract reasoning skills related to verbal intelligence influence the success of a child's socialization and are essential to the development of self-control and inhibiting childhood behaviors and impulses (Moffitt, 1993). Low verbal IQ scores are related to impulsivity, poor judgment, weak language processing, poor memory, and failure to synchronize visual information with motor actions (Lezak, 1988).

The neuropsychology of juvenile delinquency demonstrates the connection between global IQ deficits and antisocial behavior even when controlling for the compounding effects of social disadvantage, socioeconomic status, race, legal attention of delinquent acts, parental IQ, and scholastic attainment (Connor, 2004). The consistent finding of reduced verbal IQ scores relative to performance IQ scores across a number of neuropsychological studies has given rise to a theory of relative left hemisphere dysfunction in youth with early onset and persistent developmental histories of aggressive conduct problems. Antisocial youngsters are likely to have less lateralized linguistic functions and have relatively inefficient left hemisphere information processing compared to individuals who are not at risk for early onset aggressive problems (Raine, 1993).

Hanlon, Brook, Stratton, Jenson, and Rubin (2013) examined the neuropsychological and intellectual differences between types of murderers relevant to affective/impulsive versus predatory/instrumental premeditated homicide. They found differences between the affective/impulsive group with a mean full-scale IQ score of 79 versus the predatory/instrumental group with a mean IQ of 93. They had noted the research suggesting significant neuropsychological dysfunction including behavioral disinhibition and below average performance on some types of executive functioning relevant to affective and impulsive violent offenders. Interestingly they found a higher prevalence of personality disorders for the predatory/instrumental group and a higher rate of developmental disorder such as mental retardation or learning disorder in the affective/impulsive group.

Neuropsychological assessment of murderers

Hanlon (2010) studied 77 indigent murder defendants and death row inmates relevant to psychiatric diagnoses and neuropsychological functioning as well as to criminal classification. They found that the collective neuropsychological profile in the sample revealed that executive functions were significantly decreased, relative to memory functions with over half the sample demonstrating executive dysfunction. They noted their sample was consistent with other murderer samples including high rates of developmental disorders, psychopathology, traumatic brain injury, seizure disorders, and neuropsychological dysfunction. They hypothesized that there would be clinical and neuropsychological differences between offenders who committed single murders versus those who committed multiple murders. They found that multiple murderers who had killed more than one person were twice as likely to have a personality disorder compared with defenders who committed a single murder. Further, those who had committed only one murder had a higher rate of developmental disorder and were less intelligent and manifested decreased neurocognitive functioning relative to multiple murderers. The primary cognitive difference between the two groups revealed decreased processing speed of information in single murderers.

Hanlon, Coda, Cobia, and Rubin (2012) also studied psychotic domestic murder and neuropsychological differences between homicidal and non-homicidal schizophrenic male offenders. The authors studied neuropsychological features of several schizophrenic men who had murdered family members and compared them to schizophrenic men with no history of violence or antisocial behavior. The schizophrenic murderers demonstrated significantly worse neuropsychological impairment involving executive dysfunction and memory dysfunction as compared to nonviolent schizophrenic men. They found that the schizophrenic murderer group displayed more impaired cognitive flexibility, concept formation, and response inhibition, as well as memory deficits including verbal and coding relevant to both speed and amount of information encoded.

Hanlon et al. (2013) found that offenders who committed affective/impulsive murder exhibited overall poor performance on indices of attention compared to the predatory/instrumental group. They also exhibited slow completion times on tasks assessing visuomotor and attention skills, and scanning on trail tasks, as well as deficits on a sustained measure of attention and vigilance pertaining to a lower pass rate and more omission errors. Relevant to memory functioning, the affective/impulsive murderers learned fewer words on a word list task and recalled fewer words after both short-term and long-term delays. They had poor recall for narrative verbal information relevant to short story recall. Group differences on measures of visual and nonverbal recognition memory were significant but not as impaired for the affective/impulsive murderers versus the predatory/instrumental group. The two groups did not differ on a card-sorting task assessing concept formation skills, although the affective/impulsive group committed a greater number of errors. No significant difference was observed on traditional measures of response inhibition and impulsivity including the Stroop Color and Word Test (SCWT). The authors reported that the affective/impulsive murderers demonstrated significantly poorer performance than the predatory/instrumental murderers across neurocognitive domains with larger effect sizes on measures of intelligence, memory, attention, and executive functions and these differences remained significant after controlling for the influences of demographic and other background variables. Predatory/instrumental murderers showed largely intact functioning across most neurocognitive areas.

Box 32.3   PTSD and complex trauma

A mental condition that may be linked to violence is PTSD. The new *DSM-5* diagnostic criteria for PTSD in part even includes aggression as a symptom of PTSD (D1). Those afflicted with PTSD, especially war veterans, are at risk for violence in part due to the disorder as well as premorbid and lifestyle factors. A number of empirical studies documented aggressive or violent behavior toward others as a problem in a substantial proportion of veterans, especially those returning home from military service in Iraq and Afghanistan (Jakupcak et al., 2007). Many of these veterans suffer from PTSD, TBI, and/or substance abuse (Hoge et al., 2004). Having the diagnosis of PTSD has been found to be significantly related to violence, violent thoughts, anger and hostility, and ownership of deadly weapons in veterans (Beckham, Moore, & Reynolds, 2000).

There are a number of risk factors related to an increase in violence in PTSD war veterans including: pre-redeployment violence and criminal conduct; childhood antisocial conduct; having a dysfunctional family of origin, prior symptoms of PTSD; witnessing parental fighting; prior substance abuse and TBI; history of depression; history of personality disorder; and a history of physical and/or sexual abuse (Elbogen et al., 2010). It has also been shown that a diagnosis of PTSD is related to perpetrating more types of violence including physical fights, property damage, use of weapons, and/or threats (McFall, 1999).

Research on PTSD has revealed neuroanatomical brain regions including the amygdala, medial prefrontal cortex, and hippocampus (Vasterling & Berwin, 2005). The amygdala is known to be involved with the assessment of threat-related stimuli and plays a crucial role in the process of fear conditioning: those with PTSD have shown heightened acquisition of commissioned fear in some studies. The medial prefrontal cortex area sends projections to the amygdala and may be critically involved in the process of extinction, fear of conditioning, and the retention of extinction. Recent neuroimaging studies have reported reduced neuronal integrity and cortical volumes in the medial prefrontal structures in this disorder. Amygdala hyperreactivity is thought to account for heightened behavioral arousal and exaggerated responses to stimuli that are perceived to be associated with danger or threat, which often can lead to aggressive or violent acts (see Box 32.3)

Three domains of functioning are influenced by PTSD symptoms including cognition, physiological arousal, and emotions. Anger, hostility, and violence have cognitive, affective, and behavioral components that are related to the effects of PTSD. When considering neuropsychological components of violence in veterans, deficits in information processing and arousal regulation place veterans at risk for physically acting out when feeling threatened (Chemtob, Novaco, Hamada, & Gross, 1997).

Critical to the link of trauma to violence is the condition of complex trauma. Many offenders have histories of complex trauma including exposure to traumatic stressors such as polyvictimization, life-threatening accidents or disasters, and interpersonal losses. Complex trauma has been defined as exposure to traumatic stressors at an age (e.g., early childhood) or in a context (e.g., prolonged torture or captivity) that compromises secure attachment with primary caregivers (Cook et al., 2005) and the associated ability to self-regulate emotions (Ford, 2005). Complex trauma includes physical or sexual abuse or neglect, and chronic childhood victimization such as family and community violence, physical and sexual assault, and bullying (Finkelhor, Ormrod, & Turner, 2009). Complex trauma adversely affects early childhood biopsychosocial development and attachment bonding, placing the youth at risk for a range of serious problems (e.g., depression, anxiety, oppositional defiance, risk taking, substance abuse) that may lead to reactive aggression. Complex trauma is associated with an extremely problematic combination of persistently diminished adaptive arousal reactions, episodic maladaptive hyperarousal, impaired information processing and impulse control, self-critical and aggression-endorsing cognitive schemas, and peer relationships that model and reinforce disinhibited reactions, maladaptive ways of thinking, and aggressive, antisocial, and delinquent behaviors (Ford et al., 2012).

Research also supports the view that complex trauma compromises the development of core self-regulatory competences (Ford, 2005), including: 1) attention and learning; 2) sensorimotor functions; 3) working (short-term processing), declarative (verbal), and narrative (autobiographical) memory; and 4) emotion regulation and social relatedness (attachment).

Those with complex trauma and evidence of polyvictimization and witnessing and/or experiencing multiple traumas are likely to be hypervigilant and typically in survival and self-protection mode. When the brain operates in survival mode (Ford, 2009), chronic changes occur not only in psychological and behavioral functioning (e.g., hypervigilance, dysphoria, reduced tolerance for frustration and delayed gratification, impulsivity) but also in the body's central and autonomic nervous systems (Neumeister, Henry, & Krystal, 2007; Raine, 2002a, b). Such biological changes can severely compromise physical health, as well as override and reduce the functionality of key learning networks in the brain: reward and motivation systems (involving neurotransmitter dopamine), distress tolerance systems (involving the neurotransmitter serotonin), and "executive" systems (involving emotion and information processing in limbic and prefrontal cortex areas) (Raine, 2002a).

PTSD and complex trauma adversely affect brain function and structure. Childhood trauma, and especially early onset of severe and diverse trauma detrimentally affect brain development. The traumatic stress interferes with the normal death of neurons, development of neural pathways, and synaptic pruning. Trauma places a brain's neurocircuitry at risk of being frayed in connections that promote emotional, physical, cognitive, and social development. Certain areas of the brain including the hippocampus, amygdala, anterior cingulate cortex, and the orbitofrontal cortex are critical to the processing and regulating of emotion especially during times of stress.

The adverse effects of complex trauma on adolescent psychosocial functioning and risk of aggression may be due to a variety of mechanisms. The central (brain) and peripheral (autonomic) nervous system alterations associated with childhood exposure to maltreatment and violence are likely to increase stress reactivity, anger, and impulsivity, while reducing the youth's ability to inhibit these reactions and engage in effective problem solving (Weder et al., 2009; Yang, Wu, Hsu, & Ker, 2004; Yang, Shin, Noh, & Stein, 2007; Raine, 2002a).

Substance use disorders

Substance use disorders are the most prevalent diagnosed mental health conditions in forensic and correctional populations. They are the most common comorbid conditions in cases of violence and criminality (Monahan, 2001). The National Institute on Drug Abuse suggests that 50% of all violent episodes in the USA occur when the victim and/or the offender are under the influence of acute intoxication. Substance abuse likely plays a role in two-thirds of violent crimes (i.e., 62% of assault; 68% of manslaughter; 54% of murder or attempted murder; and 52% of rape or sexual assault) (National Institute on Alcohol Abuse and Alcoholism, 1990). Important to this chapter is not only the prevalence of substance use and intoxicated states in violent and sexual violent offending, but also the potential neurocognitive short- and long-term effects on the brain that substances have.

Neurological predictors for increased risk of aggression include: prior brain injury, temporal lobe dysfunction, history of pathological intoxication, and encephalopathy (Boles & Miotto, 2003). Alcohol and drugs might mediate violent behavior through effects on electrical activity in the brain (Reiss & Roth, 1993). Cocaine use may also sensitize a release of limbic/hypothalamic mechanisms for aggressive behavior (Davis, 1996). Exposure to solvents both in recreational and occupational settings has been linked to a toxic encephalopathy (Sharp, Beauvais, & Spence, 1992). Methamphetamine use has been linked to acute neuronal disruption in the cerebral cortex and limbic systems leading to impulsivity and psychotic experiences (Fabian, 2007).

Individuals with mental illness and/or neuropathological and cognitive impairment, such as TBI, are more likely to abuse substances and the combination of cognitive dysfunction and substance abuse places an individual at greater risk for violence (Fishbein, 2000). There also is a consensus with the notion of addiction as a brain disorder characterized by longstanding changes in cognitive functioning, especially in the areas of executive functioning (Goldstein & Volkow, 2002) similar to that in offender populations. Executive deficits in individuals with substance dependence are more generalized (i.e., affecting mechanisms of access, working memory, inhibition, planning, flexibility, and decision making) and are greater in magnitude. Importantly, neuropsychological dysfunction often characterizes both drug abuse and violence and may contribute to traits often cited as precursors to impulsive behaviors, poor decision making, disinhibition, and an inability to assess consequences of an individual's behaviors. Deficits in executive cognitive functioning mediated specifically by the prefrontal cortex are implicated in substance abusers and those that display violent behavior. Therefore, the offender with a tendency to aggression and violence, who is a substance abuser, is even more likely to experience structural and functional neurological impact, especially in the area of executive and attentional functions.

Prevalence rates for neurological dysfunction among aggressive offenders and drug abusers are inconsistent, however, numerous reports indicate the incidence of brain dysfunction is significantly higher within these populations as distinguished to non-aggressive offenders and non-drug abusers and to normal controls (Reiss, Miczek, & Roth, 1994; Volavka, 1995).

In summary, offenders are more likely to experience head injuries than non-offenders. Other risk factors including prior head injuries and substance abuse, neurodevelopmental disorders such as low IQ, ADHD, violent victimization, and child abuse are all correlated with their relationship to violence. While most head injuries are ruled to be mild in nature and are generally uncomplicated concussive experiences, many young offenders are prone to experience a number of these cerebral insults, which would also leave the brain more vulnerable to repetitive frontal/temporal trauma that could elevate risk of aggression and violence.

Sexual Violence, Neuroimaging, and Neuropsychological Functioning

Neuroimaging

The emphasis of this chapter is on the neuroscience, including neuroimaging and neuropsychological functioning, of violent offenders. However, much of the risk assessment conducted by forensic psychologists has to do with more recent sex offender legislation. There have been a number of high profile cases that had to do with sex offenses and sexual homicide offenses in particular, that caused concern among citizens and legislatures about community safety from sex offenders. Subsequently, legislation has been passed regarding continued confinement and even civil commitment of high risk sex offenders. Forensic mental health professionals have been involved in the creation of risk assessment tools aimed at assessing sex offender recidivism. However, the examination of sexual violence from a neuroscience perspective is scant yet imperative. Below will be a brief review on this subject matter.

Fabian (2012) provided a review on the neuropsychology and neuroscience of sexually violent predators. Similar to nonsexual violent offenders, empirical evidence suggests that sexually deviant behavior is associated with cortical and subcortical brain structures, anterior cingulate, and frontal and/or temporal lobe damage, and impairment in prefrontal–striatal–thalamic circuits (Spinella & White, 2006). The frontal and temporal lobes are very much involved with adjusting sex drive – initiation and activation of sexual behaviors – and the subcortical structures, such as the hippocampus and the amygdala as well as a septal complex and hypothalamus, brain stem, and spinal cord, are involved in the adaptation of behavior (Spinella & White, 2006). Joyal, Black, and Dassylva (2007) hypothesized that injury to the circuitry of the frontal cortex, basal temporal lobe, diencephalic structure, and limbic area leads to behavioral disinhibition, hypersexuality, and diminished mate selectivity.

Neuroimaging evidence has indicated that there is reduced blood flow in the frontotemporal areas of the brain in sex offenders as compared to non-sex offenders (Hucker et al., 1986). Empirical brain evidence has demonstrated reduced blood flow in the brain and diminished skull density in sex offenders (Hendricks et al., 1988). Similarly, researchers have found the brains of sex offenders are smaller in the left hemisphere compared to controls and pedophiles showed smaller left hemispheres and right hemispheres, where sexual aggressors were equally split between left and right asymmetries, indicating temporal horn dilation in pedophiles and sexual aggressives (Wright, Nobrega, Langevin, & Wortzman, 1990).

The two primary areas of the brain that likely receive the most attention in relationship to criminally violent and sexually violent behaviors are the temporal and frontal lobes. As noted above, the frontal lobes are responsible for higher-order executive functioning including judgment and abstract reasoning, modulating, regulating and controlling behavior, and empathy. The dorsolateral prefrontal cortex (dlPFC) is associated with cognitive functions including language, working memory, and selective and sustained attention. The ventral and polar frontal cortices assist in regulating emotions and decision making as well as social awareness. The orbitofrontal cortex appears to be related to sex offending due to its role in regulating behavior and its intimate neural circuits in connection with the limbic system (Spinella & White, 2006). This area of the brain is activated during sexual arousal and is noted to be relevant in neuroimaging studies (Redouté et al., 2000). It is also indicated as being a significant factor in overall mood regulation, impulsivity, and behavioral control, as well as aggression and violence and sexual violence. Dressing et al. (2001) examined neuronal activation with functional MRI (fMRI) in homicidal pedophiles and found activation of the attention network and of the right orbitofrontal cortex. This region is also important in the role of empathy, which sex offenders often lack. Importantly, much of the research on neuroimaging and brain function and structure with sex offenders include case studies rather than larger sample studies. Research in isolated cases is associated with hypersexuality after a thalamic infarction disrupting frontal–striatal–thalamic circuits (Spinella, 2004).

In summary, the orbital prefrontal cortex and areas such as the ventral anterior cingulate cortex are associated with motivation as well as inhibition of impulsive aggression, and dysregulation in these brain circuits that are connected with the limbic structures of the brain have been indicated in persons with impulse control disorders and problems with aggression and sexual aggression.

The temporal lobe, including the limbic system, is heavily researched regarding neuroimaging and sex offending. The areas including the temporal lobes and amygdala are responsible for processing unprovoked and exaggerated anger, memory, intellectual impairment, behavioral control, impulsivity, and receptive language impairment. The amygdala functions as a low order autonomic neural processing center and is in charge of the regulation of immediate emotional impulses. Sartorius et al. (2008) recently examined amygdala activation with fMRI imaging in pedophiles, and found that pedophilic men exhibit significantly more amygdala activation to child images than adults.

Other areas of the subcortical structures of the brain include the thalamus and hypothalamus, septum, and hippocampus and the basal ganglia, and when impaired they have been indicated to be associated with hypersexuality and paraphilic behaviors. Lesions of the septal nuclei in humans have been indicated in hypersexuality, such as inappropriate sexual language and public masturbation (Gorman & Cummings, 1992). Temporal lobes have been the subject of the most attention as being damaged and affected within heterogeneous groups of sex offenders, leading to hypersexuality and sexually sadistic behavior (Blumer, 1970; Hucker et al., 1986; Joyal et al., 2007; Langevin, 2009; Langevin and Cunroe, 2008a).

Neuroimaging has revealed temporal lobe structure and functional impairments in pedophiles and offenders who have sexually assaulted and raped adults (Cohen et al., 2002). CT and MRI brain imaging data have revealed that pedophiles and rapists experience temporal horn dilation and reduction in the temporal-frontal region of the brain along with reduced blood flow to these areas (Graber, Hartmann, Coffman, Huey, & Golden, 1982; Wright et al., 1990). Cantor et al. (2008) have found that MRI data shows significant negative associations between pedophilia and white matter volumes in the temporal and parietal lobes bilaterally. A handful of studies of MRI-based structural differences in pedophiles have been published by means of voxel-based morphometry, alterations in grey matter and white matter. In a study of 18 incarcerated heterosexual and homosexual pedophilic men with history of sex offending against prepubertal children, significantly lower grey matter volume was found in the bilateral orbitofrontal cortex, bilateral insula, bilateral ventral striatum, precuneus, left posterior cingulate, as well as superior right middle temporal, parahippocampal gyrus, and cingulate compared to 24 normal men (Tenbergen et al., 2015). In an MRI study of homosexual pedophiles, with a history of sexual offenses against children, the substantia nigra, caudate nucleus, the occipitotemporal and prefrontal cortices, thalamus, globus pallidus, and the striatum were activated in response to male child sexual stimuli (Schiffer et al., 2008). In another study, Schiffer et al. (2008) found that the orbitofrontal deactivation as shown in pedophilic participants represents a dysfunction of the neural network necessary for the appropriate cognitive component of sexual arousal processing. Langevin et al. (1985) studied pedophiles, incest offenders, sexual aggressors, and nonsexual violent offenders, and found reduced left frontal and temporal areas in sex offenders, while pedophiles displayed smaller left than right hemispheres, more so than other groups.

When turning to rapists, brain imaging studies appear to be less profound in their results than with pedophiles. Similarly, there is little research in this field that focuses on sexual homicide offenders or sexual sadists. Hucker et al. (1988) found right temporal lobe abnormalities in a sample of sexual sadists, while Langevin, Wortzman, Dickey, Wright, and Handy (1988) found abnormal CT scans in 40% of their sex killer group and 60% of their sex aggressor group, with typical impairments relative to right temporal horn dilation. Raine (1994) found significantly lower glucose metabolism in both the lateral and medial prefrontal cortex in a sample of murderers, and this was replicated in an expanded sample of subjects, with some of them being sexual murderers.

In addition to neuroimaging studies with sex offenders, brain injury is common among both pedophiles and rapists (Fabian, 2012). Langevin (2005) found that 48% of the sex offenders studied had a history of head injuries leading to unconsciousness and about 22% sustained significant neurological insults, with a major cause–effect being motor vehicular accidents. Blanchard et al. (2002) examined pedophiles, and found that they had more history of head injuries before age 13 than control groups.

The neuroimaging data suggest a connection between neuropathology and damaged frontotemporal circuitry with sexual deviance, yet these findings are consistent with those who are impulsive and antisocial and engage in nonspecific violence.

Neuropsychological functioning

While neuroimaging studies of sex offenders focus on the frontal and temporal areas of the brain, neuropsychological assessment of this unique population accordingly focuses often on executive functioning relevant to the frontal systems. Joyal et al. (2007) studied the neuropsychology of sexual deviants and found that a profile of lower-ordered executive functions including sustained attention and inhibition and verbal deficits, with intact or good capacities for higher-order executive functioning such as reasoning and cognitive flexibility, and visuospatial processing was preferentially found among sex offenders, ultimately suggesting basal frontotemporal anomalies. This group found that pedophiles were more consistently and severely impaired than rapists. They theorize that the basal frontotemporal profile is not characteristic of sexual deviance, as it is also found in association with delinquency and general criminality.

Researchers have found neuropsychological deficits in mentally disordered sex offenders, specifically to the left frontotemporal area of the brain (Gillespie & McKenzie, 2000). When considering pedophiles, Tost et al. (2004) found that pedophiles were impaired in neuropsychological functions germane to prefrontal and motor processing loops including response inhibition, working memory, and cognitive flexibility. Martin (1999) found that pedophiles were more cognitively impaired than rapists, especially in tasks of attention and memory, supporting the frontotemporal dysfunction theory. Langevin, Lang, Wright, Handy, and Majpruz (1989) examined child molesters and rapists and found that subgroups of pedophiles revealed patterns of neuropsychological impairments and that heterosexual and homosexual pedophiles exhibited verbal deficits and left hemispheric brain dysfunction, whereas bisexual pedophiles did not have similar results, and revealed right hemispheric visuospatial deficits. Other researchers such as Blanchard et al. (1999) and Cantor, Blanchard, Robichaud, and Christensen (2005) compared IQ scores, and found pedophiles to score lower than rapists of adults. Hucker et al. (1986) found that pedophiles suffer more commonly from left than right hemispheric impairments on the Halstead-Reitan Battery and the Luria-Nebraska Battery.

Deutsher (2004) further studied neuropsychological assessment in sex offenders. This author noted the neuropsychological assessments of various sex offender populations as inconsistent and inconclusive. The author investigated brain function in males convicted and incarcerated for sex offenses against children using neuropsychological assessment. The author administered neuropsychological tests to incarcerated male sex offenders, incarcerated male non-sex offenders, and a control group with no criminal history. Sex offenders performed significantly worse than the controls on all neuropsychological tests. Statistically significant differences were only found between sex offenders and the controlled group on immediate recall trials of a verbal learning and memory test and a complex figure memory test. There was insufficient evidence from the study to support the hypothesis that sex offenders have functional impairment in the frontal and temporal lobes.

Intellectual functioning has also been related to sex offending in that low IQ and especially verbal IQ is related to criminality and violence and has also been related to sexual violence (Langevin, 2005). This author found that 38% of heterogenous groups of sex offenders show at least a 10-point difference in lower verbal IQ than performance IQ, and 22.5% revealed a 15-point difference.

Langevin and Cunro (2008b) further examined neuropsychological impairments among sex offenders and found that about one-third of them were impaired on the Halstead-Reitan Battery, but did not differ significantly from non-sex offender controls. These non-sex offender controls were forensic psychiatric patients and many of them were violent and shared similar lifestyle variables of the sex offender group. The results ultimately suggest that there may be no difference between sex offender and non-sex offender criminal offenders. They did find, however, that child sex offender groups were more significantly impaired than sex offenders against adult victims such as rapists, which seems to be a common finding in the research.

In perhaps the most important and recent research study in meta-analysis of the neuropsychology of sex offenders, Joyal, Beaulieu-Plante, and de Chanterac (2014) reviewed 23 neuropsychological studies on over 1,700 participants. They found that sex offenders against children tended to obtain lower scores than did sex offenders against adults on higher-ordered executive functions, whereas sex offenders against adults tended to obtain results similar to those of non-sex offenders, with lower scores in verbal fluency and inhibition. The authors concluded that neuropsychological data on sex offenders is too scarce to confirm these trends or to test more precise hypotheses. These authors found that sex offenders performed significantly lower than non-sex offenders when all neuropsychological tasks were considered. The authors concluded from their analyses that sex offenders as a group present a significantly wide range in cognitive impairments compared with the general population. Sex offenders against children tend to score lower than sex offenders against adults on the Wisconsin Card Sorting Test (WCST) assessing deduction and cognitive flexibility, although they were significantly better on the COWAT (verbal fluency) and a Stroop Test (control of internal interference and inhibition). Both subgroups of prepubescent child molesters obtained comparable results on a trail-making test assessing mental flexibility and motor speed. They found that sex offenders against adults tended to score similarly to non-sex offenders on tasks of inhibition and verbal deficits.

Much of the research on neuropsychological functioning and sex offenders has focused on a frontotemporal notion of brain dysfunction. Furthermore, a growing number of neuropsychological and neuroimaging reports suggest that pedophiles as a group are more cognitively impaired than rapists of adults (Joyal et al., 2007).

Recent neuropsychological studies of sex offenders have focused on their executive functioning, and this recent meta-analysis certainly sheds light on the field of brain functioning in sex offenders. Overall, sex offenders against children scored lower than did sex offenders against adults in higher-order functions, and sex offenders against adults obtained results similar to those of non-sex offenders, with lower scores in

862   *J. M. Fabian*

verbal fluency and inhibition. The authors poignantly suggest that more specific neuropsychological assessments may help identify different risk factors associated with sexual offending, such as general delinquency, antisociality, impulsivity, and risk taking, or low social competency including asociality, poor social skills, and poor high order executive functioning. Perhaps the risk factors associated with sexual offending including general criminality, impulsivity, and risk taking would be related to rapists, whereas low social competence and poor high order executive functioning would be aligned with child molesters and pedophiles. Accordingly, neuropsychological assessments then could be based on more specific measures, often focusing on verbal and language skills and executive functioning skills, as well as potentially social perception and social cognitive assessment.

Forensic and Legal Applications of Neuroscience and the Law

Approaches to violence risk assessment

While the substance of this chapter has addressed the association between neuropsychological and neurological brain pathology, functioning, and structure with violence, the practice of standardized risk assessment of violence has not traditionally incorporated brain functioning. Mental health clinical and forensic clinicians are often asked to examine and determine an individual's risk of future violence and sexual violence. Violence risk assessments are examined in a wide variety of clinical and forensic situations including probation/parole decisions, death penalty evaluations, involuntary civil commitments, inpatient care decisions and discharges, sex offender risk assessments, and fitness for duty evaluations, for example.

The nature of violence risk includes a multifaceted construct that includes the type of what kinds of violence might occur, the severity and how serious the violence might be, the frequency of how often the violence might occur, the imminence of how soon the violence may occur, and the likelihood and probability that the violence might occur (Doyle & Dolan, 2008). Much of the literature and forensic mental health practice is focused on violence risk assessment in persons with mental illness (Monahan, Steadman, & Silver, 2001; Mulvey & Lidz, 1985; Scott & Resnick, 2006). There are a number of risk factors associated with violence in adults including current young age, young age at first violent offense, personality disorder, male gender, prior violence, substance abuse, access to weapons, specific psychotic symptoms such as delusions and command hallucinations, and mood disorders, among other elements (Monahan, 2001; Monahan & Steadman, 1994). However, the risk factor of neuropsychological and neurological dysfunction has not gained much attention in the process and mechanism of violence risk assessment and is often considered only on a case-by-case individual offender basis.

A brief review of risk assessment approaches

When assessing current dangerousness and violence risk and sexual violence risk in adults and juveniles, a number of risk assessment analyses and procedures may be utilized (Fabian, 2006). Standardized risk assessment includes a number of different methods such as unstructured professional judgment, structured professional judgment, anamnestic risk assessment, and actuarial approach. Briefly, an unstructured professional judgment approach is a clinically based risk assessment derived from the clinician's observations, experience, and professional judgment and overall impressions of an individual, while a structured professional judgment assessment involves an examiner focusing on empirically based risk factors to guide decisions. The anamnestic risk assessment includes the examiner reviewing past events to identify behavioral patterns of violence and aggression that may occur within a particular individual. Finally, the actuarial approach includes a more statistical method of assessment of violence risk relevant to a number of predictors or factors that are weighted as a graduated probability measure representing the amount of risk attributed to the individual. Actuarial measures are based on specific assessment data derived from group data and they have been found to be more accurate than unstructured clinical approaches. However, these approaches are non-discretionary and focus only on a number of factors grounded in research, ignoring potentially critical case-specific individual factors germane to the particular offender being evaluated, such as brain injury, stroke, ADHD, or learning disability. This approach may diminish critical individual risk factors that may not have been tested or supported by the research empirically or may be relevant to the particular offender and their pattern of violence at hand.

An example of an actuarial risk assessment tool for the assessment of violence would be the Violence Risk Appraisal Guide (VRAG) consisting of 12 items, essentially standardized from information from several hundred patients in a maximum-security hospital (Webster, Harris & Rice, 1994; Rice, Harris, & Lang, 2013). Items on the VRAG include psychopathy, prior criminal offending for both nonviolent and violent offenses, substance abuse problems, mental illness, age of offender, personality disorder diagnosis, and schizophrenia, for example. However, there is no mention specifically of neuropsychological impairments, TBI, ADHD, overall general cerebral dysfunction and brain damage, or neuropsychological/neuroimaging assessment, which are areas of concern highlighted throughout this chapter that have relationships with violence.

Similarly, when assessing sexual violence risk, the Static-99R has been deemed the most widely used and accepted actuarial instrument to assess sexual violence (Hanson, et al., 2012). This actuarial instrument, similar to the VRAG, considers a number of items that are found to be statistically correlated with sexual recidivism including, but not limited to, age at release, marital status, prior sex offenses, unrelated victims, and prior sentencing dates. Again, there is no specific consideration as to risk factors related to brain dysfunction and neuropathology or neuropsychological impairments.

The question remains as to whether actuarial risk assessment methods can actually generalize to a particular offender. The answer to this question is likely not. A particular violent or sexually violent offender with significant brain dysfunction and/or brain injury may have offending patterns that are unique and may not be well represented in the offender developmental representative samples of the actuarial measure. Actuarial risk assessments have limitations with substantial margins of error when it comes to making predictions. In essence, the average probability for the validation developmental sample does not necessarily reflect any individual case in that sample (Vincent, Maney & Hart, 2009).

Structured professional judgment is a practical approach that attempts to bridge the gap between the scientific actuarial approach and the unstructured clinical practice of risk assessment (Douglas, Cox, & Webster, 1999; Douglas, Ogloff, & Hart, 2003). Structured professional judgment approaches include a combination of a variety of risk prediction and management elements. The risk factors are grounded in empirical literature applicable to risk factors that are correlated with violence but, in addition to static factors such as prior violent acts, they also address dynamic issues such as insight into mental illness, attitudes toward treatment, and future plans. This approach recommends the process of clinical risk assessment, which is a dynamic and continuous process mitigated by changing conditions (Doyle & Dolan, 2007). Structured professional judgment involves assessment approaches that are grounded in empirical literature related to recidivism but also includes current, past, and future factors that may be related to violence and sexual violence risk.

For example, the HCR-20: Assessing Risk for Violence Instrument[3] (Pedersen, Ramussen, & Elsass, 2010) is a broadband violence risk assessment with 20 items dividing historical, clinical risk management items (Webster, Douglas, Eaves, & Hart; Pedersen et al. 2010). The items entail: historical data, such as previous violence, age at first violent offense, and history of abuse; clinical items, such as current symptomatology and psychosocial adjustment; and risk management items, such as release and treatment plan issues and exposure to destabilizers in the environment. Again, the factors do not specifically highlight or concern the importance of neuropsychological and neurological brain impairments. Rather, the clinical items emphasize mental illness and psychopathology rather than neuropathology.

Similarly, the SVR-20[4] (Sexual Violence Risk-20) is a structured professional judgment type instrument assessing sexual violence risk. This is a tool for reviewing information and incorporating empirically related risk factors for sexual violence focusing on psychosocial risk factors, sexual offense items, and future plans items (Boer, Hart, Kropp, & Webster, 1997; Rettenberger, Hucker, Boer, & Harris, 2009). Psychosocial adjustment risk factors include history and condition of paraphilia, history of abuse, employment, and criminal history, while sexual offense items comprise factors related to past offending including multiple victims, and high-density sex offending, while future plans items emphasize attitudes toward treatment. The SVR-20 is a useful tool that guides the professional in conducting a comprehensive assessment of sexual violence risk focusing on prior history, mental health concerns and conditions, and future plans and attitudes about offending and treatment. However, the instrument does not emphasize or specifically consider neuropathology and neuropsychological impairments or deficits for the sex offender, while some of the research noted above does link a connection between brain-based behavior in neuropsychological testing and sexual violence.

In essence, the criminal sex offender who has a history of ADHD and language-based learning disability with an IQ of 75, suffered multiple traumatic brain injuries as a bipolar disordered teenager and adult, and has developed chronic addictions to crystal methamphetamine and toluene (spray paint) is not well considered and represented by the Static-99R developmental samples, and his various neuropsychological factors are not addressed on the SVR-20. Therefore, it is important to note that neuropsychological and neurodevelopmental deficits, neuropathology, and cerebral dysfunction are individual risk factors that may be ignored in some cases due to their absence, yet they are likely present in the majority of cases of violent offenders.

This author recommends in these types of cases, when there may be a connection between neuropathology and brain dysfunction with violent or sexually violent behavior, conducting relevant neuropsychological assessment and neuroimaging (when accessible and affordable) to determine structure and function of the offender's brain and consulting the literature to guide the risk assessment with empirically-based studies regarding neuroscience and violence.

Toward neuroprediction in risk assessment

To date, there may be only one study addressing the neuroprediction of future arrest (Aharoni et al., 2013). These authors noted the fact that one of the strongest and most widely studied risk factors for recidivism is impulsivity and behavioral disinhibition, as well as persistent lack of restraint and consideration of consequences. They stated that risk assessments in neuropsychological measures have been utilized to assess impulsivity germane to a potential goal of predicting future antisocial behavior. These measures may only be intermediary tools for the direct assessment of the brain's inhibitory and cognitive control systems. The authors set out to utilize neuroimaging to examine an offender's brain functioning and its link with future criminal behavior. Specifically, they were concerned with the limbic region of the anterior cingulate cortex associated with error processing, conflict monitoring, response selection, and avoidance learning. They utilized fMRI with offender and non-offender groups on a number of behavioral tasks assessing behavioral impulsivity. Their follow-up procedure included re-arrest data.

The authors found that at least half of the sample was re-arrested and a larger portion of the sample was re-arrested for nonviolent offenses (41.7%) than for violent offenses (9.4%). In summary, they found that error related brain activity elicited during performance of an inhibitory task prospectively predicted subsequent re-arrest among adult offenders within four years of release. The odds that an offender with low anterior cingulate activity would be re-arrested were approximately double than that of an offender with high activity in this brain region. Ultimately, the results suggest a potential neurocognitive biomarker for persistent antisocial behavior.

Forensic neuropsychology and neuroscience and its application in legal proceedings

Forensic mental health professionals are often requested to examine a number of issues in court proceedings. When contemplating the application of forensic neuropsychology and the law, the forensic neuropsychologist expert witness could be utilized in legal proceedings addressing competency to stand trial and waive Miranda rights, not guilty by reason of insanity, sexual violence and violence risk assessments, mitigating circumstances at sentencing, and juvenile waiver/transfer cases to adult court.

Forensic neuropsychology is critically important in assessment of pretrial forensic issues such as competency to stand trial and waive Miranda rights, where neurocognitive functioning is central pertaining to one's cognitive capacity to learn and recall information in court, to process information, and to express and receive language appropriately. Similarly, in Miranda interrogations, neuropsychological skills including reading, language, attention, and memory, are critical to consider when under stressful circumstances. It is vital to take into account the neurocognitive skills of attention, executive functioning, memory, and processing information when addressing a defendant's mental state germane to insanity or diminished capacity defenses that examine a defendant's mental state, including cognitive functioning, at the time of the offenses.

Forensic neuropsychological assessment may play an important role in assessing current cognitive functioning for competency examinations and when analyzing retrospective mental state assessments.

Considering the nature of the discussion in this chapter and the emphasis on violence, mitigation investigations, sexual violence risk assessment and examination as to legal mental abnormality requirements with emphasis on serious difficulty controlling in civil commitment cases, juvenile life without parole evaluations, and juvenile transfer/waiver assessments may be most applicable in the application of neurodevelopmental issues, brain function and dysfunction, and the etiology and risk of violence. Some of these issues have been addressed by the author through review of recent court cases in the USA, see Case Studies 32.1 and 32.2.

This author looked at US Supreme Court case law upholding the civil commitment of high risk sex offenders in the US outlined in two substantial cases – *Kansas v. Hendricks* and *Kansas v. Crane* – and then practically applied forensic neuropsychological assessment to psycholegal issues (Fabian, 2012). In the former case, the US Supreme Court upheld the constitutionality of the civil commitment of high risk sex offenders after they serve their prison terms for necessary care and treatment. The Court upheld the Kansas Act (civil commitment statute) and its procedures and the definition of a "mental abnormality" as a "congenital or acquired condition affecting the emotional or volitional capacity which predisposes the person to commit sexually violent offenses to the degree that such person is a menace to the health and safety of others." The Court concurred with Kansas that the Act limits persons eligible for confinement to persons who are not able to control dangerousness. In the latter *Crane* case, the Court clarified that its earlier holding in *Kansas v. Hendricks* did not set forth a requirement of total or complete lack of control over one's sex offending behavior, but noted that the Constitution does not permit commitment of a sex offender without some lack of control determination.

Traditionally, the field of forensic psychology has taken an active role in the assessment of these cases relevant to the issues of mental abnormality and dangerousness and risk assessment. However, germane to this chapter, the field of forensic neuropsychology has become important to the assessment of mental abnormality and the often litigated *Crane* volitional issue of serious difficulty controlling. Neuropsychological assessments include some tests that may have more relevance to behavioral impulsivity and volitional impairments than other tests. The tests that are most relevant are executive functioning tests, which measure cognitive processes that deal with behavioral regulation and control, inhibition, mental flexibility, problem solving, reasoning, working memory, impulse control, risk taking, planning, abstract thinking, and concept formation.

Importantly, forensic neuropsychological assessment can be applied to the psycholegal issues of mental abnormality and the issue of serious difficulty controlling to examine whether a sex offender qualifies for civil commitment.

Case Study 32.1 Sammy – with history of sexual offenses

Sammy has a history of ADHD diagnosed by age eight. He suffered a severe head injury to his right frontal lobe area in a bicycle accident at age 13. His first sex offense of attempting to rape a nine-year old stranger girl, was his most violent offense on record, and was committed within a year of his TBI. Sammy therefore had early conditions of ADHD and brain injury and had a developing damaged brain. As a youth, Sammy suffered from significant evidence of developmental psychopathology including behavioral and emotional impairments, head injury, ADHD, speech pathology, and special education. Furthermore, his TBI resulted in problems with emotional stability and affected his relationships with peers, which lead to further peer rejection. At age 19, Sammy then committed another sexually violent offense against a five-year old girl and a sexually violent verbal threat against his girlfriend.

Neuroscience research described below has revealed that the adolescent brain does not mature until early adulthood. Adolescents and young adults process emotional information and behave more impulsively due to their early reliance on the limbic system (emotional center) of the brain. The limbic system is the neural system that is impulsive and based on immediate emotional responses rather than the consideration of consequences of behavior, reasoning, and judgment, ultimately compromising one's control over behavior. In contrast, the frontal lobes of the brain are the largest and last area of the brain to fully develop. The frontal lobes (especially the prefrontal cortex) play an important role in the "higher-order" functions; for example, planning and organizing behavior, using previously learned information to problem solve and regulate behavior, controlling impulses, establishing, changing, and maintaining a mental set, modulating and adapting behavior in light of expected consequences, and processing information. The limbic system appears to be dominant and hyperactive earlier in adolescence and young adulthood while the frontal lobes are developing and, as a consequence, adolescents and young adults are more susceptible to engaging in aggression.

Sammy's TBI was in the right frontal lobe area – which, as mentioned, plays an important role in the higher-order neurocognitive functions. Further, his ADHD resulted in a preexisting condition of developmentally impaired neurocircuitry. Together, these two neurocognitive impairments in a developing brain placed him at some risk for behavioral impairments, impulsivity, and aggression. Sammy's most recent sex offense was a non-contact child pornography possession type case at age 42. While presenting with signs of pedophilia, his earlier hands-on offending may be more rooted and engrained in damaged and developing neurocircuitry during adolescent and early adult years and his more recent offending is sexually deviant, but not violent with physical harm to victims. While he had no history of neuropsychological assessment before the current evaluation, his current testing at his civil commitment trial did not demonstrate any evidence of brain dysfunction relevant to attention, executive functioning, intelligence, memory, or language for example.

While his most recent offending of child pornography possession does not have significant etiological connection to his TBI or ADHD condition, his early sequence of ADHD, brain injury, and developing brain conditions placed him at risk for sexual violence and violence as a teen and young adult. His most recent offending was non-sexually violent, and his current neuropsychological testing

> demonstrated a healthy functioning brain with no evidence of functional executive impairments on tests of concept formation, reasoning, impulsive decision making, and disinhibition and impulse control. These data support an argument that Sammy at the time of his civil commitment trial had a relatively healthy brain, and no significant evidence of brain-based dysfunction affecting his volitional control of contact sexual offending.

The current author (Fabian, 2010) analyzed the US Supreme Court's holding in *Roper v. Simmons* (2005) outlawing the death penalty for juveniles, in great part due to ongoing research in brain development, and applied this holding to juvenile transfer and waiver proceedings. In essence, the author considered juveniles and youth brain development, risk of violence, and diminished culpability when considering the Supreme Court's holding in *Kent v. United States* (1966), addressing specific risk factors to consider in juvenile transfer including: potential risk to the community; whether the offense was committed in an aggressive, violent, premeditated, or willful manner; sophistication, maturity, and character of the juvenile; and amenability to treatment and rehabilitation in the juvenile justice system. This author questioned whether an adolescent's developmental, psychological, and neuropsychological frailties, impairments, and vulnerabilities prevented him or her from being tried as an adult. The author cited the American Psychological Association (APA) and the Missouri Psychological Association, as amici curiae that are helpful in understanding behavioral studies and neuropsychological research suggesting that juveniles are less culpable and responsible for their actions than adults. In particular, youth demonstrate deficits in psychosocial maturity affecting judgment and decision making. Factors relevant to these processes in youth include cognitive capacities and information processing, susceptibility to peer influence, attitudes toward perception of risk and consequence, future orientation, and the capacity for self-management (Cauffman & Steinberg, 2000; Grisso & Schwartz, 2000; Steinberg & Cauffman, 1996).

In *Roper*, the US Supreme Court utilized neuroscientific research indicating that the adolescent brain does not mature until early adulthood (Wiener & Miller, 2004; Aronson, 2007; Giedd et al., 1999). The author questioned whether these issues, such as brain development, deficits in information processing, judgment and decision making, impulsivity, and neuropsychological testing in part assessing these functions, could be useful and impactful in juvenile transfer evaluations.

The author questioned whether, since the US juvenile justice policy was founded on a rehabilitative and protective model of justice and if the purposes of punishment in individualized sentence schemes include retribution and deterrence, adolescents who experience impulsivity, low frustration tolerance, and an inability to consider the consequence of their actions could be adequately treated as an adult. The question was asked whether the transfer of an adolescent to adult court would on its face comply with the traditional objectives of juvenile court justice. Finally, the author questioned whether all juvenile waiver transfer evaluations should have some discretionary consideration by the judiciary given the fact that so many of these juveniles have heightened risk factors and developing damaged brains.

Case Study 32.2 Joey – a sexual and violent offender

Joey was a 16-year old defendant, with a history of abuse and neglect, multiple caregiver placements, parental substance abuse problems, his own methamphetamine addiction, and a history of ADHD, depression, and a language-based learning disability with a borderline IQ of 80. He had a prior criminal history of theft, burglary, robbery, unruly behavior, and assault. He was offered outpatient mental health and substance abuse treatments with mixed results. He had a history of probation violations and some escalation of offending. His parents were not active in his treatment and he had been removed from the home due to abuse and neglect, placed in foster homes, and with his grandmother who could not control him. Joey committed a serious juvenile offense of rape, robbery, and assault, which is the instant offense for which the prosecutor was attempting to have the juvenile judge transfer him to be tried in adult court.

Joey was examined pursuant to the holding in *Kent*, focusing on risk assessment and dangerousness utilizing structured violence risk assessment, treatment amenability, and sophistication/maturity. The author found significant deficits in neuropsychological testing pertaining to deficits in impulse control, mental/cognitive flexibility, perseverative problem solving and reasoning, sustained attention, receptive and expressive language skills, reading comprehension, auditory and verbal learning, and processing speed. Psychological testing yielded diagnoses of PTSD and depression, the former consistent with both emotional, cognitive, and behavioral sequelae. Methamphetamine, ADHD, and depression were conceptualized by the author as a tri-diagnostic condition (cognitive, psychiatric, and substance abuse disorders), with a need for a multiple-modality of treatments. His criminal offending and instant offense was described pursuant to a conglomeration of CD, brain development including neurodevelopmental conditions/impairments, low cortical arousal relevant to ADHD, deficits in impulse control and judgment, and inability to appreciate the consequences of his acts. While he posed as a significant general criminal, violent, and sexually violent risk, the issue of risk management was addressed through the state's juvenile justice correctional treatment facility, rather than through adult court, jail, and prison. Within the juvenile justice system, he could be managed in a locked facility with individual and group therapy, psychiatric medication management, and substance abuse treatment programming.

Consistent with example in Case Study 32.2, the US Supreme Court's trend recently has been to consider sentencing mitigation due to brain-related mitigating factors. Similar to the *Roper* opinion, their recent decision in *Graham v. Florida* (2010) held that juvenile offenders could not be sentenced to life in prison without parole for non-homicide offenses. The brief of the American Psychological Association, American Psychiatric Association, National Association of Social Workers, and Mental Health America as amici curiae supporting petitioners (2009)[5] outlined research recognizing developmental characteristics of adolescents, recent neuroscience research revealing that adolescent brains were not yet fully developed in regions related to higher-order executive functions such as impulse control, planning ahead, and risk evaluation, and evidence that anatomical immaturities consonant with juveniles demonstrate psychosocial immaturity.

The brief highlighted that adolescents are statistically over-represented in virtually every category of reckless behavior and are more impulsive than adults and less able to exercise self-control. The brief addressed the Court's holdings in *Roper* and *Graham* considering brain development and the degree of adolescent culpability when they commit criminal acts. Such acts often result from impulsive and ill-considered choices driven by psychosocial immaturity. The brief focused on the fact that psychosocial immaturity is consistent with emergent research regarding brain development and that recent neurobiological research demonstrates that brain systems governing many aspects of social and emotional maturity including impulse control, weighing risks and rewards, planning ahead, simultaneously considering multiple sources of information, and coordinating emotion and cognition continue to mature through adolescence and young adulthood.

Similarly, the US Supreme Court also opined in *Miller v. Alabama* (2012) that mandatory sentences of life without the possibility of parole are unconstitutional for juvenile offenders. The brief for the American Psychological Association, American Psychiatric Association, and National Association of Social Workers as amici curiae in support of petitioners (see *Miller v. Alabama*, 2012) again cited neuroscience research suggesting a potential physiological basis for recognized characteristics of adolescents and, in particular, why adolescent brains are not yet fully mature in regions and systems related to higher-order executive functions including impulse control, planning ahead, and risk avoidance.

In addition to highlighting etiological risk factors of the brain and brain functioning for adolescent type criminal proceedings, capital mitigation at sentencing is also a very relevant forensic issue for forensic neuropsychologists to partake in. A number of US states implement the death penalty and individual state legislation highlights mitigating factors that are consistent, including the age of the defendant at the time of the crime, whether the defendant acted under duress or under the domination of another person, if the capacity of the defendant to appreciate the criminality of their conduct or to conform their conduct to the requirements of law was impaired, and whether the capital felony was committed while the defendant was under the influence of a mental or emotional disturbance (North Carolina General Statutes, Chapter 15A: Criminal Procedure Act)[6].

These highlighted mitigating factors above from the state of North Carolina could all include brain dysfunction and brain development as mitigating circumstances in a capital offense and offender. For example, an individual suffering from ADHD and learning disorder as a child and adolescent, and later suffering from multiple concussions, chronic substance abuse, and addiction, while enduring a history of physical, sexual, and emotional abuse, and complex trauma would present with a number of risk factors affecting brain functioning, which could be considered as mitigating factors, especially if accompanied by past and current neuropsychological functioning and/or neuroimaging deficits in the areas related to violence and aggression (i.e., attention, impulse control, higher-order reasoning, and verbal skills).

Capital mitigation evaluations emphasize psychological and neuropsychological dysfunction and impairments because they may be considered as mitigating and reducing a defendant's moral culpability. The practicing forensic psychologist and neuropsychologist in these proceedings are not responsible for addressing aggravating factors, but rather potential mitigating factors. Therefore, neuropsychological assessment, especially in areas related to aggression and violence such as attention, language, and executive functioning, is key.

In contrast, a few states and the federal government require future dangerousness as an aggravating circumstance in order to implement the death penalty (VTCA Penal Code Section 19.03). In fact, two states – Texas and Oregon – explicitly require jurors in capital cases to consider evidence concerning future dangerousness. Twenty-one states consider a defendant's future dangerousness to be an aggravating circumstance at the sentencing phase of capital trials, although they do not make future dangerousness a necessary condition for the death penalty. Prosecutors have an objective of minimizing mitigating evidence and highlighting aggravating evidence focusing on the defendant's past violent and criminal behavior and propensity and risk for future violence. In fact, they may wish to rebut the potential of mitigating factors presented by a defense expert with their own expert who focuses on other etiological risk factors for the homicidal act and/or future dangerousness.

Accordingly, mental health evidence and issues of brain functioning and dysfunction can also be utilized by prosecutors to set forward a nexus between brain dysfunction and both past and prospective future violence leading to a recommendation for the death penalty. Prosecutors may argue that brain-related dysfunction and its connection to violence, such as head injuries affecting limbic and frontal structures or PTSD affecting limbic structures in particular, may lead certain capital offenders at risk to commit future acts of violence under various circumstances, that is, in prison settings where stress and threat are the norm.

Typically, forensic neuropsychological assessment is generally admissible and rarely questioned in forensic neuropsycholegal proceedings. There are rarely scientific challenges, at least in the USA, as to the validity, reliability, and overall general acceptance of neuropsychological testing and assessment data in legal proceedings.

In *United States v. Sandoval-Mendoza* (2006), Eduardo Sandoval-Mendoza and his brother Ricardo were indicted for conspiracy to distribute methamphetamine. At trial, Sandoval-Mendoza admitted to selling methamphetamine to government informants, but claimed that he had a large pituitary tumor compressing his frontal lobe, temporal lobe, and thalamus. According to the neurologist and neuropsychologist engaged by the defense, an MRI demonstrated that when the tumor size was reduced with chemotherapy, his frontal lobe "herniated" into the empty space and there was atrophy in the left temporal lobe and invasion of a bone separating the pituitary gland from the brain stem. Defense experts determined that Sandoval-Mendoza's performance IQ was in the borderline mental retardation range, which they attributed to the tumor, and opined that the tumor would have caused him to be disinhibited and have deficits in judgment and memory. The trial court judge did not permit Sandoval-Mendoza to call these expert witnesses, as the judge concluded that the experts had not made a causal connection between the tumor and the predisposition to commit the crime, and that the probative value of the evidence would have been outweighed by its tendency to confuse and mislead the jury and cause undue delay. The Ninth

Circuit Court of Appeals reversed this exclusion of evidence and remanded the case for a new trial, stating that the exclusion prevented Sandoval-Mendoza from proving lack of predisposition and hampered his ability to defend himself. The court opined:

> The district court concluded that the proposed medical expert opinion testimony was unreliable because it did not conclusively prove Sandoval-Mendoza's brain tumor caused susceptibility to inducement or a lack of predisposition. But medical knowledge is often uncertain. The human body is complex, etiology is often uncertain and ethical concerns often prevent double-blind studies calculated to establish statistical proof. This does not preclude the introduction of medical opinion testimony when medical knowledge permits the assertion of a reasonable opinion.

In contrast, criminal cases in the USA have addressed the application of neuroimaging in capital cases and there is heightened scrutiny on allowing neuroimaging into court versus neuropsychological assessment. In *People v. Protsman* (2001), the defendant utilized an expert to present PET scan evidence to a jury to mitigate the degree of murder. The expert testified to frontal lobe damage of a TBI. However, in rebuttal, the state's expert testified that PET scan data are not generally accepted in the medical field for diagnosing or evaluating head trauma or predicting behavioral patterns. The California Court of Appeals agreed with the state expert that the defense's application of PET scan images was not supported by the neurology and brain imaging community.

Another case, *Jackson v. Calderon* (2000), addressed PET scan evidence as having poor utility in the courts. The Court considered PET scan evidence in this case and honored the state's expert's testimony, stating that the use of PET scans to diagnosis chronic PCP (phencyclidine) abuse is not generally accepted by the scientific community. In addition, no evidence was introduced that the PET scan proved that Jackson was unable to premeditate or form a specific intent at the time of the shooting. The PET scan evidence could at best only establish that Jackson suffered from a PCP-induced brain abnormality, the effect of which on Jackson's capacity for higher thought was not demonstrated.

In *People v. Ford* (2005), Charles Watson Ford was convicted of first-degree murder and appealed his conviction on multiple grounds, including failure of the trial court to permit an expert witness to testify about a SPECT scan of his brain. At trial, the defense expert testified that Ford's long-term alcoholism and a head injury resulted in impairments or vulnerabilities of his frontal and left temporal lobes. The defense expert concluded that these impairments would affect his reasoning and planning skills, particularly when the defendant was intoxicated. The trial court excluded the SPECT evidence, finding that the technology was not generally accepted within the medical community for diagnostic purposes in a forensic setting. Ford asserted that failure to allow testimony on this SPECT scan was reversible error because it would have provided the jury with a visual image of the defendant's brain impairments and would have supported his claim that he was unable to form the specific intent to premeditate or kill. The *Ford* court upheld the exclusion of this SPECT evidence because the defense expert was still able to testify to all of his conclusions without the scan, the scan merely confirmed the diagnosis the expert otherwise formulated, and admission of the scan was therefore unlikely to have resulted in a more favorable verdict.

In *Commonwealth v. Yancy* (2003), the defendant was convicted of deliberately premeditating the murder of his girlfriend and estranged wife. In an appeal from this conviction, Yancy alleged that defense counsel's failure to call as a witness a neuroradiologist who performed a SPECT scan of the defendant's brain constituted ineffective assistance of counsel. The SPECT scan report, admitted in evidence, stated that the defendant had frontal lobe abnormalities that corresponded with bilateral areas of decreased activity in the frontal lobes, and a right temporal lobe abnormality involving the mesiotemporal cortex, consistent with the defendant's history of head trauma and a seizure disorder. The court conducted a hearing on the motion for a new trial, and took the testimony of the original neuroradiologist. The neuroradiologist testified that the defendant's frontal lobe abnormalities were "subtle" or "small," that there was diminished neuronal activity in the temporal lobe and that there was a reasonable expectation that his seizure disorder contributed to abnormal behavior. The court held that failure to call this neuroradiologist to elaborate on SPECT findings was not ineffective assistance of counsel because it did not prejudice the defendant. The court observed that the neuroradiologist "did not testify that the defendant had an organic brain defect that impaired his capacity to deliberately premeditate or specifically intend the killings" and that his testimony with respect to seizures and abnormal behavior concerned epilepsy as a whole and did not refer to the specific circumstances surrounding the killings. The court concluded that where there were multiple expressions of the intent to kill and unmistakable indicia of planning, expert opinion that the defendant was incapable of intending or premeditating was unlikely to create a reasonable doubt.

Some state supreme courts have emphasized the importance of neuroimaging examinations in capital cases. In *State v. Reid* (2006), the Tennessee Supreme Court accepted the Trial Court's admission of PET scan evidence in which the expert testified that the results indicated shrinkage and atrophy of the left temporal lobe of the defendant's brain. Further, in *State v. Hoskins* (1999) the Supreme Court of Florida ruled that the Trial Court erred in disallowing defense experts to conduct a PET scan of the defendant.

In another case, defendant Peter Chiesa was charged with the first-degree murder of two women. The prosecutor declined to seek the death penalty in light of Chiesa's age (65), diagnosis of vascular dementia, and history of seizures, but refused to negotiate a plea bargain to second-degree murder. Chiesa's defense team initiated a diminished actuality defense (similar to diminished capacity except that, instead of asserting a lack of capacity to form intent, it asserts that the defendant did not actually form the intent) claiming that SPECT scan evidence revealed that he had serious brain abnormalities that impaired his ability to exercise judgment, exert self-control, control his temper, integrate new information, and employ forethought. In support of these conclusions, he presented SPECT evidence of hypoactivity in the prefrontal cortex, temporal lobe, and cerebellum. The jury found Chiesa guilty of two counts of second-degree murder, with one juror subsequently commenting that the neuroimaging brought home the testimony that he suffered from a vascular dementia.

In *People v. Jones* (1994), the defendant was convicted of killing an intruder who was attempting to break into his home. The defendant asserted a defense of justification and requested authorization for neuroimaging, which was denied by the trial court. Jones appealed, claiming that the trial court abused its discretion by denying his application for neurological testing, subsequently referred to as "brain scans." The defendant had apparently suffered a TBI as an adolescent, had sustained unspecified deficits, and had a 30-year history of alcohol abuse. Expert witnesses were prepared to testify that cognitive limitations made the defendant's responses to the victim justifiable. In support of this conclusion, defense witnesses intended to testify that Jones was unable to think quickly and flexibly, had difficulty modifying a course of action and was impaired in his ability to act purposely. The appellate court held that Jones was entitled to present brain scans to support this testimony and remanded the case for a new trial.

In *State v. Risner* (2016), the defense utilized volumetric MRI data in a death penalty mitigation proceeding with a defendant who developed a history of brain trauma and PTSD in the Middle East war zone and then murdered a sheriff who was attempting to arrest him after a road rage incident. The neuroimaging data indicated reduced hippocampal volumes and dilated perivascular spaces. The spaces could be a consequence of TBI or due to an inflammatory process and/or vascular risk factors. The hippocampal shrinkage found in the defendant may be due to a consequence of TBI, seizure disorder, PTSD, and/or delusional disorder. The neuroimaging data also showed particular volume loss in the amygdala, and it was argued by this author/neuropsychologist that this area of the brain is particularly important to the fight and flight phenomenon in PTSD and potentially to a temporal-limbic theory and condition of paranoia and delusional disorder. Further, neuropsychological testing also indicated evidence of brain dysfunction in the dlPFC and therefore, structurally and functionally, both neuropsychological assessment and neuroimaging data were used to explain a subcortical–cortical process of reactive aggression and violence.

Central to presenting neuroimaging data in court is not only the presentation of structural neuroimaging data by neuroradiology or neuroscience professionals, but also the connection of this data to the overall neuropsychological functioning of the individual and optimally to their behavior and violent behavior if possible. The forensic neuropsychologist must know the neuroanatomical function of a particular area of brain impairment, and associate this information to particular neuropsychological tests that measure function in that area. Ultimately, the expert may address this neuroanatomical structure and neuropsychological function with neuropathology/neurological disorders and violence/homicide.

The causal connection between brain function, structure, pathology, and behavior, including violence, is a significant leap. Some courts separate expert testimony, again emphasizing neuroscientist and neuroradiologist testimony to brain structure and function while psychologists, neuropsychologists, and psychiatrists testify about behavior. The forensic neuropsychologist is able to offer brain behavior relationship testimony regarding neuropsychological testing especially in the executive functioning domain to address behavior, and potentially aggression.

Consider the case *People v. Weinstein* (1992), in which Herbert Weinstein was charged with the second-degree murder of his wife. Prosecutors alleged that Weinstein strangled his wife and then threw her from their apartment window in order to make her death appear to be a suicide. At trial, Weinstein intended to claim that he was not criminally responsible for his conduct because of a mental disease or defect, namely a large arachnoid cyst in his frontal lobes. His defense team wanted to introduce a PET scan showing the cyst and an area of abnormal enhancement surrounding part of the cyst in support of this claim. After an evidentiary hearing, the trial court admitted the PET evidence and ruled that defense experts could describe the cyst and metabolic imbalances in Weinstein's brain, but could not testify that the cyst or hypometabolism in the frontal lobes directly caused the violence alleged. After this evidentiary ruling, the defense secured a reduced plea to manslaughter. Important to this holding is the potential of a forensic neuropsychologist's role in proceedings to connect relevant neuropsychological testing, if applicable, to areas of brain functioning and structure that might lead to disinhibition, poor problem solving, and executive functioning, and ultimately to violence and aggression. Courts appear to be more lenient in neuropsychological testimony connecting testing and assessment with behavior and violence than to the link between neuroimaging and behavior.

Accordingly, in *State v. Johnson* (2009), Mr. Johnson was convicted of three counts of bank robbery. On appeal, he alleged that failure to allow a defense expert to testify that his fetal alcohol spectrum disorder (FASD) impaired his ability to form the specific intent to commit theft was an abuse of judicial discretion. The defense offered an expert in fetal alcohol disorders. This expert was permitted to use MRI scans that purportedly demonstrated severe FASD-related brain damage (unspecified), and testified extensively at trial regarding the impact of such damage on executive functioning abilities. The expert, who had never personally examined the defendant, was precluded from testifying that FASD in general impairs the ability to tell right from wrong and was not allowed to give an opinion about the defendant's ability to discern right from wrong. The Johnson court concluded that excluding such testimony was not reversible error, because the defense failed to connect the expert's general knowledge about impairments associated with FASD to the defendant's ability to tell right from wrong at the time of the robberies. Similarly, the court held that without personally evaluating the defendant, he should not have been permitted to offer the opinion that the defendant would have had great difficulty in forming the specific intent to commit a robbery. Critical to this opinion is the emphasis of expert testimony not only to brain structure in neuroimaging and function pursuant to neuropsychological assessment, but the nexus between structure, function, and neuropathology to violence.

Most recently, Adrian Raine, a researcher in the field of neurocriminology known for assessing physical, genetic, and environmental roots of violent behavior, served as an expert witness in a Colorado death penalty case.[7]). Raine examined capital defendant Donta Page, noting he was a man who had a long history of violence, severe abuse and neglect, early head injuries, learning disabilities, poor cognitive functioning, and lead exposure. Raine presented expert testimony as to Page's brain pathology, specifically a distinct lack of activation of the ventral prefrontal cortex responsible for regulating emotions and controlling impulses, coupled with environmental risk factors, ultimately persuading a three-judge panel not to execute him after he was convicted of a sexual homicide. Importantly to this case, a forensic neuropsychologist needs to educate the jury on neuroanatomical function through their neuropsychological assessment but also on other mediating psychosocial risk factors related to violence.

As we have seen, many US courts have taken the lead of the US Supreme Court in considering neuroscientific assessment and evidence in relation to criminal behavior and violence. In addition to contemplating brain functioning in the *Roper* case, the US Supreme Court also recognized in *Atkins v. Virginia* (2005) that the physical condition of a defendant's brain can implicate their capacity for moral culpability relevant to a diagnosis of mental retardation/intellectual disability. The Supreme Court held that it was unconstitutional and cruel and unusual punishment to execute an intellectually disable defendant. In *Atkins*, the Court essentially mandated a fine line diagnosis threshold of mental retardation as a bar to execution. However, recent research and commentary has questioned the broader implication of the Court's reasoning as it relates to those individuals who present with similar neurological damage or brain damage and defect but who do not qualify as mentally retarded pursuant to the decision in *Atkins* or as an adolescent under the age of 18 pursuant to the opinion in *Roper* (Sasso, 2007).

Conversely, the US Supreme Court compromised its holdings in *Roper* and *Atkins*, which relied on neuropsychological and neurological research to exclude groups from the death penalty. Consider death penalty defendant Jeffrey Landrigan, *Schriro v. Landrigan* (2007), who was granted an evidentiary hearing germane to the potential physical and neurological damage he suffered as a result of fetal alcohol syndrome, yet the US Supreme Court reversed, characterizing his brain-related mitigation evidence as weak, and opined that district courts would be forced to reopen factual disputes that were conclusively settled in state courts. The Court's description of the evidence as weak and insubstantial, despite suggesting the defendant may suffer from a serious organic brain disorder, is somewhat confusing given its holdings in *Atkins* and *Roper*. The Court in *Landrigan* failed to acknowledge the likely connection between serious brain damage and the defendant's extremely violent past (Sasso, 2007).

In contrast, the US Supreme Court in *Abdul-Kabir v. Quarterman* (2007) emphasized the importance of neurological-related mitigating evidence and childhood abuse. The Supreme Court held that federal habeas corpus relief was warranted since there was a reasonable likelihood that the state trial court's instructions prevented jurors from giving meaningful consideration to constitutionally relevant mitigating evidence, including brain damage. In essence, the Court recognized that evidence of neurological and brain damage diminishing an offender's moral culpability for his conduct can serve as mitigating evidence at the sentencing phase of his capital trial.

Conclusions

This chapter has emphasized the consideration of brain functioning and violence. It is of note that this chapter could be expanded into book form given the growing empirical research dissecting environmental conditions, psychiatric disorders, brain structure, and function outlined in neuroimaging and neuropsychological assessment and their individual and collective relationships with violence. It is observed that these links are correlative in nature, usually not plainly causative and always allowing for the elusive effects of a number of other variables such as acute effects of substances, personality disorder, and environmental circumstances to add to the explanation of violence. However, the risk for violence may be enhanced with a collective and cumulative effect of these variables in a particular offender. The legal implications of these risk factors may be applied in a number of forensic examples where human behavior encounters with the law such as insanity, mitigation, and violence risk assessment. Traditional evaluation of violence risk in accounting for how a particular offender became violent (retrospective evaluation) and violence risk assessment of a particular offender's future risk of violence (prospective evaluation) has likely been negligent in examining neuropsychological, neurobiological, and neuroscientific causes and conditions. It is the spirit of this chapter that expert witnesses in criminal neuropsychology, neurocriminology, neuroscience, and neuropsychiatry along with attorneys and judges continue to contemplate the application of neuropsychological assessment and neuroimaging to these legal questions when assessing the individual violent offender.

Notes

1 It should also be noted that Chapter 17 examines risk factors for offending in detail.
2 See https://clinicaltrials.gov/ct2/show/NCT00132249.
3 See http://hcr-20.com.
4 See http://proactive-resolutions.com/shop/manual-for-the-sexual-violence-risk-svr-20/.
5 See http://www.apa.org/pubs/highlights/spotlight/issue-73.aspx.
6 See http://www.ncga.state.nc.us/gascripts/Statutes/StatutesTOC.pl?Chapter=0015A.
7 See http://online.wsj.com/news/articles/SB10001424127887323354045784446828 92520530.

Recommended Reading

Fishbein, D. (2000). Neuropsychological function, drug abuse, and violence: A conceptual framework. *Criminal Justice and Behavior, 27*(2), 139–159. doi:10.1177/0093854800027002001. *This paper is valuable in discussing how violence shares many of the same underlying mechanisms of substance abuse given the comorbidity and commonalities in behavioral dimensions and how neuropsychological dysfunction consistently characterizes both drug abuse and violence.*

Joyal, C., Beaulieu-Plante, J., & de Chanterac, A. (2014). The neuropsychology of sex offenders: a meta-analysis. *Sex Abuse, 26*(2), 149–177. *An important meta-analysis analyzing the neuropsychological correlates to sex offending with different sex offender populations and providing valuable information on executive functioning and its link to sexual violence.*

Raine, A. (2002b). Biosocial studies of antisocial and violent behavior in children and adults: A review. *Journal of Abnormal Child Psychology, 30*(4), 311–326. *Important paper that investigates the connection between multiple social and biologial risk factors and how they interact pertaining to violent and antisocial behaviors.*

Shiroma, E. J., Ferguson, P. L., & Pickelsimer, E. E. (2010). Prevalence of TBI in an offender population: A meta-analysis. *Journal of Correctional Health Care, 16*(2), 147–159. *A meta-analysis on the rare topic of the prevalence of TBI in prisons and discussion on how researchers measure severity of head injuries.*

References

Abdul-Kabir v. Quarterman (2007) 127 S.Ct. 1654.

Allely, C. S., Minnis, H., Thompson, L., Wilson, P., & Gillberg, C. (2014). Neurodevelopmental and psychosocial risk factors in serial killers and mass murderers. *Aggression and Violent Behavior, 19*, 288–301. doi: 10.1016/j.avb.2014.04.004.

American Psychiatric Association (1994). *Diagnostic and statistical manual of mental disorders* (4th ed.) (*DSM-IV*). Washington, DC: American Psychiatric Association.

Anckarsäter, H. (2006). Central nervous changes in social dysfunction: Autism, aggression, and psychopathy. *Brain Research Bulletin, 69*(3), 259–265. doi: 10.1016/j.brainresbull.2006.01.008.

Aronson, J. D. (2007). Brain imaging, culpability and the juvenile death penalty. *Psychology, Public Policy, and Law, 13*(2), 115–142. doi: org/10.1037/1076-8971.13.2.115.

Atkins v. Virginia 536 U.S. 304 (2002).

Barkataki, I., Kumari, V., Das, M., Hill, M., Morris, R., O'Connell, P., ... Sharma, T. (2005). A neuropsychologil investigaiton into violence and mental illness. *Schizophrenia Research, 74*, 1–13. doi: 10.1016/j.schres.2004.08.001.

878   *J. M. Fabian*

Barkley, R. A. (2008). Challenges in diagnosing adults with ADHD. *Journal of Clinical Psychiatry, 69*(12), e36.

Barnfield, T. V., & Leathem, J. M. (1998). Incidence and outcomes of traumatic brain injury and substance abuse in a New Zealand prison population. *Brain Injury, 12*(6), 455–466. doi: 10.1080/026990598122421.

Baron-Cohen, S. (1991). Precursors to a theory of mind: Understanding attention in others. In A. Whiten (Ed.), *Natural theories of mind: Evolution, development and simulation of everyday mindreading* (pp. 233–251). Cambridge, MA: Basil Blackwell.

Beckham, J. C., Moore, S. D., & Reynolds, V. S. (2000). Interpersonal hostility and violence in vietnam combat veterans with chronic posttraumatic stress disorder. *Aggression and Violent Behavior, 5*(5), 451–466. doi: 10.1016/S1359-1789(98)00018-4.

Blake, P. Y., Pincus, J. H., & Buckner, C. (1995). Neurologic abnormalities in murderers. *Neurology, 45*(9), 1641–1647. doi: 10.1212/WNL.45.9.1641.

Blanchard, R., Christensen, B., Strong, S., Cantor, J., Kuban, M., Klassen, P., ... Black, T. (2002). Retrospective self-reports of childhood accidents causing unconsciousness in phallometrically diagnosed pedophiles. *Archives of Sexual Behavior, 31*(6), 511–526. doi: 10.1023/A:1020659331965.

Blanchard, R., Watson, M., Choy, A., Dickey, R., Klassen, P., Kuban, M., & Ferren, D. J. (1999). Pedophiles: Mental retardation, maternal age, and sexual orientation. *Archives of Sexual Behavior, 28*, 111–127. doi: 10.1023/A:1018754004962.

Blumer, D. (1970). Hypersexual Episodes in Temporal Lobe Epilepsy. *The American Journal of Psychiatry, 126*(8), 1099–1106.

Boer, D. P., Hart, S., Kropp, P. R., & Webster, C. D. (1997). Sexual Risk Violence-20. Psychological Assessment Resources, Inc.

Boles, S., & Miotto, K. (2003). Substance abuse and violence: A review of the literature. *Aggression and Violent Behavior, 8*(2), 155–174. doi: 10.1016/S1359-1789(01)00057-X.

Brooks, N., Campsie, L., Symington, C., Beattie, A., & McKinlay, W. (1986). The five year outcome of severe blunt head injury: A relative's view. *Journal of Neurology, Neurosurgery and Psychiatry, 49*(7), 764–770.

Brower, M. C., & Price, B. H. (2001). Neuropsychiatry of frontal lobe dysfunction in violent and criminal behaviour: A critical review. *Journal of Neurology, Neurosurgery and Psychiatry, 71*(6), 720–726. doi: 10.1136/jnnp.71.6.720.

Bufkin, J. L., & Luttrell, V. R. (2005). Neuroimaging studies of aggressive and violent behavior: Current findings and implications for criminology and criminal justice. *Trauma Violence and Abuse, 6*(2), 176–191. doi: 10.1177/1524838005275089.

Cantor, J., Blanchard, R., Robichaud, L., & Christensen, B. (2005). Quantitative reanalysis of aggregate data on IQ in sexual offenders. *Psychological Bulletin, 131*(4), 555–568. doi: 10.1037/0033-2909.131.4.555.

Cantor, J., Kabani, N., Christensen, B., Zipursky, R., Barbaree, H., Dickey, R., ... Blanchard, R. (2008). Cerebral white matter deficiencies in pedophilic men. *Journal of Psychiatric Research, 42*, 167–183. doi: 10.1016/j.jpsychires.2007.10.013.

Capaldi, D. M., & Patterson, G. R. (1996). Can violent offenders be distinguished from frequent offenders: Prediction from childhood to adolescence. *Journal of Research in Crime and Delinquency, 33*(2), 206–231. doi: 10.1177/0022427896033002003.

Cauffman, E. (2005). Psychological, neuropsychological, and physiological correlates of serious antisocial behavior in adolescence: The role of self-control. *Criminology, 43*(1), 133–176. doi: 10.1111/j.0011-1348.2005.00005.x.

Cauffman, E., & Steinberg, L. (2000). (Im)maturity of judgment in adolescence: Why adolescents may be less culpable than adults. *Behavioral Sciences & the Law, 18*(6) 741–760.

Chemtob, C. M., Novaco, R. W., Hamada, R. S., & Gross, D. M. (1997). Cognitive-behavioral treatment for severe anger in posttraumatic stress disorder. *Journal of Consulting and Clinical Psychology, 65*(1), 184–189. doi: 10.1037/0022-006X.65.1.184.

Cohen, L., Nikiforov, K., Gans, S., Poznansky, O., McGeoch, P., Weaver, C., ... Galynker, I. (2002). Heterosexual male perpetrators of childhood sexual abuse: A preliminary neuropsychiatric model. *Psychiatric Quarterly, 73*(4), 313–336. doi: 10.1023/A:1020416101092.

Commonwealth v. Yancy (2003) 440 Mass, 234.

Conners, C. K., Erhardt, D., & Sparrow, E. (2004). Conner's Adult ADHD Rating Scales: Correctional Settings, MHS.

Connor, D. F., Doerfler, L. A., Toscano, P. F. Jr., Volungis, A. M., & Steingard, R. J. (2004). Characteristics of children and adolescents admitted to a residential treatment center. *Journal of Child and Family Studies, 13*(4), 497–510.

Cook, A., Spinazzola, P., Ford, J., Lanktree, C., Blaustein, M., Cloitre, M., ... van der Kolk, B. (2005). Complex trauma in children and adolescents. *Psychiatric Annals, 35*(5), 390–398.

Davidson, R. J., Putnam, K. M., & Larson, C. L. (2000). Dysfunction in the neural circuitry of emotion regulation- A possible prelude to violence. *Science, 289*(5479), 591–594. doi: 10.1126/science.289.5479.591.

Davis, W. M. (1996). Psychopharmacologic violence associated with cocaine abuse: Kindling of a limbic dyscontrol syndrome? *Progress in Neuro-Psychopharmacology and Biological Psychiatry, 20*(8), 1273–1300. doi: 10.1016/S0278-5846(96)00126-1.

Day, R., & Wong, S. (1996). Anomalous perceptual asymmetries for negative emotional stimuli in the psychopath. *Journal of Abnormal Psychology, 105*, 648–652. doi: 10.1037/0021-843X.105.4.648.

Dein, K., & Woodbury-Smith, M. (2010). Asperger syndrome and criminal behavior. *Advances in Psychiatric Treatment, 16*(1), 37-43. doi: 10.1192/apt.bp.107.005082

DelBello, M. P., Soutullo, C. A., Zimmerman, M. E., Sax, K. W., Williams, J. R., McElroy, S. L., & Strakowski, S. M. (1999). TBI in individuals convicted of sexual offenses with and without bipolar disorder. *Psychiatry Research, 89*(3), 281–286. doi: 10.1016/S0165-1781(99)00112-2.

Deutsher, M. (2004). A Neuropsychological Assessment of Adult Sex Offenders. (Unpublished doctoral dissertation). Institute of Swinburne University, Australia.

Di Martino, A., Ross, K., Uddin, L. Q., Sklar, A. B., Castellanos, F. X., & Milham, M. P. (2009). Functional brain correlates of social and nonsocial processes in autism spectrum disorders: An activation likelihood estimation meta-analysis. *Biological Psychiatry, 65*(1), 63–74.

Dolan, M. (1994). Psychopathy – A neurobiological perspective. *British Journal of Psychiatry, 165*, 151–159.

Dolan, M., & Park, I. (2002). The neuropsychology of antisocial personality disorder. *Psychological Medicine, 32*, 417–427.

Douglas, K. S., Cox, D. N., & Webster, C. D. (1999). Violence risk assessment: Science and practice. *Legal and Criminological Psychology, 4*(2), 149–184. doi: 10.1348/135532599167824.

Douglas, K. S., Ogloff, J. R. P., & Hart, S. D. (2003). Evaluation of a model of violence risk assessment among forensic psychiatric patients. *Psychiatric Services, 54*(10), 1372–1379. doi: org/10.1176/appi.ps.54.10.1372.

Doyle, M., & Dolan, M. (2008). Understanding and managing risk. In K. Soothill, P. Rogers, & M. Dolan (Eds.), *Handbook of Forensic Mental Health* (pp. 244–266). London/New York, NY: Routledge/Willan Publishing.

Dressing, H., Obergriesser, T., Tost, H., Kaumeier, S., Ruf, M., & Braus, D. F. (2001) Homosexual pedophilia and functional networks – An fMRI case report and literature review. *Fortschritte der Neurologie-Psychiatrie, 69*(11), 539–544.

Dutton, D. G., & Hart, S. D. (1992). Evidence for long-term, specific effects of childhood abuse and neglect on criminal behavior in men. *International Journal of Offender*

Therapy and Comparative Criminology, 36(2), 129–137. doi: 10.1177/0306624 x9203600205.

Elbogen, E. B., Fuller, S., Johnson, S. C., Brooks, S., Kinneer, P., Calhoun, P. S., & Beckham, J. C. (2010). Improving risk assessment of violence among military veterans: An evidence-based approach for clinical decision-making. *Clinical Psychology Review, 30*(6), 595–607. doi: 10.1016/j.cpr.2010.03.009.

Fabian, J. M. (2006). A literature review of the utility of selected violence and sexual violence risk assessment instruments. *Journal of Psychiatry & Law, 34*(3), 307–350. doi: org/10.1177/009318530603400304.

Fabian, J. M. (2007). Methamphetamine motivated murder: Forensic psychological/psychiatric and legal applications in criminal contexts. *Journal of Psychiatry & Law, 35*(4), 443–474. doi: org/10.1177/009318530703500403.

Fabian, J. M. (2009). Mitigating murder at capital sentencing: An empirical and practical psycho-legal strategy. *Journal of Forensic Psychology Practice, 9*(1), 1–34. doi: 10.1080/15228930802425084.

Fabian, J. M. (2010). Neuropsychological and neurological correlates in violent and homicidal offenders: A legal and neuroscience perspective. *Aggression and Violent Behavior, 15*(3), 209–223.

Fabian, J. M. (2011). Assessing a Sex Offender with Asperger's Disorder: A Forensic Psychological and Neuropsychological Perspective. *Sex Offender Law Report, 12*(5), 65–80.

Fabian, J. M. (2012). Neuropsychology, neuroscience, volitional impairment and sexually violent predators: A review of the literature and the law and their application to civil commitment proceedings. *Aggression and Violent Behavior, 17*(1), 1–15. doi: 10.1016/j.avb.2011.07.002.

Farrington, D. P. (1990). Implications of criminal career research for the prevention of offending. *Journal of Adolescence, 13*(2), 93–113. doi: 10.1016/0140-1971(90)90001-N.

Fedora, O., & Fedora, S. (1983). Some neuropsychological and psychophysiological aspects of psychopathic and non-psychopathic criminals. In P. Flor-Henry, & J. H.Gruzelier (Eds.), *Laterality and psychopathology*. Amsterdam: Elsevier.

Filley, C. M., Price, B. H., Nell, V., Antoinette, T., Morgan, A. S., Bresnahan, J. F., ... Kelly, J. P. (2001). Toward an understanding of violence: Neurobehavioral aspects of unwarranted physical aggression: Aspen Neurobehavioral Conference consensus statement. *Neuropsychiatry Neuropsychology and Behavioral Neurology, 14*(1), 1–14.

Finkelhor, D., Ormrod, R. K., & Turner, H. A. (2009). The developmental epidemiology of childhood victimization. *Journal of Interpersonal Violence, 24*, 711–731. doi: 10.1177/0886260508317185.

Fishbein, D. (2000). Neuropsychological function, drug abuse, and violence: A conceptual framework. *Criminal Justice and Behavior, 27*(2), 139–159. doi: 10.1177/0093854800027002001.

Flannery, D., Vazsonyi, A., & Waldman, I. (2007). *The Cambridge handbook of violent behavior and aggression*. New York, NY: Cambridge University Press.

Ford, J. D. (2005). Treatment implications of altered neurobiology, affect regulation and information processing following child maltreatment. *Psychiatric Annals, 35*, 410–419.

Ford, J. D. (2009). Neurobiological and developmental research: Clinical implications. In C. A. Courtois & J. D. Ford (Eds.), *Treating complex traumatic stress disorders: An evidence-based guide* (pp. 31–58). New York, NY: Guilford Press.

Ford, J., Chapman, J., Connor, D., & Cruise, K. (2012). Complex trauma and aggression in secure juvenile justice settings. *Criminal Justice and Behavior, 39*(6), 694–724.

Freedman, D., & Hemenway, D. (2000). Precursors of lethal violence: A death row sample. *Social Science and Medicine, 50*(12), 1757–1770. doi: 10.1016/S0277-9536(99) 00417-7.

Gatzke-Kopp, L. M., Raine, A., Buchsbaum, M., & LaCasse, L. (2001). Temporal lobe deficits in murderers: EEG findings undetected by PET. *Journal of Neuropsychiatry and Clinical Neuroscience, 13*(4), 486–491. doi: 10.1176/jnp.13.4.486.

Giedd, J. N., Blumenthal, J., Jeffries, N. O., Castellanos, F. X., Liu, H., Zijdenbos, A., ... Rapoport, J. L. (1999). Brain development during childhood and adolescence: A longitudinal MRI study. *Nature Neuroscience, 2*(10), 861–863.

Gillespie, N., & Mckenzie, K. (2000). An examination of the rule of neuropsychological deficits in mentally disordered sex offenders. *The Journal of Sexual Aggression, 5*, 21–29. doi: 10.1080/13552600008413293.

Goldstein R. Z., Volkow, N.D., (2002). Drug addiction and its underlying neurobiological basis: Neuroimaging evidence for the involvement of the frontal cortex. *The American Journal of Psychiatry, 159*(10), 1642–1652. doi: 10.1176/appi.ajp.159.10.1642.

Gorenstein, E. (1982). Frontal lobe dysfunction in psychopaths. *Journal of Abnormal Psychology, 91*, 368–379.

Gorman, D. G., Cummings, J. L. (1992). Hypersexuality following septal injury. *Archives of Neurology, 49*(3), 308–310.

Goyer, P. F., Andreason, P. J., Semple, W. E., Clayton, A. H., King, A. C., Compton-Toth, B. A., ... Cohen, R. M. (1994). Positron-emission tomography and personality disorders. *Neuropsychopharmacology, 10*(1), 21–28.

Graber, B., Hartmann, K., Coffman, J. A., Huey, C. J., & Golden, C. I. (1982). Brain damage among mentally disordered sex offenders. *Journal of Forensic Science, 27*(1), 125–134.

Grafman, J., Schwab, K., Warden, D., Pridgen, A., Brown, H. R., & Salazar, A. M. (1996). Frontal lobe injuries, violence, and aggression: A report of the Vietnam Head Injury Study. *Neurology, 46*(5), 1231–1238. doi: 10.1212/WNL.46.5.1231.

Graham v. Florida (2010). 130 S. Ct. 2011.

Hanlon, R. E., Brook, M., Stratton, J., Jenson, M., & Rubin, L. (2013). Neuropsychological and intellectual differences between types of murderers: Affective/impulsive versus predatory/ instrumental (premeditated) homicide. *Criminal Justice and Behavior, 40*(8), 933–948. doi: 10.1177/0093854813479779.

Hanlon, R. E., Coda, J. J., Cobia, D., Rubin, & L. H. (2012). Psychotic domestic murder: Neuropsychological differences between nonhomicidal and homicidal schizophrenic men. *Journal of Family Violence, 27*(2), 105–113.

Hanlon, R. E., Rubin, L. H., Jensen, M., & Daoust, S. (2010). Neuropsychological features of indigent murder defendants and death row inmates in relation to homicidal aspects of their crimes. *Archives of Clinical Neuropsychology, 25*(1), 1–13. doi: org/10.1093/arclin/acp099.

Happe, F., Ehlers, S., Fletcher, P., Fitch, U., Johansson, M., Gilberg, C., ... & Frith, C. (1996). "Theory of mind" in the brain. Evidence from a PET scan study of Asperger syndrome. *Neuroreport, 8*(1), 197–201.

Hare, R. D. (1999). Psychopathy as a Risk Factor for Violence. *Psychiatric Quarterly, 70*(3), 181–197.

Hendricks, S. E., Fitzpatrick, D. F., Hartmann, K., Quaife, M. A., Stratbucker, R. A., & Graber, B. (1988). Brain structure and function in sexual molesters of children and adolescents. *The Journal of Clinical Psychiatry, 49*(3), 108–112.

Hinshaw, S. P., & Lee, S. S (2003). Conduct and oppositional defiant disorders. In E. J. Mash & R. A. Barkley (Eds.), *Child psychopathology* (pp. 144–198). New York, NY: Guilford Press.

Hoge, C. W., Castro, C. A., Messer, S. C., McGurk, D., Cotting, D. I., & Koffman, R. L. (2004). Combat duty in Iraq and Afghanistan, mental health problems, and barriers to care. *New England Journal of Medicine, 351*(1), 13–22. doi: 10.1056/NEJMoa040603.

Hoskins v. State (1999). 735 So. 2d 1281 (Fla. 1999) (per curiam).

Hucker, S., Langevin, R., Wortzman, G., Bain, J., Handy, L., Chambers, J., & Wright, S. (1986). Neuropsychological impairment in pedophiles. *Canadian Journal of Behavioural Science, 18*(4), 440–448.

Hucker, S., Langevin, R., Wortzman, G., Bain, J., Handy, L., & Wright, S. (1988). Cerebral damage and dysfunction in sexually aggressive men. *Annals of Sex Research, 1*(1), 32–48.

Jackson v. Calderon (2000). 211 F.3d 1148.

Jakupcak, M., Conybeare, D., Phelps, L., Hunt, S., Holmes, H. A., Felker, B., ... McFall, M. E. (2007). Anger, hostility, and aggression among Iraq and Afghanistan War veterans reporting PTSD and subthreshold PTSD. *Journal of Traumatic Stress, 20*(6), 945–954. doi: 10.1002/jts.20258.

Johansson, M., Wentz, E., Fernell, E., Stromland, K., Miller, M. T., & Gillberg, C. (2001). Autistic Spectrum Disorders in Mobius Sequence: A Comprehensive Study of 25 Individuals. *Developmental Medical Child Neurology, 43*(5), 338–345. doi: 10.1111/j.1469-8749.2001.tb00214.x.

Joyal, C., Beaulieu-Plante, J., & de Chanterac, A. (2014). The neuropsychology of sex offenders: A meta-analysis. *Sex Abuse, 26*(2), 149–177.

Joyal, C., Black, D., & Dassylva, B. (2007). The neuropsychology and neurology of sexual deviance: a review and pilot study. *Sexual Abuse: A Journal of Research and Treatment, 19*(2), 155–173.

Kansas v. Crane (2002). 534 U.S. 407.

Kansas v. Hendricks (1997). 521 U.S. 346.

Kent v. United States (1966). 383 U.S. 541.

Kuin, N., Masthoff, E., Kramer, M., & Scherder, E. (2015). The role of risky decision-making in aggression: A systematic review. *Aggression and Violent Behavior 25*,159–172. doi: 10.1016/j.avb.2015.07.018.

Langevin, R. (2005). Sexual offenses and traumatic brain injury (abstract). *Brain and Cognition, 60*(2), 206–207.

Langevin, R. (2009). Neuropsychological findings in sex offenders. In F. M. Sallah, J. Grudzinshas, J. M. Bradford, & D. Brodsky (Eds.), *Sex offenders: Identification, risk assessment, treatment, and legal issues.* New York, NY: Oxford University Press.

Langevin, R., Bain, J., Ben-Aron, M. H., Coulthard, R., Day, D., Handy, L., ... Russon, A. E. (1985). Sexual aggression: Constructing a predictive equation. In R. Langevin (Ed.), *Erotic preference, gender identity, and aggression in men: New research studies* (pp. 39–76). Hillsdale, NJ: Lawrence Erlbaum.

Langevin, R., & Cunroe, S. (2008a). Are the mentally retarded and learning disordered overrepresented among sex offenders and paraphilics. *International Journal of Offender Therapy and Comparative Criminology, 52*(4), 201–215.

Langevin, R., & Cunroe, S. (2008b). Assessing neuropsychological impairment among sex offenders and paraphiliacs. *Journal of Forensic Psychology Practice, 8*(2), 150–173.

Langevin, R., Lang, R. A., Wright, P., Handy, L., & Majpruz, V. (1989). An examination of brain damage and dysfunction in genital exhibitionists. *Annals of Sex Research, 2*(1), 77–88.

Langevin, R., Wortzman, G., Dickey, R., Wright, P., & Handy, L. (1988). Neuropsychological impairment in incest offenders. *Sexual Abuse: Journal of Research and Treatment, 1*(3), 401–415.

Langlois, J. A., Rutland-Brown, W., & Wald, M. M. (2006). The epidemiology and impact of TBI: A brief overview. *Journal of Head Trauma Rehabilitation, 21*(5), 375–378.

Långström, N., Grann, M., Ruchkin, V., Sjostedt, G., & Fazel, S. (2009). Risk factors for violent offending in autistic spectrum disorder: A national study of hospitalized individuals. *Journal of Interpersonal Violence, 24*(8), 1358–1370.

Lapierre, D., Braun, C., & Hodgins, S. (1995). Ventral frontal deficits in psychopathy:Neuropsychological testing findings. *Neuropsychologia, 13*(2), 139–151.

Lezak, M. D. (1988). IQ: R.I.P. *Journal of Clin Experimental Neuropsychology, 10*(3), 351–361. doi: 10.1080/01688638808400871.

Lilienfeld, S., & Waldman, I. (1990). The relation between childhood attention-deficit hyperactivity disorder and adult antisocial behavior reexamined: The problem of heterogeneity. *Clinical Psychology Review, 10*, 699–725.

Loeber, R., Pardini, D., Homish, D. L., Wei, E. H., Crawford, A. M., Farrington, D. P., ... Rosenfeld, R. (2005). The prediction of violence and homicide in young men. *Journal of Consulting and Clinical Psychology, 73*(6), 1074–1088.

Manes, F., Piven, J., Vrancic, D., Nanclares, V., Plebst, C., & Starkstein, S. E. (1999). An MRI study of the corpus callosum and cerebellum in mentally retarded autistic individuals. *Journal of Neuropsychiatry and Clinical Neurosciences, 11*(4), 470–474.

Martin, J. E. (1999). Assessment of executive functions in sexual offenders. Dissertation Abstracts International: Section B: The Sciences & Engineering, *59* (10-B), 5580. University Microfilms International, USA.

McFall, M. (1999). Analysis of violent behavior in Vietnam combat veteran psychiatric inpatients with posttraumatic stress disorder. *Journal of Traumatic Stress, 12*(3), 501–517.

Mednick, S. A., Gabrielli, W. F., Jr., & Hutchings, B. (1984). Genetic influences in criminal convictions: Evidence from an adoption cohort. *Science, 224*(4651), 891–894.

Miller, L. (1987). Neuropsychology of the aggressive psychopath: An integrative review. *Aggressive Behavior, 13*(3), 119–140.

Miller v. Alabama (2012). 132 S. Ct. 2455.

Milligan, K., Astington, J. W., & Dack, L. A. (2007). Language and theory of mind: Meta-analysis of the relation between language ability and false-belief understanding. *Child Development, 78*(2), 622–646.

Moffitt, T. E. (1993). The neuropsychology of conduct disorder. *Developmental Psychopathology, 5*(1–2), 135–151.

Moffitt, T. E., & Henry, B. (1989). Neuropsychological assessment of executive function in self-reported delinquents. *Developmental Psychopathology, 1*, 105–118.

Moffitt, T. E., & Lynam, D., Jr. (1994). The neuropsychology of conduct disorder and delinquency: Implications for understanding antisocial behavior. *Program of Experimental Personality and Psychopathology Research*, 233–262.

Moffitt, T. E., & Silva, P. A. (1988). Self-reported delinquency, neuropsychological deficit, and history of attention deficit disorder. *Journal of Abnormal Child Psychology, 16*(5), 553–569.

Monahan, J. M. (2001). *Rethinking risk assessment: The MacArthur study of mental disorder and violence.* New York, NY: Oxford University Press.

Monahan, J. M., & Steadman, H. J. (Eds.) (1994). *Violence and mental disorder: Developments in risk assessment.* Chicago: University of Chicago Press.

Monahan, J. M., Steadman, H. J., Silver, E., Appelbaum, P. S., Clark Robbins, P., Mulvey, E. P., ... Banks, S. (2001). *Rethinking risk assessment: The MacArthur study of mental disorder and violence.* Oxford: Oxford University Press.

Montgomery, J., McCrimmon, A., Schwean, V., & Saklofske, D. (2010). Emotional Intelligence in Asperger's syndrome: Implications of dissonance between intellect and affect. *Education Training in Autism and Developmental Disabilities, 45*(4), 566–582.

Morgan, A., & Lilienfeld, S. (2000). A meta-analytic review of the relation between antisocial behavior and neuropsychological measures of executive function. *Clinical Psychology Review, 20*(1), 113–136.

Mouridsen, S. E., Rich, B., Isager, T., & Nedergaard N. J. (2008). Pervasive developmental disorders and criminal behavior: A case control study. *International Journal of Offender Therapy and Comparative Criminology, 52*(2), 196–205.

Mulvey, E. P., & Lidz, C. W. (1995). Conditional prediction: A model for research on dangerousness to others in a new era. *International Journal of Law and Psychiatry, 18*(2), 129–143.

Murrie, D. C., Warren, J. I., Kristiansson, M., & Dietz, P. E. (2002). Asperger's syndrome in forensic settings. *International Journal of Forensic Mental Health, 1*(1), 59–70.

National Institute on Alcohol Abuse and Alcoholism (NIAAA) (1990). *Alcohol and health: Seventh special report to Congress.* Rockville, MD: NIAAA.

Neumeister, A., Henry, S., & Krystal, J. H. (2007). Neurocircuitry and neuroplasticity. In M. J. Friedman, T. M., Keane, & P. A. Resick (Eds.), *Handbook of PTSD: Science and practice* (pp. 151–165). New York, NY: Guilford Press.

Newman, S. S., & Ghaziuddin, M. (2008). Violent crime in Asperger syndrome: The role of psychiatric comorbidity. *Journal of Autism and Developmental Disorders, 38*(10), 1848–1852.

Newman, J., Patterson, C., & Kosson, D. (1987). Response perseveration in psychopaths. *Journal of Abnormal Psychology, 96*, 145–148.

Otnow Lewis, D., Moy, E., Jackson, L. D., Aaronson, R., Restifo, N., Serra, S., & Simos, A. (1985). Biopsychosocial characteristics of children who later murder: A prospective study. *The American Journal of Psychiatry, 142*(10), 1161–1167. doi: org/10.1176/ajp.142.10.1161.

Otnow Lewis, D., Yeager, C. A., Swica, Y., Pincus, J. H., & Lewis, M. (1997). Objective documentation of child abuse and dissociation in 12 murderers with dissociative identity disorder. *The American Journal of Psychiatry, 154*(12), 1703–1710. doi. org/10.1176/ajp.154.12.1703.

Patrick, C., & Verona, E. (2007). The Psychophysiology of aggression: Autonomic, electrocortical and neuro-imaging findings. In D. Flannery, A. Vazsonyi, & I. Waldman (Eds.). *The Cambridge handbook of violent behavior and aggression* (pp. 111–150). New York, NY: Cambridge University Press.

Pedersen, L., Ramussen, K., & Elsass, P. (2010). Risk assessment: The value of structured professional judgments. *International Journal of Forensic Mental Health, 9*(2), 74–81.

People v. Ford (2005). WL 236487 (Cal. Ct. App.).

People v. Jones (1994). 210 A.D.2d 904 (N.Y. App. Div.).

People v. Protsman (2001). 105 Cal. Rptr. 2d.

People v. Weinstein (1992). 591 N.Y.S.2d 715 (N.Y.).

Pincus, J. H., & Tucker, G. J. (1978). Violence in children and adults: A neurological view. *Journal of American Academy and Child Psychiatry, 17*(2), 277–288.

Raine, A. (1993). *The psychopathology of crime: Criminal behavior as a clinical disorder.* San Diego, CA: Academic Press.

Raine, A. (2002a). Annotation: The role of prefrontal deficits, low autonomic arousal, and early health factors in the development of antisocial and aggressive behavior in children. *Journal of Child Psychology and Psychiatry, 43*(4), 417–434.

Raine, A. (2002b). Biosocial studies of antisocial and violent behavior in children and adults: A review. *Journal of Abnormal Child Psychology, 30*(4), 311–326.

Raine, A., Brennan, P., & Mednick, S. A. (1994). Birth complications combined with early maternal rejection at age 1 year predispose to violent crime at age 18 years. *Archives of General Psychiatry, 51*(12), 984–988.

Raine, A., & Buchsbaum, M. (1996). Violence, brain imaging, and neuropsychology. In D.M. Stoff, & R. B. Cairns (Eds.), *Aggression and violence: Genetic, neurobiological, and biosocial perspectives* (pp. 195–217). Mahwah, NJ: Lawrence Erlbaum Associates.

Raine, A., Buchsbaum, M., & LaCasse, L. (1997). Brain Abnormalities in murderers indicated by positron emission tomography. *Biological Psychiatry, 42*(6), 495.

Raine, A., Buchsbaum, M., Stanley, J., Lottenberg, S., Abel, L., & Stoddard, J. (1994). Selective reductions in prefrontal glucose metabolism in murderers. *Biological Psychiatry, 36*, 365–373.

Raine, A., Moffitt, T. E., Caspi, A., Loeber, R., Stouthamer-Loeber, M., & Lynam, D. (2005). Neurocognitive impairments in boys on the life-course persistent antisocial path. *Journal of Abnormal Psychology, 114*(1), 38–49.

Redouté, J., Stoléru, S., Grégoire, M. C., Costes, N., Cinotti, L., Lavenne, F., ... Pujol, J. F. (2000). Brain processing of visual sexual stimuli in human males. *Human Brain Mapping, 11*(3), 162–177.

Reiss, A. J., Miczek, K. A., & Roth, J. A. (1994). *Understanding and preventing violence (Vol. 2. Biobehavioral influences)*. Washington, DC: National Academy Press.

Reiss, A., & Roth, J. (1993). *Understanding and preventing violence.* Washington, DC: National Academy Press.

Rettenberger, M., Hucker, S., Boer, D., & Harris, G. (2009). The reliability and validity of the Sexual Violence Risk-20: An international review. *Journal of Sex Offender Treatment, 3*, 1–14.

Rice, M., Harris, G., & Lang, C. (2013). Validation of and Revision to the VRAG and SORAG: The Violence Risk Appraisal Guide-Revised (VRAG-R). *Psychological Assessment, 25*(3), 951–965.

Roper v. Simmons (2005). 543 U.S. 551.

Sandel, M. E., & Mysiw, W. J. (1996). The agitated brain injured patient. Part 1: Definitions, differential diagnosis, and assessment. *Archives of Physical and Medical Rehabilitation, 77*(6), 617-623.

Saner, H., & Ellickson, P. (1996). Concurrent risk factors for adolescent violence. *Journal of Adolescent Health, 19*(2), 94–103.

Sartorius, A., Ruf, M., Kief, C., Demirakca, T., Bailer, J., Ende, ... Dressing, H. (2008). Abnormal amygdala activation profile in pedophilia. *European Archives of Psychiatry and Clinical Neuroscience, 258*(5), 271–277.

Satterfield, J. H., Hoppe, C. M., & Schell, A. M. (1982). A prospective study of delinquency in 110 adolescent boys with attention deficit disorder and 88 normal adolescent boys. *American Journal of Psychiatry, 139*(6), 795–798.

Schiffer, B., Paul, T., Gizewski, E., Forsting, M., Leygraf, N., Schedlowski, M., & Kruger, T. H. C. (2008). Functional Brain Correlates of Heterosexual Pedophilia. *NeuroImage, 41*(1), 80–91.

Schneider, K., Pauly, K. D., Gossen, A., Mevissen, L., Michael, T. M., Gur, R. C., ... Habel, U. (2013). Neural correlates of moral reasoning in autism spectrum disorder. *Social cognitive and affective neuroscience, 8*(6), 702–710.

Schriro v. Landrigan (2007). 550 US 465.

Scott, C. L., Resnick, P. J. (2006). Violence risk assessment in persons with mental illness. *Aggression and Violent Behavior, 11*(6), 598–611. doi: org/10.1016/j.avb.2005.12.003.

Scragg, P., & Shah, A. (1994). Prevalence of Asperger's syndrome in a secure hospital. *The British Journal of Psychiatry, 165*(5), 679–682.

Séguin, J. R., Pihl, R. O., Harden, P. W., Tremblay, R. E., & Boulerice, B. (1995). Cognitive and neuropsychological characteristics of physically aggressive boys. *Journal of Abnormal Psychology, 104*(6), 614–624.

Sharp, C. W., Beauvais, F., & Spence, R. (1992). *Inhalant abuse: A volatile research agenda.* National Institute of Drug Abuse (NIDA) Research Monograph 129. US Department of Health and Human Services, Public Health Service, National Institute of Health. NIH Publication No. 93-3475.

Shiroma, E. J., Ferguson, P. L., & Pickelsimer, E. E. (2010). Prevalence of TBI in an offender population: A meta-analysis. *Journal of Correctional Health Care, 16*(2), 147–159.

Shumaker, D. M., & Prinz, R. J. (2000). Children who murder: A review. *Clinical Child and Family Psychology Review, 3*(2), 97–115.

Silver, J. M., McAllister, T. W., & Yudofsky, S. C. (2011). Textbook of traumatic brain injury. Washington, DC: American Psychiatric Publishing, Inc.

Siponmaa, L., Kristiansson, M., Jonson, C., Nyden, A., & Gillberg, C. (2001). Juvenile and young adult mentally disordered offenders: The role of child neuropsychiatric disorders. *Journal of American Academy of Psychiatry and the Law Online, 29*(4), 420–426.

Soderstrom, H., Nilsson, T., Sjodin, A., Carlstedt, A., & Forsman, A. (2005). The childhood-onset neuropsychiatric background to adulthood psychopathic traits and personality disorders. *Comprehensive Psychiatry, 46*(2), 111–116.

Spinella, M. (2004). Clinical case report: Hypersexuality and dysexecutive syndrome after a thalamic infarct. *International Journal of Neuroscience, 114*(12), 1581–1590.

Spinella, M., & White, J. (2006) Neuroanatomical substrates for sex offenses. *International Journal of Forensic Psychology, 1*(3), 84–94.

Sreenivasan, S., Kirkish, P., Shotaw, S., Welsh, R., & Ling, W. (2000). Neuropsychological and diagnostic differences between recidivistically violent not criminally responsible and mentally ill prisoners. *International Journal of Law and Psychiatry, 23*(2), 161–172.

State v. Johnson (2009). 208 P.3d 1265 (Wash. Ct. App.).

State v. Reid (2006). 213 S.W. 3d 792 (Tenn.).

State v. Risner (2016). Cause No. 73250.

Steinberg, L., & Cauffman, E. (1996). Maturity of judgment in adolescence: Psychosocial factors in adolescent decision making. *Law and Human Behavior, 20*(3), 249–272. doi: org/10.1007/BF01499023.

Teicher, M. H., Andersen, S. L., Polcari, A., Anderson, C. M., Navalta, C. P., & Kim, D. M. (2003). The neurobiological consequences of early stress and childhood maltreatment. *Neuroscience Biobehavioral Reviews, 27*(1–2), 33–44.

Teicher, M. H., Ito, Y., Glod, C. A., Schiffer, F., & Gelbard, H. A. (1996). Neurophysiological mechanisms of stress response in children. In C. R. Pfeffer (Ed.), *Severe stress and mental disturbance in children*, (p. 673). Arlington, VA: American Psychiatric Association.

Tenbergen, G., Wittfoth, M., Fireling, H., Ponseti, J., Walter, M., Walter, H., ... Kruger, T. (2015). The neurobiology and psychology of pedophilia: Recent advances and challenges. *Front Human Neuroscience, 9*, 344.

Tost, H., Vollmert, C., Brassen, S., Schmitt, A., Dressing, H., & Braus, D. (2004). Pedophilia: Neuropsychological evidence encouraging a brain network perspective. *Medical Hypotheses, 63*, 528–531.

US v. Sandoval-Mendoza (2006). 472 F.3d 645 (9th Cir.).

Vasterling, J. J. (2005). *Neuropsychology of PTSD: Biological, cognitive, and clinical perspectives.* New York, NY: Guilford Press.

Vincent, G. M., Maney, S. M., & Hart, S. D. (2009). The use of actuarial risk assessment instruments in sex offenders. In M. S. Fabian, A. J. Grudzinkas, J. M. Bradford, & D. J. Brodsky (Eds.). *Sex offenders: Identification, risk assessment, treatment, and legal issues* (pp. 70–88). Oxford/New York, NY: Oxford University Press.

Vitelli, R. (1996). Prevalence of childhood conduct and attention-deficit hyperactivity disorders in adult maximum-security inmates. *International Journal of Offender Therapy and Comparative Criminology, 40*(4), 263–271.

Volavka, J. (1995). *Neurobiology of violence.* Washington, DC: American Psychiatric Press.

Volkow, N. D., & Tancredi, L. (1987). Neural substrates of violent behaviour. A preliminary study with positron emission tomography. *British Journal of Psychiatry, 151*, 668–673.

Volkow, N. D., Tancredi, L. R., Grant, C., Gillespie, H., Valentine, A., Mullani, N., ... Hollister, L. (1995). Brain glucose metabolism in violent psychiatric patients: a preliminary study. *Psychiatry Research, 61*(4), 243–253.

Wahlund, K., & Kristiansson, M. (2009). Aggression, psychopathy and brain imaging: Review and future recommendations. *International Journal of Law of Psychiatry, 32*(4), 266–271.

Weder, N., Yang, B. Z., Douglas-Palumberi, H., Massey, J., Krystal, J. H., Gelernter, J., & Kaufman, J. (2009). MAOA genotype, maltreatment, and aggressive behavior: The changing impact of genotype at varying levels of trauma. *Biological Psychiatry, 65*, 417–424.

Weeks, R., & Widom, C. S. (1998). Self-reports of early childhood victimization among incarcerated adult male felons. *Journal of Interpersonal Violence, 13*(3), 346–361.

Werner, E. E. (1989). High-risk children in young adulthood: A longitudinal study from birth to 32 years. *American Journal of Orthopsychiatry, 59*(1), 72–81.

Wiener, R. L., & Miller, M. K. (2004). Judicial notebook: Determining the death penalty for juveniles. Psychology can help measure society's evolving standards of decency. Monitor, (35), 1, 68. Retrieved from http://www.apa.org/monitor/jan04/jn.aspx.

Widom, C. S. (1989). Does violence beget violence? A critical examination of the literature. *Psychological Bulletin, 106*(1), 3–28.

Widom, C. S. (1993). Child abuse and alcohol use and abuse. In S. E. Martin (Ed.), *Alcohol and interpersonal violence: Fostering multidisciplinary perspectives.* National Institute on Alcohol Abuse and Alcoholism Research Monograph No. 24. NIH Publication No. 93-3496, (pp. 291–314). National Institute on Alcohol Abuse and Alcoholism, Bethesda, MD.

Widom, C. S. (1997). Child abuse, neglect, and witnessing violence. In D. Stoff, J. Breiling, & J. Maser (Eds.). *Handbook of antisocial behavior,* (pp. 159–179). New York: John Wiley & Sons.

Williams, D. (1969). Neural factors related to habitual aggression. Consideration of differences between those habitual aggressives and others who have committed crimes of violence. *Brain, 92*(3), 503–520.

Wright, P., Nobrega, J., Langevin, R., & Wortzman, G. (1990). Brain density and symmetry in pedophilic and sexually aggressive offenders. *Sexual Abuse: A Journal of Research and Treatment, 3*(3), 319–328.

Wong, M. T., Fenwick, P. B., Lumsden, J., Fenton, G. W., Maisey, M. N., Lewis, P., & Badawi, R. (1997). Positron emission tomography in male violent offenders with schizophrenia. *Psychiatry Research, 68*(2–3), 111–123.

Yang, P., Wu, M. T., Hsu, C., & Ker, J. H. (2004). Evidence of early neurobiological alternations in adolescents with posttraumatic stress disorder. *Neuroscience Letters, 370,* 13–18.

Yang, S. J., Shin, D. W., Noh, K. S., & Stein, M. A. (2007). Cortisol is inversely correlated with aggression for those boys with attention deficit hyperactivity disorder who retain the irreactivity to stress. *Psychiatry Research, 153,* 55–60.

Yeudall, L., & Fromm-Auch, D. (1979). Neuropsychological impairment in various psychopathological populations. In J. Gruzelier, & P. Flor-Henry (Eds.), *Hemisphere asymmetries of function in psychopathology.* Amsterdam: Elsevier/North-Holland.

33

Forensic Neuropsychology in the Criminal Court
A Socio-legal Perspective
Leon McRae

Key points

- In the chapter it is noted that, as a result of greater understanding of the relationship between the brain and antisocial behavior, neuropsychological evidence is slowly helping courts assign criminal responsibility.
- Nevertheless, lawyers have been largely silent on the implications of speaking brain science to law, with the result that advocates of the neuropsychological approach have often expressed concern that legal doctrine fails to adequately recognize and respond to individual vulnerabilities.
- This chapter addresses these issues by looking at three areas of especial concern to neuropsychologists:
  - the appropriate age of criminal responsibility;
  - the (ir)responsibility of psychopaths; and
  - whether vulnerable defendants declared fit to stand trial require greater protection.
- Two main arguments are advanced here:
  1. the complex relationship between certain brain states and behavior, as depicted in emergent, and sometimes contradictory evidence, may undermine its potential application in the courtroom; and
  2. even where neuropsychological research linking certain brain states to antisocial acts is strong, evidential assumptions about irresponsibility may be rejected. To exculpate – that is, to show or declare that someone is not guilty of wrongdoing – certain defendants, it is argued, would oppose the usefulness of the criminal law in reducing the perceived sites of abstract "risk." It would also undermine the scope of the criminal law to shape public morality according to socially constructed notions of normal and abnormal violence.

The Wiley Blackwell Handbook of Forensic Neuroscience, First Edition. Edited by Anthony R. Beech,
Adam J. Carter, Ruth E. Mann and Pia Rotshtein.
© 2018 John Wiley & Sons Ltd. Published 2018 by John Wiley & Sons Ltd.

- These limitations, it is argued in the chapter, are most evident in legal responses to "antisocial" children and criminal psychopaths.

Terminology Explained

Actus reus is the Latin term used to describe the physical element of the crime.

Criminal law case outcomes will depend upon the strength and admissibility of evidence, including physical proof, scientific evidence, and witness testimony. The rules of criminal evidence are invariably complex.

Criminal responsibility refers to both elements of the crime, *actus reus* and, usually, *mens rea* being present at the time of the alleged crime.

Doli incapax refers to the former rebuttable presumption that those between 10 and 14 years of age could not be attributed with the state of mind necessary to be convicted of a crime.

Exculpate means to show or declare that someone is not guilty of wrongdoing.

Fitness to plead is the capacity of a defendant in criminal proceedings to comprehend the course of those proceedings. The concept of fitness to plead also applies in Scotland. The US equivalent is competence to stand.

Mens rea is the Latin term used to denote that the defendant must have the respective state of mind (such as intent or recklessness) sufficient for criminal liability.

Mental capacity means being competent to make one's own decisions.

Moral agency is an individual's ability to make **moral** judgments based on some notion of right and wrong, and to be held accountable for these actions.

A **moral agent** is a live person who is capable of acting with reference to notions of right and wrong.

Psychopathy refers to those with personality characteristics that can be broadly described as: criminally minded; glib/superficially charming; manipulative; lack of remorse or guilt/conscience; pathological lying; lack of emotional depth; irresponsibility and impulsiveness; callous parasitic lifestyle; poor behavioral controls; promiscuous sexual behavior; and a history of childhood (antisocial) problems. Psychopaths also show emotional empathy deficits. Obviously, this mix of personality traits and behaviors makes it highly likely that such individuals will commit crimes: see DeBrito & Mitchell (Chapter 9) in this volume for a discussion of what is known about neuroscientific deficits of this disorder.

Introduction

In recent decades, neuropsychologists have made impressive gains in identifying and explaining the neural correlates of antisocial behavior. In the criminal law, this increasingly sophisticated understanding of the neuropsychological bases of behavior has the potential to both inform and problematize traditional notions of responsibility, and punishment. In view of these developments, this chapter focuses on the scope and limitations of applying neuropsychological evidence to the criminal law. In the first part of the chapter, the focus of responsibility, punishment, and expert evidence is situated within paradigmatic assumptions operating in the criminal law. In the second part of the chapter, the implications of applying neuropsychological evidence in the courtroom are discussed in the context of three topical case studies: 1) fitness to plead, 2) lack of age, and 3) psychopathy. In addition to discussing the relevant law and policy, the chapter will provide a conceptual lens through which we might begin to understand the marginalization of extant neuropsychological evidence indicating irresponsibility.

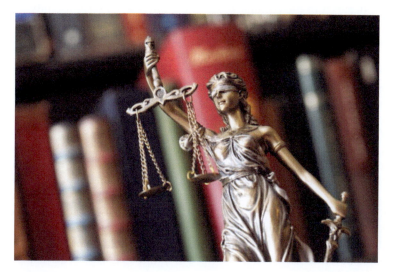

Criminal law and responsibility *Criminal punishment is the strongest formal censure that society can inflict. Those convicted of a criminal offence face a deprivation of liberty, fine, or other measure of control. The consequentialist justification for such punishment focuses on the potential to reduce crime through measures of deterrence, rehabilitation, incapacitation, and restorative justice.*
Source: © Sebnem Ragıboglu. Used under license from 123RF.

Criminal law and responsibility

Criminal punishment is the strongest formal censure that society can inflict. Those convicted of a criminal offence face a deprivation of liberty, fine, or other measure of control. The consequentialist justification for such punishment focuses on the potential to reduce crime through measures of deterrence, rehabilitation, incapacitation, and restorative justice. By comparison, the retributive justification ("just deserts"), upon which most law reform over the past 20-years has been based, more simply emphasizes that people, as responsible agents, deserve some form of punishment when they break the law. It follows that only those who are sufficiently responsible for their crimes should be subject to punishment. However, it will be shown in this opening section that the process of evidence gathering, and decisions about criminal responsibility taken in respect of that evidence, is inherently complex, and controversial.

Attributing criminal responsibility Whether a suspect is liable for a criminal law offence depends upon whether s/he is found to have committed the *actus reus* ("guilty act") of an offence with, ordinarily, the necessary *mens rea* ("guilty mind"). In some crimes, such as murder, it is perfectly clear that the criminal act has been committed, meaning guilt largely turns on the issue of whether the defendant has the necessary mental state. On a charge of murder, for instance, the prosecution is obliged to prove, beyond reasonable doubt, that the defendant "intended" to kill, or realized that death was a "virtually certain" consequence of his or her actions (*R v. Woollin*, 1999). In some instances, the suspect will have *mens rea* but raise an exculpatory defense, such as insanity (see Box 33.1). If the jury, empaneled to answer questions of fact, decides on the evidence that the defense applies, the defendant escapes liability because s/he is deemed not to have been a responsible agent at the time of their alleged crime. Further examples of defenses in the criminal law include diminished responsibility and loss of control (which reduces liability for murder to manslaughter), necessity, self-defense, consent, and intoxication.

Box 33.1   The insanity defense

The insanity defense is an "ancient and humane principle" (Home Office and Department of Health and Social Security, 1953, para. 278) founded on the belief that some people are so mentally disordered at the time of their alleged offence that the defense "not guilty by reason of insanity" (NGRI) should be available to them. Upon a finding of NGRI, the judge may impose a hospital order, and must do so in the case of murder (Home Office and Department of Health, 2005, p. 12), if the criteria for admission are met – that is, the offender has a "mental disorder" that is of a "nature or degree which makes it appropriate to be detained in a hospital for [appropriate] treatment" (section 37 of the Mental Health Act (MHA) 1983). The judge may also order supervision and treatment in the community or acquit the defendant (section 5(2) of the Criminal Procedure (Insanity) Act 1964).

In most jurisdictions, a defendant will be assessed using the M'Naghten Rules (1843). The M'Naghten Rules decree that the judge will offer the jury the opportunity to consider the defense of NGRI if the defendant can adduce psychiatric evidence proving, on the balance of probabilities, either that s/he did not know the nature and quality of their act, or, if they did, that what s/he was doing was wrong (known as the "knowledge limbs") due to a "defect of reason" arising from a "disease of the mind."

For many years in England and Wales, the individual limbs of the M'Naghten Rules have been criticized as being both under and over inclusive. The charge of over inclusivity stems from the fact that the legal definition of "disease of the mind" does not accord with psychiatric understanding of mental disorder. Examples of qualifying disorders have been hyperglycemia (caused by diabetes), sleepwalking, epilepsy, and heart disease. The insanity defense may also be under inclusive because defendants who have awareness of their actions are, strictly speaking, required to prove that they did not know what they were doing was *legally* wrong (*R v. Windle*, 1952). By comparison, in Australia evidence of insanity can be derived from the defendant's mistaken belief that his or her act was morally right according to the ordinary standards of reasonable people (*Stapleton v. R*, 1952). Similarly, in some American states, the Model Penal Code (1985) provides that a defendant may be deemed insane if s/he lacks substantial capacity to appreciate that his or her conduct was morally wrong.

In view of the limitations of the M'Naghten Rules, reform of the insanity defense has been considered for a number of years by different government-appointed committees. Most recently, the Law Commission (2013a) proposed that the NGRI verdict be replaced by "not criminally responsible by reason of a recognized medical condition." Such a verdict could be returned if it was adjudged that the defendant wholly lacked capacity to: "(i) rationally form a judgment about the relevant conduct or circumstances; (ii) to understand the wrongfulness of what he or she is charged with having done; *or* (iii) to control his or her physical acts in relation to the relevant conduct or circumstances as a result of a qualifying recognized medical condition [leading to a genuine loss of physical control]" (para. 1.93). Notwithstanding, the application of the proposed test would not be without its own challenges (see Case Study 33.3).

Whatever the applicable defense, if it is accepted by the jury, the judge will usually have some discretion as to how to dispose of the defendant. Similarly, even if the defendant has *mens rea* and offers no valid defense, provided s/he has a mental disorder, a hospital order can still be imposed at the sentencing stage. The rationale for imposing a hospital order will be that "the [respective] offender [will receive] the care and attention which he needs in the hope and expectation of course, that the result will be to avoid the commission by the offender of further criminal acts" (*R v. Birch*, 1989). If psychiatric medication is proposed by hospital doctors, it can be given even in the absence of consent (section 63 of the MHA); for psychosocial intervention, however, such as is routinely given to psychopathic and child patients, cooperation is fundamental to successful treatment. Therefore, while the hospital order settles the issue of whether legal responsibility and punishment is appropriate in the circumstances, it gives rise to a potentially problematic, if implied, issue that offenders take responsibility for their crime by engaging with treatment to address their criminogenic risk.

In neuropsychological terms, the ability to act responsibly, that is, in accordance with accepted conventions and social norms, presumes moral agency. For certain groups, such as young children and psychopaths, this presumption is problematic. For instance, psychopaths (and those with the allied conditions of anti-social personality disorder, dissocial personality disorder, and dangerous and severe personality disorder) may be completely "blind to central moral considerations" (Levy, 2007, p. 213). While this suggests they may not deserve "the full blame that attaches to moral transgressions (or, indeed, any significant amount of blame)" (Levy, 2007, p. 219), it also implies that the rehabilitative model of punishment may be unrealistic. For this group, then, the task for criminal justice policy is to carefully balance considerations of responsibility, treatability (*qua* rehabilitation) and future risk. It will be argued below that, as the evidence base grows, neuropsychology may provide better understanding of the relationship between these triumvirate and established legal precepts. It will also be argued, however, that the development of rehabilitative programs in hospitals and prisons through contemporary criminal justice and mental health policy has been consistently overshadowed by an overarching concern to secure public protection through preventive detention. At the outset, this suggests that neuropsychological evidence may only be acceptable to the criminal justice system to the extent that it contributes to the prevailing ambitions of social policy. As Ingleby put it: "professions are not their own masters, but operate by virtue of a mandate, and have to tailor their activities accordingly" (1985, p. 178).

For young children, the problematic is slightly different. In recent years, legitimate concerns have been expressed about the appropriateness of assigning moral agency to those with developing brains. Currently, in England and Wales a child can be found guilty of a criminal offence once s/he reaches the age of ten; prior to this, they have a quasi-defense of lack of age (or doli incapax, as it is sometimes erroneously known). The low age of criminal responsibility in England and Wales has been criticized by numerous international bodies (see, e.g., European Committee on Social Rights 2003–2004: Conclusions XVII-2 (United Kingdom); United Nations Committee for the Rights of the Child (para 77(a)). Rule 4.1 of the United Nations Standard Minimum Rules for the Administration of Juvenile Justice ("The Beijing Rules") provides that:

> In those legal systems recognizing the concept of the age of criminal responsibility for juveniles, the beginning of that age shall not be fixed at too low an age level bearing in mind the facts of emotional, mental and intellectual maturity.

In various other European countries (but, interestingly, not in some US states), the concept of juvenile justice has resulted in greater recognition of the potential negative impact of developing brains on decision making. For instance, in Scotland, Ireland, and the Netherlands, France, Germany, Scandinavia, Spain and Portugal, and Belgium, the respective ages are 12, 13, 14, 15, 16, and 18. Nevertheless, the underlying question facing the authorities in these countries is the same: "Can it be said that, when [children] do criminal things with [*mens rea*], they are acting as moral agents, in a sufficiently full sense?" (Ashworth & Horder, 2013, p. 140).

If we believe that children do have sufficient moral agency, they will be required to participate fully in a trial of which they may have little understanding. It has already been decided in the European Court of Human Rights that the presumption that a young child is fit to stand trial may breach the "right to a fair trial" enshrined by Article 6 of the European Convention on Human Rights (*V and T v. United Kingdom*, 1999). On the more vexed question of criminal liability, it would seem appropriate that neuropsychological evidence assist the criminal law by clarifying the relationship between childhood behavior and cognitive development.

Speaking scientific evidence to law: A socio-legal primer Before scientific evidence can be admissible in court, the respective expert witness must practice in a field that is "sufficiently well-established to pass the ordinary tests of relevance and reliability" (Tapper, 2010, p. 545). In an emergent discipline like neuropsychology, in which scientific advances are common, an expert witness will generally be permitted to rely on facts supplied by others (section 127 of the Criminal Justice Act 2003), such as those appearing in reputable research publications. What an expert witness is not permitted to do is express an opinion on the ultimate issue in a trial. An example would be an expert who is asked whether, in their opinion, a doctor accused of negligence had failed to exercise the expected standard of medical care (*Rich v. Pierpoint*, 1862), since this would encroach upon the ultimate issue of guilt to be decided by the jury (in a Crown Court) or judges (in a Magistrates' Court). In reality, the expert witness is routinely permitted to express their opinion provided "the diction employed is not noticeably the same as that which will be used when the matter is subsequently considered by the court" (Keane, 2010, p. 542).

A more theoretical way of conceiving of these complex, though ultimately permissive, rules on the admissibility of medical evidence is that science contributes to the continuing social order through an entirely different form of communication to law. In law, communication is oriented towards the binary code of guilty/not guilty; if we compare this to psychiatry, for example, the relevant binary is sane/insane (loosely construed). This phenomenon of self-reference is indispensable to a discourse, because it protects it from conceptual interference from other discourses. The result in the courtroom is that a scientific discipline typically retains the normative expectation that it holds the most advanced knowledge available based on its binary code, while the legal decision maker (judge, jury, or magistrate) is bound to "accord with the expectations [of the discourse that] one believes must be assumed for social relations to continue" (Luhmann, 1995, p. 235). Thus, if a psychiatrist, to continue the example, produces a medical report to the effect that the defendant is insane and requires hospitalization, the decision maker will typically transmute that finding into the terms of the guilty/not guilty binary, rather than engage in determined critique of the underlying scientific logic. Two, arguably idealistic, implications flow from this socio-legal position.

First, scientific discourses, including neuropsychology, must be attentive to the fact that only through its own self-reference will its normative expectations be challenged: judges, jury members, and defendants (or their counsel) are generally ill-equipped to do so. Second, and by implication, scientific discourse may be bestowed significant power in the courtroom, since it affords legitimacy to the law's binary code and enables the allocation of punishment. For example, psychiatric testimony was arguably borne of evidential problems presented by the homicidal maniac in the early 19th century. The homicidal maniac was a specific type of defendant who could give no logical account of why s/he had committed their crime, and yet they did not appear "mad." This lack of rational engagement with the court process challenged all efforts to determine precisely which punishment morally fitted the crime (Foucault, 1988, p. 151). The psychiatrist was subsequently called upon to furnish an account of the differences within and between defendants, in order that the guilty ("bad")/not guilty ("mad") distinction could be retained. Psychiatrists, through their acceptance by law, were in turn able to establish a "new domain for themselves" (p. 133).

Today, we see striking similarities between the homicidal maniac, who challenged the normative expectations of law, and the defendant with psychopathy. In Case Study 33.3, psychopathy is used to example the contribution neuropsychology is currently making, and could make, to assigning responsibility and punishment. At a time when psychiatry is struggling to give a consistent account of responsibility in relation to criminal psychopaths, neuropsychology appears well positioned to help determine questions of responsibility for the criminal law. What is not clear, however, is whether neuropsychological conceptions of responsibility will result in fair treatment of psychopaths under law, as psychiatry once ensured for homicidal maniacs. Similar doubts must be raised in respect of children and defendants who are potentially "unfit" to stand trial.

Neuropsychology in the courtroom: Applications and limitations

There continue to be examples in law reports of the application of neuropsychological evidence in the courtroom. The explanation is that scientific understanding of the neural correlates of antisocial behavior identifies which individuals should be held accountable for their actions, and in so doing helps legitimize legal decision making. In what follows, the benefits, challenges, and limitations posed by the use of such evidence is discussed in the context of fitness to plead proceedings, lack of age and psychopathy.

Case Study 33.1 Unfitness to plead and the contestable nature of scientific evidence

The criminal court, also known as the Crown Court, has, to some extent, been attentive to neuropsychological evidence for at least 30 years. A striking use of such evidence in more recent years has been to determine whether a defendant is fit to plead, that is, broadly, whether s/he can enter a plea, understand the evidence against them, instruct their solicitor, follow court proceedings and challenge a juror (*Pritchard*, 1836). While a finding of unfitness to plead does not absolve the defendant of his or her crime, it operates to protect the vulnerable defendant from having to participate in his or her trial. The disposals available to a judge sentencing a guilty defendant who was not fit to plead are the same as a NGRI verdict (see Box 33.1).

The most high-profile fitness to plead case to date involving neuropsychological evidence is *Mohammed Sharif* (2010). The issue in this case was whether the Crown Court judge had erred when finding that the defendant (charged with conspiracy to defraud) was fit to plead. In court, considerable reliance was placed on the testimony of Prof. Deakin, who, having reviewed the available evidence, concluded that Sharif presented "a clear case of malingering and that there was no psychiatric or neurological component" (para. 6). However, while on remand awaiting trial, the prison medical authorities further investigated Sharif's mental state by performing functional magnetic resonance imaging (fMRI). This time, a different expert, Dr. Launer, contended that the results showed that Sharif was suffering from atrophy of the brain (organic brain syndrome) and long-standing functional psychosis, making him unfit to plead.

At trial, Prof. Deakin was invited to revisit his opinion in light of the conflicting view held by Dr. Launer. While now expressing his view in less robust terms, he maintained that it was probable that Sharif was faking his impairments to avoid standing trial. Deemed fit to plead by the judge, the jury subsequently found him guilty. He was sentenced to three years in prison.

Sharif's conviction was subsequently referred to the Court of Appeal in light of fresh medical evidence commissioned by Prof. Tony Holland, a professor of learning disabilities and a consultant psychiatrist. Among the many medical reports received, Prof. Holland was particularly impressed with the report of Dr. Crauford, a consultant in psychiatry and neuropsychiatric genetics, who claimed that Sharif suffered from severe cerebral atrophy resulting from "a previously unrecognized autosomal recessive disorder" (para. 19). Indeed, the original expert to the case, Professor Deakin, on revisiting the evidence, "radically altered his opinion" (para. 24). For the judge, Lord Justice Maurice Kay, these findings inevitably favored the conclusion that the guilty verdict, based on the original fitness to plead proceedings, was unsafe. Sharif's conviction was quashed.

For Sharif, however, the decision to quash his conviction was academic. From the time of his original conviction, it took nine years of painstaking evidence gathering by the independent Criminal Cases Review Commission before the case was heard by the Court of Appeal. While the Court, on a finding that he had in fact been unfit to plead, was at liberty to order Sharif's complete discharge or treatment in the community (section 6(2) of the Criminal Appeal Act 1968), Sharif had already served his custodial term. Had uncontested neuropsychological evidence been presented sooner, Sharif may not have served his full term. In his judgment, Lord Justice Maurice Kay implied two general limitations of neuropsychological evidence:

> As often happens in complex medical cases ... one medical expert is reluctant to express a view without further exploration by a colleague in a slightly different discipline ... (para.18).

> The matters under investigation in this case are plainly of a highly unusual nature and it is understandable that even the most competent medical practitioners might not have been able to reach their present conclusions in 1999 on the basis of the evidence then available and the available learning (para. 24).

The first limitation espoused by the judge touches on the interdisciplinary nature of neuropsychological evidence. In *Mohammed Sharif*, psychiatrists, geneticists, neuroradiologists, ophthalmologists, and neurologists were called upon to interpret the meaning of fMRI results. Orientating these parochial interpretations into a coherent picture for legal processes requires that the court become its own expert in giving weight to medical testimony. As the various disciplines continue to build on their own paradigmatic assumptions in light of emerging evidence, the court is likely to be faced with increasing divergent accounts of the relationship between various areas of the brain and behavior. For example, despite evidence that the prefrontal cortex is involved in truth telling and deception, functional imaging experiments continue to implicate different areas of the brain in lying (see Farah, 2008). *Mohammed Sharif* encouraged an even more complicated evidential process by inviting medical professionals from different disciplines to give evidence on the possible link between deception and mild and severe cerebral atrophy of the brain. In so doing, the experts in this case highlighted the fragility of objective pronouncements based on neuropsychological "understanding" of the brain. This would suggest that the picture of medical deference to scientific opinion is not straightforward where the impact of possible brain dysfunction is at issue.

The second limitation spoken by Lord Maurice Justice Kay flows from the first: neuropsychological evidence is especially prone to recapitulation. In terms of legal certainty, the case of *Mohammed Sharif* demonstrates that, in a relatively short space of time, sound legal decisions can later appear whimsical. The impact of paradigmatic recapitulation on legal certainty has no obvious precedent: for example, the success of psychiatry as a source of expert testimony relates in part to its ability to assimilate the assumptions of allied disciplines such as psychology, neurology, genetics, and psychoanalysis into its biochemical explanation of mental illness. As *Mohammed Sharif* shows, the eclecticism of psychiatry (specifically, the importance of Prof. Holland to evidence gathering in the case) helped guarantee its centrality in the fact-finding process. Neuropsychological (or, perhaps, more accurately neuroscientific) evidence, by comparison, was presented in this case by neuroradiologists, neurologists, *and* a neuropsychiatric geneticist. One interpretation of this point is that the rise of neuropsychology in the courtroom will testify to the phenomenon of psychiatric imperialism rather than the increasing rationality of a new distinct science giving effectiveness to law.

A third, tangential limitation must be the impracticability of assigning potentially protective human rights to defendants whose claims of unfitness to plead and stand trial lack scientific credibility. The relevant human right can be found in Article 6(3)(a) of the European Convention on Human Rights, which requires that everyone charged with a criminal offence has the minimum right "to be informed promptly, in a language which he understands and in detail of the nature and cause of the accusation against him." In *SC v. United Kingdom* (2005), Article 6(3) was interpreted to mean that the accused has

> a broad understanding of the nature of the trial process and of what is at stake for him or her, including the significance of any penalty which may be imposed ... The defendant should be able to follow what is said by the prosecution witnesses and, if represented, to explain to his own lawyers his version of events, point out any statements with which he disagrees and make them aware of any facts which should be put forward to the defence.

Looking at the neuropsychological evidence accepted by the Court of Appeal in *Mohammed Sharif*, it is quite possible that Sharif did not meet the stated threshold of effective participation protected by Article 6. However, a closer look at wider case law on the issue, again, reminds us of the importance of agreement between the experts on the meaning of the evidence.

In *R v. Miller* (2006), an adult defendant was found fit to plead despite psychological evidence that he had an IQ of 65 – a score placing him in the bottom 2.5% of the population. By comparison, the defendant in *SC v. United Kingdom* was an 11-year-old boy with an IQ of 56, equivalent to the intellectual ability of a child between six and eight years old – a point of evidence the court felt to be "noteworthy" in finding him unfit to plead (para. 32). On account of the similar IQ scores, the respective decisions may seem surprising; yet, from an evidential point of view, it may be significant that in *SC* both a psychiatrist and psychologist shared the opinion that the boy's reasoning ability was restricted. This ran in stark contrast to the four psychiatrists and two psychologists in *Miller*, who were unable to give an unequivocal statement on the issue. While it is at least possible that neuropsychological evidence of brain function in relation to IQ could have led to different outcomes in these cases, the potentially unsatisfactory impact of contestable evidence pervades.

A final, more generic, explanation for the divergent approaches taken in the two cases may be explained by our inherent sensibilities towards children. For, even though the court in *SC* correctly expressed the view that proceedings must take into account the "age, level of maturity and intellectual and emotional capacities" of the defendant (para. 18), much of the analysis in the case focuses on the danger that young and immature children will experience intimidation, humiliation, or distress in court. The precedent for this emphasis appears in various statutes and policy guidelines on court procedures (see, e.g., section 24 of the Magistrates' Courts Act 1980; section 44 of the Children and Young Persons Act 1933; Practice Direction (Crown Court: Trial of Children and Young Persons) [2001] 1 Cr App R 483). For adults, the concern appears less acute: in *Miller*, a more general contention that the defendant merely "coped satisfactorily" with the whole aspect of the trial was being tested (para. 25). While neuropsychological advances may one day provide justification for placing vulnerable adults and children in fitness to plead proceedings on an equal footing, it may be that legal decisions in this context are underpinned by intuitive assumptions about the relationship between emotion instability and irresponsibility *and* young age. It may also be that a defendant who is perceived to be less capable of discerning right from wrong by virtue of their young age is more likely to evoke the procedural sympathies of the court than an adult whose responsibility is more easily assumed.

Case Study 33.2 Lack of age: Decision-making capacity on trial

Doli incapax: A reassessment

In Case Study 33.1 it was implied that the attribution of criminal responsibility to a person of 11 years old does not in itself give rise to a breach of Convention rights, provided the child is able to effectively participate in his or her trial (*SC v. United Kingdom*). Before 1998, however, there was a *rebuttable* presumption that a child between 10 and 14 years old was incapable of committing a crime on account that s/he could not tell right from wrong (doli incapax). Thus, the prosecution was required to prove the child did the act with the requisite *mens rea, and* also that s/he appreciated their conduct was seriously wrong. The rebuttable presumption has since been abolished (section 34 of the Crime and Disorder Act 1998; *R v. JTB*, 2009): only children below the age of ten are now exempt from criminal liability. For older children, recourse to unfitness to plead (see Case Study 33.1) may be their only means of avoiding the full force of the criminal law.

In procedural terms, however, in *SC* it was suggested that the standard of effective participation requires that a child be tried "in a specialist tribunal which is able to give full consideration to and make proper allowance for the handicaps under which [s/he may labor], and adapt its procedure accordingly" (at 35). This suggests that, except for serious crimes such as murder and rape, children aged between 10 and 17 should be tried by magistrates (or a district judge) in the youth court.

Despite the inevitable participation difficulties that will arise in some children with developmental immaturity, there is no test for unfitness to plead in the youth court (or adult Magistrates' Court). For imprisonable offences, a child who has a mental disorder can receive a hospital order under section 37(3) of the MHA, rather than a custodial sentence. This means that children with non-psychiatric conditions, such as learning disabilities, have no equivalent protection in law. For these children, the only way a judge can recognize their vulnerability is to stop, or stay, proceedings. The justification will be that the child is sufficiently vulnerable that s/he will not receive a fair trial if it continues. In *R (TP) v. West London Youth Court* (2005), it was stated (at 7) that, as a minimum, a child receiving a fair trial should be able to:

1 Understand what s/he is said to have done wrong.
2 Have the means of knowing what s/he did (or omitted to do) was wrong.
3 Understand what, if any, defenses are available to them.
4 Have a reasonable opportunity to make relevant representations to the court if s/he wishes.
5 Have the opportunity to consider what representations s/he wishes to make once s/he understands the issues involved.

In the subsequent case of *Crown Prosecution Service v. P* (2007), Lady Justice Smith opined that child criminal court proceedings raised a number of overlapping capacity issues yet to be resolved:

> The test for deciding upon fitness to plead bears some resemblance to the criteria set out in *SC* ... as those relevant to the question of whether a defendant is capable of effective participation in the trial. The criteria are also similar, although not identical, to those set out in the *West London* case ... relating to the essential elements of a fair trial. It should be noted however, that one of the listed requirements of a fair trial is that the defendant should know that what he is alleged to have done is wrong, which is in effect the test for *doli incapax*.
>
> (at 48).

Despite the similarities, the abolition of doli incapax in the year that *P* was decided suggests that effective participation, rather than criminal liability, is the only issue that will be answered by reference to levels of cognitive development. The impact of this distinction, however, is somewhat moot. Judges stay proceedings only in exceptional circumstances (see *Crown Prosecution Service v. P*, 2008), meaning that children charged with serious crimes may have less protection than adults tried in the Crown Court. By comparison, and by analogy to Lady Justice Smith's discussion of doli incapax, a child's representative might invite the court to acquit the defendant if s/he does not know what they did was seriously wrong according to the standards applied by the fair minded in society (points 1 and 2 above). This suggests that the important question is whether a child has sufficient capacity to be criminally liable, not whether s/he is able to participate effectively in an adversarial trial. Thus, the ability of neuropsychologists to call upon evidence of the relationship between developmental immaturity and offending behavior is immediately appealing (see Box 33.2).

Box 33.2 Criminal responsibility: A neuropsychological account

The neuropsychological basis of determining whether an individual knows right from wrong has often focused on impulse control. In one early experiment, it was shown that impulsive murderers displayed lower prefrontal cortex activity (the reflective system) and increased subcortical activity (principally the amygdala involved in the impulsive system) compared to controls (Raine et al., 1998). More recently, these correlates have been shown to exist in young boys (Boes et al., 2009). Amid the increasing evidence of insufficient impulse control in children, debate has focused on when during adolescence higher executive functions fully develop. Ages cited range from "approximately 14 years of age" (The Royal College of Psychiatrists, 2006, p. 38) to "half way through the third decade of life" (Prison Reform Trust, 2012, p. 11). To complicate matters further, it is also claimed – by analogy to the psychopath (Case Study 33.3) – that brain imaging can be used to detect characteristics predictive of antisocial behavior in children as young as seven (Raine et al., 2010).

To put this finding into context, government statistics reveal that 98,837 offenses were committed between 2012 and 2013 by children aged between 11 and 17, while 43,601 were sentenced (Ministry of Justice, 2014, p. 9). Among this age group, 77% of those receiving a "substantive outcome" (court order or pre-court disposal) were aged 15 and over. In light of the neurological evidence, many, if not most, of these children are likely to have lacked meaningful "capacity to feel guilt and shame, linked with an awareness of the implications for others of the offender's wrongful actions" (Fontin, 2009, p. 73). Does this indicate that decisions about responsibility should be guided by neuropsychological evidence?

Taking into account all the evidence, the Law Commission recognized in 2013 that proposed reform of the law of fitness to plead in respect of children might equally be approached as a general review of the age of criminal responsibility:

> [The decision in *P*] raises some questions in the light of developing [psychological] research on developmental maturity in children and adolescents, which is possibly relevant to the issue of decision-making capacity generally. In particular, there may be sound policy reasons for looking afresh at the age of criminal responsibility
>
> (Law Commission, 2013c, para. 8.57)

On June 2, 2015, the government responded to this call by introducing the Age of Criminal Responsibility Bill 2015–2016 in the House of Lords. If enacted as law, it would amend the Children and Young Persons Act 1993 so that the age of criminal responsibility would be raised from 10 to 12 years old. Lord Dholakia explains:

> [It would constitute a] more effective and more humane to deal with offenders under that age in family courts, as other European countries do. A strategy along these lines would help to move this country away from its unenviable position of having the highest prison population in western Europe. In doing so, it would help to concentrate our limited resources on the measures that are most likely to protect the public by rehabilitating offenders and reducing reoffending.
>
> (Hansard: column 330)

Contrary to the views of Lord Dholakia, raising the age of criminal responsibility to 12 is unlikely to be seen as significantly "more effective and more humane" by anyone familiar with neuropsychology. There must also be some doubt that the Bill will ever be enacted: the current Bill presently restates the proposal of its predecessor, the Age of Criminal Responsibility Bill 2012–2013. Consider that parliament is constantly forced to prioritize what it takes forward as legislation. The policy reasons favoring reforms to matters of, for example, economics and extremism can be readily justified by reference to utilitarian gain; when applied to criminal justice practice, by comparison, utilitarianism generally takes on the form of zero tolerance or "tough on crime" policies. This begs the question: what are the policy reasons that favor the status quo in relation to the age of criminal responsibility?

One such policy reason may be that neuropsychological findings are mediated by both genetic factors and the social environment making up a child's experiences. While it has for some time been patently clear that early deprivation factors impact upon brain development and future (offending) behavior (see, e.g., West & Farrington, 1973), it is equally clear that "bad luck" factors are irrelevant to decisions about responsibility in the criminal law. "Welfarist" approaches to criminal justice have been out of favor since the 1980s, largely due to a rise in conservative politics emphasizing that social welfare programs aimed at addressing deficient socialization in families are less effective at reducing crime than punitiveness. As Ronald Regan once famously said when campaigning for tough federal judges: "We don't need a bunch of sociological majors on the bench" (quoted in Rowland, Songer, & Carp, 1988, p. 194).

Garland (2001) has importantly shown that the punitive, or retributive, approach to punishment has generated a philosophy in criminal justice policy of public protection at all costs. He observes that this preoccupation is a consequence of the increasing visibility of the victim and the media's coverage of crime. In respect of children, we have become accustomed to sensationalist, and often misleading, headlines such as: "[t]he suspects behind almost 3,000 crimes, half of them arson or criminal damage, went unpunished – because they were too young to be prosecuted" (*Daily Mail*, 2007). In Garland's (2001) view, this sort of coverage demonstrates the way in which crime is now crafted as "a matter of anti-social cultures or personalities" (p. 102). One result is that crime by certain abstract groups (including children) is now seen as both normal *and* worthy of our anxiety.

It is important to note that the possible impact for neuropsychologists, and other scientists, of this revised conception of the social order is that, even if invited to provide a scientific account, in particular, of the mediatory effects of environmental factors on the expression of genes governing capacity in children, they may merely prevail upon the judge and jury "a general definition of the dangers one wishes to prevent" (Castel, 1991, p. 288). To put this differently, evidence may simply endorse the retributive response to crimes by children (who lack capacity) based on unarticulated notions of risk.

By contrast, one area in which neuropsychological involvement might prove advantageous is in sentencing mitigation. Recent sentencing guidelines on assault, burglary, and drug offences stipulate that those sentencing must take account of the offender's "age and/or lack of maturity" when passing sentence (Sentencing Council, 2011a, 2011b; Sentencing Council, 2012, p. 7). Unfortunately, some magistrates and judges claim that the maturity of offenders (be they children or adults) is already taken into account at the sentencing stage, despite little evidence of a consistent approach (Prison Reform Trust, 2012, p. 11). This indicates that guidelines are simply codifying pre-existing prejudices. For neuropsychologists, this should at the very least engender concern that the meaning of "age" and "maturity" is yet to receive a full and proper hearing in the criminal law.

Fitness to plead: A new legal test of capacity?

In recognition of the limits of the law governing fitness to plead, the Law Commission (2013c) has proposed a new test of fitness to plead based on decision-making capacity. Deriving from section 1(3) of the Mental Capacity Act (MCA) 2005, a defendant would be found fit to plead unless they could not: 1) understand the information relevant to the decisions that s/he will have to make in the course of his or her trial; 2) retain that information; 3) use or weigh that information as part of a decision-making process; and 4) communicate his or her decisions (para. 3.13). The new test would focus on factors such as emotion and volition, rather than cognitive ability, as is currently the case. However, no assumptions would be made about the capacity of children between the ages of 10 and 17.

Respondents to the Law Commission discussion paper (2013b) did not speak in one voice about whether age should be taken into account when determining capacity. Her Majesty's Council of Circuit Judges, for instance, argued: "It must surely be wrong to deal with a youth who has lived for 14 years but who has a mental age of 9 when the law would not allow the prosecution of a 9 year old" (para. 1.316). By comparison, the British Psychological Society opined that drawing on the competency of psychologists to determine "variation in cognitive functions between people of the same age" is preferable to "a simple estimate based upon age" (para 1.313). Support for the latter approach derives from the MCA itself. Section 1(3)(a) states that "A lack of capacity cannot be established merely by reference to a person's age or appearance." This suggests that calls for the new capacity test to take account of neurobiological and psychological maturity are evidence of the desire to see doli incapax reintroduced.

A further stricture proposed by the Law Commission (2013c) is that a "standardized psychiatric test" be introduced to ensure consistency in determining decision-making capacity at trial (para. 5.14). Some respondents expressed concern that a standardized test (which does not currently operate in the context of the MCA) would lead to inflexibility, while those in support of the test overwhelmingly argued that there is little justification for introducing a test that is psychiatrically-oriented. The British Psychological Society, for instance, noted that psychologists are already well-instructed on how to conduct capacity-based judgments (see British Psychological Society, 2013), and that this instruction would provide "a very functional approach to the assessment of fitness" (footnote 46, para. 1.57). In contrast, Graham Rogers, consultant educational and child psychologist, contended that:

> [Psychiatric] training does not necessarily cover the idiosyncrasies of childhood systems necessary to determine and declare a person as learning disabled. One could argue that it is the learning disabled who are most likely to struggle in terms of "fitness".

> (BPS, 2013, para. 1.187)

Notwithstanding compelling claims of the suitability of the profession to lead capacity judgments, it is improbable that (neuro)psychologists will usurp the role of psychiatrists in the process. The Law Commission (2013c) recommends that decision-making capacity be based on the testimony of at least one psychiatrist. This it justifies on the basis that an "unfit" defendant might be suitable for a hospital order under the MHA. Currently, under section 12(2) of the MHA, at least two medical practitioners must recommend hospital admission, with at least one approved by the Secretary of State as having special experience in the diagnosis or treatment of mental disorder. This will be "more easily available," the Commission states, "if there has been evidence from at least one psychiatrist at the point when the accused's decision-making capacity was determined" (para. 5.34).

Further, while welcoming a multidisciplinary approach to determinations of capacity, Graham Rogers questions whether "the political will exists to make such a process happen" (BPS, 2013, para. 1.190). One interpretation of this view is that there may be competition between psychiatry and psychology for professional currency, if a standardized assessment were to be enshrined in law. For example, in the provision of services for the mentally ill, inter-professional competition has led Nicola Glover-Thomas (2007) to argue that multi-disciplinarity is notoriously difficult to achieve. More optimistically, responses to the Law Commission's discussion paper suggest few latent tensions between the various disciplines.

A better interpretation, I would argue, can be gleaned from the many respondents who doubted that any changes to the relevant law would lead to improved treatment of children and adolescents in the criminal justice system. Nicola Padfield, for example, complained:

> There are ... some dreadful stories percolating up from the youth court: read *CPS v P* [2007] EWHC 946 (Admin). It beggars belief that the [Crown Prosecution

Service appealed against] the sensible decision of a District Judge to stay as an abuse of process criminal proceedings against a boy aged 11 with very significant problems.

(para. 1.303)

On this account, the desire to protect vulnerable children runs counter to the emphasis of risk in criminal justice policy, which has the potential to cause decision makers to emphasize "the [perceived] need for security, the containment of danger, the identification and management of risk of any kind" (Garland, 2001, p. 12). While there is almost certainly the potential to consciously resist the distorting effects of policies built on risk concerns, the problem, Foucault posits (1978, pp. 94–95), in his typically dense style, is that "it is often the case that no one is there to have invented [them], and few who can be said to have formulated [them]". The potential for false consciousness to propagate risk-infused criminal justice decision making at the expense of protecting the vulnerable orientates the strongly held view that the Law Commission's proposals on fitness to plead are "consistent with a process-driven, criminalizing system of juvenile justice," which prioritizes custodial sentencing and other methods of control "rather than providing an exit route from the criminal justice system for children [in need]" (Association of Panel Members, in Law Commission, 2013b, para. 1.309; see, more generally, Muncie, 2009, pp. 331–340).

In light of statistics showing that children aged 10 to 14 accounted for 23% of all young people sentenced in 2012 and 2013 (Ministry of Justice, 2014, p. 27), the aim of (neuro)psychologists must be to imagine a different, if not more compassionate, legal order. Protected from the pernicious influence of risk by the pursuit of scientific credibility and generalizable data, they will advocate criminal justice policies that adequately reflect the significant vulnerabilities that professionals diagnose in the courtroom. At the same time, however, it must be acknowledged that "the law is also concerned to make a diagnosis – the diagnosis of crime" (Maudsley, 1874, p. 77).

Case Study 33.3 Psychopathy and neuropsychology in an era of risk

In this final Case Study, the possible implications of speaking neuropsychology to law are discussed in the context of psychopathy. This focus is particularly apt since psychopathy, perhaps more than any other mental disorder or vulnerability, highlights the potential for incongruity between neuropsychological understanding of moral responsibility and pragmatic assertions of criminal responsibility in criminal justice policy. Consider that, on the one hand, it is now reasonably clear that structural change in the amygdala and prefrontal cortex caused by early adverse events predisposes adults to risk-taking behaviors more commonly seen in adolescents (Dillon et al., 2009). The implication is that the psychopath (like the adolescent) should not be criminally liable. On the other hand, unlike the majority of immature children, whose offences typically lack abject violence, the affective core of callous-unemotional traits common to psychopaths predisposes them to "start offending at an early age and continue across the lifespan with acts that are often predatory in nature" (Viding, Blair, Moffitt, & Plomin, 2005, p. 592). This will be of particular interest to criminal justice policy. Consider, in particular, that the rate of violent offending by psychopaths released from prison is approximately four times as great as non-psychopaths (Hart, Kropp, & Hare, 1988). With the prevalence of psychopathy in prisons at 7.7% for men and 1.9% for women (Coid et al., 2009), around 6,587 men and 1,625 women (based on a prison population of 85,554 (Howard League, 2014)) present significant risk to the public, if released from prison.

In the context of punishment and public protection, reoffending by psychopaths is most easily prevented through prison and/or hospital incapacitation. However, under Article 5(1)(e) of the European Convention on Human Rights, only offenders of "unsound mind" may be lawfully detained in hospital (*Winterwerp v. the Netherlands*) 1979); and numerous European and International instruments on imprisonment (see, e.g., United Nations Standard Minimum Rules for the Treatment of Prisoners, 1955; International Covenant on Civil and Political Rights, 1966; Committee of Ministers Recommendation Rec, 2003, 23 of October 9, 2003; the European Prison Rules, 2006) make it clear that rehabilitation should be its ultimate goal. Nevertheless, criminal justice policy has hitherto struggled to achieve a productive balance between the goals of incapacitation and rehabilitation. We have witnessed this struggle in two key policies introduced by the last Labour government in the UK: the (now disinvested) Dangerous and Severe Personality Disorder (DSPD) Programme from 2001 in hospitals and prisons and the (now abolished) Indeterminate Sentence for Public Protection (IPP) under the Criminal Justice Act 2003.

The stated aim of the IPP was to rehabilitate dangerous, including psychopathic, prisoners during their "tariff" period in prison by administering psychological and psychosocial interventions. Prisoners who did not sufficiently mitigate their risk through treatment or otherwise impress upon the Parole Board their suitability for release remained detained. The problem was that overuse of the IPP coupled with insufficient treatment resources has resulted in significant numbers of offenders experiencing incapacitation, because they have no practical opportunity to reduce their risk.

Following a decision of the European Court of Human Rights that this form of incapacitation constitutes a form of unlawful detention (*James, Wells & Lee v. the United Kingdom*, 2012; see also Article 5(1)(a) of the European Convention on Human Rights), the IPP has now been replaced with an Extended Determinate (fixed term) Sentence by the Legal Aid, Sentencing and Punishment of Offenders Act 2012 (Ministry of Justice, 2011).

Like the IPP, the ostensible aim of the DSPD program was to "provide treatment that addresses mental health need and risk" (Ministry of Justice, 2005, p. 2). Yet DSPD hospitals were often employed to preventively detain psychopaths nearing the end of determinate (fixed term) sentences by warrant of the Secretary of State for Justice, under section 47 of the MHA. In 2008, the Mental Health Act Commission (as it was) reported that:

> [a number of patients were] refusing to engage in therapy and otherwise proving to be a severe management problem due to their resentment of such late transfers. One patient told us that he had been assessed several times in prison and told that he did not have a mental disorder.
>
> (para. 7.19)

Two observations flow from this empirical evidence. First, the Labour Government appears to have responded to the impracticability of preventively detaining all offenders with mental illness by confining criminal psychopaths who are neither "mad" nor "bad" but in whose characters there exist abstract factors which postulate risk. Second, the preoccupation in criminal justice policy with eradicating risk through regimes of incapacitation leads medical practitioners to "no longer control the usage of the data they produce" (Castel 1991, p. 289). Instead, they are in danger of becoming disillusioned administrators of policies of preventive detention that succeed in giving the mere impression that they constitute "a sincere desire to help a group of people who are desperately in need of help" (Tyrer et al., 2010).

In 2011, apparently steering a different course, the Coalition Government announced that the DSPD program would be disinvested in favor of increased treatment provision in high secure prisons (Department of Health and Ministry of Justice, 2011). The announcement, appearing in the *Personality Disorder Pathway Implementation Plan* (Department of Health and Ministry of Justice, 2011), was part of a series of measures aimed at securing public protection by improving rehabilitative regimes. Specifically planned measures include identifying and assessing offenders who present "the highest risk of serious harm to others and have the most complex needs *early in their sentence*" (p. 5, emphasis added) and making pathways out of detention clearer, so as to encourages offenders to engage with treatment. Though it is still too early to be certain what effects, if any, these changes will have, it is arguable that the Coalition Government's drive to improve rehabilitation suffers from a fundamental flaw: no consideration has been given to the potential impact that the shift from the IPP to the new Extended Determinate Sentence (EDS) will have on treatment engagement.

Specifically, the EDS removes the expressive link between gaining parole and treatment engagement that predominated under the IPP. Unlike IPP offenders, EDS offenders are almost always eligible for automatic release at the two-thirds point in their sentence. Only those serving a prison sentence of ten years or more must first demonstrate to the Parole Board that they are suitable for expedited release at this point. In light of research showing that psychopaths require legal coercive pressures to engage with treatment (McRae, 2013), it is a real concern that the EDS will shore up large numbers of treatment-refusing psychopaths who, by implication, are perceived to pose a risk to the public. One side effect may be that the Secretary of State for Justice will increasingly rely on the MHA to transfer psychopathic prisoners who are due for release to hospital. To put this differently: the EDS will encourage continued reliance on the "incapacitative" model of criminal justice.

The potential for abuse of hospital transfers upon the expiry of prison sentences is an issue that could implicate neuropsychologists as providers of medical evidence forming the justification for hospital admission. A medical practitioner providing evidence in support of admission is only required to supply "some reasons which they consider adequate" (*R (on the application of SP) v. Secretary of State for Justice*, 2010, *per* Lady Justice Arden, para. 23). Impressive and irrefutable (collateral) evidence of psychopathy would clearly be provided by fMRI, even though such evidence could have been called upon earlier in the offender's sentence. Properly speaking, however, the criteria for admission under section 47 of the MHA (the offender has a "mental disorder" that is of a "nature or degree which makes it appropriate to be detained in a hospital for [appropriate] treatment") hardly requires sophisticated, and potentially expensive, neuropsychological investigations.

A better use of neuropsychological evidence would be to encourage greater use of hospital orders at the *point of sentencing* (e.g., upon a finding of NGRI: see Box 33.1). Three collateral benefits of this approach are as follows. First, the problem of treatment disengagement among disgruntled psychopathic offenders transferred to hospital late in their prison sentence is militated against, because hospital admission is less likely to be viewed as punitive. Second, earlier hospital admission may provide "substantially more effective opportunity ... to plan [the offender's] rehabilitation and eventually reintroduction into the community" than has hitherto been the case in prisons (*R v. Simpson (Jonathan Paul)*, 2008, *per* Mr. Justice Gibbs, para. 27). Third, there is the procedural benefit that a First-tier Tribunal (Mental Health) could review whether psychiatric detention remains warranted after six months (and then every 12 months renewed).

It must be borne in mind, nevertheless, that tribunals seldom order discharge unless this result is supported by the patient's medical practitioner in charge of their overall care (Responsible Clinician) (see, e.g., Peay, 1989; Dolan, Gibb, & Coorey, 1999; Richardson & Machin, 2000). Despite the fact that tribunal decision making is principally guided by risk criteria (is continued detention "Necessary for the health or safety of the patient or for the protection of other persons", section 72(1)(b)(ii) of the MHA), research reveals that in 88% to 90% of tribunal hearings, pre-decision deliberations are based more broadly on the offender's diagnosis, mental health symptoms, and cooperation with treatment (Richardson & Machin, 2000). This suggests that judgments in respect of dangerous offenders, including psychopaths, will focus heavily on whether treatment has had any benefit.

Despite significant investment by the Labour Government, the DSPD program brought us no closer to understanding whether psychopaths are amenable to treatment. Such was the focus on containment that treatment sessions were delivered infrequently, and were "very heterogeneous, often with little theoretical rationale for their application" (Duggan, 2011, p. 432). Outside the DSPD estate, however, research has shown that there is no statistically significant difference in reoffending rates among psychopaths five years after hospital discharge between treatment completers, non-completers and those expelled from treatment for rule breaking (McCarthy & Duggan, 2010). For medical practitioners working with psychopaths, an ever-attendant problem will be discerning whether the psychopath who engages with treatment does so wholly or partly in pursuit of ulterior motives.

Uncovering deception is an area in which it is possible that neuropsychologists could help. Neuropsychologists, for example, could contribute to discharge decision making by discerning truth telling from lying as a consequence of treatment received by using fMRI lie detection technology, thermal imaging, or similar technology. However, to be viable, research will have to reach a consensus on the many areas of the brain involved in lying (Farah, 2008; McCabe, Castel, & Rhodes, 2011). Neuropsychologists would also have to contend with the problem that the psychopath, as a skilled prevaricator, could employ covert countermeasures to overcome deception detection procedures (Ganis et al., 2011).

Conversely, psychopaths who are being truthful may suffer the result of false positives caused by misattributing lying to a specific area of the brain (Miller, 2010). More fundamentally, even if these problems of scientific validity could be resolved, it is important to realize that the mere administration of scientific tests looking to uncover deception may simply reinforce the bias that "immoral" psychopaths present significant risk to the public, and should remain detained. For neuropsychologists, these tensions uncover a dilemma: is it preferable for medical expertise to be used to justify measures of preventive detention or potentially reward recalcitrant psychopaths for their deceptive behaviors?

It is conceivable that some neuropsychologists, rather than directly responding to this dilemma, might remark that psychopaths are incapable of acting responsibly, and so should be exempted from criminal liability. Most discussion along these lines will focus on whether psychopaths should be able to rely on the insanity defense (see Box 33.1). Thus, it is important to appreciate that, while a finding of NGRI can result in a complete acquittal or supervision and treatment order in the community, it is more likely that the judge would impose on the psychopath a hospital order. In this context, the legal rationale behind the hospital order would shift from rehabilitation, care, and treatment to "protect[ing] society against the recurrence of dangerous conduct" (*R v. Sullivan*, 1983). The subtle implication is that psychopaths deemed to be insane at the time of their offence could face protracted detention in hospital (again, allowing for the possibility of release by the Tribunal). Unsurprisingly, the Law Commission has noted that "defendants often prefer the certainty of a [determinate] prison term to the uncertainty of a release date from hospital" (2013a, para. 1.82). Of course, if the newly introduced EDS merely results in increased use of hospital transfers once the offender reaches his or her prison release date, this outlook could change.

In support of the use of the insanity defense by psychopaths, Duff (1977) argues that psychopaths do not know the nature and quality of their acts because they do not understand the emotional and moral significance of prosocial behavior. Presumably, psychopaths also do not appreciate the wrongfulness of their actions, when compared to the fair-minded majority in society. In light of evidence that courts make little effort to distinguish between cases where the defendant does not know that his or her actions are legally wrong (as formally required in England and Wales) as opposed to morally wrong (as permitted in Australia and in some states in America) (Mackay & Kearns, 1999), the common law approach in many jurisdictions to treat psychopaths as prima facie sane seems at odds (see, e.g., *Stapleton* (Australia) and section 4.01 of the American Model Penal Code, 1985). Nevertheless, the Law Commission (2013a) in England has advocated that psychopathy (or, in its words, those with antisocial personality disorder) be explicitly rejected as a qualifying medical condition from its new proposed defense of "not criminally responsible by reason of a mental disorder":

> [it would be inappropriate] for a person to be able to rely on this defense if the accused's condition consists of a personality disorder characterized solely or principally by abnormally aggressive or seriously irresponsible behavior; in other words,

the evidence for the condition is simply evidence of what might broadly be called criminal behavior.

(para. 1.90)

At first blush, the rejection of psychopathy from the insanity defense coheres with broader medical and legal opinion that the disorder is synonymic with crime, and as such that it should be contained in the criminal justice system (reported in Duggan & Kane, 2010). But, while a criminal justice focus undoubtedly serves the goal of public protection at the heart of legal responses to psychopathy, a blanket policy of exclusion severely forestalls opportunities for experts practicing in the field of neuropsychology to inform ethical debate about the true relationship between personality and responsibility.

In the absence of ethical debate, it is probable that the approach of the Law Commission hints at a more complex, largely unarticulated, and intuitive relationship between personality, responsibility, and society. The essence of this complexity, I would argue, derives from the sociological observation that crime can never disappear in solidary societies, because "the sentiments [based on a common morality] that are offended would have to be found without exception in all individual consciousness" (Durkheim, 1895, p. 13). A corollary of this observation must be that the scope of the law to shape social morality is predicated on citizens' willingness to view crime as both "other" and unconducive to social cohesion. However, since we all differ in the extent to which we are amenable to the collective morality, by virtue of heredity and socialization, effective societies must conceive of an archetypal criminal – the psychopath – to complete the continuum and enable members of society to recognize, and integrate, the morality-shaping function of legal rules. It would be antithetical to this potential to have undue sympathy for the biologically and socially determined psychopath, even though we may understand perfectly well his or her moral limitations. As Reid (1985, p. 77) put it:

> [W]e should expand our view of the perpetrators of psychopathic ... violence to include those whose intent can be readily inferred, while excluding those whose behavior is either clinically psychotic ... or arguably altruistic (... including actions of war or political terrorism). The group which remains is broad indeed.

Reid goes on to propose that the media's focus on the victim gives rise to "healthy concern for our safety and for the feelings and safety of others whom we [conveniently] perceive to be like us" (ibid). The effect, he argues, is a "somewhat disturbing dichotomy between 'us' and 'them'" (ibid). In the forced separation of normal and abnormal violence, however, Reid warns of the two-horned dilemma of the risks to our freedom we face by containing the psychopathic so as to "liberate" ourselves:

> On the one hand, we frustratedly give up the ability to move about as we please after dark, to take that romantic walk through the woods, to send the children to play on their own. On the other, many have suggested we abridge everyone's freedom in an effort to contain the antisocial element. In doing so we may, by our own hand, become victims before we have even been victimized

(p. 79)

Forensic Neuropsychology in the Criminal Court

While it would certainly take us too far afield to test these ideas in full, there is some evidence that policy and law makers, quite selectively, marginalize expert evidence so as to communicate guilt to certain types of (stereotyped) defendant. The Law Commission, for example, gives scant consideration to the claim based on neuropsychological evidence that automatically bars psychopaths from the insanity defense is indefensible:

> Kinscherff [2010] writes that "convergent research in neurocognitive sciences and behavioral genetics has increasingly rendered meaningless any distinction between those mental disorders with a 'biological' basis and those that are 'merely' a 'psychological' disorder". We acknowledge the validity of this point: that a denial of a defense in law may be unjust if it is based on a view of the human condition which is shown by subsequent scientific developments to be invalid
>
> (para. 4.105)

This argument must fail, in my view. In addition to the fact that all mental disorders are socially constructed, the neuropsychological evidence base underpinning claims about psychopaths is as good as, if not better, than other mental disorders recognized by the insanity defense. It is conceivable that neuropsychologists, and allied professionals, might yet complain that social construction works as well on the rules of law as it does on science; and that, crucially, by marginalizing certain knowledge claims in science, legal rules risk losing legitimacy in the fair-minded debate about adult disorders of personality and responsibility.

For neuropsychologists, the marginalization of scientific claims will run in stark contrast to the historical account of the homicidal maniac, whose responsibility was effectively determined by the "psychiatrization of criminal danger" (Foucault, 1988, p. 137). However, then as now, psy-scientists cannot reproduce their findings at will in the courtroom. While neuropsychologists are certainly capable of highlighting inadequacies in the criminal law, it is the law, Talcott Parsons once noted, that "defin[es] the situation for them" (1989, p. 176).

Conclusions

This chapter has considered the potential scope and impact of affording neuropsychologists a greater role in the courtroom. Discussion has focused on three case studies: fitness to plead, lack of age, and psychopathy. The choice of these case studies was heavily influenced, in particular, by perennial concerns among neuropsychologists, and those in allied fields, that children and psychopaths should not be responsible for their crimes. For instance, scientists have often expressed concern that the removal of doli incapax in respect of children aged between 10 and 14 years failed to acknowledge evidence that moral competency develops much later in the brain (see Case Study 33.2). Similarly, psychopaths have been shown to suffer from "deficits in moral emotions and deficits in practical reason" (Maibom, 2010, p. 321). One limitation of these criticisms is that the channels of communication through which neuropsychologists and lawyers speak are very different. While legal discourse is framed according to a guilty/not guilty binary, neuropsychological discourse reflects a free will/determinism binary.

Not only is law incapable of framing criminal responsibility according to the neuropsychological binary, it would be imprudent to do so. Consider, for instance, in the era of doli incapax, the policy reason behind holding children over 14 years of age criminally responsible:

> Experience makes us know, that every day murders, bloodsheds, burglaries, larcenies, burning of houses, rapes, clipping and counterfeiting of money, are committed by youths above fourteen and under twenty-one; and if they should have impunity by the privilege of such their minority, no man's life or estate could be safe
>
> (Hale, Wilson, & Emlyn, 1778, 25; taken from *R v. JTB*, para. 11)

This historical warning suggests that criminal law responsibility has always been viewed as a predicate of dangerousness. Over the past 100 years, however, we have witnessed the replacement of dangerousness with risk, or "a combination of abstract factors which [are perceived to] render more or less probable the occurrence of undesirable modes of behavior" (Castel, 1991, p. 287). In juvenile criminal justice policy, the unimaginative response has been the "criminalizing and incarceration of young people at unprecedented rates" (Association of Panel Members, in Law Commission, 2013b, para. 1.321).

Psychopaths, by comparison, present an exceptional case study on the effects of risk discourse. On the one hand, legal commentators express concern that the diagnosis of psychopathy is tautological, insofar as the "mental disorder is inferred from anti-social behavior while the anti-social behavior is explained by mental disorder" (Wootton, 1981, p. 90). Indeed, it is for this reason that the Law Commission (2013a) rejected psychopathy as a recognized medical condition for its proposed new defense of "not criminally responsible by reason of a recognized medical condition." On the other hand, psychopaths seem indispensable to us. They are the personification of our fears that harm lurks in the shadows after dark; the actor who delivers compassionless murders to our homes through the television; the serious sexual predator who we feel to be ubiquitous. They are at once within and without us. For instance, to continue the last example, Garland (2001) is right to ask:

> Could it be that the extraordinary public fears and hostilities in respect of certain crimes against children stem from the residual guilt and ambivalence that families feel about their own choices and the vulnerabilities that they seem to cause? If so, the pedophile [is a screen] upon which [we] project our guilt as well as our anxieties.
>
> (footnote 64, p. 157)

If we could only consider that we detain at will the psychopath in order to liberate ourselves from facing our own antisocial nature, we would admit that the project to free him or her from the shackles of criminal responsibility is an altruistic goal that is, ultimately, inward looking. There must, indeed, remain a certain truth to Packer's claim, that "the law treats [people's] conduct as autonomous and willed, not because it is, but because it is desirable to proceed as if it were" (Packer, 1968, p. 75).

But, perhaps, vulnerability in the courtroom of those alleged to have committed a crime is a different matter. To abide by the mental suffering of another in this context is to delegitimize the practical benefit we all experience, if subconsciously, of diagnosing the psychopath. For the psychopath – or, perhaps more accurately, the child s/he mimics – we accept that procedural justice is important to justify criminal justice processes. Notwithstanding, despite considerable work on the insanity defense, which would exculpate such defendants, the Law Commission is right to note that "more practically-needed reform is to the law and procedures relating to *unfitness to plead*" (2013a, para. 1.10, emphasis added). In scientific terms, with the possibility that a new capacity test (borrowed from the MCA 2005) will be employed in future to uncover those who lack decision-making capacity at trial, the stage is set for multidisciplinary perspectives on both the meaning and impact of vulnerability. While it is improbable that this development will introduce neuropsychologists to an era of imperialism in matters of courtroom evidence, the speaking of brain science to law has, arguably, never been so worthwhile.

Recommended Reading

Ashworth, A., & Horder, J. (2013). *Principles of criminal law*. London: Oxford University Press. *A comprehensive, yet intelligible, canvas of substantive criminal law and theory for those interested in some of the issues raised in this chapter.*

Garland, D. (2001). *The culture of control: Crime and social order in contemporary society*. Oxford: Oxford University Press. *A seminal book explaining at a theoretical level the rise of the emergent "risk society" in England and America. While it does not provide a case study for psychopathy, it does discuss changes at the in criminal justice policy facing children.*

Keane, A. (2010). *The modern law of evidence* (8th ed.). Oxford: Oxford University Press. *A general introduction to the law governing the admissibility of (scientific) evidence in the criminal court.*

Law Commission. (2010). *Unfitness to plead: A consultation paper. Consultation Paper No 197*. London: Law Commission. *This consultation discusses the use, and weaknesses, of the current test for unfitness to plead in the criminal court. There is significant discussion of proposed reform in this area.*

Law Commission. (2013). *Criminal liability: Insanity and automatism: A discussion paper*. London: Law Commission. *This consultation discusses the insanity defense in comprehensive detail, covering both the law and relevant social policy, and proposals for reform.*

Reid, W. H. (1985). Psychopathy and dangerousness. In M. Roth & R. Bluglass (Eds.), *Psychiatry, human rights and the Law* (pp. 72–810). Cambridge: Cambridge University Press. *Despite being written some years ago, this edited collection describes in interesting detail the interplay of psychopathy and law, at both the doctrinal and theoretical level.*

References

Ashworth, A., & Horder, J. (2013). *Principles of criminal law*. London: Oxford University Press.

Boes, A. D., Bechara, A., Tranel, D., Anderson, S. W., Richman, L., & Nopoulos, P. (2009). Right ventromedial prefrontal cortex: A neuroanatomical correlate of impulse control in boys. *Social Cognitive and Affective Neuroscience, 4*, 1–9.

British Psychological Society. (2013). *Best interests: Guidance on adults who lack capacity to make decisions for themselves*. London: British Psychological Society.

Castel, R. (1991). From dangerousness to risk. In G. Burchell, C. Gordon, & P. Miller (Eds.), *The Foucault effect: Studies in governmentality, with two lectures by and an interview with Michel Foucault* (pp. 281–299). Chicago, IL: The University of Chicago Press.

Coid, J., Yang, M., Ullrich, S. Roberts, A. Moran, P. Bebbington, P., ... Hare, R. (2009). Psychopathy among Prisoners in England and Wales. *International Journal of Law and Psychiatry, 32*(3): 134–141.

Crown Prosecution Service v. P (2007). EWHC 946 (Admin).

Daily Mail. (September 2, 2007) Unpunished: The 3,000 crimes committed by the under-10s. Retrieved from http://www.dailymail.co.uk/news/article-479384/Unpunished-The-3-000-crimes-committed-10s.html.

Department of Health and Ministry of Justice. (2011). *Consultation on the Offender Personality Disorder Pathway Implementation Plan*. London: Department of Health and Ministry of Justice.

Dillon, D. G., Holmes, A. J., Birk, J. L., Brooks, N., Lyons-Ruth, K., & Pizzagalli, D. A. (2009). Childhood adversity is associated with left basal ganglia dysfunction during reward anticipation in adulthood. *Biological Psychiatry, 66*, 206–213.

Dolan, M., Gibb, R., & Coorey, P. (1999). Mental Health Review Tribunals: A survey of special hospital patients' opinions. *Journal of Forensic Psychiatry, 10*(2), 264–275.

Duff, A. (1977). Psychopathy and moral understanding. *American Philosophical Quarterly, 14*, 189–200.

Durkheim, E. (1895). *Les Règles de la Méthode Sociologique* (translated by Margaret Thompson). Paris: Alcan.

Duggan, C., & Kane, E. (2010). Developing a National Institute for Health and Clinical Excellence guideline for antisocial personality disorder. *Personality and Mental Health, 4*(1), 3–8.

Duggan, C. (2011). Dangerous and severe personality disorder. *The British Journal of Psychiatry, 198*, 431–433.

European Committee of Social Rights, Conclusions XVII-2 (United Kingdom), reference period January 1, 2003 to December 31, 2004.

Farah, M. J. (2008). Brain imaging and brain privacy: A realistic concern. *Journal of Cognitive Neuroscience, 21*, 119–127.

Fontin, J. (2009). *Children's rights and developing law*. Cambridge: Cambridge University Press.

Foucault, M. (1978). *The history of sexuality, Vol. 1: An introduction* (translated by Robert Hurley). New York, NY: Pantheon.

Foucault, M. (1988). The dangerous individual. In L. Kritzman (Ed.) *Politics, philosophy, culture: Interviews and other writings, 1977–1984*, (pp. 125–152) (translated by Alan Sheridan). New York: Routledge.

Ganis, G., Rosenfeld, P. J., Meixner, J., Kievit, R. A., & Schendan, H. E. (2011). Lying in the scanner: Covert countermeasures to disrupt deception detection by functional magnetic resonance imaging. *Neuroimage, 55*, 312–319.

Garland, D. (2001). *The culture of control: Crime and social order in contemporary society*. Oxford: Oxford University Press.

Glover-Thomas, N. (2007). Joint working: Reality or rhetoric in housing the mentally vulnerable. *Journal of Social Welfare and Family Law, 29*(3), 217–231.

Hale, M., Wilson, G., & Emlyn, S. (1778). *Hale's history of the pleas of the Crown*. London: T. Payne and others.

Hart, S. D., Kropp, P. R., & Hare, R. D. (1988). Performance of male psychopaths following conditional release from prison. *Journal of Consulting and Clinical Psychology, 56*, 227–232.

Home Office and Department of Health and Social Security. (1953). *Royal Commission on Capital Punishment* (Butler Committee). Cmnd 8932. London: Home Office and Department of Health and Social Security.

Home Office and Department of Health. (2005). *Dangerous and Severe Personality Disorder (DSPD) High Secure Services for Men: Planning and Delivery Guide*. London: Home Office and Department of Health.

House of Lords. (2015). Hansard. June 2. Retrieved from http://www.publications.parliament.uk/pa/ld201516/ldhansrd/text/150602-0001.htm#15060223000413.

Howard League. (2014). Weekly prison watch. Latest prison population figures. Retrieved from http://www.howardleague.org/weekly-prison-watch.

Ingleby, A. (1985). Mental health and social control. In S. Cohen & A. Scull (Eds.), *Social Control and the State* (pp. 141–191). Oxford: Blackwell.

James, Wells & Lee v. the United Kingdom (2012) (application nos. 25119/09, 57715/09, and 57877/09).

Keane, A. (2010). *The modern law of evidence* (8th ed.). Oxford: Oxford University Press.

Kinscherff, R. (2010). Proposition: A personality disorder may nullify responsibility for a criminal act. *Journal of Law, Medicine and Ethics, 38*(4), 745–769.

Law Commission. (2013a). *Criminal liability: Insanity and automatism: A discussion paper.* London: Law Commission.

Law Commission. (2013b). *Unfitness to plead: Analysis of responses.* London: Law Commission.

Law Commission. (2013c). *Unfitness to plead: A consultation paper.* Consultation Paper No 197. London: Law Commission.

Levy, N. (2007). The responsibility of the psychopath revisited. *Philosophy, Psychiatry and Psychology, 14*, 129–138.

Luhmann, N. (1995). *Social systems.* Stanford: Stanford University Press.

Mackay, R., & Kearns, G. (1999). More fact(s) about the insanity defence. *Criminal Law Review, Sept*, 714–725.

Maudsley, H. (1874). *Responsibility and mental disease.* New York: Appleton.

Maibom, H. L. (2010). Moral unreason: The case of psychopathy. *Mind and Language, 20*(2), 237–257.

McCabe, D. P., Castel, A. D., & Rhodes, M. G. (2011). The influence of fMRI lie detection evidence on juror decision–making. *Behavioral Science and the Law, 29*, 566–577.

McCarthy, L., & Duggan, C. (2010). Engagement in medium secure personality disorder services: A comparative study of psychological functioning and offending outcomes. *Criminal Behaviour and Mental Health, 20*, 112–128.

McRae, L. (2013). Rehabilitating antisocial personalities: Treatment through self–governance strategies. *Journal of Forensic Psychiatry and Psychology, 24*(1), 48–70.

Mental Health Act Commission. (2008). *Risk, rights, recovery. Twelfth biennial report.* London: Mental Health Act Commission.

Miller, G. (2010). fMRI lie detection fails a legal test. *Science, 328*(5984), 1336–1337.

Ministry of Justice. (2011). *LASPO amendments: Review of Indeterminate Sentences for Public Protection (IPPs); clarifying the law on self-defence; and increasing the Magistrates' Court fine limit.* London: Ministry of Justice.

Ministry of Justice. (2014). *Youth justice statistics 2012/13, England and Wales.* London: Youth Justice Board and Ministry of Justice.

Mohammed Sharif (2010). EWCA Crim 1709.

Muncie, J. (2009). *Youth and Crime* (3rd ed.). London: Sage.

Packer, H. L. (1968). *The limits of the criminal sanction.* Stanford: Stanford University Press.

Parsons, T. (1989). *On institutions and social evolution: Selected writings.* Chicago and London: University of Chicago Press.

Peay, J. (1989). *Tribunals on trial: A study of decision-making under the Mental Health Act 1983.* Oxford: Clarendon Press.

Prison Reform Trust. (2012). *Old enough to know better?* London: Prison Reform Trust.

Pritchard (1836). 7 C&P.

R v. Birch (1989). 11 Cr App R(S) 202 (CA).

R v. JTB (2009). UKHL 20.

R v. Miller (2006). EWCA Crim 2391.

R (on the application of SP) v. Secretary of State for Justice (2010). EWCA Civ 1590.

R v. Simpson (Jonathan Paul) (2008). 1 Cr App R (S) 111.

R v. Sullivan (1983). 2 All E.R. 673.

R (TP) v. West London Youth Court (2005). EWHC 2583 (Admin).

R v. Windle (1952). 2 QB 8260.

R v. Woollin (1999). 1 AC 82.

Raine, A., Lee, L., Yang, Y., & Colletti, P. (2010). Neurodevelopmental marker for limbic maldevelopment in Antisocial Personality Disorder and psychopathy. *British Journal of Psychiatry, 197*(3), 186–192.

Raine, A., Meloy, R. J., Bihrle, S., Stoddard, J., LaCasse, L., & Buchsbaum, M. S. (1998). Reduced prefrontal and increased subcortical brain functioning assessed using position emission tomography in predatory and affective murderers. *Behavioral Science and the Law, 16*(3), 319–332.

Reid, W. H. (1985). Psychopathy and dangerousness. In M. Roth & R. Bluglass (Eds.), *Psychiatry, human rights and the law* (pp. 72–81). Cambridge: Cambridge University Press.

Rich v. Pierpoint (1862). F. & F. 35.

Richardson, G., & Machin, D. (2000). Judicial review and tribunal decision making: A study of the Mental Health Review Tribunal. *Public Law, Autumn*, 494–514.

Rowland, C. K., Songer, D., & Carp, R. A. (1988). Presidential effects on criminal justice policy in the lower federal courts: The Reagan judges. *Law and Society Review, 22*, 191–200.

Royal College of Psychiatrists. (2006). *Child defendants: Occasional paper, OP56*. London: Royal College of Psychiatrists.

SC v. United Kingdom (2005). 1 FCM 347.

Sentencing Council. (2011a). *Assault: Definitive guideline*. London: Ministry of Justice.

Sentencing Council. (2011b). *Burglary offences: Definitive guideline*. London: Ministry of Justice.

Sentencing Council. (2012). *Drug offences: Definitive guideline*. London: Ministry of Justice.

Stapleton v. R (1952). 86 CLR 358.

Tapper, C. (2010). *Cross and Tapper on evidence* (12th ed.). Oxford: Oxford University Press.

Tyrer, P., Duggan, C., Cooper, S., Crawford, M., Seivewright, H., Rutter, D., … Barrett, B. (2010). The successes and failures of the DSPD experiment: The assessment and management of severe personality disorder. *Medicine, Science and the Law, 50*, 95–99.

United Nations Committee on the Rights of the Child. Retrieved from http://www2.ohchr. org/English/bodies/crc/docs/AdvanceVersions/CRC.C.GBR.CO.4.pdf

V and T v. United Kingdom (1999). 30 EHRR 121.

Viding, E., Blair, J. R., Moffitt, T. E., & Plomin, R. (2005). Evidence of substantial genetic risk in psychopathy in 7-year-olds. *Journal of Child Psychology and Psychiatry, 46*, 592–597.

West, D. J., & Farrington, D. P. (1973). *Who becomes delinquent?* London: Heinemann.

Winterwerp v. the Netherlands (1979). 2 EHRR 387.

Wootton, Baroness. (1981). *Crime and criminal law*. London: Stevens.

34

Forensic Neuropsychology
Social, Cultural, and Political Implications
Jessica Pykett

Key points

- Particular forms of crime, such as antisocial behavior, are high priorities for public policy makers in neoliberal societies.
- Sociological and geographical accounts of crime, criminal behavior, and "the criminal landscape" offer an alternative approach to brain-based explanation.
- Forensic neuropsychology emphasizes the cognitive, psychological, biological, and genetic drivers of behavior as well as how these interact with *environmental* or *situational* factors.
- By contrast, sociologists and geographers focus on the *spatial* contexts in which criminal behaviors are enacted and policed, the intersections of space, power, and the law, and the spaces of imprisonment.
- These differences in explanation have far-reaching implications for the very definition of criminality as well as the solutions offered.

Terminology Explained

Geo-historical context is the social, political, cultural, and economic attributes of a location and era (e.g., 18th-century Europe; 21th-century USA). This is opposed to "situation" or "environment," which might describe a smaller scale configuration of space (as in situational crime prevention), or the effect of factors external to the body/brain on behavior (as in gene-environment interaction).

Micro-politics is an approach to understanding power relations, which emphasizes the "bottom-up" everyday sociologies of power, often in institutional settings. This approach does not ignore the larger scale importance of power relations but makes space for resistive and transgressive challenges to the social norms set by prevailing rationalities.

Neoliberal is a market-oriented form of "laissez-faire" political and economic organization, which emphasizes freedom of choice, often characterized by privatization,

---

The Wiley Blackwell Handbook of Forensic Neuroscience, First Edition. Edited by Anthony R. Beech, Adam J. Carter, Ruth E. Mann and Pia Rotshtein.
© 2018 John Wiley & Sons Ltd. Published 2018 by John Wiley & Sons Ltd.

deregulation, and the use of market principles in every sphere of social life. This evolved from the "Chicago School" of economics in the 1980s, and is described as socially conservative and morally authoritarian.

Neuroliberal, like neoliberal, is a form of rationality that shares a commitment to freedom of choice and a market-oriented society but refers to the specific dominance of the brain sciences in providing explanations for the limits of human agency and the legitimacy of neuropsychologically informed forms of governing. The term was originally coined by Engin Isin (2004) to refer to the management of anxieties as a form of neoliberal rule.

Panoptical is the term for Jeremy Bentham's 18th-century prison designs, which were described by Foucault as a spatial arrangement that enabled maximum surveillance of prisoners. It was the sense of being watched that had a disciplining effect on prisoners rather than any explicit form of control. The term has since been used to describe phenomena such as CCTV.

Punitive state is a mode of social regulation that recognizes the role of the prison system within social welfare and the governance of behavior by the state. The term is also used to draw attention to the exponential growth in prison populations (particularly in the USA) and the use of punishing or disciplining techniques and rationalities within the welfare system or other state encounters with citizens.

Rationalities are the underlying reasons that account for particular geo-historical contexts but are inseparable from the forms of power that are used to establish this rationality as the dominant form of truth in any given place or time. They provide a rationale for particular modes of social regulation.

Social norms are a set of accepted and acceptable behaviors specific to and constructed within a particular geo-historical context. These norms pose particular behaviors as transgressive or undesirable. This is opposed to behavioral accounts, which see social norms as inherent in human nature.

Subjectification is Foucault's account of the role of disciplinary practices in producing particular subject positions. In the prison, this referred specifically to the way in which prison architecture and spatial practices produced prisoners who were subject to particular relations of power.

Introduction

This chapter examines sociological and geographical theories relating to the causes of crime, criminal behavior, and the contextual factors in which these are enacted. In so doing it raises a distinction between *criminal responsibility*, understood as individual culpability for a particular crime, and *criminal justice*, as a set of social, cultural, and political issues surrounding the fairness or otherwise of the practices of policing, law, and punishment. The chapter highlights the potential unintended consequences of forensic neuropsychology in terms of focusing public and expert debate on crime at the scale of the brain, gene–environment interactions, and "situational" factors, at the expense of more structural, socio-spatial explanations of crime and criminal behavior. In so doing, the chapter moves beyond exploration of the policy implications of forensic neuropsychology and rather identifies the broader political impact of brain-based explanations of crime.

Antisocial and Pro-Social Behavior in Recent Public Policy

Prison populations in the UK reached a record level of 88,179 after the "summer riots" of 2011, having approximately doubled since 1993.[1,2] Hence understanding the causes of crime and "what works" in terms of prevention, treatment, punishment, and rehabilitation has arguably never been more important. Under the New Labour administration (1997–2010), Tony Blair had launched the "Respect Agenda," set up explicitly to tackle what was deemed to be a new wave of "antisocial" behavior and a general lack of respect for fellow citizens, particularly among young people. Controversially, in 1998 the government introduced a new legal instrument, the Anti-Social Behavior Order (ASBO), to tackle a wide array of incidents including noise pollution, graffiti, street drinking, and several other offences. Critics were quick to condemn ASBOs as effectively criminalizing children and young people (Crawford, 2009), introducing too many vague new offences (Millie, 2008), and being a form of social exclusion (Muncie, 2006). Others pointed out how ASBOs victimized marginalized and vulnerable children who have already experienced abuse and neglect (Batmanghelidjh & Gaskel, 2005). As such, policies relating to antisocial behavior cast a wider net over the kinds of actions and behaviors which were deemed criminal, and re-invigorated cultural and political debates over a certain "underclass" displaying "yobbish" behaviors at the expense of society as a whole. Prison populations continued to rise steadily. Subsequently, widespread disturbances took place throughout several cities in the UK in the summer of 2011, involving thousands of public order offenses and tens of thousands of participants. The "summer riots," as they became known, re-invigorated public debate concerning youth crime, with over half of those convicted of offences being aged between 10 and 17 years old.[3] Several explanations were offered, ranging from overarching themes such as poverty, disadvantage, and inequality, to specific cuts to the Educational Maintenance Allowances paid to encourage young people to stay on at school and speculations about the role of race in sparking the initial disturbances. *The Guardian*'s Zoe Williams (2011) argued that young people bombarded with advertising have felt disenfranchised from a society in which identity is bound up with consumerism. The tabloid press, by contrast, sought to expose the apparent stupidity and selfishness of specific rioters and looters with personal interest stories dominating their headlines. At the heart of these popular conceptions of the predominately "low-level" criminality was the notion of deficiencies in moral character that had led to looting, criminal damage, and, in more serious cases, violence.

It is evident, then, that policies and practices relating to crime, policing, and the judicial system can be influenced by specific political agendas, high profile events, and changing cultural values, all of which are represented, interpreted, and mediated by the press, broadcast media, and increasingly by social media technologies. Meanwhile, the backdrop of antisocial behavior, along with a decline in deference and a perceived sense of political and social apathy (particularly among young people), has led to an increasing interest among public policy makers in new approaches to fostering "pro-social behavior," specifically by investigating the neurobiology of the "social brain." Pro-social can refer to the shaping of behavior which will promote such grand ideals as the progress of wider society (Taylor, 2007), through more everyday forms of engaged citizenship and participation in civil society, for instance. Or it can mean more specifically the cultivation of certain behaviors and dispositions towards empathy, reciprocity, altruism, cooperation, or simply helping others. In the UK, the RSA think tank has been a prominent contributor to political debate heralding the need for pro-social behavior in a contemporary era characterized as avowedly secular, democratic, individualistic, and suffering from environmental degradation, social pathology, and family breakdown (Taylor, 2007). Confronting these landmark issues, it is argued, requires new **social norms**, and for people to act more responsibly. The solutions proffered here are not structural but behavioral, and the RSA's appeal to the neurosciences for understanding how the social brain can potentially dissolve some of society's stickiest problems has been well documented (see the RSA's Social Brian Project,[4] and a critique by Raymond Tallis, 2012). Significant advances in the neurobiology of pro-social behavior have been reported, gaining increasing currency within a public policy realm searching for new, effective, and cost-efficient ways of changing behaviors for the "social good." For instance, neuroscientists have posited that introducing higher levels of the neurotransmitter, serotonin (by introducing citalopram (a selective serotonin reuptake inhibitor) to research subjects, is associated with improving pro-social behaviors and empathy (Crockett, Clark, Hauser, & Robbins, 2010). Conversely, geneticists have been examining the antisocial brain for some time, with the influence of a deficiency of monoamine oxidase A (MAO-A) on serotonin uptake and aggressive behaviors being a significant research program (Brunner, Nelen, Breakefield, Ropers, & van Oost, 1993). A state-of-the-art review of the neurobiology of social and antisocial behaviors is provided by Beech, Nordstrom, and Raine (2012) (also see Chapter 19 in this volume).

In terms of translating this complex set of debates around the neurological drivers of antisocial behavior and gene–environment interactions into implications for policy (e.g., the RSA's Social Brain Project), it appears that some very specific findings about antisocial personality disorder (ASPD), aggression, and psychopathy can too readily be muddled up with some more general assertions about the neurobiological drivers of antisocial behavior. This is an explanatory leap made even by those who are fiercely opposed to ASBOs and the Respect Agenda as policy tools to deal with those deemed antisocial. For instance, Batmanghelidjh and Gaskel (2005) claim that "This science [of neurobiology] argues that children who have experienced poor or ruptured attachments, who have been exposed to chronic stress, develop a poor ability to control their impulses and regulate their levels of frustration and rage" (p. 2). It is not clear why it is necessary to invoke a neurobiological argument to illustrate that neglect, abuse, and lack of care are detrimental to the lives of children, and, in doing so, the argument becomes individualized and pathologized in a way that the authors may not have wished. Indeed, neuroscientists themselves are well aware of the risks of reductionism and scientism in their approaches to explaining criminal responsibility. In a report by the Royal Society, an eminent set of neuroscientists warned that:

> An attitude of scientific reductionism to forensic uses of neuroscience might lead to a one-dimensional legal approach which would be less likely to serve the requirements of justice or due process. Overly scientistic approaches to subjective fact-finding disregard the many complex factors that feed into legal and judicial decision-making.
>
> (Royal Society, 2011, p. 79)

Sociological Accounts of Criminal Behavior

Sociology is famously a discipline born out of Emile Durkheim's (1858–1917) seminal studies of suicide, written in France during the 1890s. By studying the prevalence of suicides with recourse to demographic data for different societies, these studies sought to challenge the prevailing psychological accounts of suicide, by showing how suicide could be understood – in part, at least – as a "social fact." While not denying that there may be individual reasons for suicide, Durkheim introduced a radical concept – particularly given that suicide was a criminal act across Western Europe up until fairly recently – that the predispositions for suicide had social causes relating to variations in religious practice, family norms, occupation, economic trends, and the cultural and moral characteristics of particular societies. A sociological approach therefore offers a quite different scale of explanation for apparently obvious individual pathologies. For sociologists, social theorists, and human geographers alike, context is crucial for understanding behavior, including criminal behavior. This cannot be easily reduced to "environmental" factors, situations, or gene-/brain–environment interactions. Instead, it refers to a much broader **geo-historical** context in which we must not only take into account the specific conditions that shape criminal behaviors, but also understand how those conditions produce certain kinds of scientific, psychological, forensic knowledge that provide dominant explanations for antisocial and criminalized behaviors. These explanations are closely bound up with particular **rationalities** of governing citizens, which are specific to those contexts (see Box 33.1).

A second key figure in the development of sociological accounts of crime, punishment, and the uses of psychological knowledge in governing populations is the French philosopher Michel Foucault (1926–1984). His work provides key lessons for our understanding of the relationship between psychology and crime, and – by extension – the contemporary significance of forensic neuropsychology. In *Discipline and Punish* (1975), Foucault charts the historical emergence of the Western European prison during the 19th century, contrasting its distinctive regulatory environment and spatial **panoptical** form with more violent, public forms of punishment and torture popular in the 18th century. While many historians had reported the birth of the prison as a reformist moment in the history of crime and punishment, Foucault took issue with this notion of humanitarian progress, arguing that the prison signified a continuation of forms of **subjectification**, discipline, and control – albeit by less explicitly physically violent means. His broader point was that the 19th-century prison signified a new form of disciplinary power, which was of relevance as much to the penal system as it was to schools, asylums, factories, and modern industrial society itself. The disciplines of medicine, psychology, criminology, and pedagogy/tutelage themselves could be understood as part of the institutionalization, professionalization, and scientific legitimization of these new forms of control. Crucially, through using these kinds of knowledge to shape the behavior, dispositions, and bodily movements of the prisoner, Foucault described how the prison itself produces delinquency, through isolating inmates, forcing them to undertake useless work, pursuing arbitrary abuses of power, creating an environment in which "antisocial clubs" of prisoners can educate the young first-time offender in a life of crime, placing them under conditions of constant surveillance, and indirectly placing the prisoners' families into poverty by preventing productive, paid work (Foucault, 1975, pp. 266–268). While there have been improvements in prison education programs, mentoring schemes, and support on release since the late 19th century, the ever-increasing rise in the prison population and ongoing problem of recidivism in countries such as the UK appear to confirm Foucault's thesis that the modern penal system is counter-productive in terms of reducing crime.

While this aspect of Foucault's work focused specifically on crime, disciplinary power, and the prison system, his most important influence has arguably been on understanding the role of psychological knowledge in shaping behavior and cultivating behavioral norms, through his works such as *Madness and Civilization* (1967), *The Birth of the Clinic* (1973), and *The History of Sexuality* (1978). This strand of social theory has been taken up and developed at length by the sociologist Nikolas Rose (1947–), and is of direct relevance to examining the social, cultural, and political implications of forensic neuropsychology. Rose (1998) is well known for showing how the discourses and techniques of the "psy" disciplines such as psychology and psychiatry have shaped how we come to see ourselves and act as persons in the specific geo-historical context of modern Western Europe and North America. This modern self, as Rose depicts, was a "coherent, bounded, individualized, intentional, the locus of thought, action, and belief in the origin of its own actions, the beneficiary of a unique biography" (Rose, 1998, p. 2), and the self by which transgressions from the norm were judged, and social differences categorized, controlled and managed.

In so doing, and in contrast to Durkheim, Rose seeks to show how "psychology is a profoundly *social* science" (Rose, 1998, p. 19), whose very emergence and importance as a discipline is linked to the prevailing political and social needs of the time – for instance, the construction of programs of social welfare and the apparatus of social work. As a discipline, it serves to render people governable, not through coercion, authority, or manipulation, but by creating the conditions in which the ideal person is set as a social norm around which social and governmental institutions, conventions, and practices are shaped. This ideal someone is responsible, autonomous, self-managing, and productive – the "pro-social" individual to which the antisocial person is counter-posed. Rose goes on to highlight how the coherence of the modern "private" self, if it ever truly existed, is under question, challenged by genetic technologies such as fertility treatments, organ transplants, pacemakers, and equally by our understandings of the socially constructed nature of our gendered, racialized, classed identities (Rose, 1998, p. 5).

In more recent work, Rose has specifically explored how developments in human genetics and neuroscience have brought forth new concerns at the intersection of criminal responsibility and criminal justice. These concerns are not necessarily those shared by "neuroethicists" relating to legal responsibility, for instance the use of psychological evidence and brain imaging techniques in the criminal courtroom. For Rose, the philosophical notion of free will, the autonomous agent, and the legal principle of *mens rea* – the guilty mind enshrined in law – are not under threat from neuroscientific explanations of intentionality, mental disorders, and the drivers of behavior. Anglo-American legal systems, as he points out, have been overwhelmingly resistant to accepting neurobiological evidence, and continue to conceive of the accused as "individuals with minds, or mental states, who intend the acts they commit, and who foresee the outcome to the extent that any reasonable person could do so" (Rose & Abi-Rached, 2013, p. 178). There may be specific circumstances where the accused can plead not guilty by reason of insanity, or claim diminished responsibility, but these relate to the particular causes of the actual crime committed rather than any general probabilities conveyed by "known" genetic or neurological risk factors. Should we therefore feel secure that the notion of criminal responsibility will remain intact? While Rose and Abi-Rached contend that the principle of *mens rea* will prevail, they also carefully examine the broader sociological, cultural, and political implications of the neurobiological accounts of personhood, which they argue have developed in earnest since at least the late 19th century. What should concern us, then, from a sociological point of view, is the impact that forensic neurobiology (neuroscience and genetics alike) has on our conceptions of assessing risk, prevention, and pre-emption of criminal dispositions – what Rose terms the imperative to "screen and intervene" (2010, p. 79). Where neurobiological accounts will have the most impact will be in policies aimed at identifying risky persons, the management of psychopathy, the investigative process, the determination of sentences, prison release decisions, and in the probation services (Rose, 2010, p. 180). It is in these spheres, and in the sphere of early intervention, family control, and the management of antisocial behavior that a radical shift can be identified, signifying:

> a new relationship between psychiatric genetics and neuroscience, in which they would work together to identify the neurobiological pathways that accounted for the variations in susceptibility or resilience between individuals to environmental insults
> (Rose & Abi-Rached, 2013, p. 188)

Examining solely the specific spaces of criminal justice, policing, the courtroom, and the prison – while these may be important – misses out on many of the significant implications that developments in forensic neuropsychology have for wider society. Forensic neuropsychology provides the impetus, rationale, and techniques for controlling "impulsive" and aggressive behaviors more generally, and for intervening in parenting and family relationships. It reimagines contextual factors such as poverty, housing, and unemployment as environmental determinants of antisocial behavior, internalized in the susceptible brain and the inherited body, as opposed to contributing to a broader structural inequality, which for many social scientists proves to be the root cause of several variants of crime (e.g., Wilkinson & Pickett, 2010, p. 135). This is not to say that examining the specifics of policing, criminal law, and the many aspects of punishment and/or treatment are not crucial endeavors, as the chapter will go on to investigate. Instead, the sociological approach outlined here demands that close attention is paid to the particular (historical, national, cultural, social, and political) contexts in which forensic neuropsychology is deployed as an explanatory framework for understanding and intervening in the criminal mind.

Understood in these terms, the rise of forensic neuropsychology is bound up with our contemporary fears of insecurity, the tyranny of "public" norms as opposed to antisocial exceptions (criminals imagined through the media as monstrous, evil, "insane"), and the **neoliberal** imperative to manage risk, whether in economic decisions or social life. It does not simply signify a trajectory of logical and rational developments in science, methods, imaging technologies, and knowledge. Rather, as Table 34.1 shows, various historical accounts (here provided by Beech et al., 2012; Davies, Beech, & Hollin, 2012; Rose & Abi-Rached, 2013) of scientific developments relating to the criminal mind since the 19th century in Western Europe and North America can be characterized by their specific geo-historical rationalities. We are not necessarily getting closer to the truth of the criminal mind itself, in this sense; rather our conceptions of the criminal mind, and the place of the forensic neurobiology in understanding it,

Table 34.1 Shifting truths of the "criminal mind" through history, and their rationalities and/or unintended consequences

Timeline	Development of forensic neuropsychology (Beech et al., 2012; Davies et al., 2012)	Development of neurocriminology (Rose & Abi-Rached, 2013)	Rationality/unintended consequences
1820s–1830s		Phrenology – criminal mind is observable in skull shape, *Franz Joseph Gall, 1822*	Setting moral **norms** and exposing transgressors
1870s–1890s	Physiognomy – criminality is inherited and reflected in face shapes, *Cesare Lombroso*	Brain size – criminal mind is smaller than average, *Paul Broca* Moral degeneracy – related to "low physical and mental characteristics," *Henry Maudsley* Cerebral localization and hemispheric functioning – left brain as a civilizing and rational and right brain as savage, impulsive, mad, *David Ferrier* Criminal anthropology – "objective measures" of delinquency, criminality and feeblemindedness, *Havelock Ellis*	Crime **prevention** **Enlightenment** science Challenges to religious doctrine End of "free will" **Subordination** of "inferior groups" with inferior brains (women, lower classes, non-whites, criminals)
1900s–1930s	Evidence fails to confirm the claims of physiognomy, phrenology, and crude brain measurements, *Charles Goring*	Brain science seen as the basis for correct sociology, *August Forel* Structural and functional brain mapping – "newer" parts of the evolved brain, i.e., the cortex controls lower impulses, and the criminal brain said to have a diminished third cortical layer, *Oscar Vogt* Genetic drivers of brain pathology, *Hugo Spatz and Julius Hallervorden, Kaiser Wilhelm Institute for Brain Research (KWIBR)*	"Positive" **eugenics** through planned human breeding (Vogt) **Nazism** – criminals and mentally ill killed in concentration camps and their brains sent to KWIBR for use in research

1960s–1980s	Attachment theories – biological need to be close to parents/primary carers and impact on stress levels and brain development, *John Bowlby* Personality – certain types more or less likely to learn (from their social environment) antisocial or criminal behaviors, *Hans Eysenck* Operant learning (behaviorism) – behavior produces good or bad consequences for an individual, who experiences reward/reinforcement or punishment/aversion, *B. F. Skinner* Social learning theory – internal thoughts and emotions can be shaped, modified, learnt, *Albert Bandura* Cognitive behavioral therapies developed Cognitive development – achievement of moral reasoning is learnt through the life course, *Lawrence Kohlberg* Rational choice theory – criminality seen as personal gain and avoiding detection		Socialization Learning Treatment Situational crime prevention Punishment
1980s-1990s	Clinical diagnoses of criminality – e.g., ASPD, *Robert Hare*	Neuroimaging techniques used on violent criminals – EEG, PET, and CT scans showing activity in left temporal regions, *Nora Volkow and Lawrence Tancredi* Violent brain as visually observable – EEG and brain scanning used to determine localized activity and brain defects/mental illness, *Daniel Martell*	Neoliberalism – potential criminals should learn to modulate impulses and self-manage; they are governed through their freedom in market-oriented societies Zero-tolerance policing

(*continued*)

Table 34.1 (Continued)

Timeline	Development of forensic neuropsychology (Beech et al., 2012; Davies et al., 2012)	Development of neurocriminology (Rose & Abi-Rached, 2013)	Rationality/unintended consequences
		Brain abnormalities – Lesions on ventromedial frontal cortex lead to abnormal social conduct and lack of impulse control, Antonio Damasio The "mean gene" – revival of biological and genetic causes of criminal behavior, MAOA deficiencies, Adrian Raine, Hans Brunner	"Designing out" crime through urban planning and urban entrepreneurialism Treatment
2000s	Gene–environment interactions – ACE model of genetic, shared family environment and environmental risk factors – e.g., head injury, Henrik Larsson et al. Genetic predispositions can be modified for better or worse through social experience Gillarth et al. Identification of risk factors – male gender, living in a "criminogenic environment," where a parent is a criminal, smoking, childhood maltreatment Social brain and antisocial brain neural network theories – e.g., role of insular cortex in emotional responses, the orbital prefrontal cortex in emotional regulation, the anterior cingulated cortex in "maternal behavior," said to include communication, cooperation, and empathy, the role of the amygdala in aversive conditioning, i.e., responses to emotional stimuli, Joseph LeDoux	Aggression determined by specific neural circuits and adaptive (mal)functions, shown in neuroimaging and animal studies, Klaus Miczek Gene–environment interactions – exposure to early (childhood) stress changes long-term levels of norepinephrine, serotonin, and dopamine, with effects moderated by genetic predispositions, Avshalom Caspi and Terrie Moffitt Antisocial personality as inheritable clinical disorder – callous-unemotional traits (AS-CU) in children as predictor of adult psychopathy, Essi Viding, Terrie Moffitt et al.	Diagnosis Pre-emption and screening Risk-reduction Early intervention Neuroliberalism – the brain sciences are used within market-oriented societies to govern freedom through shaping the brain, pre-empting risk, and identifying criminal susceptibilities Production of "carceral subjects" (pre-emption and intervention before criminal activity, affecting particular social groups and individuals differentially)?

Social, Cultural, and Political Implications 927

are evolving with the times. In this regard, it is possible to identify how developments in neurobiology have evolved with prevailing social, cultural, and political norms, from its phrenological roots, though the inception of Enlightenment ideals, a dark period of eugenics, an era of punishment coupled with prevention, and more recently a shift from the neoliberal emphasis on techniques of self-management to a **neuroliberal** focus on the governing of freedom through shaping the brain, pre-empting risk, and identifying criminal susceptibilities. In light of these accounts, a geographical approach to policing, law, and punishment gives a new perspective on the political impacts of forensic neuropsychology, as the next section demonstrates.

Geographies of Criminality

It is commonly accepted that there are clear spatial patterns to incidences of crime, and there is an increasing public and policy interest in using geographic information systems (GIS) to map crime hotspots and plan policing strategies.[5] But geographers are equally concerned with understanding the spatial processes that produce crime, and the everyday experiences of criminality, fear, and crime prevention, particularly within urban spaces (Evans, Fyfe, & Herbert, 1992; Pain, 1991). In this sense, the focus of research for geographers of crime is already clearly divergent from that of forensic neuropsychologists, not just in terms of the scale of explanation (not the brain but the city), but also in terms of the sociological theories that are mobilized in explaining the social and spatial determinants of crime. For instance, during the 1980s and 1990s social geographers of crime were influenced by Giddens' notion of structuration, exploring how individual acts are structured by established cultures, institutions, and social norms which are specific to geo-historical contexts (Evans et al., 1992, p. 3). While several geographers have analyzed policing practices in specific cities and nations, others have focused on the intersections of space, power, and the law, and the spaces of imprisonment. This section briefly reviews some of the main issues at stake for geographers in each of these three areas, before drawing some conclusions together to identify how criminality and the criminal mind are reimagined through a geographical perspective – a perspective which significantly problematizes some of the key assumptions of forensic neuropsychology.

Policing and criminal spaces

Some facets of policing lend themselves easily to a geographical reading, for instance, the way in which the police control crowd behaviors, use strategies of "kettling" in public protests, and build explicit control mechanisms in to urban spaces, such as CCTV surveillance, automatic number plate recognition technologies, and iris and facial recognition. Murakami-Wood (2007) – again informed by Foucault's *Discipline and Punish* – has argued that our surveillance society has built a new "basic neural infrastructure for the city" (p. 37), which integrates biomarker datasets with policing practices in order to map risk and contain potential threats. Others have argued that UK urban design itself has become dominated by a military discourse of securitization; that regeneration schemes and urban planning are now preoccupied with controlling access and movement, protecting private property, and crime prevention (Coaffee, Murakami-Wood, & Rogers, 2008; Minton, 2009).

Herbert and Brown (2006) have even argued that criminological studies themselves have been driven by neoliberal discourses underwritten by a fear of the "other," a sense of threat, and a need to exclude outsiders. They identify the popular "broken windows" theory of Wilson and Kelling (1982), the ideas of situational crime prevention (Mayhew, 1976), and defensible space (Newman, 1972), as examples of policing approaches based on an assumption that criminality can be encouraged by a lack of environmental quality. These theories have been highly influential both in the USA and UK. The former is in evidence in the "zero-tolerance" policing strategies pioneered by New York Mayor Guiliani during the 1990s, while situational crime prevention is an approach which has been taken up by the UK Home Office since the 1980s, reflected in reports such as Clarke and Mayhew's *Designing Out Crime* (1980), *Crime Prevention Through Environmental Design* (Crowe 1991/2000), and more recently *Safer Places. The Planning System and Crime Prevention* (ODPM, 2004).

Geographers have shown how 1980s European discourses of economic regeneration and urban entrepreneurialism (the "urban renaissance") became bound up with strategies for social regulation in which policing, the control of conduct, and the setting of moral standards were the lynch pins for urban policy and design (Helms, Atkinson, & MacLeod, 2007, p. 267). Hence, commentators have noted how the gated communities, panoptical shopping malls, and "interdictory spaces" of contemporary European and North American cities have become commonplace features of advanced capitalist cities (Christopherson, 1994; Davies, 1990; Flusty, 2001). Urban design and architecture in this sense become part of the police apparatus for regulating social conduct. Clearly this is a departure from previous accounts of environmental psychology and environmental criminology, which are now largely considered too determinist, mechanistic, and individualistic in their explanations of criminal spaces. Rather, policing itself can be seen as counter-productive in the setting of behavioral norms of respect and civility, as many have argued is the case with the Respect Action Plan and its failure to distinguish between children and young people's annoying behaviors and more serious crimes that cause real harm to others (Bannister, Fyfe, & Kearns, 2006, p. 928). The key contribution of this strand of work on the geographies of policing has been to demonstrate just how far policing itself is bound up with political and economic imperatives which privatize, polarize, and preserve urban spaces to serve particular interests in ways that socially exclude. Here it is context, and not environment, that shapes behavior, and we are thus urged to interrogate the political, social, and economic rationalities, which inform the production of particular spatial forms.

Yet it is the relatively narrow definition of environmentally-determined crime (mapping the "known" predictors of criminality such as socio-economic class, areas of deprivation, the nature of family relationships) that is predominantly used when forensic neuropsychologists discuss the interaction of genetic, neural, and environmental drivers of criminal behavior. A crucial middle-scale level of explanation is arguably missing from such analyses. This is the scale at which we might begin to better understand geography not as a variable but as *constitutive* of the criminal landscape. For instance, we must consider how the broader dynamics of "uneven development; racial segregation; and the social production of fear" (Herbert & Brown, 2006, p. 757) are deeply implicated in the geographical distribution and socio-spatial processes underpinning urban crime.

Law, space, and power

While a focus on criminal landscapes has much to contribute to understanding contemporary forensic practice and the causes of crime, there has been much less geographical work relating to criminal law, the legal process, and jurisprudence. The work that has been done has focused on the contested legal spaces of urban life, property, and territory more generally (Blomley, 1994). Or it has explored key geographical trends such as globalization and urban capitalism as drivers behind legal change, for example, the anti-homeless legislations in US cities, which served to exclude poor people from the public space of the city (Mitchell, 1997).

Although not specifically addressing the geographies of criminal law per se, the subfield of legal geographies highlights some crucial intersections between law, the state, and power, which have broader implications for understanding the political dimensions of crime and punishment in specific state contexts. The principal proponent of legal geographies is Nicholas Blomley, whose writings since the 1990s have explored critical legal discourse and have developed a concern for the way in which the law "structure[s] the very manner in which we experience and understand social life" (1994, p. 12). He has challenged the idea that spaces and places are simply the canvas on which legal life is played out. Instead, he argues that space plays an active role in constituting the law, while at the same time legal instruments and their consequences produce particular kinds of spaces. This is considered to be particularly important in managing urban change (1994, p. 45), for instance, through housing legislation, rules of ownership, place-specific legal knowledge, and the locally-specific interpretations, applications of, and resistances to laws. Put simply, law as a "force in the world causes things to happen"; it "makes" *institutions* such as nation states, corporations, markets, and families, as well as *relations and identities* such as "husband, boss, owner, citizen, felon, slave, neighbor, debtor, judge" (Delaney, Ford, & Blomley, 2006, xv).

This constitutive power of law is an idea that has been taken forward by political geographer Joe Painter (2006) in his analysis of the everyday reach of state power as invoked by ASBOs in the UK. In these terms, the ASBO law is never simply a legal tool or method of policing but signifies a specific social and power relation between the state, certain local neighborhoods, and "problematic" citizens. While the ASBO itself may be (albeit vaguely) defined in legal language, it takes on new meanings associated with general "yobbishness" through the actions and interpretations of the police, newspapers, citizens, and politicians. It is these *prosaic* meanings, representations, and social practices that have actual effects in terms of making state power real.

In a content analysis of the White Paper *Respect and Responsibility – Taking a Stand Against Anti-Social Behavior* (Home Office, 2003), Painter showed how responsibility for this new legislation falls far beyond the hands of the police. He described how 277 different actors (people and institutions) are identified as crucial to combatting antisocial behavior. These include young people, local authorities, police officers, various actors within the justice system, and social officers, teachers, and housing officers. For Painter, this is ample evidence "that it is impossible to draw a line between 'state' and '(civil)' society" (2006, p. 767). But the complex coming together of various civil and criminal "state" and "non-state" actors, policies, and practices is not always pulled off, and Painter discovered that ASBOs have been concentrated geographically in particular cities, with 24.5 ASBOs per 100,000 residents in Greater Manchester, 8.7 in Merseyside, and 4.5 in Greater London (between April 1999 and September 2004)

(Painter, 2006, p. 769). Therefore, it is not a legal instrument that is geographically "innocent" in the sense of being evenly applied. A specific law such as the ASBO, which itself blurs the boundaries between criminal and civil legislation, indicates the intensification of state power and the "statization" or enrolment of a wide range of social actors and agencies in the achievement of government aims. The insight that the law and state power can be so intricately intertwined might therefore urge criminologists and forensic neuropsychologists to look beyond specific neural processes, beyond individual and social behaviors, and towards more geographically specific analyses of *state responses to crime*.

Prison, hyperincarceration, and the punitive state

This chapter has so far examined several geographical issues relating to policing and the law. The third area of interest is spaces of punishment, in particular recent insights from human geography that have deepened our understandings of the relationship between the **micro-politics** of the prison space and the wider notion of the **punitive state**. While prison sociologists and criminologists have been arguably preoccupied with the experiences of "doing time," a new sub-disciplinary focus on "carceral geography" (Moran, Pallot, & Piacentini, 2011; Moran, 2013a) is emerging as a means for exploring the importance of space both in and beyond the prison situation. The theoretical influence of Foucault can be clearly traced in the project of carceral geography, just as it could be with Rose's work on the impact of neurobiological knowledge on reframing and managing the criminal mind, and equally with the idea of a surveillance society, which has informed geographical conceptions of the urban criminal landscape. The endeavors of carceral geography have been multi-faceted (for a full review of this work see Moran, 2013a). Geographers have debated Foucault's idea that the spatial arrangements of the prison render prisoners' bodies docile, have examined patterns of prison location and their impact on communities, and have widened the conception of the "carceral" to imply a state of embodiment that outlives a prisoner's release (Moran, 2013b), or to denote a distinctive mode of social regulation also described as the punitive state (Peck & Theodore, 2009).

Some of this work is explicitly concerned with prison architectures, the organization and regulation of prison spaces (and movement between spaces), and the impact that these spaces can have on prisoners' embodied experiences, sense of agency, and (dis)empowerment. Moran (2013a, p. 180) has, for instance, explored how, why, and in what circumstances prison visitations and spaces of visitation in particular have a successful impact in reducing reoffending. The geographical theorization of space here is important in that it reflects the idea that space is both the product of and productive of social relations, leading Moran to scrutinize prison visiting spaces as liminal spaces in which visitors are temporarily imprisoned and prisoners temporarily "at home." The different configurations of such spaces can be both transformative in the sense of helping to reintegrate prisoners into the routines and behaviors of everyday domesticity, and yet they are often highly controlled, shaping conduct and intimacy in particularly restrictive ways.

Perhaps the most significant value of the carceral geographical approach is its ability to navigate between vastly different scales of explanation from the management of the body to the management of whole populations. The ideas of the punitive state and of hyperincarceration are key to this latter purpose, and diverge dramatically from

Social, Cultural, and Political Implications 931

brain-based explanations of criminality. With reference to the USA, geographers Peck and Theodore (2009) have powerfully argued that:

> the prison system has come to assume the role of a significant (urban) *labor market institution*, the regulatory outcomes of which are revealed in the social production of systemic unemployability across a criminalized class of African–American males, the hypertrophied economic and social decline of those "receiving communities" to which thousands of ex-convicts return, and the remorseless rise of recidivism rates
>
> (p. 251, emphasis added)

They identify a clear continuum therefore between the prison system and the welfare system, demonstrating how prisons provide a ready repository of "low-skill" laborers living at the margins of a low-wage and informal economy – with short, repetitive prison stays becoming the norm in the most marginalized segments of particular communities in US cities. This reflects long-running concerns from sociologists and social policy scholars alike that the US prison system in particular, whose population dwarfs that of the UK (6.98 million prisoners in the USA in 2011, or 1 in 34 people (2.9% of the US adult population[6]), compared to just over 88,000, or 0.1% of the UK population), has become (or continues to be) a means to *manage poverty* rather than serve criminal justice. Loïs Wacquant (2000) has argued that the spatial context of the black US ghetto has become inextricably bound to the prison system in a

> *carceral continuum* which entraps a redundant population of younger black men (and increasingly women) who circulate in closed circuit between its two poles in a self-perpetuating cycle of social and legal marginality
>
> (p. 384, original emphasis)

Meanwhile, Schram, Soss, Houser, and Fording (2010) have argued that social welfare structures are themselves increasingly deploying punitive logics and sanctions and imposing behavioral controls on claimants:

> Welfare systems have become more thoroughly entwined with carceral systems, and their disciplinary operations have shifted toward a more penal logic characteristic of the "culture of control" in an "era of mass incarceration"
>
> (p. 125)

What these contributions from a range of disciplinary perspectives convey is the importance of viewing debates on criminal responsibility, the criminal mind, and the forensic sciences which shape practice in the spheres of policing, criminal law, and imprisonment, in the broader context of the geo-historical epochs in which criminal justice is or is not served. Such perspectives highlight that there may be macro-economic, macro-social, and macro-political explanations for criminality; scales of explanation that are not readily adopted by methods more suited to understanding neurons, cognition, and possible/probable behavioral outcomes.

Hence, while one of the great achievements of forensic neuropsychology may be to reframe criminal responsibility as an issue of public health, the work of geographers outlined here has shown criminality to be actively produced by the prevailing political-economic doctrines of the times. For these researchers, rapidly increasing prison populations, the increasingly authoritarian policing of a myriad of antisocial behaviors, and the exclusionary logics of new urban "defensible spaces" are all part of a specific culture of "hyperpunitiveness" congruent with the contemporary neoliberal state (Herbert & Brown, 2006). The dismantling of welfare and the collapse of demand-side economic management has opened up a gap between the responsible, economically rational, self-governing citizen and the irresponsible individual whom the former must fear as a potential threat (Herbert & Brown, 2006, 769). In these terms, mass incarceration "hides a growing unemployed class," politically reframes the victims of a neoliberal regime (where the state has increasingly withdrawn from welfare) as disorderly threats, and exacerbates the exclusionary effects of racial segregation and class inequality endemic to the urban landscape, particularly in the US context. It is not simply the case that we live in neoliberal times, but that the spaces we have produced – at the scale of welfare regimes, urban landscapes, physical features of the built environment – are complicit in producing what we understand to be criminality.

Conclusions

Examining the historical evolution of the discipline of forensic psychology and neuropsychology is illuminating insofar as it places the workings and reworkings of this scientific endeavor within the social histories and specific contexts in which certain notions of the criminal mind have gained traction. We have seen how criminality has shifted to a certain extent from an immoral form of behavior in need of punishment, through a mental health problem in need of treatment, toward a set of genetic-neural predispositions in need of prevention, pre-emption, and intervention. The chapter has considered how forensic neuropsychologists might tackle the thorny issue of brain–environmental and gene–environmental interactions, and new insights on the social brain. Finally, the chapter has reviewed sociological accounts of the effects of psychological and neurosciences in reimagining personhood, criminal responsibility, and notions of risk, and geographical research on policing the criminal landscape, the law and state power, criminal justice, and carceral space.

Notes

1 *Story of the prison population 1993–2012 England and Wales.* London: Ministry of Justice, January 2013. Retrieved from https://www.gov.uk/government/publications/story-of-the-prison-population-1993-2012.
2 Berman, G. (2012). Prison population statistics standard note SN/SG/4334. 24 May. London: House of Commons Library. Retrieved from http://www.parliament.uk/briefing-papers/sn04334.pdf
3 National Youth Agency (2012). Summer Riots. Summary of existing literature and key observations. Retrieved from http://www.nya.org.uk/briefings.
4 See http://www.thersa.org/action-research-centre/learning,-cognition-and-creativity/social-brain.
5 For example, http://www.crimemaps.org.uk.
6 Glaze, L. E., & Parks, E. (2012). Correctional populations in the United States (2011). U.S. Department of Justice, Bureau of Justice Statistics. Retrieved from http://www.bjs.gov/content/pub/press/cpus11ppus11pr.cfm.

Social, Cultural, and Political Implications 933

Recommended Reading

Choudhury, S., & Slaby, J. (Eds.). (2012). *Critical neuroscience. A handbook of the social and cultural contexts of neuroscience.* Oxford: Wiley-Blackwell. *This handbook examines the difficulties involved in translating laboratory experiments to policy and practice. It shows how putting neuroscience back in its geo-historical context raises new questions about the significance of so called "neuro-hype" and addresses the issue of reductionist scientism.*

Rees, D., & Rose, S. (Eds.). (2004). *The new brain sciences. Perils and prospects.* Cambridge: Cambridge University Press. *Neurobiologists, philosophers, psychologists, geneticists, legal scholars, and sociologists provide accounts of ethical, political, and social problems posed by the rapid expansion of the neurosciences during the 1990s and identify some of the limits of neurobiological explanation.*

Rose, N., & Abi-Rached, J. M. (2013). *Neuro. The new brain sciences and the management of the mind.* Oxford: Princeton University Press. *This book traces how the neurosciences claim authority in producing knowledge about personhood and the expert management of behavior and investigates the impact of the neurosciences on culture, politics, and society, with chapters on the social and antisocial brain.*

Thornton, D. J. (2011). *Brain culture: Neuroscience and popular media.* London: Rutgers University Press. *An excellent account of how neuroscientific ideals sit with the prevailing neoliberal economic orthodoxies of advanced Western societies.*

References

Bannister, J., Fyfe, N., & Kearns, A. (2006). Respectable or respectful? (In)civility and the City. *Urban Studies, 43,* 919–937.

Batmanghelidjh, C., & Gaskel, C. (2005). *"Named and shamed": A psycho-political response to anti-social behavior orders.* London: Kids Company and Liberty. Retrieved from http://www.geog.qmul.ac.uk/docs/staff/4405.pdf.

Beech, A. R., Nordstrom, B., & Raine, A. (2012) Contributions of forensic neuroscience. In G. Davies & A.R. Beech (Eds.), *Forensic psychology. Crime, justice, law, interventions* (2nd ed.). Chichester: John Wiley & Sons.

Blomley, N. (1994) *Law, space and the geographies of power.* New York, NY: Guilford Press.

Brunner, H. G., Nelen, M., Breakefield, X. O., Ropers, H. H., & van Oost, B. A. (1993). Abnormal-behavior associated with a point mutation in the structural gene for monoamine oxidase A. *Science, 262,* 578–580.

Christopherson, S. (1994). The Fortress city: Privatized spaces, consumer citizenship. In A. Amin (Ed.) *Post-Fordism: A reader.* Oxford: Blackwell.

Clarke, R. V., & Mayhew, P. M (Eds.). (1980). *Designing out crime.* London: H. M. Stationery Office.

Coaffee, J., Murakami-Wood, D., & Rogers, P. (2008). *The everyday resilience of the city: How cities respond to terrorism and disaster.* Basingstoke: Palgrave Macmillian.

Crawford, A. (2009). Criminalizing sociability through anti-social behavior legislation: Dispersal powers, young people and the police. *Youth Justice, 9*(1), 5–26.

Crockett, M. J., Clark, L., Hauser, M. D., & Robbins, T. W. (2010). Serotonin selectively influences moral judgment and behavior through effects on harm aversion. *Proceedings of the National Academy of Sciences of the United States of America, 107*(40), 17433–17438.

Crowe, T. (1991/2000). *Crime prevention through environmental design* (2nd ed.). Woburn, MA: Butterworth-Heinemann.

Davies, G., Beech, A., & Hollin, C. (2012). Introduction. In G. Davies & A. Beech (Eds.) *Forensic psychology: Crime, justice, law, interventions.* Chichester: John Wiley & Sons Ltd.

Davies, M. (1990). *City of quartz: Excavating the future in Los Angeles*. London: Verso.

Delaney, D., Ford, R. T., & Blomley, N. (2001). Preface: Where is law? In N. Blomley, D. Delaney, & R. T. Ford (Eds.), *The legal geographies reader* (pp. xiii–xxii). Oxford: Blackwell.

Engin, I. (2004). The neurotic citizen. *Citizenship Studies, 8*, 217–235.

Evans, D., Fyfe, N., & Herbert, D. (Eds.). (1992). *Crime, policing and place: Essays in environmental criminology*. London: Routledge.

Flusty, S. (2001). The banality of interdiction: Surveillance, control and the displacement of diversity. *International Journal of Urban and Regional Research, 25*(3), 658–664.

Foucault, M. (1967). *Madness and civilization*. London: Tavistock.

Foucault, M. (1973). *The birth of the clinic*. London: Tavistock.

Foucault, M. (1975). *Discipline and punish: The birth of the prison*. London: Penguin.

Foucault, M. (1978). *The history of sexuality. Vol 1*. London: Penguin Books.

Helms, G., Atkinson, R., & MacLeod, G. (2007). Editorial: Securing the city: Urban renaissance, policing and social regulation. *European Urban and Regional Studies, 14*(4), 267–276.

Herbert, S., & Brown, E. (2006). Conceptions of space and crime in the punitive neoliberal city. *Antipode, 38*(4), 755–777.

Home Office. (2003). *Respect and responsibility- taking a stand against anti-social behavior*. Norwich: Home Office, The Stationary Office.

Mayhew, P. (1976). *Crime as opportunity*. London: HMSO.

Millie, A. (2008). Anti-social behavior, behavioral expectations and an urban aesthetic. *The British Journal of Criminology, 48*(3), 379–394.

Minton, A. (2009). *Ground control. Fear and happiness in the twenty-first century city*. London: Penguin Books.

Mitchell, D. (1997). The annihilation of space by law: The roots and implications of anti-homeless laws in the United States. *Antipode, 29*(3), 303–335.

Moran, D. (2013a). Carceral geography and the spatialities of prison visiting: Visitation, recidivism and hyperincarceration. *Environment and Planning D: Society & Space, 31*(1), 174–190.

Moran, D. (2013b). Between outside and inside? Prison visiting rooms as liminal carceral spaces. *GeoJournal, 78*(2), 339–351.

Moran, D., Pallot, J., & Piacentini, L. (2011). The geography of crime and punishment in the Russian federation. *Eurasian Geography and Economics, 52*(1), 79–104.

Muncie, J. (2006). Governing young people: Coherence and contradiction in contemporary youth justice. *Critical Social Policy, 26*(4), 770–793.

Murakami-Wood, D. (2007). Securing the neurocity. *Criminal Justice Matters, 68*(1), 37–38.

Newman, O. (1972). *Defensible space: Crime prevention through urban design*. New York, NY: Macmillan.

ODPM. (2004). *Safer places. The planning system and crime prevention*. London: Office of the Deputy Prime Minister.

Pain, R. (1991). Space, sexual violence and social control: Integrating geographical and feminist analyses of women's fear of crime. *Progress in Human Geography, 15*(4), 415–431.

Painter, J. (2006). Prosaic geographies of stateness. *Political Geography, 25*(7), 752–774.

Peck, J., & Theodore, N. (2009). Carceral Chicago: Making the ex-offender employability crisis. *International Journal of Urban and Regional Research, 32*(2), 251–281.

Rose, N. (1998). *Inventing our selves: Psychology, power, and personhood*. Cambridge: Cambridge University Press.

Rose, N. (2010). "Screen and intervene": governing risky brains. *History of the Human Sciences, 23*(1), 79–105.

Rose, N., & Abi-Rached, J. M. (2013). *Neuro. The new brain sciences and the management of the mind*. Oxford: Princeton University Press.

Royal Society, The. (2011). *Brain waves 1: Neuroscience, society and policy.* London: The Royal Society. Retrieved from http://royalsociety.org/policy/projects/brain-waves/society-policy/.

Schram, S. F., Soss, J., Houser, L., & Fording, R. C. (2010). The third level of US welfare reform: Governmentality under neoliberal paternalism. In J. Pykett (Ed.) *Governing through pedagogy. Re-educating citizens* (pp. 123–138). London: Routledge.

Tallis, R. (2012). *Aping mankind. Neuromania, darwinitis and the misrepresentation of humanity.* Durham: Acumen.

Taylor, M. (2007). Pro-social behavior: The future – it's up to us. Retrieved from http://www.thersa.org/action-research-centre/expertises/pro-social-behavior.

Wacquant, L. (2000). The new "peculiar institution": On the prison as surrogate ghetto. *Theoretical Criminology, 4,* 377–389.

Wilkinson, R., & Pickett, K. (2010). *The spirit level. Why equality is better for everyone.* London: Penguin Books.

Williams, Z. (2011). The UK riots: the psychology of looting. *The Guardian,* August 9. Retrieved from http://www.theguardian.com/commentisfree/2011/aug/09/uk-riots-psychology-of-looting.

Wilson, J. Q., & Kelling, G. L. (1982/1997). Broken windows. In R. Dunham & G. Alpert (Eds.), *Critical issues in policing* (pp. 424–437). Prospect Heights, IL: Waveland Press.

Part VII
Conclusions

35

Explanation in Forensic Neuroscience

Tony Ward and Carolyn E. Wilshire

Key points

- The chapter explains why neuroscience must not be seen as a stand-alone explanation for criminal behavior.
- Even if research shows an association between a brain structure/process and criminal behavior, or can document altered brain functioning with subgroups of people who have committed certain types of crime, this does not mean that the brain structure/process has caused the criminal behavior.
- Instead, neuroscience explanations should be seen as compositional or part-causal; and should be carefully integrated with biological, social, and psychological components to create a theory of criminal behavior that is multilevel and inter-field.
- A proper theory of criminal behavior must then identify all the parts and processes at the different levels of the mechanism, and depict their inter-level relationships.
- It is of note that human beings are as much creatures of culture as of biology.

Introduction

Forensic neuroscience is a rapidly developing area of research and promises to yield new ways of explaining and responding to crime and its associated problems. For example, some researchers have explored the relationship between alterations in brain structure and deviant sexual preferences in males diagnosed with pedophilia (e.g., Cantor et al., 2008), while others have investigated the impact of developmental adversity on the brain structures underlying emotional regulation (e.g., Creeden, 2004). The identification of the molecular and neurological processes underlying offending related phenomena such as impulsivity may offer practitioners opportunities to alter individuals' criminal dispositions and reduce reoffending rates.

The Wiley Blackwell Handbook of Forensic Neuroscience, First Edition. Edited by Anthony R. Beech, Adam J. Carter, Ruth E. Mann and Pia Rotshtein.
© 2018 John Wiley & Sons Ltd. Published 2018 by John Wiley & Sons Ltd.

However, demonstrating a significant association between the behavioral (and psychological) features of offenders and brain structures or processes is not sufficient to establish the nature of causation, or to arrive at a comprehensive explanation. First, we don't know whether the causal direction is top-down (i.e., from behavioral level to brain level), bottom-up (i.e., brain processes generate the behavioral features), or if both are the product of a third factor. Second, it is necessary to be clear about the type of neuroscience explanation being offered (Craver, 2007). That is, whether an explanation is intended to be 1) an *etiological* explanation where a set of causal processes (mechanism) results in a subsequent, downstream effect (e.g., empathy failure, deviants sexual arousal, and intimacy deficits plus relevant contextual factors cause an initial deviant offense) or 2) a *compositional* explanation where the aim is to describe the components of a single mechanism and their interactions, which are responsible for the occurrence of a phenomenon (e.g., empathy failure, with its constituent parts and processes at multiple levels described and their interactions outlined). Furthermore, it is important to state if an explanation is intended to be fundamental (reductionistic) in nature or multilevel. This point reflects the former claim that some levels of analysis are more important than others, and therefore should be the primary level of explanation. Third, before a model or theory is formulated it is necessary to clearly describe what phenomenon is the focus of an explanation. All these issues should be considered at the front end of a forensic neuroscience research project.

The Neuroscience Perspective

Once it is accepted that the nature of human beings is formed from the dynamic interplay between biology, culture, and social experience it is obvious that traditional criminology can only offer a partial understanding of normative breakdowns (Durrant & Ward, 2015). Social variables such as poverty, unemployment, and inequality may set the scene for antisocial behavior but on their own cannot explain it. In part, this is because individual differences in capacities such as emotional regulation and cognition underpin criminal dispositions (Andrews & Bonta, 2010). However, the major reason why social causes are insufficient to account for offending is the acknowledgement that as embodied and evolved organisms, individuals' actions can only be explained by the consideration of biological as well as social and psychological causes (Durrant & Ward, 2015). The molecular and brain systems levels are as important as the social and psychological; in fact, collectively they form an explanatory mosaic, contributing distinct and necessary parts of any satisfactory theory of human behavior (Bechtel, 2008; Craver, 2007; Craver & Darden, 2013). The various disciplines comprising neuroscience offer unique perspectives on human functioning, which can be combined into *multilevel* (i.e., focus on the various components of a mechanism and their constituent processes) and *inter-field* (i.e., include the unique viewpoints of different disciplines and sub disciplines) explanations of psychological and social phenomena such as crime. Craver (2007) captures the multifaceted aspect of neuroscience and its explanatory strategies well:

> Explanations in neuroscience refer to the behaviors of organisms, the processing functions of brain systems, the representational and computational properties of brain regions, the electrophysiological properties of nerve cells, and the structures and conformation changes of molecules.
>
> (p. 9)

neuroscience is unified not by the reduction of all phenomena to a fundamental level, but rather by using results from different fields to constrain a multilevel mechanistic explanation.

(p. 231)

According to Craver, neuroscience should seek to describe and develop accounts of phenomena through the lenses of the different disciplines comprising it, converging on comprehensive and unified explanations. The resulting product will be an integrated, multilevel mechanistic explanation of phenomena such as intimacy deficits or empathy failures. Unfortunately, there is a temptation for researchers and practitioners to privilege one level over another, for example, arguing that molecular explanations are more fundamental and therefore ground the other levels. They are viewed as the "real" ones and levels such as the behavioral or social are considered to be merely pragmatically useful; the entities and processes referred to at these higher levels are thought to not exist. Ultimately, the eliminitavist argument goes, they will be replaced by molecular or neuropsychological models. We believe that this approach to neuroscience explanation is mistaken and unlikely to result in cogent models of phenomena such as long-term memory, learning, or decision making (Craver, 2007), let alone something as complex as crime.

Forensic Neuroscience and the Explanation of Crime

The focus of inquiry

It is pointless developing explanatory theories of crime until you have clearly described the phenomenon of interest; description should always precede explanation (Haig, 2014). A problem in the forensic and correctional domains is that frequently insufficient attention is paid to this methodological requirement. At times, the focus of inquiry is something as vague as sexual offending or violence, or dynamic risk factors. Crimes within a particular category can vary in terms of the offenders' motivations and intentions, their severity, and context – so focusing inquiry on a particular type of crime is likely to result in overly general explanations. What is of more value at the start of a research project is the identification and description of the relevant problems associated with a crime, such as emotional loneliness, deviant sexual desires, sadistic behavior, impulsive behavior, feelings of rage, a need for revenge, and so on.

A related problem is that constructs such as criminogenic needs (dynamic risk factors) are sometimes recruited as possible causes of crime when in fact they are composite constructs that contain causal, contextual "symptoms" within them (Ward, 2016; Ward & Beech, 2015). Relying on these constructs for explanations will result in conceptual confusion and poor explanatory theories because of their problems of incoherence (due to their composite nature), lack of specificity (too many causal possibilities included within one dynamic risk factor), and referential failure (because of their high level of abstraction). An important research task is to deconstruct them and identify what are phenomena requiring explanation and what are possible causal factors.

While descriptions of phenomena are frequently refined and enriched throughout the research process it is crucial to begin with at least some sense of what the explanatory target is. In forensic neuroscience, it is likely to be a behavioral or psychological feature of individuals who commit crimes, for example, problems with emotional regulation, cognitive biases, or empathy failures.

Causal mechanisms

Explanation in the life sciences and psychology differs from fundamental sciences such as physics by virtue of its focus on mechanisms rather than universal laws (Craver & Darden, 2013). The reason for this stress on mechanisms is that the functioning of biological organisms is strongly influenced by contextual and local causal factors, and therefore universal biological laws that apply across all times and places do not exist. In addition, organisms are comprised of multiple, interacting causal systems that are hierarchically organized and very sensitive to developmental and contextual variables. For example, the circulation system is comprised of the heart, arteries, veins, and blood, all of which are constituted by subsystems of their own. Each system depends on the others for its capacity to function adaptively and problems in any of the components and their processes are likely to compromise the integrity of the whole system. Furthermore, the presence of contextual problems such as environmental toxins can damage the various components of the relevant system and impair its functioning.

In the life sciences (including psychology) the scientific goals of prediction, explanation, and control are advanced by the discovery of the mechanisms that underpin phenomena (Craver & Darden, 2013). References to mechanisms help to explain both normal and maladaptive functioning, and it is expected that disease or psychopathology (and the psychological and social problems associated with some types of crime) are produced by disrupted or damaged mechanisms and their relevant systems. Craver and Darden speaking in the context of the life sciences state that:

> Biologists seek mechanisms that produce, underlie, or maintain a phenomenon. Stated most generally: Mechanisms are entities and activities organized such that they are productive of regular changes from start or set-up to finish or termination conditions.
>
> (2013, p. 15)

The significant implications of this definition arise from the dynamic and integrated (i.e., organizational) nature of mechanisms. They are organized hierarchically in the sense that each mechanism is comprised of multiple levels. Each level has its own parts and processes, which are (sub)mechanisms in their own right but which are also collectively components of the next level. Thus, the levels constituting a mechanism span the molecular to the brain to the behavioral level; all within a single mechanism. For example, in Beech and Mitchell's (2005) model of intimacy deficits in sex offenders, there are submechanisms at a number of different levels that constitute the overall mechanism producing intimacy problems. These levels range from the neurobiological to the psychological mechanisms constituting attachment style, such as beliefs concerning trustworthiness of others, the perceived value of the self, and strategies to secure a sense of safety. Mechanisms are responsive to local, contextual factors, and consist of parts, processes, and their interrelationships and rely on their various components running smoothly in order to adequately perform their functions. Mechanistic explanations therefore ought to include reference to the internal and external contexts within which they occur, and identify the triggers that initiate, maintain, and terminate their functioning.

If you accept that psychological explanations revolve around the identification of causal mechanisms then this should be reflected in the theories in question and their component concepts. In addition, it is to be expected that approaching human behavior from a neuroscience perspective means constructing multilevel, inter-field explanations. The methodological theory underpinning the search for multilevel explanations is *integrative pluralism*. A methodological implication of the embodied nature of human beings is that explanations of psychological or behavioral phenomena need to be formulated at a number of distinct levels (Zachar & Kendler, 2007). This may take the form of constructing models focused on single mechanisms explaining something like empathy deficits, or constructing a theory that spans a series of related phenomena such as sexual offending and its associated problems. In the latter case, the resulting explanation will consist of multiple models that are loosely linked, each focused on a particular domain and its associated mechanism; for example, in the case of sexual offending, relational problems, crime supportive beliefs and attitudes, self-regulation difficulties, emotional regulation problems, and deviant sexual interests (Ward, 2014). Referring to the broader type of theory Kendler (2005) states that:

> In integrative pluralism, by contrast, active efforts are made to incorporate divergent levels of analysis. This approach assumes that, for most problems, single-level analyses will lead to only partial answers. However, rather than building large theoretical structures, integrative pluralism establishes small "local" integrations across levels of analysis.... Our field may be in particular need of integrative pluralism, where scientists, without abandoning conceptual rigor, cross borders between different etiological framework or levels of explanation.
>
> (p. 437)

Theories referring to causal processes at each level of a mechanism should be consistent with each other and provide a set of constraints for subsequent theory development. It is unlikely that it will be possible to reduce one level to another within a model of specific mechanisms (i.e., each level adds value and collectively they provide a coherent account of a phenomenon), and certainly unrealistic when it comes to comprehensive explanations that span multiple domains and their respective mechanisms.

Explanation in forensic neuroscience

In light of the above argument, theories of crime ought to be based on the identification and description of psychological and social *mechanisms* that underlie problems associated with crime. These problems typically include issues such as aggressive inclinations, deviant sexual desires, emotional loneliness, crime supportive cognitions, impulsive behavior, and substance dependence (Ward & Beech, 2015) depending on the domain of interest (e.g., sexual or violent offending). In a robust mechanistic model, explanatory concepts should be clearly described, the parts and interrelated processes of the relevant mechanisms carefully outlined, and some account given of what constitutes maladaptive functioning of the mechanisms and their associated systems. Mechanistic theories vary in their degree of precision and epistemic status, and range from loosely linked sets of concepts denoting entities and their activities that are vaguely described – often using "filler" terms such as "interaction," "activate," "process" and so on – to rich, detailed depictions of the constituents of the phenomenon.

In the remainder of this chapter, we would like to stress three points. First, theorists should be careful to specify what type of explanation they are intending to construct: 1) an *etiological theory* composed of multiple mechanisms, at different levels, that collectively (a multifactorial theory) cause crime and its associated problems, or 2) a *compositional account* of a mechanism underpinning a phenomenon. It is our impression that this distinction is rarely made and there is a danger that researchers often conflate the theoretical tasks they are engaged in and, by doing so, create confusion. For example, it makes no sense to state that the components of a mechanism underlying a phenomenon actually cause it. This is because a cause necessarily precedes an effect, and given that the phenomenon is constituted by the components of the mechanism – at various levels – it cannot cause itself (Craver, 2007; Illari & Russo, 2014). Attention to the different types of explanation will help therapist and practitioners to avoid the mistake of thinking that brain processes (or neurobiological processes at the molecular, cellular level, etc.) cause a phenomenon when in fact what they mean is that they are (partly) constitutive of it.

Second, forensic neuroscience explanations should be multilevel ones and not be built around what are viewed as *fundamental* levels. This is partly a legacy of the fact the mechanisms are composed of parts and their activities, which are hierarchically nested. For example, the mechanism constituting the phenomenon of spatial navigation in mice consists of orientating behavior within a specific context, the capacity of the hippocampus to generate a spatial map, neurons within the hippocampus that induce long-term potentiation, and changes in the structure of NMDA receptors (example taken from Craver, 2007, p. 166). It is necessary to identify all of the parts and processes at the different levels of the mechanism, and to depict their inter-level relationships in order to provide a satisfactory account of the mechanism and its associated phenomenon. Put simply, the behavioral level (and also the intentional level in human beings) is a crucial part of the mechanism and should not be ignored or its role down played.

Third, it is necessary to rule out the influence of common causes, confounds, and irrelevant factors, when seeking to trace the relationships between brain-level components and processes and the psychological or behavioral features of a phenomenon. This means being aware of the limitations of brain-level methods of data collection, such as the fMRI or CAT scans, or neurological interventions that alter the functioning of a mechanism in some way (Bechtel, 2008). It is well accepted that simply documenting altered brain functioning within a certain diagnostic group or in individuals following an experimental procedure does not warrant inferences about its relationship with psychological capacities. Once a phenomenon of interest has been carefully described, models of the mechanism should be developed, taking care to include all the relevant levels and their associated parts and processes. Research should be theory directed and aimed at understanding the nature of specific mechanisms. Once this has been achieved, it will be easier to construct etiological theories of crime and its associated problems (Ward & Fortune, 2016); such theories will be pluralistic and integrative.

Conclusions

In this chapter we have argued that forensic neuroscience can provide an important, multi-disciplinary contribution to the understanding and management of crime. However, if it is to do so then greater attention needs to be paid to the construction of multilevel, mechanistic explanations of offending. Ideally, such theories will integrate molecular, cellular, neuropsychological, behavioral, and contextual levels of explanation within a single, albeit complex, structure. The development and elaboration of

Explanation in Forensic Neuroscience 945

forensic neuroscience mechanistic theories will require the allied efforts of researchers from a number of different scientific disciplines, each offering a unique perspective. Doctrinaire appeals to the superiority of any level of analysis is likely to frustrate this project and ultimately fails to grasp the fact that human beings are as much creatures of culture as biology. The following quote from Craver (2007) illustrates the above points well:

> Finally, whereas reduction models emphasize the importance of explanatory reduction to fundamental levels, the mosaic view can be pluralistic about levels, recognizing the genuine importance of higher-level causes and explanations. The mosaic unity of science is constructed during the process of collaboration by different fields in the search for multilevel mechanisms.

(p. 271)

Recommended Reading

Craver, C. F. (2007). *Explaining the brain: Mechanisms and the mosaic unity of neuroscience.* New York, NY: Oxford University Press. *This book presents a nuanced, neuroscience-informed theory of explanation based on the distinction between etiological and compositional perspectives. The compositional perspective provides an understanding of the different types of nested mechanisms that underlie behavior and encourages a multilevel, nonreductive view of human actions. From this viewpoint any human action, including crime, is the result of multiple systems operating at different levels of analysis. An adequate explanation of crime should seek to understand how the different systems interact rather than build theories at only one level (e.g., biochemical, neurological, phenomenological, or behavioral.*
Magnus, P. D. (2012). *Scientific inquiry and natural kinds: From planets to mallards.* New York, NY: Palgrave Macmillan. *This book provides an excellent overview of classification in science (i.e., categories that pick out entities and their core properties and relationships) and the degree to which classification systems correspond to real patterns in the world as opposed to artificial ones. It raises some interesting questions about whether or not classifications of offenders are better understood as artificial categories that provide little scientific information other than reoffending estimates and a narrow set of offence related concerns.*

References

Andrews, D. A., & Bonta, J. (2010). *The psychology of criminal conduct.* New Providence, NJ: Anderson Publishing.
Bechtel, W. (2008). *Mental mechanisms: Philosophical perspectives on cognitive neuroscience.* London: Routledge.
Beech, A., & Mitchell, I. (2005). A neurobiological perspective on attachment problems in sexual offenders and the role of selective serotonin re-uptake inhibitors in the treatment of such problems. *Clinical Psychology Review, 25,* 153–182. doi:apa.org/?uid=2005-01239-002.
Cantor, J. M., Kabani, N., Christensen, B. K., Zipursky, R. B., Barbaree, H. E., Dickey, R., ... Blanchard, R. (2008). Cerebral white matter deficiencies in pedophilic men. *Journal of Psychiatric Research, 42,* 167–183. doi:10.1016/j.jpsychires.2007.10.013.
Craver, C. F. (2007). *Explaining the brain: Mechanisms and the mosaic unity of neuroscience.* New York, NY: Oxford University Press.
Craver, C. F., & Darden, L. (2013). *In search of mechanisms: Discoveries across the life sciences.* Chicago, IL: University of Chicago Press.

Creeden, K. (2004). The neurodevelopmental impact of early trauma and insecure attachment: Re-thinking our understanding and treatment of sexual behavior problems. *Sexual Addiction & Compulsivity, 11*, 223–247.

Durrant, R., & Ward, T. (2015). *Evolutionary criminology: Towards a comprehensive explanation of crime and its management.* New York, NY: Academic Press.

Haig, B. D. (2014). *Investigating the psychological world: Scientific method in the behavioral sciences.* Cambridge, MA: MIT Press.

Illari, P., & Russo, F. (2014). *Causality: Philosophical theory meets scientific practice.* New York, NY: Oxford University Press.

Kendler, K. S. (2005). Toward a philosophical structure for psychiatry. *American Journal of Psychiatry, 162*, 433–440. doi:10.1176/appi.ajp.162.3.433.

Kendler, K. S., Zachar, P., & Craver, C. (2011). What kind of things are psychiatric disorders? *Psychological Medicine, 41*, 1143–1150. doi: 10.1017/S0033291710001844.

Ward, T. (2014). The explanation of sexual offending: From single factor theories to integrative pluralism. *Journal of Sexual Aggression, 20*, 130–141. doi:10.1080/13552600.2013.870242.

Ward, T. (2016). Dynamic risk factors: Scientific kinds or predictive constructs? *Psychology, Crime, & Law, 22*(1–2), 2–16. doi:10.1080/1068316X.2015.1109094.

Ward, T., & Beech, A. R. (2015). Dynamic risk factors: A theoretical dead-end? *Psychology, Crime & Law, 21*, 100–113. doi:10.1080/1068316X.2014.917854.

Ward, T., & Fortune, C. A. (2016). From dynamic risk factors to causal processes: A methodological framework. *Psychology, Crime & Law, 22*, 190–202. doi:10.1080/1068316X.2015.1117080.

Zachar, P., & Kendler, K. S. (2007). Psychiatric disorders: A Conceptual taxonomy. *American Journal of Psychiatry, 164*, 557–565. doi:10.1176/appi.ajp.164.4.557.

36

Considerations for the Forensic Practitioner

Adam J. Carter and Ruth E. Mann

Introduction

In this concluding chapter, we consider how forensic practitioners might use the contents of this book to inform and help their practice. In bringing together consideration for a number of different areas of relevance to forensic practice, this book has aimed to demonstrate how neuroscience can inform the work of the forensic practitioner. Our job in this chapter is to integrate these insights and clarify how they can be used by those in forensic practice – assessing, managing, or working therapeutically with clients who have committed crime. We hope that forensic practitioners will have a better understanding of emerging neuroscience findings to improve their practice and, ultimately, help with the prevention of crime and better care for their clients.

Of course, neuroscience is not everything. No one in this book has claimed that the neuroscientific contributors to criminal behavior mean that a person who commits a crime had no choice about what they did. And similarly, as Beech and Fisher noted in Chapter 1, we are not in a position where brain scans should be used by a parole board in determining whether an individual should be released from prison. Crime, and our policy and practice in response to it, must involve a wider consideration than neuroscience that incorporates genetics and evolutionary understanding as well as social factors – including adverse or impoverished upbringing, current level of social capital, and the influence of others – and psychological factors, such as personality, identity, life goals, attitudes, beliefs, and self-efficacy. This wider focus is necessary to understand both why people commit crime and how we may help to prevent people acting criminally to begin with.

The chapters, particularly in Part II, of this book describe how our knowledge of a map of the brain is developing. We have an increasing understanding of the key areas of the brain in terms of their structure and neurological functioning. In Chapter 1, Beech and Fisher introduced those parts of the brain considered integral to motivation and our ability to control emotions. Beech and Fisher observed that these areas, collectively named the social brain, have until recently received relatively little attention in terms of investigating neurobiological and neurochemical understanding and their relevance to criminal behavior. This book has set out to provide an overview of how neuroscientific study, especially the neurobiological and neurochemical functioning

---

The Wiley Blackwell Handbook of Forensic Neuroscience, First Edition. Edited by Anthony R. Beech, Adam J. Carter, Ruth E. Mann and Pia Rotshtein.
© 2018 John Wiley & Sons Ltd. Published 2018 by John Wiley & Sons Ltd.

of the social brain, can add to our understanding of why people commit crime and engage in antisocial behavior.

For example, we have seen in this book how dysfunction in the structure and functioning of the social brain (e.g., the amygdala, anterior cingulate cortex, orbital prefrontal cortex, and the insular) can increase the propensity for violence and antisocial behavior. Of course, this dysfunction on its own does not account for why people commit violence and aggression. There is a myriad of different factors involved in every violent act. Neuroscience is expanding our understanding of the etiology of different types of offending, but this understanding comprises many different components. However, we can see across many chapters of this book that how, and the degree by which, the neuroscientific components contribute, as well as how they interact with social, environmental, and other components, is varied and complex. For example, we have seen how changes to gene expression following birth can be caused by environmental factors that include stress and being subjected to trauma and sexual abuse. Even though not everyone who experiences an impoverished or abusive childhood goes on to commit offences and not everyone who offends has had an impoverished and abusive childhood (although many do), these insights are important in our understanding of crime.

Outside of how neuroscience can help us understand culpability, less controversially it can inform how practitioners can better engage with forensic clients. As the earlier chapters in this book illustrate, there is growing evidence that impairments in some key areas of the brain are associated with a number of difficulties in cognitive functioning, such as deficits in the ability to plan, empathize with others, and resist impulses. Alongside this, there is evidence that trauma can disrupt the ability for the brain to regulate emotions and generate appropriate emotional responses (see Chapter 26). We have also seen that these impairments and accompanying dysfunction are particularly prevalent in forensic populations. Better knowledge about these impairments can help us understand why someone behaves impulsively and makes poor decisions, and consequently to respond in a way that is appropriate and helpful. In other words, understanding impulsivity and poor emotional regulation as impairment of brain development rather than character deficiencies may make it easier to sustain a coaching response when someone struggles or lapses.

In this book, we have examined how neurological impairments are associated with various kinds of offending including acquisitive and impulsive/reactive aggression. They are also helpful for understanding psychopathy and why people sexually offend (see Chapters 9 and 13 respectively). Familiarity with some of the main areas of the brain, their functions, and consequences of dysfunction is therefore invaluable for forensic practitioners, and this is the purpose of Chapters 1 and 2. Knowledge and understanding of methods to determine when neurological impairments are present (see Chapter 15) will help us to provide the right kind of rehabilitative and engagement approach and support to our forensic clients.

Part III progresses to neuroscientific understanding concerning specific conditions, disorders, or types of offending. Again, these insights emphasize that it is important not to consider brain and neurotransmitter functioning in isolation if we are to better comprehend the presentation and behavior of the people in our forensic populations. Awareness of how factors like upbringing interplay with brain and neurotransmitter functioning is necessary to develop an insight into why people present as psychopathic or have attention deficit hyperactivity disorder (ADHD). This understanding and learning should then inform case assessment and formulation.

Part IV focuses on risk factors. Risk can be understood in terms of the factors that can raise the likelihood of criminality for people as a group and the factors that raise an individual's risk. Forensic practitioners are used to identifying risk factors, but may not be so used to considering their origins, and this part of the book therefore provides some rich explanations about how many well-known risk factors, including alcohol and drug abuse, can have neuroscientific components. This realization then leads to a recognition that a neuroscientifically informed response may help with reducing the potency of some key risk factors. Accordingly, Part V on rehabilitation describes the neurological basis for certain types of interventions that may not usually be seen as part of a rehabilitative package for forensic populations, such as eye movement desensitization and reprocessing (EMDR), exercise, mindfulness, and meditation (See Chapters 25, 26, and 29, respectively).

Editing this book has made us, as practitioners, think more deeply about the question of culpability and how this is understood in history, politics, and sociology as well as science. As Jessica Pykett points out in Chapter 34, the cause of criminal behavior is usually conceptualized in one of two ways: the immoral individual versus the divided unequal society. The immoral individual is portrayed by the media as a lawless, aggressive, surly, "other" who commits crime because of a disregard for social norms. The assumption here is one of characterological deficiency and dangerousness. On the other hand are explanations that people who behave criminally are products of a divided society that over values consumerism and, in doing so, produces a disadvantaged and alienated subgroup who can only reach the higher echelons of consumerism's goals through crime. In her chapter, Pykett cautions against the use of neuroscience to merely add to the "one-dimensional" pathologizing of individual human beings (see Royal Society, 2011) and reminds us powerfully of ways in which the concept of a criminal brain can lead to acts of inhumanity. While an understanding of neuroscience offers a way to gain deeper insight into a person's behavior, it should not be used to further demonize people who commit crime by taking the notion of culpability to its extreme and concluding that a brain development deficit means any person is inherently and irrevocably dangerous.

We will now look at some of the implications of the different parts of this book in more detail and how they can practically inform formulation, assessment, and diagnosis, as well as treatment and supervision.

General Neurobiology Research and the Forensic Practitioner

Part II on general neuroscience shows that a variety of biological techniques have been employed to study the underlying neurobiological basis of aggressive and antisocial behavior (see Chapter 3). Foell and Patrick outline how studies of twins have been used to identify genetic and environmental factors that affect human propensity for violence. That environmental factors can determine whether a gene is expressed demonstrates that neurobiological insights must be considered in conjunction with evolutionary perspectives and social and psychological factors to help explain the causes of criminal and antisocial behavior.

Given that sexual offences represent a breach of socially acceptable behavior, Mokros (Chapter 13), argues that sexual offending is not dependent upon identifying brain dysfunction linked with sexual offending – and it would appear that, in the majority of cases, sexual offences are committed by people without such dysfunction.

While not sufficient in isolation to explain crime, neurological dysfunction has been linked to certain crimes and these could be helpful to the forensic practitioner. Part II also demonstrates how neurobiological insights can help understand processes of offending. Foell and Patrick (Chapter 3) discuss how aggressive individuals can be differentiated according to the type of violence they perpetrate, stemming from different contributory processes. Here, aggression termed impulsive/reactive differs from premeditated/instrumental aggression. In Chapter 9, De Brito and Mitchell provide a helpful overview of how psychopathy has been defined and assessed as well as highlighting some misconceptions commonly held about this condition. De Brito and Mitchell also refer to variants of psychopathy. The primary and secondary psychopath commit violence similar to Foell and Patrick's impulsive and instrumental aggressor respectively.

Identifying these different neurological processes has implications for rehabilitative efforts. *Psycho education* for forensic clients that explains how the brain functions could help them to understand why particular techniques are being suggested and the possible benefits to them of participating in these processes. *Emotional regulation training* may be of more benefit for impulsive aggressors and secondary psychopathic offenders, as described above, than for instrumental aggressors. Likewise, *meditation* for impulsive aggressors could lead to better emotional regulation by increasing the activity of the prefrontal brain regions. *Mindfulness techniques,* including simple affect labeling tasks, have been shown to increase prefrontal control over the amygdala (Cresswell, Way, Eisenberger, & Leiberman, 2007). Teaching this approach could help to counter the overactive amygdala and underactive prefrontal cortex that characterize the impulsive/reactive aggressors.

Abu-Akel and Bo (Chapter 20) outline neurobiological characteristics of schizophrenia, personality disorder, and autism, all of which can elevate the risk to behave violently. While our understanding of the neurobiology of aggression for these mental health conditions is limited, and further research is needed, Abu-Akel and Bo considered evidence that the brain regions involved in a propensity for violence are also involved in the handling of socio-cognitive functioning. They proposed that these shared circuitries in acts of violence and governing socio-cognitive functions make disruption to the social brain a helpful model for understanding the physiology of aggressive behavior. From the forensic practitioner perspective, understanding dysfunction in both brain regions and neurochemical functioning can provide frameworks to help inform the use of *medication* to ameliorate these difficulties and to develop therapeutic approaches that *enhance socio-cognitive functioning.*

Risk Assessment: A Neuroscientific Perspective

The need to identify the subgroups of perpetrators of crime, that create particular problems in society because they cause significant emotional and/or physical harm, is well recognized. Typically, risk assessment can take what has been termed a "pincushion" approach (Ward, Mann, & Gannon, 2006) – listing out the factors that need to be removed, like pins from a cushion, in order for risk to be reduced. Usually an assessor compiles this list using a structured process. The outcome of this approach to risk assessment can be reported without any need for consideration of how or why the risk factors arose. On the one hand, this makes for a clear, objective, account of the issues that need to be tackled in order for any individual's risk to be lowered. On the other hand, the lack of context to the process, and the lack of explanation of how risk factors develop, can mean that the risk assessment process is alienating to the person being assessed. In the limited literature available on the client's perspective of risk assessment, it appears that risk assessment is a process that they fear and dislike because it feels reductive and impersonal (Attrill & Liell, 2007; Maruna, 2011). It therefore could be valuable both for the purpose of engagement and to aid decision making if the risk assessor devoted some time to considering possible neurobiological origins of the risk factors they identify in an individual. This consideration could be the key that links the individual's experience of childhood trauma, neglect, abuse, or other impoverishment to brain abnormality and associated characteristics that lead to crime.

The neurobiological components of risk factors that are amenable to change is starting to take shape. Importantly, neuroscience could improve early identification of people at risk of developing disorders associated with raised risk of violence and criminal behavior; for example, those adolescents with conduct disorder (CD) and high levels of callous-unemotional traits who advance to meeting the diagnosis of psychopathy (see Chapters 9 and 18). Chapters 10 and 16 explain the neurobiological stance on the irritability, disobedience, sensitivity to threat, and proneness to reactive aggression that characterize oppositional defiant disorder, CD, and antisocial personality disorder (ASPD). These traits are heritable and brain imaging studies are beginning to identify the abnormal brain structures and functions that explain them. Understanding CD and antisocial behavior in terms of brain abnormality may lead practitioners to adopt a different approach to describing their clients, in reports and so forth, which could help decision makers choose the most appropriate courses of action. For example, as Chapter 16 touches upon, adolescents with CD show increased sensitivity to reward and lack of sensitivity to punishment, which may, in part, explain why justice system processing is often iatrogenic for young people who have committed crime (Petrosino, Turpin-Petrosino, & Guckenburg, 2010). We have also seen how co-morbidity, when substance abuse further complicates an already demanding condition such as ADHD, CD, impulsivity, or psychopathy, can be relevant to risk of violence and is therefore an important consideration in risk assessment.

Managing and Supervising Forensic Clients: A Neuroscientifically Informed Approach

People who have committed crime are often compelled to reside in institutions such as prisons or secure hospitals, or to live their lives under the supervision of probation or parole officers in the community. For many forensic practitioners therefore the challenge is not only to assess and treat clients, but also to manage them to live their lives without harming others or themselves. For example, prison staff have to maintain order and control in prisons as a prerequisite to any successful rehabilitation goal of the institution. Probation officers have to assist their clients to live meaningful lives while at the same time holding responsibility for protecting the public from any potential harm. How can a neuroscientific perspective help people carry out these duties effectively?

A common mistake that practitioners make with those in their care is to assume that their clients think like they do: that they weigh things up rationally, consider the consequences before they do something, and understand how their behavior affects other people. This assumption can lead to frustration and often punitive approaches when their charges instead behave in ways that seem unreasoned, unpredictable, destructive, or callous. For instance, why would a man in prison who has a possibility of early release on parole commit an assault on a member of staff? To those who think "normally," this kind of act seems so irrational that it is easy to label the man or woman in question as "aggressive" or "dangerous" and impose a more restricted environment on them. Prisons are places to which people are sent for punishment and the cloud of punitiveness that hangs over them is easily translated into sanction-oriented behavior-management policies within the institution.

However, many people in prison are neurobiologically wired so that punishment has little effect on them. They can be punished and then repeat the problem behavior, leading staff to conclude that they are so dangerous they cannot be corrected. New restrictive solutions then pile on: isolation, physical restriction of movement, deprivation of fresh air, social company and exercise, and so forth. These "solutions" continue to have no effect but, once stuck in a cycle of punishment, many institutions are so aligned to layperson intuitive thinking (and not surprisingly, given that the punitive ideal is continually reinforced by the media) that they believe they must simply up the ante – punish more harshly until some change is seen.

For people on probation, a similar situation can develop. A person fails to adhere to some part of his/her probation conditions – maybe they are late for an appointment, or they lose their job, or they get drunk. One response would be to sanction them – restrict conditions, put them on a warning, or even return them to prison. While many probation officers would prefer to take a more rehabilitative approach, sometimes their guidelines or their concerns about public protection make this difficult, and the pressure of living in a punitive society can take its toll.

What neuroscience research teaches us is that those with under-developed regulatory functions respond better to reward than punishment. However, a systematic and organized rewarding approach is very rarely found in prisons or with clients on probation. To many correctional practitioners, reward is something that you deliver only on exceptional occasions. You do not reward someone for doing just what they should be doing (i.e., causing no disruption and staying out of trouble).

But, one of the comforts that neuroscience research brings is its recognition of the apparent plasticity of the brain. People have the potential to continue to grow, in neurological terms, even after they have reached adulthood. Rewarded learning, especially when paired with neuropsychologically informed psychological coaching (see rehabilitation section) is one of the most effective ways to create new links within the brain, enhancing pro-social behaviors and emotional regulation capability.

Additionally, as this book explains, understanding people at a neuropsychological level enables practitioners to recognize impulsivity and aggressiveness as behaviors with a different meaning than simply "dangerousness," and lack of perspective taking is not now synonymous with "callousness." Instead these features of a person's behavior are understood as signals of underlying neurological dysfunction, and this understanding should lead to a different rehabilitation and management approach. Thinking about prisoners in this way leads to ideas of whole-prison approaches to coaching and rewarding prisoners in the skills of emotional regulation, perspective taking, goal setting, future planning, impulse management, and problem solving. In this kind of institutional environment, staff both model and coach the above skills, and there is a policy of rewarding people for showing signs of development in these areas, rather than punishing them for not doing so.

Case Formulation: Adding a Neuroscientific Component to the Picture of an Individual

Neuroscience is helping us to better understand how many factors that raise the risk of someone engaging in criminality impact upon the development and functioning of the brain (see Chapters 12, 15, 23, and 32). While these insights are only one component, they are nevertheless an important part of the picture when carrying out case formulation. Neuroimaging studies are helping us to build our understanding of impairments in brain structure and functioning associated with violent and antisocial behavior. In Chapter 14, Nee proposes that knowledge about the neurocognitive disruption that can underpin what has become established behavior in our forensic clients alongside the ability to make assessments that take into account individual manifestations of this disruption is necessary to tailor rehabilitative efforts and provide appropriate support. There are also techniques and tools to help inform assessment. As Amen and Willeumier have demonstrated (Chapter 23), if used in conjunction with a comprehensive history, identification of neural activity can inform assessment and rehabilitative approaches. Single photon emission computed tomography (SPECT), has a role in case formulation (e.g., identifying alterations in neural functioning associated with alcohol consumption to make formulations about violent behavior or uncovering traumatic brain injury (TBI) otherwise not known or recorded). Shug, Feiger, Geraci, and McLernan, in Chapter 12, outline neuropsychological research showing how deficiencies in aspects of intelligence and executive functioning may be indicative of brain and neurological dysfunction for violent offending and particular differences more relevant to certain cohorts of perpetrator. Although more research is needed, establishing specific deficits of intelligence or executive functioning linked to violence could inform targeting in treatment programs for this client group.

Engaging and Connecting: Neuroscience and Relationships

The principle of "responsivity" within the most evidence-based model of correctional rehabilitation (the risk-need-responsivity model, Andrews & Bonta, 2006) is concerned with how best to respond to the particular needs of the individual. Jackson and Beaver (Chapter 25) refer to how *styles and modes of treatment are employed that are capable of influencing criminal needs.* To date, while biomedical methods have been found to have value (Bradford, 2008; Grubin, 2008), cognitive-behavioral methods have been considered the best approach to change criminal needs (Lösel & Schmucker, 2005). We have seen how cognitive-behavioral techniques may not adequately take into account neuroprocessing obstacles that many forensic clients are likely to face (see Chapter 22). The evidence base for methods and techniques employed in treatment programs is yet to be fully established (Carter & Mann, 2016). Fountaine, McCrory, and Viding (Chapter 18) conclude that we need to better identify those parts of treatment that are of benefit to addressing problem areas specific to antisocial youth with callous-unemotional traits. They point to a promising study that demonstrated the benefit of having emotional recognition therapy accompany standard interventions as being beneficial to positive outcome. In Chapter 16, Fairchild and Smaradhi outline the role that neuroimaging could play in helping us understand the components of interventions that account for change in antisocial behavior. Fairchild and Smaradhi also propose that neuroimaging techniques could help determine those most likely to benefit from particular approaches by using them to evaluate change prior to and during the treatment process. We know that the skills and competencies of the staff facilitating groups can be important to fostering a cohesive environment and the process of change (e.g., Beech & Fordham, 1997; Marshall et al., 2003). As suggested earlier in this chapter, insights from neuroscience to help us change our assumptions about why forensic clients behave the way they do and the techniques that may be better suited to clients with dysfunction in the structure and functioning of the social brain. This may help therapists to show the qualities that help individuals to change, such as instilling hope, displaying empathy, and warmth. Neuroscience can help us tailor techniques to influence and change criminal need and also provide psycho education to help staff work more effectively with forensic clients. Psycho education for clients will also help them to see the value of certain approaches and monitor how well they are working.

Rehabilitation: Neuroscience and Change

As noted already, the good news from neuroscience research is that the brain is apparently malleable even in adulthood. Programs (individual or group) that train individuals in cognitive skills to overcome impulsivity (such as problem-solving, perspective-taking, and decision-making skills) and regulate emotions have been repeatedly shown to be associated with reduced reoffending (e.g., Travers, Wakeling, Mann, & Hollin, 2013). When people have the opportunity to learn these skills, especially if the learning takes place in a fun and lively environment, and when they are reinforced for practicing them, they have the potential to overcome early neuropsychological development deficits.

Worthy of particular note in terms of rehabilitation is EMDR therapy (see Chapter 29). As this chapter demonstrates, EMDR has an impressive evidence base, forged through numerous high quality evaluation studies and meta-analyses. Although its mechanism of change is not fully understood, it has been demonstrated that the eye movement component of EMDR is an important one, and this indicates that EMDR works through a neurobiological mechanism. EMDR has been shown to eliminate symptoms of post-traumatic stress disorder (PTSD) (and likely other disorders too), indicating that it is possible to change the way the brain stores and retrieves memories of traumatic past experiences. This research, often ignored by the more traditional academic community because of the seemingly bizarre nature of EMDR (as explained in Chapter 29 and also in Russell, 2008), provides further indication that neuroscientifically based approaches to rehabilitation hold real potential for forensic populations.

Another example of how neurobiological understanding points to a specific treatment approach for a particular forensic population can be found in Chapter 27 on the use of anti-libidinal medication with people convicted of sexual offences. In this chapter, Don Grubin explains how, perhaps self-evidently, problematic sexual behavior is often a consequence of sex drive, sexual preoccupation, or sexual fantasy. Underlying sexual behavior are the serotonergic and dopaminergic neural systems, as well as testosterone. For some people, these systems create sexual arousal that is hard to control, while for others, sexual drive is relatively weak and easily regulated. Hence, for some people whose sexual behavior has been problematic or harmful, and where that behavior is driven in part by a strong sexual drive, selective serotonin reuptake inhibitors

(SSRIs) and anti-androgens can greatly assist in self-management and, potentially, risk reduction. Grubin stresses that prescription of such drugs must be predicated on a certainty that these neural/hormonal systems are implicated in the problematic sexual behavior. They should not be prescribed simply because someone is considered to be high risk. In the UK, at least, doctors have shown some reluctance to prescribe medication in this way, fearing that they are being asked to prescribe as a form of social control rather than because of medical need (as may be indicated in the favored media term "chemical castration"). Grubin's chapter explains why this reticence is misplaced, while acknowledging that the basis for using medication in this way is built more on neurobiological theory and clinical case studies than on the usual medical standard of double blind randomized trials.

Future Directions

Within the chapters of this book there are many examples of how neuroscience can and has been used to understand aggression and antisocial behavior or disorders and illnesses that have been linked to an increased likelihood of violence. Biologically informed models to explain violence or personality disorders linked to an increased risk of antisocial and violent behavior, such as psychopathy, can help with guiding more targeted interventions like medication to help address neurochemical dysfunction. In terms of where we might go next, many of the chapters conclude with areas that require further research. There is also the call that a universally accepted definition of violence and agreement on how this is operationalized is required to help with consistency and coherence across research. We have also seen that, while promising, a number of rehabilitative efforts in forensic settings for addressing neurological vulnerabilities such as yoga, mindfulness, physical exercise, and meditation need to be subject to robust empirical investigation. Given the costs associated with imprisonment and that recidivism can be high for particular cohorts, future directions should also focus upon how neuroscience can help with preventative measures. As discussed in this book (see Chapters 12 and 19), preventative interventions by way of providing advice and guidance to improve the health and wellbeing of more socially disadvantaged pregnant women and their unborn child have been shown to reduce the likelihood of the child being arrested and convicted on follow up in comparison to a control group. Efforts to use nutrition to improve brain health through a diet rich in omega-3 fatty acids and preventing smoking during pregnancy also look promising (Chapter 19). Earlier in this chapter we mentioned that the benefits of a more detailed understanding of the structures and neurological functioning of parts of the brain associated with certain violent acts can inform models to understand violent processes and inform treatment approaches. Longitudinal studies that take into account crime trajectories and desistance and the relationship with neurological functioning and gene expression will provide insights for considering prevention and rehabilitation of forensic clients. We have also seen reference within this book to a need for better understanding about what it is about people who don't offend despite certain gene vulnerability and experiences and upbringing associated with violence and antisocial behavior can help us to learn more about building resilience and having strength-based interventions for forensic clients. It is also clear throughout this book that that our understanding of crime using neuroscience must be carried out in conjunction with sociological and *psychological* understanding, and what Pykett (Chapter 34) terms *structural and spatial explanations of crime and criminal behavior.*

Conclusions

While we hope that this book will have wide appeal to a range of people connected to forensic practice, a key objective of producing this text was for it to encourage more practitioners in this field to engage with the evolving neuroscientific evidence base concerning criminal and antisocial behavior. For those who already draw upon knowledge of the neurobiological and neurochemical functioning of the brain and other insights from neuroscience to understand, assess, and undertake rehabilitative work with forensic clients, we hope that this will be a useful resource. Box 36.1 shows our "bottom line" recommendations for how forensic practitioners, including psychologists, psychiatrists, social workers, probation officers, and prison officers, could accommodate neuroscience into their work.

Box 36.1   The basics of incorporating neuroscientific knowledge into practice

1 Develop a basic familiarity with the structures and functions of the social brain and their impact on social behavior.
2 Be aware of the ways in which childhood adversity – such as trauma, violence, abuse, or neglect – can impede the development of the brain and how this affects behavior in adolescence and adulthood.
3 Always consider your clients' childhood experiences and any possibility of head trauma; reflect on how the impact of these experiences may be playing out in current behavior. And talk to your clients about how their early experiences might have affected their brain development.
4 Define your approach with your clients as building strengths and skills that improve pro-social brain functioning, rather than removing risk factors.
5 Become familiar with "brain friendly" methods of working with people.
6 Create rehabilitative environments and interactions that recognize the plasticity of the brain but also the limitations of those who may be deficient in certain capabilities. In particular, develop environments that use coaching and reinforcement to encourage people to utilize new skills. Do not expect punishments to change behavior.
7 Augment cognitive-behavioral psychological interventions by considering other activities or therapies that might benefit your clients, such as mindfulness, nutrition, physical exercise, EMDR, or medication.
8 Be patient when people struggle. The pro-social ways of behaving that you probably learned effortlessly, they are learning the hard way.

Working with forensic clients is often challenging. The characteristics that can make these clients vulnerable to offending and behaving in a way that is antisocial (e.g., difficulties forming attachments, poor problem solving, and difficulties regulating emotions) can create obstacles for them to engage with forensic practitioners. As discussed in this chapter, many aspects of the criminal justice process, particularly imprisonment, are demanding and even harmful, rather than naturally rehabilitative. For forensic practitioners and their clients, we hope that this handbook will help the process of assessment, care, support, and change to be a rewarding process for all concerned.

Recommended Reading

Rosier, J. (2015). What has neuroscience ever done for us? *The Psychologist, 28*(4), 284–287. *This article examines why the abundance of neuroscientific research over the last quarter of a century has not yet translated into new and better-informed treatment for people with mental health problems. It discusses whether this is about to change and whether we will now see innovation and enhanced treatment resulting from a collaboration of neuroscientific understanding and practice.*

References

Andrews, D. A., & Bonta, J. (2006). *The psychology of criminal conduct* (4th ed.). Newark, NJ: LexisNexis/Anderson.

Attrill, G., & Liell, G. (2007). Offenders' views on risk assessment. In N. Padfield (Ed.), *Who to release? Parole, fairness and criminal justice* (pp. 191–201). Cullompton, Devon: Willan.

Beech, A., & Fordham, A.S. (1997). Therapeutic climate of sex offender treatment programs. *Sexual Abuse: A Journal of Research and Treatment, 9,* 219–237.

Bradford, J. M. W. (2008). The biomedical treatment of sexual sadism and associated conditions. In A. J. R. Harris & C. A. Pagé (Eds.), *Sexual homicide and paraphilias: The correctional service of Canada's Experts Forum 2007* (pp. 167–212). Ontario: Correctional Service of Canada.

Carter, A. J., & Mann, R. (2016). The strengths of treatment for sexual offending In D. R. Laws & W. O'Donohue (Eds.), *Treatment of sex offenders: strengths and weaknesses in assessment and intervention* (pp. 157–174). Cham, Switzerland: Springer International Publishing.

Cresswell, J. D., Way, B. M., Eisenberger, N. I., & Lieberman, M. D. (2007). Neural correlates of dispositional mindfulness during affect labeling. *Psychosomatic Medicine, 69,* 560–565.

Grubin, D. (2008). The use of medication in the treatment of sex offenders. *Prison Service Journal, 178,* 37–43.

Lösel, F., & Schmucker, M. (2005). The effectiveness of treatment for sexual offenders: A comprehensive meta-analysis. *Journal of Experimental Criminology, 1,* 117–146.

Marshall, W. L., Fernandez, Y., Serran, G. A., Mulloy, R., Thornton, D., Mann, R. E., & Anderson, D. (2003). Process variables in the treatment of sexual offenders: A review of the relevant literature. *Aggression and Violent Behavior, 8,* 205–234.

Maruna, S. (2011). Why do they hate us? Making peace between prisoners and psychology. *International Journal of Offender Therapy and Comparative Criminology, 55,* 671–675.

Petrosino, A., Turpin-Petrosino, C., & Guckenburg, S. (2010). *Formal system processing of juveniles: Effects on delinquency.* Oslo, Norway: The Campbell Collaboration.

Royal Society, The (2011). *Brain waves 1: Neuroscience, society and policy.* London: The Royal Society. Retrieved from http://royalsociety.org/policy/projects/brain-waves/society-policy/.

Russell, M. C. (2008). Scientific resistance to research, training and utilization of eye movement desensitization and reprocessing (EMDR) therapy in treating post-war disorders. *Social Science and Medicine, 67,* 1737–1746.

Travers, R., Wakeling, H. C., Mann, R. E., & Hollin, C. R. (2013). Reconviction rates following a cognitive skills intervention. *Legal and Criminological Psychology, 18,* 48–65.

Ward, T., Mann, R. E., & Gannon, T. A. (2006). The good lives model of offender rehabilitation: Clinical implications. *Aggression and Violent Behavior, 12,* 87–107.

Index

Page references for illustrations are in italics (e.g. *512*). Page references for tables and notes have 't' and 'n' added (e.g. 512t, 21n).

5-HTTLPR (serotonin-transporter-linked polymorphic region), 456, 463–5, 544
5-hydroxytryptamine (5-HT), 19, 46, 47, 48, 97, 240–3, 361, 366–8, 463–7, 497, 522, 539–40, 542, 545, 660, 665–6, 667, 669, 708, 712–13, 717
9/11 terrorist attacks, 559

Abe, N., 182
Abel, L., 395
abnormal sensation, 292
Abramowitz, C., 681
Abu, Z., 201
Abu-Akel, A., 539, 542
acetaminophen, 156–7
acetylcholine, 46
acquired brain injury (ABI), 373, 375–6, 385–412, 519–20, 544, 577–94, 608–10, 631–52

acquisitive/impulsive offenders, 359–78
see also impulsivity
Adams, R. B., 153
Adaptive Information Processing (AIP) Model, 756–7, 760–2, 770
ADHD (attentional deficit hyperactive disorder), 32–3, 235–6, 278, 373–5, 376, 390, 431, 434, 580, 660, 662, 665, 666
Adi, Y., 717
adolescents, 396–7, 421–44, 783–807
adverse childhood experiences (ACEs), 243, 247, 250, 287, 370–1, 390, 394, 401, 439–40, 507, 515–17, 579–81, 584–5, 681, 730, 768, 784, 788–90
age-crime curve, 423–4, 426–8
callous-unemotional traits (CU), 422, 425, 428,

435–6, 440, 443–4, 483–502, 503n
conduct disorder (CD), 229–55, 421–44
comorbid disorders, 234–8, 286–7, 390, 429–31, 434, 680–1
definition, 4, 230, 385, 422, 484, 508
developmental taxonomic theory, 431–9
genetic studies, 483–502
recidivism risk assessment, 439–41
treatments, 500–2
diminished-capacity standards, 118, 138
emotion regulation, 686, 687, 690–1
language skills, 580–1, 584–5
peer relationships, 110–11, 371–2
physical fitness, 661–3
recidivism risk assessment, 439–41, 792–3

The Wiley Blackwell Handbook of Forensic Neuroscience, First Edition. Edited by Anthony R. Beech, Adam J. Carter, Ruth E. Mann and Pia Rotshtein.
© 2018 John Wiley & Sons Ltd. Published 2018 by John Wiley & Sons Ltd.

960 Index

adolescents (*Continued*)
  risk-taking behavior,
    105–18, 371–3, 427,
    635, 665
  sex differences, 234, 241,
    424–5, 428–33,
    492–3
  sexual offenders, 783–807
adoption studies, 239–40,
  465, 523
adverse childhood
  experiences (ACEs),
    243, 247, 250, 287,
    370–1, 390, 394,
    401, 439–40, 507,
    515–17, 579–81,
    584–5, 681, 730,
    768, 784, 788–90
aerobic exercise, 564–6, 583,
  659–70
affect regulation, 344, 395–6
affective decision making,
  192
affective empathy, 279
African-Americans, 241,
  254–5
Aftanas, L. I., 563
age-crime curve, 423–4,
  426–8
aggression, 61–76, 365,
  437–43, 615–20,
  631–52, 711–12,
  727
  and alcohol abuse, 455–68
  risk assessment, 18–19,
    75–6, 465–7,
    531–43, 634–5,
    637–41
  sex differences, 234, 401,
    428–33, 439, 463
  treatments, 76, 99, 397,
    641–52
Ågmo, A., 86, 88
Aguilar, R., 520
Aharoni, E., 160, 216, 440,
  441
Albert, D., 110–11
alcoholism, 249, 397,
  455–68, 606–8
  alcohol outcome
    expectancies (AOE),
    458–9

fetal alcohol spectrum
  disorders, 49, 374,
    391–3, 508, 511–12
Alderman, N., 635, 636,
  637, 640–1, 642, 645
Aleman, A., 686
alexithymia, 554
Allaby, D. B., 316
Allely, C. S., 392
Allen, D., 288, 292
Allen, M., 564
Alm, P. O., 201
Almvik, R., 314
Alpern, L., 519
Alzheimer's disease, 601–2,
  609–13
Amen, D. G., 394, 606–8,
  609, 616
American Psychological
  Association, 558
amnesia, 407
amygdala, 13, 27, 35–6, 40,
  42, 49, 53, 127, 202,
  203–4, 245–6, 282,
  290, 337, 341–2,
  363–4, 365, 372,
  394, 428, 430, 435,
  440–1, 462, 463,
  510, 542, 544, 563,
  579, 580, 681, 682,
  683–4
Anastassiou-
  Hadjicharalambous,
  X., 159
Anckarsäter, H., 275, 618
Andershed, H., 493–4, 496
Anderson, C. A., 130
Anderson, G. C., 97
Anderson, I., 307
Andrews, D. A., 362, 556
androgen deprivation
  therapy, 337, 704,
  715–17
angular gyrus, 333
animal studies, 49
  aggression, 463–5, 466–7
  emotion regulation, 127
  empathy, 147–9
  impulsivity, 367–8
  sexual behavior, 85, 86–7,
    88–9, 91–3, 95–8,
    342–3

Aniskiewicz, A. S., 159
A-not-B task, 359, 369
anterior cingulate cortex,
  13, 37, 112, 127,
  129, 176, 311, 343,
  363, 365–6, 370,
  372, 376, 438,
  440, 510, 544, 664,
  686
anterior insula, 109
anterior prefrontal cortex,
  174–6
anti-androgens, 705,
  715–17, 718–19
antidepressants, 46–7,
  361, 613–14, 615,
  620
anti-psychotic medication,
  717–18
antisocial personality
  disorder, 180–1, 202,
  229–55, 346, 390,
  423, 427–8, 543–4,
  634, 661
  comorbid disorders,
    234–8, 248, 250,
    680–94
  definition, 230, 385–6
  developmental taxonomic
    theory, 431–9
  genetic studies, 483–502
  treatments, 677–94
Anwar, S., 535
anxiety disorder (AD), 127,
  236, 278, 620,
  680–94
Apgar score, 507
apoptosis, 31
appearance-reality task, 360,
  369
Arango, C., 320
arborization, 372–3
Arden, J. B., 579–80
Ardila, A., 401
Ariely, D., 336
Arnett, P. A., 198
Arntz, A., 239
aromatization, 84, 95
arousal, 690, 747
  fear response, 365, 428,
    663, 682, 690, 729,
    732, 764–5

Index

sexual arousal, 90–1, 334, 336, 339–40, 342, 343–5, 684, 705–7, 710–19
arsonists, 287, 535
Ashburner, J., 212
Asperger, H., 279
Asperger syndrome, 531, 542
associative learning *see* conditioning (associative learning)
attachment, 507–8, 514, 518–19, 522, 727, 734–5, 740, 787–8
attention, 406–7, 460, 744–5, 747, 769
auditory learning, 585, 587–8, 801
autism spectrum disorder (ASD), 49, 179–80, 273–94, 532
  comorbid disorders, 278, 286–7, 293, 541–2
  definition, 273
autonomic nervous system, 4, 42–3, 56, 66–9, 197–9, 677–8
avoidance, 743
Awh, E., 132
Aykac, V., 691–2

Babcock, J. C., 69
Bachevalier, J., 127
Baguley, I. J., 634–5
Bailey, D., 460
Baker, C. I., 582–3
Banissy, M. J., 155
Barbaree, H. E., 336, 344, 345
Barber, F., 316
Barkataki, I., 307, 308, 314, 316, 317
Barkley-Levenson, E. E., 112–13
Barnett-Walker, K., 433
Barnfield, T. V., 388
Barona Index, 406
Baron-Cohen, S., 279, 284–6
Barrett, L. F., 29
Bartels, A. A. J., 208

Bartz, J. A., 155
basal ganglia, 13, 37, 301, 360, 365, 376, 510, 579
basic emotion hypothesis, 29
basolateral complex, 13
Batson, C. D., 157
Baudrexel, S., 245
Bauer, D., 501
Baum, M. J., 95
Baxter, M. G., 127
BDNF (brain-derived neurotrophic factor), 554, 566, 659, 667–9
BDSM, 335
Beauchaine, T. P., 67, 690–1
Beauregard, M., 134, 684, 768
Bechara, A., 152, 363, 466
bed nucleus of the stria terminalis (BNST), 127
Beech, A., 243, 340, 735
Beeney, J. E., 153
Beer, J., 73
behavior modification, 28
behavioral neuroscience, 29–30
Beissner, F., 245
Beitchman, J. H., 201, 498t
Belau, D., 520
Béliveau, L., 662
Belopolsky, A. V., 132
Ben-Ami Bartel, I., 147, 148
Ben-Aron, M. H., 393
Benning, S. D., 74, 195
Berchtold, N. C., 668
Bergmann, U., 768
Bernardez Sarria, M. S., 147, 148
Bernardi, L., 689
Berner, W., 394
Bernstein, H.-G., 127
Berntson, G. G., 149
Bertelsen, P., 539, 542
Berthiaume, C., 662
Bertsch, K., 250
beta-endorphins, 666
Bhatt, S., 176
Bielau, H., 127
Bigio, E. H., 612
Bihrle, S., 16, 305, 306

Bilby, C., 759
Billstedt, E., 286, 288
biofeedback, 678, 688–92
Birbaumer, N., 17
Biron, L., 11
bisexuality, 96–7
Bishop, S. L., 685
Bjork, J. M., 665
Blackburn, R., 320
Blair, R. J., 152, 159, 202, 203, 204, 206, 294
Blake, P. Y., 319–20, 394
Blakemore, S.-J., 152
Blanchard, R., 338
Blase, K. A., 28
Blasi, A., 150
Bliss-Moreau, E., 29
Blonigen, D. M., 494
Bloom, P., 151
Bo, S., 195, 539, 542
Boccardi, M., 211
body language, 589
Bogerts, B., 127
Bohman, M., 523
BOLD imaging, 26, 172, 301, 564
Bond, V., 520
Bonsall, R. W., 95
Bonta, J., 556
Bonte, F. J., 612
Book, A. S., 19
Booth, R. D., 281
borderline personality disorder (BPD), 236–7, 687–8
Born, J., 770
Borysenko, J., 768
Boswell, C. P., 177
bottom-up processing, 132
Botvinick, M. M., 157
Bouman, Y. H. A., 558
Bourgouin, P., 134, 684
Bowen, S., 567
Bowlby, J., 735
brain development, 30–3, 107–10, 114, 234, 249–50, 281, 282, 315, 426–7, 507–23, 579–80, 730, 801–6
  critical periods, 32, 249, 278, 322, 378, 768
  developmental lesions, 49

brain development
(*Continued*)
effects of malnutrition,
511, 513, 515, *520*,
580
and emotion regulation,
136–8, 632–3, 681
and empathy, 150–3, 636
impulse control, 362,
368–73, 378, 635
perinatal development,
514
prenatal development, 31,
49, 361, 374, 375,
390–3, 509, 511–13,
579
schizophrenia, 251–4
and sexual behavior, 337
synaptic pruning, 372–3,
422, 509
and treatment, 783–807
brain structure, 33–49
and alcohol abuse, 466–7
antisocial personality
disorder, 244–54,
440–1, 544, 661
autism spectrum disorder
(ASD), 281–4
cellular structure, 43–9
conduct disorder (CD),
244–54, 427–8,
433–9
emotion regulation,
126–9, 438, 544,
618, 636, 644,
677–94
and impulse control,
107–10, 114, 363–6,
438, 465–6, 563,
615, 635–6, 665
lesions, 7–8, 49–51, 95–6,
127, 128, 129,
201–4, 342–3,
364–5, 373, 375–6,
385–412, 461, 544,
577–94, 608–13,
615–16, 634–5,
637–41
neuroplasticity, 65, 347,
378, 522, 561,
582–3, 664, 668–9,
767–8

and physical fitness, 566,
583
psychopathy, 250–1, 544
and sexual behavior, 95–6,
97, 337–8, 789
tumors, 338, 401
violent offenders, 303–11
brainstem, 33–4
Bramen, J. E., 337
Bratt, M. A., 687
Braun, J. M., 244
breathing exercises, 745–6
Brennan, J., 201, 501
Brennan, P., 390–1, 514
Brickman, D., 162
Briken, P., 394
Brink, J., 637
Brislin, S., 212
British Crime Survey, 336
Broadbent, D. E., 177
Brodmann's areas, 26,
173–4
Brooks, J., 640–1
Brooks-Gordon, B., 759
Broomhall, L., 314
Brower, M. C., 389
Brown, M., 558
Brownell, C. A., 151
Bruce, K. E., 94
Bruce, V., 28
Bryan, K., 580–1
Bryant, R. A., 389
Bryden, D. P., 99
Buchsbaum, M., 306,
308–9, 320, 395
Buddhism, 554, 555, 562,
728
Bunge, S. A., 133, 684
Burdette, J. H., 664
Burgess, P. W., 638, 642
Burke, J., 181
Burnett, S., 209
Burt, S. A., 438
Bushman, B. J., 130
Buss, K. A., 137
Byrd, A. L., 242
Byrnes, J. P., 108

CA1/CA3 neurons, 659,
664
Cacioppo, J. T., 149
Cacioppo, S., 67

Cajal, S. R. *see* Ramón y
Cajal, S.
Calcedo Barba, A., 320
Calcedo Ordóñez, A., 320
Calhoun, V. D., 213
callous-unemotional traits
(CU), 74–5, 422,
425, 428, 435–6,
440, 443–4,
483–502, 503n
Caltran, G., 150
Cambridge Study in
Delinquent
Development, 18
Campbell, C., 561
Cantor, J. M., 346–7, 556
Capasso, D. R., 460
caring, 737–41 *see also*
empathy
Carlson, E., 519
Carlson, S. M., 179
Carmody, J., 687
Carpenter, M., 151, 152
Carr, V. J., 537
Carrere, R. C., 773
Carter, A. J., 581
Casanova, M. V., 17
Caspi, A., 19
Castellanos, M. A., 148
castration, 704, 713–14
CAT scans (computerized
axial tomography),
15, 386, 410–11
catechol *O*-methyl-
transferase, 540
Cauchi, A. J., 501
caudate nucleus, 302
Cauffman, E., 661
Cavanaugh, D., 790
Cavanna, A., 334
cavum septum pellucidum
(CSP), 386, 390–3
Cazzell, M., 116
Cederlund, M., 284, 288
cellular neuroscience,
43–9
central amygdala nucleus,
35–6
central motive states, 84, 87,
95–6
central nervous system,
33–42

central sulcus, 41
centromedial complex, 13
cerebellum, 37, 282
cerebral cortex, 39–42
Chaddock, L., 664
Chan, C. C., 114, 116
Chang, J. K., 313
Chang, Y. K., 662
Chapman, M., 150
Checknita, D., 243
Chein, J., 110–11
chemical castration, 704
Chen, C., 208
Chen, H.-Y., 150, 157
Cheng, J. Y. J., 132
Cheng, K., 131
Cheng, Y., 150, 157, 158, 159
Cheung, C. K., 137
Chhabra, P., 236
Chiavegatto, S., 463–4
Chiesa, A., 686
children, 421–44
  acquisitive/impulsive offenders, 362, 368–73, 378
  adverse childhood experiences (ACEs), 243, 247, 250, 287, 370–1, 390, 394, 401, 439–40, 507, 515–17, 579–81, 584–5, 681, 730, 768, 784, 788–90
  anxiety disorder (AD), 680–1
  conduct disorder (CD), 229–55, 421–44
  comorbid disorders, 234–8, 286–7, 390, 429–31, 434, 680–1
  definition, 4, 230, 385, 422, 484, 508
  developmental taxonomic theory, 431–9
  genetic studies, 483–502
  recidivism risk assessment, 439–41
  treatments, 500–2

emotion regulation, 690–1
physical fitness, 661–3
violent offenders, 392–3
Choden, 735
Choi, C., 338
Choi, W., 137
Chomsky, N., 7
Chou, K.-H., 157
Chrisjohn, R. D., 11
Christ, S. E., 173–4
Christman, S. D., 767
Chung, A., 86
Chung, H. Y., 313
Chung, S., 313, 317
Church, R. M., 147
Cibrian-Llanderal, T., 97
Ciccone, J. R., 401
Cikara, M., 157
Cima, M., 195, 200, 203, 239
cingulate cortex, 36–7
  see also anterior cingulate cortex
Cipolotti, L., 202
Clare, I. C. H., 288
Clark, K., 563
Clark, L., 759–60
Clarke, E. J., 244
classical conditioning, 28, 84, 89, 90–1, 97
Clay, Z., 148
Claycomb, S., 320
Cleckley, H., 194, 195
Clements, C. B., 17–18
Cloninger, C. R., 523
cluster B personality disorders, 333–4
Cobia, D., 316
cocaine, 367–8
Coccaro, E. F., 72, 310
Coda, J. J., 316
cognitive behavioral therapy, 583–94, 643–4, 646–7, 678, 689, 748, 759, 772
cognitive empathy, 279–80
cognitive function, 311–17
  coping skills, 590–1, 592t
  developmental stages, 178–80, 363–4, 365, 368–73, 426–7, 785–92

executive function, 284, 305, 314–17, 345, 365–6, 368–71, 458–62, 520, 541, 554, 565–6, 579, 590–1
foundation skills, 784, 790–1, 801–2
intelligence, 312–14, 346–7, 405–6
language skills, 405–6, 580–1, 584–5, 643–4
learning disabilities, 582, 583–91, 593, 643–6, 789
memory, 364–5, 368–71, 407, 459, 522, 565, 586, 589, 611–12, 617, 663, 664, 756–8, 760–76
neurobehavioral disability, 633–52
and physical fitness, 564–6, 583, 659–70
social information processing, 460–2, 539
cognitive reappraisal, 125, 133–4, 137, 679–80, 693, 749
Cohen, L. J., 337, 345
Coid, J., 233, 238, 680
Colantonio, A., 609
Cole, S. W., 149
Coleman, E. M., 587, 593
Colletti, P., 16, 211, 213, 305, 390
comorbid disorders, 234–8, 248, 250, 278, 286–7, 293, 373, 390, 429–31, 536–8, 541, 680–1, 708
compassion-focused therapy, 725–49
Comprehensive Health Assessment Tool (CHAT), 378
computerized tomography (CT) scans, 15, 386, 410–11
COMT enzyme, 540, 545

conditioning (associative learning), 27–8, 84, 89, 90–1, 97, 638–9
conduct disorder (CD), 229–55, 421–44
  comorbid disorders, 234–8, 286–7, 390, 429–31, 434, 680–1
  definition, 4, 230, 385, 422, 484, 508
  developmental taxonomic theory, 431–9
  genetic studies, 483–502
  recidivism risk assessment, 439–41
  treatments, 500–2
conflict resolution tasks, 365–6
confluence model of sexual aggression, 335–7
congenital brain lesions, 49
connectivity analysis, 53, 136, 137, 281
Conrod, P., 681
continuous performance tasks, 406–7
Contreras-Rodriguez, O., 206, 207
Convit, A., 319, 320
Cook, C. L., 132
Cooke, D. J., 194
Cooper, J., 635
Cooper, P. F., 177
Cope, L. M., 213
coping skills, 590–1, 592t
Corman, M. D., 460
corpus callosum, 247, 274, 282, 508
cortisol, 4, 19, 200, 433, 580, 684
Côté, G., 236, 237
Cowell, J. M., 162
Cozolino, L., 593, 735
Craig, M. C., 214
Craissati, J., 518
Cramer, V., 233
cranial nerves, 34
Cranston, J., 460
Creeden, K., 580, 582, 585, 593, 788, 790
Creswell, J. D., 686
Crisford, H., 759

Crook, J. H., 736
Crossman, A., 180
Crowe, J. A., 392
CT scans (computerized tomography), 15, 386, 410–11
Cuijpers, P., 770–1
Cullen, F. T., 670
Cummings, J. L., 612
cyberball, 62, 67, 137, 156
Czobor, P., 319

Dabbs, J. M., 19
Dadds, M. R., 201, 204, 501
Dalle Ore, G., 343
Dalley, J., 368
Damasio, A. R., 8, 152, 363, 364
Damasio, H., 8, 152
D'Amato, F. R., 148
Danesh, J., 634
Daniels, M., 588
Dao, T. K., 692
Daoust, S., 316
Dapretto, M., 152–3
Dare, H., 759
Davidov, M., 151
Davidson, M. L., 133–4
Davidson, P. R., 770–1
Davidson, R. J., 67, 72, 75
Davis, M., 72
Davis, P., 771
Dawel, A., 207
Day, A., 686
De Bellis, M. D., 789
De Brito, S. A., 195, 202, 213, 236, 246, 248–9
de Meirleir, K., 666
de Oliveira-Souza, R., 212
de Ruiter, C., 558
de Silva Ramos, S., 581
de Visser, L., 116
de Waal, F. B. M., 148
Deakin, W., 307
deception, 171–83
Decety, J., 146, 147, 148, 150, 152, 157, 158, 159–60, 162, 163, 206–7, 208
Decker, S. A., 200

Deeley, Q., 206, 207
default mode network, 53
deficient mentalizing model, 279–80
degenerative brain damage, 46, 50, 181–2, 565, 601–2, 609–13
Deichmann, R., 245
delay discounting, 106
dementia, 50, 565, 601–2, 609–13
den Boer, J. A., 208
Denney, R. L., 542
DePaulo, B. M., 460
depression, 127, 129, 236, 278, 589, 634
  comorbid disorders, 708
  treatments, 46–7, 97, 613–14, 615, 620, 667, 713, 717
Derryberry, D., 163
Desmarais, S. L., 637
Detre, T., 621
developmental studies, 136–8
developmental taxonomic theory, 431–9
Developmental Treatment Model, 793–800t
deviant sexual interest/preference, 334, 335, 336–7, 339–44, 394, 707, 708–9, 718–19
DeVincent, C. J., 292
Devous, M. D., 616
DeWall, C. N., 157, 730–1
Diagnostic and Statistical Manual of Mental Disorders (DSM), 21n, 230–1, 274, 275, 334, 340, 431, 436, 485, 532, 603, 613, 707, 758
dialectal behavior therapy (DBT), 687–8
Diamond, P., 408
diathesis-stress model, 537
diffuse axonal injury (DAI), 376
diffusion tensor imaging (DTI), 15, 62, 71–2, 302, 434–5

Index

dihydrotestosterone (DHT), 84, 91, 95
Dimeff, L., 688
diminished-capacity standards, 76, 118, 138, 293–4, 349–50, 403
Dinov, I. D., 612
Dishman, R. K., 666
disinhibition (externalization), 62, 508, 514
dismantling studies, 756, 767, 770
distress tolerance, 738–9
Dobrowolny, H., 127
Dolan, C. V., 284
Dolan, M. C., 180, 248, 307, 313
Domes, G., 155
domestic violence, 68, 69, *321*, 456–7, 467
Dondi, M., 150
Donnellan, M. B., 438
dopamine, 19, 46, 47, 48, 242–3, 360, 366–8, 369, 374, 462, 463–4, 466, 537, 539–40, 542, 660, 662, 665–6, 667, 669, 704, 709, 712–13
dorsal striatum, 127–8
dorsolateral prefrontal cortex (dlPFC), 128, 290, 306, 369, 376, 662
dorsomedial prefrontal cortex (dmPFC), 42
Drabant, E. M., 133
Drabick, D. A., 292
drama therapy, 588
Drellich, M. G., 94
Drevets, W. C., 152
drug abuse, 235, 250, 605–8, 634
and impulsivity, 366–8, 374–5
and mental illness, 536–7, 541
and sexual behavior, 97–8
Drummond, P. D., 767, 769, 771

dual systems model, 107
dual-process model of emotion, 132
Dugan, Brian, 348–9
Dunbar, R. I. M., 12
Dunedin Multidisciplinary Health and Development Study, 422, 432–3
Dunn, D., 72
Durbin, C. E., 75

Earle, J., 316
Eastman, N., 561
echo planner imaging (EPI), 53
Ecker, C., 281
ecological validity, 637–8
economic trust game, 146
Egeland, B., 519
Egner, T., 133, 135–6
Ehde, D., 388
Eisenberger, N. I., 152–3, 156, 686
Ekman, P., 29
El Masry, Y., 204
electrodermal activity, 56, 172, 176–7, 198–9
electroencephalography (EEG), 15, 26, 54–5, 62, 410, 411, 566, 682, 683
aggressive behavior studies, 69–71, 317–20
serial killers, 401–2
electromyography (MEP), 56
Eley, T. C., 437–8
Ellis, M. L., 17–18
El-Sheikh, M., 67
emotion recognition, 283, 428, 442–3
emotion regulation, 125–39, 438, 544, 618, 632–3, 636, 644, 677–94, 725–49
emotional go/no-go task, 126, 129, 136, 137
emotional Stroop task, 126, 135–6, 137

empathy, 145–63, 207–9, 279–80, 286, 428, 485, 539, 612–13, 636, 739
Enayati, J., 287
endogenous hormones, 84, 91–5, 200–1, 666
endorphins, 666
environmental toxins, 244, 279, 508, 511–13, 605–8
epigenetics, 4, 19–20, 230, 243–4, 248, 279, 322, 368, 373, 496–7, 500, 522–3, 730, 768
epilepsy, 343, 397–9, 411, 613–14, 616–18
episodic dyscontrol syndrome, 635–6
episodic memory, 765–6
ERASOR (Estimate of Risk for Adolescent Sexual Offender Recidivism), 784, 792
Erickson, K., 309, 566, 583, 664
Ermer, E., 213
Ernst, M., 108
estradiol, 84, 91, 95, 96
ethical issues
aggression, 75–6
diminished-capacity standards, 76, 138, 293–4, 349–50, 403
treatment of sexual offenders, 713–14, 720
etiological research methods, 64–5, 375–6, 437–8, 483–502
Etkin, A., 132, 133, 135–6
European Institute for Crime Prevention and Control, 303
Evangeli, M., 759
Evans, J. R., 319, 320
event-related potential (ERP), 62, 172, 563
evolutionary psychology, 147–9, 158, 727–30, 732–3, 742–3

Ewing-Cobbs, L., 789
executive function, 284, 305,
    314–17, 345, 363,
    365–6, 368–71,
    458–62, 520, 541,
    554, 565–6, 579,
    590–1
exercise, 564–6, 583,
    659–70
explicit (declarative)
    memory, 364–5
explicit ER (emotional
    regulation), 126,
    132–5
expressive suppression, 126,
    133, 134–5, 137,
    246, 680
externalization
    (disinhibition), 62,
    508, 514
extinction tasks, 192
eye movement
    desensitization
    reprocessing therapy
    (EMDR), 755–76
eye-tracking studies, 30,
    339–40
Eysenck, H. J., 10–11
Eysenck, S. B. G., 11

Fabian, J. M., 348
Fabiano, E. A., 371
facial emotion recognition,
    28, 29–30, 283, 428,
    442–3, 563
Fairchild, G., 213, 428, 430
Fallon, J. H., 394
false belief tasks, 360, 369
families, 233–4, 240, 241,
    243, 245, 247,
    254–5, 439–40,
    496–7, 501, 515–19,
    521, 727, 728,
    734–5, 787–8, 805–6
Fann, J. R., 388
Farah, M. J., 636
Farahany, N., 5
Farmer, L., 692
Farrington, D. P., 11, 18
Fazel, S., 287, 398–9, 535,
    634, 635
Fazio, R. L., 542

fear response, 365, 428, 663,
    682, 690, 729, 732,
    764–5
Fehr, E., 155
Felitti, J. J., 515–16
Fellows, L. K., 636
Felmingham, K., 635
Fenton, G. W., 308
Fenwick, P. B. C., 308
Feresin, E., 348, 349
fetal alcohol spectrum
    disorders, 49, 374,
    391–3, 508, 511–12
fetishism, 91, 394
Finger, E. C., 214
Finzi, R., 519
Fischbacher, U., 155
Fisher, J., 772
Fiske, S. T., 157
Fisler, R., 765
Fitzgerald, P., 177
Fix, R. L., 686–7
Fix, S. T., 686–7
Fixsen, D. L., 28
flanker task, 360, 366, 554,
    565–6
fMRI (functional magnetic
    resonance imaging),
    15–16, 26, 52–3, 63,
    410–12, 428, 462,
    563, 602, 608, 683–4
Fodor, J. A., 7
follicle stimulating hormone
    (FSH), 704, 710
Fontaine, N. M. G., 493,
    494, 501
Ford, J. M., 155
forebrain, 37
Forsman, M., 493–4, 496
Fortescue, D., 581
Foster, H. G., 320
foundation skills, 784,
    790–1, 801–2
Fowler, T., 498t
Fox, J., 567
Fox, P. T., 116
Frady, R. L., 19
Frank, R., 8
Franklin, R. G., 153, 156
Frazzetto, G., 19, 522
Freedman, D., 388
Freer, J., 580–1

Freud, S., 10
Frewen, P. A., 686
Frick, P. J., 17–18, 196–7,
    234, 240, 433, 497,
    501
Friesen, W. V., 29
Friston, K. J., 212
Frith, U., 279, 280, 281
Fritz, A. S., 369
frontal lobe, 41, 304–7, 370,
    389–90, 394–5,
    406–7, 412, 544, 579
frontal lobe dysfunction
    theory, 290–1
frontotemporal dementia,
    609–10, 612–13
Fudge, J. L., 108
Fullam, R. S., 180, 181, 313
Fulton, J. J., 244
functional near-infrared
    spectroscopy (fNIRS),
    53
Furlong, C., 580–1
fusiform gyrus, 192, 302,
    334, 342

GABA (gamma-
    aminobutyric acid),
    47–8, 455, 461,
    464–5, 466–7
Gabbard, G. O., 76
Gabrieli, J. D. E., 133, 174,
    684
Gadow, K. D., 292
Gage, Phineas, 7–8, 50
Gainer, P., 147
Galaburda, A. M., 8
Gale, S., 135–6
Gall, Franz Joseph, 6–7
Galvan, A., 116
galvanic skin response
    (GSR), 56, 172,
    176–7, 198–9
Galveston Orientation and
    Amnesia Test
    (GOAT), 407
gambling, 112–13, 114,
    116, 128
game-based learning,
    589–90
Gammon, C. B., 460
Gannon, T. A., 558, 759–60

Gao, J. H., 116
Gao, Y., 70–1, 196, 198, 200
Garakani, A., 689
Gardiner, P., 662
Garnett, S., 342
Gatze-Kopp, L., 67, 320, 690–1
Gazzola, V., 208
Gebbia, P., 392
gender identity, 743
general intelligence, 311–14, 346–7, 405–6
generalized anxiety disorder (GAD), 127, 680–94
genetics, 26, 64–5, 559
  alcoholism, 465
  antisocial personality disorder, 239–43, 254–5, 437–8
  autism spectrum disorder (ASD), 278–9
  callous-unemotional traits (CU), 483–502
  gene polymorphisms, 19, 230, 456, 463–5, 497–500, 522, 540, 544, 727
  impulsivity, 367, 368
  telomeres, 508, 516
  XYY syndrome, 5, 12
genotype, 26, 65
Gentile, B., 730–1
George, D. T., 467
Georgopoulos, A. P., 765
Gerring, J. P., 376
Geshwind, R., 399
Gevirtz, R., 692
Ghaziuddin, M., 288, 292–3
Ghaziuddin, N., 288
Giancola, P. R., 458–62
Gilbert, F., 209
Gilbert, P., 735, 736, 737, 743, 744, 747
Gillberg, C., 275, 284, 287, 288
Gillberg, I. C., 288
Gillespie, S. M., 30
Gilman, J. M., 665
Gizewski, E., 337
Glenn, A. L., 200, 208, 211, 213, 309
glial cells, 20n, 45

glucose metabolism, 17, 395–6, 615–16
glutamate, 47
GnRH agonists, 704, 715–16
Godefroy, O., 161
Godleski, S. A., 180
Goethals, I., 309
Golden, C. J., 399
Goldin, P. R., 134–5
Goldin-Meadow, S., 589
Goldsmith, H. H., 137
gonadal hormones, 84, 91–5, 97–8, 704–5, 709–12, 713–15
gonadotropin releasing hormone (GnRH), 704, 710
go/no-go task, 334, 360
González-Salvador, T., 320
good lives model (GLM), 558, 646, 650, 651
Goodall, J., 729
Gordon, A., 646
Gottmann, J. M., 68, 69
Gould, J., 277
Grabowski, T., 8
Graham, K., 460
Granger, D. A., 200
Granholm, A. C., 669
Grann, M., 287, 398–9
Green, A. I., 537
Green, H., 234
Green, J., 319
Green, M. J., 537
Gregory, S., 212, 250
Grey, N., 637
grey matter, 5, 52, 155, 245, 246, 282, 337–8, 372–3, 394
grief, 740–1
Grier, M. M., 99
Gross, J. J., 130, 131, 132, 133, 134, 135, 679–80, 684
Guastella, A. J., 204
Guay, M. C., 662
Guillin, O., 667
guilt, 736–7, 749
Gulati, G., 535
Gunnar, M., 363

Guyer, M., 76
Gyurak, A., 132

Haaven, J., 586, 587, 593
habenula, 13–14, 127
Habermann, N., 394
Habermeyer, B., 337, 346
Haddlesey, C., 581
haemodynamic response, 26
Hagberg, B., 284, 288
Hall, J. R., 195
Haltigan, J. D., 433
Hamann, S., 133
Hamlin, J. K., 151
Han, S., 157
Hancock, M., 315–16
Handy, L., 393
Haney-Caron, E., 250
Hanlon, R. E., 316
Hansen, A., 521, 689–90
Hanson, J. L., 789
Hanson, K. R., 338–9
Happé, F., 209, 281
Haque, S., 76, 408
Hardy, K. R., 90
Hare, R. D., 158, 193, 195, 280
Hare, T. A., 137
Harenski, C. L., 160–1, 208, 341–2, 343
Harenski, K. A., 160–1
Har-Even, D., 519
Harger, J., 67
Harini, A. R., 133
Harmon-Jones, E., 70, 247
Hart, S. D., 195, 789
Harvey, J. A., 513
Harvey, O. J., 162
Haskins, A. L., 134
Hassett, A. L., 692
Hauser, M. D., 195
Hawes, D. J., 201, 501
Hawes, S. W., 239, 346
Hawkley, L. C., 149
Hayden, B., 460
Hayman, G. C., 767
Heard-Davison, A., 95
heart rate, 18, 56, 65, 198, 678, 688–92
Heiman, J. R., 94, 95
Hein, G., 157
Heinrichs, M., 155

Heinz, A., 466, 467, 468
Hemenway, D., 388
Hendrie, C. A., 89–90
Hennessy, J. J., 393
Henning, K., 341
Herbert, J., 18
heritability, 19–20, 230, 239–43, 465, 483–502, 559
Hermans, E. J., 200
Herpertz, S. C., 309–10
Hibbeln, J. R., 513
Hill, A., 394
Hillbrand, M., 320
Hillman, C. H., 565–6
Hinckers, A. S., 465
hippocampus, 36–7, 40, 50, 290, 291, 308–9, 347, 361, 365, 394, 522, 554, 566, 580, 582, 583, 663–4, 668, 669
Hirono, N., 612, 618
Hirsch, J., 135–6
Hirt, M., 320
history (medical history), 407–9
Hix, H. R., 179
Hoaken, P. N. S., 316
Hockenhull, J. C., 76
Hodgins, S., 195, 236, 237, 251–4, 313
Hoek, H. W., 513
Holland, A. J., 288
Holmes, S., 586, 587, 591
Holz, N., 242
Hölzel, B., 322
Homberg, J., 116
homeostasis, 42–3
homicides see murderers
Hommer, D. W., 665
homosexuality, 96–7
Hong, C. J., 667
Hong, J. P., 313
Hood, W. R., 162
Hoon, P. W., 94
Hoppenbrouwers, S. S., 214
Horman, R. W., 616
hormones, 18–19, 84, 91–5, 97–8, 192, 193, 200–1, 433, 580,

666, 704–5, 709–12, 713–15, 726, 733, 734
Howells, K., 686
Howlin, P., 274
Howner, K., 291
Hoyer, J., 344
HPA (hypothalamic-pituitary-adrenal) system, 684
HRV (heart rate variability) biofeedback, 678, 688–92
Hucker, S. J., 338
Huebner, T., 16, 307
Hughes, B. L., 133–4
Huizinga, M., 284
Hung, A.-Y., 159
Hurley, A. D., 586
Huskens, B., 280
Hux, K., 520
hyperfusion, 602, 613–14, 620
hypersexuality, 705, 707
hypoperfusion, 602, 605–13, 615–16, 620
hypothalamus, 37–8, 85, 92, 95–6, 403
hypoxia, 390–1

identity, 730–3, 742, 743, 746–7
Iguchi, M. Y., 513
IMAGEN study, 422, 427
imagery, 747
impaired delay discounting, 466
implicit (procedural) memory, 364–5
implicit ER (emotional regulation), 126, 132, 135–6
impulsivity, 108, 344–6, 359–78, 438, 465–6, 563, 615, 635–6, 665
definition, 362–3
Ingalhalikar, M., 247
Ingnatiff, M., 729
Inoue, Y., 151
insula (insular cortex), 13, 42, 109, 343, 428, 434, 510, 522, 544

integrated emotion systems model, 290–1
integrative neuropsychiatric model, 337
intelligence, 311–14, 346–7, 405–6
intermittent explosive disorder (IED), 302, 306, 310, 462
internal drive hypothesis, 87–8
interoception, 27, 422
intimate partner violence, 68, 69, 321, 456–7, 467
Iowa gambling task, 192, 202, 302, 361
Ireland, C. A., 586
Ishikawa, S. S., 198
Ishiwara, T., 320
Itakura, S., 151

Jackson, D. C., 682
Jacobs, A., 608–9
Jacques, S. C., 513
Jaffee, S. R., 240
Jage, R. E., 634
Jambrak, J., 201
Janet, P., 765
Jeffries, F. W., 771
Jelicic, M., 200
Jensen, E., 801
Jensen, M., 316
Jeon, D., 148
Jerome, G. J., 565–6
Jiang, W., 181
Johnsen, B. H., 689–90
Johnson, D. F., 93
Johnson, J. G., 543
Johnson-Bilder, A., 17
Jones, A. P., 209, 240, 497
Jonson, C., 287, 670
Joyal, C. C., 342, 343, 348, 541
Jung, J., 313
Jurkovic, G. J., 19

Kaba, F., 408
Kabat-Zinn, J., 685, 687
Kafka, M. P., 717
Kalisch, R., 133
Kanai, R., 155
Kanakogi, Y., 151

Kandel, E. R., 135
Kanner, L., 277, 279, 293
Kaplan, H. S., 94
Karavidas, M. K., 692
Karmiloff-Smith, A., 136
Karpman, B., 196
Kawashima, R., 583
Kaylor-Hughes, C. J., 182–3
Kazama, A. M., 127
Kearns, A., 288
Kelly, G., 635
Kempes, M., 290
Kennealy, P. J., 19
Kerlin, K., 17–18
ketamine, 47
Keysers, C., 208
Kiecolt-Glaser, J. K., 149
Kiehl, K. A., 160–1, 205–7,
    208, 210, 213, 308,
    309, 348–9
Kim, H., 666
Kim, J. M., 613
Kim, S. H., 133
Kim-Cohen, J., 237, 275
kinaesthetic learning, 585,
    588–90, 801
Kinchloe, B., 94
Kingham, M., 759–60
Kirby, K., 367–8
Kitazaki, M., 151
Kleinschmidt, A., 16–17,
    310
Klüver-Bucy syndrome,
    342–3
Knight, C., 641
Knoch, D., 116
knowledge-based long-term
    memory, 364–5
Knutson, B., 467
Kober, H., 29
Koch, Julius, 10
Koenigs, M., 193–4, 203,
    210
Koerner, K., 688
Kogut, T., 161
Kolko, D. J., 500–1
Kolts, R. L., 747
Koole, S. L., 135
Kopp, C. B., 137
Korach, K. S., 95
Korenyok, V. V., 563
Korn, D. L., 762

Kosfeld, M., 155
Kosofsky, B. E., 513
Kosson, D. S., 681
Kozasa, E. H., 563
Kraepelin, E., 9–10
Kramer, A. F., 565
Kramer, L. A., 789
Krebs, A., 16–17, 310
Krell, D., 127
Kringlen, E., 233
Kristiansson, M., 287
Kronenberger, W., 72
Krueger, R. F., 239
Krueger, T. H. C., 337
Kruepke, M., 193–4
Kruesi, M. J. P., 17
Kucuk, N. O., 606
Kuffel, S., 95
Kumari, V., 305, 310–11
Kupfer, D. J., 621
Kuruoglu, A. C., 606

Laakso, M. P., 16, 210
LaCasse, L., 16, 305, 308–9,
    320, 390
Lacefield, K., 730–1
Lai, M. C., 276
Lamm, C., 155
Lane, R. D., 689, 690
Langevin, R., 320, 393
Langford, D. J., 148
Langhinrichsen-Rohling, J.,
    68
Långström, N., 288–9, 293,
    398–9, 542
language skills, 405–6,
    580–1, 584–5, 643–4
Larson, C. L., 67
Larsson, H., 493–4, 496
Lashley, L., 399
Lawing, K., 501
Lazar, S. W., 522
lead poisoning, 244, 279
learning disabilities, 582,
    583–91, 593, 643–6,
    789
learning styles, 585, 588–90,
    801
Leary, M. R., 147, 153
Leatham, J. M., 388
LeBlanc, M., 11
Lee, C. W., 767, 769, 770–1

Lee, K., 181
Lee, L., 390
Lee, S.-L., 150
Lee, T. M., 114, 116
Leeds, A. M., 764
legal issues
    admissibility of
        neurological evidence,
        348–50
    diminished-capacity
        standards, 76, 118,
        138, 293–4, 349–50,
        403
    traumatic brain injury,
        403–4
    vulnerable defendants, 291
Lehrer, P. M., 691
Leibenluft, E., 108
Leitenberg, H., 341
Lelard, T., 161
Lencz, T., 16, 305
Leonard, K., 459–60
Leroy, R. F., 616
lesion studies, 7–8, 49–51,
    95–6, 127, 128, 129,
    201–4, 342–3,
    364–5, 373, 375–6,
    461, 544, 608–13,
    615–16, 634–5,
    637–41
Leslie, A. M., 279
Leung, A. W., 116
Levander, S., 314
Levenson, R. W., 135
Lévesque, J., 134, 137, 684
Levy, K. N., 153
Lewis, D. A., 621
Lewis, D. O., 388
Lewy body dementia, 610
Li, L., 116
Li, T. Q., 72
Lichtenstein, P., 275, 398–9,
    437–8, 493–4, 496
Lieberman, M. D., 686
Lilienfeld, S. O., 194–5,
    315, 520
limbic system, 4, 12–14, 38,
    127–8, 309–10, 315,
    372, 389, 427,
    632–3, 636
Lin, C. P., 157
Lin, Z. J., 116

Lindberg, N., 320
Lindner, P., 247
Lindquist, K. A., 29
Lindquist, M. A., 133–4
Lindsay, W. R., 587
Lindstrom, E. M., 545
Linehan, M. M., 688
Linford, L., 579–80
Little, J. T., 620
Liu, H., 116
Liu, J., 515
Lobbestael, J., 239
locked-in syndrome, 34
Lockwood, P. L., 159, 209
Loeber, R., 181, 309
Loewenstein, G., 336
Loktev, K. V., 563
Lombroso, C., 8–10
Loney, B. R., 17–18
Long, Bobby Joe, 401–2
long-term memory, 364–5
Lorber, M. F., 66, 198, 199
Lorberbaum, J. P., 155
lordosis, 85, 86–7, 91, 96
Lorenz, M., 456
Lottenberg, S., 395
Lowings, G. R., 580
Lubahn, D. B., 95
Lubbe, S., 287
Lucas, Henry Lee, 400, 402–3
Luders, E., 563
Lumsden, J. J., 308
Lundström, S., 289
Luria, A. R., 370
Luria-Nebraska Neuropsychological Battery, 389
Lussier, P., 344
luteinizing hormone (LH), 705, 710
Luu, P., 163
Ly, M., 213
Lykken, D. T., 317
Lyons-Ruth, K., 519

Ma, D., 730–1
MacDonald, G., 147, 153
MacDonald, R., 408
Machado, C. J., 127
Machiavellianism, 180

magnetoencephalography (MEG), 16, 27, 55, 63, 765
Maguire, E. A., 347, 582
Major, G., 640–1
Malamuth, N. M., 335–6
Maletzky, B. M., 716
Malik, A. I., 201, 499t
malnutrition, 511, 513, 515, 520, 580
Mann, R. E., 558, 581
Mannheim, G., 17
Mannion, H. D., 89–90
Manuck, S. B., 133, 242
Marchese, V., 393
Marcus, D. K., 244
Marian, D. E., 134
Mark, G., 685
Mark, V., 398
marker studies, 65–6
Markus, H. R., 371
Márquez, C., 243
Marsa, F., 787–8
Marsee, M. A., 197
Marsh, A. A., 17, 159, 161, 204, 209
Marshall, W. L., 336, 344, 345, 558
Martin, G. B., 150
Martinson, R., 660
Mason, P., 147, 148
Masserman, J. H., 148
Masten, C. L., 152–3
Mather, M., 114
Mathews, V. P., 72
Mattern, C., 93
maturational imbalance theory, 107
Maughan, B., 275
Mauss, I. B., 132
Max, J. E., 376
Maxfield, L., 767
McBurnett, K., 197
McClure, E. B., 108
McClure, S. M., 127
McFarland, B., 716
McGuire, J., 254
McGuire, R. J., 339
McKie, S., 180
McMurran, M., 759
McRae, K., 133
Mead, H. K., 67, 691

Mechelli, A., 212, 213
Mechta, P. H., 73
medial amygdala nucleus, 36
medial nuclei, 13
medial preoptic area, 85
median longitudinal fissure, 40
medical history, 407–9
meditation, 322, 554, 555, 561–4, 567, 678, 685–8, 692–4, 745, 747, 748
Mednick, S. A., 390–1, 514
Meek, S. W., 177
Meerwijk, E. L., 155
Meeusen, R., 666
Meffert, H., 208
Mega, M. S., 612
Melnyk, W. T., 767
Meloy, J. R., 305–6, 395–6, 544
Melser, J., 558
memory, 364–5, 368–71, 407, 459, 522, 565, 586, 589, 611–12, 617, 663, 664, 756–8, 760–76
Mendez, M. F., 612
mental illness, 531–43, 559
   anxiety disorder (AD), 127, 236, 278, 620, 680–94
   depression, 46–7, 97, 127, 129, 236, 278, 589, 613–14, 615, 620, 634, 667, 708, 713, 717
   obsessive-compulsive disorder (OCD), 278, 602, 613, 708
   post-traumatic stress disorder (PTSD), 682, 692, 755–76
   schizophrenia, 182–3, 237, 251–4, 307, 308, 309, 310–11, 313, 316, 317, 318–19, 320, 394, 532, 535–41, 637
   schizophrenia spectrum disorders, 532

Index

mentalization (theory of mind), 178, 179, 274, 279, 361, 369, 428, 532, 539, 544, 748
Merry, S. N., 589
mesolimbic system, 632–3
methodology, 49–56
  animal studies, 49, 85
  control of variables, 249, 496
  emotional tasks, 126, 129, 135–6, 137
  etiological approach, 64–5, 375–6, 437–8, 483–502
  experimental methods, 29–30
  eye-tracking studies, 30, 339–40
  forensic assessment *see* risk assessment
  Iowa gambling task, 192
  neuroimaging, 15–16, 51–5, 62–3, 71–3, 214–15
  neuropsychology, 49–51
  passive avoidance learning task, 249
  placebo-controlled studies, 461, 467
  psychophysiological measures, 55–6, 62, 65–6, 176–7
  reliability, 66, 117, 214–15, 233–4, 388–9, 408, 638–41
  response reversal tasks, 192, 249
  sampling techniques, 388
  self-report measures, 388–9
  validity, 214–15, 282, 407–10, 558, 637–41
Meyer-Lindenberg, A., 242
Meyers, C. A., 202
Mezzacappa, E., 690
Michael, R. P., 95
Michie, C., 194
Miczek, K. A., 462
midbrain, 34–5
Mier, D., 207
Miller, A. R., 181

Miller, D. C., 108
Miller v. Alabama (2012), 138
Mills, S., 304, 397
mindfulness meditation, 322, 554, 555, 561–4, 567, 678, 685–8, 692–4, 745, 747, 748
Miner, M. H., 340
Mini-Mental Status Examination (MMSE), 405
Minnesota Multiphasic Personality Inventory (MMPI-2), 407–8
Minnesota Twin Family Study, 487t
mirror neurons, 14
Mishkin, F., 612
Mitchell, I. J., 201, 735
Miura, H., 315
M'Naughten rules, 274, 293
Mobbs, D., 245
modal model of emotion, 129–30, 678–80
Modinos, G., 686
Moffitt, T. E., 240, 286, 430–3, 437–8, 497
Mohammed, A. H., 669
Monahan, J., 556
Monahan, K. C., 433
monoamine oxidases (MAO), 4, 46–7, 241–2, 243, 463, 509, 522
monoamines, 46, 659, 664–6, 705
Montague, P. R., 127
Montalan, B., 161
Monuteaux, M. C., 438
Moore, A. A., 240
Moore, E. A., 537
moral behavior, 9–10, 291, 293–4, 729
  and empathy, 145–63, 207–9, 485, 612–13, 636, 739
  and guilt, 737, 749
Moretti, M. M., 493
Morgan, A. B., 315, 520
Morrison, H., 403

Morse, S. J., 349
Morton-Bourgon, K. E., 338–9
Moser, J. S., 75
Moses, L. J., 179
Motzkin, J. C., 210, 214
Moul, C., 498t
Mouras, H., 161
Mouridsen, S. E., 287, 288
MRI scans (magnetic resonance imaging), 15, 51–2, 63, 410–12, 563–4, 602, 608, 683–4
Mueck-Weymann, M., 691–2
Mulcahy, M., 86
Müller, J. L., 206, 212, 309
Mullins, A. D., 180
Multiaxial Assessment System, 532
multi-modal learning, 585–90
murderers, 305–6, 307, 312–14, 317, 318–19, 320, 385–412, 535, 615–16, 619–20
Murphy, D., 281
Murray, E. A., 127
Murray-Close, D., 67
Murrie, D. C., 289
music, use in therapy, 587–8
myelination, 41–2, 315, 369–70, 372, 426–7, 435, 509
myopia hypothesis, 459–60

Nagy, G., 370
Naidu, K., 86
Nair, M. S., 76
narcissism, 180
Narr, K. L., 213
Narr, L., 563
narrative memory, 765–6
Nasby, W., 460
National Child Traumatic Stress Network, 788
National Institute of Mental Health (NIMH), 618–19
negativity bias, 732, 733–4

Nelson, E. E., 108
Neria, Y., 764
Nestor, P. G., 314
Neugebauer, R., 513
neurobehavioral
    rehabilitation, 632,
    641–52
neurodevelopmental
    disorders, definition,
    275
neuroimaging, 15–16, 51–5,
    62–3, 71–3, 303–11
  admissibility in court, 76
  as diagnostic tool, 410–12,
    440–3, 578, 601–22
neurons, 43–5, 65
neuropeptides, 48–9, 146,
    154–5
neuroplasticity, 65, 347, 378,
    522, 561, 582–3,
    664, 668–9, 767–8
neuroscience, 3–57
  definition, 4
  history of, 6–12, 27–9
neurotoxins, 244, 279
neurotransmitters, 19, 45–9,
    65, 240–3, 366–8,
    369, 374, 461–2,
    463–7, 522, 539–40,
    542, 554, 659, 660,
    664–6, 667, 669,
    704, 705, 708, 709,
    712–13, 717
neurotrophic factors, 554,
    566, 660, 667–9
Newberg, A., 609
Newman, J. P., 193–4, 210
Newman, S., 292–3
Newton, N., 289–90
Nicholls, T. L., 637
Nichols, S. R., 151
Nieuwenhuis, S., 771
Nilsson, K. W., 242
Nock, M. K., 234
non-judgmentalism, 739,
    745, 748
noradrenalin, 46
Nordstrom, B. R., 66
normal pressure
    hydrocephalus
    (NPH), 611–12
Norman, G. J., 148, 149
Norris, J., 397, 400, 403

North American Adult
    Reading Test
    (NAART), 406
Nowrouzi, B., 201
nucleus accumbens, 46, 106,
    108–9, 128, 532,
    545, 665
Nusbaum, H., 589
Nyalakanti, P. K., 213
Nyden, A., 287

Oaten, M., 131
Obradovic, J., 363
O'Brien, B. S., 197
O'Brien, L., 110–11
obsessive-compulsive
    disorder (OCD), 278,
    602, 613, 708
occipital lobe, 40
Ochsner, K. N., 133–4,
    679–80, 684
O'Connor, M.-F., 156
O'Connor, P. J., 666
oddball tasks, 63, 177
Oddy, M., 581
Odgers, C. L., 432, 433, 493
O'Donohue, W. T., 772
offenders, typology of, 8–9,
    635–6
Ogawa, S., 95
Ohio State University TBI
    Identification, 409
Okumura, Y., 151
Olds, D., 322
Olegård, R., 392
omega-3 fatty acid
    supplementation, 521
O'Nions, E., 209
Oosterveld, P., 280
operant conditioning, 28,
    638–9
oppositional defiant disorder,
    180
orbitofrontal cortex, 12–13,
    109–10, 112, 116,
    246, 290, 337–8,
    372, 376, 430, 438,
    682–4, 789
orbitoprefrontal cortex
    (vmPFC), 42, 50,
    129, 193, 201–3,
    290, 306–7, 315,
    364–5, 366, 372,

376, 427, 428, 430,
    434, 462, 510, 520,
    522, 544, 682–4
Ormel, J., 686
Ortiz, J., 66, 690
Oscar-Berman, M., 249
Ostrosky-Solís, F., 401
Ostrov, J. M., 180
Oswald, P. A., 159
Otnow-Lewis, D., 400–1,
    402
ovariectomy, 85, 91, 93, 94
Overt Aggression
    Scale-Modified
    (OAS-MNR), 632,
    638–9, 641, 648,
    649–50
Overt Behavior Scale (OBS),
    639
Owen, A. M., 174–6
Owett, T., 94
oxytocin, 48–9, 154–5, 192,
    201, 713, 726, 733,
    734
Oyserman, D., 371

P300 response, 63, 70–1,
    172, 181, 554, 565–6
pain, 740–1
Palermo, M. T., 292–3
Pallone, N. J., 393
panic disorder, 689
Panksepp, J., 147, 153
Papageorgiou, C., 130
parahippocampus, 394
paraphilia, 85, 91, 99, 334,
    340–1, 343, 394,
    707, 708–9, 718–19
parasympathetic nervous
    system, 42–3, 56
Pardini, D., 181, 216, 309,
    440–1, 500–1
parenting, 233–4, 240, 241,
    243, 245, 247,
    254–5, 439–40,
    496–7, 501, 515–19,
    521, 727, 728,
    734–5, 787–8, 805–6
parietal lobe, 40–1, 109,
    302
Park, N. S., 319, 559
Parker, K. C., 770–1
Parkes, K. R., 177

Index

Parkinson's disease, 46, 51, 181–2, 712, 713
Parr, L. A., 148
Pasalich, D., 201
Passamonti, L., 72, 246, 428
passive avoidance learning task, 249
Patel, P., 349
Patel, S. J., 116
Patrick, C. J., 19, 74, 75, 194–5
Paulus, M. P., 114, 115
Pavlov, I. P., 28
Pavlov, S. V., 563
Pavlovian conditioning, 28, 84, 89, 90–1, 97
Pavone, F., 148
Payne, E., 759
PCL-R (Psychopathy Checklist Revised) *see* Psychopathy Checklist Revised (PCL-R)
pedophilia, 91, 98–9, 334, 336–8, 339–40, 342, 343–8
peer relationships, 110–11, 371–2
Peraza, D. M., 135
Pérez, M., 401
perfusion, 602, 605–22
perinatal brain development, 514
peripheral nervous system, 4, 42–3, 55–6
personality, 10–11
  alexithymia, 554
  callous-unemotional traits (CU), 422, 425, 428, 435–6, 440, 443–4, 483–502, 503n
  and risk-taking, 115–16
  strengths, 559
personality disorder, 708
Petee, T. A., 314
Petersen, E., 579
Petersen, S., 579
Peterson, C., 559–61
Petrowski, K., 691–2
Petry, N., 367–8
Pettersson, E., 275
Pfadt, A. G., 586
Pfaff, D. W., 95, 96
Pfeifer, J. H., 152–3

Pham, T. H., 198, 669
Phan, K. L., 72
phenotype, 26, 64–5, 75, 230, 726, 727–8, 730
Philip, R. C. M., 283
Phillips, M. C., 177
Phoenix, C. H., 93
photon emission tomography (PET), 602
photoplethysmogram (PPG), 85
phrenology, 5, 6–7, 71, *72*
physical fitness, 564–6, 583, 659–70
Pieters, T., 290
Pietz, C. A., 542
Pillmann, F., 319
Pimental, A., 790
Pincus, J. H., 390, 392–3, 394–5
Pine, D. S., 108
Pinel, Philippe, 10
Piquero, A. R., 433, 661
Pitman, I., 581
placebo-controlled studies, 461, 467
Plomin, R., 240, 497
Ploughman, M., 668
Polaschek, D. L. L., 194–5
Polier, G. G., 236
Polisois-Keating, A., 342, 343
polygenic threshold model, 430
polygraphy, 172, 176–7
Pope, K., 210
Popper, K., 29
Porges, S. W., 747
positive neuroscience, 553–67
positive psychology, 558–61
positron emission tomography (PET), 15, 53–4, 386, 410, 411, 542, 615–16
Posner, M. I., 579
post-central gyrus, 40–1
post-traumatic amnesia (PTA), 407
post-traumatic stress disorder (PTSD), 682, 692, 755–76

Potter, S., 376
Poustka, A., 17, 310
Pouw, L. B., 280
poverty, effect on brain development, 19, 234, 511, 513, 728
Poythress, N., 196
Prasad, M., 789
precuneus, 302, 334
prediction errors, 128
pre-eclampsia, 361, 390, 508
prefrontal cortex, 41–2, 115–16, 127, 128–9, 174–6, 201–3, 290, 305–7, 365, 366, 369, 372, 394, 395, 400–1, 427, 434, 438, 461–2, 544, 545, 563, 608, 612–16, 620, 662–3, 669, 681, 686, 789
Prehn, K., 209–10
prenatal brain development, 31, 49, 361, 374, 375, 390–3, 509, 511–13, 579
Prentky, R., 790
Preuschoff, K., 115, 157
Price, B. H., 389
Price, C. J., 212
primates
  aggression, 464–5, 466–7, 727, 729
  emotion regulation, 127
  empathy, 148–9
  sexual behavior, 89, 91–2, 95, 97, 342–3
Prison Yoga Project, 567
process model of emotion, 130–1, 132–3, 134–5
process studies, 66
progesterone, 85, 91, 96
Propper, R. E., 767
Proulx, J., 344
pseudodementia, 611
psychopathy, 158–61, 180–1, 191–216, 235, 250–1, 280, 290, 308, 346, 348, 365, 396–7, 428, 483–502, 537–8, 543–4, 616, 737

Psychopathy Checklist Revised (PCL-R), 230, 231, 346, 616
psychophenomenology, 705, 707–9
psychophysiology, 55–6, 62, 65–6, 176–7, 767
Pujara, M., 210
pupillometry, 172
Purisch, A. D., 389
Putkonen, A., 541
Putman, P., 200
Putnam, K. M., 67
pyramidal neurons (cells), 39, 44–5

Quinsey, V. L., 19

Radke-Yarrow, M., 150
Rafter, N., 6–7
Raine, A., 14, 16, 17, 18, 66, 69, 70–1, 74, 196, 198, 200, 210–11, 213, 214, 251, 290–1, 304, 305–6, 308–9, 314, 317, 320, 389, 390–1, 395, 396–7, 403, 430, 439, 514, 515, 615–16, 661
Ram, A., 519
Ramirez, Richard, 399
Ramnani, N., 174–6
Ramón y Cajal, S., 43, 767–8
Ranft, K., 127
rape, 99, 335–6, 349, 729
rapid eye movement (REM) sleep, 756, 769–70
Rasch, B., 770
Rasmussen, K., 314
reappraisal (cognitive reappraisal), 125, 133–4, 137, 679–80, 693, 749
recidivism risk assessment, 439–41, 556–61, 646, 714, 716, 792–3
Redding, R. E., 388, 403
Rees, G., 155
rehabilitation *see* treatments
Reidy, D. E., 200
Reif, A., 242

Reiner, R., 691
relational aggression, 234, 429, 439
reliability, 66, 117, 214–15, 233–4, 388–9, 408, 638–41
REM (rapid eye movement) sleep, 756, 769–70
Repacholi, B., 519
Repucci, N. D., 493
response modulation (suppression), 126, 133, 134–5, 137, 246, 680
response reversal tasks, 192, 249
restorative justice, 737
Reva, N. V., 563
reward circuitry dysfunction model, 537
reward sensitivity, 105–18, 127, 128, 209–10, 361, 363–78, 427, 465–6, 537, 632–3, 665, 733
Reynolds, C. F., 621
Reynolds, M., 108
Rhee, S. H., 240
Rhodes, M., 162
rhythmic breathing, 745–6
Ricci, R. J., 759
Rice, G. E., 147
Rice, M. E., 347
Rieffe, C., 280
Ries, E. E., 180
Rinne, T., 290
risk assessment, 18–20, 289–92, 338–47, 362, 378, 403–12, 556–61, 742, 791–3
aggression, 18–19, 75–6, 463, 465–7, 531–43, 634–5, 637–41
recidivism, 439–41, 556–61, 646, 714, 716, 792–3
RNR model (risk-needs-responsivity), 556–7, 558, 646, 660, 692, 793
structured assessment guides, 784, 792–3

risk management, 553–67
risk-taking behavior, 49, 105–18, 128, 202, 209–10, 302, 371–3, 374, 391–3, 427, 465–6, 508, 511–13, 635, 665
risky-gains task, 114
Ritov, I., 161
Rizvi, S. L., 688
Robbers Cave Experiment, 162, 163n
Roberts, A., 233
Roberts, N., 307
Robertson, B., 349–50
Robins, L. N., 231, 238
Robinson, R. G., 634
rodents
aggression, 463–4, 466–7
empathy, 147–8, 149
impulsivity, 367–8
sexual behavior, 86–7, 88–9, 91, 95, 96–7, 98
Rodgers, D. A., 147, 148
Rogers, J., 586
Rogers, J. C., 246
Rogers, P., 759
Rogers, R., 556
Roiser, J., 368
Roisman, G. I., 433
Romero, T., 148
Rosenfeld, J. P., 181
Rösler, A., 716
Ross, R. R., 371
Rossiter, R., 586, 587, 591
Rothermund, K., 135
Roth-Hanania, R., 151
Rothstein, P., 30
Rowe, R., 235, 436
Roy, E., 583
Rubia, K., 250, 789
Rubin, L. H., 316
Rudorf, S., 115
Rueda, M., 373, 378
rule-use paradigm, 361, 370
Rusch, H. L., 764
Rushton, J. P., 11
Rutter, M., 240, 275
Ryding, E., 545
Ryland, H., 376

Sack, M., 767
Sadeh, N., 497, 498t
sadism, 338, 341–2, 347, 348, 729
sadness, 740
Saltaris, C., 519
sampling methods, 388
Samuels, J., 238
Samuelson, M., 687
Sanger, D., 520
Santana-Vargas, D., 401
Santarnecchi, E., 563–4
Sarkar, S., 214
Sato, J. R., 215
Saus-Rose, E., 690
Sbordone, R. J., 389
scaffolding, 136–7
Schaefer, S. M., 683
Schatzberg, A. F., 621
Schein, M. W., 97
Schene, A. H., 558
Schiavi, R. C., 94
Schiffer, B., 245, 251, 337, 345
schizophrenia, 182–3, 237, 251–4, 307, 308, 309, 310–11, 313, 316, 317, 318–19, 320, 394, 532, 535–41, 637
schizophrenia spectrum disorders, 532
Schmidt, M. F. H., 151
Schneider, F., 206
Schneider, K., 10
Schofield, C., 558
Schreiner-Engel, P., 94
Schubert, S. J., 771
Schug, R. A., 198, 200, 320
Schumann, G., 427
Schurtz, D. R., 730–1
Schutter, D. J. L. G., 200, 247
Schwartz, B., 790
Schwartz, J. M., 768
Seara-Cardoso, A., 215
Sebastian, C. L., 137, 209, 246
Segal, Z. V., 685, 748
Seidel, E. M., 67
selective serotonin reuptake-inhibitors

(SSRI), 467, 667, 705, 713, 717, 718–19
self-harm, 533
self-regulation, 108, 344–6, 359–78, 748–9, 794
Seligman, M. E. P., 559–61
semantic networking theories, 459
Senju, A., 542
sensation seeking, 18, 105, 111–12, 371
sensory assessment, 784, 792–3
Seo, D., 19
serial killers, 390–1, 397–412
serotonin, 19, 46, 47, 48, 97, 240–3, 361, 366–8, 463–7, 497, 522, 539–40, 542, 545, 660, 665–6, 667, 669, 708, 712–13, 717
Serretti, A., 686
Seto, M., 343–4
sexual abuse, 243, 247, 250, 287, 516–17, 788–90
sexual behavior, 83–99, 516
    arousal, 90–1, 334, 336, 339–40, 342, 343–5, 684, 705–7, 710–19
    definition, 86–7
    and developmental issues, 786–90
    deviant sexual interest/ preference, 334, 335, 336–7, 339–44, 394, 707, 708–9, 718–19
    homosexuality and bisexuality, 96–7
    sadism, 335, 338, 341–2, 347, 348, 729
sexual incentive motivation theory, 85, 87–91
sexual offenders, 287–8, 333–50
    and alcohol abuse, 456–7
    comorbid disorders, 708
    murderers, 390–1, 393, 394, 397–403
    risk assessment/ management,

338–47, 516–17, 556–7
    stalking, 287–8, 289–90
    treatments, 99, 337, 587, 703–20, 759, 783–807
    violent offenders, 99, 335–6, 349, 711–12, 729
Shah, A., 281
Shamay-Tsoori, S. G., 280
shame, 727, 729, 730, 736–7, 739, 748–9
Shane, M. S., 160–1
Shapiro, F., 756–7, 760–2, 770, 772–3
Sherif, C. W., 162
Sherif, M., 162
Shevich, J., 588–9
Shimamura, A. P., 134
Shnitt, D., 519
Short-Term Assessment of Risk and Treatability (START), 640–1
Shvil, E., 764
Siepman, M., 691–2
Sigvardsson, S., 523
Silani, G., 157
Silberg, J., 240
Silver, H., 317
Silverthorn, P., 433
Simion, F., 150
Simpson, G., 338
Singer, T., 157, 279
Singh, J. P., 540
Singh, N. N., 687
single photon emission tomography (SPECT), 15, 54, 394, 410, 411, 601–22
Siponmaa, L., 287
Skeem, J. L., 194–5, 196
Skelly, L., 206–7
Skinner, B. F., 28
Skinner, S., 520
Slaughter, B., 388
sleep, 756, 769–70
slot machine task, 113
slow wave sleep (SWS), 756, 770
Small, D. M., 127

Smeets, T., 200
Smith, A., 589
Smith, A. L., 662
Smith, H., 94
Snook, E. M., 565–6
social anxiety disorder, 278
social brain hypothesis,
     12–14, 275, 283,
     731
social information
     processing, 460–2,
     539
social-cognitive model/
     theory, 455, 458–62
socioeconomic status, 19,
     234, 511, 513, 728
Soderstrom, H., 308–9, 616,
     618
Sollers, J. J., 689–90
Solomon, R. M., 770
somatic marker hypothesis,
     363–4
somatosensory system, 42,
     56
Sommerville, J. A., 151
Southern California Twin
     Project, 488t
Southwick, L., 459, 460
SPARX (game), 589
spatial resolution, 678, 683
spatial/performance
     intelligence, 314
Spiers, H. J., 582
spouse abuse, 68, 69, *321*,
     456–7, 467
Sprokay, S., 593
Sripada, C. S., 72
Sroufe, A., 519
St Andrew's-Swansea
     Neurobehavioral Scale
     (SASNOS), 639, 648,
     650
Stachen, N. M., 588–9
Stadler, C., 16–17, 310
stalking, 287–8, 289–90
Stanley, J., 395
Stapp, H. P., 768
startle response, 199
Starzyk, K. B., 19
Stauffacher, K., 180
Steele, C. M., 459, 460

Steinberg, L., 107, 110–11,
     138, 661
Stenvik, K., 689–90
Sterzer, P., 16–17, 310
Stevens, M. C., 250
Stickgold, R., 767, 769–70,
     776
Stiglmayr, A., 349
Stix, G., 5
Stochholm, K., 12
Stockmann, L., 280
Stoddard, J., 306, 395
Stokes, M., 288, 289–90
Stone, M. H., 397, 399, 400
stoplight driving game,
     110–11
strengths-based treatments,
     553–67, 646–50,
     651, 741–9, 785–807
stress, 19, 462, 465, 580,
     682, 692, 755–76
striato-thalamo-cortical
     network model, 337,
     545
striatum, 46, 127–8
Stroop task, 366, 563
structural MRI (magnetic
     resonance imaging),
     52, 410–12, 426–7,
     563–4, 608
structured assessment guides,
     784, 792–3
substance abuse, 235, 250,
     605–8, 634
  alcoholism, 49, 249,
     374–5, 391–3, 397,
     455–68, 606–8
  and impulsivity, 366–8,
     374–5
  and mental illness, 536–7,
     541
  in pregnancy, 49, 374,
     391–3, 508, 511–13
  and sexual behavior, 97–8
  smoking, 511, 512–13
suicide, 533, 615
Sullivan, G. M., 764
superior colliculus, 35
superior temporal gyrus, 428
suppression (expressive
     suppression), 126,

     133, 134–5, 137,
     246, 680
Supreme Court, 138
Susman, E. J., 200, 433
Susser, E., 513
Sutherland, A. M., 94
Sutherland, R. J., 692
Suzuki, K., 291
Svetlova, M., 146, 151
Swedish Twin Study of Child
     and Adolescent
     Development,
     488t–9t, 496
sympathetic nervous system,
     42–3, 56
sympathy, 738
synaptic pruning, 372–3,
     422, 509
systems neuroscience, 27

't Hart-Kerkhoffs, L. A., 287
Tackett, J. L., 437
Takeuchi, H., 583
Talwar, V., 180
Tan, G., 692
Tangney, J. P., 736
Tani, K., 320
Taren, A. A., 561
Tarullo, A., 363, 378
Tateno, A., 634
Tavares, M. C., 93
Taylor, G., 771
Taylor, S., 459–60
Taylor, V. A., 693
Teaching Family Model, 28
Teasdale, J. D., 685, 693,
     748
Teicher, M. H., 516,
     579–81, 585
telomeres, 508, 516
temporal lobe, 40, 192,
     307–8, 370, 389–90,
     402–3, 406–7, 428,
     544, 566, 608,
     616–18, 789
temporal lobe epilepsy,
     397–9, 411, 613–14,
     616–18
tensor-based morphometry
     (TBM), 789
teratogens, 508, 511–13

Terris, W., 148
Terzian, H., 343
testosterone, 18–19, 84, 85, 93, 94–5, 97–8, 99, 200, 704, 705, 709–15
thalamus, 5, 37–8, 310–11, 376
Thayer, J. F., 689–90
Theeuwes, J., 132
theory of mind, 178, 179, 274, 279, 361, 369, 428, 532, 539, 544, 748
Thibaut, F., 719
Thomas, C., 582–3
Thompson, R. A., 130
Thornton, D., 340
threat focus, 732, 733–4
thyroid, 193, 200–1
tics, 274
Tiihonen, J., 212
Timbers, G. D., 28
Timonen, M., 376
Toga, A. W., 213, 563
Tolan, P. H., 716
Tomasello, M., 151, 152
Tomasulo, D. J., 586
Tomaz, C., 93
Tonnaer, F., 195
top-down processing, 132
Topic, B., 93
Torgerson, S., 233
Tost, H., 337
Toupin, J., 237
toxins, 244, 279, 508, 511–13, 605–8
trail making test, 302
Traksman-Bendz, L., 545
Tranel, D., 152
transcranial direct current stimulation (tDCS), 50–1
transcranial magnetic stimulation (TMS), 50–1
traumatic brain injury, 373, 375–6, 385–412, 519–20, 544, 577–94, 608–10, 631–52

Traumatic Brain Injury Questionnaire (TBIQ), 408
treatments, 577–807
acquired brain injury (ABI), 641–52
acquisitive/impulsive offenders, 375, 377–8
ADHD (attentional deficit hyperactive disorder), 375
adolescent offenders, 442–3, 783–807
antisocial personality disorder, 241, 254–5, 442–3
anxiety disorder (AD), 620
breathing exercises, 745–6
cognitive behavioral therapy, 583–94, 643–4, 646–7, 678, 689, 748, 759, 772
compassion-focused therapy, 725–49
conduct disorder (CD), 254–5, 442–3, 500–2
depression, 46–7, 97, 467, 589, 613–14, 615, 620, 667, 708, 713, 717
diagnostic neuroimaging, 410–12, 440–3, 578, 601–22
emotion regulation, 677–94
exercise, 564–6, 583, 659–70
game-based learning, 589–90
HRV (heart rate variability) biofeedback, 678, 688–92
malnutrition, 521
meditation, 322, 554, 555, 561–4, 567, 678, 685–8, 692–4, 745, 747, 748
music and drama therapies, 587–8

neurobehavioral rehabilitation, 632, 641–52
parent training programs, 254–5, 521
post-traumatic stress disorder (PTSD), 682, 692, 755–76
sexual offenders, 99, 337, 587, 703–20, 759, 783–807
strengths-based approach, 553–67, 646–50, 651, 741–9
strengths-based treatments, 785–807
violent offenders, 76, 99, 397, 467, 542, 641–52
Treiman, D. M., 398
triadic model, 108
triarchic model of psychopathy, 74–5
triidothyronine (T3), 193, 201
Trimble, M. R., 334
Tsai, L., 288
Tucker, D. M., 163
Tuiten, A., 95
tumors, 401
Twenge, J. M., 730–1
twin studies, 19–20, 64–5, 239–40, 278–9, 286, 437–8, 465, 486–97, 559
Twins Early Development Study, 484, 489t–91t, 495, 499t
Tyler, N., 759–60
Tyrer, P., 233

Uchino, B. N., 149
Uckert, K., 110–11
Ullrich, S., 233, 680
Ullsperger, M., 127
uncinate fasciculus, 246–7, 422, 435
Unterdörfer, J., 691–2
Urbach-Wiethe disease, 27, 49
Urry, H. L., 684

Vaish, A., 151, 152
VAK (visual-auditory-kinaesthetic) learning styles, 585–90, 801
validity, 214–15, 282, 407–10, 558, 637–41
Values in Action (VIA) project, 559–61
van den Bos, R., 116
van der Gronde, T., 290
van der Kolk, B. A., 765–6
van der Molen, M. W., 284
van El, C., 290
Van Honk, J., 200
Van Horn, J. D., 8
Van Leijenhorst, L., 112–13
Vaschillo, B., 691
Vaschillo, E., 691
vascular dementia, 602, 609–10
Vasey, P. L., 96, 97
vasopressin, 48–9
Vassileva, J., 681
Veit, R., 206
Vélez-García, A., 401
Venables, N. C., 74
Venables, P. H., 69–70
Vendemia, J. M., 176, 177
Venters, H., 408
ventral striatum, 46, 106, 108–9, 128, 290, 374, 466
ventrolateral prefrontal cortex (vlPFC), 129
ventromedial hypothalamus, 85, 92, 95–6
ventromedial prefrontal cortex (vmPFC), 42, 50, 129, 193, 201–3, 290, 306–7, 315, 364–5, 366, 372, 376, 427, 428, 430, 434, 462, 510, 520, 522, 544, 682–4
verbal intelligence, 314
Verheul, R., 688
Verrett, C., 662
Vessantara, 728
victimisation, 239
Viding, E., 209, 215, 234, 240, 246, 428, 497, 499t, 500

Vignaux, T., 349–50
Violence Reduction Program (VRP), 646–51
violent offenders, 301–22, 345, 346, 349, 615–20, 727, 729
  ADHD (attentional deficit hyperactive disorder), 373
  and alcohol abuse, 455–68
  antisocial personality disorder, 238–9
  arsonists, 287, 535
  autism spectrum disorder (ASD), 287–92
  dementia, 612–13
  murderers, 305–6, 307, 312–14, 317, 318–19, 320, 385–412, 535, 615–16, 619–20
  risk assessment, 75–6, 403–12, 531–43, 556–61, 634–5, 637–41
  self-harm and suicide, 533, 615
  sex differences, 401, 428–33
  traumatic brain injury, 385–412
  treatments, 76, 99, 467, 542, 641–52, 677–94, 711–12
Vipassana meditation, 555, 562
virtual lesions, 50–1
visual learning, 585–7, 747, 801
Volavka, J., 69, 319, 397, 398
Volkow, N., 306, 307
Vom Saal, F., 18–19
von Cramon, D. Y., 127
von Knorring, A., 523
Vonlaufen, C., 345
voxel-based morphometry (VBM), 212, 422
vulnerable defendants, 291

Wager, T. D., 29, 133–4
Wagner, E., 150

Wagner, S. M., 589
Waldman, I. D., 240
Walsh, A., 314
Walsh, C. K., 561
Walsh, V., 155
Wang, P.-Y., 150
Wang, X., 157
Wang, Y., 72
Ward, T., 558
Warden, D., 159
warrior gene, 19, 509, 522
Watt, A., 759
Waxenberg, S. E., 94
Way, B. M., 686
weak central coherence theory, 281
Weber, B., 115
Webster, S. D., 558
Wechkin, S., 148
Wechsler adult intelligence scale (WAIS), 302, 313, 406
Weiner, E. H., 612
Weinfield, N. S., 519
Weinstock, R., 76
Weiss, S. J., 155
Weizman, A., 519
Welch, S. S., 688
Wells, A., 130
Wells, H., 759
Wells, L. J., 30
Wenzel, S. L., 513
West, Frederick, 400
Whalen, P. J., 72, 127
White, B. J., 162
White, C. L., 612
White, D., 94
White, N. A., 433
White, S. F., 207, 210, 212, 501
white matter, 5, 40, 52, 246–7, 282, 369–70, 372–3, 426–7, 434–5
Whitlock, F. A., 10
Whitman, Charles, 401
Whitson, S. M., 67
Wicks, B., 580
Wide Range Achievement Test-Revised (WRAT-R), 406
Williams, F., 581
Williams, H., 646

Williams, J. M. G., 685, 748
Williams, K. D., 137
Williams, M., 69–70
Williams, W. H., 376, 634
Wilson, B. A., 637
Wimalaweera, S., 204, 501
Winblad, B., 669
Wing, L., 277, 286
Wisconsin Card Sorting Test (WCST), 302, 314, 412
Witvliet, C. V. O., 748
Witztum, E., 716
Wolf, M. M., 28
Wolf, R. C., 247
women
  abuse survivors, 243, 247, 250, 401
  antisocial personality disorder, 234, 241, 242, 247, 249, 254, 424–5
  risk-taking behavior, 49, 116, 374, 391–3, 508, 511–13

sexual behavior, 89–91, 93–6
violent offenders, 401, 428–33
Wong, M. T. H., 308, 309, 319
Wong, S. C. P., 646
Wood, R., 645
Woodbury-Smith, M. R., 288
Woollett, K., 347, 582
Wootton, J. M., 197
working memory, 172, 177, 365, 368–71, 565, 586, 589, 769
World Health Organization (WHO), 303, 763
Wright, P., 393
Wu, J. C., 609
Wynn, K., 151

X-ray computed tomography (X-ray CT), 15, 386, 410–11
Xu, X., 157
XYY syndrome, 5, 12

Yang, M., 233
Yang, Y., 211, 213, 215, 251, 306, 307, 308, 309, 348, 389, 390, 394
Yanowitch, R. N., 72
Yaralian, P. S., 213
Yates, P. M., 558
Yoder, K. J., 206–7
yoga, 563
York, M. K., 127
Yoshi, N., 320
Young, A., 28
Young, S., 373

Zahn-Waxler, C., 150, 151
Zai, C. C., 201
Zak, P. J., 155
Zanolie, K., 112–13
Zen Buddhism, 555, 562
Zenchak, J. J., 97
Zuckerman, S., 93
Zumpe, D., 95
Zuo, X., 157

Printed and bound by CPI Group (UK) Ltd, Croydon, CR0 4YY
29/04/2022
03122050-0001